BRISTOL CARS

Compiled by R M Clarke

ISBN 1 85520 5637

BROOKLANDS BOOKS LTD.
P.O. BOX 146, COBHAM,
SURREY, KT11 1LG. UK
sales@brooklands-books.com

A-BRQP

Printed in China

ACKNOWLEDGEMENTS

We started our Gold Portfolio series about fourteen years ago and amongst the first subjects covered was Bristol cars. It sold well and went out of print some six years later. It was then updated with further articles to bring the story up to 1992 and now, some eight years further on, it has gone out of print again. A recent visit to our archive unearthed another 50 stories which we have incorporated here in the hope that it will make this book an even more useful source of reference for Bristol aficionados.

We have always enjoyed a great deal of support from the Bristol Owners Club. In the early days from their Oxford section and, more recently, from club member, Andrew Blow, who has generously loaned us photographs from his vast collection. These include our front cover photograph and the top four pictures on the back cover.

We have also had invaluable help over the years from Tony Crook of Bristol Cars Limited who has furnished us with the bottom two photographs on our back cover. As well as this he has kindly written the knowledgeable introduction below, which expertly leads us through the Bristol story over the last 55 years.

Finally, our thanks go to the publishers of the world's leading motoring journals who for over 40 years have allowed us to reissue their informative copyright stories in our 'road test' portfolios. Our thanks go in this instance to the managements of *Autocar, Automobile Topics, Autosport, Car, Car and Driver, Car Life, Cars Illustrated, Cars of the World, Classic & Sports Car, Classic Cars, Light Car, Motor, Motor Manual, Motor Sport, Motor Trend, NZ Classic Car, Performance Car, Road & Track, Road & Track Specials, Sporting Motorist, Sports Car Annual, Sports Car World, Sports Cars Illustrated, Top Gear, Wheels, World Cars, World Car Catalogue* and *World Car Guide* for their continued support.

R.M.Clarke

INTRODUCTION

"I am often asked which is my favourite Bristol. Answer - the current one at the time. I believe each model has been an improvement. I do not think we ever made a bad car, although our inspectors were horrified by the workmanship of the coachwork on the handful of early chassis we were persuaded to sell without coachwork in Italy and Switzerland soon after the company opened. Highlights for me include my inaugural drives in the first 400 (I have still got it) - the very first car. It was certainly not just a pre-war BMW made post-war in England. During World War 2 I owned a number of 2-litre BMWs, and very good they were too, but the Bristol 400 was not only an entirely new, different, more roomy shape but also bristled with new technical features and was made to the highest aircraft standards and very well soundproofed. So different was it that it was a pity we copied the BMW radiator grille! Then there was the 401/403 series; streamlined, wind tunnel tested body, making other contemporary cars look 'old hat'. The 405, our only four door ever made, suffered perhaps from doors which were too small, but how well the car held the road and so relaxing, in part due to the new overdrive reducing the rpm/mph ratio. With production of the 405 model running at three cars per week we also made a total of 50 in all of the short chassis 404, our only two seater and so rare that one newspaper commented that the only way to have a chance of seeing one was

to catch my car (MPH 100) in the paddocks of racing circuits! Incidentally this model 404 was the only car for which we produced production figures. Many inaccurate guesses and estimates of production figures for other Bristols have been made - all wrong! - as we have not used, for instance, consecutive chassis numbering. Suffice to say that in 55 years of production we have made less cars than one luxury car manufacturer has produced in a few months. No wonder our cars are so rarely seen, and are thus so exclusive.

The luxurious 406 model was a highlight because we, along with Jaguar, were the first manufacturers in the world to fit disc brakes. The additional weight of the 406 was offset by a slight increase in engine size. Rocket age performance came with the 407, our first V8, which was more than twice the engine size of the 406 2.2-litre, with coil spring suspension replacing the former transverse leaf spring. After exhaustive testing we brought out the 410, the first car we made with power steering. The additional speed of the larger engined 411 surprised the boy racers in the hatchbacks which were appearing. The greatest radical body shape change came with the introduction of the 412, the versatile coupé/saloon, and the 603 series which were both newly styled models. These proved as fast as previous models because they were fitted with further developed, smaller and lighter engines, and there was a general weight saving of the cars overall. They ran on unleaded fuel.

Testing the pre-production Beaufighter was most stimulating - the first British car, and second only to Saab, to be turbocharged. The first car was completed in the middle of one night and I only drove it for 400 miles in the dark before handing it over to *The Motor* first thing in the morning. With only 400 miles on the clock, a rather tight engine and only 'guess tuned', it swooped from 0-60mph in 6.7 seconds. When run-in the car was even faster and the fuel consumption was halved by the time we later lent it to the next magazine.

A while later the 603 and 412, (by that time the 412/S2,) series was replaced by three new models; the Britannia saloon, the turbocharged Brigand saloon and the turbocharged Beaufighter semi-convertible. Most road tests have been knowledgeably carried out, although some of the acceleration figures have been hand timed. There are a few howlers, such as that on one test the driver complained about wind noise on a 603, simply because he had wrongly used the air vent system.

Recently I visited our factory in Bristol where Bristols of all ages are attended to, or renovated, by the operators when they can be spared from the latest car production line. What memories!! I took out our very first car, my 1946 Type 400, then stepped into our latest car, the Blenheim 3, concluding that our fundamental aim to produce a fast, 'well mannered', roomy and safe, compact four-seater had not changed one iota. Nor have we had to make the cars any bigger outside. The Blenheim 3 is only one inch longer, and two inches wider, than the 401's of 1949 but it is a far more compact car than other manufacturers offering the same or less interior space.

After more than two and a quarter million miles on road and track, I am happy indeed to reflect that so many of them have been done with my involvement in every Bristol model since we started 55 years ago."
Tony Crook

CONTENTS

7	The Bristol 400	*Motor*	Nov	6	1946
11	Bristol Enterprise	*Autocar*	Jan	9	1948
14	2-Litre Bristol Type 400 Saloon Road Test	*Autocar*	Jan	9	1948
16	Anglo-Italian Accord	*Autocar*	Dec	5	1947
17	The Bristol Type 401	*Motor*	Nov	24	1948
20	West Country Specialities - 401	*Autocar*	Nov	26	1948
24	The Bristol 2-Litre Saloon	*Motor*	May	19	1948
26	The Bristol 2-Litre Model Mechanically Unchanged	*Motor*	Oct	13	1948
27	Bristol at New York Show - 401	*Motor*	Apr	5	1950
27	Evolution of the "401"	*Motor*	July	19	1950
32	Bristol Development - 401	*Autocar*	Oct	12	1951
33	The Bristol Type 401 Road Test	*Motor*			1952
36	Bristol 401 Saloon Road Test	*Autocar*	Mar	7	1952
39	By Bristol to Brescia - 401	*Motor*	May	28	1952
43	The Bristol 401 Road Test	*Motor Sport*	Jan		1953
46	The 2-Litre Bristol "401" Road Test	*Autosport*	Aug	1	1952
49	The Bristol 403 Saloon	*Motor*	May	13	1953
52	Bristol Evolves Still Further - 403	*Autocar*	May	15	1953
56	More Power for Bristol - 403	*Wheels*	June		1953
59	Bristol 403	*Automobile Topics*	Aug		1953
60	The Bristol "403" Road Test	*Autosport*	Aug	28	1953
63	A Modern Sports/Racing Car: The Bristol 450	*Motor Sport*	Aug		1953
65	Plucked From The Air - 1947 Bristol 400	*Wheels*	June		1988
66	The Bristol That Wouldn't Die - Bristol Farina	*Classic Cars*	Nov		1998
72	Aerodyne Bristol - 1951 Bristol 401	*NZ Classic Car*	July		1998
76	Plane Clothes - 402 Drophead	*Classic & Sports Car*	Dec		1987
81	The Bristol 403 Road Impressions	*Light Car*	Dec		1953
82	An Exciting New Bristol - 404	*Autocar*	Sept	25	1953
86	The "404" Bristol Coupé	*Autosport*	Oct	16	1953
89	The Bristol Type 404	*Motor*	Sept	30	1953
92	Bristol Fashion! - 403	*Autocar*	Mar	12	1954
93	Bristol Cream - Supercharged 403	*Autocar*	Apr	30	1954
94	Arnolt-Bristol	*Car Life*	Mar		1954
95	Collector's Piece - 404	*Autocar*	May	28	1954
100	The Lister-Bristol Road Test	*Autosport*	Aug	27	1954
102	The Bristol 450	*Car Life*	Aug		1954
103	Goodwill Mission - 403	*Autocar*	Sept	10	1954
107	A Four-Door Saloon from Bristol - 405	*Motor*	Oct	6	1954
110	Andean Episode - 401	*Autocar*	Nov	12	1954
111	Next in Sequence, the Bristol 405	*Autocar*	Oct	8	1954
114	To Spain in a Bristol - 403	*Motor Sport*	Dec		1954
118	The 1955 Lister Sports-Racing Car	*Autosport*	Mar	11	1955

120	Think of a Number! - 405	*Autocar*	May	20	1955
124	Arnolt's Sports Car	*Road & Track*	Mar		1955
125	Arnolt-Bristol & Bristol - 405	*Sports Car Annual*			1956
126	Arnolt-Bristol Driving Impressions	*Motor Trend*	Oct		1955
128	Bristol: Businessman's Express	*Sports Cars Illustrated*	Nov		1955
132	New For Fall - Arnolt-Bristol Coupé	*Road & Track*	Oct		1955
133	Looking at Lakeland Passes with a Bristol 405	*Motor Sport*	Feb		1956
136	The Arnolt-Bristol for Competition Road Test	*Road & Track*	Feb		1956
138	The Bristol 405	*Motor Trend*	Oct		1956
140	SCI Tests the Arnolt-Bristol Road Test	*Sports Cars Illustrated*	July		1956
145	Bristol 405 Drophead Coupé	*World Cars*			1957
145	Bristol - An "Export Only" 2¼-Litre Type 406	*Motor*	Oct	2	1957
146	Arnolt-Bristol Driving Impressions	*Motor Trend*	June		1958
149	The New Bristol 406	*Motor*	Aug	27	1958
153	Bristol 406 with Four-Wheel Disc Brakes	*Sports Cars Illustrated*	Oct		1958
154	Seventh of the Line - 406	*Autocar*	Aug	29	1958
158	Bristol - 406	*Cars of the World*			1960
159	Used Cars on the Road - 1952 Bristol 401	*Autocar*	Jan	29	1960
160	New Cars - 407	*Sporting Motorist*	Oct		1961
161	Best of Both Worlds - 408 & Jensen C-V8 Mk II	*Classic & Sports Car*	Dec		1984
164	Bristol Sixes - 400 to 406	*Classic & Sports Car*	Oct		1990
172	Club Class - 406 & Alvis TF21	*Classic & Sports Car*	Aug		2000
177	Bristol 407	*Autocar*	Sept	8	1961
180	The Bristol 407	*Motor*	Sept	6	1961
183	Bristol 407 Road Test	*Autocar*	Oct	6	1961
187	Bristol Gets a V8 - 407	*Motor*	Sept	13	1961
188	The Bristol 407 Road Test	*Motor*	Sept	13	1961
192	Bristol 450: Great Unknown	*Car and Driver*	Feb		1962
196	Close-Up: Bristol's 407 GT Zagato	*Sports Car World*	May		1962
200	Bristol Build - But Air Inspired	*Sporting Motorist*	Oct		1962
206	Automatic GT - Forecast for the Future	*Road & Track*	Feb		1962
208	Bristol 407 Road Test	*Autosport*	Jan	4	1963
210	Bristol 407	*World Car Catalogue*			1963
211	Bristol 408	*Autocar*	Sept	27	1963
212	The Bristol 408	*Motor*	Sept	25	1963
213	Used Cars on the Road - 1960 Bristol 406	*Autocar*	Nov	27	1964
214	Bristol 408	*World Car Catalogue*			1964
215	Bristol 408 Road Test	*Cars Illustrated*	Dec		1964
218	A Lighter Swifter Bristol - 409	*Motor*	Oct	23	1965
219	Bristol 409	*Autocar*	Oct	22	1965
220	Bristol 409	*World Car Catalogue*			1967
221	Not-so Fashionable Bristol	*Car*	Sept		1967

224	The Bristol 410 Road Test	*Autosport*	Dec	8	1967
226	Bristol 410	*World Car Catalogue*			1969
227	The Bristol 411	*World Car Guide*	Dec		1969
228	Fastest True Four-Seater Touring Car - 411 Road Test	*Autosport*	Aug	20	1970
230	British as Boiled Beef - Bristol 411	*Wheels*	Feb		1973
234	And Now a Quick Look at Setright's Bristols	*Car*	Jan		1974
238	Bristol: Simple Superiority? - 412	*Car*	July		1975
241	Flat-Out, Blow-Out	*Motor*	Mar	1	1975
242	Bristol 412 Convertible	*Bristol Cars*			
243	New Bristol 412	*Motor*	May	17	1975
244	Bristol of Filton	*Motor Sport*	Aug		1975
247	Convertible Bristol - 412	*Motor Manual*	Aug		1975
248	Bristol Fashion 412 Road Test	*Motor*	Mar	5	1977
253	Western Expansion 411 Replaced by New-Style 603	*Autocar*	Oct	16	1976
253	Long, Narrow and British	*Autosport*	Oct	14	1976
254	The Hypertourers - Bristol 412 vs. Ferrari 400 Auto vs. Aston Martin Lagonda Comparison Test	*Car and Driver*	June		1977
260	Bristol 603 - S3 Road Test	*Motor*	Sept	2	1978
266	Bristol 412 Convertible V8	*Car*	June		1977
267	Bespoke Express - 603	*Motor*	Nov	27	1977
268	Return of the Beaufighter Feature Test	*Autocar*	Jan	12	1980
270	The Blown Bristol Beaufighter Road Test	*Motor*	Jan	12	1980
273	Bristol Beaufighter	*Motor Sport*	Oct		1981
275	The Brigand Flies In	*Autocar*	Oct	16	1982
276	Exclusivity in Extremis! - Brigand	*Motor Sport*	Jan		1984
278	New from Bristol...	*Autocar*	Oct	23	1982
279	Bristol Beaufighter	*Road & Track Specials*			1985
282	Rule Britannia	*Motor*	Nov	1	1986
289	The Beaufighter Turbocharged Convertible	*Bristol Cars*			
290	Bristol Fashion	*Performance Car*	June		1991
292	New Bristol Shock! - Blenheim	*Autocar*	Sept	15	1993
296	A Bristol Man	*Autocar*	Apr	17	1985
297	Bristol Fashion is Still Shipshape - Blenheim	*Autocar*	Aug	7	1996
298	Blenheim Palace	*Top Gear*	Aug		1998
300	Lap of Luxury - 411 & R-R Silver Shadow	*Classic & Sports Car*	Jan		1999
304	Bristol Cream - Types 407 to 411	*Classic & Sports Car*	May		1986
310	Souls of Discretion - All Significant Models	*Classic & Sports Car*	May		1996
316	Bristol Unveils Beefier Blenheim	*Autocar*	Oct	20	1999
317	Bristol Blenheim 3	*Bristol Cars*	Nov	10	1999
318	Bristol Fashion - Fighter	*Autocar*	Dec	1	1999

The Bristol 400

A two-litre car of outstanding qualities and performance

GOOD-LOOKER. — This two-door four-seater saloon body of the new Bristol is a good example of modern coachwork form. It will be supplemented in the range by a cabriolet having similar lines.

The outstanding statistical feature is undoubtedly the remarkable figure of 77 b.h.p. per ton, this being over 40 per cent. better than the average of comparable cars listed in "The Motor" specifications Indeed, the margin of superiority is so great that it would be suspect if it were derived entirely from abnormal power output In fact, however, the car represents a very acceptable compromise on this score, for whereas the figure of 2.67 h.p. per sq. in. of piston area is 26.5 per cent. better than average, it is not so high as to cause any difficulties on the score of loss of tune or unreliability On the other hand, the dry weight figure of 22 cwt. is remarkably low, and has only been achieved by the utmost study of detail, as will be disclosed in the ensuing technical description.

The combination of 85 b.h.p. with this low weight enables outstanding performance to be realized. The 1939 edition of this power unit would, for instance, propel a closed car at over 90 m.p.h., whereas the average speed for all British cars in the same category was 73 m.p.h. Perhaps of even greater value in year-to-year running is the fact that at 2,500 f.p.m piston speed the Bristol is cruising at 77.5 m.p.h., whereas the class average (again according to "The Motor" 1946 speci-

I T is often said that the automobile industry of the world has reached a point where it is no longer possible successfully to introduce an entirely new type of car. There are, however, certain exceptions to test this rule both in this country and on the Continent, a remarkable example in Europe being the development of a design laid down by two young Austrians for the B.M.W. Co. This development reached its apotheosis in the period 1939-40, in which the sports version of this design with inclined overhead valves ran fifth in the Le Mans 24-hour race of 1939 with a remarkable average speed of 82.5 m.p.h., the same type of car subsequently averaging 103.59 m.p.h. and over 17 m.p.g. to win the Italian 1,000-mile race on the Brescia circuit in 1940.

It is, of course, well known that slightly modified versions of these cars, known as the Frazer-Nash-B.M.W., achieved remarkable successes in this country, not only in speed events but also in reliability trials over very rough going. Every automobile enthusiast must, therefore, have rejoiced to read the announcement made some time ago that the Bristol Aeroplane Co were making plans to continue production in England through the medium of A.F.N., Ltd., in which they now have a majority shareholding.

Some Impressive Figures

The pro and con of putting into production, after a lapse of eight years, an existing type, as compared with starting from a clean sheet of paper, has been frequently argued, but in individual cases the decision must obviously be determined by the merit of the design under review and its relation to comparable current automobiles It may, therefore, be of interest to set out the data for the Bristol design in relation to the average cars between 1½-litres and 2½-litres capacity which are now marketed.

BRISTOL DATA

Model	400 Saloon	Model	400 Saloon
Engine Dimensions		Prop. shaft	Hardy Spicer
Cylinders	6	Final drive	Spiral bevel
Bore	66 mm.		
Stroke	96 mm.	**Chassis Details**	
Cubic capacity	1,971 c.c.	Brakes	Lockheed
Piston area	31.8 sq. ins.	Brake drum diameter	11 ins.
Valves	Inclined overhead	Friction lining area	147 sq. ins.
Compression ratio	7.25 : 1	Suspension : Front	Independent transverse leaf
Engine Performance		Rear	Live axle with torsion bar
Max. b.h.p.	85	Shock absorbers	Bristol
at	4,500 r.p.m.	Wheel type	Pierced disc
Max b.m.e.p.	138	Tyre size	5.50 by 16
at	3,000 r.p.m.	Steering gear	Rack and pinion
B.H.P. per sq. in. piston area	2.67	Steering wheel	Spring spoke, 17 ins. diameter
Peak piston speed, ft. per min.	2,835	**Dimensions**	
Engine Details		Wheelbase	9 ft. 6 ins.
Carburetter	Triple S.U.	Track : Front	4 ft. 4 ins.
Ignition	Coil	Rear	4 ft. 6 ins.
Plugs : Make and type	A.C., 10 mm.	Overall length	14 ft. 2 ins.
Fuel pump	U.G.	Overall width	5 ft. 5 ins.
Fuel capacity	12 gallons	Overall height	5 ft.
Oil filter (make, by-pass or full flow)	Tecalemit full-flow filter	Ground clearance	6½ ins.
Oil capacity	10 pints	Turning circle	36 ft.
Cooling system	Fan and pump	Dry weight	22 cwt.
Water capacity	17 pints	**Performance data**	
Electrical system	72 amps.	Piston area, sq. in. per ton	29 sq. ins.
Battery capacity	20 hrs.	Brake lining area, sq. in. per ton	134 sq. ins.
Transmission		Top gear m.p.h. per 1,000 r.p.m.	19.5
Clutch	Borg and Beck, 8 ins.	Top gear m.p.h. at 2,500 ft./min. piston speed	77.5
Gear ratios : Top	3.9	Litres per ton-mile, dry	2,755
3rd	5.07		
2nd	8.48		
1st	16.77		
Rev.	13.43		

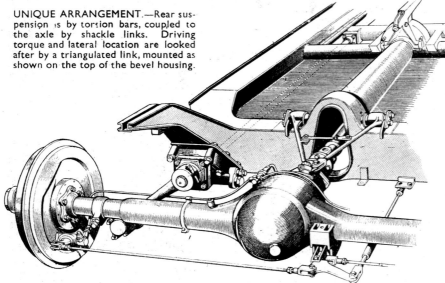

engine has a more direct inlet porting system than the Bristol, but it is of equal importance to observe that cooling on the exhaust side has been given careful attention. There is water around the full circumference of both the exhaust port and the guide, and heat transfer from the seat is materially aided by the use of a light-alloy casting for the head, This in turn involves the use of shrunk-in inserts for the valve seats and a threaded insert for the rather deeply masked sparking plug. This is of 10 mm. diameter, and the mask, it is interesting to note, is the full diameter of the thread

The general layout of the head also offers a secondary advantage which is not lightly to be disregarded, viz., that by carrying the main casting up to the level of the rocker shafts, its depth

fications tables) is 64.2 m.p.h. In other words, the safe sustained speed of the Bristol is not only 13 m.p.h. more than average for the class, but, even more remarkable, is 4½ m.p.h. higher than the average maximum of 1938-39 models. When one adds that the basic design is renowned for lightness and accuracy of control, reliability and extreme length of life, it is obvious that the new Bristol can start life with unusually strong claims to be entitled a car of the first order.

An Ingenious Mechanism

Turning now to the engine and chassis details, it will be found that, well proved as they are, they show a number of departures from the orthodox.

The power unit, for example, has a single chain-driven camshaft mounted in the block, but also embodies valves inclined at 60 degrees in the cylinder head. Each inlet valve is worked directly through a push rod and rocker, but the exhaust-valve mechanism includes, in addition, transverse push-rods carrying the motion from the camshaft across the head. This ingenious mechanism is fully disclosed in a perspective drawing of the engine, from which one can at the same time observe the remarkably good flow characteristics of the paired induction ports. These breathe through three downdraught S.U. carburetters, and although the engine is conservatively rated for road use, it is easily possible by carburetter adjustments to raise the m.e.p. to well over 130 lb. per sq. in. at 5,000 r.p.m. It is safe to say that no other

is sufficient to afford great stiffness as a beam, and hence distortion, with subsequent irregular running or even gasket failure, is avoided.

Saving Weight

Stiffness is also a keynote of the cylinder block, although at the same time every effort has been made to keep the dimensions to a minimum, with a view to weight saving. It is, indeed, somewhat remarkable that with the cylinder bores accounting for an aggregate of 15.6 ins. the total length of the block is only 20 ins., although there is a reasonable water space between each pair of cylinders; that is, above each main bearing. It can, of course, be deduced from these figures that the four main bearings themselves are somewhat narrow (1 in. at the centre and 1.25 ins. approximately at the ends), but ample bearing area is provided by virtue of having a shaft

2 ins. in diameter. The shaft is hardened, and the bearings are the copper-lead strip type produced by Vandervell.

The steel connecting rods are short (stroke × 1.71), and are drilled to provide full-pressure lubrication right up to the gudgeon pin.

The pins are mounted somewhat lower in the piston than is usual and are retained by circlips. The pistons in themselves are also of interest, for they are made by Specialloids from pressings, a construction which offers particular advantages in light weight, with metal of excellent grain flow and consequent high strength, particularly at elevated temperatures

"Oil Cooling"

The lubrication system is very thoroughly carried out and includes a full-flow filter and a temperature stabilizer. The latter consists of a finned tube placed the full length of the water intake, which is low down on the exhaust side of the cylinder block. In normal running, and particularly when starting from cold, the cooling fluid imparts heat to the oil, thus promoting a reasonable viscosity in the lubricant, whilst under conditions of prolonged high-speed running the heat balance tends to change over, thus preventing any excessively high oil temperature without involving the use of a separate external oil cooler.

The crankshaft is fully counter-weighted, and damped torsionally by a disc at the front end, which is rubber bonded on to a pressing of slightly larger diameter, which, in turn, is connected to the fan-belt pulley.

Other interesting constructional features of the engine are the use of a Bristol designed and made disc-type air filter and silencer, to which are connected the breather pipes of the engine, fumes being absorbed in this way, and the inlet-valve guides provided with a slight oil mist.

The engine, complete with dynamo, starter and flywheel, weighs only 353 lb. The derived figures of 4.15 lb. per h.p. and 179 lb. per litre both being exceptionally good, the latter particularly so on this size of power unit.

The clutch, which is a conventional single-plate type, transmits the torque into a four-speed gearbox, which is again completely constructed by the Bristol organization. Synchromesh engagement is provided for all the upper three ratios, which have helical teeth, but it is interesting to observe that first gear has

FULL WIDTH.—As a consequence of using sliding windows the door can be curved, giving valuable extra body space. The length of the door is sufficient to provide easy entry to the rear seats

straight teeth. Moreover, the construction is such that when (and only when) first gear is engaged a free wheel is operative. It is thus possible to engage first gear instantly at any road speed, irrespective of engine speed and without necessarily touching the clutch pedal. This feature can be of particular importance, not only in trials work, but also under emergencies of mountain climbing and other extreme touring conditions.

Chassis Details

The gearbox in itself is notable for having a centre main bearing, the casing being split vertically to permit assembly, a feature rarely found on modern cars. The transmission embodies yet another interesting detail in the offtake shaft internally splined, and the propeller shaft is mated to it, the splines thus being enclosed and running constantly in oil.

The bevel drive and rear axle casing do not in themselves call for any special comment, but the location of the axle on the frame and the rear suspension are special to this design of car. As neither leaf spring nor a torque tube is employed, it is necessary to locate the axle laterally and also to provide some means of driving the car. Both of these functions are embraced by a short triangulated link which has its apex on the bevel housing and terminates in two swinging bearings mounted on the rear end of the frame. At first sight one would feel that these bearings would be very heavily loaded, but the construction has now been tested for many years and has fully justified itself as a light and simple solution of an often difficult problem. The roll centre of the car at the rear is, of course, somewhat higher than usual.

The rear suspension itself is by a single arm on each side of the car connected to a torsion bar 0.805 in. in diameter and 59.4 ins. long, the remote anchorage of which is a splined member placed approximately in the middle of the frame.

The hydraulic shock absorbers, which are of piston type and of Bristol manufacture, are directly operated by the suspension arms. Similarly, dampers are incorporated in the front suspension, which consists of a pair of upper wishbones, the lower link being provided by a transverse leaf spring grooved

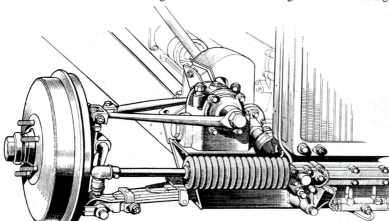

SIMPLICITY.—The I.F.S. and control gear has a minimum number of parts, direction being provided by a rack and pinion gear and suspension by a transverse spring grooved to reduce weight.

for the dual purposes of weight and cost reduction.

The wheels are directionally controlled by the increasingly popular rack-and-pinion mechanism, which is placed forward of the wheel centre. A fabric universal joint is interposed between the pinion and the steering column, thus isolating the latter from any slight distortions. The frame is, in point of fact, immensely stiff both as a beam and in torsion.

As shown in a drawing, the side members, together with the front and rear cross members, are fully box sectioned, and although of only 14 gauge, the frame is 6.5 ins. deep over the centre section, and has two tabular cross bracing members at its mid-point. It is of interest that the main part of the frame stops short approximately 15 ins. ahead of the rear axle and has two light pressings extending backwards as body supports.

The installation of steering, engine and pedals is such that either right-hand or left-hand drive can be offered, the hand brake being centrally mounted. This connects to the rear wheels through rods in tension, the pedal operating a Lockheed system with two leading shoes.

Specially designed Lucas electrical equipment is employed, including a starter in which a solenoid places the pinion in mesh with the flywheel before the starter motor is activated.

Body Types

Two standard types of body will be offered in the range, the saloon shown in the photographs and a cabriolet having similar lines. It will be seen that its shape is the modern cleaned-up type, in which the drag is sensibly reduced (by immersion of the head lamps into the wings, for example), although true aerodynamic form has not been sought.

Constructionally, the body is of interest in the use of light-alloy panelling to reduce weight, and it also incorporates many features which will appeal to the enthusiastic driver. For example, speedometer and tachometer have plainly read circular dials, and the whole front of the panel can be quickly removed to expose the instruments for removal or service if required. A radio set is an integral feature, as is an electrically driven ventilating fan which can draw cold air from the nose of the car, or hot air from a muff around the exhaust pipe, at the choice of the driver.

The two-door body allows reasonable access to the rear seats, and although the luggage accommodation is somewhat impaired by stowing the spare wheel internally, this feature will be considered by many justified on the grounds of appearance.

From what has been said it will be evident that, even though the Bristol 400 may be said to have its origins in a pre-war design, it is nevertheless an entirely up-to-date car of very high performance. The basic design is well-tried, and the 1946 version has behind it all the war-time experience of the Bristol Aeroplane Co. with light structures and high-output internal-combustion engines, experience which no other British firm can claim to possess over such a wide field.

This is a car which, in respect of bodywork, chassis features and performance, should have an international appeal, and both A.F.N., Ltd., and Bristol Aeroplane

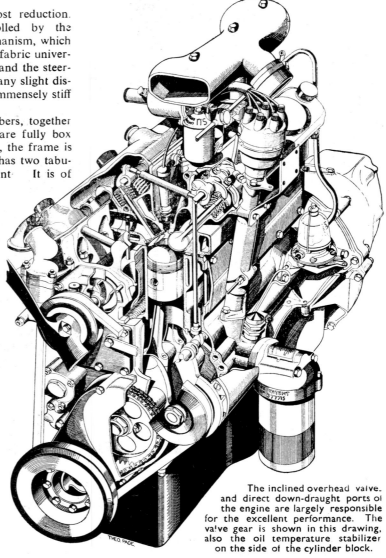

The inclined overhead valve. and direct down-draught ports of the engine are largely responsible for the excellent performance. The valve gear is shown in this drawing, also the oil temperature stabilizer on the side of the cylinder block.

Co., Ltd., are to be congratulated on their initiative in getting it into production so quickly. Deliveries will commence in the early part of 1947, meanwhile, intensive road testing of pre-production models is continuing, both in this country and under the arduous conditions of Continental travel.

In addition to the Bristol 400, A.F.N., Ltd., and The Bristol Aeroplane Co., Ltd., are to produce a sports 2-seater Frazer-Nash. The same engine unit is employed in both cars, but in the sports version the compression ratio is 8.5 to 1, this and other detail changes increasing the power output to 100 b.h.p. at 5,000 r.p.m.

The sports Frazer-Nash model uses a tubular chassis frame, the wheelbase of 7 ft. 10½ ins. and the track of 4 ft. being appreciably below the dimensions of the Bristol saloon and cabriolet. The weight of the Frazer-Nash is only 16 cwt., and, geared to 21.4 m.p.h. per 1,000 r.p.m., this model promises to have a quite outstanding performance. The figure of 3,450 litres per ton mile, in conjunction with an engine developing a peak b.m.e.p. of 150 lb. per sq. in., guarantees remarkable top-gear acceleration, while the fact that 2,500 ft. per minute piston speed corresponds to a cruising speed of 85 m.p.h., shows that speed has not been sacrificed to acceleration.

The subject of this article, the Type 400 2-litre Bristol coupé, with another member of the family, the Brigand torpedo bomber.

BRISTOL ENTERPRISE

How a World-famous British Aircraft Firm Has Turned Its Abilities to Making an Outstanding Quality Car : Production and Driving Impressions

BOTH in this country and in the United States, which are the two greatest producers of aircraft in the world, not excepting Russia, there has been the fundamental difficulty on the reversion to peacetime conditions of maintaining the capacities of the huge aircraft establishments built up so laboriously and at such cost for the war. Government contracts for thousands of fighters and bombers have ceased. Civilian air liners are needed only in hundreds. And so the aircraft world has inevitably turned to other fields in engineering. One of these has been cars.

In the United States, government contracts were cancelled automatically by the end of the war and there was a scramble to find alternative engineering outlets. Thus North American and Lockheed tried somewhat unsuccessfully to turn to the private aircraft. Consolidated now make marine engines, buses and even a combined car and aircraft. Northrops formed satellite companies to make jet engines, motor scooters, and artificial limbs. There was considerable unemployment; yet none dared to try to produce a new make of car.

In Britain the changeover has been less harsh and somewhat better planned by the more gradual reduction of contracts. Also, because of our preference for an individual type of car, at least one firm, the Bristol Aeroplane Company, has been able to divert some of its skill and experience to the manufacture of a new make of car on a small production scale. Needless to say, this is not the only novel post-war activity of that extensive concern, one of whose factories is mass-producing pre-fabricated houses; whilst the aircraft divisions (engines and airframes) are even more in the public eye with the Brabazon, Britain's largest landplane, due to fly this year, and with the development of their helicopter. Other interests include British Messier and—with Rolls-Royce—Rotols.

In a recent article in *Flight* on the air transports of today and tomorrow, H. F. King gave an authoritative commentary on the Brabazon air liner as follows:—

." In the Brabazon we shall have the most advanced, if not strictly the largest, of the big landplanes, and what is most important, one designed for the specific task of maintaining a transatlantic service. By far the largest landplane to be constructed in Great Britain (there are people who firmly predict that no larger will ever be built), it was planned to provide totally new standards in performance, load capacity, and passenger comfort. The Bristol design staff have boldly addressed themselves to immense technical problems. . . ."

Faced with the almost national responsibility of making a success of such a unique undertaking—failure is inconceivable—Bristol's doubtless turned to what has sometimes been regarded as another very stormy sea, the business of making and selling cars, with comparative equanimity! The car project was first announced in 1945 and a complete technical description followed the next year (*The Autocar*, September 9, 1946). Deliveries began in mid-1947 and now production is well into its stride. Already the 2-litre Bristol fixed-head coupé is beginning to be seen on our roads (only one model is made) and in this issue the first road impressions and performance data are given.

Let it be said straight away that although Bristol's have not attempted to create a unique car design, they are already in production with an outstanding British car in the quality field. That was their object, and it has been achieved in a comparatively short time.

Of course, when the bulk of the production of a new firm goes overseas it is difficult for the average motorist in

In this final assembly shop, body frames and panels are fitted before passing to upholstery trim. On the right are chassis with extra sub-frames to take special coachwork.

this country to estimate its progress. Few Bristols have been seen about and people were inclined to wonder what was happening with the new car. The truth is that plenty of Bristols are going through in the various parts of the aircraft factory now allotted to this purpose and an expanding organization is being built up.

A visit to the aircraft and car factory, which covers several square miles on a hill-top on the outskirts of Bristol city, reveals something of the complication of starting production of a completely new car. When that factory also works to aircraft standards of metallurgy and of inspection, and sets out to build almost all parts itself, then that task is increased. But equally such a policy is likely to pay in the long run, although only a firm with very large financial and engineering resources could undertake it. Bristol's have both these necessities.

Major components not made by Bristol's are the Lucas electrical equipment, the Borg and Beck clutch and Lockheed brakes, the propeller-shaft and tyres. Finally, it has already been found in practice that when difficulties of construction or of research are met, consultation with their own aircraft division can often find a rapid solution, as just that problem may have been the subject of lengthy research for aircraft, especially in the usage of light alloys.

Distinguished Company

The car engines are assembled in a plant adjoining the aero engine works, where the huge radials in the Hercules and Centaurus series are built. Complex casting is a subject about which a firm making 2,600 h.p. aircraft engines, including turbo-jets, knows plenty and the initial difficulties with the car engine's aluminium alloy twin rocker-box head and the cast iron cylinder block have been strenuously tackled. Crankshaft balancing machinery was installed and in general personnel from the aircraft side have taken readily to their various new tasks.

The carburettor installations available are a single Solex system or three S.U.s with the S.U. electric starting carburettor. The gear box casing, which splits vertically and not horizontally, as is usual but less convenient for assembly, is of aluminium alloy, but apart from the engine and gear box there is not an unusual use of light alloys. The all-steel chassis, which has side members of generously proportioned welded-up box section joined by a tray making it a unit is most sturdy, but as a result of its short, square proportions is not unduly heavy.

The body design is entirely Bristol's own. It is really a fixed-head two-seater, but, instead of devoting the space behind the seats to luggage only, fully upholstered rear seats are provided for two more passengers. Although leg room is limited there was no complaint from two passengers who tried the rear seat over twenty miles or so, when the car was driven on the road by the writer. The body frame is of ash covered with steel sheet. The very short chassis frame, which is all contained within the wheelbase, has no rear overhang; so in order to accommodate special coachwork, such as the Pinin Farina drop-head coupé (*The Autocar*, December 5, 1947), an extended subframe is added both at the rear and at the sides to carry fashionable full-width coachwork.

The standard fixed-head coupé, the frame, panelling and upholstery trim are all carried out at Bristol, and quite a number of engines, chassis and bodies can be seen going through at all stages, as the photograph above of the final assembly shop shows. A large-scale production is not envisaged, as the conception of the car is as a hand-built one for the connoisseur and one that will maintain British reputation for thorough quality. If an estimate were to be made, one does not envisage a peak production of more than four figures.

In some ways it was a surprise not to find more obvious application of aircraft engineer's thinking applied to cars. Perhaps this will come when the new Car Division has more experience, and then this country will be able to join in the development of a lightweight, streamlined, stressed skin car of the future, which seems bound to come. However, one can sympathize with the manufacturer starting out on this industrial adventure for not taking on too much at once. Bristol themselves call their design "a commonsense compromise." And one must acknowledge the real excellence of the result, which is based on so well-tried and admirable a chassis as the B.M.W., but which, for the moment, somewhat sacrifices weight considerations to durability and serviceability.

Weight, incidentally, is nearly 26 cwt, which, considering that the engine would previously have been rated as a sixteen, says much for a design which can do an easy 85 m.p.h. with four up.

The feeling obtained in trying the Bristol over more

The ability behind the construction of the Bristol car can be measured by the type of project on which the Bristol Aeroplane Company is engaged. This exclusive photograph poses the new car beside one of the greatest engineering ventures in Britain today, the Brabazon 224 - seater transatlantic air liner, to have eight engines, a wing span of 230 feet and to weigh 128 tons. In other workshops on the hill behind this enormous hangar, Bristol cars are already coming off the line.

The cars are made by a separate Car and Light Engineering Division of the aircraft company. Chiefly responsible are Major George Abell (right), the general manager, who was once with Invicta, and Mr. George White (left), assistant managing director of the holding company and son of Sir Stanley White, Bart., the chairman. Both are keen and active motorists and are seen with a model of the twin 20mm cannon turret for which their new division is also responsible.

than 500 miles of fast driving was that the specification had been chosen by people who like fast cars of the style appealing to the most discriminating of motorists. Thus it is interesting to find as general manager of the Car and Light Engineering Division of the Bristol Aeroplane Company Major George Abell, who, before he joined B.A.C. in 1933, was managing director of Invictas in the days when they were making that famous and still so much admired low-slung 100 m.p.h. model. Also closely associated with him now are two keen and young motorists, George White and W. R. Verdon Smith, who are on the board of the Car Division and who are also assistant managing directors of the main holding company.

The Bristol is the sort of car which one looks forward to driving as a special and pleasurable experience. The essence of its quality is its road-holding ability, which is excellent. The chassis and suspension are surely an outstandingly successful piece of design. It has become a cliché to refer to accurate steering over the proverbial sixpence, but the Bristol can be placed with exactness when cornering, probably largely because of the effectiveness of the independent front-wheel suspension in reducing the unsteadying effects of camber and uneven road surfaces. The ride is firm but not harsh, and the front seats are deep and comfortable. But they seem set rather low because of the low roof line and high waistline of the "intimate" body, which, with its sliding (not winding) windows and curved rear window, gives something of the impression of an aircraft cabin.

Much of the mileage covered was at night, and with the powerful lamps and with car radio and heater operating, long distances were driven tirelessly, especially as the engine gives a wide range of cruising speeds up to and even beyond the seventies.

With the roads freer than previously as a result of the basic petrol cut, it was possible to get near to maximum on several occasions, and, as stated above, 85 m.p.h. was reached easily even with four up. To better 90 m.p.h. requires rather more road than is usually available among normal traffic. The highest reading, on a *slow* speedometer, was 89 m.p.h. at about 4,300 r.p.m.

As to average speeds obtained, the best section at night was between Newbury and London on the way from the works to Town, when 51 miles were covered at an average of 43 m.p.h., and again on another occasion just south of Stratford-on-Avon, when 22 miles were covered in the half-hour. The best run in daylight was from Broadway into London, in two hours: 86 miles, which included stops to take some photographs, and yet gave a 43 m.p.h. average. The best daylight section was nearly 26 miles in half an hour, or 51 to 52 m.p.h. At these high maintained speeds the petrol consumption was between 21 and 22 m.p.g. But such commonplace average speeds for a fast car could be improved on considerably if complete concentration were given to obtaining performance only.

Without doubt the Bristol Aeroplane Company at the first attempt have produced an outstanding British car.

J. D.

No. 1343

2-LITRE BRISTOL

TYPE 400

SALOON

The Autocar ROAD TESTS

DATA FOR THE DRIVER

2-LITRE BRISTOL TYPE 400

PRICE, with two-door fixed-head saloon body, £1,525, plus £848 14s 6d purchase tax, total £2,373 14s 6d.

RATING : 16.2 h.p., six cylinders, overhead valves, 66 × 96 mm. (1,971 c.c.) **TAX,** £10.

BRAKE HORSE-POWER : 80 at 4,200 r.p.m. **COMPRESSION RATIO :** 7.5 to 1.

WEIGHT, without passengers, 25 cwt 1 qr 2 lb. **LB. PER C.C. :** 1.44.

TYRE SIZE : 5.50 × 16in on bolt-on steel wheels.

LIGHTING SET : 12-volt. Automatic voltage control.

TANK CAPACITY : 12 gallons, approx. fuel consumption range, 22-26 m.p.g.

TURNING CIRCLE : 37ft 6in (L. and R.). **MIN. GROUND CLEARANCE :** 7in.

MAIN DIMENSIONS : Wheelbase, 9ft 6in. ; track, 4ft 3½in (front) ; 4ft 6in (rear).
Overall length, 15ft 3in ; width, 5ft 4in ; height, 4ft 11in.

ACCELERATION

Overall gear ratios	From steady m.p.h. of		
	10 to 30	20 to 40	30 to 50
3.90 to 1	13.8 sec.	13.6 sec.	13.8 sec.
5.07 to 1	9.1 sec.	8.7 sec.	8.7 sec.
8.48 to 1	5.6 sec.	5.6 sec.	—
16.77 to 1	—	—	—

From rest through gears to :—

30 m.p.h...	..	.. 5.6 sec.
50 m.p.h...	..	.. 13.5 sec.
60 m.p.h...	..	.. 19.1 sec.
70 m.p.h...	..	.. 28.6 sec.

Steering wheel movement from lock to lock : 3 turns.

Speedometer correction by Electrical Speedometer : 10 (car speedometer) = 10.5 ; 20 = 20.5 ; 30 = 30.5 ; 40 = 40.5 ; 50 = 50.5 ; 60 = 60.5 ; 70 = 71 ; 80 = 82.

Speeds attainable on indirect M.p.h. gears (by Electrical Speedo- (normal meter) .. .. .. and max.)

1st	..	..	..	16—22
2nd	..	..	..	33—43
3rd	..	..	..	55—68

WEATHER : Mild, wet surface, fresh wind.

Acceleration figures are the means of several runs in opposite directions.

Current model described in " The Autocar " of September 6, 1946.

PROLONGED road experience of the 2-litre Bristol has been awaited with especial eagerness. As is well known, this car, built by the Car Division of the Bristol Aeroplane Company, with all the resources behind it that are implied, follows the design of the pre-war Frazer Nash-B.M.W., which had a considerable following among those who appreciate the finer points of motoring.

The British-built version, now in production, retains all those characteristics which then appealed—the easy high-speed performance on an exceptionally high top gear ratio, fine road holding, and an outstanding factor of safety. In addition, it has, of course, a British body made by Bristol's themselves and British equipment. Under present conditions the car cannot be other than expensive, carrying as it does the burden of double purchase tax, but in return the buyer obtains a connoisseur's car, attractive to look upon, comfortable to ride in and a constant delight to handle because of the accuracy of control and responsiveness of the performance. The 2-litre Bristol is a car which can live with almost anything on the road, a machine far removed from the ordinary run of cars. It is, too, a design of proved efficiency.

From the first moment of acquaintance one realizes that here is a high-spirited, extremely willing performer of sports character, but at the same time a car which is tractable given reasonable use of the gear box. The six-cylinder engine is silkily smooth and has a sufficient suggestion of exhaust note when revved up to make the car sound "interesting," but not enough to cause it to attract unwelcome attention ; at speed there is some mechanical and wind noise.

The Bristol can be cruised at any speed up to 80 m.p.h. without sense of effort, a characteristic upon which passengers as well as the driver remark, and it will achieve an extremely high average even over roads that are not specially helpful. Sheer maximum speed is not by any means everything, but it is none the less satisfying that during _The Autocar_ Road Test a speed in excess of 90 m.p.h. was achieved by electrical speedometer—in point of fact, 91-92. This was on virtually level ground in the favourable direction of the wind. It is a fine performance which would indicate that aerodynamically the shape of the car must be efficient.

It is to be particularly noted that the speedometer read _slow_ throughout the range of speed, and even when the Bristol was being shown by _The Autocar's_ fifth-wheel-driven master speedometer to be exceeding 90 m.p.h. the car's own speedometer did not go beyond 89. The car was not specially prepared in advance with *The Autocar* Road Test in prospect, and it is to be emphasized that weather conditions, with wet surfaces, were decidedly adverse to the recording of the performance figures, especially the through-the-gears acceleration.

An ignition setting control enables a position to be obtained for town running where there is no pinking even on the present fuel; towards and at the fully advanced position there is noticeably greater liveliness of the engine and some pinking then occurs, though not to an excessive extent. At no time was running-on experienced.

During various phases of this long-distance test by *The Autocar*, extending over nearly a fortnight, the Bristol was handled by various members of the staff, in addition to those who normally conduct the Road Tests. It has been driven in London traffic, and has been used under everyday conditions; it has been taken on straightaway fast main road journeys.

From all this varied use the Bristol emerges in such a way as more than to confirm preconceived opinion based on knowledge of its predecessor. In other words, it is a "real car," safe, swift and completely under control whatever the circumstances. It holds the driver's interest all the time, even in traffic, and yet does not make undue demands on him, though flexibility at low speed would not be expected on a top gear ratio as high as 3.9 to 1. It is a joy to start in the morning—to hear the efficient-sounding engine come to life, and throughout a run, fast or slow—though naturally fast, such are the car's capabilities—it gives motoring on the highest plane.

Steering, braking and road holding are just as the enthusiastic driver of fast cars would specify. The rack and pinion steering, though light, has at all times the desirable positiveness to afford a feeling of confidence. There is good self-return action after taking a corner. Yet the steering is so light as to make manoeuvring really easy, in conjunction with a good lock. The Lockheed hydraulic brakes perform in the manner expected of this system; the latest two-leading-shoe type is fitted in front. On several occasions during the testing when rapid deceleration had to be effected very high marks were given to the braking for the smooth and sure manner in which the speed was brought down. A fly-off type of hand brake lever is placed most conveniently between the front seats. As regards road holding the car feels exactly right and can be cornered extremely fast without roll or any feeling of insecurity. Yet the suspension—independent in front by means of a transverse leaf spring—is never harsh, and the

A bonnet-ful of efficient engine, with its three S.U. carburettors. The appearance of a twin overhead camshaft is given by the rocker boxes in V formation, but the valve operation is by push rods. The reservoir for the one-shot chassis lubrication and connections for the interior heater will be noticed.

car rides in a particularly level way at high speed over surfaces that a few years ago would have been treated with respect.

The gear change is light and quick with good synchromesh on second, third and top, and a free-wheel for first gear. This free-wheel arrangement has decided uses in town driving, for with just a normal depression of the clutch pedal immediately before coming to rest at traffic lights and so forth, first gear can be slipped in ready for the getaway. The indirect gears are quiet. The clutch pedal action is light, and an excellent point is that there is ample space to the left of this pedal for even a tall driver's leg. Left-hand steering is available. The spring-spoked steering wheel is telescopically adjustable, and in general the driving position is very satisfactory; the separate seat gives good support to the back. In addition to the normal adjustment the seat back rests are adjustable for angle.

One sits well down in the car, and visibility to the front is good, a driver of average height being able to see the near-side wing by just lifting his head. It is possible to put one's head out of the sliding type window to see behind for reversing, though this is not particularly convenient. The two-door body is in effect a fixed-head coupé with rear seats for occasional use, these being comfortably upholstered but limited in leg room. There is altogether exceptional luggage space in the tail; the spare wheel is mounted in the lid of the locker.

Matching rev counter and speedometer are key items of the neat and practical instrument layout, whilst in a grouping to the right of the steering column are water and oil temperature gauges, oil pressure, ammeter, fuel gauge and electric clock. With white markings and needles against black faces the instruments are particularly easy to read, and they are well illuminated at night. H.M.V. Radiomobile radio is a standard fitting, but the very effective Clayton Dewandre interior heating system fitted to the car that has been tested is an extra. De-misting and de-icing vents are provided. The doors close with an expensive, specialist coachbuilder sound, and the interior trimming is attractive in light-coloured leather of excellent quality. The exterior finish is also of high quality.

First-press starting from cold was experienced throughout the test. There is a normal mixture-enriching control in connection with the three S.U.s and, in addition, an S.U. auxiliary starting carburettor is fitted for ease of starting in very cold weather. The engine will pull at once from cold, although it is desirable to treat an engine of this quality with respect as regards revs until some movement of the oil temperature needle is seen. Warming up is greatly assisted by thermostatically controlled radiator shutters. A warning light shows when the head lamps are in the undipped position, and can be useful when running into areas with street lighting. Built-in lamps give a good but not outstanding beam.

The bonnet catches could be more positive in action; an unusual point is that the bonnet can be locked. A rear window blind would be appreciated. An excellent view behind is given by the driving mirror. One-shot chassis lubrication is a valuable feature, leaving few points to be dealt with by hand.

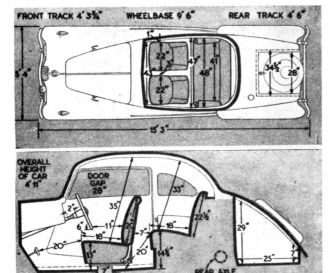

Measurements are taken with the driving seat at the central position of fore and aft adjustment. These body diagrams are to scale.

Anglo-Italian Accord

The lovely lines of the Farina-bodied Bristol are seen to advantage in this photograph of the car.

Modified Bristol with Pinin Farina Drop-head Body

THE beautiful lines and excellent detail work of the bodies exhibited by the leading Italian coachbuilders at Geneva and Paris caused something of a sensation. Many will therefore be interested to learn that, as a result of an agreement recently signed by A. F. N., Ltd. with Carrozzeria Pinin Farina S.A. of Turin, a modified version of the 2-litre Bristol will in future be available with a Farina drophead coupé body.

At the Frazer Nash works at Isleworth the Bristol chassis is extended rearwards to carry a new 18-gallon fuel tank behind the rear axle. It will be remembered that on the standard chassis the 11-gallon fuel tank is mounted above the rear axle, where it would occupy valuable space in the luggage boot of the Farina body, hence the modification. The new tank resembles a saddle tank set on its side, the spare wheel fitting into the semi-circular arch thus formed. The chassis is also fitted with a substan-

tial scuttle built up of spot-welded pressed steel sections; various other detail modifications are also made before it is shipped to Italy.

An inspection of a completed car revealed a close attention to detail that was delightful. The bonnet catches, for instance, are operated by a substantial lever under the instrument panel on either side of the body. When the catches on one side of the bonnet are released those on the other side act as a hinge, whilst if both catches are released the bonnet may be lifted clear of the car. A little blue light in the instrument panel lights up as soon as any of the lights are switched on. Should any of them fail it goes out; thus the driver can tell at once if a side or tail light should misbehave. The car has an overall length of 15ft and is 5ft 5in wide and 4ft 8in high with the hood raised. The weight is 21½ cwt. Like so many other beautiful things this car will, alas, be available only for export.

Similarly a small red bulb glows so long as either of the direction indicators is in use. These may seem small points in themselves but they do illustrate the very practical approach of the designers, for in this type of body with all lights built-in none of them is directly visible from the driving seat.

- -

Left: Particularly ingenious is the bonnet locking mechanism. In this illustration the right-hand locks have been released by the right-hand lever under the facia and the bonnet top swung open on the left-hand locks, which then act as hinges. **Right:** Very business-like is the driving compartment, which has something of the fascination of an aircraft cockpit. It is also very comfortable.

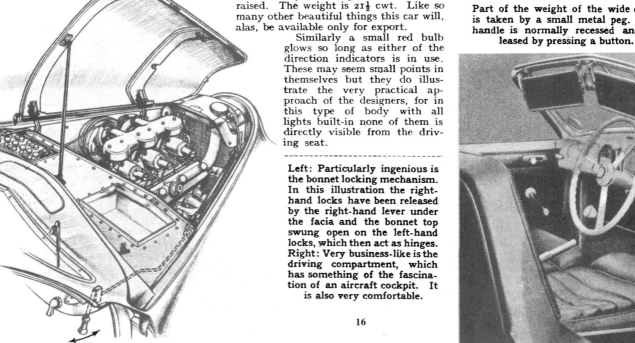

Part of the weight of the wide doors is taken by a small metal peg. The handle is normally recessed and released by pressing a button.

The BRISTOL TYPE 401

Unusual Body Construction Methods Used in New Export Versions of a High-performance 2-litre Car

AMONG the cars which were first announced to the public on the opening day of the Earls Court Motor Exhibition were two new versions of the 2-litre Bristol. Comprising a two-door saloon, and a somewhat similar convertible model, these cars which were illustrated in "The Motor" of October 27 are the result of collaboration between the Bristol Aeroplane Co., Ltd., and Carrozeria Superleggera Touring of Milan. Constructed and designed entirely in this country, the bodies benefit from the considerable experience gained by the Italian coachbuilding company with the constructional methods used.

The new bodies represent an attempt to meet the particular requirements of certain export markets. The existing type 400 saloon also continues in production, this type of close-coupled coachwork suiting the requirements of most people who buy the high-performance Bristol for use on the congested roads of Britain. In America and elsewhere, however, the demand is for roomier cars, and there are differing tastes in detail equipment, which requirements the Bristol 401 is designed to meet.

Keeping Down the Work

To increase the useful size of bodywork on a car, without impairing performance or making increased demands on the engine, is a difficult feat, and success has resulted from careful attention to both structural and aerodynamic aspects of the new design. In regard to obtaining the lowest possible air resistance compatible with roominess and the demands of fashion, the Bristol company are able to draw on a vast fund of experience gained with high speed aircraft. To produce the larger bodies without increase in weight, they have adapted to their purposes unusual constructional methods which have been developed to very high standards by Superleggera in Milan.

It is only necessary to study the new bodies under construction at Bristol to appreciate what a sturdy structure they, in conjunction with their chassis, form. Aluminium panels conceal a jig-welded framework of steel tubes which provide the strength of the body. Collaboration with the Italian originators of this form

has given the Bristol company the benefit of experience which brings weight to a very low level without any sacrifice of necessary strength.

The chassis is modified only in detail to accommodate the new coachwork, changes relating to such matters as the scuttle structure and the provision for fuel tank mounting. It is formed of box section members, braced by cross-members and a steel floor, and, apart from the inevitable upswept extension passing over the rear axle, is of simple form, giving that rigidity which is desirable with flexible suspension for moderate weight. Supplementing this strong basis, the new full-width bodies are based upon distinct body side rails of box-section steel, deep but of light gauge, set parallel to and outside the chassis longerons. Rising from these body side rails are four sturdy box-section steel pillars, one upright on each side carrying a wide forward-hinged door, the other pair serving as corner posts for the body rear section.

Two distinct bodies are founded upon this same basis, one a saloon and the other a convertible coupé. The two cars having so much in common, it will suffice to describe the saloon and make reference to leading features of the alternative model.

Out of Contact

The artist's drawing of the 401 saloon shows, more clearly than can any words, the way in which the body panels are moulded around a lattice structure of curved tubes. There is, however, no direct metal-to-metal contact between panels and framework except at the edge area of each sheet.

In such parts as the roof, the tubular members are bound with hessian material, prior to being externally panelled and concealed (by trimming) from passengers inside the car. The body panels are of aluminium alloy, and are held in position by the simple method of swaging the edges over angle-section strips which in turn are riveted to the body members. This method of securing light alloy panels over the steel framework is used throughout the body, doors, and wings of both saloon and convertible models.

A great deal of thought has been put into the detail

equipment of these cars, and many parts which are more often purchased ready-made by other car manufacturers have in this case been made specially to the required high standards of quality. A detail which is immediately evident on approaching the car, for example, is that there are no door handles, but only neat, recessed buttons, pressure upon which unlocks the door and causes it to open a few inches. Provision for door opening from inside the car is similar, the press-buttons being leather covered to match the interior body trimming: duplicate buttons on each of the wide doors are convenient for front and rear passengers respectively (the latter set can be omitted if it is desired to eliminate all risk of children opening the doors by mistake), and check springs prevent the door flying open so far as to be likely to hit a garage wall or other obstruction.

The facia takes the form of a Tufnol panel, which may be removed to give access to the wiring of switches and instruments. Comprehensive instrumentation is built around matched speedometer and tachometer, these and the other instruments having dials which are almost rectangular in form yet retain precise and even calibrations. A specially made two-spoke steering wheel, with moulded finger-grips on spokes and rim, is telescopically mounted on the sharply raked column, and is surmounted by a matching form of switch for the trafficators.

The body is a spacious four-seater, with a low floor level, and with doors of such a size that entry to front or rear is very much easier than is the case with the Type 400. There is a capacious luggage locker in the tail of the body, protection against theft taking the form of dual catches which can only be released from within the car: similar protection is afforded to the petrol tank, the filler of which is only revealed when a catch inside the car is released. When the luggage locker is open, a catch may be released, allowing a counterbalanced tray accommodating the spare wheel to hinge down on to the road.

American automobiles are the standard form of transport in many countries where the Bristol 401 will be sold, and the very practical bumper equipment has been designed fully to match transatlantic standards. Heights have been selected with this in view, bumper depth suffices to minimize risk of over-riding, and inset rubber strips serve as neat rubbers. Further, study of the drawing will reveal that each bumper bracket incorporates a massive rubber-in-shear buffer unit, which can cushion impact loads with a movement of more than 2 ins. before metal-to-metal stops come into action.

All lights are inbuilt on the new models: thus, in addition to the usual pair of head lamps, there are also two recessed-fitting flat-beam lamps which, located outboard of the head lamps, incorporate the parking side lamps. Tail and stop lamps are recessed into the rear bumper, on either side of the number plate.

Excellent Opening

The alternative convertible body is notably handsome, having the rear seat set slightly farther forward than on the saloon, but is nevertheless a genuine four-seater. Remarkable success has been achieved in combining the open and closed states. With the hood raised, there are very smooth roof contours, but both hood and frame fold completely down below the level of the body sides into a space behind the rear-seat squab to produce an open four-seater. A further practical point is that a tonneau cover is provided which will either cover the rear compartment when this is unoccupied, or will cover all the seats if the car is parked during showery weather.

As has been indicated already, the mechanical details of these cars do not differ appreciably from those of the Type 400, which was fully described in "The Motor" of November 6, 1946, and formed the subject of a "Motor" road test report published on May 9, 1948. It will, therefore, suffice to give a brief recapitulation.

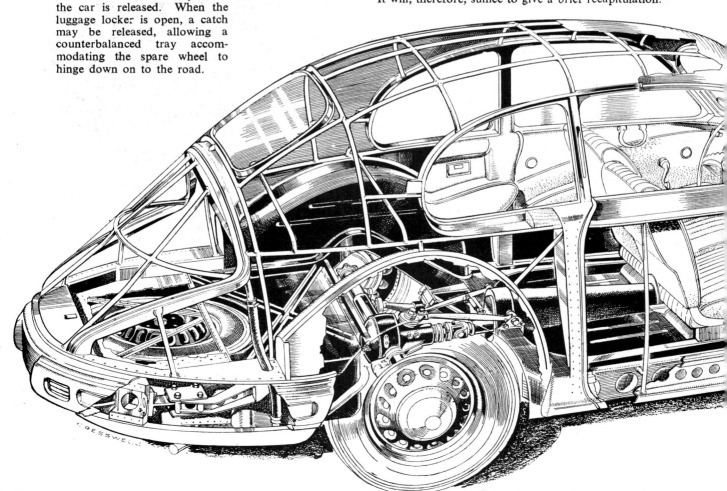

The Bristol power unit is a 2-litre "six," with inclined push-rod-operated valves in hemispherical combustion chambers. Alternative manifolding arrangements are available according to a purchaser's desire for emphasis on speed or flexibility, the most favoured version being a triple downdraught carburetter layout quoted as giving 85 b.h.p. at 4,500 r.p.m. It will be recalled that the Type 400 saloon road tested by "The Motor" attained a mean maximum speed of 94.1 m.p.h. with this engine.

The single dry-plate clutch, and four-speed synchromesh gearbox, are orthodox in general conception, as are the open propeller shaft and spiral-bevel rear axle. The front wheels of the 114-in.-wheelbase chassis are independently sprung, by a transverse leaf spring steadied by Bristol hydraulic shock absorbers, and are steered by high-efficiency rack-and-pinion gear. Rear suspension is by longitudinal torsion bars.

The two new additional body types extend the appeal of the Bristol 2-litre to a very wide field of purchasers. Attractive as the cars are, in a showroom or on a brief demonstration run, we have seen enough of their construction and of their behaviour under trying conditions to say confidently that big mileages will render owners ever more appreciative of their inbuilt quality.

LHU 613

DETAIL. — Tail lamps and number plate are recessed into the sturdy rubber-mounted light-alloy bumper, and the spare wheel is in a tray which may be lowered from below the luggage locker.

TOUT ENSEMBLE.—Integration of the aluminium panelled, steel-framed body with the strong box-section chassis is evident from this "Motor" drawing. Carefully planned external shape, and constructional methods new to this country, have allowed roomier bodywork to be provided in a model with smart appearance and the promise of unimpaired high performance.

NEW CARS DESCRIBED

West Country

1949 Bristols Have Roomier Bodies of New Appearance with Many Practical Improvements

YEAR by year the development of the modern car shows that the body is no longer entirely a matter for the coachbuilder as his craft was understood originally, but more and more an integral part of the chassis, equal with it in importance, and designed as an engineering whole. This tendency is admirably illustrated in the latest models of the Bristol car, Types 401 and 402, as seen at the recent London Show. Since the announcement of the machine late in 1946 experience has proved that the chassis will do its work well, and so the modifications to it are very slight indeed, the principal one being concerned with the rear of the frame, and then only because of the new body design. But a great deal has been done with the body, which now has more room for all its passengers and an immense amount of detail improvement, all resulting from experience gained during the long-distance fast touring for which this car is intended.

The body is now built on a very light tubular frame, and, as befits a firm whose knowledge of aircraft is almost unlimited, light alloy is used wherever possible with advantage. Then, as the accompanying illustrations show, the exterior lines have been improved out of all knowledge, and the car has that grace which comes of modern design, but fortunately is not very much wider or longer—two current tendencies which conflict with limited garage space. The instrument board has been tidied and its controls have been made much neater ; incidentally, a feature of the car is the

considerable number of controls, as befits a sports-type machine. The wheel now has two spokes, pleasantly curved, which somehow make it seem more logical than the three-spoked wheel of the past, although that gave a clear view of the instruments ; and the wheel, with its spokes and boss, has a clean and stylish effect.

Roller blinds are fitted above the V-shaped windscreen, to be used when driving into a low sun, and they are wide enough to be really effective. The two cupboards in the instrument board both have good locks, and there is

The new Bristols can be described as sports cars de luxe, for they provide performance with the maximum of driver and passenger comfort. Push-button operation of body fittings has been taken to the utmost limit, as this series of sketches shows. This drawing by *The Autocar* artist is of the Type 401 saloon, a most desirable car for either home or overseas.

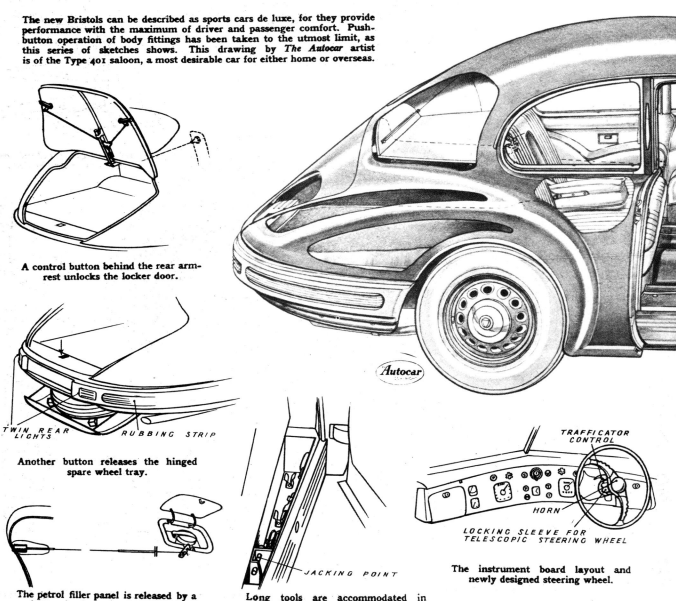

A control button behind the rear armrest unlocks the locker door.

TWIN REAR LIGHTS   RUBBING STRIP

Another button releases the hinged spare wheel tray.

The petrol filler panel is released by a button in the near-side arm-rest.

JACKING POINT

Long tools are accommodated in valance lockers on either side.

TRAFFICATOR CONTROL

HORN

LOCKING SLEEVE FOR TELESCOPIC STEERING WHEEL

The instrument board layout and newly designed steering wheel.

Specialities

interior lighting, by which it is easy to read a map at night without incommoding the driver. Both doors contain good, capacious pockets, covered, so that when the door is opened in rain the contents do not become wet, and so arranged that the arm-rests for the front seats are part of the cover concerned. Both doors look very solid. They are, in fact, long, but, being much lighter than their appearance suggests, do not overload the hinges, nor are they carried so low that the normal kerb of a pavement would prevent them from opening. The locks are controlled by neat discs sunk in the panels, the operation being mechanical, though the push-button control suggests an electrical system.

A small mirror mounted on the centre strut of the windscreen gives an excellent view astern, leaving only one very

The Type 401 has an extremely well-balanced appearance. Its curves have been reduced to the minimum consistent with aerodynamic aims and the front of the car is nicely "clean." The radiator grille is augmented by grilles in the bumper structure.

½" RETRACTION TRAVEL FOR BUMPER

Both bumpers are permitted sliding travel—an underside view.

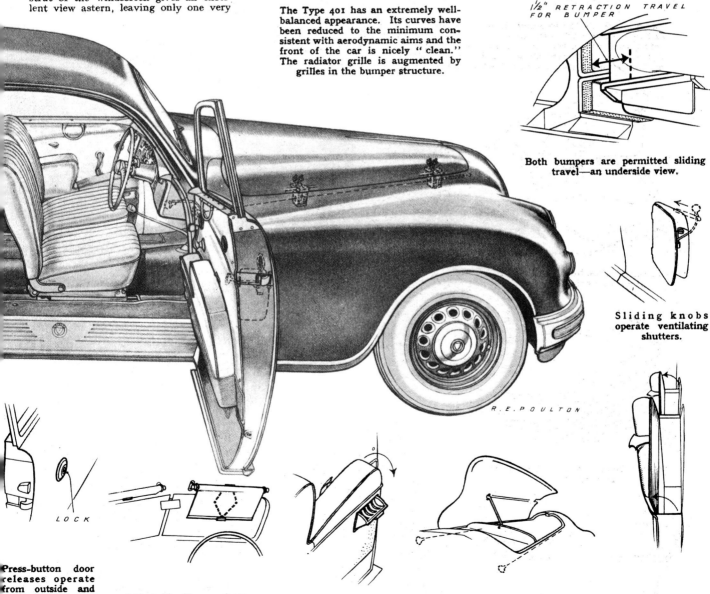

R. E. POULTON

Sliding knobs operate ventilating shutters.

Press-button door releases operate from outside and inside.

Adjustable silk sun visors.

Ash trays in either door and in rear quarters.

Press-buttons permit the bonnet to be opened at either side or removed.

Hinged arm-rests provide access to map pockets.

LOCK

SPECIFICATION

Engine.—6 cylinders, 66×96 mm, 1,971 c.c. Overhead valves operated by push rods from camshaft in crankcase. Pump cooling. Pressure lubrication. Compression ratio, 7.5 to 1.

Transmission.—4-speed gear box with synchromesh. Central gear lever. Single-plate clutch. Overall gear ratios: Top 3.9, third 5.5, second 8.5 and first 16.8 to 1. Open propeller-shaft. Spiral bevel final drive.

Suspension.—Independent front with half-elliptic transverse spring. Normal rear with torsion bars.

Brakes.—Lockheed hydraulic two-leading-shoe.

Fuel System.—17-gallon tank at rear with mechanical pump feed.

Tyres and Wheels.—Dunlop 5.50 × 16in tyres on steel wheels.

Electrical Equipment.—Lucas 12-volt starting and lighting. Coil ignition. Flush fitting sealed reflector head lamps.

Main Dimensions. — Wheelbase, 10ft 4in. Widest track, 5ft 2⅞in. Overall length, 15ft 10in; width, 5ft 7in. Ground clearance, 7in. Turning circle 37½ft. Weight 2,632 lb (23½ cwt).

Prices.—Saloon and 2-4-seater, £2,085, plus £1,128 3s 4d purchase tax. Total, £3,213 3s 4d.

small blind spot. A blind is fitted to the rear window, its cord control coming through the roof lining just above the driver. When the doors open they disclose sockets for the jacks, and at the side of the seat, below the carpet, there is a long and most useful box, sunk into the floorboards, which holds the jack and its accessories and which would be very useful for many other items of the gear one carries for long-distance runs. The new Leveroll seats automatically come back to the correct

position after being pushed back to give more clearance at the doors.

Inside the driving compartment, also, are the controls by means of which the lid of the bonnet is locked or unlocked, the arrangement being unusual because, though this lid appears to be of the crocodile type, it is not, but can be raised from either one side or the other, then locked in the open position by sliding a special strut into a catch. There is a great deal to be said for this arrangement, more especially as the lid can be lowered gently and will still lock, whereas many bonnets of this type need a comparatively heavy blow before they are secure. Inside the bonnet and on the structure of the scuttle are deep bins having at the top trays which will carry tools retained in rubber housings, the lockers coming in useful again for spare parts and odds and ends. When the doors are locked the bonnet cannot be raised and the door locks cannot be wrenched open, because there is no handle over which to fit a lever.

Ample Luggage Space

There is more space than in the original Type 400 body for the rear passengers, the seats for whom are deep and very comfortable. Behind these seats, at the level of the rear window, is a useful tray that takes quantities of parcels during a shopping excursion. In the tail is a magnificent luggage compartment—one would say almost the most capacious ever fitted to a machine of this type—and its lid is locked by mechanism controlled from within the body, so that nothing can be removed from the luggage when the machine is parked and locked. The lid of the tail compartment is well balanced, needing no effort to raise or to close. Moreover, it is quite easy to extract the spare wheel

Front and back—the former characteristic, the latter roomy and convenient for luggage.

from its compartment below the tail, for pressure on a button causes the wheel carrier and wheel to drop, thus making it quite easy for the wheel to be rolled out of position. It is equally easy to replace a wheel with a punctured tyre and to pull the wheel carrier back to the locked position.

The fuel filler, which has a very neat little snap catch, is covered over, so that it is both safe and does not break the line of the car. This also is controlled from within the body and, therefore, is locked when the doors are locked.

While retaining the characteristic features of the Bristol—the radiator grille and the special badge—the front of the car has been com-

The promise in the frontal appearance is fulfilled at the back, where the body terminates in a swept tail. The Bristol nameplate is the sole "ornament."

Door trimmings, amongst which hinged arm-rests conceal deep pockets.

The 2-litre six-cylinder engine fills the bonnet. Note the two tool trays which form the lids of extra under-bonnet receptacles.

Mouth-watering controls for the driver who " enjoys every minute." The wheel is quite unusual and has finger-grips on the spokes.

and should appeal very much indeed to the driver who wants a real sports car possessing many of the characteristics of a racing machine but also the tractability that allows it to be used on shopping and normal runs.

The chassis characteristics will bear repetition. The engine is a six-cylinder of just under 2 litres. The four-speed synchromesh gear box is in one unit with the crankcase and has a rear extension in which is housed a shaft leading to the first universal joint of the open propeller-shaft. A normal rear axle has torsion bar suspension, while at the front independent suspension is arranged, each wheel assembly having a wishbone lever and one end of a single transverse leaf spring. The frame is of box section, very deep and very stiff, the extension at the rear having been modified to take the tail of the new body, together with the fuel tank. One of the features of this car is its stability, especially when cornering fast, while the suspension is excellent—so good, in fact, that it is exceedingly difficult to judge whether the road surface is good or bad, even when driving at very high speed; and, of course, a car of this type can cruise without apparent effort at speeds up to 70 m.p.h.

pletely remodelled, the very substantial bumpers being effective as such. All lamps can be adjusted, and the normal side light has given place to a comparatively large lamp, as the illustrations show. Very great care has been taken to prevent water finding its way into either the bonnet or the luggage compartment, the lid joints of the latter being provided with a quite elaborate system of guttering and water drainpipes. Ventilation has also been improved considerably.

In addition to the Type 401 saloon, a new open model, Type 402, has been produced, very much on the same lines, but, because it is an open car, with much more instinctive suggestion of high speed. The hood is concealed, but balanced in such a way that it can be raised with very little effort, while windows wind out of the doors as requisite. This is a most workmanlike machine,

Nothing is stinted in the back seats, which are comfortable and divided by an arm-rest. The quarter-lights are hinged.

THE BRISTOL 2-LITRE SALOON

Outstanding Performance Combined with Economy and Refinement

THE Bristol 2-litre model which was recently submitted to a 2,000-mile test by "The Motor" is a car with quite exceptional ability to suit itself to the mood of driver and passengers. If haste is required, it will give speed and road holding which might be the envy of many a super-sports model. If, on the other hand, the mood is leisurely, it will drift quietly along in the most comfortable touring fashion.

The car submitted for test incorporated an engine to the latest specification, with three downdraught carburetters, and had a compression ratio high enough to call for either gentle use of the throttle, or some use of the manual ignition control, at low speeds. The rather better grades of petrol available in Belgium, and notably Araline of those tried out, largely eliminated pinking, however, and it is worthy of mention that the acceleration figures published were measured after the car had covered 1,100 miles in our hands, no amount of hard work seeming to worry the engine.

ON CONTINENTAL TEST.—The new Bristol is a first-rate car for European motoring, being well up to prolonged punishment by bad roads. This picture was taken in the Grand Duchy of Luxembourg, at the village of Esch-le-Trou.

High-priced Quality

The Bristol is frankly an expensive car, but quite apart from the performance and comfort which it offers, there is no lack of those detail refinements which are expected of a quality car. Waiting in the customs shed at Dover, we found that to change over the lighting system from keep-left to keep-right dipping was the work of only a moment, requiring no tools whatever, but merely interchange of two accessible under-bonnet plugs. In 2,000 hard miles, the only attention given to the car was to adjust a noisy tappet (the work of very few minutes), add two quarts of oil, inflate the tyres, and occasionally press the lubrication pedal situated above the accelerator—and after 90 m.p.h. driving over cobbled roads, not a squeak or rattle was audible anywhere.

The figures printed on the data page are fully adequate testimony to the performance of the car. In our post-war series of road tests, only two larger cars have bettered the mean maximum speed of 94.1 m.p.h., and only one of these has bettered the Bristol's time of 19.7 seconds for the standing-start quarter-mile. The fact that this performance is not obtained extravagantly is indicated by a petrol consumption which is moderate by any standard, better than 30 m.p.g. at 50 m.p.h. cruising speed and not falling to 20 m.p.g. until the pace is raised substantially above 80 m.p.h.

On the road, the combination of good performance and handling qualities makes the Bristol almost without equal for safely high average speeds. A red marking on the revolution counter dial implies that the continuous cruising speed should not appreciably exceed 80 m.p.h. on motor roads, but on ordinary highways no ill effects seem to result from frequent use of considerably higher speeds.

The steering of the Bristol is extremely light and quick in response, yet transmits only very moderate road wheel reaction even under extreme conditions, and there is a notably compact turning circle. High-speed driving induces an absolute minimum of fatigue, partly because of the small physical effort involved in controlling the car, but also because there is no mental strain involved in placing it accurately on either straight or curving roads. The luggage locker is so exceptionally large that there is every temptation to load the car to a tail heavy state, but even so and with unaltered tyre pressures the wet-road speed can be pushed up to 80 m.p.h. before the weight of baggage really begins to make itself felt.

Fast, but Tidy, Corners

The car clings tenaciously to the road when cornered fast on a dry surface, any roll which takes place being imperceptible inside the car. Forced to the absolute limit, it yields in a fully controllable rear-wheel slide, but normally the car may be said to corner fast and tidily however long the curve. Wet roads reduce the possible cornering speeds, of course, but do not show up any vices.

Combined with these good handling qualities is a quite exceptional standard of comfort in riding over bad roads— exceptional by absolute standards and not merely for a small car. The transverse leaf front spring and torsion bar rear springs, with their Bristol double-acting hydraulic shock absorbers, give excellent cushioning of shocks without allowing undamped motion to build up at any time. The combination of level riding, steady cornering, and seats which give good support in all planes,

CONVENTIONAL ACCESS to the engine is afforded by a longitudinally hinged bonnet. Adequate air-silencing is provided for the three Solex carburetters.

contributes towards it being quite unusually comfortable; it is even possible for a passenger to write or sleep while astonishing numbers of miles are being covered in an hour.

The riding and handling qualities of the Bristol are attained with weight distribution which puts slightly more than half the weight on the driven rear wheels. While our tests did not include actual trials-type hills, sufficient muddy farm lanes were covered for us to confirm that there is no lack of traction on slippery surfaces.

Something to be Desired

The transmission system is, perhaps, the feature of the car most open to criticism, as falling below an otherwise extremely high standard. The clutch dragged occasionally, so that engagement of bottom gear from rest was not silent, and while behaving well in normal use it slipped when racing gearchanges were essayed as an aid to even better acceleration figures.

The gearchange, too, while light to operate and with a well-sited central lever, lacks the smooth feel of the best modern synchromesh mechanisms. Taken in leisurely fashion, however, all changes of gear were quiet and easy, bottom gear incorporating a free-wheel mechanism and all other ratios having synchronized engagement. Current production models have a slightly higher third-gear ratio than the test car, which should be advantageous for open road driving. The minimum non-snatch speed in top gear on level road is approximately 20 m.p.h., the manual ignition timing control requiring to be used for the taking of acceleration figures from below this speed.

The hydraulic brakes proved fully fit for use on a fast car, remaining effective after usage which would have put many cars into a service station. The hand brake, too, of fly-off racing type mounted accessibly between the front seats, has very adequate power. Two rear-tyre failures which occurred after spells of fast driving on winding roads revealed the effectiveness of the side-jacking arrangements, although an improvement in access to the spare tyre valve for periodic inflation would appear very desirable and not difficult to arrange.

No amount of hard driving seemed to worry the engine, which invariably idled steadily, or stopped instantly when switched off, after full-power driving. Underbonnet temperatures always appeared moderate, though warming up was rapid, thanks to thermostatic shutters in front of the radiator; and although rather high oil temperatures could be reached at times, there was never any lack of oil pressure. During our test the engine always started from cold instantly, and would soon run without the choke, and starting from hot was quite sure, provided the throttle was opened.

The Bristol body is unusual in appearance, but it has great practical merit and seemed very pleasing to owners of American types of large car. Aerodynamically it is evidently of good form, as witness the moderate fuel consumption of the car at high speeds, and the exceptionally direct flow of rain and mud backwards along the bonnet and mudguards.

The generous accommodation in the rear luggage boot has already been mentioned, and this is supplemented by a locker on the facia, and by door pockets which are vast in capacity yet have easy access for removal of small objects. The hursnn passengers are also very comfortably housed. the front of the car being really roomy, thanks to the low floor and the doors which are recessed to give extra elbow room. The rear seats are not especially accessible, but once entered they are unexpectedly comfortable.

Interior Comfort

The interior is very pleasantly furnished and thoroughly soundproofed, only the particular adjustable steering wheel used being out of keeping with the prevailing high standard of wood and leather work. Visibility from the driving seat is adequate, despite the high level of the scuttle, and there is good vision sideways as well as through the large curved rear window. The car is quiet internally, and the ventilation by sliding windows, hinged quarter lights, and forward facing scuttle panels, was sufficient for spring-time weather conditions. A driver appreciates having an adjustment for the rake of the squab, as well as being able to slide the seat, and finds very comfortable foot space to the left of the clutch pedal.

The facia carries a comprehensive array of instruments, fully worthy of a quality sports car, and in top gear there is a pleasing unison of movement between speedometer and r.p.m. indicator needles.

Our test of the Bristol was comprehensive and arduous, while circumstances brought it into direct comparison with the products of various other countries. Alternating between this and other cars during a busy fortnight, we developed great, and ever increasing, respect for the Bristol, which contrived to combine first-class touring standards of comfort with extremely high performance, and showed an immense capacity for hard work without requiring any maintenance attention.

GENEROUS STOWAGE.—The luggage boot is quite remarkably roomy, as this picture shows. An efficient and conveniently workable jack is carried clipped to the back of the luggage space, and the spare wheel is mounted outside. Great saving in space is made by placing the petrol tank forward of the boot, behind the rear seats.

1949 CARS

The BRISTOL 2-litre Model Mechanically Unchanged

A High-performance Car with Six Cylinders, Inclined o.h.v. and Torsion Bar Suspension

ALTHOUGH chassis-carrying bodies styled especially to suit export markets will be exhibited at Earls Court, the Bristol Type 400/85 saloon is being continued without alteration for sale to British buyers during 1949. This model, it may be recalled, was subjected to a 2,000-mile Continental Road Test by "The Motor" early this year, and apart from revealing excellent riding and handling qualities plus a vast appetite for hard work, attained a maximum speed in excess of 94 m.p.h., yet could cover more than 30 miles on a gallon of fuel at a steady 50 m.p.h.

The essential features of the Bristol car are a chassis of modern layout built to an unusually high standard of detail refinement, a high efficiency 2-litre six-cylinder engine which is powerful without being extravagant of fuel, and a close-coupled steel saloon body of low weight and wind resistance. The result is a car which can cover short or long distances comfortably in outstandingly quick time.

Inclined overhead valves, actuated from a single camshaft by an unusual but well-proven arrangement of push rods, are combined with vertical induction ports to give unusually high specific power output. Alternative induction arrangements are offered, with triple downdraught carburetters for maximum power, or a dual-choke instrument for utmost flexibility.

Box-section chassis longerons are linked by a steel floor, and by tubular and other cross-members, to form an extremely rigid frame which contributes to good road holding and to long body life. Front suspension is independent, by a gaitered transverse leaf spring and a pair of wishbones which actuate the Bristol-built hydraulic shock absorbers. A forward-mounted rack-and-pinion gear gives precise steering with a minimum number of wearing parts.

Rear suspension is by longitudinal torsion-bar springs, hydraulically damped, and a rigid axle beam. Positive location of chassis relative to axle, under all conditions of acceleration, braking and cornering, is provided by the torsion-bar arms plus a triangulated member amidships.

The Type 400 body is a compact four-seater saloon of two-door type, offering ample space in all directions for the front passengers and adequate accommodation for two passengers in the rear seat. Unusually generous luggage accommodation for long-distance motoring is a commendable point.

Lockheed hydraulic brakes are fitted, brake drums of 11-in. diameter accommodating the generous areas of friction lining desirable on a fast car. Ventilated steel disc wheels of dished formation provide generous cooling air flow for dissipation of heat from the brakes.

BRISTOL 400 SALOON DATA

Engine Dimensions			**Transmission—contd.**	
Cylinders	6		Prop. shaft	Hardy Spicer
Bore	66 mm.		Final drive	Spiral bevel
Stroke	96 mm.		**Chassis Details**	
Cubic capacity ..	1,971 c.c.		Brakes	Lockheed
Piston area	31.8 sq. ins.		Brake drum diameter..	11 ins.
Valves	Inclined overhead		Friction lining area	147 sq. ins.
Compression ratio ..	7.25 : 1		Suspension : Front ..	Independent transverse leaf
Engine Performance			Rear ..	Live axle with torsion bar
Max. b.h.p.	85			
at	4,500 r.p.m.		Shock absorbers ..	Bristol
Max. b.m.e.p.	138 lb./sq. in.		Wheel type	Pierced disc
at	3,000 r.p.m.		Tyre size	5.50 by 16
B.h.p. per sq. in. piston area	2.67		Steering gear	Rack and pinion
Peak Piston speed, ft. per min.	2,835		Steering wheel ..	Spring spoke, 17 ins. diameter
Engine Details			**Dimensions**	
Carburetter	Triple S.U.		Wheelbase	9 ft. 6 ins.
Ignition	Coil		Track : Front	4 ft. 4 ins.
Plugs : Make and type	AC 10 mm.		Rear	4 ft. 6 ins.
Fuel pump	U.G.		Overall length	14 ft. 2 ins.
Fuel capacity	12 gallons		Overall width	5 ft. 5 ins.
Oil filter (make, by-pass or full flow) ..	Tecalemit full-flow filter		Overall height	5 ft.
			Ground clearance ..	6¼ ins.
Oil capacity	10 pints		Turning circle	36 ft.
Cooling system	Fan and pump		Dry weight	22 cwt.
Water capacity	17 pints			
Electrical system ..	—		**Performance data**	
Battery capacity ..	72 amps. 20 hours.		Piston area, sq. ins. per ton	29
Transmission			Brake lining area, sq. ins. per ton	134
Clutch	Borg and Beck, 8 ins.		Top gear m.p.h. per 1,000 r.p.m. ..	19.5
Gear ratios : Top ..	3.9		Top gear m.p.h. at 2,500 ft./min. piston speed	77.5
3rd ..	5.07			
2nd ..	8.48			
1st ..	16.77		Litres per ton-mile, dry	2,755
Rev. ..	13.43			

BRISTOL at New York Show

Produced by:
Bristol Aeroplane Co., Ltd.
Filton, Bristol, England

THE Bristol Aeroplane Co. was founded as long ago as 1910, and in the past 40 years has been responsible for many important developments in the aeronautical world, including the adaption of the single sleeve valve gear to the air-cooled radial engine and, more recently, the development of propeller-cum-gas turbine prime movers. The possibility of using part of the company's capacity for the construction of both engines and aircraft in the manufacture of motorcars was contemplated in the closing period of the war, and the decision to go forward was made in June, 1945. The use of a famous European design as a basis saved much time in experimental and development work, and the car exhibited at New York can justly claim to be a remarkable example of European co-operation, in which the best of English workmanship and materials are allied to a chassis and body which incorporate years of practical road experience. The six-cylinder engine embodies a unique design of valve gear in which both vertical and horizontal push rods are used so as to give inclined overhead valves with a single camshaft located in a conventional position.

The porting of the head is also unusual with direct downdraught passages, which promote efficiency to the extent that although the nominal capacity is only half that normal to the U.S. car, the engine develops some 85 b.h.p

A Body for Speed

The body is very carefully shaped so as to reduce wind resistance losses, and this power suffices to drive the car at a genuine 95 m.p.h., whilst by using a very light tubular framework with a light-alloy skin the weight of the car is kept down to such a low figure that it will reach 60 m.p.h. in only 15 seconds, and will climb a 5 per cent. gradient at considerably more than 80 m.p.h.

An unusual detail is incorporated in the transmission system In addition to the conventional synchro-change between the three upper gear ratios, a free wheel is auto-

matically unlatched on the emergency low gear, and thus literally no skill is required to engage this ratio. This obviously forms a safety feature, and it should also be mentioned that very positive steering is provided by means of rack and pinion gear, and that the rear axle is joined to the frame through a link motion, torsion bars being used for the rear suspension.

Finish and Equipment

Some idea of the care taken in constructing this car may be inferred from the fact that some 16 coats of primer and finisher are used when cellulosing the body, whilst each mechanical component is individually tested, even the spring dampers, as well as engines and gearboxes. The body equipment is also well worth inspection; the doors open themselves at the push of a button, and both the rear luggage boot door and the flaps covering the filler caps are opened by controls situated within the body, so that theft is virtually impossible. The direction indicator switch is mounted on the almost horizontal steering column, where it can be reached through the two-spoke steering wheel, and very full provision is made for carrying small personal packages in accessible positions.

SUMMARY OF EXHIBITS

Six-cylinder 85 b.h.p. two-door saloon, type 401

BRISTOL 401	
Weight : 2,576 lb.	Wheelbase : 114 ins.
Capacity : 120 cu. ins.	Track : front, 51¾ ins.
	rear, 54 ins.

This manufacturer's decision to exhibit became known too late for inclusion in the special supplement in the centre of this issue.

STAND No. 22

EVOLUTION

LATEST.—The Type 401 Bristol in current production form.

of the

"401"

How an Outstanding Bristol Model has Benefited by a Two-year Process of Continuous Development.

By Harold Hastings

IN factories where weekly output is measured in hundreds and production flow is a prime consideration, design modifications inevitably come under the heading of necessary evils. As such, they are liable to be subdivided into two broad classes, according to urgency. In the first class are those which serve to rectify some initial design fault and are put into effect at the earliest possible moment as a matter of necessity. In the second, are alterations which represent pure improvements and, as such, can be delayed until it is possible to incorporate several together at an appropriate moment (such as a motor show) to produce a new or improved model.

To the specialist car manufacturer, on the other hand, the question of production flow is of far less moment and improvements can much more readily be incorporated immediately they have passed the development stage. Thus progress emerges in the form of a series of steps in the one case and as a more or less continuous process of evolution in the other.

It is unfortunate, perhaps, that where the latter applies, numerous worthwhile improvements are apt to creep in unheralded and unsung and the progressive policy tends to escape due appreciation. A quite notable example of this is the case of the Bristol "401," which has been steadily and quietly improved in innumerable details since its original introduction in the autumn of 1948.

To an outsider, the "401" appears much as it did when it first appeared and it is only if one is privileged—as I was recently—to sit in the drawing office and thumb steadily through the "mods" file, that the great progress made in detail work can be fully appreciated. The more important of these detail changes are well worth reviewing, both as examples of progressive policy by a specialist manufacturer and as matters of general interest concerning a very notable car.

In the general layout of the 85 b.h.p., 1971 c.c. six-cylinder engine, with its clever arrangement of inclined o.h. valves operated by push rods from a single camshaft, no change has been made. To such wear-resisting refinements as direct oil feed to the little ends, and a nitride-hardened crankshaft, however, cylinder liners have now been added.

These are of the dry type, made in Brivadium and, besides giving increased resistance to wear, have the further merit that, when wear does eventually call for attention, replacement liners are fitted instead of the block having to be rebored.

At the same time, additional water holes have been provided to give improved cooling in the block, in which the circulation is by thermosiphon action. Circulation in the head is, of course, by pump and, although not new, the fact that the pump and fan unit is dynamically balanced is worth mentioning as a further example of the thorough detail work which justifies the admittedly high price of the Bristol.

Another small example of this same thoroughness lies in a very minor alteration it had been thought worthwhile to make to the oil relief valve. Because the original design produced a slight tendency to flutter as the plunger uncovered the relief passage, a series of staggered holes which are uncovered progressively by the plunger have now been introduced to relieve excessive pressure evenly.

Of much greater interest to those who drive hard (even by Bristol standards) or whose motoring is done in tropical countries, is the introduction of an oil-cooler as an optional extra. This takes the form of a six-bar gilled-tube unit which fits neatly in front of the base of the radiator and is inserted in the oil circulation system by connection to the unions of the full-flow filter.

Silencing Problems

In a high output engine such as the Bristol, problems of efficient silencing without the creation of back pressure are by no means easy to solve and, when an apparently satisfactory solution has been obtained, the system may be found to be subject to periodic effects under certain conditions. In the case of the "401" some suggestion of such periodic noise effects was traced to the Y-junction where the two down pipes from the manifolds united into a single pipe before entering the silencer of the original system. This effect has been eliminated by carrying the two pipes through individually to a new type of Burgess silencer which has been specially designed for the "401." The new system, together with the internal details of the new silencer, can be seen in one of the accompanying drawings.

Another exhaust modification is an excellent example

28

WOOL TUFT TESTS.—These two pictures show an alternative method of studying the aerodynamic qualities of the body. In this case, actual cars are being driven at speed down an aerodrome runway, with wool tufts and linen tapes affixed to the body surface. The direction of the air flow at any point is shown by the line assumed by the appropriate tufts.

of the old saying about an ounce of practice being worth a lot of theory—and incidentally, emphasizes the fortunate position of the makers in having access to the 1¾-mile runway of the Bristol Aeroplane Co., Ltd., for test purposes. One or two complaints were received of exhaust fumes finding their way into the interior of the body in cases where careful examination of every possible source of leakage had disclosed no fault.

Mystified, the experimental department decided that the only way to get to the root of the trouble was to make the exhaust gases visible and *watch* where they went. So the crude but entirely effective expedient of giving the engine a near-fatal overdose of upper-cylinder lubricant was adopted and the car driven at various speeds up and down the runway, with observers both in the car and in a second vehicle driven alongside.

It then became apparent that the trouble lay, not in any faulty joints, but simply in the fact that the unit pipe discharged into a low-pressure area behind the tail, where the gases were sucked along with the car instead of being dispersed into the air stream. A slight modification was accordingly made to the tail pipe (which now discharges

at an angle instead of directly to the rear) and the trouble disappeared.

Considerable detail work has, however, also gone into the question of improved sealing of the engine bulkhead as a precaution against both fumes and heat.

In the transmission, the oversize (9-in.) release block used for the 8-in. Borg and Beck clutch is now of an improved coppered-carbon type, a soft gear-lever knob (which is both more pleasant to handle and oddly enough, cuts out any tendency on the part of the lever to "sizzle" after prolonged mileage) has been adopted and dirt seals of a more efficient type have been devised for both clutch and brake pedals.

Other modifications have been more of the constructional (as opposed to design) type and include such points as a longer screwed sleeve on the pinion bearing assembly of the final drive to obtain greater stability of adjustment and the use of bolts, instead of studs, to secure the front of the rear axle casing to the banjo. This is a direct result of racing experience, since the Mille Miglia revealed that,

INDEPENDENT.—The entire i.f.s. and steering assembly forms an independent unit which is assembled and tested separately before being bolted to the chassis. Innovations include the fitting of a safety link (shown parallel to the spring), modified spring eyes and improved shock absorbers. The sketch also shows the connections for the one-shot chassis lubrication system.

DETAIL.—Several improvements are visible in this drawing which shows the new spare wheel tray fasteners, the counter-balanced support for the internally-locked boot lid, the new-style bumper (with its clever concealed rubber mounting), the modified exhaust tail pipe and the latest type of road wheel. Note the construction of the locker lid which is on the same principle as the remainder of the body.

although studs had given no trouble in normal usage, the safety factor was hardly equal to the ill usage of long-distance racing. Ergo, trouble *might* arise in the hands of normal owners and must be forestalled.

Although steering and suspension have always been outstanding features of all Bristol models, the makers' guiding principle that even the best can be improved has been applied here, as to every other part of the car.

Amongst external differences in the latest design are the use of a new steering arm and a slight modification to the eye of the transverse leaf spring, the master leaf now being shaped so that the axis of the hole is in the same plane as the master leaf. The combination of these alterations has provided improved steering geometry over wide deflections and, in this connection, it is interesting to note that each front suspension assembly is individually tested for both camber angle and toe-in before being fitted to the chassis. The test rig (which is shown in an accompanying illustration) is arranged so that, when the suspension unit is bolted in place and steel discs are fitted in place of the wheels, both settings can be checked at any spring deflection, the latter being controlled by the hydraulic rams.

Another suspension innovation since the "401" was introduced, is a safety link which is provided on each side parallel with the leaf spring to guard against possible effects of a broken master leaf. In addition, the front end-plate attachment of the whole unit has been strengthened and the front shock absorbers are now easier to remove.

The shock absorbers themselves, both at front and rear, have also been improved in detail, notably in the provision of a new type of recuperating valve and spring. The disc of the valve is now faced with Tufnol and the seat itself has also been modified, both with the object of making the valve completely silent in operation. The shock absorbers, which are of Bristol design and manufacture, are all pre-set on a test rig before fitting and the setting adopted has been modified as the result of extensive experiments to provide an even better ride without loss of the handling characteristics for which the Bristol is rightly famous.

At the rear, the suspension is little changed, although certain small detail improvements, such as the use of more efficient oil seals, have been incorporated.

To revert to the evolution process, other mechanical improvements include the use of new road wheels of better appearance and greater strength (which are, incidentally, individually balanced to within fine limits), a new type

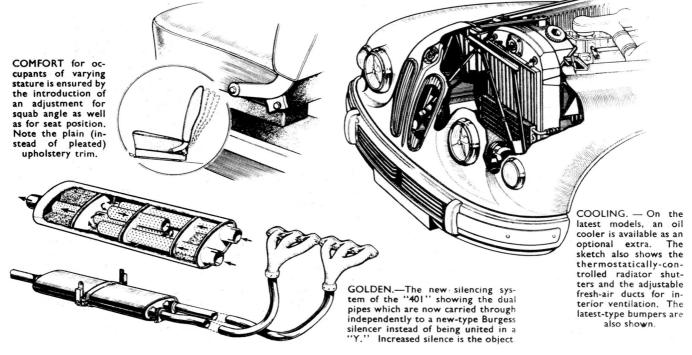

COMFORT for occupants of varying stature is ensured by the introduction of an adjustment for squab angle as well as for seat position. Note the plain (instead of pleated) upholstery trim.

GOLDEN.—The new silencing system of the "401" showing the dual pipes which are now carried through independently to a new-type Burgess silencer instead of being united in a "Y." Increased silence is the object.

COOLING. — On the latest models, an oil cooler is available as an optional extra. The sketch also shows the thermostatically-controlled radiator shutters and the adjustable fresh-air ducts for interior ventilation. The latest-type bumpers are also shown.

Evolution of the "401"

of ratchet with double teeth of improved contour for the fly-off handbrake and minor alterations to the internal construction of the fuel tank to avoid erratic behaviour of the feed when the level is low.

The body of the "401" is of unusual construction, in which the aim has been to achieve an optimum compromise between the conflicting requirements of strength and lightness. To this end, an aluminium shell is built up on a light but strong tubular steel framework, to which the shell is attached by swaging its edges over angle-section strips riveted to the framework; except along these edges, there is no metal-to-metal contact and, in the case of such areas as the roof, Hessian binding (concealed by interior trim) is used to provide insulation.

This form of construction is already familiar (through previous descriptions) to most readers. What is not generally appreciated is that, to avoid saddling the car with any unnecessary weight, the gauge of the aluminium is varied according to the strength required. Thus, the tops of the front wings (a favourite resting spot for mechanics' elbows!) are of 16 gauge as also is the bonnet top and so forth, the remainder of the body being of 18 gauge.

Similarly, the hardness of the alloy (which is of the work-hardening type) is chosen according to the amount of panel beating involved so that, when the shell is complete, an approximately equal degree of hardness is obtained throughout.

Good Form

The contours of the body reflect the very careful attention to the combined requirements of good appearance, practical comfort and good aerodynamic form, the last-named a matter in which the makers are in the particularly fortunate position of both having access to wind-tunnel facilities and (as mentioned earlier) to a runway particularly suitable for high-speed observations. Some of the use to which these facilities have been put in the case of the "401" can be gathered from the accompanying photographs showing wind tunnel smoke tests with a model and wool tuft and tape tests of an actual car on the runway. In the latter, small wool tufts or lengths of tape are affixed liberally to the body and the direction of the air stream at various points detected by the position they can be seen to have assumed at high speeds in photographs obtained from a car driven alongside.

As the photographs show, the results (bearing in mind the slightly uncomplimentary scale effects in evidence with small models), are excellent indications of the good aerodynamic form achieved. Faults there undoubtedly are (and the makers are fully conscious of them) but when it is borne in mind that the "401" is designed as a high-speed touring car, and not as a one-purpose record breaker, the makers can justifiably congratulate themselves on the excellent wind-cheating characteristics achieved.

To turn to bodywork details, the most noticeable internal change is probably the adoption of a high-grade wood facia board in place of the metal type previously used. The general arrangement is much the same, but the alteration has made a pronounced difference to the general appearance of the interior. A small point, but one which again illustrates the general attention given to detail, is that the peak formed by the continuation of the scuttle above the facia panel has now been made more pronounced for the sole purpose of preventing light from the instruments reaching the sloping screen.

TEST RIG.—Before attachment, each front-suspension assembly is checked on this test rig which enables camber and toe-in to be tested under various conditions of spring deflection. Pneumatic rams control deflection and measurements are obtained by bringing horn plates into contact with steel discs bolted to the brake drums and taking readings on a scale.

The upholstery is now carried out in plain (instead of pleated) leather, which gives a distinctly improved appearance besides avoiding traps for dirt, whilst the front seats are now fitted with the very simple but effective adjustment for rake shown in one of the drawings; this is, of course, in addition to the normal sliding adjustment for position. As before, push-button locks for the doors are provided, but the leverage has been modified for easier operation and, in addition, the internal buttons are now visible instead of being hidden by the upholstery trim.

Bumpers on the latest cars are of light metal as before, but, in place of being chromium plated with rubber contact inserts, are now painted to match the car and have plated steel contact strips and over-riders, an alteration which has the double merit of improved resistance to damage and greater restraint in appearance. The very notable feature of mounting these large bumpers so that they appear integral with the body although, in actual fact, they are carried on hidden rubber mountings which permit a considerable degree of individual movement on contact, has been retained.

At the rear of the body, several detail modifications are to be found. The excellent system of carrying the spare wheel in a let-down tray is continued, but more positive fasteners of the toggle type are now used, whilst the boot lid is now fitted with a central telescopic bracket which is spring loaded to provide a counter-balanced effect. In addition, small spring-loaded plungers are provided at the base which serve to spring the locker lid open approximately $\frac{3}{8}$ of an inch when the lock is released from inside the car; the result is to enable the lid to be grasped easily without the need for an external handle. A similar plan is provided for the bonnet top which, as will be recalled, is ingeniously arranged so that it can be swung open from either side of the car or quite readily detached entirely.

So far as equipment is concerned, head lights of the latest P770 long-range type are now used, a socket for an inspection lamp or trickle charger is now fitted on the engine side of the scuttle bulkhead, the adjustable steering column is now provided with three positive positions and various minor details such as a new horn button and improved rubber sealing for the screen and windows have been adopted.

Thus an outstandingly good car has been made progressively better by a continuous process of evolution which reflects the greatest credit on the skill, technical ability, and, above all, enthusiasm, of those responsible for its design.

Revisions to the elegant Bristol 401 include improved seat shapes and bumper modifications to provide for towing.

BRISTOL DEVELOPMENT

PROCESS OF GILDING THE LILY CONTINUES

NO large-scale changes would be expected, or are in fact being made, in the one model produced by the Car Division of the Bristol Aeroplane Company, the 2-litre Type 401. The policy behind this car is one of steady evolution and changes of a subtle rather than of a drastic nature to a fine basic design.

Among current modifications of interest resulting from this policy, and incorporated in the latest cars, is curvature given to the back rests of the separate front seats, thereby providing firmer support to the occupants, which is so desirable in a car of this character which can be cornered fast. Already adjustment is provided for angle of the back rests. By the simple modification of holes drilled in front and rear bumper overriders provision is now made for the car to be towed in an emergency or to give towing assistance to another vehicle, and the overriders are secured by a three-bolt attachment to give the necessary increased strength.

A simple form of screw adjustment is now provided for the rear suspension

torsion bars and the gear box now has closer ratios of 3.9, 5.05, 7.12 and 14.0 to 1. The synchromesh used is the Borg-Warner mechanism. Increased leverage, and therefore lighter pedal pressure, results from redesigning the brake pedal lever.

Finish of the facia, with its fine, practical array of well-arranged instruments, formerly French polished, is now in a hard gloss lacquer, whilst a new body colour has been introduced, a distinctive dark green.

SPECIFICATION
BRISTOL 401

Engine: 6 cyl, 66 × 96 mm (1,971 c.c.), 85 b.h.p. at 4,500 r.p.m. Overhead valves. Compression ratio 7.5 to 1. Three Solex downdraught carburettors with Vokes air silencer. Vokes oil filter. Impeller pump water circulation.

Transmission: Dry single-plate 8in diameter Borg and Beck clutch; 4-speed gear box with free wheel on first gear. Overall gear ratios: Top 3.9, third 5.05, second 7.12, first 14.0 and reverse 11.22 to 1. Spiral bevel final drive.

Suspension: Independent transverse spring front; torsion bar rear.

Reinforced bumper over-riders and a large luggage locker at the rear of the Bristol 401.

Steering: Rack and pinion.

Brakes: Lockheed, two-leading-shoe hydraulic; 11in diameter drums.

Wheels and Tyres: Perforated steel disc wheels with 5.75-16in tyres on wide base rims.

Fuel System: Tank capacity 17 gallons, including two gallons reserve. Camshaft-operated AC fuel pump.

Electrical Equipment: 12-volt 51-ampère-hour battery.

Main Dimensions: Wheelbase 9ft 6in. Track (front) 4ft 3½in; (rear) 4ft 6in. Overall length, 15ft 11½in; width, 5ft 7in; height, 5ft 0in. Ground clearance 6½in. Turning circle 37ft 6in.

The BRISTOL Type 401

A Medium-sized Car Offering Very High Standards of Comfort and Performance

AERODYNAMIC FORM.—Smooth contours appropriate to a product of the Bristol Aeroplane Company are shown off in this photograph, taken in the Belgian Ardennes.

IN applying their proven craftsmanship as builders of aeroplanes and aero engines to the task of building cars, the Bristol Aeroplane Company have worked on the principle that a vehicle of high quality need not necessarily be a large one. The type 401 Bristol saloon which we drove for some 1,500 miles recently is essentially a comfortable four seater the dimensions of which are compact enough to suit country lanes, and a high initial purchase price is explained by high performance, notable refinement, and the promise of unusual durability rather than by bulk.

Although many eyes will have turned already to performance figures printed on the opposite page, the matter which asks to be put first in this test report is comfort, this matter having very evidently been foremost in the minds of those responsible for the development of the model.

It is first realised that the seating arrangements are very comfortable, notably but not solely in the front compartment, two individually adjustable seats having shaped backrests with simple cams permitting adjustment of their rake: convenient, when there is not room to open a front-hinged door fully, is the ease with which either seat can be slid back to facilitate exit from the car: slightly annoying on the test car however, was a hard ridge (concealed by the upholstery) across the base of the seat squab. The back seat with its folding armrest is restful, amply roomy, and not unduly difficult to enter by two-door saloon standards, whilst the elbow width available in the front of the car is very generous indeed. Good provision for miscellanea is provided by glove lockers, door pockets, and a shelf beneath the rear window.

Matching the comfortable body, there is a suspension system which is arranged to give excellent riding at high speeds or low. Inevitably some compromise has had to be struck between comfort and

controllability, but without being harsh on potholed roads negotiated slowly, the suspension is nevertheless well enough damped to suit all but the most awkward surfaces when the car is travelling fast. Whilst the passage of time and the rapid change in standards of comparison on matters of riding ease make it dangerous to refer back to the Bristol model 400 (with different weight distribution and shock absorbing) tested 4 years ago, it seems that the latest car has gained in respect of ability to ignore increases in the passenger and luggage load carried, but lost slightly in respect of rear seat riding smoothness.

In respect of controllability, the prime virtue of the Bristol is the extreme mechanical excellence of its steering, which is very quick and precise in normal use, and is self-centring yet free equally from excessive friction or substantial road reaction. Handling characteristics at high speeds tend towards the "oversteer", perhaps because of the far-forward centre of pressure of a truly aerodynamic body; maximum speed testing in a cross wind on a slippery road showed up exaggerated steering sensitivity. In normal use, however, the car is a delight to handle, the steering calling for very little effort, and the wheel playing gently back through the driver's fingers to the straight-ahead position as the throttle is opened for acceleration out of a corner. The car is virtually free from roll, and quite automatically puts up high average speeds on either open or winding roads.

The driving position behind a steeply raked steering wheel is well suited to most tastes, the two-spoke steering wheel having nicely moulded finger grips on both rim and spokes. The gear lever (a conventional central lever of modest length) is well positioned for instant

INTERIOR ROOMINESS.— Very ample headroom, elbow width and length, for four people, are available inside the two-door body. Cams provide easy selection of four different backrest angles for each front seat.

PILOT'S PLACE.—A curved facia panel of polished wood is surmounted by a hood which prevents reflection of the instruments in the sloping windscreen. Also visible here are the comfortable, steeply raked steering wheel and the well-placed gear and handbrake levers.

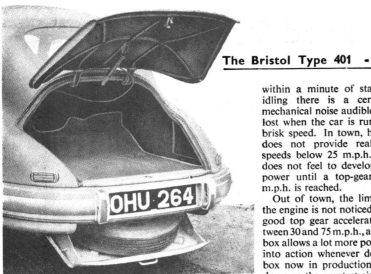

LUGGAGE CAPACITY.—A luggage locker of great depth is provided, unobstructed by the spare wheel which is separately accommodated on an easily accessible tray as shown here.

The Bristol Type 401 · · ·

availability, and the handbrake lever set between the seats has its tip almost too close to the gear lever. The two points of mild criticism are a shallow foot-well in the floor, which is positioned just to the left of the accelerator and so involves mild ankle-twisting, and a roller-blind type of sun visor on the top of the steeply raked windscreen which is so near to the driver's forehead as to irritate some people. It is also slightly unfortunate that, although a full set of precise instruments is provided on a wooden facia panel which is excellently finished like the rest of the interior, circular dials have not been chosen for the speedometer and matching tachometer.

In respect of performance, the abilities of the Bristol in the hands of a keen driver are very considerable. Only a handful of closed cars (of greater engine size) can equal a 0-50 m.p.h. acceleration time of 10.2 seconds, and a true maximum speed of more than 97 m.p.h. as the mean of runs in opposite directions is again remarkable amongst comfortable saloon cars.

Willing Performance

Providing a really useful 85 b.h.p. from only 2-litres displacement, the 6-cylinder Bristol engine gives no indication that it is working hard, the oil consumption in fast driving remaining at around 1-2 pints per 1,000 miles. This engine is also notably economical, as witness the fuel consumption of 27½ m.p.g. at a steady 50 m.p.h. and the overall consumption figure of 20.8 m.p.g. for 320 far-from-slow miles. There has, however, been a considerable sacrifice of pulling power at low r.p.m., as the price of maximum performance.

The engine starts instantly from cold, and the choke can be forgotten completely

within a minute of starting up, but at idling there is a certain amount of mechanical noise audible, this noise being lost when the car is running at its usual brisk speed. In town, however, top gear does not provide real smoothness at speeds below 25 m.p.h., and the engine does not feel to develop its true pulling power until a top-gear speed of 40-45 m.p.h. is reached.

Out of town, the limited flexibility of the engine is not noticed, there being very good top gear acceleration available between 30 and 75 m.p.h., and use of the gearbox allows a lot more power to be brought into action whenever desired. The gearbox now in production must be written down as the greatest single improvement made in the Bristol car since it was first introduced: its ratios are well chosen (only with a 5th ratio would it be possible to fill the gap between a 2nd ratio giving well over 50 m.p.h. and a bottom gear permitting starts on steep hills !) and the action of the gearchange is now excellent, selection of the upper three ratios being aided by a good modern synchro-mesh mechanism, and 1st gear having a free-wheel to facilitate its engagement.

On open roads, the fast 2nd and 3rd gears are delightful for overtaking or acceleration out of corners, being commendably quiet. In town, use of the gears is a must, and although the car can be started from rest in 2nd one should, in fact use 1st gear whenever the car speed is brought low. The excellent handling qualities of the car allow wet and slippery town streets to be treated with only mild respect, but the rising torque curve of the engine means that if wheelspin starts it will very readily become spectacular !

The overall noise level inside the car is, very consistently indeed, low. At high speeds, the really smooth body does not create much wind noise, except for one or two details such as imperfect window edge sealing. On rough going, the tubular-framed aluminium-panelled body has the freedom from major rattles or squeaks usually associated with welded construction (and, presumably, the ability of this type of rigid body to protect passengers from injury in many kinds of crash) combined with the absence of resonances to road or power unit excitation which the coachbuilt body can still claim as its especial virtue. Such detail rattles as were evident, from the facia panel and the hinged rear window catches, were duly noted by a Bristol engineer who accompanied the car

whilst we were using it on a variety of Belgian by-ways.

A substantial disappointment concerning the Bristol type 401 was in respect of the braking system. The car always pulled up absolutely squarely whilst in our hands, and although not indulging in a deliberate fade test we never found the brakes inadequate for individual hard applications during fast driving. The pedal pressures required to produce either gentle or powerful retardation were quite unusually high, however, and rather tiring for the muscles of the right leg. Downhill, the 3rd or 2nd gears can be used to provide that braking effect which, with a small engine and smooth bodywork, is not marked on the overrun in top gear; 1st gear is not usable for this purpose, because of the free wheel.

No Greasing

The lighting system provided is appropriate to a fast car, a speed of 70 m.p.h. or more being comfortable on straight roads at night. The headlamp beams are very narrow, however, and on winding roads it is preferable to switch over to the pair of flat-beam auxiliary lamps of much shorter range which are also provided. Commendable also is the bright interior lamp, with its switch mounted on the facia panel.

Quite beyond price for the long-distance tourist who does not wish to spend time having maintenance work done on a car is the centralized chassis lubrication system, operated by a pedal above the accelerator. The light yet rigid lids of the engine compartment and the extremely deep luggage locker (the latter with a very thief-resistant concealed catch) were pleasing to handle, and the windscreen de-misting system worked very effectively. An owner would soon cease to notice window winders which seemed to the testers to work back-to-front, but we cannot regard the interior heating arrangements provided as being up to 1952 standards of power or controllability.

For the motorist who covers long distances, whose time is valuable, and whose passenger carrying requirements on business or private journeys are met by a four seater saloon with a large luggage capacity, a Bristol is a very understandable ambition. Built to give long service without either wearing out or becoming outmoded, and with a very restrained thirst for fuel, it is a luxury certainly, but not by any means such an extravagance as a purchase price of £2,270 might suggest.

UNBROKEN LINES. — Details of an exceptionally smooth body include built-in bumpers of proven sturdiness, and neat press-button catches, flush with the panelling, which release the door locks.

The Motor Continental Road Test No. 3C/52

Make : Bristol **Type : 401**

Makers : Bristol Aeroplane Co., Ltd. (Car Division), Filton, Bristol

Dimensions and Seating

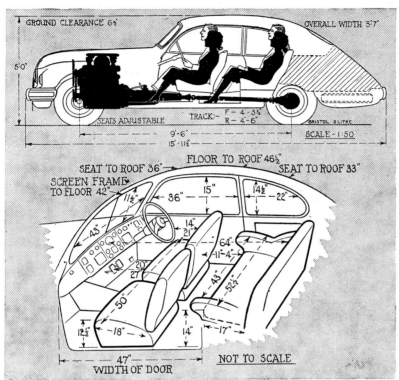

GROUND CLEARANCE 6½   OVERALL WIDTH 5'7"

5'0"

SEATS ADJUSTABLE   TRACK:- F – 4'-3¾"   R – 4'-6"   Bristol 2 Litre

9'-6"

15'-11½"   SCALE · 1:50

SEAT TO ROOF 36"   FLOOR TO ROOF 46½"   SEAT TO ROOF 33"

SCREEN FRAME TO FLOOR 42"   11½"   36"   15"   14½"   22"

43"   14"   21"   64"   11'-4"

20"   27"   43"   52½"

50"

12½"   18"   14"   17"

47"   NOT TO SCALE
WIDTH OF DOOR

In Brief

Price £2,270 plus purchase tax £1,262 12s. 3d., equals £3,532 12s. 3d.	
Capacity	1,971 c.c.
Unladen kerb weight	24½ cwt.
Fuel consumption	20.8 m.p.g.
Maximum speed	97.3 m.p.h.
Maximum speed on 1 in 20 gradient	82 m.p.h.
Maximum top gear gradient	1 in 11.7

Acceleration
10-30 m.p.h. in top. .. 17.8 secs.
0-50 m.p.h. through gears 10.2 secs.
Gearing 20.25 m.p.h. in top at 1,000 r.p.m. 80.5 m.p.h. at 2,500 ft. per min. piston speed.

Test Conditions

Cold weather with strong cross wind. Smooth, damp concrete surface (Ostend-Ghent motor road). Belgian premium-grade (approx. 80 octane) pump fuel.

Test Data

ACCELERATION TIMES on Two Upper Ratios

	Top	3rd
10-30 m.p.h.	17.8 secs.	10.8 secs.
20-40 m.p.h.	14.4 secs.	9.0 secs.
30-50 m.p.h.	12.2 secs.	8.6 secs.
40-60 m.p.h.	12.6 secs.	9.0 secs.
50-70 m.p.h.	13.9 secs.	10.7 secs.
60-80 m.p.h.	17.5 secs.	—

ACCELERATION TIMES Through Gears

0-30 m.p.h.	4.4 secs.
0-40 m.p.h.	7.2 secs.
0-50 m.p.h.	10.2 secs.
0-60 m.p.h.	15.1 secs.
0-70 m.p.h.	20.6 secs.
0-80 m.p.h.	30.2 secs.
Standing Quarter Mile	19.9 secs.

MAXIMUM SPEEDS

Flying Half Mile
Mean of four opposite runs .. 97.3 m.p.h.
Best time equals .. 98.8 m.p.h.

Speed in Gears
Max. speed in 3rd gear .. 80 m.p.h.
Max. speed in 2nd gear .. 57 m.p.h.

WEIGHT

Unladen kerb weight	24½ cwt.
Front/rear weight distribution	50/50
Weight laden as tested	28 cwt.

INSTRUMENTS

Speedometer at 30 m.p.h.	accurate
Speedometer at 60 m.p.h.	1% fast
Speedometer at 90 m.p.h.	1% fast
Distance recorder	3% slow

FUEL CONSUMPTION

27.0 m.p.g. at constant 30 m.p.h.
27.5 m.p.g. at constant 40 m.p.h.
27.5 m.p.g. at constant 50 m.p.h.
25.0 m.p.g. at constant 60 m.p.h.
23.0 m.p.g. at constant 70 m.p.h.
20.5 m.p.g. at constant 80 m.p.h.
Overall consumption for 320 miles, 15.4 gallons, equals 20.8 m.p.g.

HILL CLIMBING (at steady speeds)

Max. top gear speed on 1 in 20		82 m.p.h.
Max. top gear speed on 1 in 15		71 m.p.h.
Max. gradient on top gear		1 in 11.7 (Tapley 190 lb/ton)
Max. gradient on 3rd gear		1 in 8 (Tapley 275 lb/ton)
Max. gradient on 2nd gear		1 in 5.4 (Tapley 410 lb/ton)

BRAKES at 30 m.p.h.

0.95g retardation (=31½ ft. stopping distance) with 160 lb. pedal pressure.
0.63g retardation (=48 ft. stopping distance) with 100 lb pedal pressure.
0.30g retardation (=100 ft. stopping distance) with 50 lb. pedal pressure.

Specification

Engine

Cylinders	6
Bore	66 mm.
Stroke	96 mm.
Cubic Capacity	1,971 c.c.
Piston area	31.8 sq. in.
Valves	Inclined o.h.v. (pushrods)
Compression ratio	7.5/1
Max. power	85 b.h.p.
at	4,500 r.p.m.
Max. b.m.e.p.	134 lb./sq. in.
at	3,500 r.p.m.
Piston speed at max. b.h.p.	2,835 ft. per min.
Carburetter	3 Solex 32BI downdraught
Ignition	Lucas coil
Sparking Plugs	10 mm. K.L.G. P.Ten.L50
Fuel Pump	AC mechanical
Oil Filter	Vokes full-flow

Transmission

Clutch	Borg & Beck s.d.p. type 8.A6.G
Top Gear (s/m)	3.9
3rd gear (s/m)	5.05
2nd gear (s/m)	7.12
1st gear (freewheel)	14.0
Propeller shaft	Hardy Spicer, open
Final drive	Spiral bevel

Chassis

Brakes	Lockheed hydraulic, 2 l.s. front
Brake drum diameter	11 ins.
Friction lining area	148 sq. ins.
Suspension	
Front	I.F.S. (Transverse leaf spring and wishbones)
Rear	Torsion bars and rigid axle
Shock absorbers	Newton telescopic
Tyres	Dunlop, 5.75 x 16

Steering

Steering gear	Bristol rack and pinion
Turning circle	37½ feet
Turns of steering wheel, lock to lock	3

Performance factors (at laden weight as tested)

Piston area, sq. in. per ton	22.7
Brake lining area, sq. in. per ton	106
Specific displacement, litres per ton mile	2,080

Fully described in "The Motor," November 24, 1948.

Maintenance

Fuel tank: 17 gallons, including 2 gallons reserve. **Sump:** 10 pints, S.A.E. 30 (or, below freezing point, S.A.E. 20; over 90° F., S.A.E. 40). **Gearbox:** 3 pints, S.A.E. 50. **Rear axle:** 6 pints, S.A.E. 140 E.P. gear oil. **Chassis lubricant reservoir:** 2 pints S.A.E. 50 oil. **Radiator:** 10 pints (2 drain taps). **Chassis lubrication:** By grease gun every 3,000 miles to 2 points. Depress lubrication pedal in car every 70 miles. **Ignition timing:** T.D.C. static. **Spark plug gap:** 0.018 in. **Contact breaker gap:** 0.010—0.012 in. **Valve timing:** I.O., 10° b.t.d.c.: I.C, 50° a.b.d.c.: E.O., 50° b.b.d.c.: E.C., 10° a.t.d.c. **Tappet clearances:** Inlet and exhaust, cold 0.002 in., hot 0.012 in. **Front wheel toe-in:** 0—0.100 in. (car unladen). **Camber angle:** 2°—2¾° (car unladen). **Castor angle:** ¼°—1¼° (car unladen). **Tyre pressures:** Front 24 lb., rear 28 lb. **Brake fluid :** 1 pint, Lockheed Orange. **Battery:** 12-volt, 51 amp.-hr. Lucas G.T.W. 9A. **Lamp bulbs:** 12 volt. Headlamps Lucas No. 302, 48/48 watt: Passlamps, 2 x Lucas No. 162, 36 watt: Sidelamps and number plate, 4 x Lucas No. 989, 6 watt: Stop/tail lamps, Lucas No. 353 24/6 watt. Ref. B/20/52.

The Bristol has a very smooth exterior, not broken even by protruding door handles or hinges. Easily the most noticeable projection is the aerial for the optional radio. Perforated wheels and open rear wheel arches help to keep the brakes cool.

No. 1458 : BRISTOL 401 SALOON

MANUFACTURERS of motor vehicles have sometimes transferred their interests to the production of aircraft or of aero engines, but seldom does the reverse take place. However, with the Bristol Aeroplane company this has happened, as the car division at Filton was not formed until just after the war, whereas the company have been producing aircraft for many years. This fact is a very important one, as it influences the outlook of the company on car design as a whole. As a passing instance, when the car was demonstrated to *The Autocar* before it was handed over for Road Test it was remarked by a technical representative, "To increase the cabin ventilation air flow can be increased by opening the rear quarter light." The Bristol has a cabin, while other cars have a passenger compartment.

The aircraft influence is again shown by the keen interest taken in problems connected with the reduction of wind resistance or "drag." The success of this policy of producing a car that is genuinely streamlined is reflected by the high maximum speed, as well as by good petrol consumption at high speeds, while using an engine of only 2-litre capacity. There is little doubt that this is one of the fastest four-seater saloons in production with an engine of this size ; in fact, disregarding engine size there have been few saloon cars tested by this journal that have shown as good a performance. The accompanying data were recorded on the Belgium motor road, as is the practice of *The Autocar* with cars of the Bristol's performance potential.

But the 401 is not intended to be a super sports mount with performance as its prime function, for such a car often leaves something to be desired when used for general motoring. Decidedly that is not so with the Bristol, which com-

— DATA —

PRICE (basic), with saloon body, £2,270.
British purchase tax, £1,262 12s 3d.
Total (in Great Britain), £3,532 12s 3d.
Extras : Radio £55 4s 6d.
Heater £35.

ENGINE : Capacity : 1,971 c.c. (120.25 cu. in.).
Number of cylinders : 6.
Bore and stroke : 66 × 96 mm. (2.598 × 3.78in).
Valve gear : o.h.v. by push rods.
Compression ratio : 7.5 to 1.
B.H.P. : 85 at 4,500 r.p.m. (59.5 B.H.P. per ton laden).
Torque : 106.8 lb ft at 3,500 r.p.m.
M.P.H. per 1,000 r.p.m. on top gear, 19.83.

WEIGHT (with 5 galls fuel), 24¾ cwt (2,786 lb).
Weight distribution (per cent) : 49.5 F ; 50.5 R.
Laden as tested : 28⅝ cwt (3,200 lb).
Lb per c.c. (laden) : 1.6

TYRES : 5.75—16in.
Pressures (lb per sq in) : 22 F ; 26 R.

TANK CAPACITY : 17 Imperial gallons.
Oil sump, 8½ pints.
Cooling system, 18 pints (plus 2 pints if heater fitted).

TURNING CIRCLE : 37ft 6in (L and R).
Steering wheel turns (lock to lock) : 3.

DIMENSIONS : Wheelbase 9ft 6in.
Track : 4ft 3½in (F) ; 4ft 6in (R).
Length (overall) : 15ft 11½in.
Height : 5ft 0in.
Width : 5ft 7in.
Ground clearance : 6½in.
Frontal area : 21 sq ft (approx).

ELECTRICAL SYSTEM : 12-volt 51 ampère-hour battery.
Head lights : Optional single or double dip, 48-watt double filament.

SUSPENSION : Front, independent, transverse spring.
Rear, torsion bars.

— PERFORMANCE —

BRISTOL 401
ACCELERATION : from constant speeds.
Speed, Gear Ratios and time in sec.

M.P.H.	3.9 to 1	5.04 to 1	7.12 to 1	14.08 to 1
10—30	—	11.9	7.3	—
20—40	15.2	10.2	6.3	—
30—50	14.8	9.5	6.9	—
40—60	15.7	10.5	—	—
50—70	16.6	11.9	—	—

From rest through gears to :

M.P.H.			sec.
30	..	..	5.0
50	..	..	11.7
60	..	..	17.4
70	..	..	23.2
80	..	..	35.7

Standing quarter mile, 20.2 sec.

SPEED ON GEARS :

Gear			M.P.H. (normal and max.)	K.P.H. (normal and max.)
Top	..	(mean)	93.4	150.3
		(best)	93.75	150.87
3rd	..	..	60—78	97—126
2nd	..	..	40—52	64—84
1st	..	..	20—28	32—45

TRACTIVE RESISTANCE : 29.7 lb per ton at 10 M.P.H.

TRACTIVE EFFORT :

	Pull (lb per ton)	Equivalent Gradient
Top	155	1 in 14
Third ..	230	1 in 9.8
Second.. ..	358	1 in 6.2

BRAKES :

Efficiency	Pedal Pressure (lb)
84 per cent	138
69 per cent	100
31 per cent	50

FUEL CONSUMPTION :
22.7 m.p.g. overall for 590 miles. 12.4 litres per 100 km.
Approximate normal range 20—24 m.p.g. (14.1—11.8 litres per 100 km).
Fuel : Pool petrol and Belgian premium grade (approximately 80 octane).

WEATHER : Fresh cross wind ; dry surface. Air temperature 38 degrees F.
Acceleration figures are the means of several runs in opposite directions.
Tractive effort and resistance obtained by Tapley meter.
Model described in *The Autocar* of November 26, 1948.

SPEEDOMETER CORRECTION : M.P.H.

Car speedometer ..	..	10	20	30	40	50	60	70	80	90	96
True speed ..	..	10	19	29	39	48	57.5	67	77	87.5	93.75

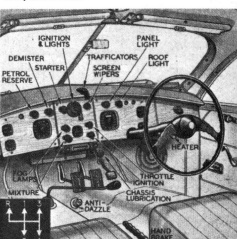

Combined side and fog lights are placed on each side of the built-in head lights. The one-piece bonnet can be opened from either side, or removed completely.

Very good protection is provided by the curved rear bumpers which wrap round the 401's sloping rear quarters. The flush-fitting petrol filler cover is released from inside the body.

bines most if not all of the qualities asked for by the driver who wants a car that is beautifully functional, designed on sound engineering principles. The Bristol has more than that: it has a great deal of a certain something that makes people want to drive it. For example, in the hands of *The Autocar* well over fifteen hundred miles were covered in a little over a week, and most of that outside normal working hours, because experienced drivers, who from their opportunities of comparative experience can be called connoisseurs of cars, enjoyed driving it far above the average.

Effortless cruising with 80 on a speedometer more nearly accurate than is common is a very useful way of getting from place to place in comfort, and it enables long distances to be covered in a very short space of time. What is more, at the end of a journey little fatigue is noticed, while averages of much nearer fifty than forty miles in the hour are quite easily achieved. To obtain the best results this car must be driven: for example, there is perhaps less power available at the bottom end than with some engines of a similar capacity, but a very effective four-speed gear box is fitted, possessing well-chosen ratios, and is there to be used. It is unusual in that a free wheel operates on first gear, and this is very useful for town driving, even more so perhaps than synchromesh on first, as it enables clutchless changes to be made in circumstances that frequently arise in towns.

Although all main road hills capable of being approached briskly can be taken on top gear, the use of third gear is sometimes advantageous. In town work, too, third gear is very useful, whilst second gear offers an extremely useful range for quick acceleration into the fifties. The gear change mechanism, of the type known as conventional before the almost universal adoption of the steering column control, consists of a central lever that is well placed and very light to operate. It is quite slender but it does not vibrate unduly, nor is there an excessive travel from gear to gear.

The Bristol is not a large car, yet the design is not in any way cramped; the wheelbase, for example, is considerably longer relative to the overall length than in some cars. Thus, it has that desirable feature of "a wheel at each corner"; and this feature alone can have a considerable effect on the whole character of a car, as it means that all the passengers are well within the wheelbase. This in turn enables the overall height to be reduced, which provides a reduction in frontal area consequently in drag.

Not only does the Bristol make economical high-speed travel possible, it also seems to like going fast. As already suggested, it will cruise at around eighty with no fuss or bother, and there is a feeling of safety and stability equalled by very few cars indeed. It has a slight tendency to oversteer, but this is not in any way pronounced. Also, the use of rack and pinion steering gear ensures that there is virtually no lost motion in the mechanism, a fact combining with the precision of the steering to give handling qualities very much above the average. This car has the feel of a thoroughbred; it is light and lively and seems to know what is expected of it.

The central fold-down arm rest in the rear seat covers the luggage locker lid release. There is a wide shelf behind the rear seat back rest. Hinged extractor rear windows permit draught-free ventilation with, if desired, the wide main windows closed.

The separate front seats, with the hand brake lever placed ideally between them, are instantly adjustable for back rest angle. Instruments—in a curved polished timber facia—and minor controls present an impressive and practical array. A peak formed by the top of the scuttle prevents the instruments from being reflected.

There is plenty of luggage space in a compartment that is of a useful shape. A hinged lower tray released from above houses the spare wheel.

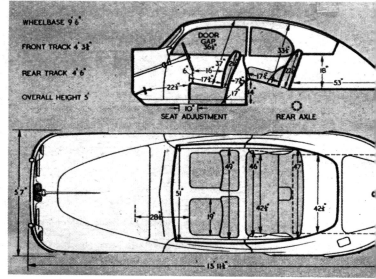

Measurements in these ⅛in to 1ft scale body diagrams are taken with the driving seat in the central position of fore and aft adjustment and with the seat cushions uncompressed.

The suspension, too, is very satisfactory and earns full marks. It is soft enough to cope with really bad surfaces such as Belgian pavé, yet at high speed there is no suspicion of float. On bends the behaviour is good and there is very little roll, and a general feeling of well-being is induced. Inside the car the road noise level is low, no matter what type of surface is being traversed. Wind noise, too, because of the body shape, is not appreciable, although there is a considerable sound if the main window in either of the wide doors is wound open about half an inch; yet further opening reduces this noise. Insulation from both draughts and engine noise is good.

The brakes are one of the very few units of this car that can be criticized, on account of the pedal pressures required being heavy by current standards. In no case did they fail to stop or slow the car as required and in fact the maximum braking figures show a good efficiency.

A good driving position is of the utmost importance in

Comfort at the Wheel

any car, and even more so in a car that goes fast. The Bristol leaves very little room for improvement in this respect; the front seats have ample fore and aft adjustment, in conjunction with the best form of Leveroll mechanism, while the back rests are also adjustable for angle. The combination of these two variables results in a car that is tailor made for most figures, and very comfortable indeed. Increased leg support by means of a longer seat cushion would be useful to some drivers—according to their build—on long journeys. From the driving seat the forward view is satisfactory; the wing line on the passenger side cannot be seen, but the central bonnet strip forms a useful "foresight." Slimmer windscreen pillars and a slightly larger rear window would still further increase the good general visibility.

All the controls are very well placed. The steering wheel in particular deserves mention as, apart from being at just the right angle, it is not cluttered up with minor controls; the two spokes are leather covered and notched. The pedals come just where they are wanted and have a quality feel; the throttle in particular has a very smooth action and is well placed. The driver's left foot is also well provided for, extra room being arranged by placing the dip switch below and between the clutch and brake pedals instead of to the left of the clutch as is usual. Most of the minor controls are grouped around the instruments; they are all within easy reach of the driver, yet sufficiently far apart to prevent confusion. Among them is an overriding ignition setting control, useful for dealing with varying grades of fuel, though in its full advance position there was virtually no pinking, even on Pool petrol. Chassis lubrication is performed by a "one shot" system operated by

the driver's foot, an arrangement, now rare, that is a boon to the busy owner and one that, incidentally, represents a substantial economy in the course of a year.

The interior of the 401 is well finished and very comfortable, and it conveys an air of quality found in few cars today. There is not an excessive number of interior fittings, these being limited to the useful ones such as extensible blind sun vizors, a rear blind—now so rare and appreciated by many drivers—and lockable facia cupboards. There is also a useful complement of ash trays. Much more valuable is the provision of a reserve fuel supply of about three gallons, switched in from the facia. The optional heating system is efficient without becoming overpowering and exceptionally effective for demisting. Instrument lighting is good and can be controlled by means of a rheostat, a useful fitting now seldom found on cars produced in this country.

As well as the powerful head lamps, of which the range is fully adequate, the Bristol is fitted with twin fog lamps; these can be switched on in the usual way as required, or they can operate as pass lights under the control of the dip switch. The horns have a pleasing tone. Starting from cold was instantaneous and very little use of the choke was necessary; also the engine holds heat for longer than usual when standing; thermostatically operated radiator shutters, another modern rarity, are fitted.

The Bristol is a car in a class of its own. It is expensive, but it gives the experienced driver the strongest possible impression that the purchaser is getting for his money a car that is really something, with a fine performance, an "atmosphere" in detail and in road behaviour that belongs to only a select few cars, and with highly practical equipment of a nature not found on many modern cars of lower price.

The six-cylinder engine well fills the space under the bonnet. General accessibility—including that of the battery—is very good. The three carburettors are fed by a single air cleaner. A screen wash unit can be conveniently mounted as an extra.

By
BRISTOL
to
BRESCIA

*With some musings on the
Mille Miglia*

BEFORE moving a yard in the Bristol Type 401 it is clear that the men responsible for it are acutely aware of the needs of the private motorist who uses his car for long-distance touring; lest it be imagined that this is normal, let me say that I can think of not more than half-a-dozen companies in the world who display a similar apprehension. It was therefore with a rarely enjoyed pleasure that I found that the door pockets on the Bristol would support a Michelin guide in the vertical position, that they were divided into two halves so as to prevent a mad jumble when one accelerated or braked hard; that the back of the seats could be given four differing degrees of rake; that there were two lockable cubbyholes and that the rear luggage locker would contain nearly all the luggage needed by two people travelling for two weeks across Europe.

To turn from the general to the particular, this rear locker, which is an epitome of the car as a *voiture de grande tourisme*, will comfortably hold a case of spare parts, a gallon tin of oil, two suitcases, one hat box and three small handbags, leaving the rear seat free for a medium-sized cabin trunk.

The installation of such equipment was not, so to speak, a dummy exercise, but real provision for a trip that I was fortunate enough to make recently in the company of my wife to "cover" the Turin Motor Show and to observe (but not report upon) the XIXth Mille Miglia.

Bishop Wordsworth, who has the remarkable distinction of being the founder of both the Boat Race and the 'Varsity Cricket Match, once noted in his diary :

"In all societies it is advisable to associate with the highest; not that the highest are always the best, but because if disgusted there we can at any time descend, but if we begin with the lowest to ascend is impossible. In the grand theatre of human life a *box ticket* takes us through the house."

Over and above the material benefits accruing to the Technical Editor of a leading motoring journal, it is perhaps the *box ticket* which is the most prized perquisite of the position, and when it is manifested in the shape of a Bristol at one's disposal for three weeks, a lordly reception at Turin, and a well-nigh fuedal life at Brescia, I for one will not challenge the validity of this proposition.

In the first few miles from London to Dover the Bristol showed itself to be a true car of quality. It showed immediately that elusive quality of a response which warms the heart of

CONTRAST IN TUNNELLING.—The Type 401 Bristol is one of the few British cars which has had the benefit of wind-tunnel testing, making use of $\frac{1}{10}$th and other scale models in an 18 in. diameter throat. The car is appropriately pictured near to the French O.N.E.R.A. at Modane which uses hydraulic power to feed one of the largest tunnels in the world in which speeds of up to 675 m.p.h. can be realized in a throat diameter of $26\frac{1}{4}$ ft. The French automobile industry can make use of the 6,000 h.p. tunnel at Chalais Meudon which provides a speed of up to 110 m.p.h. in a throat 53 ft. in diameter.

any man who seeks to drive a car rather than be driven by it, and although (in England particularly) full use must be made not only of third but also of second gear, so smooth and positive are the changes which one can ring from the centre gear lever that one is tempted to use the box even when it is not strictly necessary so to do.

The brakes demand a rather heavier pedal pressure than one would willingly accept, but the steering is so responsive and accurate that there are many occasions where one can, as it were, slip through the eye of the needle where on a larger or less manageable vehicle braking would be the only safe act.

An Illegal Immigrant

Our passage across the Channel by the ever-efficient Townsend Ferry, was on a sea as smooth as a mill pond, but, nevertheless, disturbed somewhat violently in the last half hour before reaching Calais by the discovery that Pomeroy's wife was attempting to enter France with a passport already one week out of date. The prospects looked gloomy, but the immigration officer took mercy upon us and upon a promise (duly fulfilled) to have the offending document renewed by a British Consul at the earliest possible moment, we were allowed to continue our joint progress. As the British Consular service is not open to the public during the weekend this meant deviating slightly from our set route in order to present ourselves at Lyons at the earliest possible moment on the following Monday, and during the journey south we had one of the first many pleasant surprises which was finding that our fuel consumption was at the rate of 22.6 m.p.g.

If one seeks a full four-seater car which will cruise at 80 m.p.h., and do better than 20 m.p.g., choice is limited

By LAURENCE
POMEROY, M.S.A.E.

RECORD VICTORY.—Bracco is shown here winning the Mille Miglia on his 2.7-litre Ferrari, having made a record speed despite extremely bad weather. His margin over the runner-up, Kling, on the new SL Mercedes-Benz was the very small one of 0.28 secs. per mile.

irrespective of the country of origin. Restricted to an English car one is in the position of Mr. Hobson; it is Bristol or nothing. Nor should the benefits of, say, 22½ m.p.g. as against, say, 17½ m.p.g., be dismissed as small. In the 2,000-odd miles covered by the Bristol in fourteen days the difference is between roughly 90 and 115 gallons and at an average price of, say, 5s. 6d. per gallon one has a difference of some 10s. per day. To anyone motoring constantly abroad the gain will be upwards of £50 a year which is equal to the interests on capital sum of over £1,500, even neglecting the incidence of tax.

Credits and Debits

But when considering cars costing over £2,000, economies of running are of little worth if accompanied by major disadvantages in operation or in passenger comfort. In respect of the former one continues to be conscious that the Bristol is a largish car in relation to its engine size and although second gear is rarely needed in Europe, third gear may most profitably be employed in the speed range of 50/70 m.p.h. and thus becomes of particular value in the winding roads that are found in the lower reaches of mountainous country. On mountain climbs second gear is a most excellently-chosen ratio and the presence of a free wheel on first makes it possible quickly to select the lowest gear without bothering with clutch movement when right up against a climbing hairpin corner. It is difficult to restrain enthusiasm for the excellence of the gearbox and the delicacy of the gear change, but unequivocal admiration of the steering and handling of the car in England must be slightly modified after Continental experience.

The car is by nature an over-steerer, and in England and on winding Continental roads gives the driver the very satisfactory experience of responding to the slightest nudge on the wheel, indeed all but the sharpest corners can be taken merely by a flick of the wrist. But on long, straight roads there is some loss of directional stability as the speed rises, particularly should there be a cross wind. Moreover, the high mechanical efficiency in the steering gear, which imparts the desired lightness and delicacy of control, also admits a kick-back on to the steering wheel of considerable magnitude on the rough roads. Here again effects are exaggerated in the upper part of the speed range, and control which is super-responsive on winding roads at below 65 m.p.h. becomes hypersensitive on straight rough roads at over 80 m.p.h. The Bristol is therefore a car which makes definite demands on the driver's skill if it is to be driven fast, although only in respect of the brakes does it call for the exertion of any noticeable physical effort. Roll and pitch are mercifully almost entirely absent, but by the standards which are to-day reached by the leading Continental constructors the suspension is firm, indeed the unkind critic might well call it hard.

In sum, the Bristol is the delight not of a back-seat passenger but of the keen driver, and although it required

watchfulness and concentration I personally enjoyed every kilometre of the road from Calais to Brescia through Turin, and from Brescia through Milan to Dunkirk.

The sensitivity of the car was such that the difference between the French and Italian road surfaces was just as apparent as was the case between England and France. I was also interested to observe that whereas French super carburant at the equivalent of 6s. per gallon was not greatly better than British Pool, the Italian premium fuel

THOROUGH PREPARATION.—The Mercedes-Benz team for the Mille Miglia was accompanied by 20 mechanics, and each of the three drivers had the opportunity of making 14 prior laps of the circuit. This picture shows a small section of the well-organized system of spare parts which accompanied the cars.

as exemplified by the "Esso Extra" which I consistently used, completely eliminated pinking over the whole range of engine speed at the equivalent of a nominal 7s. 10d. per gallon. This, however, was reduced to 5s. 7d. per gallon by taking advantage of the tourist rebate.

In respect of creature comfort I found the seats and driving position to be excellent; forward visibility first class; the wind noise at 80 m.p.h. low; and the whole structure of the body and chassis remarkably rigid—which doubtless made it possible to cover 2,000 high-speed miles without a murmur or a rattle from any part except an experimental air scoop beneath the sump.

So far as performance is concerned, I found that one could cover 96 miles in two hours in adversity, e.g. narrow mountainous valley roads (Chambery to North of Bourg) in extremely wet weather, and 120 miles (Avalion to Orly) in two hours under good conditions, and 400 miles in the day could thus readily be accomplished without an excessively early start or late finish, and without cutting unduly short the luncheon interval.

I suspect, incidentally, that prices for food in France are declining somewhat compared with last year, but they remain higher than those of neighbouring European countries (with the exception of Belgium) and uncomfortably high by British standards. The medium-priced French lunch is to-day 500 frs. or little over 10s. as a starting price, with coffee and tips, etc., to be added, and even in a simple country inn I found that soup for two, one ravioli, a pork chop, vegetables, cheese, fruit, coffee and half a bottle of wine, made up a total of 1,932 frs. or almost £2. In Italy a similar sum provided a considerably grander meal or alternatively one could do reasonably well at about two-thirds the price even in a large city such as Turin, the capital of Piedmonte.

I have already recorded my impressions of the Show which is, *inter alia*, remarkable for a very fine Press service organized by Dott. Giovannetti, and, by tradition, a most enjoyable Press luncheon laid on by Dott. Pestelli of Fiat.

BRITISH HOMEWORK.—Three of the five Aston Martin cars in the Mille Miglia ran as a works team, and here the cars of Parnell and Abecassis are being worked upon in the garage of the Casa Maggi which was an open house for the entire British contingent.

Although by force of external circumstance I arrived in the closing week there were many other foreign journalists there at the same time who were, like myself, on the way to Brescia to deal with the XIXth Mille Miglia. For this remarkable, indeed, unique race, Count Maggi (who will be remembered as a leading Bugattisti in pre-war days) and his charming wife, extend an equally remarkable and unique hospitality to the British competitors and their associates. In the week before the race the Casa Maggi, large as it is, was filled to overflowing, and on the Friday before the event a really large party was held at which the Mayor of Brescia presented awards won by British competitors last year. This was a good omen, for of the house guests in training for the XIXth event, Prince Metternich won the 1,100 c.c. production sports-car class; Mackenzie rode with Leslie Johnson in the Nash-Healey which was fourth in the over 2-litre sports class, and the

first British car to finish; whilst Wisdom and Parnell were first and second in the over 2-litre Grande Tourisme class. Even Stirling Moss, who was forced to retire at Bologna, must have been well pleased by the fact that he was at that time lying third in a British car which was intervening in the age-long struggle between Germany and Italy.

The Mille Miglia has much in common with the Isle of Man Tourist Trophy races. The T.T. has been run 33 times over a long and difficult circuit, but the Senior has been won only twice by a non-British make, only once by a foreign rider, and in the English-speaking world it is regarded as the race of races. The Mille Miglia commenced as recently as 1927, but the principle of a long, town-to-town race over normal roads stretches back to the dawn of motoring competition, the net racing distance of the Paris-Marseille-Paris race of 1896 being, for example, 1,062.5 miles, and the winner's time 67 hrs. 42 mins. 58 secs. !

As with the Tourist Trophy, so with the Mille Miglia, the event has only been won once by a foreign driver (Caracciola on the Mercedes-Benz in 1931) and as a further similarity the Italians regard it as the greatest race in the world.

It is beyond question the most popular, for 502 cars were released from the starting ramp between 11 o'clock on Saturday night and 6.30 on Sunday morning, more than a hundred of them anticipating a drive extending over more than 16 hours.

The finest technical performance was certainly by Lancia, for their short-chassis 2-litre models took third, fifth, sixth and eighth positions in the General Classification. Fagioli, the fastest of them, actually beat his Grand Prix contemporary Caracciola, by 8 mins. 20 secs. From a moral viewpoint, however, all was subsidiary to the duel between Mercedes-Benz and Ferrari.

Opening a Window

Dr. Nallinger, the Technical Director of Mercedes-Benz, is a modest and sensible, as well as a most competent man, and during the course of the race he made some modest, sensible, and competent remarks to the international Press. He asked us not to suppose that Daimler-Benz were returning to racing on the pre-war scale but rather to realize that since the war they had had first to rebuild the bomb-blasted works and then to bring forward a post-war programme for cars and commercial vehicles. Only last year, said Dr. Nallinger, were they able to give attention to a racing car project, and they had been very

COMMUNICATION CAR.—Owing to a breakdown in organization photographs for the Mille Miglia report had to be delivered at the last moment by hand to Milan Airport, and the Le Mans Type SL Mercedes-Benz used for this journey covered 86.5 miles within 60 minutes of leaving the square in Brescia in which it is shown parked next to the Type 401 Bristol.

By Bristol to Brescia - - - Contd.

conscious that the 12 years of 1939-1951 had been the longest period in Daimler-Benz history in which they had not engaged in active competition. They were aware that the conditions and technique of racing had changed and developed in their absence, and their present policy was merely to open a window through which they could observe current conditions.

Some of us who were present could assess the size of this window, in the knowledge that the Company now has 40 mechanics in the Racing Car Dept., half of whom were present in Italy to look after the three competing cars and one spare car. The drivers, moreover, had spent about two months in Italy practising on the course, both with normal cars and the SL competition model.

Some Fast Motoring

The latter is obviously one of the fastest sports-cars in the world, and by a stroke of apparent misfortune I was able to get a very good picture of its performance on the road. As my witness of the Mille Miglia was in itself a last-minute accident, prior arrangements had been made for an editorial report and for the supply of photographs which were to be motored from Brescia to Milan airport during the morning of the race. Having confirmed on my arrival that these schemes were well founded I was more than mildly surprised to be told mid-day on Sunday that there was no question of sending photographs to England before Tuesday—48 hours too late for them to appear in "The Motor." I had myself taken some amateur snaps with a cheap camera but it seemed impossible to reach Milan in time to get them on the aeroplane, until Uhlenhaut, who was with me at the moment when I was confronted with this apparently insoluble problem, said, "All is not lost, I will take you in the spare SL." Jumping in through the Le Mans type doors, we departed from the Square of Brescia (where it was parked next to the trusty Bristol) and 60 minutes later turned off the Autostrada to the airport with 86.5 miles behind us. This fails by over 10 miles to equal the distance I covered in one hour in a Lagonda on the German autobahn in 1939, but on the Italian trip we not only had a cloudburst of such severity that lights had to be put on, but also a major detour through Bergamo caused by a broken bridge. In these circumstances it was, I thought, a staggering effort by a superb driver, who took not the shade of a risk during the entire performance.

Despite at least 200 h.p./ton, the combination of I.R.S. with Z-F differential inhibits wheelspin, and the extremely stiff multi-tubular frame, which weighs only 110 lb., makes it possible to cover roads, so rough as to bring a normal car down to 40 m.p.h., at over double this speed without discomfort. The maximum speed is known to be over 150 m.p.h., but on the Autostrada we eased along at a bare 135/140 m.p.h., a violent cross wind making it necessary

for Uhlenhaut to give full attention to the steering. The brakes on "our" car had an unduly high proportion of effort on the rear wheels, but I was interested to learn that the team were using Ferodo VG 95 brake linings cemented to the shoes by the Redux synthetic glue produced by Aero Research at Duxford.

At the time, the ride of Paul Revere and bringing the news to Ghent seemed minor episodes in history compared to despatching the photos to Temple Press, and it was a good thing for my temporary sense of self-esteem that not until I returned to England did I learn that the aeroplane was running 3½-hrs. behind schedule.

In the meanwhile, I had witnessed Bracco winning the XIXth Mille Miglia amidst scenes of hysterical enthusiasm after a drive of almost unimaginable virtuosity for a man of over 50 years of age.

This result, after so much German preparation, underlines the exceedingly difficult task confronting any foreign participant in this great race, but it may also be noted that failure to win at a first attempt is very much in the Mercedes-Benz tradition. The cars of this company were, for example, 10th and 11th in the 1906 G.P. de l'A.C.F., 10th in the 1907 event, and they won in 1908. Returning after five years they were third in the 1913 G.P. de France, and 1st, 2nd and 3rd in the 1914 G.P. de l'A.C.F. Reappearing again in 1921 a Mercedes was second in the Targa Florio and first in 1922, and in the 750 kg. Formula races of 1934 et seq. no car finished the first race in which they were entered, but they were runners-up in the second and they won the last two of the season. The following year Mercedes-Benz cars won five of the seven Grands Epreuves. With Le Mans almost upon us the question every enthusiast will be asking is whether the SLs will be victorious in their second appearance in a major race, or whether they will have to wait until their second year.

While pondering upon this it may be interesting to break down the Bracco versus Kling struggle into relative speeds between various Controls. This can best be done by setting out a table :

RELATIVE TIMES AND DISTANCES : BRACCO AND KLING 1952 MILLE MIGLIA

Control	Total distance covered	Cumulative Margin of Bracco
Ravenna	189 miles	+05 mins. 27 secs.
Aquila	455 miles	—13 mins. 32 secs.
Rome	576 miles	——11 mins. 58 secs.
Sienna	718 miles	—12 mins. 00 secs.
Florence	761 miles	—04 mins. 40 secs.
Bologna	828 miles	+09 mins. 39 secs.
Brescia	965 miles	+04 mins. 32 secs.

From this we can deduce Bracco's performance in relation to Kling between the Controls thus :

BRACCO'S TIME PER MILE cf. KLING IN 1952 MILLE MIGLIA

Stage	Stage length	Bracco's time, cf. Kling per mile
Brescia-Ravenna	189 miles	Gain 1.73 secs.
Ravenna-Aquila	266 miles	Loss 4.3 secs.
Aquila-Rome	121 miles	Gain 5.9 secs.
Rome-Sienna	142 miles	Loss 0.14 secs.
Sienna-Florence	43 miles	Gain 10.45 secs.
Florence-Bologna	67 miles	Gain 4.47 secs.
Bologna-Brescia	137 miles	Loss 2.24 secs.

From these tables it is apparent that, although Bracco put his superior local knowledge of the Futa and Raticosa Passes (which lie between Florence and Bologna) to good use, the race was really decided between Sienna and Florence. As Kling took nearly 50 minutes to cover only 43 miles he presumably stopped upon the way; but not even a "box ticket" enables a man to observe every mile in a thousand.

THE BRISTOL 401

A High-Efficiency 2-litre Saloon Possessing Outstanding Qualities of Performance, Comfort and Control. Driving an Epicurean Pleasure in this Near-Perfect Car for the Connoisseur.

UNDER wintry conditions last November we realised a patiently-awaited experience, that of road-testing the Bristol 401. We have always held the Bristol in high esteem, approving of the famous aeroplane company's decision to make a beautifully-appointed, extremely comfortable, fast car of only 2-litres capacity and, consequently, a car which pays dividends to a keen driver and which is essentially a high-efficiency sports saloon and not an over-engined luxury carriage. It would have been easy for the Bristol engineers, Car Division, having got a firm footing in the luxury-car market, to have followed the Bristol 400 with a car having an engine of twice its capacity which would have done all its work in top gear or even hydramatically. But such a temptation, if indeed it ever arose, was resisted, and the Bristol 401 retains its high-efficiency 85-b.h.p., 2-litre engine, compact dimensions and a gear-change that needs to be used and is a delight to handle.

Our test of the 401 extended to a four-figure mileage and the present writer completed 633 miles in the car. Incorporated in this mileage was a journey from Hartley Wintney in Hampshire to Land's End accomplished at an average speed of over 50 m.p.h. The entire out and home run, a distance of 502 miles, with only 20 minutes' rest, was accomplished in a running time of 11 hours, although much of the return journey was done after dark, some of it restricted to 40 m.p.h. over icy surfaces, and all of it made between the hours of 9.30 a.m. and 9.30 p.m. when the roads carried normal traffic. The extreme effortlessness of Bristol-fashion travel was nicely emphasised by this journey, undertaken with no thought of ultra-fast driving, or "dicing," but as any other driver used to fast cars would have made it. On this run the overall fuel consumption was 20 m.p.g., a remarkable economy at these speeds, and after over 500 almost continuous miles the driver felt only moderately tired and mentally alert for many more hours behind the wheel.

Thus, although it is true that a 2-litre engine in a car weighing over 24 cwt. and pulling a 3.9 to 1 top gear calls for considerable frequency of gear-changing, this does not tire the driver, but contributes, if anything, to the *joie de vivre* of his motoring.

A number of good qualities combine in the Bristol to make possible safe, effortless, very comfortable average speeds in the 50/60 m.p.h. range. The view of the un-ornate bonnet, uncluttered by mascot or dummy filler cap, pleases, and although the near-side wing is invisible, a driver unfamiliar with the 401 is immediately happy cleaving a way through narrow traffic gaps. The deep front seat, with its firm yet comfortable upholstery and high curved squab adjustable for rake, leaves the elbows free and provides the utmost comfort. The pedals are well placed and solid. Above the walnut facia is a decked-ledge to keep reflections from the windscreen. The facia itself, as will be seen later, is very fully equipped, with neat pull-out or push-in knobs as minor controls.

In this luxuriously-appointed "office" the driver is able to enjoy the epicurean pleasure afforded by the Bristol's performance and handling characteristics. The six-cylinder, three-carburetter engine is smooth but is an engine which demands assistance from the driver, who will thus use third gear frequently in traffic and up main road hills, and will almost as frequently drop into second gear. If speed falls really low second gear will give only mediocre acceleration at first, but a drop into bottom will provide a very vivid "step-off."

The gearbox, then, is there to be used but as the long central lever is absolutely rigid, has a delightful "grip," and can be whipped rapidly from ratio to ratio without effort, helped if need be by excellent synchromesh, anyone who professes to like driving will respond with pleasure to this call for the lower ratios. Even the change out of second into bottom gear is rendered a lightning operation by the employment of a free-wheel, on the lowest ratio only. This first gear free-wheel can be usefully employed for inching forward in thick traffic. The indirect gears are completely unobtrusive and so can be used for as long as the driver desires; they provide

maxima of 25, 50 and 70 m.p.h. without hurrying the engine unduly.

Acceleration is very smooth and purposeful once the engine speed builds up in any gear, and a cruising speed of 80 m.p.h. (4,000 r.p.m.) becomes habitual on ordinary main roads, maintained up hill and after passing obstructions by free use of those delightfully spaced and easily engaged indirect gears.

It is after holding this speed for a while that the occupants become aware of a remarkable and very desirable aspect of the Bristol saloon. Eighty miles per hour gives the impression of little increase over 50 m.p.h., and it dawns on the fortunate owner that the aerodynamic lines of the handsome two-door closed body are really and truly aerodynamic, *i.e.*, that the wind-tunnel tests made on the Bristol have resulted in a car which, so far as wind-noise is concerned, is all but completely silent at all speeds up to 90 m.p.h. As the speedometer needle creeps from 90 to over 100 m.p.h. a slight increase in sound is perceptible, but it is very slight. Complete silence in this respect is marred only by a slight whistle of air round the area of the front screen pillars and even this is inaudible in the back compartment.

This lack of wind-noise is one of the main factors in the Bristol's effortless running, leaving the occupants fresh after many hundreds of miles at high cruising speeds, as our winter-day's drive to Land's End and back so nicely emphasised.

This clean aerodynamic form gives rise to the impression, even at low speeds, that the car has a free-wheel (which is actually operative in first gear only), so that the driver feels he must rely on his brakes more than usual. It also permits engine noise, which is to be expected from a high-efficiency 2-litre unit, to be heard in the lower gears to a greater extent than would be the case in square-rigged cars; in any case, the engine note is not in any way excessive and is not accompanied by so much as a trace of exhaust noise, while the aerodynamically-efficient form undoubtedly contributes to a fuel consumption of a genuine 20 m.p.g. under conditions when we would have been well content with 5 m.p.g. less.

In top gear the Bristol runs with the smoothness and silence of the true luxury car. As the engine idles at 600 r.p.m. in neutral it is virtually inaudible.

The cornering and roadholding qualities are fully in keeping with the Bristol's easy, vivid performance.

The steering, which on the car tested showed about $\frac{1}{16}$ in. free movement in the rack-and-pinion mechanism, is smooth and quite light, but acts against a strong castor action, which not only spins the wheel straight after corners, but renders control a taut, positive action. The front wheels can be "felt" almost unconsciously by the driver and on some surfaces cause the wheel to rock but not kick through his hands—good, sensitive steering. It feels extremely high-geared, although, in fact, calling for three turns from one generous lock to the other. No vibration is conveyed to the pleasant thick-rimmed wheel and, to sum up, this is steering which enables the Bristol to be taken down the camber at 70 m.p.h. and past a lorry with only inches to spare with complete nonchalance and no conscious effort, while it gives great confidence when the sheen of sheet-ice is mistaken for the glint of rain-soaked tarmac.

The Bristol goes round corners fast with neither over- nor understeer characteristics and with a minimum of roll. Such roll as there is takes the form of a slight lurch, killed at the outset before the back end breaks away. Rain has little effect on the splendid roadholding, but if the back wheels do break away a flick of the sensitive steering wheel corrects the incipient slide. The tyres make practically no sounds of anguish during fast cornering or brisk negotiation of traffic roundabouts. The nose of the car can be made to dip slightly under very heavy braking but this is particularly firm suspension, yet one which gives a luxurious ride—there is no other term for it—over the vilest surfaces. The wheels are also very well damped, and a sudden excursion onto an unmade road verge has no effect on the accuracy of control, which is another feature of the Bristol's seven-league boots. Before we dismiss the transverse leaf-

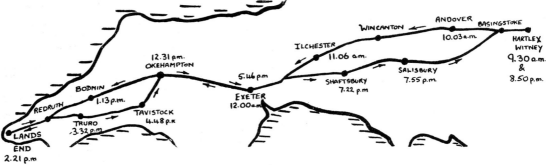

500-MILE JAUNT. —The Bristol 401, in which a run of over 500 miles was comfortably accomplished within 12 hours total time, seen on the left at the start at Hartley Wintney on A30, well known to V.S.C.C. supporters of "Phoenix" evenings, and on the right outside the Land's End Hotel (shut for the winter) which it reached in 4 hr. 51 min., although this was a gentle run, not a record-attempt! The map may be of interest to others who make this journey west.

spring i.f.s. and torsion-bar rear suspension, it must be remarked that no noise from the Michelin-shod wheels over varying road surfaces was transmitted to the occupants' ears.

To this general picture of the 401, difficult to set down but adding up to an ability to go far, fast, with a maximum of pleasure to those travelling in it, can be coupled some more detailed observations on performance.

The Bristol is not intended as a top-gear car, although the lazy need have no qualms; it will accelerate smoothly from 20 m.p.h. in top gear. Use that delightful gearbox and cruising speeds that would not disgrace a car of twice the engine size come up like magic. The body is substantially made and completely rain- and draught-proof. The doors, for example, possess that solid construction which denotes the luxury car, while the equipment is truly generous. Yet 60 m.p.h. from rest comes up in under 17 seconds, 70 m.p.h. in 23 seconds or less. Some performance figures are included in the data panel but we must emphasise that they were taken on a wet road, and on Pool petrol, so that the engine would take very little ignition advance; the clutch was also prone to slip. Incidentally, there was noticeable free-play in the transmission.

The poor weather conditions precluded a maximum speed check, but this can be put at about 97-98 m.p.h. Twice the speedometer indicated well over 100 m.p.h. and, what pleased us more, was to see it at over 90 m.p.h. up an appreciable main-road hill! The Bristol 401, for all its refined manners, does not lack real performance. (It is a stimulating mental exercise to visualise a short-chassis "Gran Sport" version with alloy-shell saloon body and the 132-b.h.p. Bristol engine used in the Le Mans Replica Frazer-Nash!)

The 11-in. Lockheed hydraulic brakes are so powerful that all four wheels can be locked and they are in themselves vice-free. However, they call for determined pressure on the pedal when fully arresting the car. This rather "solid" vintage-style retardation is quite pleasant but proves tiring on a long run and as the leg muscles tire it becomes increasingly difficult to gauge the braking effect. Moreover, a lady would hardly enjoy such braking and at times we felt the car lacked sufficient stopping power, although for a crash stop, given sufficient effort, the safety factor would prove ample. For mere slowing down from high speeds these are good brakes. The horizontal central hand-lever has a good hand-grip topped by a release button, and works impeccably.

Clutch and accelerator are light to operate. The gear-lever is sprung away from the reverse location.

The three-carburetter engine proved difficult to start under low-temperature conditions but, once started, pulls well with minimum use of the mixture control and without falter. It ran too cool,

blanking of the grille still failing to send the water temperature over 80 deg. C.; the oil temperature stayed at 50 deg. C. The oil pressure varies somewhat with speed, to a maximum of about 70 lb./sq. in. We noticed that Castrol oil was in use; only a pint was needed throughout the test and the radiator did not require topping up. The engine pinks viciously at full advance, but there is a sensitive, slide-out ignition control as an antidote, a similar control providing hand variation of engine speed from 600-2,800 r.p.m. The engine does not run-on, not a trace of fumes enters the car, and the Bristol feels as if it would do over 500 miles within 12 hours day after day without loss of engine or chassis tune.

Although the saloon has such good aerodynamic contours the interior is spacious, with plenty of leg and head room for everyone and an unusually deep luggage locker. The sloping rear window poses no problem of rear-view visibility and the rear windows, which open slightly to extract warm air, give a fine view.

The Bristol in Detail

The 401 is such a magnificently appointed car that a brief description of those features which make it such a desirable personal possession will be of interest.

The built-in Lucas 770 headlamps give a long but not sufficiently concentrated beam; this may be because they had yellow bulbs. They are supplemented by excellent, but dazzling, fog-lamps, automatically extinguished as full headlamp beam is selected. The doors are opened internally and externally by flush push-buttons, the driver's having a Yale lock. There are rope "pulls" on the doors and four ash-trays. The driver's door button was far too stiff and resulted in a sprained thumb, although it became easier to operate with use. The doors each have deep, "rigid," very useful, two-partition wells, and there is a deep shelf behind the back seat.

The walnut facia carries large knobs which control the concealed panel lights (rheostat control of intensity), starter, mixture, throttle, ignition, de-mister, roof-light, petrol reserve, and wipers. There are neat windows for headlamp beam, fuel reserve and ignition lamps.

The horn button is part of the steering-wheel boss and the indicator switch is on the screen sill—it works rather too lightly and the self-cancelling action is too rapid. The lamp dipper is under the clutch pedal; we prefer a steering-wheel switch. In place of visors there are neat pull-out stiff blinds for both front-seat occupants. The sloping V-screen with central rib is free from reflected light; the wipers function well but are not self-parking. The screen sprays work splendidly; the lamps control is normal. A nice touch is the tiny "Bristol 2-litre" badge attached to the ignition key ring.

At each end of the facia is a good cubby-hole with matching

44

G.A. OF THE 401.—A view of this very fine 2-litre which shows the high-efficiency engine, massive doors and exceedingly comfortable seating, etc.

walnut lid having a Yale lock. The interiors are lined to match the roof, in washable material, and the lids have leather " keeps."

The doors stay fully open as set; the locker lid is light to lift and is released by a knob concealed beneath the rear-seat central armrest when this is stowed. After the locker has been opened the catches which release the spare-wheel tray and allow it to be opened are revealed. Another clever anti-thief device is a knob in the near-side rear-seat armrest which releases the flap covering the quick-action fuel filler. This location keeps its operating Bowden cable short but would be more convenient on the facia.

A rear-window blind with a " wire " cord within reach of the driver is provided; it did not quite eliminate dazzle from lamps close behind, but at least this warned of a closely-following vehicle. The radio is that impeccable set, His Master's Voice, with external non-adjustable roof aerial. The heater has a stopcock within reach of the driver and volume controls (providing cool air with the heater off) for both front-seat passenger and driver. The heater took time to come into operation but was then very effective. There is rheostat control of de-mister heat and the fan is quite quiet.

The door windows wind easily and their handles have rotating finger-knobs, but the action is opposite from conventional, tending to a locked car with open windows! The back windows hinge slightly open to give an extractor effect.

The instruments comprise an accurate fuel gauge, Smith's speedometer with trip and total mileometers, Smith's rev.-counter, combined oil and water thermometers, clock, ammeter, and oil gauge. All are steady-reading, high-grade " square-dial " instruments with white needles. The speedometer suffered only slight needle-float while the rev.-counter took some time to " settle "; the former was virtually accurate at 30 and 60 m.p.h. The petrol gauge reads zero before the two reserve gallons have been consumed.

Above the accelerator is the pedal for working the useful Enoto one-shot chassis lubricator, to be used rather frequently—every 70 miles. The bumpers provide excellent protection of wings and tail. The light bonnet top panel opens on either side by operation of the appropriate pull-out knob, or can be removed entirely. It can be propped open with a crude but effective stay. There is no screen de-froster. A reversing lamp is selected automatically as the gear-lever engages reverse.

The front seats have slides which give a wide choice of positions, while four-lobe cams enable the angle of the squabs to be pre-set to any one of four positions before the occupants enter. As these cams are not interconnected some delay can result in getting them synchronised. These seats also slide forward to give very reasonable access into the comfortable back seat. These bucket-type front seats with their curved-back squabs are a commendable feature of a fast-cornering car. The upholstery is of the finest crushed-grain leather over Dunlopillo and the head-lining is of soft, washable material, while the floor is covered with a deep carpet over a felt underlay.

Battery, dip-stick, etc., are decently accessible when the bonnet is raised. The coachbuilt, aluminium-panelled body is free from rattles, and its fine construction is complementary to the Bristol's refined manner of running.

Conclusion

In conclusion, the Bristol 401 appeals not on account of a single outstanding characteristic, but because a combination of good qualities renders it an outstandingly pleasant car on long runs when time presses or the driver seeks to go fast for the sheer pleasure of driving. Responsiveness of control and the high degree of aerodynamic silence stamp the 401 as a fine car, perhaps to a greater

degree than its acceleration and speed abilities, excellent as these are. The fascinatingly complete equipment and the craftsmanship evident in the specification and construction are truly refreshing in this age of standardisation and chromiumed tin shrouds. This, indeed, is the car for the true connoisseur. It can only be modesty on the part of the Bristol publicity boys which has prevented them from quoting as the 401's slogan " The Best Car in Britain."—W. B.

THE BRISTOL 401 SALOON

Engine : Six-cylinder, 66 by 96 mm. (1,971 c.c.). Push-rod o.h.v.; 7.5 to 1 compression ratio; 85 b.h.p. at 4,500 r.p.m.
Gear ratios : 1st, 14.08 to 1; 2nd, 7.12 to 1; 3rd, 5.04 to 1; top, 3.9 to 1.
Tyres : 5.75 by 16 Michelin on bolt-on steel disc wheels.
Weight : 24 cwt. 1 qtr. (less occupants but with one gallon of petrol).
Steering ratio : Three turns, lock to lock.
Fuel capacity : 17 gallons (including 2 gall. in reserve). Range approx. 340 miles.
Wheelbase : 9 ft. 6 in.
Track : Front, 4 ft. 3¾ in. Rear, 4 ft. 6 in.
Overall dimensions : 15 ft. 11½ in. by 5 ft. 7 in. (wide) by 5 ft. (high).
Price : £2,000 (£3,112 12s. 3d. with p.t.).

PERFORMANCE DATA

Speeds in gears :

1st	... 25 m.p.h.	3rd	... 70 m.p.h.
2nd	... 50 m.p.h.	Top	... 98 m.p.h.

Acceleration (on wet road) :
Through gears :

0-30 m.p.h. in	5.0 sec.	0-60 m.p.h. in	16.4 sec.
0-40 ,,	,, 7.6 ,,	0-70 ,,	,, 23.0 ,,
0-50 ,,	,, 11.2 ,,	0-80 ,,	,, 33.0 ,,

        s.s. ¼-mile in 20.7 sec.

Second gear :

10-30 m.p.h. in 5.8 sec.	30-50 m.p.h. in 5.4 sec.
20-40 ,, ,, 5.6 ,,	

Third gear :

20-40 m.p.h. in 7.4 sec.	40-60 m.p.h. in 8.0 sec.

Top gear :
    30-50 m.p.h. in 11.0 sec.

Makers : The Bristol Aeroplane Co., Ltd., Filton, Bristol.

1. Petrol Reserve Switch.	11. Bonnet Release.
2. Demisting Switch.	12. Air Inlet Contro Ventilation.
3. Starter Switch.	13. Fog Lamp Switch.
4. Lighting Switch.	14. Mixture Control.
5. Trafficator Switch.	15. Throttle Control.
6. Ignition Switch.	16. Ignition Advance and Retard
7. Wiper Switch.	Control.
8. Panel Light Switch.	17. Head Lamp Dip Switch.
9. Roof Light Switch.	18. Door Release Button.
10. Diffuser Ventilating System.	

upper three ratios, and a free wheel incorporated in the first speed pinion, nobody need be afraid of making proper use of the gearbox.

It should be made clear at this point that the engine is quite flexible, and will pull away smoothly from the lowest speeds in top gear. Driven thus, though, the car gives no hint of its latent performance, and only moderate acceleration is available. In any case, it is rare indeed to find

(Above) . . . Fully controllable at all times; the Bristol during some fast laps at Silverstone.

(Right) As distinctive a closed carriage as anyone could desire.

THE Bristol is a most unusual car, in fact it is entirely different from anything else on the British market. In spite of its relatively recent introduction, it has already acquired an almost legendary fame, and he (or she) who drives a Bristol gains considerable prestige thereby.

More than anything else, it is the body of the "401" that determines its character. It is a full-sized five-seater saloon, equipped and finished in a style that stands out even among cars of the highest class. Every imaginable refinement is provided for the comfort of the passenger, and this is a most luxurious conveyance. There is ample luggage accommodation, and such installations as heating, ventilation, and radio are unobtrusively built in. The traditional wooden instrument panel carries every sort of dial and control that the enthusiastic driver could desire.

Without sacrificing a single cubic inch of interior space, the designers have enclosed all this in an envelope of truly aerodynamic shape. This has been achieved by long and tireless experiments in the wind tunnel, and naturally aircraft technique has been called upon extensively. The fully streamlined form endows the car with a high maximum speed, but it also renders the employment of a relatively small engine quite impractical, and one thus enjoys two-litre economy with four-litre luxury and performance.

On the road, it takes a few miles before one is accustomed to these unusual characteristics. Once one realizes, however, that the two-litre, high-efficiency engine works better in the upper range of crankshaft speeds, the true pleasure of handling the machine becomes apparent. With such a car, the behaviour of the gearbox is immensely important, and in this component, the Bristol engineers have excelled themselves. One soon forms the habit of making frequent gear changes, almost without realizing that one has touched the lever; which, thank heavens, is mounted in the proper place on the floor, and not hidden under the steering wheel. With effective synchromesh on the

a roomy saloon that provides racing maximum on the indirects, and I found myself using that delightful lever at any possible excuse.

It is on the open road that this car really comes into its own. At low speeds, the engine and gearbox are not completely silent, but at an easy cruising gait of 80 m.p.h., no car runs more quietly. At 90 m.p.h. there is still not the slightest sign of stress, and I am sure that that pace could be happily maintained for as long as road conditions permitted. Seventy m.p.h. may be exceeded in third before the valve gear becomes audible.

A truly streamlined body, allied to an engine that has many of the

RISTOL "401"

ater Closed Car
on 100 m.p.h.

The facia panel shows definite traces of being the work of an aircraft-construction concern, all instruments being clearly calibrated and placed in the best possible position for quick reading.

virtues of a racing unit, must pro-duce a rapid vehicle. Nevertheless, mere speed, without good roadhold-ing, is almost valueless, and that is another problem that has been tackled from first principles.

Complete rigidity is the main essential, and the Bristol starts off with a well braced box-section frame. The steel floor is a stressed member, and so are the tubular body supports. The whole structure is designed for maximum stiffness, and every component plays its part to that end. When one sees these chassis being built up, one realizes that such perfection can never be cheap, for the complete framework is of considerable complexity. All the panels are of light alloy, and do not touch any other member, except where they are "wrapped" at their edges.

The front suspension is by a trans-verse leaf spring, which is located beneath a pair of wishbones. The steering is rack and pinion. At the

rear, torsion bars, running forward parallel with the frame, are coupled to the ends of the axle through arms and short shackles. A positive lateral positioning is secured by a triangular link in the axle centre. There are large telescopic dampers all round.

In practice, the roadholding and suspension represent a good compro-mise, and the steering is truly excel-lent. Pitching and swaying are entirely absent, and the ride, while fairly firm, is comfortable and untir-

ing to all the occupants. Under some conditions, there is a suspicion of over-steering, though excessive rear-end breakaway does not take place. Naturally, one is conscious of the length of the vehicle when negotiating sharp bends, but I put in some fast laps of the Silverstone and Brands Hatch circuits, and the car was fully controllable at all times.

It is most noticeable that, at the higher speeds, the Bristol will coast

(Right and below) The perfect aero-dynamic body con-tours are empha-sized in these two views of the beauti-ful Bristol 401. The shape was the result of intensive wind-tunnel testing.

★

★

for considerable distances with a closed throttle, due to the aero-dynamic efficiency of the body. This of course, means that the brakes have a particularly hard task to per-form during fast driving. Even after repeated violent applications, no serious fading can be engendered, though the smell of hot linings be-comes evident. Powerful braking is always available, but the pedal

The Bristol 401—*continued*

pressure is greater than is normal these days.

The six-cylinder, inclined-valve engine feels as though it revels in hard work and high averages, and that gear-lever just asks to be used. It is on long, fast journeys, rather than in the stopwatch figures of the data panel, that the true worth of this car shows itself. I found that, even when I was tired, I continued to reel off the miles in effortless ease, and did not long for the journey to end.

In spite of all its technical excellences, the Bristol would not sell readily at its admittedly high price if its appearance did not inspire pride of ownership. In this respect, the functional simplicity of the low-drag form pays dividends, and it has not been marred by garish decorations. It is regrettably true that, among expensive cars, mere vulgar opulence is usually the styling *motif*. In marked contrast, the Bristol presents a well-bred purity of line that causes it to stand out in any company.

I was privileged to inspect the factory where these cars are built, and was able to confirm that the brilliance of the design is fully backed up by high standards of engineering at all stages of manufacture. The experience behind the finest British aircraft is employed as a matter of course, and it is this superb craftsmanship, above all, that gives the car its intrinsic value.

Perhaps you are the kind of AUTOSPORT reader who cares only for the one-and-a-half-seater open sports-car that is full of sound and fury. I sometimes feel that way myself. I must admit, though, that as I left Silverstone, exhausted after an

Three downdraught carburetters are used on the Bristol 401 engine, which, in modified form, is used on Frazer-Nash, Cooper-Bristol and E.R.A. The detail work is to the highest engineering standards.

unequal struggle with recalcitrant broadcasting machinery, it was good to have the door of the Bristol swing noiselessly open at the touch of a button, and to sink into that comfortable seat. As I inched my way through the heavy traffic, I relaxed in air-conditioned ease, listening to the kind of music I like. I am only human, and it was fun to collect an admiring crowd when I stopped at an hotel for refreshment.

Later, as the roads emptied, 90 m.p.h. was exceeded again and again, but this was a "ninety" with a difference, for no wind noise marred our flight. The adjustable instrument illumination glowed brightly, since a clever shield prevents all reflection in the sloping screen, and the light, accurate steering seemed to transfer my thoughts

straight to the road, without any mechanical intervention. It was one of those journeys that live long in the memory, and whether you regard the Bristol as the most sybaritic of sports-cars, or as a luxurious magic carpet with an incidental turn of speed, the result is such *de luxe* transport for five people and their luggage as one never thought that a car of only two litres could provide.

* * *

THE INVACAR

AFTER my recent road-test of the Bond Minicar, a correspondent suggested that I should try the Invacar invalid carriage, which is propelled by the same type of 196 c.c. engine. I have, therefore, made a short test of one of these machines, and I must say that the performance is quite astonishing. Acceleration from a standstill to 30 m.p.h. takes only 10 seconds, and most hills are climbed easily on top gear.

Whereas the Bond is wide and low, being a full 2/3-seater, the Invacar is a narrow single-seater, and I must admit that at its terminal velocity, which approaches 50 m.p.h., I was very frightened indeed. Actually, the tiller steering is much better than one would expect, and the brakes, which work through a lever on which one rests one's arm, are quite reasonably effective. The little car is great fun to drive, and I am very glad that such a delightful means of transport is now available to invalids.

JOHN V. BOLSTER.

* * *

VILLORESI'S FERRARI

CONTRARY to general belief, the 4½-litre Ferrari which Luigi Villoresi drove at Silverstone was not one of the Indianapolis cars. It was a new experimental model with rubber-controlled rear suspension. Excessive bouncing made it difficult to handle, but it is said to be the most powerful Ferrari ever built.

SPECIFICATION AND PERFORMANCE DATA

Car Tested: Bristol "401" model saloon, price £2,270 (£3,532 12s. 3d. with P.T.).

Engine: Six-cylinders, 66 mm. x 96 mm. Pushrod operated inclined valves in light alloy head. 85 b.h.p. at 4,500 r.p.m. 7.5 to 1 compression ratio. Three downdraught Solex carburetters. Coil and distributor with automatic advance, plus hand control.

Transmission: 8 in. Borg and Beck clutch. 4-speed gearbox with central control; ratios 3.9, 5.51, 8.48 and 16.77 to 1. Hardy Spicer propeller shaft. Spiral bevel rear axle.

Chassis: Box section frame, reinforced with integral steel floor and tubular body frame. Independent front-suspension by transverse leaf spring and wishbones. Rear suspension by torsion bars. Newton telescopic dampers

all round. Bolt-on pierced disc wheels, fitted 5.50 in. x 16 in. tyres. Lockheed hydraulic brakes.

Equipment: 12-volt lighting and starting. Speedometer, revolution counter, ammeter, water temperature, oil temperature, oil pressure, and fuel gauges, heating, demisting and radio.

Dimensions, etc.: Wheelbase, 9 ft. 6 ins. Track, front, 4 ft. 3¾ ins., rear, 4 ft. 6 ins. Overall length, 15 ft. 10 ins. Turning circle, 36 ft. Weight, 25 cwt.

Performance: Maximum speed, 97 m.p.h. Speeds in gears, third, 80 m.p.h., second, 55 m.p.h. Acceleration, standing quarter-mile, 20¾ secs. 0-50 m.p.h., 11⅜ secs. 0-60 m.p.h., 18 secs. 0-70 m.p.h., 25 secs.

Fuel Consumption: Driven hard, 23 m.p.g.

The BRISTOL 403 Saloon

Mechanical Improvements, Greater Comfort and Increased Power are Features of the Latest 2-litre Model

THROUGHOUT their relatively brief history the products of the Car Division of the Bristol Aeroplane Company have been highly individual machines intended for a discerning and individual customer. Despite a slight change of policy in 1948 in favour of a full four-seater saloon instead of a close-coupled coupé style, the emphasis has remained on quality and comfort in a fast and essentially modern car. In short, the Bristol offers luxury high-speed motoring in the highest class.

With this short but effective tradition, and still more, with the resources of the parent company behind it in the field of aeronautical and aerodynamic research, it is not surprising that the latest in the Bristol line, the 403, should retain the outward appearance and general construction of its predecessor, while incorporating a number of important mechanical modifications and detail refinements.

Briefly, the major changes include higher power from the 2-litre engine, improved braking and suspension units, an alteration to the transmission to give smoother running at low speeds and attention to passenger comfort in the shape of a heater system equally efficient in town use and on the open road.

It is some time since the Bristol was fully described in *The Motor*, and the latest improvements may be better appreciated in conjunction with a resumé of the basic features of the design.

Most readers will be familiar with the six-cylinder 1,971 c.c. engine, which has combustion chambers of the classic hemispherical shape, and valves operated by lightweight pushrods and rockers. In the latest version both power and engine speed have been stepped up, the '100A' giving

100 b.h.p. at 5,250 r.p.m. against 85 b.h.p. at 4,500 r.p.m. for the previous type—an increase of over 17%. The crankshaft has nitride-hardened journals running in four lead-copper strip type main bearings of increased diameter, and the shaft is now fully balanced statically and dynamically by bolt-on counterweights.

The aluminium alloy cylinder head has been redesigned to allow the use of larger inlet valves, which are of chrome nickel steel alloy, while the exhaust valves are of austenitic chrome steel. A new camshaft gives an increased overlap which while putting peak revolutions up by 750 r.p.m. does not, it is claimed, impair the flexibility or fuel con-

BRISTOL 403 DATA

Engine Dimensions			Chassis Details		
Cylinders	... ...	6	Brakes	... ...	Lockheed hydraulic (2LS front)
Bore	... ...	66 mm.			
Stroke	... ...	96 mm.	Brake drum diameter		11 in.
Cubic capacity	...	1,971 c.c.	Friction lining area		148 sq. in.
Piston area	...	31.8 sq. in.	Suspension: Front	...	I.F.S. (Transverse leaf spring and wishbones)
Valves	...	Inclined o.h.v. (pushrods)		Rear	Torsion bars and rigid axle
Compression ratio		7.5/1	Shock absorbers	...	Newton telescopic
Engine Performance			Wheel type	...	Pierced disc
Max. b.h.p.	...	100 b.h.p.	Tyre size	...	5.75 x 16
at	... ...	5,250 r.p.m.	Steering gear	...	Rack and pinion
Max. b.m.e.p.	...	147 lb. per sq. in.	Steering wheel	...	Two-spoked
at	... ...	3,500 r.p.m.			
B.H.P. per sq. in. piston area	...	3.14	**Dimensions**		
Peak piston speed ft. per min.	...	3,305 ft. per min.	*Wheelbase	...	9 ft. 6 in.
			Track: Front	...	4 ft. 3¾ in.
Engine Details			Rear	...	4 ft. 6in.
Carburetter...	...	3 Solex downdraught	Overall length	...	15 ft. 11¼ in.
Ignition	... ...	Lucas coil	Overall width	...	5 ft. 7 in.
Plugs: make and type		K.L.G. 10 L100	Overall height	...	5 ft.
Fuel pump	...	AC mechanical	Ground clearance	...	6¼ in.
Fuel capacity	...	17 gallons	Turning circle	...	36 ft. 6 in.
Oil filter (make, by-pass or full-flow)...		Vokes full-flow	Dry weight	...	24 cwt.
Oil capacity	...	12 pints			
Cooling system	...	Fan and pump			
Water capacity	...	21 pints	**Performance Data**		
Electrical system	...	Lucas 12-volt	Piston area, sq. in. per ton	...	26.5 sq. in.
Battery capacity	...	51 amp./hr.	Brake lining area, sq. in. per ton	...	123.3 sq. in.
Transmission			Top gear m.p.h. per 1,000 r.p.m.	...	20.25
Clutch	... ...	Borg and Beck s.d.p.			
Gear ratios: Top	...	(s/m) 3.9	Top gear m.p.h. at 2,500 ft./min. piston speed		80.5
3rd	...	(s/m) 5.04			
2nd	...	(s/m) 7.12	Litres per ton-mile, dry...	... ...	2,425
1st	...	(free wheel) 14.08			
Rev.	...	11.27			
Prop. shaft	...	Open			
Final drive	...	Spiral bevel			

Bonnet flashes and a silvered radiator grille distinguish the 403 seat squabs, wide door pockets and two-spoke steering wheel optional extra.

The Bristol 403 Saloon - - - Contd.

sumption, 24 m.p.g. being quoted as an average figure on the open road. As before, three downdraught Solex carburetters are used, with a large air cleaner and silencer. A margin of safety for the higher loads is provided by the bigger capacity of the oil pump and sump, which now holds 12 pints.

Central Gear Lever

Transmission is by single dry plate clutch and Bristol gearbox, with a long extension rearwards to reduce the length of the open propeller shaft. Very easy gear changing is possible with the central gear lever, Borg Warner syncromesh being provided on the three upper gears, while bottom gear has a free wheel. The balanced propeller shaft is now fitted with "Layrub" rubber universal joints at either end to give a cushioned drive at low speeds. The banjo-type rear axle uses semi-floating shafts driven by a spiral bevel crown wheel and pinion and two star differential.

No change has been made in the general construction of the Bristol, or in the aluminium panelled, steel-framed body closely integrated with an immensely strong steel box-section frame. The aerodynamic shape of the body is, of course, largely owed to experiments in the wind tunnel at Filton.

The suspension also follows the same lines as that of the 401, with small but important changes which are reflected in the improved roadholding. The front wheels are independently sprung by wishbones above a single transverse leaf spring, with a safety link as a safeguard against breakage of the master leaf. A torsion anti-roll bar has now been added, mounted beneath the main chassis members. The spring and all joints are protected against mud and dirt by water-resistant gaiters, and there is one-shot lubrication of the joints by a pedal on the toe-board.

Fine Roadholding

Rear suspension is by longitudinal torsion bars, and the axle is located laterally by a triangular bracket on top of the differential casing. Large double-acting telescopic shock absorbers are fitted front and rear, with revised settings to improve the ride, particularly over bad surfaces. A short drive in the 403 on some twisty minor roads near Filton offered convincing proof of the roadholding ability of the new model, which gives complete confidence for fast driving even on first acquaintance. There is very little roll, and the Bristol rack and pinion steering is light and precise.

With the performance now available (there seems every

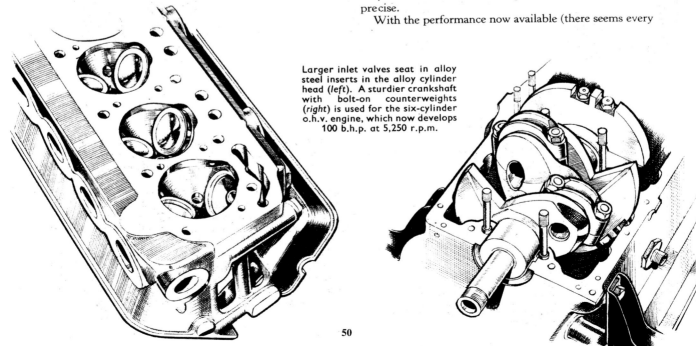

Larger inlet valves seat in alloy steel inserts in the alloy cylinder head (left). A sturdier crankshaft with bolt-on counterweights (right) is used for the six-cylinder o.h.v. engine, which now develops 100 b.h.p. at 5,250 r.p.m.

reason to believe the claim for a maximum of over 100 m.p.h.) braking becomes a matter of still greater importance, and two changes here are an alteration of the brake pedal leverage to reduce the effort required, and the fitting of Alfin light alloy drums, which have bonded alloy cast iron liners. Both front and rear drums are finned for better cooling.

Quality in the Bristol is not confined to the mechanical design and construction, passenger comfort receiving the same meticulous attention. No pretence is made of carrying more than four in the leather-covered, Dunlopillo

seats, and those at the front are adjustable both for reach and for the angle of the squabs. The equipment is comprehensive, and the walnut instrument panel includes such rare items as an oil thermometer and a warning light for the petrol reserve which is operated by a switch on the panel.

The interior heating system has been modified to cope with all conditions by the provision of an extra control for recirculating hot air in very cold weather or when driving in town. Fresh air is normally taken in through ducts just in front of the radiator by the ram effect of the car's passage (eliminating fan noise), and passes through heat exchangers before entering the passenger compartment at floor level on either side of the car. Air from the upper half of one of the heaters can, if needed, be tapped off and blown on to the windscreen or downwards towards the driver's feet by an electric fan. When the outside temperature is very low, or the speed of the car is insufficient to let in enough warm air, the ducts are closed and the blower draws air back through the lower half of the heater and then through the upper half and directs it to the windscreen and feet. Further silence has been achieved by repositioning the windscreen wiper motor under the bonnet.

A most unusual fitting these days is a rear window blind, raised by a cord-pull conveniently placed in the centre of the roof above the front seats. An automatic

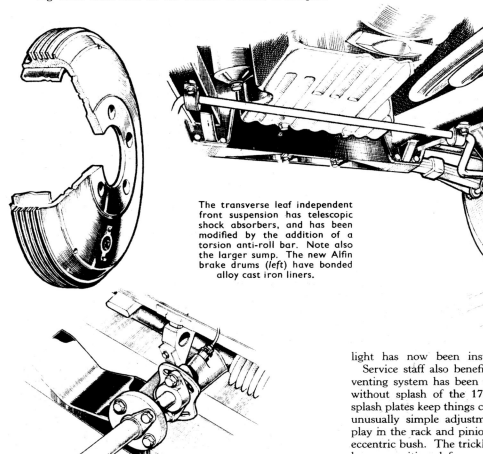

The transverse leaf independent front suspension has telescopic shock absorbers, and has been modified by the addition of a torsion anti-roll bar. Note also the larger sump. The new Alfin brake drums *(left)* have bonded alloy cast iron liners.

Typical of Bristol attention to mechanical detail is this simple adjustment for taking up wear in the rack and pinion steering. An eccentric bush is turned by slackening the two bolts and moving the slotted plate. Behind the plate can be seen the connection from the one-shot lubrication system.

light has now been installed in the luggage locker.

Service staff also benefit from the improvements; the venting system has been altered to allow quicker filling without splash of the 17-gallon petrol tank, and anti-splash plates keep things clean in the engine bay, while an unusually simple adjustment makes it easy to take up play in the rack and pinion steering gear by means of an eccentric bush. The trickle charger in the engine bay has been repositioned for easier access.

Externally, the new Bristol is distinguished from its predecessor by silver-enamelled front grilles and red medallions, and '403' flashes on the bonnet sides. The very high quality of finish comes in fifteen combinations of interior and exterior colour schemes.

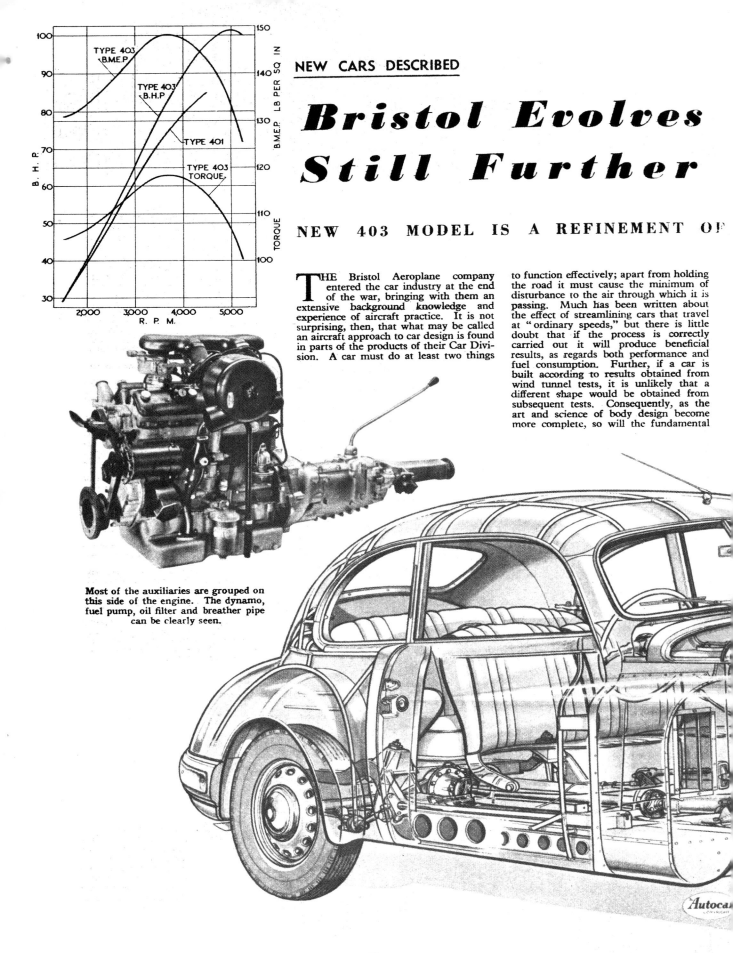

Bristol Evolves Still Further

NEW 403 MODEL IS A REFINEMENT OF

THE Bristol Aeroplane company entered the car industry at the end of the war, bringing with them an extensive background knowledge and experience of aircraft practice. It is not surprising, then, that what may be called an aircraft approach to car design is found in parts of the products of their Car Division. A car must do at least two things to function effectively; apart from holding the road it must cause the minimum of disturbance to the air through which it is passing. Much has been written about the effect of streamlining cars that travel at "ordinary speeds," but there is little doubt that if the process is correctly carried out it will produce beneficial results, as regards both performance and fuel consumption. Further, if a car is built according to results obtained from wind tunnel tests, it is unlikely that a different shape would be obtained from subsequent tests. Consequently, as the art and science of body design become more complete, so will the fundamental

Most of the auxiliaries are grouped on this side of the engine. The dynamo, fuel pump, oil filter and breather pipe can be clearly seen.

The clean lines of the Bristol are completely free from frills. The 403 motif is mounted on the side of the bonnet.

A FIRST-CLASS DESIGN

shape of cars designed for a certain purpose emerge. The Bristol 401 was built as a result of wind tunnel tests and consequently its successor, the 403, now announced, is almost identical in general appearance.

The process of development has been taken one stage further and a number of modifications have been made to the basic design to improve performance and handling. If it is desired to build a car that has a performance above the average for its class and yet provides comfort and convenience as well as a high degree of detail refinement and finish, the task is difficult. In designing the Bristol the aim has been to build just that type of car—one that is interesting and fun to drive, but that also provides the comfort and refinement desired by the connoisseur. The new features incorporated in the 403 include a number of modifications, of

which the first four, those to the engine, brakes, suspension and heating systems, are perhaps the most important.

Power unit output has been increased from 85 b.h.p. at 4,500 r.p.m. to 100 b.h.p. at 5,000 r.p.m.—a very worthwhile gain. To do this it has been necessary to modify some of the major engine components while other alterations have been made not so much to increase the power output as to ensure reliability at high speeds. The six-cylinder engine has a cast-iron cylinder block and crankchamber that is both light and rigid. It is also dimensionally compact, the overall height being reduced by finishing the crankchamber at the crankshaft centre line. The bores are water-jacketed almost completely on the exhaust side, but only for a distance of about 2½in on the inlet side. This is to provide the necessary clearance to insert the tappets. Brividium dry liners are used to increase cylinder bore life and it is usual practice to replace these rather than to rebore the engine.

Two slots are cut in the bottom of the bores so that the connecting rods can be raised to permit assembly or removal of the pistons or rings without removing the crankshaft, as would otherwise be necessary. The crankchamber is divided into three sections by means of the webs which support the two inner main bearings of the four-bearing crankshaft.

The most important change in the

bottom part of the engine affects the crankshaft, as, apart from increasing the diameter of the main bearing journals from 2in to 2⅛in diameter, and using copper-lead steel-backed bearing shells on the nitrite hardened journals, the system of balance weights has been modified and bolted-on weights are now used to im-

SPECIFICATION

Engine.—6 cyl, 66 × 96 mm (1,971 c.c.). Compression ratio 7.5 to 1. 100 b.h.p. at 5,000 r.p.m. Maximum torque 117.3 lb ft at 3,500 r.p.m. Four-bearing crankshaft. Hemispherical combustion chambers. Side camshaft operating inclined overhead valves by push rods and rockers.

Clutch.—Borg and Beck 8in diameter six-spring dry single plate.

Gear Box.—Overall ratios : Top 3.9; third 5.04; second 7.12; first 14.08 to 1; reverse 11.27 to 1. Synchromesh on top, third and second gears; free wheel on first gear.

Final Drive.—Spiral bevel two-pinion differential. Ratio 3.9 to 1.

Suspension.—Front, independent by transverse leaf spring and wishbones. Rear, longitudinal torsion bars and telescopic dampers. Suspension rate (at the wheel), front, 122 lb per in; rear, 190 lb per in.

Brakes.—Lockheed two-leading-shoe front; leading and trailing rear. Drums 11in diameter, 1¾in wide front and rear. Total lining area 148 sq in (74 sq in front).

Steering.—Bristol rack and pinion.

Wheels and Tyres.—Dunlop Speed 5.75-16in on wide base rims. Five-stud steel disc wheels.

Electrical Equipment.—12-volt; 51 ampère-hour battery. Head lamps, single dip; 48-48-watt bulbs.

Fuel System.—17-gallon tank (including 2-gallon reserve). Oil capacity 12 pints; full-flow filter.

Main Dimensions.—Wheelbase 9ft 6in. Track, front 4ft 3½in; rear 4ft 6in. Overall length 15ft 11½in. Width 5ft 7in. Height 5ft 0in. Ground clearance 6½in. Frontal area 21 sq ft. Turning circle 37ft 6in. Weight (in running trim with 5 gals fuel), 25¼ cwt. Weight distribution 48.75 per cent front; 51.25 per cent rear.

V.R.BERRIS

The Bristol 403 has a high output 2-litre six-cylinder engine mounted in a fine modern chassis. Part of the tubular framework supporting the light alloy body can be seen.

Bristol Evolves Still Further
—continued—

prove balance. Weights are placed on each side of the two intermediate bearings and on the inside of the front and rear main bearings. To reduce unnecessary weight the big-end bearing journals are hollow. A torsional vibration damper is mounted on the front of the shaft.

Like the main bearings, the big-end bearings are steel-backed copper-lead and the connecting rods are split at right angles to the longitudinal centre line of the rod. The caps are located by fitted portions on the studs. A central drilling enables lubricant to pass to the gudgeon pin; consequently the rod is of a modified H-section with the central web thickened locally. A bush is provided for the little-end bearing and the fully floating gudgeon pin is located in the piston by means of circlips. Three compression and one oil control ring are used on the aluminium alloy domed-top piston; the top ring is chromium plated.

The next important bottom end modification is a new Hoburn Eaton oil pump which has a capacity of 195 gallons per hour at 3,000 r.p.m. engine speed, compared with 130 gallons per hour at the same speed for the previous double gear type pump. A new light alloy sump is also used, which increases the oil capacity

from 8½ pints to 12 pints. Oil from the pump passes through drillings in the block to the full-flow oil filter and back via further drillings to the main oil gallery. The relief valve is placed between the pump and the filter. From the gallery, drillings connect with the main bearings, while holes in the crankshaft (which are offset so that tubes are not required, as with the previous engine, in spite of the fact that the big-end journals are drilled) convey the lubricant to the big-end bearings and, via the connecting rods, to the gudgeon pin bearings.

Further drillings in the block allow lubricant to pass to the four-bearing camshaft, the rear bearing of which is cross-drilled to provide an intermittent feed to the overhead valve gear by means of further drillings in the cylinder block and an external pipe which forms the connection between the block and the head. A gear on the camshaft drives the vertical shaft, the lower end of which drives the oil pump via a square-ended shaft (to provide some measure of flexibility or permit slight misalignment), while the upper end drives the ignition distributor shaft and also the tachometer (or rev counter) by a further pair of gears housed in the vertical extension which supports the distributor. These gears are lubricated by another external pipe connected to number 2 camshaft bearing.

Top End

The modifications mentioned so far have been to increase the reliability and

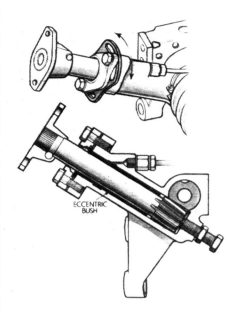

The pinion bearing on the steering box is mounted on an eccentric bush to permit fine adjustment.

to provide an engine "bottom end" still more capable of standing up to hard work. How, then, is the increased performance obtained? The main change in the bottom half of the engine is in the camshaft; the cams have been modified to give an increased overlap and the inlet valve opens 15 deg before, and the exhaust valve closes 15 deg after, top dead centre, while the exhaust opens and the inlet closes 65 deg before and after bottom dead centre respectively. Previous figures were 10 and 50 deg. The induction and exhaust periods have thus been increased from 240 deg to 260 deg.

In conjunction with the new camshaft modified tappets are used, the object of the modification being to reduce the reciprocating mass. This has been achieved by reducing the skirt thickness on the piston type tappet and machining a groove 0.15in wide on the outside of the solid or bottom portion. Three radial drillings connect with this groove so that oil is not trapped in the base of the tappet around the push rod.

Although a single side camshaft is used the engine has inclined overhead valves and hemispherical combustion chambers. The inlet valve is operated directly by the vertical push rod and rocker, while the exhaust valve is operated by means of bell-cranks and additional push rods across the engine, which operate the exhaust valve by a rocker. In conjunction with the modified valve timing a new cylinder head is used with larger inlet ports, the inlet valve diameter being 1.54in compared with 1.425in on the previous engine. The port diameter at the valve throat is 1.40in inlet and 1.17in exhaust. As a light alloy cylinder head is used, valve inserts are fitted to all ports. Both the inlet and exhaust valve springs remain unchanged but they are individually packed on assembly to give a uniform load when fitted. To provide a more uniform distribution of loading it will be noticed that the large diameter inlet valve is operated directly by one push rod and rocker, while the relatively small diameter exhaust valve is operated by the auxiliary cross push-rod arrangement. The re-

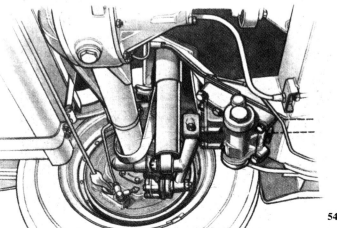

The front suspension unit complete with steering gear is attached to the frame members by eight bolts. An anti-roll bar is fitted behind the front cross member.

Longitudinal torsion bars are used at the rear. The axle is located by a central A bracket and the torsion bars are connected by means of links.

ciprocating mass of the valve gear has been reduced by redesigning the push rods and rocker adjusting screws. Instead of having a cup at the top of the inlet push rod, both inlet and exhaust vertical push rods are provided with ball ends at the top; they are located by cups in the bell-crank lever or by a redesigned cup type of rocker adjusting screw. A similar arrangement is used on the auxiliary push rod which operates the exhaust valve rocker. Although these minor changes may appear insignificant to the casual observer, they are of very great importance, particularly at high operating speeds.

Carburation

A mechanical pump driven from the camshaft supplies fuel to the three Solex downdraught carburettors; these are bolted to the top of the cylinder head so that one instrument feeds each pair of cylinders. A single belt and crankshaft pulley drives the water pump dynamo and magnesium alloy two-blade fan.

Very few changes have been made to the transmission and the drive is transmitted by means of an 8in dry single-plate clutch to the four-speed and reverse gear box. The layout of the box is interesting, as both main shaft and layshaft are provided with centre bearings; in consequence the box is split in the vertical plane to permit assembly. Normal Borg Warner synchromesh is used on top, third and second gears, and a free wheel is incorporated in the first gear. An internal splined adaptor is attached to the rear of the main shaft; this supports the front end of the gear box extension shaft and provides the necessary amount of movement in place of a splined slider on the propeller-shaft. A duct cast on the inside of the gear box extension directs oil to lubricate the splines. From the gear box the drive is through a Layrub propeller-shaft to the spiral bevel rear axle.

Suspension

The front suspension unit is unchanged and consists of a transverse leaf spring and wishbones. These, together with the inclined telescopic dampers and rack and pinion steering unit, are all mounted on a box section cross member (the leaf spring being housed inside the box), which is attached to the main chassis frame by eight bolts, four on each side. The most important change is the addition of an anti-roll bar; this is mounted behind the front cross member and attached to the wishbones by means of short vertical links. This should eliminate the slight oversteer tendency noticed on the 401. Tubular extensions welded to the cross member project forward to support the front bumper. To simplify adjustment a minor modification has been made to the steering box and a flange is now fitted to the eccentric pinion bush, which can be adjusted by slackening the two clamping bolts.

If the performance of a car is increased it is also usually necessary to improve the brakes and on the 403 several modifications have been made to these important components. Ribbed Al-fin drums are used to improve the thermal conductivity, while the brake pedal ratio has been increased from 3.5 to 1 to 4.6 to 1. These alterations should reduce fade as well as give the brakes a nicer feel.

As well as possessing good streamline characteristics, the body is designed to provide a structure that is strong, light and quiet. The main framework consists

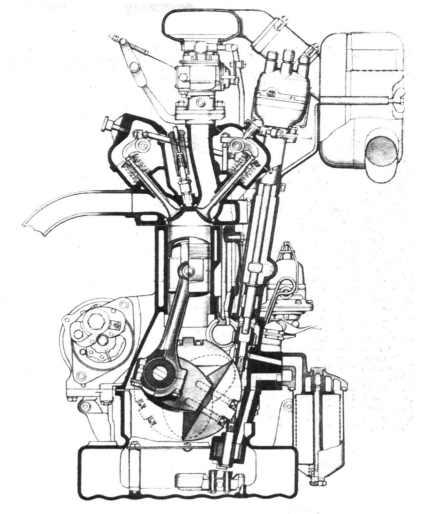

The Bristol 403 engine has hemispherical combustion chambers and inclined valves operated by a single side camshaft.

of ¾in and ⅝in diameter steel tubes welded up to form a skeleton structure. Before the light alloy panels are attached the tubes are bound with fabric to prevent chafing and to provide some measure of resilience. In the rear compartment the steel floor is welded direct to the main chassis frame members, but at the front the floor, scuttle, and toeboard are made of aluminium faced plywood. Aluminium is used for the luggage locker floor. There is very little timber in the body structure, although some is used on the sides of the doors and on the lower edges of the rear window. This is not intended as part of the structure, but to prevent accidental damage that might occur with an unsupported panel.

The interior of the body is very well trimmed, the seats being Dunlopillo with hide upholstery. The general layout of the interior is unchanged, but the battery

trickle charger socket has been repositioned so that it is accessible from either side of the car. Other minor modifications include a light in the luggage locker, and moulded windscreen wiper blades, which, it is claimed, give a more effective wipe than the type used previously. There are very few changes to the appearance of the car, but the aluminium radiator grille is now finished in silver stove enamel; the Bristol medallion is in red and the car wears 403 flashes on the sides of the body. Fitted as standard on this car, the heater system, which is designed by Bristol's, has been modified to permit recirculation of the air when required, as well as the normal fresh-air arrangement.

The modifications that have taken place considerably improve the car as regards performance, road-holding, and comfort. The Bristol is not cheap, but there is a lot built into the design.

This view shows the bolted-on crankshaft balance weights and the duplex chain camshaft drive. The tube from the rear main bearing cap is a drain from the crankshaft thrower.

MORE POWER FOR BRISTOL

With an increase of 15 b.h.p. the aerodynamic 403 saloon will comfortably exceed 100 m.p.h.

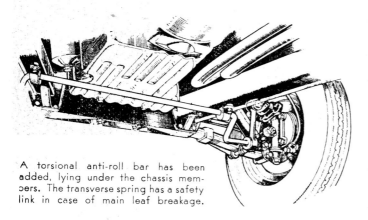

A torsional anti-roll bar has been added, lying under the chassis members. The transverse spring has a safety link in case of main leaf breakage.

A MORE powerful 2-litre engine which develops 100 b.h.p. at 5,200 r.p.m. is the biggest change in the new Bristol. This is an increase of 15 b.h.p. from 85 at 4,500 r.p.m., the output of the later versions of the 401 series engine.

There is no increase in all-up weight of the 403 saloon. The extra power improves the performance and the car now exceeds 100 m.p.h.

Balanced light-alloy drums are fitted to improve the braking, better leverages have reduced pedal pressures, and an anti-roll bar is fitted to the front suspension to improve stability.

The air-conditioning system has been re-designed to circulate warm air in the interior of the car while the engine is running slowly in traffic or under very cold conditions.

In its latest form the car should be a potent performer. The conception of a six-cylinder, 2-litre engine tuned to give 85 b.h.p. (and now 100 b.h.p.) propelling an aerodynamic shape of 24 cwt. proved highly successful. The car had brilliant acceleration and approached 100 m.p.h., and now goes comfortably into three figures.

The tubular steel and aluminium-panelled body accommodates four people and a large amount of luggage.

A different cam shape with more overlap is largely responsible for the increased power. Inlet valves are bigger and with the exhausts operate into hemispherical combustion chambers which were a feature of previous models.

Other engine features are an alloy head and a statically and dynamically balanced crankshaft with bolt-on counterweights and a torsional vibration damper at the forward end.

Bore and stroke is 66 mm. and 96 mm. At 5,200 r.p.m. piston speed is 3,500 ft./min., and at the cruising limit of 2,500 ft./min. the speed of the car is 80.5 m.p.h. at approximately 4,000 r.p.m. in top gear.

A central direct lever controls the four-speed, close-ratio gearbox. Ratios are 3.9, 5.04, 7.12 and 14.08, with freewheel on first.

A wealth of detail is incuded in the four-light body. It has been wind-tunnel tested and there are no external fittings to break the air flow.

A gearbox extension reduces the length of the fully-balanced tailshaft and a new fitting is the rubber universal joints designed to smooth out the transmission at low speeds.

Meticulous construction is evident right through the car. The back axles are machined for their entire length and the seal areas are specially ground to ensure oil tightness.

Steering is by rack and pinion, with an adjustable wheel for the driver. A simple device for taking up wear in the box is provided by an eccentric bush which can be rotated.

Eleven-inch drums with two leading shoes in front give powerful braking. A substantial pull-up handbrake between the seats operates on the rear wheels.

Independent front suspension is by wish-bone arms and a transverse multi-leaf spring with a safety link to guard against main leaf failure, and anti-roll torsion bar has been added. Gaiters to protect spring and suspension are retained.

Rear suspension is by longitudinal torsion bars with larger shock absorbers than those fitted to the front.

The two-door four-light body is luxuriously furnished. The twin seats in front are adjustable for reach and squab rake and the rear seat has a folding armrest. Upholstery is in good leather on Dunlopillo cushions and squabs.

There are four ashtrays, assist pulls in the rear and the doors are opened from inside and out by flush-fitting push-button locks.

Instrumentation is comprehensive and occupies most of the polished walnut facia. Besides the rev. counter and speedometer there are gauges for oil pressure, oil and water temperature and fuel contents. An ammeter, clock, ignition warning light, headlamp beam indicator and petrol reserve warning light are included. There is a lockable glove box on each side of the facia.

Other small articles are accommodated in door pockets. The head lining cloth is washable, and the attention to detail goes so far as a carpeted floor in the immense luggage locker.

Lubrication is by the one-shot system, with a pedal in the driver's compartment.

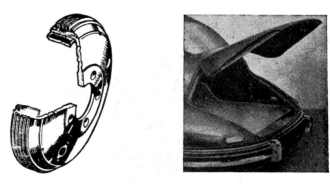

Bonded iron-alloy liners are fitted to the finned light-alloy brake drums (above). The floor of the boot is carpeted (right).

Six cylinders, 7.5 : 1 compression ratio, inclined valves, three Solex carburetters and hemispherical heads give the engine its power (right). Piston area is 26.5 sq. .ins. per ton. Left: the 403 body.

BRISTOL 403

*. . . High in Quality
and Performance*

BODY STYLING for new Bristol is unchanged from previous model, as it has proved aerodynamically sound. Wheelbase is 114 inches. Car is produced by British aircraft firm.

THE makers of the Bristol state that this British car is designed and sold as "a product for the connoisseur." Its record of high performance and increasing popularity throughout Europe tend to back up this statement. Certainly, it is not an average automobile.

Recently introduced is a new Bristol model, the "403", which is identical in most respects with the former 401 model, except for a considerably improved 6-cylinder engine, fully-balanced light aluminum brake drums and certain suspension refinements.

This new car is intended to compete in the American market particularly, and is expected to pull some of the "Jaguar and MG dollars" into Bristol coffers. The firm is quite young, in terms of actual years of car production, the first 400 model having been conceived only in mid-1945 and put on the British market in 1947. It could be said the car was developed primarily because several executives of the Bristol Aeroplane Company found themselves with some "spare time" when the boom of aircraft production slowed following World War II.

Obviously, this group of engineers and enthusiasts experienced in aircraft design methods had a different approach to the problem of developing a new car than typical automotive engineers. Styling of the aluminum alloy body was arrived at, not by a series of pleasing sketches and clay models painted pretty colors, but by countless wind-tunnel tests with wooden mock-ups. The resulting pleasant body lines were decided upon purely for their lack of wind resistance.

Because the body design has been proved aerodynamically sound, the new model retains it, with some detail improvements inside for passenger comfort. Push button door handles are flush-mounted and the bumpers are built into the body.

Layout of the Bristol engine is derived from the pre-war German BMW unit. It has 80-degree inclined overhead valves operated by a unique cross-over push rod system, providing high efficiency, as does the cast aluminum cylinder head. The cylinders have steel liners and three large downdraft carburetors are utilized. Developing 100 brake horsepower, compared to 85 for the previous 401 model, the new engine should allow outstanding acceleration and top speed, since total car weight is only 2700 lbs. (approx.).

New light aluminum finned brake drums of 11-inch diameter are used on the 403, bonded to cast iron friction surfaces, specially ground. Each brake assembly is carefully balanced.

A transverse semi-elliptic leaf spring and wishbones are employed for independent front suspension, with an anti-roll bar incorporated to further improve the Bristol's cornering and road-holding ability. Rear suspension is by torsion bars located parallel to the frame side members. Chassis and

TRIPLE CARBURETORS supply mixture for the 6-cylinder, overhead-valve Bristol engine. In present form, it offers 100 h.p. at 5000 r.p.m., has 1971 cc. (120.3 cu. in.) displacement. Valves are inclined at 80 degrees, giving hemispherical combustion chambers.

suspension parts are lubricated by a one-shot system operated by foot pedal.

Attention to detail is apparent in the interior of the Bristol 403. In typically good British fashion, the instrument panel is of highly-polished walnut, has two large glove compartments, and includes the following instruments: speedometer, tachometer, oil pressure gauge, oil temperature gauge, water temperature gauge, fuel gauge, ammeter, clock, ignition warning light, fuel reserve warning light, and headlight indicator.

An exclusive Bristol air conditioning system is also worth remark. Based on the ram principle, it uses the recirculating principle of maintaining comfortable temperatures at slow car speeds.

Crushed grain leather upholsters the two individual bucket-type seats which are adjustable for reach and back-angle, and the headliner is of a special washable material.

It seems there are no "extras" to buy for the Bristol 403, since nearly every desirable accessory is fitted to the car at the factory. With a reported gas mileage figure of 20-21 m.p.g., the 403 should find popularity among American automotive "connoisseurs."

The island of Fidra, near North Berwick in the Firth of Forth, forms a rugged background to the superb lines of the Bristol "403".

JOHN BOLSTER TESTS

THE BRISTOL "403"

Many Chassis Improvements — 100 b.h.p. and 100 m.p.h. in Worthy Successor to "401" Model

JUST a year ago, the Car Division of the Bristol Aircraft Co., Ltd., submitted their "401" model for an extended road test. Recently, they presented their new "403"-type car for similar treatment, and I have just returned it to them. As many AUTOSPORT readers will remember my article on the earlier version, and others are familiar with the car from their own experience, it might be as well, straight away, to compare the two machines.

I think that it would be helpful, at this point, to inject a purely personal note. When I had tested the "401", I marked it off in my mental card index as a very interesting car of high quality, from which I obtained considerable pleasure. On relinquishing the "403", on the other hand, I recorded it as one of the few really great cars that I have handled, and which I would definitely buy for myself if I were in a position to do so. It is, in fact, much better in almost every important respect than the already excellent "401", and it is astonishing that so great an improvement could be achieved in such a short time. If this is the result of the maker's entry into racing, then it is indeed a powerful argument on behalf of competition work as a rapid means of development.

Among the many improvements that have been incorporated in the latest car, the new engine comes high on the list. It is of similar specification to the preceding unit, being a six-cylinder two-litre with inclined valves in a light alloy head. The valve operation

is still by vertical pushrods, from a single camshaft, with additional rockers and horizontal rods to transfer the motion to the exhaust side. By numerous small changes, the power output has been increased from 85 b.h.p. at 4,500 r.p.m. to 100 b.h.p. at 5,000 r.p.m. More important, however, is the improvement in the power curve from 2,500 r.p.m. upwards, and a far greater degree of smoothness and silence. The slight suspicion of a carburation flat spot which one sometimes noticed on the "401" engine has been eliminated, and the new unit weighs no more than the one which it replaces.

The gearbox has benefited from the refining process, too, though I do not know how this has come about. Suffice it to say that the change, with synchromesh on the three upper ratios and a free wheel for the bottom speed pinion, is even lighter and easier than it was before. Gear noise, of which I was a little critical last year, has been entirely eliminated, and it is literally true that complete silence has now been obtained on all four speeds. I note that, on the occasion of the previous test, I thanked heavens that the gear lever was on the floor, instead of being hidden under the steering wheel, and I now beg leave to repeat that pious remark.

Again referring to my earlier article, I see that I accused the "401" of having a suspicion of oversteer. That defect has been entirely eliminated by the incorporation of an anti-roll torsion bar with the independent front suspension. Furthermore, damper modifications have given a softer ride in spite of increased stability. In principle, however, the box-section chassis remains the same, with a transverse front spring plus wishbones, and torsion bars for the rear axle. As before, the steel floor and the tubular body supports are stressed members, from which the aluminium outer panels are insulated as far as possible.

The actual body shape is unchanged. It was evolved after an immense amount of aerodynamic research, and in consequence it has a phenomenally low drag coefficient for a full five-seater saloon. To alter its lines merely to make the new model look different would be quite indefensible, but it can be distinguished by a silver radiator grille, red "Bristol" medallions, and the figures "403" on the sides of the bonnet.

In some ways, the most important alteration is a revised braking system. Much lower pedal pressures and better heat dissipation were sought, and entirely new light alloy drums have been incorporated. The better a car is streamlined, the more work the brakes have to perform, and so the Bristol takes a good deal of stopping from the high speeds which it may habitually attain. This is just another department in which the "403" excels the "401".

How does all this work out in practice? On taking over the new car, I decided to waste as little time as possible on the aerodrome routine and get right down to the job for which it was designed—ultra-high speed long-distance touring. A few test figures were obtained, however, to complete the data panel, and they are of immense interest.

First of all, it was found that the speedometer was just about dead accurate, an almost unheard of thing these days, but one that increases one's respect for any car. Then, the acceleration figures were so much better than those of the earlier car that they are in a different class altogether. Finally, the maximum speed was up from 97 to 104 m.p.h., and 100 m.p.h. was exceeded again and again on quite short straights. That new engine was certainly justifying itself!

SPECIFICATION AND PERFORMANCE DATA

Car Tested: Bristol "403" model saloon, price £2,100 (£2,976 2s. 6d. with P.T.).

Engine: Six cylinders, 66 mm. x 96 mm. Pushrod-operated inclined valves in light alloy head. 100 b.h.p. at 5,000 r.p.m. 7.5 to 1 compression ratio. Three downdraught Solex carburetters. Coil and distributor with automatic advance, plus hand control.

Transmission: Borg and Beck clutch. Four-speed gearbox with central control; ratios 3.9, 5.51, 8.48, and 16.77 to 1. Hardy Spicer propeller shaft. Spiral bevel rear axle.

Chassis: Box-section frame reinforced with integral steel floor and tubular body frame. Independent front suspension by transverse leaf spring and wishbones. Rear suspension by torsion bars, Newton telescopic dampers all round. Bolt-on, pierced disc wheels fitted 5.50 in. x 16 in. tyres. Lockheed hydraulic brakes.

Equipment: 12-volt lighting and starting. Speedometer, revolution counter, ammeter, water temperature, oil temperature, oil pressure and fuel gauges, windscreen wipers and washers, heating, demisting and radio.

Dimensions, etc.: Wheelbase 9 ft. 6 ins. Track, front 4 ft. 3¾ ins., rear 4 ft. 6 ins. Overall length 15 ft. 10 ins. Turning circle 36 ft. Weight 25 cwt.

Performance: Maximum speed, 104 m.p.h. Speeds in gears, third 85 m.p.h., second 60 m.p.h. Acceleration, 0-50 m.p.h. 10⅘ secs., 0-60 m.p.h. 13⅔ secs., 0-70 m.p.h. 17⅛ secs.

Fuel Consumption: 20 m.p.g.

(Above) Typical aircraft practice, featuring a vertical panel and read-at-a-glance instruments, is employed on the Bristol.

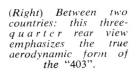

(Right) Between two countries: this three-quarter rear view emphasizes the true aerodynamic form of the "403".

The Bristol 403—*continued*

I would dearly have loved to take the Bristol on a Continental tour, but as the next best thing, I undertook a flying visit to Scotland, with the editor and the chief photographer aboard, to cover the Charterhall race meeting. Journalists are always in a hurry, and it was certain that more than a thousand miles would be covered in a week-end, without any time for nursing or servicing the car.

What a delightful week-end that was! The Bristol has no cruising speed, for it is just as silent at 90 m.p.h. as at 80 m.p.h., or even 100 m.p.h. for that matter. The miles fairly stream beneath its wheels, and this is the most effortless motoring imaginable. The suspension is truly excellent, and fast corners may be taken at high speed without any tendency for the rear end to break away. On certain types of road surface, a modicum of tyre scream can be produced by the front wheels if very fierce handling methods are employed, but this is not normally evident. The steering is higher geared than is usual, in spite of which it is light to handle, though the rapid negotiation of very sharp corners requires a little more effort. Even at its maximum speed, the car runs dead true, and requires no conscious direction from the driver.

An Inviting Gear Lever

Although the engine is entirely flexible down to a crawl in top gear, the real performance can only be enjoyed by the intelligent use of the gear lever. With ultimate maxima of 85 and 60 m.p.h. respectively on third and second speeds, one has every opportunity of keeping the willing power unit in its most efficient revolution range. If the gear change were less than perfect, this could prove irksome, but in fact it is so light and easy that one cannot resist exercising it as often as possible. The free wheel for bottom gear renders the engagement of this ratio quite foolproof, and encourages one to use it frequently for sudden spurts in heavy traffic. Although smooth in action, the clutch is well up to the demands of a racing getaway, and the positively located rear axle is entirely free from any judder or "winding up".

On the trip to Scotland, I employed the gearbox to the full, generally engaging top speed at around 70 m.p.h. I found that this actually made the journey less tiring, for it added interest to the driving. The engine and gearbox are so astonishingly quiet that my continuous use of that delightful lever did nothing to mar my passengers' enjoyment of the built-in radio. This, by the way, has two speakers, one in the roof and one in the shelf behind the rear seat, and the results are very good.

Even when travelling at high speed, the windows may be opened without causing any draught. This is one of the benefits of a truly streamlined shape, and the complete absence of any wind noise is another. All the controls are well arranged, and the pedals are ideally situated for "heel and toe" operation. As well as scorning the steering column gear lever, the makers have also eschewed the equally obnoxious "umbrella handle" brake. The hand lever is positioned horizontally between the seats, and is easily capable of locking the rear wheels. The foot brake is smooth and progressive, but requires far less pedal pressure than formerly for an emergency stop. I used the brakes a good deal, including several heavy applications at three-figure speeds, but fading troubles are not experienced.

One excellent feature of the aerodynamic body is the large luggage compartment which the streamlined tail provides. The lid is released by a remote control inside the car, and is balanced by a spring counterpoise. Lights within the boot assist the stowage of luggage at night. The petrol filler cover and the bonnet are also released from within the car, so when the doors are locked, no interference is possible by unauthorized persons.

Graceful Form

The whole car is beautifully finished, both inside and out. The body has most delightful lines, and while the appearance is quiet and unobtrusive, it impresses by its sheer artistic purity of form. Ample adjustment is available to accommodate the tallest drivers, and the seats and upholstery are most comfortable. The car is so well equipped that one would be hard put to it to think of a single useful accessory with which it is not provided.

The Bristol car has such a world-wide reputation for quality that one can hardly believe that the first model, the type "400", was not produced until 1946. With the "401" in 1948, a new conception of high-speed luxury motoring, allied with moderate running costs, was evolved. Now, the "403" has put the Bristol very high indeed among the world's best cars, and as an extremely fast machine of immense refinement and superb handling qualities it is probably unique. We should indeed be proud of this fine example of British craftsmanship.

A MODERN SPORTS/RACING CAR:
The Bristol 450

THE new Bristol 450 coupé which won its class in the Reims 12-hour race and finished fifth in general classification has a 2-litre six-cylinder in-line engine with overhead valves. The bore is 66 mm. (2.598 in.), the stroke 96 mm. (3.779 in.), capacity 1,971 c.c. (120.3 cu. in.). The chrome-iron cylinder block is fitted with "Brivadium" high nickel content alloy steel dry-liners. A special aluminium-alloy cylinder head with centrifugally cast "Austenitic" alloy steel inserts for valve seats and bronze insert for sparking plug boss is used. Large overhead valves are inclined at 80 deg. and operated by the unique type of push-rod mechanism common to Bristol engines. The extra-large inlet valves are of chromium-nickel steel alloy and the exhaust valves of special "Austenitic" chrome-steel. All valve gear is of strong but ultra light construction, with a high surface-finish and there are highly polished, hemispherical combustion chambers. The camshaft is mounted on four large pressure-lubricated bearings. The 10-mm. vertical sparking plugs have h.t. leads and plug tops shrouded to exclude dampness. Three Solex multiple-jet downdraught carburetters are employed, fitted with efficient but non-restrictive silencers. The A.C. fuel pump is camshaft-operated. Pressed, forged aluminium-alloy pistons, "diamond turned," are each fitted with three compression and one oil control rings. The piston skirts taper and are oval-ground. Special forged-steel connecting rods are used. The massive crankshaft is statically and dynamically balanced and supported on four extra-large main bearings, with all crankshaft journals nitride hardened. The bearings are copper-lead, steel-backed strip type. A torsional vibration damper is fitted. Centrifugal pump cooling makes use of extra-large water passages round the exhaust valves. A full-flow oil cleaner is incorporated in the lubrication system, and an extra-large capacity sump assists cooling of the lubricant.

The gearbox incorporates four forward speeds and reverse with "non-crash" synchromesh on top, third and second speeds. Helical-cut gears are used, hardened and ground. All free-running gears are mounted on needle-roller bearings. Ratios are selected by a light and efficient centrally-placed lever. The multi-plate dry clutch is 7¼ in. in diameter.

Lockheed hydraulic brakes operate through separate master-cylinders for front and rear, with two leading shoes on the front wheels. The brake drums are fully machined all over, with specially-ground friction surfaces of 12 in. diameter and 2¼ in. wide. All the drums are scientifically balanced and cooling air is ducted to the front one. The hand-brake operates on the rear only, via rods, and is centrally situated between the seats.

The chassis frame is of steel-tube construction and of extra-rigid section, with four cross-members. A large-capacity, centrally-mounted petrol tank is fitted. Independent front suspension,

de Dion rear suspension, rack-and-pinion steering and light-alloy 15-in. wheels with demountable rims feature in the chassis specification. The wheelbase is 8 ft. 1½ in. ; track 4 ft. 3 in. front and rear ; ground clearance 5¾ in. and turning circle 39 ft. on both locks.

Lucas 12-volt electrical equipment, with constant-voltage control and fully ventilated large-capacity dynamo is employed with ignition by Lucas coil or magneto as required. The lamps, so vital in after-dark races, are built-in, long-range Lucas 700s, backed by twin pass-lights and twin rear lamps incorporating twin stop-lights. Twin large-arc silent windscreen-wipers are operated electrically or manually.

The two-seater aerodynamic Bristol sports saloon body employs a steel-tube structure and light-alloy panelling. The one-piece bonnet is hinged along the rear edge and the spare wheel stowed behind the seats. The instrument-panel carries 5 in. diameter tachometer and ampmeter, oil and water temperature gauges, oil pressure gauge, and lighting switches ; there are built-in ventilators. The external oil filler cap shuts magnetically.

OFFICE.—The driving compartment of the Type 450 Bristol. Note the hooded instruments, purposeful steering-wheel and handy Pyrene.

The 'Bristol'

404

...a new Bristol 2-litre model

Sports coupé

The 404 has individual bucket type front seats adjustable for both rake and reach. Main instruments are grouped together in front of the driver and are cowled to eliminate reflection.

The rear luggage shelf of the 404 folds up, as shown here, to provide back-rests for the two occasional seats.

Offering the same superlative comfort and high performance, and with beauty of line similar to that which makes the " Bristol " 403 2-litre saloon one of the world's outstanding cars—the 404 2-litre sports coupe is a new " Bristol " model which combines the ultra high performance of competition motoring with the docility and grace of a town carriage.

THE CAR DIVISION OF THE BRISTOL AEROPLANE CO. LTD., BRISTOL, ENGLAND · London Showrooms: 80 Piccadilly, W.1.

RETROSPECTIVE

PLUCKED FROM THE AIR

World War II aircraft design gave birth to the 1947 Bristol 400

BEFORE revealing the intricacies of the car's heating and fresh-air system, one of the early Bristol owner's manuals recommends that the reader should have a grasp of the basic principles of aerodynamics. These the manual then proceeds to deliver. It's just another reminder that Bristols belong to a group of unusual cars – Saabs, for instance, or Voisins – built by companies closely linked with aircraft.

Like Saab, Bristol recognised that the end of World War II would mean a sharp drop in the demand for planes and aero engines, and the production of motor cars could be a useful way to employ the existing plant and workforce. Unlike Saab, which set out to build an all-new, low-cost people's car, Bristol aimed upmarket. It was quickly successful because, where Saab had to start from scratch, Bristol springboarded from an exist-

ing design, the brilliant pre-war 326, 327 and 328 BMWs.

As war reparations, Bristol acquired a large number of BMW drawings and the personal services of BMW's chief pre-war automobile designer, Dr Franz Fiedler. This was achieved largely through the initiative of H. J. Aldington of Frazer Nash, a member of the Bristol board since before the war and importer of BMW cars and Messerschmitt aircraft.

Ironically, Bristol and BMW aero engines must have had innumerable hostile encounters between 1939 and 1945. But the post-war association of Bristol and Fiedler was highly productive. A Bristol-built clone of the 328 BMW engine was running by mid-1946, and a complete Bristol car was on sale in 1947 – the 400, a two-door close-coupled four-seat coupe with clear chassis and links to the 326 and 327 BMWs.

The Bristol 400 was almost

entirely Bristol-built. Specialist items as diverse as the steel and alloy panelled bodywork, the leather upholstery and trim, the piston-type shock absorbers and the alloy-cased, four-speed gearbox were all manufactured within the giant factory at Filton, near the city from which the car took its name.

Nonetheless, the BMW parentage was always visible, if only reluctantly acknowledged by the British press of the time. The engine, incorporating useful Bristol knowledge in metallurgy, was largely an imperial-dimensions continuation of the two-litre (66 mm x 96 mm) BMW 328, now with three SU carburettors above its distinctive downdraught inlet ports. This tall engine produced 63 kW (85 bhp) at 4750 rpm, an outstanding figure for a flexible road engine in the 1940s. The chassis was clearly derived from the BMW 326, having deep box-section

side members, rack and pinion steering and careful location of the torsion-bar sprung rear axle.

This in a 1150 kg car offered great potential for competition. Bristol touring cars were very successful in racing and rallying in the late '40s and early '50s, and purpose-built sports versions of the Bristol engine in sports-racing Bristols, ACs and Frazer Nashes won the two-litre class at Le Mans six times in 11 years from 1949.

Bristols were even more successful, however, in their original purpose of providing fast transport for the discriminating and well-heeled enthusiast. There was a complete change of body styling with the 401 in late 1948, and another change with the 404 in 1953, but the mechanical specification introduced with the 400 was continued without major change until 1961, and the last of the Bristol-engined models, the 2.2-litre 406. The Bristol 407 then introduced the Chrysler V8 which Bristols use today – in a chassis closely related to that of the original 400.

Bristol has never been concerned with high-volume production. Total production since 1947 is less than 4000 units. Current output is around three cars each week, all of them the 200 km/h (145 mph) V8s of which there are only a handful in Australia. On the other hand, from the total production of about 450, between 90 and 100 Bristol 400s were sold in Australia, and of them about 75 are understood to survive.

The 400 illustrated here was rebuilt by its present owner from a partially stripped car kept for spares by another Bristol enthusiast. It runs a later Bristol engine in production sports trim, a wonderfully busy-sounding, free-spinning engine which delivers around 100 kW (135 bhp) and a top speed of some 25 km/h beyond the 150 km/h (95 mph) of a normal 400.

There is a fine view down the long bonnet from the high seat behind the adjustable three-spoke wheel, and there is plenty of leg-room – although six-footers would find the back seats squeezy. If there is any obvious aircraft influence it is not in the timber dash with its seven dials, or even in the sliding windows of the slim curved doors. Rather it is in the attention to detail in all the fittings and controls, and the way in which everything works.

Graham Howard

Its bare chassis went over the Alps to get a Pinin Farina body. It was rallied, then driven into the ground by a mad collector and left rotting in a South London yard for 25 years. Lloyd McNeill now welcomes back...

The Bristol that wouldn't die

ELDERLY OWNER BRINGS UNIQUE EARLY Bristol to specialist for a no-expense-spared full restoration – it was like a dream come true. The Car – the second ever production Bristol chassis, fitted with a gorgeous Pinin Farina drophead body and a prototype Frazer Nash specification Bristol engine – had been standing uncovered in a garden in Streatham, London for more than 25 years. It should have made a classic rags-to-riches story but, as with all the best tales, there was a twist. The owner ➤

Rare Bristol Farina is back on the road for the first time in 35 years. No wonder restorer Spencer Lane-Jones can't stop driving it

wanted it back in six months. 'I'd love to be able to say that we merely rolled up our sleeves and got the job done,' says Spencer Lane-Jones, the specialist in question. 'But life just isn't like that. In some respects, this story doesn't have a happy ending at all. Antony Manual, the owner, was elderly when he brought the car to us, and I think he sensed he didn't have much longer left to enjoy it. He was right – within a year of him approaching us he was dead.'

The Bristol's tale, however, was far from over. Having realised how rare the car was, Spencer was desperate to finish its rebuild.

'I persuaded my mother to buy the car from the Manual family as an investment. Mother is 87 years old now and not really a car person, but she

appreciates beautiful things and would be interested to see a piece of history being recreated. I vowed to finish the restoration in our workshops as time, space and cash flow permitted.'

Before launching himself full tilt into the restoration, Spencer took time to learn more of the car's history. The chassis number confirmed that this was the second production Bristol made – there were four earlier prototypes, of which three survive. The car had been driven as rolling chassis to Pinin Farina's Turin carrozzeria (coachbuilders) to be fitted with a cabriolet body. It is believed that production chassis No 1 also made the trip, although this is not confirmed. On the way back to Bristol's factory, chassis No 2 suffered continual overheating over the Alpine passes due

to a cut-down radiator to accommodate the lowered bonnet line. This troublesome radiator was still in Spencer's car, although it apparently worked well in normal conditions provided no thermostat was fitted.

Production chassis No 1 has long since disappeared, but Spencer's car enjoyed a high-profile life. It appeared in publicity pictures, then went on to be campaigned in rallies throughout 1948 and 1949 by Bristol director HJ Aldington, with Bristol service manager Eric Storey as his co-driver.

'The car was reasonably successful,' says Spencer, 'achieving class wins in several rallies including the 1949 Alpine Rally. When its competitive career ended, the Bristol passed into the hands of Mr Manual, a renowned collector of

not be said of the steel frame beneath.'

Spencer's team set about welding countless lengths of steel box section into the rotten chassis, cutting out the deck behind the passenger compartment and the entire front of the car below the headlamp centres to make sure that all the rust was eradicated. Some aluminium panels were then re-made with a wheeling machine.

'Doing the bodywork was hard work but straightforward because panels were hand-made originally,' says Spencer. 'Pinin Farina never used anything so high tech as a wheeling machine. I've seen pictures where panels are being beaten to shape over a selection of tree stumps. The Bristol's panels look perfect from the outside, but on the inside you can see every hammer mark.'

After the bodywork, Spencer rebuilt the mechanics. The running gear is standard Bristol, so most components were either still available from stocks or easily refabricated. Despite being strengthened for rallying, the rear differential housing had cracked – a fault which Spencer believes finally forced the car off the road. He replaced it with a standard item. Even new shock absorbers were built to the original specification by JWE Banks Ltd (tel 01733 210316). When he came on to the engine, Spencer quickly realised that he had something special.

'Despite years of neglect, every nut spun loose with equal torque, and the inside of the crankcase plus all internal components were highly polished like chrome. It turned out the engine was the prototype Frazer Nash specification unit, lovingly put together by the Bristol factory's aircraft engineers. This was fitted early in the car's life, possibly

rare and unusual cars. He clearly loved driving the car an awful lot, because mechanically it was utterly spent by the time he took it off the road. I'm amazed that it could be driven with so many components damaged and broken.'

Things were to get worse when the car was taken to a house in Streatham, where it was meant to be kept in dry store. Unfortunately, the Bristol never made it into its garage. Instead it stood exposed to the elements for 25 years with only a hood for protection.

'When we started the stripdown, the car literally fell to pieces,' continues Spencer. 'The hood had rotted, as had the interior, and there was almost nothing left of the electrics. While the aluminium body panels appeared to be intact, the same most definitely could

> ‘ *The car was utterly spent when it was taken off road. We started the stripdown and it fell to pieces* ,

during its rallying career. Bristol later supplied similar specification engines to Frazer Nash on a customer basis.'

The engine was significantly damaged. Its pistons were seized, the crank was cracked and the block corroded and frost damaged. Specialists Metalock ➤➤

Bristol Farina: from £2500 to £85,000

Engine	Six-cylinder in-line, 1971cc, OHV fuel system, triple Solex downdraught carbs
Gearbox	Four-speed manual, freewheel on first
Brakes	Drums all round
Suspension	Front: independent with transverse leaf spring and upper wishbones Rear: live axle with torsion bars and telescopic shock absorbers, location by central A-frame
Body	Aluminium over steel frame, separate chassis
Length	4724mm
Width	1600mm
Height	1346mm
Weight	1150kg (approx)
Power	125bhp @ 5250rpm
Top speed	110mph (approx)
Consumption	27mpg
Cost new	£2500
Cost now	Insured for £85,000

The Bristol Farina is the biggest challenge restorer Spencer Lane-Jones has faced since launching his company in 1987. The Wiltshire-based operation (tel 01985 847133) tackles any job on any Bristol, from a simple oil change to a full body-off rebuild

The Bristol's engine is as special as its Farina bodywork. It's the Bristol prototype built to Frazer Nash customer spec

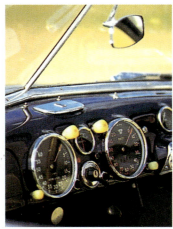

> *Charlie worked at the electrics for two weeks. He daren't stop in case he forgot anything*

UK stitched, ceramic-sealed and pressure-tested the block. After machining, all the rotating parts were balanced before Spencer's team rebuilt it.

With the engine and bodywork done, most restorations would be over the worst hassles. But Spencer's problems were only just beginning.

'We couldn't decide on a colour,' he says. 'The old press shots were black and white, so we knew only that the car was a light colour. Most Bristol cognocenti agreed it was probably ivory, but I had seen a later Bristol drophead in ivory and decided it wouldn't suit my car. Silver wasn't a possibility because the aluminium trim would be hidden. The answer came when a Scottish customer insisted her car be sprayed a shade of dark blue – a Rover colour, I think. We liked it so much we copied her.'

The electrics were equally troublesome. Much of the wiring was either rotten or had been messed around with during the car's life. Spencer decided the whole car should be rewired using 1940s colour coded braided cable – a job entrusted to his colleague Charlie.

'We used discreet modern relays and fuses where necessary to protect circuits,' says Spencer, 'and retained the original horn, wipers, screen washers and heater. We also tried to use as many of the original Italian-made electrics as possible. Charlie worked solidly at this for a couple of weeks – he daren't stop in case he forgot anything. His head was spinning by the end.'

Something Charlie couldn't obtain was replacement Carello headlamps. The car had been sporting crudely modified Lucas P770 lamps when it arrived, but these were unavailable too. Charlie looked at Porsche and VW lamps, plus various units from Italian cars, but none were suitable. In the end he used modern Bosch lamps from a Volvo 240 fitted into the original bowls. The chrome shrouds were modified slightly to fit the lamps and replated.

At last, Spencer fired the engine and took the Bristol on its first tentative ➤➤

From prefabs to helicopters: how the Bristol was born

AFTER THE Second World War, the planet's largest manufacturer of aeroplanes – Bristol Aeroplane Company – was faced with making large-scale redundancies. To avoid inflicting economic disaster on the city of Bristol, the directors of BAC diversified their production. The company made pre-fabricated houses, the first economically successful helicopter and a passenger airliner. They also decided to produce a high-quality motor car.

One of Bristol's directors, HJ Aldington, had imported BMWs before the war through his company Frazer Nash Cars. He seized BMW designs and partially complete cars as war reparations, and sprung BMW's ace engine man Fritz Fiedler from a POW camp to act as a consultant. By 1946, four prototypes had been built, incorporating the best aspects of BMW's pre-war production – engines based on the 328, bodies styled on the 327 and chassis similar to the 326.

Full production followed, with an agreement that sporting models, some with stylish bodies by Pinin Farina and Touring, would be badged as Frazer Nash-Bristols and saloon versions as 2-litre Bristols. It was a short-lived arrangement – by the time the first cabriolet returned from Farina's carrozzeria in Turin, the British companies had divorced. The split was put down to differing philosophies. Bristol, used to dealing with the aristocracy and Air Ministry, believed in making cars to exacting engineering standards, while Frazer Nash was prepared to do anything to sell cars and survive.

Bristol continued to supply uprated engines to Frazer Nash for sports cars, and is making luxury saloons to this day. But what of the early Farina-bodied cars? Nobody knows exactly how many cars went to Turin, or if any others survive. What we do know is that Spencer's car, the second production chassis, is a special piece of history preserved.

There's just time for an Alpine photoshoot after Italian body fitting

Bristol also made Belvedere helicopters and Britannia airliners

Spencer hates restored cars that look great but drive terribly. That's why the Farina handles more like a Seventies car than a Forties one. Doesn't look too shoddy either

Since getting the Bristol back on the road, Spencer's most memorable drive has been taking his elderly mother out for the first time in her 'investment'.

'Mother thought it was fabulous,' he grins. 'She has no sense of mechanics; all she could talk about was how pretty it was, so curvacious and beautifully painted in her favourite shade of blue.

'Now, of course, she is beginning to think of a return on her investment. But I'd quite like to drive and enjoy the Farina a little longer. The hood isn't finished yet, and I haven't been chasing the trimmer too hard because then there'll be no more excuses. I'm a businessman at the end of the day, so I can't afford to be too sentimental. But this car has nearly broken my resolve. I think it's the most beautiful car I've ever seen. I was besotted from the moment I set eyes on it, and I suspect I always shall be.'

Lloyd McNeill *owns a Westfield 7 and Standard Ten. Favourite supercar? Jaguar XK SS.*

journey across the workshop and yard. 'That was a special moment,' he recalls. 'From the first turn of the wheel I could tell the car was beautifully taut and balanced – more like a car from the Seventies or even the Eighties.'

Final fitting-up would be Charlie's responsibility, testing his skill and ingenuity. 'We had the locks repaired by a specialist,' says Charlie, 'but I had to make much of the latch mechanisms myself. I even used a length of sprung steel packing case strapping to make the handles pop out. I hunted everywhere for springs to hold the boot lid open, and finally used some from a New Holland combine harvester, which always raises a few eyebrows.'

The car's unique badges and decals were beautifully restored by Pamela David Enamels (tel 01769 581122). Then, after a local cabinet maker had rebuilt the wooden seat frames and specialist David Nightingale had trimmed the entire interior in attractive cream leather, Charlie applied the finishing touch by remaking the aluminium trim pieces from lengths of extrusion. These are held on by countersunk screws fixed into the trim, the heads of which Charlie lovingly polished. He challenged me to see how many I could spot. Of the dozens used, I spotted only two, and one of those was a guess.

Spencer is philosophical when asked about restoration costs. 'The raw materials were fairly cheap – I think the most expensive bits were the hides for the interior. Labour was another matter. All in, it must be around £80,000.'

> "I hunted everywhere for springs to hold the boot lid open and finally used some from a combine harvester"

Resurrection of perfection

Bristol stood forlorn in a back yard for over 25 years. But who's that girl?

Spencer made new aluminium panels from scratch before the respray

Wiring was completely remade, along with worn door latch mechanisms

Coachtrimmers rebuilt the seats and interior. Only the hood is left to do

Bristol's first car, the 400, took the motoring world by storm in 1947, quickly gaining a reputation for its superb design, performance and construction.

Respect for this new company grew too, as a 400 won the 1948 Polish International Rally and followed this by a third placing (and first British car home) in the 1949 Monte Carlo Rally. Other successes followed – all achieved by utilising engineering expertise acquired during years of making aeroplanes.

The Bristol Aeroplane Company had been heavily involved in aircraft manufacturing during WW2, but, with the war over, Bristol found themselves with a great deal of spare capacity. Even before the end of the war, a small team of Bristol staff had been working on designs and prototypes for a possible Bristol car.

A test model of rather radical design was built but serious handling flaws led the team to rethink their approach to entering automotive manufacture. The most obvious practical solution was to adapt an existing design.

Although this may seem to lack pioneering zeal, the reality facing postwar Britain, with shortages of both cash and raw materials, meant that entering the luxury car niche with no previous automotive experience was just too risky. What was needed was a good base model that could be adapted and improved.

The answer was close at hand in the form of H J Aldington, a director of the Bristol Aeroplane Company. Aldington also shared ownership of AFN Ltd – manufacturers of Frazer Nash Cars and prewar British marketing agents for BMW.

The BMW connection

During the 1930s, BMW had made huge strides forward in both car and engine design, an achievement which also led to many racing successes. RHD versions of the BMW 326, 327 and 328, marketed as Frazer Nash-BMWs, sold very well in Britain and even after the war their reputation remained secure.

However, the end of the war saw BMW themselves in trouble – with much of their plant machinery now located in the new, Russian-dominated East Germany! (Incidentally, BMW's equipment was used to produce cars again, starting with lookalikes of prewar BMWs, and from 1956 the two-stroke Wartburg small cars!)

BMW were unable to produce cars, Bristol were keen to develop their existing designs and Aldington was in the perfect position to be the marriage celebrant.

It was actually not difficult, as both BMW and the War Reparations Board were in favour of the plan. Aldington was able to 'procure' BMW designs and hardware as well as arrange for the release from military arrest of Dr Fiedler – the mastermind behind BMW's innovations.

1951 Bristol 401

Mark Sizer climbs into the cockpit of a car built with all the finesse you'd expect of a plane

The small BMW-type grille fits neatly into the frontal curves

The dash is all wood and the layout, all dials and switches, is also very reminiscent of an aeroplane

Like something from a spy story, Dr Fiedler, BMW plans and equipment all arrived at Bristol's Filton home-base. The basic plan was to combine the chassis design of the 326, install the high-performance engine of the 328 and clothe it in a body similar to the *Autenreith* coupe used on the 327.

In simple terms, BMW's best suspension, best engine and best body would be combined to produce the elegant and radical Bristol 400.

Apart from the body, our feature model 401 is very similar to the 400 and both feature a rigid box section chassis, which still forms the basis of the modern Bristol. Front suspension is independent with a single leaf spring mounted transversely across the chassis. Wishbones are directly connected to double acting dampers of Bristol's own design.

The whole structure is detachable and lubricated by a one-shot, pedal-operated system. Rear suspension is by torsion bars accompanied by hydraulic dampers as on the front.

Advanced ohv engine

The motor is unusual to say the least. Its cylinder head differs from normal designs in that the combination chambers are

hemispherical so as to permit opposing valves at 80° to each other, with the spark plugs mounted slightly off centre between them.

Such a layout would normally be associated with twin overhead camshafts but this system uses conventional pushrods to operate the inlet valves – with transverse pushrods in tunnels that go between the two sets of rocker gear to operate the exhaust valves on the far side. To make room for all these pushrods (18 in all), the inlet passages descended vertically between the two banks of valves. With triple down-draught carburettors, breathing is superb.

The engine as a whole is tall in height, short in length and very slender – being both small bore and long stroke (as well as having vertical siamesed inlet ports). In addition four main crankshaft bearings sufficed instead of the seven normally used by high-performance, six-cylinder engines. The advanced design BMW engine had proved to be very successful pre-war, but

Bristol felt they could make improvements, using the company's considerable experience and knowledge of metallurgy in aircraft engineering.

The crankshaft was aircraft steel, the cylinders were of Brivadium (an alloy steel designed for the powerful and reliable Centaurus aero engine), the main and big end bearings were fitted with Vandervell steel-backed, lead-indium-bronze liners and the head is alloy.

Finally, all the tiny moving parts in the valve gear and top end were precision made and highly polished to produce an engine that was both different and

The car has been sprayed in a stunning metallic dark green – every curve gleams with the depth of the shine

dependable. In this form the 400 model continued to be produced until 1950.

The 400's body, built using aircraft techniques, was made from a steel frame covered with a combination of steel and aluminium panelling to produce a light but strong structure.

Bristol 401

The 401, originally released in 1948, was a far more modern model than the earlier 400 and, true to Bristol's aircraft experience, was both beautiful and a model of aerodynamic efficiency.

With *superleggera* body construction, consisting of small-diameter, welded steel tubing covered by hand-beaten aluminium panels, the 401 was the epitome of aerodynamic styling.

In this, Bristol were years ahead of most of their rivals, and the 401 had an extremely low drag co-efficient of 0.35. However, all this sophisticated engineering meant that the 401 was hardly a cheap proposition – £3000 when new, the Bristol cost the equivalent of three Jaguars or ten Ford Anglias! However, Bristol did not appear to have any problem selling them, even at that price.

Feature car

Even though the 401 is now 50 years old, I was amazed at the smooth, graceful and curvaceous lines of Richard Langridge's car, especially when you consider that many of the 401's contemporaries were still using running boards, protruding headlights and high angular styling.

Long and sleek, everything on the 401 curves and there is no external clutter. Not even door handles protrude from this car – a spring loaded, flush-fitting push button opens the door for you – another aircraft feature.

Minimal chrome, no bonnet mascot, body-hugging bumpers, modern-style petrol-filler flap and, apparently, nothing to open the boot with! At the front, the headlights are very low and the small BMW-type grille fits neatly into the frontal curves.

This 1951 model is one of only eleven in

the country and Bristol Club president Lane Smytheman says there are only about 40 Bristols of all models here in New Zealand. The previous owner of our test-car used to do business with Richard, and pressed the 401 into service as an everyday car with the result that some restoration was eventually required.

Work began on the car but the cost and enormity of the task left the car sitting for a long time. Richard hated seeing a car such as this gradually deteriorating but offers to buy it were always being turned down.

Then, out of the blue, the Bristol owner rang up – he wanted to go to the 1992 Olympics and needed the cash. The Bristol changed hands for $7500; the body of the Bristol, its stripped motor and boxes of parts were brought into Richard's comprehensively equipped workshop and a $30,000 in-house restoration began.

The motor was fully rebuilt – twice – as there was a knock in it after the first reconditioning. New pistons came from Australia and other parts from the Bristol Car Company in England

The body also needed a full rebuild – extensive bogging had been used to repair a misaligned rear end, the result of an accident, and when this was removed it proved extremely difficult to get everything right. The finished result is beautiful, with the car sprayed in a stunning metallic dark green – every curve gleams with the depth of the shine. The body was not removed from the chassis – that is apparently a very difficult task, and the general condition of this car did not warrant this treatment. Only the upholstery was sent out, and the cream leather used is a perfect contrast to the colour of the car.

Low flying

Richard, whom I had never met before, handed me the keys and invited me to take the 401 for a test-drive. Once inside, the first thing you notice is how high off the ground the floor of the car is. The door is

Technical Specs
1951 Bristol 401

Engine	Six cylinder, in-line
Capacity	1971cc
Bore/Stroke	66mm x 96mm
Valves	ohv (see text)
Max Power	85bhp @ 5000rpm
Max Torque	107lb/ft @ 3500rpm
Fuel System	3 x down-draft Solex (32 B1)
Transmission	Bristol 4-speed manual
Body/Chassis	Steel chassis, aluminium panels
Brakes	Lockheed hydraulic drums
Suspension	front:Independent by transverse leaf spring, upper wishbones and hydraulic dampers
	rear: Longitudinal torsion bars, radius arms, A-bracket and hydraulic dampers
Steering	Rack and pinion
Wheels	16" steel disc
Tyres	5.50 x 16
	Dimensions:
O/all Length	15ft 10ins
Width	5ft 7ins
Height	5ft
Kerb weight	25 cwts (1270 kg)
	Performance:
Max Speed	97.8mph
Mpg	23.5 mpg (at average speed of 50 mph)

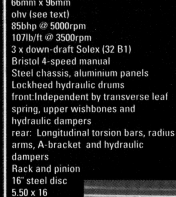

Bristol 401 Production 1948-53: 650

much lower than the inside, with a large alloy panel covering the area that the chassis occupies.

You step up and sit down on a seat that is both firm and comfortable. The car still smells of new leather – just the right ambience for a classic car lover! There are no frontal armrests but very generous storage pockets are provided on each side. The dash is all wood and the layout, all dials and switches, is very reminiscent of an aeroplane. Speedo, rev counter, amps, oil pressure, clock and dual water and oil temperature are joined by ten different switches, several warning lights and twin gloveboxes (one at each end). For a large car, the cabin is not that roomy – you sit close to the windscreen and, as the windows are not very tall, the interior lacks spaciousness and light.

The rear seat is very comfortable but fairly cramped. Rear visibility is poor – a combination of tiny back window, huge rear pillars and a small interior mirror. Despite this, I still found the interior very appealing.

On the road, the Bristol is surprisingly easy to drive. Steering, with no power assistance, is light and positive, as is the clutch. The gear lever is long but very easy to use and with first being available without stopping the car (courtesy of Bristol's 'free-wheeling' system), Auckland's rush hour traffic presented few problems.

Once clear of the traffic this car cruises very well and is very peppy when the accelerator is pushed down. Due to time available, I did not have the opportunity to take it out on the motorway but Richard assures me that the Bristol excels in this environment – being designed for all-day, high-speed driving.

The ride is firm and supportive with excellent road holding. Bristol put a lot of time into suppressing road noise and this is still very noticeable as there is only a steady tick from the motor when driving. The brakes are heavy but stop the car firmly when applied.

Bristol eccentricities

Back in the workshop, I noted some of the 401's unusual features – for example, an overhead knob in the cabin controls the angle-

At the front of the Bristol the headlights are very low and the small BMW-type grille fits neatly into the frontal curves

mounted aerial, allowing it to be swivelled around in order to receive the strongest radio signal.

The boot is opened via a knob revealed when the centre arm-rest is pulled down. Not very convenient, but definitely burglar proof.

The petrol flap is also operated by remote, this time from just inside the passenger's door, to the right beside the rear seat squab.

The side-hinged bonnet also opens from the inside, with the handle in a more conventional place. Inside the generously sized boot, two small handles control a drop tray underneath the car which contains the spare wheel – all discreetly hidden away.

Do not be deceived by the small rear lights – these contain stoplights, night lights, indicators and reversing lights. I have to mention the sun-visors – they are the old, pull-down blind variety – pure nostalgia! Bristol are still making cars, although subsequent models featured more conventional styling and the superb ex-BMW engine was supplanted in 1961 by a Chrysler V8.

The company has been run for many years by Sir Anthony Crook, a one-time WW2 fighter pilot, successful racing driver, and Bristol test driver, who is now over 80. His company never advertises, has no overseas agents, won't give out production figures (but it is around 80 per year), and sells everything they make!

On top of this, should you need to service or restore your Bristol, parts are still available for cars right back to 1948, direct from the UK.

A new Bristol is still very expensive and a Bristol Blenheim will currently set you back around £120,000 – considerably more than a Jaguar XK8!

NZ Classic Car lists a Category A Bristol 401 at $55,000, but this may be a bit high on today's market and Richard thinks around $35,000 is a more realistic price. He has spent more than this restoring his car and has no intention of selling it.

One of his passions is to bring cars back from the dead, restoring them for us all to enjoy. Bristols have always been built with pride and huge attention to detail, and Richard's restoration reflects those same standards – preserving the elegance of yesterday for another generation.

MARK SIZER

(I would like to thank the owner, Richard Langridge plus Lane Smytheman of the Bristol Car Club for their time and help with this article.)

The Bristol is both beautiful and a model of aerodynamic efficiency

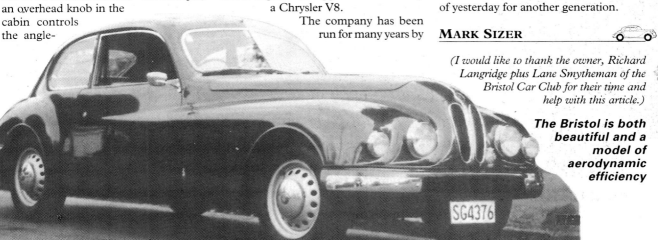

PLANE CLOTHES

On this brilliant but chilly morning, a gusty wind whitening the wave tops in the bay below, the Rusting Renault and I are lost in a labyrinth of winding Cornish lanes. We proceed cautiously between the high banks and round the blind corners, ever hopeful of a sight of the landmark that tells us we are getting warmer. It does not appear. The bearded postman in his van rescues us and sends us back the way we had come. After making the turn we should have made the first time we are suddenly there. A weatherbeaten figure is building a beautiful stone wall, at the end of which are a drive, a white garage and inside – its long, curving tail glinting in the hard rays of the sun – the splendid Bristol we have come to meet.

At last, the elusive Bristol 402, all sixteen-and-a-half handmade feet of it and, hand raised in welcome, its owner for 29 years now, Ian McDavid.

This most exclusive and well-bred of cars is the last of only twenty 402 dropheads made between 1949 and 1950 by the Bristol Aeroplane Company. For its ancestry we look back to BMW in the late thirties to the 326 and 328 which so impressed British sporting motorists and which were imported into Britain by H.J. Aldington of AFN, who sold them as Frazer Nash-BMWs. After the war the Bristol Aeroplane Co decided to diversify into car manufacture and Aldington, a director, obtained the design rights to the pre-war BMW range.

From the BMW 328, Bristol took the engine for its car. It was a six-cylinder of 2-litre capacity, long in stroke and small of bore, with a four-bearing crankshaft. The combustion chambers were hemispherical and the valves were inclined at an included angle of 80deg, but where most engines of this configuration would have had twin overhead camshafts the BMW made do with a single side-mounted one, actuating the valves via no less than 18 pushrods, of which six crossed the head to operate the valves on the far side. Triple carburettors were mounted above the engine and fed it via vertical passages between the banks of valves. The breathing was excellent, and the four-bearing crankshaft allowed plenty of revs.

The Bristol Aeroplane Company built just 20 of the elegant 402 drophead. Using the BMW 2-litre 'six' engine it had a lightweight body. Charles Herridge went to Cornwall to drive one; photos by Andrew Morland

This remarkable engine was mated to the chassis from the BMW 326, consisting of massive box sections and having transverse-leaf independent front suspension, and rear suspension by longitudinal torsion bars. These elements formed the basis of the Bristol 400, launched at the Geneva Motor Show in 1947, which bore the familiar BMW grille and carried a graceful two-door body largely panelled in aluminium. It accelerated to 60mph in the then good time of under 15sec, would reach 94mph and achieved many competition successes, including an outright win in the 1948 Polish International Rally, third in the 1948 Monte Carlo Rally, second in the touring class of the 1949 Targa Florio and third in the touring class in the 1949 Mille Miglia, driven by Aldington himself and the celebrated Count 'Johnny' Lurani.

The 400 was joined in 1949 by the 401, bearing a new streamlined body built on the Superleggera system of small-diameter welded steel tubes clad in aluminium. The 401's type 85C engine gave 85bhp at 4500rpm against the 400's 80bhp at 4200rpm, and Solex carburettors replaced the 400's SUs. It would achieve 100mph and was slightly quicker to 70mph. Contemporary road-testers wrote of the extraordinarily high standards of engineering and manufacture of the Bristol. They praised its performance, its appointments and its comfort, its ability to cruise at 80mph and return over 20mpg. Above all they liked its engine's tireless response and willingness to rev, though most were less happy about the high pedal pressure required by the brakes and about the car's tendency to oversteer. The drophead coupé 402 also appeared in 1949, substantially the same under the skin as the 401. It looked great, and went like a Bristol, but problems were experienced with the enormously long doors, and there was talk of scuttle shake as well. Stewart Granger and his wife Jean Simmons bought a pair, but only 18 others found homes, and the 402 disappeared from the catalogue in 1950. Ten are known to survive.

In his long ownership of the 402, Ian McDavid has found little to complain of, however. He first saw a 402 in 1955, when a visiting friend drove up in one.

Handbuilt quality is obvious in every detail. Facia (above) has black-faced dials and ivory knobs, plus plethora of dials. Engine (left) has been rebuilt only once, with new block at 107,000 miles, 14 years ago. Car has twice been repainted original azure blue colour – there are problems with paint on aluminium bodywork, but little corrosion. This 402 has won every club award going

Ian decided then and there that it was the right kind of car for him, and when he saw one in Anthony Crook's Hersham showroom in 1958 he did not hesitate. Mr Crook, now of course the owner of Bristol Cars, gave him £310 for his Hillman Minx, and a further £585 saw Ian driving out of the showroom. For eight years the Bristol was used as the family's only car, a function which it fulfilled without complaint. It took the McDavids and their two sons twice to the South of France on holiday – a previous owner had, also twice, taken it to Sicily. When Ian bought it it had covered some 55,000 miles with four owners. In 1966, when a company car arrived, it went into the garage for use on sunny days, but the next year a crack appeared in the water jacket, to be repaired by Ian, after various highly technical methods had failed, with a piece of canvas, which kept the water in the cooling system for six years. In 1973 a replacement 85C block was bought for £30, triggering the only major overhaul the car has ever undergone – at 107,000 miles. The replacement block was resleeved, the crankshaft reground and camshaft bearings, valve guides and gearbox bearings were renewed. New parts and machining were supplied by Bristol Cars, but the rebuilding of the engine was carried out by G.E. Jennings of Camberley, Surrey, for whom Ian has the highest praise. This lot cost some £422 – it would be thousands of pounds today – and now, 7000 miles later, the engine is nicely run in.

The body was painted in azure blue when new, which had become a lightish green when Ian became the owner. Ian has twice had it repainted the original colour, most recently by Mike Tregonning of Padstow, Cornwall, with excellent results. Over the years there have been problems with the adhesion of paint to the aluminium, but the only serious corrosion affected the front bumper valance, which crumbled away. Bristol Cars' John Dennis came up with a secondhand replacement.

For eight years, the Bristol was used as the family's only car, a function which it fulfilled without complaint

Recently the car has been tended by Bristol-trained Aubrey White at Newlyn East, near Newquay. As for the interior, the seats were recently professionally re-covered in black leather, while the rest of the trim was skilfully replaced by Ian and his wife Jean.

It is a major tribute to Ian's care of his car that over the years it has won every trophy awarded by the Bristol Owners' Club for which the car was eligible. Today he uses the car less than he would like, mostly because it is precious and the surrounding lanes are perilous, but it regularly travels to club meetings and took a proud place at the 1985 Motorfair.

Now it is time to go outside again and climb aboard. I press a large button flush with the door panel – there is no handle – and the door obligingly springs open. Ian pulls out an ivory knob marked 'M' and presses another marked 'S'. The engine fires instantly, with a healthy, sporting note. We're off, and after Ian has briskly negotiated a few miles of the terrible lanes out on to the highway, he pulls over and invites me to take the controls. Facing me as I settle into the generous pilot's seat is a dash panel covered in black leather, with ivory knobs and black-faced dials as far as the eye can see. To the right of the wheel, oil pressure and combined oil and water temperature. To the left of the wheel a large speedometer, a central petrol gauge and, in front of the passenger, tachometer, clock and ammeter. The steering wheel is an elegant affair with two leatherbound spokes in a down-turned crescent shape, and on top of the column just beyond it is a

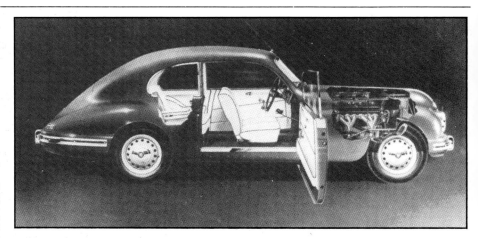

402 was mechanically identical to the tin-top 401, pictured (right) in cutaway form. Below right: Anthony Crook, then only a Bristol salesman, taking his 401 from Lympne to France, where he covered 104.78 miles in one hour. Bottom right: The 403 had 'hotter' camshaft, and Alfin brake drums

unique rocking device that activates the turn indicators. One of the many knobs, marked 'R', offers a three-gallon petrol reserve.

The pedals are reassuringly large, but my feet are even larger. I cannot rest my left foot beside the clutch pedal because my right one is in danger of brushing the accelerator when pressing on the brake. The gearlever is a long, slender wand emerging from the transmission tunnel some way forward and cranked sharply back. A fly-off handbrake lies between the seats, ready to trap the unwary, including me. The clutch is light and very smooth and the gearchange, with longish but precise movements, is just so. The accelerator action is silky and the engine's response instant. In fact, so instant that we are already rushing along.

Because all the controls work so well, this is in no way a difficult car to drive, but a few things take a bit of getting used to: on a couple of occasions, when moving to change from second or top, my hand fails to find the gearlever, for in these positions the knob is very close to – almost touching – the floor. At the first road junction I apply the brake but find it needs quite unexpectedly high pressure to shift it; we stop in time, but I have learnt my lesson.

The Bristol will do 50mph in second and nearly 80 in third, but who needs to show off? We are barrelling along at between 50 and 70mph on a splendid road that is all bends and hills, with occasional straight squirts in between, and the Bristol is, like me, enjoying itself. It doesn't roll on the corners, but sits well down. It swoops eagerly up the hills, and soaks up the bumps without a tremor. No flapping wheels, pattering tyres, lurches or wallows, unlike so many of its lesser contemporaries. For its period, the Bristol's ride is fabulously smooth and steady. Only on the straights, as the speed rises, do I notice that the steering, ever light and precise – it's rack and pinion – needs correction. It's a windy day, but I'm not sure that's the whole story.

Most of all, the Bristol is asking to be driven. It just doesn't want to dawdle languidly along. The engine wants to work. It rewards you for your efforts with a solid rising tenor note and, when you rev to change down, a hint of a delicious r-r-r-rip.

Getting the best out of a Bristol 2-litre involves keeping the revs up. It is well enough balanced and carburated to pull smoothly and uncomplainingly from 1000rpm in top but it begins to go from just under 3000. That means frequent use of third gear, and sometimes second, on the open road, the gearbox being no deterrent at all to repeated changing, snicking cleanly into the next ratio. With this kind of treatment the engine, not a big one for the size and weight of the car, seems to give more than its quoted output of 85bhp as it pulls you insistently along, ever ready to respond, untiringly, to your next wish.

So there we are, the car's long curved nose pushing through the air at a happy 70, rev counter at 3500, a steady drone from the stern, the wind in our hair and a welcome blast of warmth from the heater. Not a rattle, not a squeak, certainly no shaking of the scuttle. Come to think of it, where's that fabled Bristol symphony of knitting needles as a hundred intricate pieces of valve gear do their work? On Ian's car it's just not there.

Back in the drive I get down to have a look underneath. There are the massive front dampers,

Bristol's own, whose arms form the upper wishbone, the gaitered leaf spring forming the lower, the web of small-bore pipes of the one-shot lubrication system, the deep chassis. At the back, those big dampers again but, surprise, also a pair of telescopics. Under the bonnet, the engine is very short in length for a six but also very tall, with the Solexes on top. The overriding impressions are of quality, of functionality, of good engineering sense, of everything having been well thought out and well done.

It is interesting to compare the Bristol with some of its British contemporaries in the 'quality' drophead market: the AC 2-litre, rather ugly, still cartsprung all round, a design betraying its age, but also well engineered, with the ohc six, and very stable; the Riley 2½-litre, with its thumping four and 'sporting' ride, heavy to drive; the Alvis 3-litre, torquey and a good roadholder, but not asking to be driven like the Bristol. Overall, none of these was as advanced as the Bristol in aerodynamics, engineering or performance. It really was a rather special car.

Sadly, Ian McDavid has decided to sell the 402. He is worried about the long-term effects on it of living only 400 yards from the sea, and the surrounding lanes restrict its usefulness. In view of the car's pedigree, rarity and superb condition the price will be 'substantial', and serious enquirers should write to Ian c/o CLASSIC AND SPORTSCAR.

The
BRISTOL 403

Similar in outline to the earlier Type 401, the recently introduced 403 Bristol has a more powerful 2-litre engine, improved braking and an anti-roll bar at the front. Recognition features: chromed type numbers on bonnet and boot, and a red radiator medallion.

FOR most of us who have enjoyed our sporting motoring in a somewhat stark two-seater there comes a time when the demands of a family call for a vehicle with more room, comfort and civilized amenities. The few cars which offer all this plus high speed, sports car handling and are really fun to drive are pearls of great price. Such a one is the Bristol Type 403.

This is a car which is built almost regardless of cost with the sole purpose of providing the sporting driver with all the performance he wants—in luxury. It is a car in which one is equally at home doing the shopping in Mayfair and the knots up the Great North Road.

The recent Type 403 is an improved version of the earlier and very successful Type 401. It was with understandable alacrity, therefore, that we accepted the invitation of Anthony Crook Motors, Ltd., of Caterham Hill and Esher, the Surrey distributors, to borrow MPH 100 for a weekend.

Externally there is little difference between the 401 and the later model, but identification is made simple by type numbers on bonnet sides and boot panel and by the red-enamelled name-plate on the radiator grille. The interior of the two-door saloon coachwork is unaltered and is everything that an English car of quality should be. The individual front seats and the 44-in. rear bench are upholstered in hide-covered Dunlopillo and their shape and comfort contribute much to the lack of fatigue experienced at the end of a long run.

Deep, comfortable seats, a fully-equipped instrument panel and good visibility are features of the Bristol.

Visibility from the driving seat is almost faultless, although the nearside front wing is below the bonnet line. The deep rear window makes reversing a simple manœuvre and the side windows are low enough to enable back-seat passengers to see out without leaning forward.

So much for the bodywork which for comfort, convenience and tasteful simplicity could hardly be improved. It is under the bonnet, however, that the 403 is a different car. The well-tried 2-litre, six-cylinder engine, with its three carburetters and unusual valve gear, now develops 100 b.h.p. at 5,000 r.p.m.

Handling on the road has been further improved by the addition of an anti-roll bar at the front and by revised shock absorber settings. Braking, too, has received attention, and light alloy finned drums are now used in conjunction with Lockheed operation. The close-ratio gearbox has ratios of 3.9, 5.04, 7.12 and 14.08 to 1, the first three being synchronized: a freewheel is inbuilt into bottom gear, permitting quick and smooth changes and unusually snatch-free driving in conditions of heavy traffic.

The gearbox is one of the major delights of the Bristol, giving speeds of 50 m.p.h. in second, and 85 m.p.h. in third—speeds with which most of the opposition on a fast run can be disposed of. The relatively high top-gear ratio encourages the hearty use of the box when high average speeds are in mind but the considerable engine power confers full flexibility in top at speeds of less than 20 m.p.h.

The light, precise, rack and pinion steering and the powerful brakes make high-speed cruising a delight. Even on the roads of England in heavy rain it is possible to maintain a steady 80 m.p.h. wherever conditions permit without incurring the raised eyebrow from the passengers. With good visibility, 5,000 r.p.m. (100 m.p.h.) is easily and quickly reached. We found, in a drizzle of light rain and a strong side wind, that 106 m.p.h. was feasible, although the combination of gustiness and the oversteer characteristics of the car demanded our full attention to the matter in hand.

Whether one is in leisurely mood or committed to covering long distances in a hurry the 403 Bristol is an ideal conveyance. It is amongst the most restful of high-speed touring cars; driven hard the fuel consumption will not fall below 20 m.p.g. (24 m.p.g. at 60 m.p.h.) and it meets any demand made upon it in the most satisfying manner.

The beautifully-shaped tail provides 17 cu. ft. of luggage space as well as room for a 15-gall. petrol tank. Both boot and fuel filler are locked from inside the car.

THE 404, A HIGH PERFORMANCE SHORT WHEELBASE COUPÉ

IN May this year the Bristol Aeroplane Company announced the Bristol 403, a car of much improved detail design, although basically similar in general conception and appearance to the 401 model. This latter model was designed to provide high-speed, luxury transport for up to four persons at low fuel cost. A new model has now been introduced, known as the 404; it does not supersede the 403 but is complementary to it, as a limited production model of very high performance—a very smart, streamlined, closed two-seater car, popularly known in prototype form at Bristol as "The Business Man's Express."

It is the aim of the Bristol company's designers to provide a car that is not just good in one particular feature, but rather a vehicle that combines as many of the best features as it is possible to build into one unit. This policy results in an expensive product, and the result is also very much of what may be called a technical compromise. For example, it is necessary to decide just how much insulating and protective material can be provided without increasing the weight to the detriment of the acceleration; how much power can be extracted from the engine without tuning to the extent of excessive roughness under town driving conditions; how much body space can be provided without increasing the frontal area to the detriment of maximum speed and fuel consumption. All these and many other problems do not arise if one is building a car where everything is sacrificed in order to produce the ultimate in one feature such as maximum speed or fuel consumption. Bristol cars combine as many of these desirable features as possible without sacrificing to any marked degree any one feature in the process.

The general arrangement of the six-cylinder 2-litre engine as in the 403 (*The Autocar*, May 15) remains unchanged except that the compression ratio is 8.5 to 1 as compared with 7.5 to 1 in the 403 model, with the result that the engine used for the latest introduction develops 105 b.h.p. at 5,000 r.p.m. An alternative engine can also be supplied with a sports camshaft with increased overlap, giving the valve timing shown in the diagram on page 411, but still with a compression ratio of 8.5 to 1, and 125 b.h.p. at 5,500 r.p.m. is then developed. Other minor modifications include lowering the intake

silencer and air cleaner, and using a cast six-branch exhaust manifold with a single pipe in place of the two three-branch manifolds fitted to the 403. A 2in diameter exhaust pipe is used, silenced by two Burgess silencers in tandem.

A single casting forms the cylinder block and crankcase. It extends down as far as the crankshaft centre line, the bottom of the crank chamber being enclosed by a deep sump. Brividium (high nickel content) dry liners are fitted to the bores. The four-bearing crankshaft has bolted-on balance weights and a torsional vibration damper at the front end. All crankshaft journals are nitrite hardened and are supported in steel-backed copper

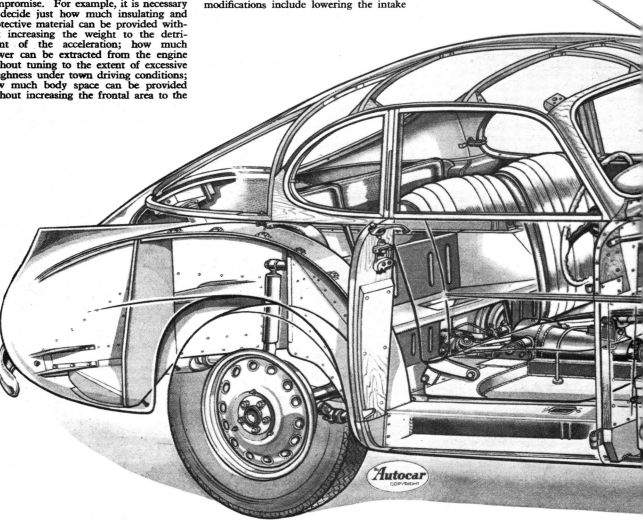

The neat, compact layout and general structural members of the body frame are apparent. The battery, together with other electrical equipment, is mounted in a compartment in the right-hand front wing.

BRISTOL

ADDED TO THE RANGE

lead bearings. The light alloy cylinder head has hemispherical combustion chambers with large overhead valves inclined at 80 degrees, inserts being used for the valve seats. A single side camshaft operates both inlet and exhaust valves, the inlet valves directly by means of push rods and rockers, and the exhaust valves via an additional set of horizontal push rods and bell crank rocker levers.

No change has been made to either the gear box or the final drive ratios. However, an improved type of clutch is used and a central remote control lever is fitted to the gear box. The gear box is of straightforward design, but owing to the use of ball and roller races to support the shafts it has been necessary to split the casing in the vertical plane. Centre bearings are fitted to both the main shaft and the layshaft, a ball and roller race being used respectively. A conventional arrangement of synchromesh is provided for second, third and top gears, while a free-wheel arrangement is provided on

The new Bristol coupé has a body style that is not only aerodynamically efficient, but also particularly beautiful. Small tail fins accentuate the rear wings.

Viewed from any angle, the 404 has very pleasing lines. The bright strip on the front wing covers the hinge line for the compartments which hold the spare wheel and battery.

V. R. BERRIS

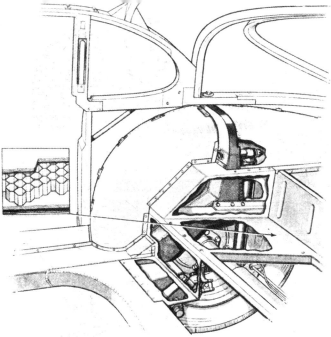

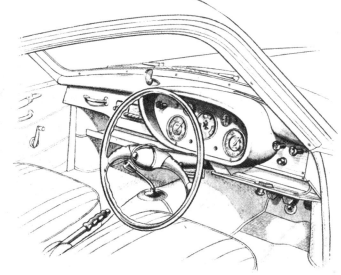

All the instruments are neatly grouped in a cowled panel in front of the driver. There is a grab rail on the passenger side, and both the hand brake control and the gear lever are conveniently placed.

A strong and light construction is obtained by using a composite structure of steel, wood and light alloy for the body frame. The rear spring damper is also seen.

AN EXCITING NEW BRISTOL . . . . continued

first gear. To cater for variations in the propeller-shaft position because of spring deflection, the main shaft extension is splined and slides in an internally splined ring attached to the rear end of the main-shaft at the front end of the gear box rear extension, as distinct from the once more conventional arrangement where the slid-ing mechanism is fitted at the rear end of the gear box extension. In place of the central gear change lever working directly in the gear box top casing, a cen-trally mounted remote control lever is used on the 404, which provides a short robust control, conveniently placed.

Detail changes have been made to the suspension and brakes; for example, the spring rates have been modified to suit the difference in loading and general weight distribution; the dimensions of the front brake drums have been increased from 11in by 1¾in to 12in by 2¼in. Alfin brake drums are used, and these are specially designed to provide a large surface area to dissipate heat as well as provide the neces-sary clearance between brake drum and front wheel. A conventional arrangement of two-leading shoe front, and leading and trailing shoe rear, brakes is adopted, but tandem master cylinders are used so that in effect the car is fitted with two com-plete hydraulic systems, one for the front and one for the rear brakes. In order to distribute the braking correctly between the front and rear wheels, a 1⅛in diameter master cylinder is used to operate the

front brakes, the rear brakes being operated by a 1in diameter cylinder. Modifications have also been made to the front hubs, which on the 404 are sup-ported on taper roller bearings in place of ball bearings used on previous models.

The production methods used for the chassis frame enable the pressings for the side members to be assembled and welded up by the Bristol company themselves, as distinct from being supplied complete by a chassis frame manufacturer. Thus the 404 frame is being produced without the need for many new and expensive jigs and fixtures. In detail, the main side mem-bers are 14-gauge top hat section press-ings placed on their side with closing plates welded to the outer edges so that the whole forms a box section 6½in deep and 4½in wide. Because of a reduction in chassis length (the wheelbase is 18in less than that of the 403) and the resulting increase in rigidity it is not necessary to use two intermediate cross members as with the 403; instead, a single centre cross member is used, consisting of a 3in diameter tube welded to the side members some 43in from the attachment points for the front cross member, which is attached to the side members by means of four bolts on each side. This cross member supports the complete front suspension and steering unit, the transverse leaf spring being housed inside the box section as with the 403.

The main frame members are very

short, having a total length of only 79.4in, for the frame as such finishes at the rear cross member, which is a massive box-section structure flared at its outer ends to form a stiff bracing. The depth of the section is increased locally at the centre of the cross member, which is pierced to allow the final drive shaft to pass through it. Two additional struts, parallel to the centre line of the frame, are attached be-tween the centre and rear cross members, while the floor and propeller-shaft tunnel are also welded in place to form a single rigid structure. Lugs to hold the "A" bracket which transversely locates the rear axle casing are attached to the top of the rear cross member, and lightweight swan-neck extensions project back from the main frame side members to form the attachment points for the rear telescopic spring dampers, the lower ends of which are attached to the axle casing, whereas on the 403 they are fixed part-way along the torsion bar arms.

The general geometry of the rear sus-pension remains unchanged. The anchorage points for the front ends of the longitudinal torsion bars are attached to the centre cross member, although the method of attachment has been simplified in order to save weight.

Body Construction

The main body framing is a composite structure of steel, wood and light alloy, each material being used where its par-ticular characteristics are most suitable. Light frames welded to the main chassis frame support the scuttle structure, which consists of a bulkhead suitably braced and boxed by means of two side plates which form the inner panels for the spare wheel and battery compartments. A sub-frame running in front of the main front cross member, and suitably braced by diagonal tubes, connects with horizontal members running from the scuttle to the front of the car, which in turn are con-nected to the light alloy wing valances. To these are attached the necessary sup-port points for the aluminium alloy body panels. Both front side panels and the complete front body panel are welded and worked to form a complete unit before

The simple air intakes give the car a very businesslike frontal appearance. The large rear glass area is also evident in this view.

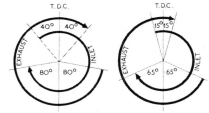

These diagrams show (right) the general valve timing for the standard engine, together with (left) the increase in overlap given by the alternative sports camshaft.

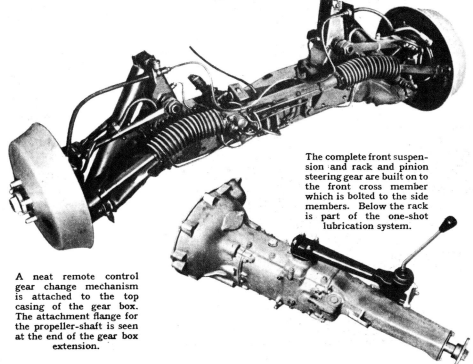

The complete front suspension and rack and pinion steering gear are built on to the front cross member which is bolted to the side members. Below the rack is part of the one-shot lubrication system.

A neat remote control gear change mechanism is attached to the top casing of the gear box. The attachment flange for the propeller-shaft is seen at the end of the gear box extension.

they are attached to the framework. The size of the resulting panel is reduced and construction is simplified by an ingenious arrangement of hinged body side panels which form cover plates for compartments behind the front wheel arches that house the spare wheel and electrical components.

At the rear the main body structure is supported on the wheel arches, which are riveted to form a solid light structure. Light alloy girders attached to the insides of the wheel arch form the rear extension and attachment points for the rear body panels. In order to save weight the floor at the tail of the car is composed of honeycomb paper core faced with plywood, with a thin metal lower panel. To protect the interior of the main rear body panels a stoneguard is attached to the inside of the wheel arch by means of bolts and cage nuts at the top, and rivets around the lower edge. It is possible to remove this panel to gain access to the inside of the main panels, should this be necessary in the event of accidental damage to the wings.

Strength and Lightness

Hardwood is used for the majority of the framework of the upper part of the body, all the wooden section being built up as a unit and attached to the main body frame by means of sockets at the front and rear of the doors, the whole being suitably braced by light metal struts where necessary. The outer faces of the wooden structure are covered with felt. This method of construction is simple and very light in weight.

Unlike some cars in which everything is sacrificed in order to obtain the ulti-

The spare wheel is housed in a compartment behind the left-hand front wheel.

mate performance, the Bristol 404 is completely trimmed and fully equipped. All the instruments are centrally grouped around the steering column and provided with a substantial cowl to prevent reflections in the curved windscreen. The top of this cowl, and in fact the whole of the facia top, is covered with leather, and a foam rubber crash pad is incorporated on the passenger side. The seats, which are of Dunlopillo trimmed with leather, have the usual Bristol form of adjustment for both leg length and squab rake. The space behind the front seats is fully trimmed with carpet and is provided with two very occasional seats, the rear section of which hinges down to give access to the luggage compartment.

A drop-head version of the 404 will also be available.

SPECIFICATION

Engine.—6 cyl, bore 66 mm, stroke 96 mm, 1,971 c.c. Compression ratio 8.5 to 1. 105 b.h.p. at 5,000 r.p.m. Maximum torque, 123 lb ft at 3,750 r.p.m. (With sports camshaft 125 b.h.p. at 5,500 r.p.m. Maximum torque 127.5 lb ft at 4,200 r.p.m.) Four-bearing crankshaft. Hemispherical combustion chambers. Side camshaft operating inclined overhead valves by push rods and rockers.

Clutch.—Borg and Beck 8 in diameter six-spring dry single plate.

Gear Box.—Overall ratios : Top 3.9; third 5.04; second 7.12; first 14.08 to 1; reverse 11.27 to 1. Synchromesh on top, third and second gears; free wheel on first gear.

Final Drive.—Spiral bevel two-pinion differential. Ratio 3.9 to 1.

Suspension.—Front, independent by transverse leaf spring and wishbones. Rear, longitudinal torsion bars and telescopic dampers. Suspension rate (at the wheel): Front, 182 lb in; Rear, 169 lb in. Static deflection: front 6.24 in; rear 7 in.

Brakes.—Lockheed two-leading-shoe front; leading and trailing rear. Tandem master cylinders. Drums: 12 in diameter, 2¼ in wide front; 11 in diameter, 1¾ in wide rear. Total lining area : 168 sq in (94 sq in front).

Steering.—Bristol rack and pinion.

Wheels and Tyres.—5.50-16 in on 16 by 4½ in wide-base rims. Five-stud steel disc wheels.

Electrical Equipment.—12-volt, 51 ampere-hour battery. Head lamps, single dip; 48-48 watt bulbs.

Fuel System.—16-gallon tank (including 2½ gallons reserve). Oil capacity 12 pints; full-flow filter.

Main Dimensions.—Wheelbase 8 ft 0½ in. Track; front, 4 ft 4.36 in; rear, 4 ft 6 in. Overall length, 14 ft 3½ in; width, 5 ft 8 in; height, 4 ft 7¾ in. Ground clearance, 6½ in. Frontal area, 18.75 sq ft. Turning circle, 32 ft 10 in. Weight (with 5 galls fuel), 20½ cwt (2,296 lb). Weight distribution, 52 per cent front, 48 per cent rear.

Price.—Basic £2,500, plus £1,042 15s 10d British purchase tax. Total £3,542 15s 10d.

The main frame members are very compact and rigid. Two cross members are welded to the main frame, the front cross member being attached by bolts. Swan neck extensions on the rear of the frame support the wheel arches and provide anchorages for the rear spring dampers.

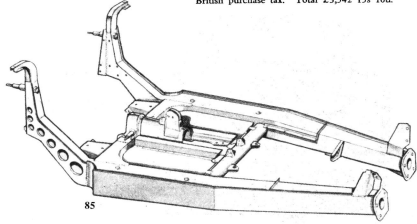

(*Right*) *The low build of the latest Bristol is emphasized by the writer standing behind the car. (Below) Essentially modern, the 404 can be regarded as one of the most handsome closed cars on the British market.*

John Bolster Tests

THE "404" BRISTOL COUPÉ

WHEN I tested the Bristol "403" recently I was most impressed. Here was a luxurious 4/6-seater car of great refinement, which was capable of exceeding the magic century whenever road conditions permitted. Its handling qualities were a great improvement on those of the previous "401" model, and altogether this was one of the most delightful machines that one could wish to drive.

Nevertheless, there exists a market, among well-to-do connoisseurs, for a more compact car than the "403". It is to fill this demand that the new "404" has been introduced. To give an idea

of its purpose, the phrase, "the business man's express", has been coined; in other words, this is first and foremost a silent and comfortable touring car, but it has been designed from the outset to operate continuously and effortlessly at almost racing speeds.

Naturally, I could not expect to have this entirely new model for an extended road test during the motor show season; that is a treat which is still in store. However, by courtesy of James Watt, the Bristol sales manager, I was able to borrow the Paris show demonstration car for an afternoon, and for that I am duly grateful.

Briefly, the "404" has a very similar specification to the "403", but it is 1 ft. 5¾ ins. shorter in the wheelbase, and no less than 20 per cent. lighter. In spite of this reduced weight, the front brakes are considerably larger than those of the "403", so there is a great reserve of braking power during even the hardest driving.

The short box-section chassis is stiffened by the steel floor and propeller shaft tunnel. The front suspension, by a transverse spring and wishbones, is assisted by an anti-roll bar. At the rear, the positively located axle is suspended on torsion bars. The engine, with inclined

★

The power-unit of the 404 is basically similar to the successful Bristol racing engine, with fully - hemispherical combustion chambers, unique "cross - over" o.h.v. operation by push-rods, three d/d Solex carburetters, and six-port exhaust system.

★

valves in a light alloy cylinder head, is similar to that of the "403", except for a higher compression ratio. It can also be had with a "hotter" camshaft, which gives 125 b.h.p. at 5,500 r.p.m., but at the cost of a little less low-speed flexibility. The vehicle under test did not have this competition-type camshaft.

The gearbox has synchromesh on the three upper ratios, and a free-wheel for bottom speed. It has a new type of remote control gear lever, which is ideally situated in the centre of the driving compartment. As there is a long extension at the rear of the gearbox, the dynamically balanced propeller shaft is shorter than on the majority of cars.

Naturally, the famous Bristol wind tunnel has played a great part in the proportioning of the stream-lined body. This is of coachbuilt construction, with light alloy panels. It looks low and compact, but there is adequate head room and plenty of luggage accommodation. The spare wheel is enclosed in the near-side front wing and the battery in the offside one. In both cases, hinged panels provide instant accessibility. The appearance is very pleasing, and the low-drag radiator inlet duct carries no useless decoration.

When one takes the wheel, one is immediately impressed with the good all-round visibility conferred by the curved screen and rear window. All the controls are well placed, and the driving position could not be bettered. The engine idles smoothly and, on moving off, it is at once obvious that this car has fiercer acceleration than any previous Bristol. The new remote control gear change is delightful to handle and, as with all cars of this make, high maxima may be attained on the indirect gears. I did, in fact, touch 85 m.p.h. before engaging top speed, but I soon found that the excellent engine performance in the middle range of revolutions renders

The spare wheel on the Bristol 404 is housed in a readily accessible compartment in the near-side front wing.

The individual bucket-type front seats are adjustable for rake and reach. Main instruments are cowled to eliminate reflection.

the frequent use of the gear lever much less necessary than with the "401" or "403".

It might seem peculiar that the speed model of the range is the most flexible, but on consideration it makes sense. In spite of a considerable weight reduction and a slight increase in engine power, the axle ratio remains the same, and so it is not surprising that the machine accelerates strongly from quite low speeds in top gear. However, there is still a great temptation to use that lever, because it does move so beautifully, and the gears really are silent.

Silence, in fact, is one of the most noticeable virtues of this car. I found that I normally cruised around the 100 m.p.h. mark, and at that useful velocity a conversation may be carried on without any raising of the voice. Due praise must be given to the body for this state of affairs, since the lack of wind noise is just as apparent as is the absence of mechanical clamour. The highest speed that I attained was 113 m.p.h., but even more impressive was the way in which a full 110 m.p.h. was held up appreciable main road gradients.

SPECIFICATION

Car Tested: Bristol "404" model coupé, price £2,500 (plus £1,042 15s. 10d. P.T.).

Engine: Six cylinders, 66 mm. x 96 mm. (1,971 c.c.). Pushrod operated inclined valves in light alloy head. 105 b.h.p. at 5,000 r.p.m. 8.5 to 1 compression ratio. Three downdraught Solex carburetters. Lucas coil and distributor.

Transmission: Borg and Beck clutch. Four-speed gearbox with central remote control; ratios 3.9, 5.04, 7.12 and 14.08 to 1. Hardy Spicer propeller shaft. Spiral bevel rear axle.

Chassis: Box section frame with integral floor and propeller shaft tunnel. Independent front suspension by transverse leaf spring and wishbones.

Rear suspension by torsion bars. Newton telescopic dampers all round. Rack and pinion steering. Bolt-on pierced disc wheels fitted 5.50 ins. x 16 ins. tyres. Lockheed hydraulic brakes, 2 L.S. in front, in Alfin drums, 12 ins. x 2¼ ins. front, 11 ins. x 1¾ ins. rear.

Equipment: 12-volt lighting and starting, speedometer, revolution counter, ammeter, water temperature, oil pressure and fuel gauges. Heating, demisting and radio.

Dimensions, etc.: Wheelbase, 8 ft. 0¼ in. Track, front, 4 ft. 4⅜ in.; rear, 4 ft. 6 ins. Overall length, 14 ft. 3½ ins. Turning circle, 32 ft. 10 ins. Weight, 20½ cwt.

The stability is first class at all speeds, and the steering is superb. The short wheelbase gives the feeling that the car may be thrown about with great ease. It was an ideal vehicle for coping with the vicissitudes of Paris traffic, and the radiator did not run hot under those conditions. During slow driving on bad roads, the suspension feels a little harder than that of the "403", but at the higher velocities both cars are equally comfortable.

The Bristol is an expensive car, but it gives that indefinable feeling of quality that only big money can buy. The upholstery and interior trim, the walnut dashboard with its array of accurate instruments, the excellent finish of every little detail —all these things make this vehicle worth its price to the man who must have the best. In the realm of performance figures, I am sure that, with the competition camshaft fitted, this car would be in the very select band of machines that can exceed a timed 120 m.p.h. For a long, fast journey à deux, the "404" is a magic carpet indeed.

DEBUTANTES of 1953

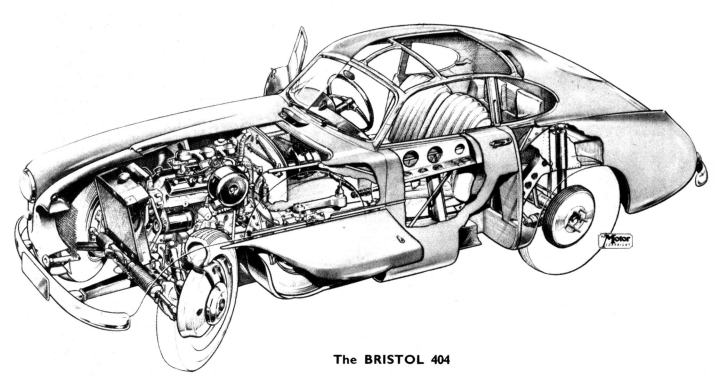

The BRISTOL 404

£2,500 is the basic price of the latest Bristol, a two/four-seater coupé of exceptionally high performance. The body form has been carefully studied in the Bristol wind tunnel, and weight is kept to a minimum by the use of light alloy panelling, whilst alternative engines are offered: 105 b.h.p. for touring, or for competition use an engine with a special camshaft giving 125 b.h.p. The chassis is orthodox, with independent front suspension by a transverse leaf spring and a rigid rear axle with torsion bars. The back of the two occasional rear seats may be folded down to make more luggage space.

LOW build and aerodynamic shape contribute to the performance of the new coupé, seen here in front of the Bristol Brabazon hangar at Filton.

1954 Cars

The BRISTOL Type 404

An Entirely New 2-4 seater, High Performance Car Available with Either 105 b.h.p. or 125 b.h.p. Engine

FOR the past three years, since the original Type 400 close-coupled saloon was discontinued, the production of the Bristol Aeroplane Company's Car Division has been concentrated on the well-known aerodynamic four-seater car, first as the 401 and more recently as the 403, with a more powerful engine and several important improvements to suspension and brakes (fully described in *The Motor*, May 13, 1953). The latest addition to the range, the 404, is new altogether, for although it uses many of the components of the 403, it is intended primarily for very fast motoring for two people, with two very "occasional" seats in the back. Its basic price is £2,500.

The basis of the new Bristol is an extremely rigid box-section frame in 14-gauge steel, similar to that of the 403 but 18 in. shorter, giving a wheelbase of only a fraction over 8 feet. Tapering sharply from about the mid-point to the front, the frame has side members 6¼ in. deep, and measures 47 in. across at the widest point. The box section is continued for the front and rear cross members, while extra rigidity is provided in the centre by a 3-in. diameter steel tube, which incidentally carries the rear extension of the combined engine, clutch and gearbox assembly.

From the widest point the side of the frame is continued rearwards, in drilled girders of smaller section, sweeping upwards over the rear axle as in the 403, but instead of extending behind the axle, it is carried vertically upwards immediately above the "arch" to provide an anchorage for the very large telescopic shock absorbers. The whole chassis is further strengthened by an integral floor, welded to the frame.

This emphasis of stiffness, which is of course helped by the reduced length of the chassis, is necessary because the 404 Bristol, unlike most saloon cars, and the Type 403 in particular, does not derive any of its strength from the body. Whereas the four-seater saloon is built up on a complex arrangement of small diameter tubes with box-section steel side pillars, the new car is panelled in 18-gauge light alloy on a body frame of pitch pine, while the wide and very light doors have alloy frames. In this way the dry weight has been kept down to 20½ cwt., which promises an excellent performance with either the standard engine, developing 105 b.h.p., or the alternative 125 b.h.p. sports engine.

As with all Bristols, the body design shows many traces of aircraft influence, being developed largely in the wind tunnel at Filton, and despite the full-width style, the frontal area is small. The bonnet is exceptionally low, so that there is a separate bulge and intake duct for the three downdraught carburetters, and the overall height of the car is only 4 ft. 7¾ in.

THE BRISTOL TYPE 404

Engine dimensions		Type 404/100B
Cylinders	... ...	6
Bore	... ...	66 m.m
Stroke...	... ...	96 mm.
Cubic capacity		1,971 c.c.
Piston area	... ...	31.8 sq. in.
Valves	... ...	Inclined overhead
Compression ratio	...	8.5 : 1
Engine performance		
Max. power	... ...	105 b.h.p. *
at	... ...	5,000 r.p.m. *
Max. b.m.e.p.	...	154 lb./sq. in. *
at	... ...	3,750 r.p.m. *
B.H.P. per sq. in. piston		
area	... ...	3.30 *
Peak piston speed ft.		
per min.	... ...	3,150 *
Engine details		
Carburetter	... ...	Solex 32 BI.
Ignition	... ...	Coil
Plugs: make and type		K.L.G. P Ten L80
Fuel pump	... ...	AC Sphinx
Fuel capacity	... ...	16 gallons
Oil filter	... ...	Vokes full flow
Oil capacity	... ...	12 (sump)
Cooling system	...	Pump circulation
Water capacity	...	17 pints
Electrical system	...	12 volt
Battery capacity	...	51 amp -hr.
Transmission		
Clutch	... ...	Borg & Beck. BB8/81
Gear ratios: Top	...	3.9
3rd	...	5.04
2nd	...	7.11
1st	...	14.10
Rev.	...	11.28
Prop. shaft	... ...	Open Layrub
Final drive	... ...	Spiral bevel 3.9 : 1

Chassis details		Type 404/100B
Brakes	... ...	Lockheed hydraulic
Brake drum diameter		Front 12 in. Rear 11 in.
Friction lining area	...	168 sq. in.
Suspension: Front		Independent by transverse leaf spring
Rear		Torsion bar and radius arms
Shock absorbers: Front		Telescopic
Rear		Telescopic
Wheel type	... ...	Bolt-on pierced disc, wide base rims
Tyre size	... ...	5.50-16
Steering gear	...	Rack and pinion
Steering wheel	...	2 spoke. 17 in.
Dimensions		
Wheelbase	... ...	8 ft. 0.25 in.
Track: Front	...	4 ft. 4.36 in.
Rear	...	4 ft. 6 in.
Overall length...	...	14 ft. 3.25 in.
Overall width	...	5 ft. 8 in.
Overall height...	...	4 ft. 7.75 in.
Ground clearance	...	6¼ in.
Turning circle	...	32 ft. 10 in.
Dry weight	... ...	20½ cwt.
Performance data	...	
Piston area, sq. in. per ton	...	31.1
Brake lining area, sq. in. per ton	...	164.3
Top gear m.p.h. per 1,000 r.p.m.		19.83
Top gear m.p.h. at 2,500 ft./min. piston speed		78.6
Litres per ton-mile, dry		2910

* With 100/C Sports Engine:—125 b.h.p. at 5,500 r.p.m. Max. b.m.e.p. 160 lb./sq. in. at 4,200 r.p.m. B.H.P. per sq. in. piston area, 3.93. Peak piston speed, 3,465 ft. per min.

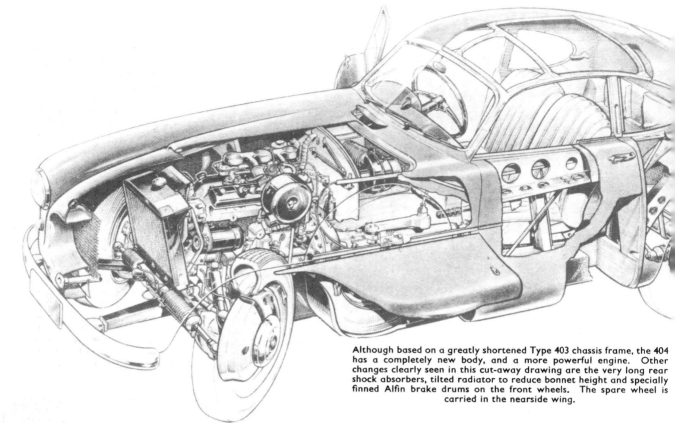

Although based on a greatly shortened Type 403 chassis frame, the 404 has a completely new body, and a more powerful engine. Other changes clearly seen in this cut-away drawing are the very long rear shock absorbers, tilted radiator to reduce bonnet height and specially finned Alfin brake drums on the front wheels. The spare wheel is carried in the nearside wing.

The Bristol Type 404 - - - •

The suspension differs only in detail from the previous arrangement. At the front a built-up bracket at each corner of the frame carries a single, slightly inclined and slightly trailing wishbone, between the arms of which passes the telescopic damper, hinged at the bottom to the outer end of the single transverse leaf spring. This has more leaves than on the larger car, but is actually rather softer because of the reduced weight. An orthodox torsion anti-roll bar is carried in rubber bushes below the chassis frame, and the spring and all joints are protected by water-resisting gaiters.

As before, the rear suspension is by longitudinal torsion bars running forward to an anchorage in the tubular cross member, and the axle is located by these and by a tri-angular stabilizing bracket mounted on top of the differential casing. All the friction surfaces in the rear suspension are lubricated automatically from the rear axle, while the remainder of the chassis has a one-shot system worked by a pedal on the toe-board.

Well-established Engine

Alternative engines are available for the Type 404, the difference lying in the design of the camshafts to give either the maximum output for competition and high-speed touring, or a more flexible performance for every-day road use. Both are fundamentally the same as that fitted to all Bristol cars and recently adopted for a number of Formula II racing cars.

The six cylinders have a swept volume of 1,971 c.c. with overhead valves inclined at 80° in hemispherical combustion chambers and operated by lightened and polished pushrods and rockers. The cylinder block is of chrome iron with alloy steel dry liners, and the aluminium alloy head has inserts for valve seats and sparking plug bushes. An outstanding feature of the Bristol engine is the free gas passage afforded by the combustion chambers, of classic shape, in conjunction with the three down-

draught Solex carburetters, which makes possible excellent fuel economy in an engine which will run freely at 5,500 r.p.m. The four-bearing crankshaft is statically and dynamically balanced by bolt-on counterweights, and forged steel connecting rods are drilled to supply oil to the gudgeon pins. With a compression ratio of 8.5/1 the normal engine, known as the 100B, develops 105 b.h.p. at 5,000 r.p.m., and the 100C sports type has an output of 125 b.h.p. at 5,500 r.p.m. A small change has been made in the exhaust system for the 404, which has a six-branch manifold with a single 2-in. diameter pipe leading to a straight-through silencer.

Considerations of space under the low bonnet have led to the unusual forward-tilting attitude of the radiator which, like the engine, is rubber mounted and actually gives slightly better cooling than it would in a vertical position.

A modified Borg and Beck 8-in. single dry plate clutch transmits power to the Bristol four-speed gearbox, which is fitted with an exceptionally smooth and positive remote control change, bringing the short, stiff lever back to the ideal position under the driver's left hand. The Borg Warner syncromesh for second, third and top gears is retained, together with a freewheel in bottom, which

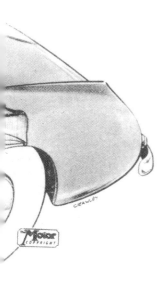

can be engaged while the car is on the move, without the need for double declutching. The extension behind the gearbox which forms one of the engine mountings also makes possible a very short propeller shaft, fully balanced and provided with Layrub universals to cushion the drive.

To cope with the very high speeds which should be obtainable not only on long open roads but under ordinary give-and-take conditions, special attention has been given to heat dispersal and long life from the brakes. A new design of "Alfin" drum is fitted at the front, with a bonded, cast-iron liner and a single large cooling fin which is dished to the shape of the pierced disc wheel. The front drums measure 12 in. by 2¼ in. and the brakes are of the two-leading shoe type, with automatic adjusters to take up wear. Single-leading shoe brakes operate in 11 in. by 1¾ in. Alfin drums on the back wheels, and all linings are of anti-fade material, ¼ in. thick. A Lockheed tandem master cylinder is now used, so that there are two balanced but independent braking systems, on front and rear brakes. A pull-up handbrake between the seats works on the back wheels only.

The steering is of the usual Bristol rack and pinion type, and so arranged that the car can easily be produced with either right- or left-hand drive.

The 404 has been designed for extremely fast driving, but it remains in the Bristol tradition as a fast car with every conceivable comfort. The two Dunlopillo bucket seats are leather covered, and individually adjustable for rake and reach, and a good driving position is possible for any shape of driver with an excellent view over the bonnet and wings. All the instruments are grouped on a raised and hooded panel of polished walnut, immediately in front of the driver, and include a speedometer and rev counter, oil and water thermometers, oil-pressure gauge, ammeter and fuel gauge. In addition a warning light indicates when the level in the 16-gallon petrol tank falls below 2.5 gallons, there are warning lights for the ignition and high-beam headlamps, and a fourth, spare, light for any other purpose at the owner's wish. Two-speed windscreen wipers are supplemented by a windscreen washer which is a standard fitting, and a heater is also standard equipment.

The electrical system is of course 12-volt, with long-range headlamps, separate side lamps and a reversing lamp automatically switched on when reverse gear is engaged. The brightness of the instrument panel illumination can be controlled with a rheostat, and the trafficators are returned by a time switch.

The thickness of the doors is used for two large pockets, and there is a lockable glove box in the facia on the driver's side, but the major space for luggage is on a platform under the very large rear window. When only two passengers are carried, this space can be considerably enlarged by folding down the back of the occasional seats.

The light alloy fuel tank is mounted below this platform, behind the rear axle, and has a central filler with a cap released from inside the car. There is no other opening at the rear, for the spare wheel has been ingeniously fitted in the near side wing, just behind the front wheel arch, and is reached by swinging the whole of this panel, below the chromium rubbing strip, out and upwards to a vertical position. On the offside a similar weatherproof compartment encloses the 51 amp.-hr. battery.

While the Bristol 404 breaks new ground for that company in the luxury, ultra-high performance field, the four-seater 403 saloon continues in production for 1954 with the 100 b.h.p. engine, identical to that of the new car except for a compression ratio of 7.5/1. This model, itself capable of speeds around the 100 m.p.h. mark, has only one modification in the adoption of a remote control gear lever, instead of the previous long central lever working directly on the gearbox.

(Above) The back of the occasional seats may be folded down to provide extra luggage accommodation. (Left and extreme left) Front and rear views show the air intake bulge for the carburetters in the low bonnet, large rear window and "fins" on the continuation of the rear wings. Above the Bristol medallion on the tail is the central petrol filler cap, which is released by a control beside the driving seat. Twin fog lamps and radio are an optional extra fitting.

BRISTOL FASHION!

LONDON TO PARIS IN JUST OVER FIVE HOURS

FAST motoring and flying between them are rapidly reducing the world's distances. A quite remarkable journey was accomplished on a recent Sunday by three enthusiasts and a Bristol 403. This party left Marble Arch, in London, at breakfast time, drove to Lympne airfield and boarded a Bristol Freighter operated by Silver City, flew the Channel to Le Touquet and continued to Paris, arriving at 3.30 p.m. The running time for this journey, including thirty-five minutes of aircraft formalities and the cross-Channel flight, became five hours and five minutes. This is a quite strikingly fast journey from London to Paris for a party with a car; although it is possible to travel unaccompanied between the two capitals faster still by air, and to make a very good journey by train, until the cross-Channel air ferry service began the car journey was a quite slow one.

The three occupants of the Bristol, in the true spirit of the enthusiast, were out to break no records even had they existed. They were merely making a fast run for the fun of it. In fact, the weather at that time made no small effort to eliminate the element of fun. London was in the grip of a biting wind and the Bristol had not travelled far in the direction of Folkestone before it ran into snow. At Lympne there was more sleet than snow, but conditions were by no means bad enough to intimidate the Silver City pilots, and the aircraft took off to time. It left the snowstorm over the Channel as it entered a high-pressure area over the Continent and the Channel beaches of France were sunlit. None the less, on the high speed straights between Le Touquet and Paris there was icy slush, through which, however, the Bristol continued to make good time.

Eight-hour Day

Four hours after leaving Le Touquet, and seven hours thirty minutes after leaving Marble Arch, the party reached the Arc de Triomphe. The difference in running time and elapsed time was accounted for by stops for photography and lunch.

Start and finish ; the Bristol poses before the Marble Arch (top left) and before the Arc de Triomphe (above).

So often when runs such as this are accomplished the participants claim with some solemnity that their efforts have resulted in a significant addition to man's knowledge; there is an engaging lack of such portentousness in the attitude of the Bristol party. "Steadfast in our naïve refusal to take the wonders of modern travel for granted, we thought it might be rather exciting to prove to ourselves, and to anyone else interested, how simple it is, in the year 1954, to breakfast in London and to have lunch at quite a reasonable hour in Paris—and to take your car with you." There speaks the true adventurer.

Throughout the journey spring-like weather alternated with wintry conditions. Near Poix there had been a heavy fall of snow. Below : Bristol 403 into Bristol Freighter ; the 403 is signalled into the aircraft's enormous maw.

A spherical fine mesh gauze filter is fitted on the inlet side of the carburettor and the manifold pipe between the carburettor and blower is water jacketed to keep up the temperature of the mixture. The Drok lubricator, which has been slightly modified, for the supercharger is attached to the left of the bulkhead and has a capacity of approximately one pint.

BRISTOL CREAM

EXPERIENCES WITH A SUPERCHARGED BRISTOL 403

GIVEN a six-cylinder overhead valve engine producing 100 b.h.p. at 5,000 r.p.m., installed in an aero-dynamically shaped four-seater saloon, one would expect a quite high performance. The Bristol 403 has in its standard form a reputation for being a quality car with behaviour above the average for its size. Its predecessor, the 401, which had a power output of 85 b.h.p. at 4,500 r.p.m. was no sluggard and whilst having a maximum speed in the region of 93 m.p.h., would reach 50 m.p.h. from rest in 11.7 sec and 80 m.p.h. in 35.7 sec.

It is therefore reasonable to assume that the current 403 with its improved output would have the legs of the earlier model on a journey of any length, but when a supercharger is added to the engine of the 403 the driver then expects to be able to hold his own with other cars of even bigger cubic capacity. This is indeed so with a Bristol 403 which has been fitted with an Arnott supercharger by Friary Motors, Ltd., of Straight Road, Old Windsor, Berkshire.

Intentions

The main object of fitting the supercharger to the Bristol engine was to improve the acceleration without seriously upsetting the fuel consumption, and with this in mind the maximum blower pressure is no higher than 2½lb per square inch. The installation does not involve any structural alterations to the engine itself. The three Solex carburettors are replaced by a single Zenith 36 VHG unit mounted at the front right-hand corner of the engine and connected to the blower by a water-heated induction pipe. The belt-driven Arnott blower runs at engine speed and the belt is kept at the correct tension by an adjustable jockey pulley. From the output side of the blower the mixture passes through a 1½in diameter tube to the distribution branch. This in turn is connected direct to the three inlets in the centre of the cylinder head, to which normally are bolted the three carburettors. A blow-off valve is incorporated in the layout.

The supercharger bearings are lubricated by oil fed separately from a Drok reservoir, the feed from which is connected to the rear of the blower. On the car tested the oil consumption for the blower lubrication was in the region of one pint every 500 miles. The installation of the supercharger and the necessary connecting manifolding rather complicates the operation of tappet adjustment, but as, obviously, this is not a weekly task, the disadvantage is not serious. The sparking plugs can be removed by the standard box spanner of the Bristol tool kit.

To sit in the driving seat of this Bristol brought back, in some degree, memories of a certain Bugatti, a 2-litre blown Lagonda and a 540K Mercedes-Benz. At once it was obvious that the modern Arnott supercharger was as quiet as the high pitched scream of the Bugatti and Mercedes blowers had been noisy. It was only when the throttle was opened with the car stationary that the Arnott unit became evident, and the note fits in well with the character of the 403. Starting from cold presented no difficulty provided that the throttle pedal was not played about with. The car in question was running without the fan and there was some over-heating in heavy traffic, but outside built-up areas the water temperature remained steady at about 80 deg C.

One is naturally tempted with a car of this nature to use the performance and this particular Bristol, which, incidentally, was fitted with 6.00 – 16in Michelin X tyres, gave some exhilarating motoring. The blower pressure of 2–2½lb begins to show at just below 2,000 r.p.m., and at 3,500 r.p.m. in second gear the engine note rises, the car seems to take off, and then a very quick change to third and again as the engine speed rises the rev counter needle seems to jump round the dial; before you know where you are there is an indicated 80 on the very accurate speedometer and top gear is engaged. The 403 seems to waft along at this speed with no blower pressure indicated until the throttle pedal is depressed and the 2-litre, very efficient engine builds up speed as required.

Its great advantage in this form is perhaps the ease with which it is possible to take advantage, with safety, of gaps in a stream of vehicles. The car's ability to accelerate in third gear from 50 to 70 m.p.h. in 9.2 sec is representative of its performance and it would accelerate from rest to 60 and 80 m.p.h. in 14.4 and 25.9 sec respectively. Owing to these capabilities there was a lessening of frustration normally felt on a certain regular journey. The maximum speed was not ascertained, but it reached a reading of 105 m.p.h. with speed still increasing and 100 m.p.h. was held for a short distance with a full complement of passengers and fifteen gallons of fuel on board. All this with two litres.

Docility

At the lower end of the speed range flexibility does not appear to have been lost for the sake of improved performance. In congested traffic this 403 was quite happy in top gear at 30 m.p.h. and would pull away from 18-20 m.p.h. in this gear without excessive jerkiness. An uninterrupted drive through a built-up area allowed top gear to be used much of the time. By using a cruising speed in the region of 70 m.p.h. it was possible to achieve a fuel consumption of well over 20 m.p.g., and during a period in which 189 miles were covered, some of them in dense traffic and the rest at high cruising speed, the consumption was 22.2 m.p.g. Considering the rejuvenating performance—to a keen driver—of the blown 403, this latter figure is excellent.

This modification can be carried out by Friary Motors, Ltd. for approximately £100 and it is, of course, applicable to the Bristol 401 as well.

ARNOLT-BRISTOL

American sport car enthusiast combines with English auto firm and Italian body designer to build a new sport car for the U. S. market.

AT THE International Motor Sport Show in New York City February 6-14, S. H. Arnolt, Inc., planned to present the new Arnolt-Bristol Car. This 2-liter sport car, weighing less than 2,000 pounds and developing 130 BHP, is the result of the collective efforts of S. H. Arnolt of Warsaw, Ind., sportsman and importer of European automobiles, the Car Division of the Bristol Aeroplane Company, Ltd. of England and Carozzeria Bertone, body designer of Turin, Italy.

The body is correct from a standpoint of aerodynamic principals and has a tendency to stay close to the road when cornering, as well as on a straightaway in heavy cross-wind. All the valuable attributes of a competition car, as well as a comfortable ride.

It has a wheelbase of only 96 inches; turning circle is 32 feet, 10 inches; overall length 14 feet, 3¼ inches; overall width 5 feet, 8 inches; the overall height is 4 feet, 7¾ inches.

Average fuel consumption at a cruising speed of 60 miles per hour is 24 miles per gallon. The high power to weight ratio makes the Arnolt-Bristol exceptionally well suited for competition purposes.

The deep-cushion bucket-type seats afford perfect body support for fast cornering. The deluxe versions are richly upholstered in the finest quality of crushed grain leather in colors to harmonize with the exterior of the car.

The headlamps are inset in the tapered front end of the car, which is an integral part of the fenders. The parking lamps are inset in the fenders. The sloping hood and sweeping contour of the fenders, flowing as they do past the windshield to the rear, assure the most efficient air flow over and around the car. This design combines maximum efficiency with low frontal area, the result of wind tunnel tests.

The disc wheels are pierced to permit adequate ventilation of the Lockheed hydraulic brakes.

The front wheels are independently sprung, employing wishbone arms and a transverse multileaf spring. An anti-roll bar is incorporated in the design. All joints are automatically lubricated by one-shot chassis lubrication system, operated by foot pedal. Torsion bars running fore and aft support the body at the rear. The rear axle is located by torsion bar arms and special triangulated stabilizing bracket at top of rear axle banjo. Large hydraulic double-acting telescopic shock absorbers on both front and rear wheels aid in keeping road shocks from driver. ☆ ☆

Arnolt-Bristol 2-Liter, 120 bhp, sport car.

By
Michael Brown

After a fast run the Bristol
would be spattered with insects,
but its shape is such that birds
were carried harmlessly up and
over the roof.

COLLECTOR'S PIECE

THE STORY OF A RARE MOTORING EXPERIENCE :
ABROAD WITH A BRISTOL 404

VERY occasionally, the wine of experience overflows the
glass of expectation and the would-be connoisseur is
aware that he has approached perfection. Nearly two
thousand miles with a Bristol 404 has left me the memory
of one of those rare satisfactions. For this is, perhaps above
all, the car for the driver; a car that, in unfeeling hands,
could easily be tortured, but which, recognizing a sympa-
thetic personality behind the wheel, responds with unin-
hibited generosity, blossoming into a very queen of the road.

It is funny how the feeling persists that the Bristol 404's
personality is feminine, although a closer analysis of its
make-up supplies good reasons. There is a real beauty in
the styling of the car; there is also a complete absence of
brute force under the bonnet. Instead, there is a reserve
of stamina, an ability to go on giving its best, which instils
confidence in the driver that the 1,971 c.c. engine will still
be revving happily when more brutal units have exhausted
their energy. It is only from the rear that masculinity wins
the 404; from there the shape is wicked, rakish, with
shoulders consciously hunched in the knowledge of the
car's powers.

As a lesson in power extraction, Bristol outputs are remarkable. At 5,000 r.p.m., the 403 (the normal saloon) has
100 b.h.p. available. The 404 can have two stages of tune;
the lesser gives 105 b.h.p. at 5,000 r.p.m., and the other,
in conjunction with a special camshaft, 125 b.h.p. at 5,500.
What the formula 2 exponents were getting last year is only
hearsay, but probably about 150 b.h.p. at 6,200 r.p.m.
Remarkable, in all the stages. PHY 404, the car concerned
in this article, has 105 b.h.p. at the behest of its driver, on
a compression ratio of 8.5 to 1, and a maximum torque of
123 lb ft at 3,750 r.p.m.

You will recall that the Bristol engine is an in-line six
with hemispherical combustion chambers and overhead
valves. The chain-driven side camshaft, with dual sprockets,
operates long vertical push-rods and rockers whose subsidiary
lobes transmit reciprocation to the auxiliary cross push-rods
which open the exhaust valves. These operate through true
exhaust rockers over on the other side of the head. The
interim spindle also carries the inlet rockers, which operate

The front is shapely and sensible, the air intake being
unadorned. The windscreen is sharply raked and curved.

directly on the valve stems. It is a long-stroke engine
(96mm), and the bore is 66mm, with three carburettors
(Solex 32BI) keeping it supplied with mixture. A good
deal of individual attention is obviously given to Bristol
engines for the sake of good breathing, and the 404 aspiration
is assisted by a six-branch exhaust manifold and a large-
bore pipe (2in) interrupted by two silencers in tandem. The
interruption is such that the resultant note is wholly

In Holland the garlands of tulips and daffodils parallel the *léis* of Honolulu, though no one sings " Aloha Ohe " ! The 404 shows itself off alongside the Jabbeke autoroute on the way home through Belgium.

pleasant, and unfailingly induces a true double-declutch for the pure pleasure of catching the thrum of the quick crescendo as the layshaft is speeded up.

There is a roadside advertisement in France which claims that Vittel, the product concerned, is a water that sings and dances. So does the Bristol engine, for it has that hall-mark of the high-performance unit, the instant response to the throttle and the smooth running up and down through the rev range which sends the needle dancing over the black and white scale in front of the driver. Amongst many influences, one supposes that first-class carburation is the chief factor in permitting this. It is wholly a virtue, for the driver of a 404 must use the gear box to justify his occupying such a driving seat; the flexibility of the engine is such that he *could* employ pottering tactics, get into top gear at 25 m.p.h. and stay there. One *could* drink champagne from an enamel mug, but the world of the 404 is a civilized one.

Moreover, this is a gear box to give pleasure for its own sake. Coming behind a six-spring clutch that has been specifically adopted to suit 404 characteristics, its lever is short and cranked, providing remote operation of the selectors and forks. The action might be jewelled. Having started by taking a fistful of gear lever knob, the 404 driver finds after a dozen changes that he is using the tips of three fingers, and one other transmission feature causes him to throw his inhibitions to the winds and extract the utmost pleasure from his sense of timing. This is the freewheel incorporated in bottom gear, which permits changes into the lowest gear to be made with even greater facility than is possible with synchromesh. Thus first

becomes usable more as a low second, and to permit even a ghost of a tinkle from the high-compression head is disgrace indeed; at least, on British premium spirit. Over in France the *super-carburant* must have a much lower anti-knock rating; in Belgium also, while Holland's petrol is nearly as bad as Spain's. Across the Channel, therefore, the hand ignition control supplements the gear box to keep the song of the engine as happy as a lark's.

Overall ratios are, like the 403's, 3.9 to 1, 5.05, 7.12 and 14 to 1, with reverse 11.22. In the two middle gears—the ones that matter in acceleration—a driver selects his r.p.m. figures for the point of change almost by instinct. In normal usage of the 404, I found myself changing at about 3,500 r.p.m., but when driving fast this point moved up a thousand to 4,500, by which time the matching speed indication was 50 m.p.h. in second and 70 m.p.h. in third. It could, of course, have been higher still, but I have never been able to set my teeth and torture an engine up to valve bounce just to see where the point is, any more than I could twist an arm until the victim cried out in pain.

Apéritif

One had settled into such figures after very few miles from the Bristol factory at Filton. With their aid, I covered eight miles of the Bath Road in seven minutes on a spring morning, and that glass of expectation became even more highly polished, for a passage was booked on the cross-Channel ferry; Brussels motor road, Eifel Mountains, the Ballon d'Alsace and the roads of France . . . this year's Tulip Rally, in fact, as a follower in a car that could play ducks and drakes with the rally main road average.

But engine performance must have its concomitants for full enjoyment. Road-holding heads the list of these. The Bristol is one of the few cars of its type that retains a "conventional" frame, and if the weight implied takes something away from the accelerative possibilities the com-

COLLECTOR'S PIECE

From every angle the shape is a pretty one, as is evident from this casual photograph of the car on a hillside near Troyes, its doors open to keep the inside temperature down.

The good does not quarrel with the good, and the neo-classical shape of the 404 is in harmony with the classical arch of the church of Baume les Dames, near Besancon.

. . . . . continued

pensation is more than provided by the solid sit of the car on the road. I know the sensation intimately, and shall regret the day that it disappears. So far, the substitute falls short in an indefinable way. Perhaps rigidity plus weight breeds a virtue in combination which is missing from any other. This, plus the reasonably stiff-feeling action of the front suspension, obtained by an underslung and gaitered transverse leaf spring in conjunction with wishbones, anti-roll bar and angular-mounted telescopic dampers, results in seemingly roll-free cornering at tremendous speeds; speeds on which there is a bonus from Michelin X tyres, fitted as standard. The virtues of these extraordinary tyres outweigh their disadvantages for me, though I try always to keep in mind the immense store of kinetic energy which they are holding in check (centrifugal force is proportional to the square of the vehicle speed). In other words, if such a tyre loses adhesion it must release more stored " centrifugal energy " than the tyre which skids more readily, and the car must, in consequence, be even less capable of control in its tangential slide. So steady was PHY 404 on fast corners that I realized with something like surprise that what seemed a flat road surface was actually giving the whee-whee-whee of tyre scream that one hears on the racing circuit but not often on the road. I looked at the speedometer, to see 80 m.p.h. where I should have expected 65.

The steering is what one requires with such suspension. It is rack and pinion and superlatively a means of delicate transmission to the driver of what is happening at the front wheels. You feel the road; you feel the set of the wheels, and the response to movements of the steering wheel is positive and instantaneous. In only three turns these front wheels move from one excellent lock to the other (the car could be turned round almost in a dog kennel) and if the road were peppered with sixpences you feel that you could flatten them one and all. Somewhere at Filton I imagine an absolute connoisseur of cars and little groups of men all

over the factory huddled in corners, looking furtively over their shoulders and whispering, " But will it get past *him*? " He knew what was what in steering.

The precision in chassis and suspension matters is not made woolly at the edges by the body construction as performance merges into creature comfort. An ash frame and a walnut facia of some thickness contribute the remarkable firmness of timber, and the aluminium panels which cloth the ash are minimum in number. The roof and rear section appears to be in one, continuing right down to the base of the screen pillars. The interior trim, in a dove-grey leather, with carpeting and a nylon roof-lining to match, was richly in keeping, and had there been any vibration to absorb the deep, superbly shaped twin seats would have absorbed it. As it was, they absorbed every peculiarity of the human frame so successfully that nights asleep in their embrace during the rally were of quite reasonable comfort. For my liking the luggage space behind them is ample, though I daresay some owners would object to extraction of suitcases through the doors, over the rip-up seat backs.

Controls

Everywhere in the car is the reminder that precision is a *sine qua non* of quality, and nowhere more obviously than in front of the driver. My immediate liking for the facia layout is excusable because it quite strikingly approximates to an "ideal" layout which I postulated in an article about a year ago. The three main dials—speedometer, that containing oil and water thermometers, oil pressure gauge and fuel gauge, and the rev counter—are housed in the foam

" Motorists, be careful! We are working for you." An engaging road sign encountered in Eastern France.

Daffodils in the Vosges. The foothills of these wooded mountains are carpeted with the Lenten lily in the spring. The 404 has halted near Gerardmer.

Filling up on the 404 involves release of the trapdoor by a trigger at the base of the hand brake, and then of the spring cap. The orifice is therefore locked away.

COLLECTOR'S PIECE . . . .

. . . continued

Important instruments are grouped in a shrouded panel immediately ahead of the driver. Subsidiary dials and switches occupy the rest of the facia. Starting controls fall readily to the right hand.

rubber shrouded vital panel ahead of the driver and visible through the twin-spoked steering wheel; the panel also holds certain switches and indicators. To its right are mixture and ignition controls, with the starter. To the left are the radio and incidentals, one or two of which are located at a lower shelf level. The absence of symmetry is extraordinarily restful after the strain that is perceptible in its achievement in so many layouts; I am intolerant of false styling effects and am at a loss to see why one dial should match another, and why switches should necessarily be ranged, lead-soldier fashion, on either side of an r.p.m. fortress. Logic, to me, demands control above all in a fast car, and therefore I want my instrument layout to be designed purely for control.

Sharp chromium needles sweep the big dials of m.p.h. and r.p.m. on the 404, and very handsome the instruments are; yet functionally they still are not quite up to the standard of the vehicle they serve; the interfering hand of the stylist is evident, for instance, in the endeavour to make the painted indicator mark for the fives look like a shaped protuberance. It isn't. The multiple central dial is frankly fussy. But these are, of course, criticisms based on idealism; by all normal standards the crisply clicking switches, the rheostatically controlled lighting, the use of black and white instead of pastel shades and chromium, are beyond criticism. One does not judge Toscanini by the standards of the village brass band.

Those whose good fortune it is to drive many cars know well how the really good car reveals itself. First, they are at home with it in fifty yards; secondly, it is tolerant of driver errors, usually extricating him from the consequences of a mistake. PHY 404 lived up to the quality reputation in these respects, its driver being able to "do what he liked with it" almost before it had nosed out of the factory gate. (It is fair to record that most of this experience was on dry roads.) At the first opportunity one tests the brakes from speed, and one expected much with self-adjusting front brakes, Al-Fin drums and wheels perforated for brake cooling. One got it; not, perhaps, at first touch of the pedal, but progressively as the pedal went down, until at full pressure a giant hand reached out of space, seized the flying 404, and arrested it as if momentum were a plaything. It would do that time after time, equally efficiently, without sign of fade, and the robust hand brake took hold of the stationary car and restored some of the confidence that umbrella handles and the term "parking brake" have dissipated. The pedal, I am convinced, was craftily placed in relation to the throttle, for heel and toe technique (simultaneous operation of brake and throttle) was deliciously easy. "He" probably saw to that.

This was the car, then, that took us first across Belgium

10·35	13,107	
11¼	13,125	
11·14	13,138	
11·30	13,151	600
11·35	13,155	100
12·½	13,177	
12·5	13,182	106
12·28	13,204	
12·35	13,207	
12·55	13,220	100
1·5	13,235	103
1·35	13,271	

Log of the run from Belfort to beyond Troyes, with supplementary notes of three-figure readings.

to the Nurburgring, and then far to the south, attracting attention wherever it went. And well it might, for if ever there was a dainty but efficient shape, the 404 has it. The driver sees the two wing pressings, straining out ahead like greyhounds neck and neck; the outsider sees a set of curves in a lovely harmony with the surroundings, whatever they may be. From a distance, you feel that the 404 could be picked up and thrown, dart fashion, on a true path through the air. Intimately, you are made aware that the shape is one that has been strictly dictated by aerodynamic principles. Its ease of passage provides one lesson; more graphically, what happens to birds that fly into the front. In nearly two thousand miles of fast going we did not kill a single bird; time and again they would fly down to the region of the air intake. Time and again they would be borne up, wings stretched, riding the air current that flowed up and over the roof peak, keeping a few inches from the body, passing harmlessly back to freedom.

We asked the Dutch rally official if we might go over the closed Ballon d'Alsace climb; he looked at the car and grinned assent. We must keep competitor's speed and not overtake or stop, and so we were able to do a carefree climb over a closed col, six miles of hairpin bends. In fact, the car ahead was not one of the faster ones, with the result that we held second gear and used the ignition control on some of the bends rather than go down into first at high revs; but the climb gave one time to think. I do not

Spring in the Doubs Valley. The Bristol poses unselfconsciously, high above the tumbling river.

remember detecting a slide in spite of damp patches on the bends, and neither did we experience one on the timed descent over the other side of the col. As anyone who has chased, say, 750 Renaults down a col knows, the small car takes some catching when engines do not matter very much, and the descent was hectic, especially as the last three hundred yards involved a bonus for rally competitors that was multiplied by ten. We enjoyed every minute of it, for we kept station, though farther back than on the climb. It would have been undignified to have dropped back at the last, fastest, stage. On this type of road the ability to cross hands and go round a hairpin with a minimum shifting on the wheel rim is invaluable. Control is preserved.

To talk cruising speeds with such a car on the Continent is absurd. Select the right road and you take your choice. On N44 into Rheims from the south we amused ourselves by selecting high speeds to hold for a given number of miles—and succeeded in each case. The high-speed run on which a log was kept (it is reproduced in these pages) was sterner stuff, over a route that I reckoned was fairly give and take; indeed, Michelin marks it mediocre in places, and elsewhere *routes bombées*. It ran from Belfort through Vesoul, Langres and Chaumont to beyond Troyes, starting in the hills and winding through built-up areas, and finishing towards the great plain, with straights appearing, of good surface. The hourly totals reflect the conditions; the first was 48, the second 52 and the third 64. After that we tired of chasing figures and stopped for lunch, and the day finished at Valenciennes, on the Belgian border, 328 miles away, with an overall average of 41 m.p.h.

Over 100 m.p.h.

The highest reading seen was 106 m.p.h., and Bristol's tell me that the oversize tyres result in a 4 per cent error on the low side, so that the true speed might well have been around 110 m.p.h. It was my wife's first experience of motoring at 100 plus. "It doesn't seem much faster than eighty," she commented. The tribute to the car is implied, because 100 m.p.h. on the road remains very fast indeed, especially on a route where frost damage warnings needed watching for, and where such damage was occasionally bringing us down to the fifties. It was a glorious, sunny day in spring, and everything contributed to exhilaration. There is a fine savour to fast driving on such a day, in such conditions, at the wheel of such a car, especially through a country so well loved and beautiful as France. As we sat on the hillside eating our lunch, with the Bristol opened up, to keep down the heat of the sun, a French peasant passed us with his horse and harrow. It was the abrupt contrast, and we greeted him as from across a century; not for him a brain full of internal combustion figures—100, five-two, oil temperature 60, water 75-80, pressure O.K. And yet we could feel that he, too, belonging as he did to France, had an equal appreciation of living.

One must pay for the really good things in life, and in first cost the Bristol 404 is expensive, for it is priced at £2,500 list, which is increased by a thousand pounds or so in British purchase tax. You don't get a Rembrandt for tuppence. On the other hand,

Baume les Dames, near Besançon, glimpsed through the arch against which the Bristol was seen in a previous picture.

all that the 404 gave us was given at a petrol consumption of 22.3 m.p.g., and this was, no doubt, slightly higher than it should have been as the result of a persistent leak at a pump union. The litre of oil which I put in was almost a courtesy topping-up, and the drink of water . . . well, it was a hot day, and the Senegalese pump attendant wanted to see the engine.

How does one sum up a machine that gave us ten days of bliss? One tries to put it soberly: this is the car for the man who has made up his mind as to what constitutes good living. It was, perhaps, appropriate that PHY 404's colour was that of a fine red burgundy.

The shape of the car is obviously aerodynamic, and the fact is emphasized by several factors. The tail fins, vestigial as they appear, exert a stabilizing influence at very high speeds.

TEST PILOT: Archie Scott-Brown winning his heat at the recent Daily Telegraph Brands Hatch meeting.

ALL of us will long remember Archie Scott-Brown's performance in the sports car race at the Silverstone Grand Prix meeting. He not only won the 2-litre class, but soundly trounced the 3½-litre brigade. The Lister-Bristol which he drove on that occasion has been prominent on many circuits this year, and so it was a great privilege for me to take over the car for a few days recently.

The Lister is now in production, and several orders have already been accepted. For various reasons, it has been found preferable to let the customer

JOHN BOLSTER TESTS

THE LISTER - BRISTOL

Cambridge-built Competition 2-litre a stable and tractable 130 m.p.h. Sports Car

supply his own engine, and body panelling is also carried out by any chosen coachbuilder. Similarly, the tyres are the owner's responsibility, because he is usually a racing driver who can get them at a specially reduced rate. The machine will generally be sold in chassis form, therefore, but as "my" Lister was a complete car I shall treat the rest of this report as a normal road test.

The basis of the vehicle is a tubular frame, of which the two main members swell outwards at the centre. They approach each other again at either end, where they join the fabricated uprights that carry the suspension units. In front, there are equal length wishbones, and at the rear, a de Dion axle. Suspension all round is by helical springs and telescopic dampers. The rear brakes are inboard mounted and the hypoid unit is a Salisbury.

The engine is set well back in the frame, and, since the wheelbase is only 7 ft. 6 ins., this means that the rear of the crankcase must come alongside the driver's feet. As the body is wide, this is of no consequence, and it makes possible the use of a delightfully short and rigid lever, mounted directly in the

lid of the gearbox. The radiator block is a Morris Oxford unit, carried very low and with a small separate header tank. There is also an oil radiator.

The power unit is the competition version of the 2-litre Bristol. This is called the BS4, and has a camshaft with considerable overlap, driven by gears instead of the usual chain. The running is somewhat bumpy below 3,000 r.p.m., but from that speed onwards the engine "takes hold" in a most refreshing manner. In racing, 6,000 r.p.m. is frequently employed, but I contented myself with 5,500 r.p.m. throughout my tests, except when timing the maximum speed, which entailed something in the region of 5,800 r.p.m. in top gear.

During the time that I had the car I covered a considerable mileage. London was crossed from end to end twice, Oulton Park was visited and lapped, and the usual timed tests were also made. On the road, the machine is reasonably quiet at moderate revolutions, and I had no trouble with noise, over-heating, or oiling up. This competition car makes a perfectly good hack, in fact, though the engine is obviously happier when it is allowed to turn over briskly.

This is a small car, and only weighs 12 cwt. Yet it is entirely stable at the very high speeds of which it is capable. I felt no qualms in driving at 130 m.p.h. with one hand while operating the stop watch with the other, which proves that the steering and suspension are about right. The springing is not hard, but the dampers have a fairly firm setting. Even at maximum speed the car rides perfectly level, and it is unaffected by gusts of wind, which cannot be said of many modern "all-enveloping" jobs.

The driving position is curious. One sits very low down and the body comes up almost to one's shoulders. Yet there is none of the difficulty in placing the car that one might expect. The steering is very light, and corners can be taken fast without any sawing at the wheel. This is very much a machine for the more advanced driver. It is like the modern racing car, inasmuch as it has extremely high cornering power but does not, by rolling, screaming of tyres, or other signs of distress, give warning that the limit is being approached. Yet one seems to develop a sixth sense—to get in the groove, so to speak—and corners can then be taken at very high speed in absolute safety and certainty. I admit that I spun off the new banked bend at Oulton while acquiring the technique, but that is another story!

I was warned that the brakes were due for servicing after several hard-fought races, but they remained powerful throughout my test, albeit with increased pedal travel. Only an occasional suspicion of judder confirmed that attention would soon be required. No fading was ever experienced, a most essential requirement if that tremendous performance were to be exploited in safety.

The gearbox is an absolute delight. Although there is effective synchromesh in the three upper ratios, this does not prevent the very quickest changes being made. The acceleration figures speak for themselves, and it will be seen that the graph goes up like a lift. I would say

COMPACT dimensions, with a 7 ft. 6 ins. wheelbase, and 4 ft. 2½ ins. track, feature in the Lister tubular chassis, which utilizes helical spring suspension all round with de Dion rear end.

FRONT END, showing the fabricated vertical members supporting the upper suspension wishbones and the helical spring for each wheel.

REAR END, detailing the Lister's de Dion layout, the helical spring suspension, the inboard brakes and Salisbury hypoid drive unit.

that the racing successes of this car stem almost as much from its acceleration as from its exceptionally fast cornering.

The de Dion axle is a very obvious asset. It has parallel radius rods each side, and a sliding block looks after the lateral location. Once one has driven a car like this, one does not wish to return to the conventional axle with its many disadvantages. It is of considerable interest that equal length wishbones have been adopted for the front suspension, and that there is no anti-roll bar. The car is so low, however, that the adoption of a system with a roll centre at ground level has no apparent penalty, and the freedom from gyroscopic manifestations must be beneficial.

heart, but I am sure that I shall have Lister printed on my posterior for many weeks to come!

The accessibility of the mechanical components is first-class. The whole of the front of the body forms the bonnet, and when it is swung open the engine is entirely free of obstructions. A large door in the rear of the body renders the de Dion assembly equally easy to service. This is of immense value for racing, but it would be of advantage even under the more leisurely conditions of normal use.

The Lister is a well-built competition car of superb handling qualities and very high performance. With a cover over the

(Continued on page 117)

ACCELERATION GRAPH OF THE LISTER-BRISTOL

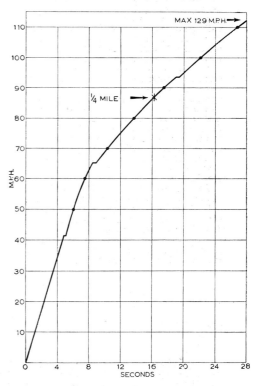

It is often alleged these days that the cars in sports car races are merely "specials", and of no use for serious touring. I disproved this with the Lister, for I drove it about like a normal saloon (only much faster!). It starts instantly at all times, and although no hood was fitted, the body deflected the wind over my head, and most of the rain was carried away. A fair amount of engine heat is retained inside the shell, and I seldom wore an overcoat even in cold weather. If the general standard of comfort met with my approval, one exception was the seat. We have heard of the queen with Calais printed on her

THROUGH SCOTT - BROWN'S VIZOR: (Above) The view forward from the driver's seat showing the stubby gear-change lever. A fuel tank is seen on the left.

POWER - PACK: The BS4 competition - type 2 - litre Bristol engine is set well back in the Lister frame.

The Bristol 450

By GARRICK M. LIGHTOWLER

During 1950-51 the British firm of Jaguar Cars, Ltd., designed and built a LeMans winner. During the same period they achieved what to many seemed the impossible, and introduced at the October Motor Show in London the now-famous Mark VII Saloon. This rapid transfer of a model from drawing-board to the center of International limelight has again been performed by a British manufacturer. Scarcely six months elapsed between the time the draughtsmen at the Bristol Aeroplane Company's works had put pencil to paper to design the '450' Sport Coupe and the finished product's first major victory. It was at the 1953 Twelve Hours Sports Car Race at Rheims (France) that the fruits of victory fell to the latest of British sport cars.

The Bristol '450' was a conclusive first in its Class (700 cc. to 2,000 cc.), with a Bristol--engined Frazer Nash placing third. The race, run between midnight and noon, was won on general classification by a 1953 Le Mans-type Jaguar 120C, followed by a French Talbot, an American Cunningham, a further 120C, and then the Bristol '450,' beaten, in fact, only by cars of much greater capacity running in the over 2 liter bracket. With the winning Jaguar's average speed of 105.5 mph., for the twelve hours, the Bristol's 92.7 mph. is creditably compared when it is considit-that the Bristol has nearly 1½ liter less engine capacity. On the same basis and compared against the largest-engined car in the race, which came in third, the result is even more startling —a result which does not altogether favor the Florida product.

The object of developing and racing the '450' sport coupe in a modest season's program is not for the purpose of prestige or for advertisement. It is part of the Car Division's research policy into engine design and body forms for their marketed high-performance sedans. This is a true case of improving the breed under race conditions and passing on to the public the lessons learned.

To say that outwardly this model is unusual is to make a typical British understatement—already it has been dubbed "the Car from Mars." It is worth, therefore, having a more detailed look at its technicalities. For although it is highly unlikely that this type as such will ever go into quantity production, many of its points will in the near future be embodied in the normal Bristol sedans.

The two-seater aerodynamic body is built with a steel-tube structure covered with light alloy panelling and is made, as regards size, to suit the individual driver. The low rakish lines terminating in twin stabilizing fins, and the nose with built-in lights and wide air intake for the engine, give it a most purposeful and businesslike appearance.

Weight, which is the curse of all sport car manufacturers, has been attacked with vigor, and the chassis of steel-tube construction, with an extra rigid section and four cross members, has received much attention in this sphere.

Suspension in the rear is DeDion, whilst in the front, fully independent. Steering is by means of a rack and pinion system.

Braking is dependent upon Lockheed hydraulics which are operated with separate master cylinders for front and rear, with special two leading shoe type on the front wheels. The 12-inch diameter drums with a 2½-inch width have specially ground friction surfaces; all four are scientifically balanced.

The gear box is exclusively Bristol and gives four forward speeds and one reverse, with special 'non-crash' synchromesh in top, third, and second. Selection of gears is by means of a short, light lever centrally mounted in the floor.

The motive power is supplied by the now well-tried 1,971 cc. Bristol engine, the same unit which has been so successfully fitted in the 'Cooper-Bristol' Formula II racing car, and the 2-liter Frazer-Nash. Fuel is fed to the six-in-line cylinders by three Solex multiple jet down-draught carburetors, which are fitted with efficient but non-restrictive silencers. The 'con' rods are made to an individual Bristol pattern; and the induction and exhaust parts are of a highly scientific design to promote the absolute maximum and efficient aspiration. The massive crankshaft, which is statically and dynamically balanced, is supported on four extra large main bearings. All crankshaft journals are nitride hardened. Potential seizing is eliminated by high pressure forced lubrication to all engine bearings by way of a full flow oil cleaner. Truly, it is a most powerful precision engine of very reasonable size.

For those of the uninitiated who ask "what good is motor racing?" here is proof positive. Here with the Bristol type '450' sport coupe is the actual example of a car with its roots embedded in the race field—due, in time, to blossom into the classic popular car of tomorrow.   ☆☆

The Bristol 450 Sport Coupe won a major victory (at Rheims, France, in 1953), scarcely six months after its designers first began work on the drawing board.

Bristol 403 into Bristol Freighter; the departure from Southampton on Friday, August 27. The take-off was delayed for $2\frac{3}{4}$ hours by fog which, when it cleared, left a brilliantly sunny day.

GOODWILL MISSION

A JOURNEY BY BRISTOL
FROM BRISTOL TO BORDEAUX

By . . . . . PETER GARNIER

IN these days of comparative peace, when one half of the world looks menacingly at the other, it is heartening to realize that there still exist direct bonds of friendship between towns in this country and on the Continent—bonds which, in several cases, were formed or fostered by the last war. The close friendship between Bristol and Bordeaux is in that category. The relationship has existed for centuries through the wine trade, but it was on August 28, 1944, when the last of the occupying forces had been driven from the French town, that the friendly spirit of the people of Bristol took the form of "adopting" Bordeaux to assist in its rehabilitation. Currently, in addition to the shipment of wine, there is an interchange of school children between the towns, each learning the other's language and way of life. In Bordeaux there is a Bristol-Bordeaux committee and a similar body exists in Bristol.

It was in keeping with this relationship between the two towns that, on August 28, 1954, the tenth anniversary of the liberation of Bordeaux, it was decided to send a message of greeting from the Lord Mayor of Bristol to his counterpart across the Channel. It was fitting that the message should be carried by products of the workpeople of Bristol; a Bristol 403 car was used, crossing the Channel from Southampton to Cherbourg in a Bristol Freighter aircraft operated by Silver City Airways. An additional object of the trip was to demonstrate that, although some 550 miles separate the two towns, in time and by modern transport they are not so very far apart.

In charge of the mission was C. B. Bailey-Watson, public relations manager of the Bristol Aeroplane Company, previously technical editor of *Flight* and a former colleague; also carried were Ray Densham, of the B.B.C. television service (with heavy television camera and equipment), the Bristol company's photographer, Ted Ashman (whose equipment was hardly less weighty), and the author. Miraculously, the car's locker accommodated all our luggage and cameras. Michelin X tyres were used, with the rear pressures 4lb per sq in above normal, and the considerable weight seemed to have no appreciable effect on the handling of the car, though the rear springs "bottomed" once or twice.

The 70 miles from Bristol to Southampton were covered at an average speed of 42 m.p.h., which included the time

Long shadows, and reflections on La Rochelle harbour in the thin, morning sunshine.

taken to change a wheel after a puncture. After sitting fog-bound at Eastleigh aerodrome for nearly three hours, the Bristol Freighter bore Bristol 403 aloft at 12.45 p.m., placing it safely on French soil 38 minutes later. By 1.35 p.m. we were clear of the Customs and away.

The Bristol soon proved itself an admirable car for the faster, traffic-free conditions of Continental travel. Such are the torque characteristics of the engine (1,971 c.c. six-cylinder, three carburettors, 105 b.h.p.) that up to about 3,500 r.p.m. the engine does not fully come to life. Above this speed the car fairly leaps away, building up 90 m.p.h., and more, surprisingly quickly. It is desirable, therefore, to use the gear box freely—operation of the short, central lever is smooth and very quick. The engine is happiest turning over quickly and it is a joyous experience to drop into the very useful second gear to overtake slower traffic. The Bristol proved itself to have a wonderful ability to cover the miles, doing so in the gentlemanly and well-mannered way one expects of such a quality car. No difficulty was found in writing a legible log and notes at speeds approaching an indicated three figures.

Good Pull-in

Including a halt to buy unaccustomed peaches, 49 miles were covered in the first hour across the Channel. In the hope of having a quick lunch, a stop was made at the French equivalent of a "Joe's Café" in Granville. Unfortunately, it was a bad choice, Joe being unaccustomed to providing food. It took nearly an hour to cook an omelette and about two minutes to eat it before we were away again. Spurred on by this delay, we put 55 miles into the second full hour's running.

The speedometer was kept at a steady 85-90 m.p.h. whenever conditions allowed and, at this rate of progress, it did not take long to learn one or two important points about Continental driving. The very easily read pictorial road signs are not put up unless there is a very definite reason for their presence. Particularly worthy of note when one is using a high cruising speed is the sign depicting the double-humped upperworks of a Bactrian camel. A considerable reduction in speed is necessary unless one wants to leap from peak to peak like a chamois.

In spite of his apparently forceful driving methods, indicated by persistent horn blowing, the French driver is generally less forceful than one expects. This was particularly noticeable when we overtook, with due judgment, in the face of oncoming traffic. The oncomer invariably

shook his fists, turned on his head lamps, blew his horn and used every available method of indicating annoyance, though, in fact, there was not the least danger. Not without his responsibilities towards the quick progress of the car is the front seat passenger. It is he, in a right-hand drive car in a right-hand side of the road country, who has the best view of the road ahead when the car is held up behind a *camion*, and he can be invaluable in advising the driver when it is safe to overtake.

Agricultural Countryside

It was pleasant hurrying along the uncrowded, straight roads in the sunshine. Occasionally we passed farm carts drawn by patient, slow-moving oxen, yoked together uncomfortably across the horns. Sunburned and weathered people worked in fields of a size that seemed impossible to cultivate without mechanization. There was the curious Doppler effect of a rise and fall in pitch of the wind horns of the *camions* as they met us, hooting at some object on the distant horizon. Occasionally there was the clatter of the camera as Ray Densham committed to celluloid some interesting part of the route, or the magic three figures indicated by the speedometer. Somehow progress gives the impression of being (and, in fact, is) quicker on the Continent because the distances are given in kilometres which, being shorter than miles, are covered more quickly. So the hours passed—52 miles in the third, only 33 in the fourth because of a delay in Nantes caused by the knocking-off of hundreds of factory workers, and 49 in the fifth.

We stopped at La Rochelle at 8.15 p.m. for dinner and,

GOODWILL MISSION . . . .

after our lesson at Joe's in Granville, tried the railway station. It was a great success from all points of view; we fed well and were away in ten minutes under the hour. Our cruising speed was reduced for the rest of the run by fog and darkness, though we put 41 and 45 miles into each of the next two hours, reaching Bordeaux at five minutes to midnight. Since leaving Cherbourg, 10 hours and 20 minutes had elapsed; of this, eight hours and 20 minutes had been spent on the move. We had covered 399.5 miles, giving a running average of a little under 48 miles in each

Straight roads reaching away to the horizon. A stretch of N137 on which the Bristol cruised for mile after mile at an indicated 90 m.p.h., despite its considerable load.

hour. It was indicative of the comfortable travel provided by the Bristol that none of us felt any undue signs of weariness, and we spent the next half-hour exploring a town which seemed in no mood to go to sleep.

The following day, Saturday, was mainly occupied in learning our part in the celebrations, carrying it out, and lunching with M. Attané, the deputy mayor. At 10 a.m. we assembled in the Hôtel de Ville and, assisted by Mlle Beauvais of the British Consulate when linguistic difficulties became insuperable, learned that the Bristol was to play an important part. Arrangements were made that an *agent de police* should call for us at our hotel at 11.40 a.m. and escort us to the Place de la Comédie, the scene of the ceremonial handing over of the Lord Mayor of Bristol's greetings. We returned to the hotel, arranged for the car to be washed (there was a divergence of opinion as to whether it should remain in its travel-stained state, indicating the hazards through which it had borne its message, or that it should do credit to its creators—the latter won), and had breakfast.

Pomp and Circumstance

The ceremony was impressive. The square was surrounded by people, and troops and members of the Resistance forces stood to attention in the centre. A band played; the Bristol drove sedately into the square and drew up at the steps of the Parthenon-like front of the Grand Théâtre. The message was handed to M. Attané by C. B. Bailey-Watson. The latter was presented to Général Druille, who had commanded Bordeaux at the time of the liberation,

More elegant and larger than its Cornish counterpart, Mont St. Michel suffers from an excess of tourists.

. . . . **continued**

Général Humbert, the present commander, M. Henri Binaud, who represented the Bristol-Bordeaux committee, and others. M. Attané read the message in French through the public address system and the sombre and moving Oath of the Resistance was read by M. Jean Duboué.

Its task completed, the Bristol drove away in company with two official Citroens to the Chapon Fin restaurant, where its crew were entertained to lunch. This was a meal that will live in the memories of four people, at least, for a very long time. Cantaloups and blue Bristol glass finger-bowls in honour of the occasion, dating, perhaps, from some long-distant trading voyage of the past; Chateaubriand steak and *cepes*, curious local mushrooms without the radial fins on the underside; *fraises du bois* with whipped cream and kirsch, and, above all, wines from one of the great vineyards owned by M. Binaud's family; finally, a bottle of 1893 Armagnac. It was a memorable meal and, like all such meals where the wines are good and well chosen, it left us mellowed but far from drowsy.

The afternoon was spent sightseeing in company with Mr. G. S. Robertson, the British vice-consul, who told us that there was a 5-litre Bugatti for sale in the town for only £60. We pressed him for further details and, from the description he gave, the car appeared to be a Type 50 4.9-litre with open Le Mans body. Why, we thought, should there be such things as import duty? At 4.23 p.m. we bade him goodbye and set off on the

return journey. The decision to leave on Saturday evening was made reluctantly, but we had to be at Cherbourg at 4 p.m. on Sunday and it would have meant a very early start if we were to do the whole run on Sunday.

We decided to spend the night at La Rochelle and, with only 113 miles to do, we did not hurry. The roads were not as clear as they had been the day before, though the weekend traffic was nothing like as bad as it is in England —despite the sunny weather. The French weekender suffers from faults similar to those of his English counterpart and drives at 30 m.p.h. on the crown of the road. A characteristic which the British motorist does not share, however, is the tendency to load his vehicle with as many people as possible. We passed motorized bicycles bowling along, the rider's girl-friend on the carrier; Lambretta scooters with the pillion passenger attractively travelling side-saddle and a child wedged between. Herds of biscuit-coloured cows wandered, well trained, along the sides of the roads at milking time. A useful accessory was noted on the rear of a Berliet coach. By means of red, amber and green lights the driver signalled to following traffic whether it was safe to overtake. We reached La Rochelle at 7.30 and garaged the Bristol in company with a 1909 Model T Ford, on the back of which was painted a notice saying that it had been retired in deference to the Vedette.

In brilliant early morning sunshine we left the hotel just before 8 a.m. on Sunday and passed the glassy harbour, with its motionless reflections of the yachts and the old forts at the entrance. A stronghold of the French Protestant

On the return journey; the Bristol poses beside the 15th-century castle at Nantes.

GOODWILL MISSION
continued

M. Attané, deputy Mayor of Bordeaux (obscured by the 403) and M. Binaud, greet C. B. Bailey-Watson, representing the Lord Mayor of Bristol.

faith and scene of many sieges, La Rochelle is a beautiful place. We left the town on N22 and, at Usseau, turned on to N137. There was little traffic about at this hour and we hurried through countryside which in some ways is like the Cotswolds with its dry walling of a similar stone. We reached Aisne at 8.28, having covered 20 miles in 20 minutes. Unlike the British Sabbath, on which blood sports are discouraged, the French seem to reserve this day for such activities. We passed a number of cyclists carrying sporting guns and towing box trailers containing dogs. A Fiat 1100 was overtaken, carrying four huntsmen whose necks were encircled by curious but attractive hunting horns.

The Bristol's progress continued well; at the end of the first hour we had covered 55 miles. We learned the significance of the road sign *Chaussée Deformée*. Deformed is a masterly understatement; the sign very often means that the surface is atrocious and can be taken only at a crawl.

Patches of fog slowed us during the second hour; this, and a pause for photography at Nantes, brought our mileage down to 38. The countryside here was undulating and uninteresting, but the straight and well-surfaced N137 was ideal for fast travel. Towards Rennes, where we left N137, it became more interesting from the point of view of driving. The straight, featureless road gave way to pleasant fast bends and twisting climbs up which the car soared in second gear. By Rennes, at the end of the third hour, we had put a further 55 miles behind us.

Sightseeing

With time in hand, we decided to make a detour to see Mont St. Michel. It was interesting, as we passed through St. Aubin d'Aubigné, to note the link between this district and St. Michael's Mount in Cornwall; the family name of Lord St. Levan, who recently presented the Cornish Mount to the National Trust, is St. Aubyn. Here we had one of several amusing experiences. We halted and, in my best French, I asked the way from a passer-by. In stammering French, with an American accent, he directed us. Congratulating myself that I should have fooled anybody as to my nationality, I put him out of his misery by saying that I, too, could speak English.

Mont St. Michel, though infinitely more elegant and larger than its Cornish counterpart, was a disappointment because of its tripper appeal. The car produced cries of appreciation from the mechanically informed French; "*Voyez, le Bristol,*" was heard on several occasions. At 12.24 we stopped sightseeing and moved on, stopping at Avranches for lunch. In this part of France it was noticed how extremely popular the Peugeot 203 seems to be—in a normal saloon form, also as an estate car and, less common, a convertible. There were, inevitably, endless 2 c.v. Citroens, their little engines singing away as they took a full load of passengers to the seaside.

So we hurried on—Granville, Coutances, Lessay, Colomby, Valognes, and Cherbourg at 3.38 p.m. The day's run of 291 miles had been covered at a running average of 48.2 m.p.h. and, including stops of 1½ hours, an all-in average of 38.8 m.p.h. Truly the Bristol had proved the second object of the journey to be true, and had carried out its mission splendidly.

Its task completed, the Bristol stands in the Place de la Comédie while M. Attané reads the message from the Lord Mayor of Bristol.

A true four-seater of attractive lines, the new Bristol has also considerable luggage space within an aerodynamic body. The engine is the well-known Bristol 2-litre.

A Four-door Saloon from Bristol

Type 405 is a High-performance Four-seater Developed from the 404 Coupé

FROM the Bristol Aeroplane Company, old-established in the aircraft industry but "young" where cars are concerned, there was announced last week the most promising model of the Car Division's six years of existence.

Though it has, basically, the chassis and technical specification which are now widely known, and substantially the same 2-litre engine, the Type 405 Bristol marks a new departure in policy as a four-seater, four-door saloon. Simple in itself, the change is sufficient to bring the Bristol into a wider market where performance and quality are not by themselves enough, and convenience is essential. As an alternative, a convertible body by Abbott will be available on the same chassis. Apart from the body, an innovation this year is the use of Laycock-de Normanville overdrive to provide a five-speed transmission.

Aircraft Practice

Reference to the photographs on these pages will show more than a slight resemblance between the new car and the two-seater 404 coupé introduced last year. The two are, in fact, identical forward of the scuttle; interestingly enough, the 404 has been subjected to the process known among aircraft manufacturers as "stretching," but the story goes back farther than that. The type 403 two-door saloon which has been the mainstay of Bristol production for several years formed the basis of the 404, the box-section chassis frame being shortened by 18 in. in the middle, and cut short at a point above the rear axle. In the latest four-seater the wheelbase has grown once more to 9 ft. 6 in., but with the new-style, unstressed body, a composite riveted structure has been built on to the rear end, very strong in itself and forming a really large luggage boot.

The chassis of the 405 thus has three stout cross-members, with some useful extra stiffening in the tail. Of 14-gauge sheet steel, the frame has fully boxed side rails $6\frac{1}{2}$ in. deep, front and rear cross-members of similar construction carrying the suspension, and a central bracing of 3-in. steel tube.

The body which is carried upon this rigid base is of very light construction—so light, in fact, that the whole car is said to scale only 2,660 lb. without liquids. From the scuttle forwards, 18-gauge and 16-gauge alloy are used, upon a light sheet-steel framework. The habitable part of the car is outlined in ash frames, covered in 18-gauge alloy. Only the luggage compartment and fuel tank mounting, the central door pillars and the doors are metal braced, the latter again in light alloy.

Intended strictly for four people, the interior nevertheless has quite generous space in the vital directions, a reduction in height of $2\frac{1}{2}$ in. compared with the 403 being achieved without loss of comfort by placing the seats lower in the chassis. There is a distinct step down

BRISTOL 405 DATA

Engine dimensions	
Cylinders	6
Bore	66 mm.
Stroke	96 mm.
Cubic capacity ...	1,971 c.c.
Piston area	31.8 sq. in.
Valves	Inclined overhead
Compression ratio ...	8.5 to 1
Engine performance	
Max. power	105 b.h.p.
at	5,000
Max. b.m.e.p. ...	154 lb./sq. in.
at	3,750 r.p.m.
B.H.P. per sq. in. piston area ...	3.30
Peak piston speed, ft. per min. ...	3,150
Engine details	
Carburetters ...	Three Solex downdraught
Ignition	Coil
Plugs	K.L.G. P.10 L.80
Fuel pump	AC Sphinx
Fuel capacity ...	16 gallons (including 2-gallon electrically operated reserve)
Oil filter	Vokes full-flow
Oil capacity ...	12 pints (sump)
Cooling system ...	Pump circulation
Water capacity ...	17 pints
Electrical system ...	12-volt
Battery capacity ...	51 amp./hr.
Transmission	
Clutch	Borg & Beck s.d.p.
Gear ratios:	
Overdrive... ...	3.28
Top	4.22
3rd...	5.46
2nd...	7.71
1st	15.24
Rev.	12.20
Prop. shaft	Hardy Spicer
Final drive	Spiral bevel, 4.22 to 1

Chassis details	
Brakes	Lockheed hydraulic, 2 L.S. front
Brake drum diameter	Front 12 in., rear 11 in.
Friction lining area	168 sq. in.
Suspension:	
Front	Independent by transverse leaf spring
Rear	Torsion bars and radius arms (rigid axle)
Shock absorbers:	
Front	Telescopic
Rear	Telescopic
Wheel type	Bolt-on, pierced disc, wide-base rims
Tyre size	5.75 – 16
Steering gear ...	Rack and pinion
Steering wheel ...	Two-spoke, 17 in.
Dimensions	
Wheelbase	9 ft. 6 in.
Track:	
Front	4 ft. $4\frac{3}{8}$ in.
Rear	4 ft. 6 in.
Overall length ...	15 ft. $9\frac{1}{4}$ in.
Overall width ...	5 ft. 8 in.
Overall height ...	4 ft. $9\frac{1}{2}$ in.
Ground clearance ...	$6\frac{1}{4}$ in.
Turning circle ...	37 ft. 6 in.
Dry weight	$23\frac{3}{4}$ cwt.
Performance data	
Piston area, sq. in. per ton	31.1
Brake lining area, sq. in. per ton ...	141.5
Top gear m.p.h. per 1,000 r.p.m. ...	Overdrive, 24.4; top, 19.0
Top gear m.p.h. at 2,500 ft./min. piston speed	Overdrive, 96.8; top, 75.3
Litres per ton-mile, dry...	Overdrive, 2,040; top, 2,620

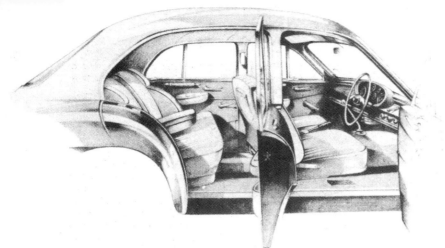

High-grade leather is used to trim the interior and to cover the Dunlopillo seats. Instruments are housed within a nacelle directly in front of the driver, and there is a short, remote-control gear lever centrally placed. The overdrive switch is on the facia by the driver's right hand. By building the boot (right) out into the rear wings, a total capacity of 17 cu. ft. is attained, and long objects such as golf clubs can be easily carried. A second speaker for the optional radio may be fitted in the wide parcel shelf beneath the rear window.

from the door sills to the floor of the interior, which incidentally is integral at the rear with the chassis frame, but the forward view from the driving seat is considerably improved over the earlier saloon by the lower sloping bonnet.

For those whose needs have not previously warranted a study of the Bristol design, some of the mechanical details may be recalled. Rubber mountings carry the six-cylinder, 1,971 c.c. engine of unusual design, with pushrod-operated overhead valves inclined at 80 degrees in hemispherical combustion chambers. The inlet valves are opened by direct pushrods and rockers in the orthodox way, the exhaust valves by additional rockers from horizontal pushrods across the top of the aluminium alloy cylinder head. Three separate downdraught Solex carburetters are used, the arrangement of the ports giving remarkably free gas passages, which contribute to the high output of 105 b.h.p. at 5,000 r.p.m. In the latest version, two three-branch exhaust manifolds have separate downpipes, meeting in a common silencer.

Five Forward Speeds

An 8-in. single-dry-plate clutch transmits power to the Bristol four-speed gearbox, which has synchromesh engagement for the three upper ratios and a freewheel on the lowest gear, so that the latter can be engaged without adjustment of the engine speed while the car is on the move. A short, remote-control gear lever is located by the driver's left hand on top of the propeller-shaft tunnel.

A new feature in the 405 is the use of a Laycock-de Normanville overdrive unit allied to the gearbox, giving a fifth ratio with clutchless finger-tip control from the instrument panel. By this means it has been made possible to lower the final drive ratio to the figure of 4.22/1, giving a lively performance in direct top. A lightly-loaded toggle switch on the panel adjacent to "two-o'clock" on the steering wheel operates the overdrive solenoid, the switch being held on by a smaller solenoid which releases it if top gear is disengaged. The

A Four-door Saloon from Bristol - -

upwards progression through the gears is thus always the same, so that it is impossible to change from third to overdrive top.

A Hardy-Spicer open propeller shaft is now used, with a spiral bevel final drive. Longitudinal torsion bars form the suspension medium and their arms help to locate

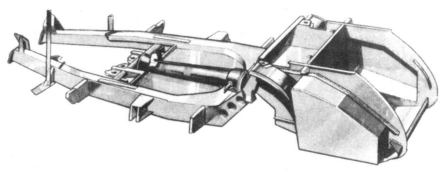

Similar to that of the 404 coupé, but allowing 18 in. longer wheelbase, the chassis frame has a strong riveted structure built on to the rear to carry the lightly built body and form a 17 cu. ft. luggage boot.

the back axle, which is also positioned by a triangular bracket on top of the differential casing. The front suspension consists of wishbones and a single transverse leaf spring, all four wheels being damped by direct-acting telescopic shock absorbers. Steering is by rack and pinion, and Lockheed hydraulic brakes are fitted, with two leading shoes in 12-in. Al-Fin drums of special shape at the front. The rear brakes, in common with those of the most recently produced 404 models, have 11 in. Chromidium drums. A single master cylinder is now used. An interesting point is that the standard tyres specified for the Bristol are of the Michelin "X" pattern, of special design with flexible side walls and a steel-reinforced tread. Especially tenacious roadholding is claimed for this type.

The interior of the Bristol, in contrast with some sports saloons and even with a number of family cars, is notable for the useful room available, as well as for the quality of the finish and appointments. There is adequate leg room

Slim and tapering in line, the 405 has the comparatively long wheelbase of 9 ft. 6 in. External door handles are used to replace flush-fitted push buttons.

for both front and rear passengers, and Dunlopillo cushions and squabs are used for all seats, which are covered in crushed grain hide of high quality. The upholstery shop is indeed one of the most impressive in the Bristol works. The front seats follow the practice of former cars, with high, supporting back-rests and a simple cam adjustment for rake as well as reach. At the rear, the single-piece seat has a definite hump in the middle, tailoring it to fit two people so as to provide the greatest possible comfort without their being thrown about in the fast driving for which the car is intended. There is a central folding armrest.

Reasonably easy access to the back seats, very easy to those in the front, is provided by the light doors. In contrast with the 403, external door handles are fitted in place of a recessed push-button release, and a feature which is practical as well as structurally convenient is the overlap of the rear doors, preserving a large clean area of the wheel arch over which the clothes of passengers getting into the car are bound to trail. Both front and rear doors have hinged ventilating panels as well as winding windows. The windscreen is of laminated glass, and all other glass, including the large wrap-around rear window, is of Triplex toughened material. The floor is covered with underfelt and pile carpet, and the head lining is of washable plastic material.

Comfort and Quality

Leather trim is used for the interior of the doors, with metal cappings, and chromium finish around the windows. For the driver and front passenger there are arm-rests adjustable for height, and the leather trim is extended to the two spokes of the steering wheel, adjustable to three different positions for column length. An alternative rake for the column may be specified when the car is ordered.

The comprehensive range of instruments is grouped in a nacelle immediately in front of the driver, cowled to avoid windscreen reflection. A speedometer with trip-reading odometer is balanced by a rev. counter, with oil pressure gauge, oil and water thermometers, ammeter and fuel gauge taking up most of the intervening space, complemented by warning lights for headlamp main beam, ignition, low fuel level and the flashing direction indicators worked from a switch on top of the scuttle. The polished walnut of the instrument panel is repeated in the facia on which are the minor controls, amongst which are switches for fog and spot lamps, heater and demister, and dual windscreen washers, all included in the specification of the car. There is a wide parcel shelf as well as the door pockets, further pockets in the front seat squabs, and a very large space available for parcels beneath the sloping rear window. H.M.V. Radiomobile or Ekco radio are available as optional extras, with loudspeakers fitted into the head lining above the windscreen, and into the rear parcel shelf.

Clever design has made possible a remarkably large luggage compartment despite the small overall width of the car and the 16-gallon fuel tank. The capacity of the riveted "box" is usefully increased by additional sections extending outwards behind the rear wheels, and in particular this allows such awkwardly shaped items as golf clubs to be carried with ease. Two handles, with a separate lock from that of the ignition and door, are used to fasten the door of the boot, and there is a third key for the cover of the petrol filler, high up in the body side. The battery is neatly disposed of in an easily reached compartment inside the offside front wing, while in the corresponding position on the near side is the spare wheel, and the tool roll is in a box on the scuttle, beneath the bonnet.

Other Models Continue

Appealing probably to a more limited public than the new four-seater, the 404 coupé continues with a few detail modifications, by which it is standardized on the 405. Thus the rear brakes, mentioned earlier, no longer have Al-Fin liners, the instrument panel follows the new pattern, and locking arrangements for the spare wheel cover are slightly different. Only the "touring" 105 b.h.p. engine will now normally be available. For those who still prefer a two-door, four-seater saloon, the Type 403 remains in production, the only alteration of note being external side lamps on top of the front wings, which have the advantage of visual indication that they are working properly.

The basic prices of Bristol models, with prices inclusive of purchase tax in brackets, are:

403 two-door, four-seater saloon, £2,100 (£2,976 2s. 6d.).
404 two-seater coupé, £2,350 (£3,330 5s. 10d.).
405 four-door, four-seater saloon, and four-seater convertible, £2,250 (£3,188 12s. 6d.).

Scale 1 to 30
(1 in. = 2 ft. 6 in.)

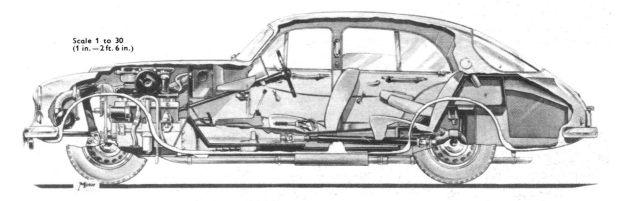

Right: Observing the rule of the road, a llama passes the Bristol soon after La Oroya, a mining town set high in the Andes at 12,000ft.

Below: The Bristol pauses on the indifferently surfaced road on the approach to the snow line and the Ticlio Pass of the Carretera Central, almost 16,000ft above sea level.

A N D E A N
E P I S O D E

TO THE "ROOF OF THE WORLD" WITH A BRISTOL

SOME cars get the breaks in life—others the knocks. My Bristol 401, I feel, has had some knocks and the fact that it is still a willing worker after five years of hard life is the reason for this account of another episode in its career. An account of a trip across Canada was published by *The Autocar* on April 27, 1951.

In May, 1953, I brought the Bristol to Peru. Whereas in Canada my daily commuting was restricted to some six traffic-ridden miles each way, which is no sort of life for a self-respecting engine, in Peru the twenty miles to and from the office, fairly free of traffic on a paved road, albeit from and to a suburban altitude of 2,000 feet above office level, must be just what Bristols are built for. A year of it hasn't caught my 401 napping at the call to duty, and its sterling qualities in the face of the unpredictable practices of the tenants of other vehicles, and the somewhat slap-dash surface of the road, are truly comforting.

Llamas graze unconcernedly beside the car in the Eastern Highlands of the Andes.

But this episode relates to the "roof of the world," the Ticlio Pass of the Carretera Central, 15,895 feet above sea level, over which a friend and I travelled to a business meeting at La Oroya, a mining centre which lies at some 12,000 feet just over the brow of the Andes.

I had made the trip before in a Fordomatic with no trouble other than the tendency of the gear mechanism to make up its mind at the wrong moment on certain gradients, so I knew the road. I also knew something of the problems of carburation and cooling at altitude but, mainly through laziness, decided to put the Bristol at it "as is." Thus we started, at 5.45 a.m., with not quite a full tank of 70 octane petrol and a vacuum flask of coffee. No preparation of the car at all, not even to clean the Canadian butterflies out of the radiator.

All went so well that there is really no story to be told— but 15,895 feet is quite a height. At that altitude I felt the loss of power more than the car. Reactions became slower and the legs became heavy when working clutch and brake —the latter important with a pot-holed and corrugated, gravelled surface, and the many hairpin bends. Naturally the car felt it too, but, provided one kept the revs up, there was still plenty of "oomph."

We arrived at La Oroya, after 120 miles, at 9 a.m. and left again at 2 p.m. on the return journey. It should be stated that in La Oroya we took on no petrol, air or water, and added a quart of oil only because the dip-stick showed a pint short on a contrary camber.

The return journey took a little longer as we engaged in dusty pursuit of trucks bearing produce from the central valley for the Lima market the next morning. We were home by 5.45 p.m., though the last 40 miles on the new tarmac highway had to be taken rather carefully owing to pronounced brake-fade—a not unnatural phenomenon after dropping down a gradient of about 1 in 11 at up to 70 m.p.h.

Worthy of note, perhaps, is the performance: 34 m.p.h. average speed and 21 m.p.g. (Imperial) on a tortuous and, for all but a short distance, unsurfaced road with an average gradient of just under nine per cent. Nevertheless the Bristol has resumed, without any objection or revision, its faithful function of commuting, but it will no doubt be asked to poke its bonnet farther into the lesser-known highways and byways of this country in due course.   J. L.

The Bristol 405 follows the general lines of the 404 as regards the front and rear end treatment, although the wheelbase is, of course, longer to accommodate the four-door body.

NEXT IN SEQUENCE . . . THE
BRISTOL 405

Four-door Quality Sports Saloon Forms Logical Development of 403 and 404

IN May and September, 1953, the Bristol Aeroplane Company announced two new models: the 403, a four-seater two-door saloon similar in appearance to the Type 401 but with improved engine performance, and the Type 404, a closed two-seater sports car on a short-wheelbase chassis, powered by an engine similar in basic design to that used for the 403 but running on a higher compression ratio. Its power output of 105 b.h.p. compared with 100 b.h.p. for the 403. An alternative engine was also available for the 404, having a modified camshaft which increased the output to 125 b.h.p. at 5,500 r.p.m. Now comes the 405—a logical development.

The 405 has been developed very closely along the lines of the 404, but like the 403 it has a four-seater body, this time with four doors, which is a new feature for Bristols. The mechanical components are similar to those of the two-seater, and except for a change in the exhaust system the power unit is unaltered. It will be remembered that this six-cylinder unit is of rather unusual design, utilizing a system of cross push rods which enable the inclined exhaust valves to be operated by a camshaft located on the opposite side of the engine. The combined cylinder block and crankcase is short; it terminates at the crankshaft centre line. The lower chamber is divided into three compartments by the two webs which support the intermediate main bearing shells. The cylinder bores are fitted with Brivadium dry liners, and the water jackets run the entire length of the bore on the exhaust side, but on the inlet side the jacket length is reduced to provide clearance for the tappets, which are inserted through a hole in the side of the crankcase. This is enclosed by a cover plate.

Copper-lead steel-backed bearings support the crankshaft, which has nitride-hardened journals. Bolted-on balance weights are used and these are placed on each side of the intermediate main bearings, and on the insides of the front and rear main bearings. There is a torsional vibration damper at the front of the shaft. The bottom of the crank-chamber is enclosed by a deep, light alloy sump which has a capacity of 12 pints.

Hemispherical combustion chambers are formed in the aluminium alloy cylinder head. Both the inlet and exhaust valves are inclined at an angle of 40 deg to the vertical line so that the included angle between the valves is 80 deg. Because of the material used for the head construction, seat inserts of centrifugally cast austenitic steel are used for both inlet and exhaust valves, and bronze inserts are provided for the 10mm sparking plugs which are in the top of the chambers between the valves. As before, the three downdraught Solex carburettors each supply a pair of near-vertical inlet ports. The exhaust gases are directed out through six ports in the side of the head, but in place of the six-branch manifold and single pipe used on the 404, the 405 has two three-branch manifolds with dual pipes running to a single silencer located amidships. A single tail pipe sweeps out diagonally at the right-hand rear corner of the car.

As with the other models, the drive is transmitted via an 8in-diameter clutch to the four-speed gear box, which has synchromesh on top, third and second gears; first gear is fitted with a free wheel. The gear box casing is split on the vertical centre line to permit the use of intermediate centre bearings for both the main and layshafts. A new feature is the inclusion of a fifth ratio, provided by the Laycock-de Normanville overdrive unit. This is built into the rear of the gear box casing in place of the previous extension. After direct top gear has been selected by the central remote control gear lever, overdrive can be engaged by raising the control lever of the switch on the right-hand side of the facia; this energizes a solenoid which effects the change. The change down from overdrive to direct top gear can be made by depressing the facia switch lever in the normal way. But if the driver changes down from overdrive to any of the indirect ratios, by operating the gear lever in the normal way, the overdrive engagement circuit is automatic-

Instruments are surrounded by a large cowl trimmed with leather, while the minor controls are grouped below the centre section of the facia, and on the right-hand side. The lever for the overdrive switch can be seen just to the right of the cowl, and to the left of the screen wash button.

ally broken and the facia switch drops to the direct top gear position; this means, therefore, that when the driver moves the gear lever back into top gear, direct top and not overdrive will be selected.

A short Hardy Spicer propeller-shaft, with a sliding joint on the front end, continues the drive to the semi-floating spiral bevel rear axle. As on the 404, this is located transversely by an A-bracket pivoted to the frame, the apex of the A being ball-jointed to the centre section of the casing. Longitudinal torsion bars form the rear springs, and levers attached to the rear ends of these are coupled to the other ends of the rear axle casing via short connecting links. It is, of course, necessary to use these short links to compensate for the change in position of the centre around which the axle pivots in relation to the torsion bar fulcrum point.

The front suspension is similar to that used on the 404 apart from a change in rate of the transverse leaf springs which form the lower suspension members. The complete front cross member, together with the spring, upper wishbones, stub axles, brakes and rack and pinion steering unit, is built up as a sub-assembly and attached to the front tuning-fork-shaped frame by means of two flanges, each having four bolts. This arrangement not only assists assembly but is also very useful in accidental damage or servicing.

Alfin Drums

The brake drum dimensions are similar to those of the 404, and the large Alfin brake drums first seen on that model are also retained, but in place of twin master cylinders, both front and rear brakes are operated by a single unit.

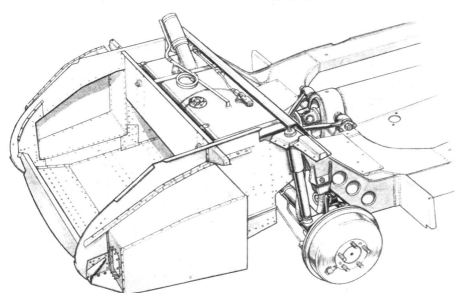

Like that of the 403, the wheelbase of the 405 is 9ft 6in but the chassis frame is modelled on that used for the short-wheelbase 404, with side members extended some 18in to cater for the increased wheelbase. The side members are about 6½in deep and are of box section formed by welding a vertical external closing plate to the flanges of a "top-hat" section; 14-gauge material is used for the side members, the 3in-diameter cross member, and the rear box section cross member, the front cross member being of 12-gauge steel.

The tops of the rear dampers are attached to the frame extensions, which sweep up at the axle. The fuel tank is mounted high up and well forward in the luggage compartment, so that there is luggage space beneath it.

To the rear of the main frame is attached a rear extension of composite structure consisting of steel brackets and light alloy sheet. This takes the form of two diaphragms spaced at the top by the petrol tank chamber and at the bottom by the luggage locker floor, around the rear ends of which the rear portion of the body shell is clinched. To increase luggage locker space the centre section of the diaphragms is in the form of box section panniers built out on each side of the structure. The remainder of the body structure is of composite construction, the front section being very similar to that used on the 404. It is built up of steel and light alloy.

With the exception of the door centre pillars, all the structural members above the waistline are formed from ash, solid ash being used for the screen pillars while a resin-bonded laminated construction is used for most of the other members. To this composite structure consisting of ash framework, light alloy and steel, is attached the main body skin, produced from 18-gauge aluminium alloy. To provide increased strength locally, the skin material is increased in thickness to 16 gauge for about 4in from each side of the front wing crown line.

Well-furnished

The interior of the Bristol is beautifully trimmed in best quality crushed grain hide, with Wilton carpet on the floor. The seats are formed of ash frames and are upholstered with Dunlopillo supported on elasticized webbing. The general cockpit layout is very well arranged. The instruments are grouped right in front of the steering wheel and are surrounded by a deep cowl to prevent reflection in the screen at night. This

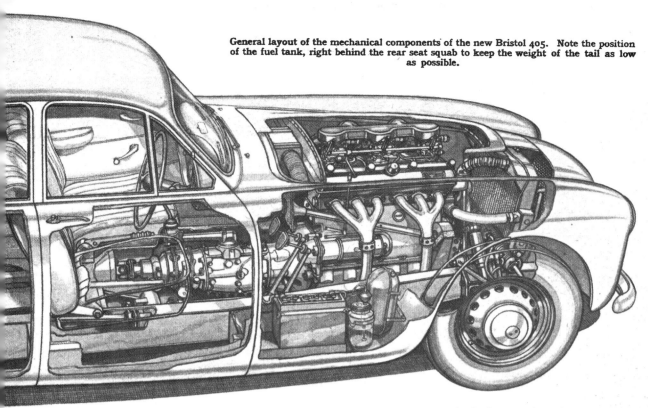

General layout of the mechanical components of the new Bristol 405. Note the position of the fuel tank, right behind the rear seat squab to keep the weight of the tail as low as possible.

tendency is still further reduced by trimming the cowl and top part of the facia with a very businesslike dull black leather, while the panel and lower facia are in polished hardwood.

In producing the 405 the engineers of the Car Division of the Bristol Aeroplane Company have produced a four-seater car with a frontal area only 0.13 sq ft greater than that of the 404 two-seater, while the weight of the new four-door car is rather more than half a hundredweight less than that of the 403 (which has only two doors). As regards weight distribution, both the 404 and 405 cars have approximately 52 per cent of weight on the front wheels, a feature which helps to improve directional stability.

The 405 is an expensive car, but a close examination of both the mechanical components and the bodywork indicates that the manufacturers of this streamlined sports saloon are out to produce a vehicle that is as good as the best.

A four-seater drophead coupé with body by Abbotts of Farnham is also available.

SPECIFICATION

Engine.—6 cyl, 66 × 96 mm, 1,971 c.c.: Compression ratio 8.5 to 1. 105 b.h.p. at 5,000 r.p.m. Maximum torque 123 lb ft at 3,750 r.p.m. Four-bearing crankshaft. Hemispherical combustion chambers. Inclined overhead valves operated by push-rods and rockers, with additional cross push-rods for the exhaust valves. Single side camshaft.

Clutch.—Bork and Beck, 8in diameter, dry single-plate. Six springs. Carbon thrust withdrawal mechanism.

Gear Box.—Overall ratios: Overdrive 3.28 to 1; top 4.22; third 5.46; second 7.71; first 15.24 to 1. Reverse 12.2 to 1. Synchromesh on top, third and second gears; free wheel on first.

Final Drive.—Spiral bevel axle 4.22 to 1 (9 : 38). Two-pinion differential.

Suspension.—Front, independent by transverse leaf spring and upper wishbones; rear, live axle, longitudinal torsion bars. Telescopic dampers. Suspension rate (at the wheel): front, 88 lb per in; rear, 132 lb per in. Static deflection (fully laden), front 7.8in; rear 6.5in.

Brakes.—Hydraulically operated, two-leading shoe front; leading and trailing shoe rear. Drums: 12in diameter, 2¼in wide, front; 11in diameter, 1¾in wide, rear. Total lining area: 168 sq in (94 sq in front).

Steering.—Rack and pinion. Three turns from lock to lock.

Wheels and Tyres.—Michelin X, 5.75-16in on 16 × 4½in wide-base rims. Five-stud perforated disc wheels.

Electrical Equipment.—12-volt, 51-ampère-hour battery. Head lamps, double-dip 60-36-watt bulbs.

Fuel System.—16-gallon tank (including 2 gallons reserve). Oil capacity 12 pints. Full-flow filter.

Main Dimensions.—Wheelbase 9ft 6in, track (front) 4ft 4.36in, (rear) 4ft 6in; length 15ft 9¼in, width 5ft 8in, height 4ft 9½in; ground clearance 6½in. Frontal area 21.36 sq ft; turning circle 37ft 6in. Weight (without fuel) 2,712 lb; weight distribution 52.3 per cent front.

Price.—Basic £2,250; purchase tax £938 12s 6d; total £3,188 12s 6d (saloon and drophead coupé).

The spare wheel is housed on the left-hand side of the body, just behind the front wheel. A similar compartment on the right of the car is provided for the battery, electrical equipment and screen wash bottle.

TO SPAIN IN A BRISTOL

An Account of a " Motoring " Trip to the Barcelona Grand Prix

THE Earls Court Motor Show clashing with the Spanish Grand Prix, time suddenly became a little short and distances seemed very long, so that the reporting of the Barcelona race needed some careful planning. Being averse to air-liners and their depressing habit of depositing you in a strange country with no means of transport other than a thumb, and also believing that if enthusiasts cannot always race, at least they can motor, the trip to Spain was planned round a motor car. There being four of us in the party, the offer of a Bristol 403 was eagerly accepted, for having tasted the joys of long-distance motoring in England with a 401 from the same firm, the Continent and 403 seemed an admirable mixture. Time was going to be short, as I was eager to reach Barcelona as soon as possible in order to see the new Lancia Grand Prix team during practice. There would be little time for sight-seeing on the way down through France, but the two ladies in the party politely agreed that they were only interested in a holiday in Spain. As they settled themselves in the back seats of the Bristol I silently hoped they would not complain too loudly as we " pressed on," for we intended to cover more than 300 miles before stopping for the night and we were leaving after lunch, crossing the Channel, and losing an hour due to the alteration of the time in England, compared with the Continent.

The Bristol was a perfectly standard 403 saloon, with 17,000 miles on the speedo., and 8.2 to 1 compression, set up on Esso Extra and running on Michelin " X " tyres—in fact, a delightful specification for any motoring, let alone 900 miles across Europe. With the friendly Townshend Ferry about to retire for its winter overhaul, and time being short, we made use of Silver City Airways. The delightful personal attention given to travellers was greatly appreciated after the dreary queues one experiences when travelling by boat in company with upwards of 50 other cars. The Bristol's only companion in the aircraft was a Vauxhall Velox on its way back to Switzerland, and in no time at all the Bristol Freighter put us down at Le Touquet and we were on our way. The flight had taken 20 minutes—the organising at both ends a total of under 40 minutes—and after correcting for daylight saving we left the aerodrome at 3 p.m. and headed south. Paris being such a terrible time-waster, like all big towns, our route lay to the west, and the Bristol was soon into its stride, cruising at 80 m.p.h. at 3,800 r.p.m., with all the needles on the various instruments indicating that all was well. We had filled the tank before leaving England and we did not anticipate buying any more fuel until we finished for the night, and down through Abbeville towards the city of Rouen the Bristol ate up the kilometres. At this time of the year the sugar beet industry in Northern France is at its height and the delightful triangular road signs that depict a saloon car spinning off the road were borne in mind. The French move hundreds of tons of beet from field to factory by means of horse and cart, and the amount of mud deposited on the roads can be very treacherous in damp weather. Fortunately for us the afternoon was dry and, with a strong wind blowing across the bleak Somme countryside, one was reminded of paintings of the French Revolution; in fact, one could almost see the cloaked horsemen galloping furiously across the horizon. Through the villages, such as Blangy and Neufchâtel, where the uneven *pave* enforced a 30-m.p.h. speed limit, without recourse to police-traps or speed-cops, one could practically hear the rumbling of the tumbrils, while some of the old village women would surely have delighted at the sound of the guillotine falling.

Descending into Rouen our passengers were rewarded with an excellent aerial view of the spindly-looking cathedral, and after bumping over the appalling cobbled road surface of some of the streets we were back to our 80-m.p.h. cruising speed once again. It said much for the back-seat comfort that the passengers were able to write notes and make little sketches. As it was their first trip to the land of the free there were many impressions to be gained, and the large side windows of the 403 allowed them an excellent view of the surroundings. After Rouen we made a slight detour in order to visit the Circuit des Essarts, where the Grand Prix races are run once a year. The surface of the downhill section after the concrete pits and grandstands was magnificent. Following N138, our aim being Tours, we gradually pushed the cruising speed up to 85 m.p.h. The only sound was the " spilling " of the air round the windscreen pillars and a pleasant hum from the engine. One of the great joys of the Bristol 403 bodywork is its air-flow and consequent lack of wind-roar, so that normal conversation can be

SPANISH TOURING.—Typical of the journey from Barcelona back to France is this splendid coastline, with the road running along the edge. Winding and twisting in and out of the numerous bays, with the Mediterranean breaking on the rocks below, the route is magnificent for the passengers. For the driver, hazards such as this slow-moving donkey cart, and blind corners, keep the eyes on the road, with only fleeting glimpses at the passing beauties.

carried on between all four passengers, unlike some British cars in which 60 m.p.h. precludes all further conversation. As darkness descended we began to see the magic name of Le Mans appearing on the signposts, for our route led through the " 24-Hour " country, while the flashing orange lights, that indicate a cross-roads worth some consideration by the high-speed motorist, began to be more visible. Those delightful little " islands " at town road-junctions, which are a few inches high with enough room for an *agent de Police* to stand on, began to flash orange warnings as well. In daylight these " super manhole covers " can easily be missed, and to hit one would ruin a wheel; to drive astride them is considered to be in very poor taste! We stopped for a change of drivers and to fit some yellow covers over the lamps, not wishing to be pushed in the ditch by an irate Berliet lorry. We reached Le Mans by 7.30 p.m., feeling that the time had arrived for dinner, for though we were in a hurry we were not in *that* much of a hurry, and anyway the Bristol was proving capable of putting well over 50 miles into each hour with no effort at all, and the schedule had been estimated on an all-in 45-m.p.h. average, which included stops and hold-ups.

After having the sort of meal that only France can produce, in one of those quiet restaurants where the only interest is good food and not rooking the tourist, we left Le Mans, which looked strangely quiet and sleepy, and headed for Tours, on N158, the Mulsanne straight actually being part of this main road. As we held an easy

WELL KNOWN.—The smooth-contoured outline of the Bristol 403 is well established, and its efficiency is really appreciated when cruising at high speed. Here the car used by MOTOR SPORT *is seen about to leave the French frontier at the beginning of N9, the Route Nationale that runs from Spain up through the centre of France. Behind the car is the excellent signboard at the entrance of the town of Le Perthus, typical of the very fine signposting throughout France.*

90 m.p.h. down the length of the famous straight, the headlamp beams picking out familiar objects that I saw last June while reporting that epic 24-hour race, we tried first to visualise a Jaguar or Ferrari going past at 170 m.p.h., and then to put ourselves in their position and see our tail-lights ahead, not being able to tell that we were doing only 90 m.p.h. We mopped our brows when Mulsanne corner appeared and were thankful that we could go straight on and not have to do it for many hours of darkness, while a hope was made that no one would enter lightheartedly for the 1955 Le Mans with a car that was not fast for its capacity. Tours was made nicely by bedtime, and before putting the car away the tank was refilled and some arithmetic showed an honest 18 m.p.g.

Thursday morning dawned bright and clear and our objective was Barcelona, all things being equal and the roads permitting. We left at 8 a.m.—a not unduly early hour even for tourists, let alone anyone in a hurry—and we headed for Châteauroux, through the Loire Valley country, with its long sweeping hills and undulating roads. As we approached that town we had the fascinating glimpse one gets of the great church, which for a brief moment appears to be built in the centre of the road, the way actually turning to one side just in time. High up on our right were the ruins of the Castle of Châteauroux, and here we joined N20 and really got down to some steady motoring. When one talks glibly of cruising at high figures there is a tendency to refer to the speed you reach between corners or on quick rushes downhill, but in the 403 cruising meant sustained speed, uphill, downhill or even round swerves. On the section from Châteauroux to Argenton we amused ourselves by checking the speedometer, with a stop-watch, against the excellent French kilometre posts, the little white 100-metre stones making the arrival of the end of the kilometre a simple task. At 80 m.p.h. we found the Smiths instrument 2½ m.p.h. fast and at 90 m.p.h. only 2 m.p.h. fast, and such was the pace that we were able to check, with time to decide which kilometre would be a good one on which to time the car, to make sure of a clear run and avoid having to drop to an indicated 85 m.p.h. due to having to give a little thought to traffic conditions. Meanwhile our passengers were happily writing post-cards to their friends, for we had insisted on an 8-a.m. start. As we climbed up the winding hill out of Argenton—the rev.-counter showing 4,200 in second gear—the sun was shining on the vast, gilt, religious statue that overlooks the town, giving it a strangely ethereal look. We passed quickly through Limoges, with its famous porcelain wares spread out on the pavements to attract the tourist with time and money to spare, and headed into the hilly country that forms the foothills of the Massif Central. The road began to wind and undulate once more, and here the cornering of the Bristol made itself really felt. With Michelin " X " tyres the rear-end breakaway, built into Bristol cars, was reduced to a minimum, and the car could be cornered on 60-70-m.p.h. bends with the tyres gently wailing and the rear ones at a slightly greater slip-angle so that just the smallest amount of pressure was exerted on the steering wheel in the opposite direction to the corner, to retain a nice balance. Had there been any free play in the steering mechanism one could have merely taken it up on reverse lock. As it was, there was none, so a fast corner was merely a question of reversing the load on the teeth of the rack-and-pinion steering and yet still have the tyres

whistling gently, even though we had increased their pressure by 2 lb. all round, in view of the sustained speed and load. While the driver enjoyed the continuous fast swerves that go on for hour after hour when crossing the Massif Central, the passengers enjoyed the sights, among them the first ox-drawn cart, the two great beasts leaning heavily on each other as they plodded along, their heads yoked together. This was a sure sign that we were getting south, and through Uzerche and Brive a distinctly Spanish, or even Algerian, influence began to make itself noticeable in the local architecture, while life itself appeared to have slowed considerably. In Brive the French were at lunch, and there is nothing so deserted and empty-looking as a town in the Dordogne country at lunchtime. We, too, began to think about lunch, but seeing that Cahors was approaching and it was claiming to be a Gastronomique Centre, we pressed on. Continuous 50 or more miles into each hour had got us well into the South of France by 1 p.m., and most of them had been in the order of 53-54, the best being 56 miles in the hour. Cahors was certainly an excellent Gastronomique Centre and, considering that it is a small town in the middle of nowhere, its restaurants and food are remarkable. Lunch took us longer than we anticipated and we were some way behind our schedule when we left, but once more the performance of the Bristol was brought in to recover lost minutes. The roads continued to be of the " dicing " variety and tyre scream and 4,500 r.p.m. in second and third enabled us to keep up our running average of 50 plus m.p.h., except for a delay at a level crossing. We had seen the train crossing a viaduct high to the right of our road and had noticed it to be loaded with Simca Aronde and 2 c.v. Citroën cars. The countryside in this part of France is such that it was not many kilometres farther on that we reached the level of the railway, to find the two long " barber's poles " that form Continental crossing gates, lowered in front of us.

Since mid-morning we had been on roads that were unbelievably deserted, even of local traffic, but running into Toulouse by half-past four, we met a lot of heavy traffic, which seemed quite a novelty. In the town we were held up by a lorry that had broken its back axle in the middle of the tram tracks, which did not seem to have worried the French in the slightest degree. Along the fast roads to Carcassonne and Narbonne, through delightful grape-vine country, the autumn tints on the leaves containing every colour from yellow to purple, there was unduly heavy traffic for the time of the year and we had difficulty in putting 46 miles in the hour. This was only achieved by combined driving by the two people in the front seats, one operating the controls and the other " spotting " and making decisions, for it will be realised that right-hand drive when driving on the right of the road has its disadvantages when in a hurry with main-road traffic. During this section we encountered our first " competition," in the form of a very persistent Peugeot 203 which profited from every traffic check that the Bristol suffered to keep up with us for many miles, even though we were continually around the 70-m.p.h. mark, or more, whenever the roads were clear for a minute or two. Crossing the bridge into Carcassonne afforded a marvellous view of the ancient city, away to the right, modern Carcassonne having moved down to the level of the great river Aude. Turning down N9 at Narbonne darkness was beginning to fall, and some fast cruising in the dark brought us to Perpignan by 7 p.m., with time for some refreshments before heading towards the Spanish frontier. As we had been motoring pretty consistently for 11 hours we wondered if our lady passengers would prefer to spend the night at Perpignan, for we were now in sight of Barcelona, by Continental travel standards, and were well up on schedule. They assured us that 11 hours in the back of the Bristol, with only a break for lunch, had not tired them nearly as much as the previous day's exertions of preparing to leave home for a week, a 'plane journey and the first experience of Continental motoring. As our arrival at Barcelona was expected, we agreed to continue, though there was less hurry now, especially as we were told the frontier did not shut until midnight. We took our time about leaving Perpignan, taking on petrol and one pint of oil, as well as buying chocolates and sweets, and leisurely motored out into the darkness towards the Pyrenees, but were soon on the winding road through the lower slopes of the mountains, where they run down to the Mediterranean at Cerbere. Our frontier was Le Perthus and the last six or seven miles were really winding mountain roads, where the driver was encouraged to go fast just for the fun of the cornering power of the Bristol and the delightful surge in second gear at corners. The passengers added to the " dice " by recounting stories of how the top Rally drivers average 33 m.p.h. over such going. Arriving at the frontier with the tyres smelling a little hot we learned that the Spaniards shut their front gate at 9 p.m. not 12 p.m., and we had four minutes to spare. Making the quickest frontier crossing

Continued on next page

TO SPAIN IN A BRISTOL

I have ever experienced in seven years of Continental motoring, we were in Spain, and the driver was warned to look out for unlit bullock carts, large holes in the road, river beds crossing the road, and a general poor standard of surface that would reduce the cruising speed to 60 m.p.h. We had not reckoned with the Bristol suspension and were soon cruising at our normal speed, and in many places were reaching 90 m.p.h., the headlights, now white once more, being able to pick out obstacles with adequate warning.

The last leg of the journey which we had imagined would be tedious saw 44 miles being put into the hour in spite of getting lost in Gerona, for here we encountered a Fair laid out all over the main road, with no room to get between the show booths and the pavement. Fortunately for us the Fair was closed, though as we drove in and out of the mass of temporary buildings we hoped we would not bump into the tiger's cage. Eventually, after bumping over boards, ropes and trestles, we got through this maze and continued on our way. Another delay was caused by the main street through Arenys de Mar, where a river bed crosses the road, the dried-up river having the best surface. With such an obstacle crossing their main road it was not surprising that the Spaniards did not bother to build a foundation to the main street. Crawling in bottom gear, the surface felt worse than an English farm track, but once out of the town things improved. As the outskirts of Barcelona appeared we encountered another " competitor " in this journey to the Grand Prix. Yet again it was a Peugeot 203, this time a drophead with Paris registration numbers, and it was in a great hurry, sitting on our tail at an honest 75 m.p.h., and eventually going past on a bumpy section where we had more respect for our torsion-bars than he had for his leaf-springs. Barcelona was reached by 11.15 p.m. and a short tour of the town was inadvertently indulged in before arriving at our hotel. We had covered 560 miles in the day in complete comfort, still averaging 18 m.p.g., and with no one feeling as though they had sat in the car for 15¼ hours, with three hours off for eating.

The Grand Prix at Barcelona was well worth attending, as reported in last month's MOTOR SPORT, even though it was supposed to be a job of work for the writer, but when you go to work in a Bristol 403 it is difficult to view Grand Prix racing as work. With the Motor Show still in progress and the Editor holding the fort, a quick return was called for, not quite so quick as the outward journey, however, as we had until midday on Wednesday to reach Le Touquet. So, leaving Barcelona on Monday morning, we returned along the same route, being able to enjoy the Spanish scenery that we had missed on the outward journey on account of the darkness. It was with great reluctance that we forked left away from the sea just before Blanes, for it meant missing the superb scenery of the Costa Brava. Now that the tourist season is over, that coastline of Spain is at its best, and for sheer breath-taking beauty of rugged coastline the journey through Tossa, San Feliu, Palamos and along the appalling roads through Pals and la Escala to Figuras, cannot be bettered. However, those roads are for people with plenty of time to spare and preferably driving a horse and cart, so we had to be content with the lower slopes of the Pyrenees, through the cork tree plantations, with the piles of cork drying in the sun, that was still hot by English standards. Lunching in Perpignan on local delicacies and *vin du pays*, we then retraced our route as far as Narbonne, and there followed the Mediterranean eastwards, our return route being up through the very centre of France, following N9. This was a slower road than our outward route, but it was agreed that a journey through such wonderful country was worth all the time that might have been spent in Paris had we returned by the faster route.

The afternoon was warm and sunny as we got back into what had become known as the Bristol-stride, which is to say 80 m.p.h., or 84 on the speedometer, and while lazily cruising along the fast stretch after Narbonne we suddenly experienced that fascinating feeling when the car in front of you does not get any closer, even though you are indicating 85 m.p.h. I say *we* experienced, but actually only the writer and one of the ladies in the rear enjoyed the next few miles, for the others were fast asleep and remained so. The grey saloon in front of us was a 1900 Alfa-Romeo so we pulled our gloves on a bit tighter and surged forward. It also had a passenger asleep in the back and, having overtaken it at just over the 90-m.p.h. mark, its Italian driver " played bears " with us for the next 35 miles, and we pitted 2 litres from Bristol against 2 litres from Milan. Fortunately for us it was only a standard model and it dropped behind at about 87 m.p.h., while the Bristol went on up to an honest three-figure speed, " just to show the Eye-ties "—of course, had it been a T.I. Alfa-Romeo 1900 saloon we should have had to have turned sharp left, for I've seen that particular model lap Montlhéry at 114 m.p.h. Having satisfied myself that the Italian could not get so near the cornering limit of his car as I could with mine, we

left the coast road and headed north, the passengers only now waking up and being furious at missing the fun.

The hilly country of the Herault " department " from Pezanas has earth of a remarkable maroon colour. The road ran in a straight line as far as the eye could see, and it looked just like an M.G.M. colour film of Mexico, with outcrops of rugged rocks rising out of the highly-coloured soil, there being very little vegetation. It was getting dark as we got into the mountains, after passing through Lodeve, and the last few kilometres over the peaks before Millau were done with the beams of the headlamps lighting up the valleys. As we descended the winding road we could see the lights of Millau twinkling far below us—seeming to stay the same distance no matter how many hairpin bends we negotiated. Rain was falling and there was a woody tang in the air when at last we reached the Grand Hotel de Commerce in the centre of this lovely little town nestled at the foot of the mountains. After the noise and pandemonium of Barcelona the quiet restfulness of Millau was almost enough to make us stop motoring for ever.

Tuesday morning saw a brisk start at 8 a.m. running on wet roads, though rain was not actually falling. The route out of Millau to St. Flour and Clermont-Ferrand was one long Prescott hill-climb and descent, rising as high as 3,500 feet, where the clouds were down below road level. Until this point I had begun to wonder about the advantages of Michelin " X " tyres, but the three hours of almost continuous cornering on wet roads, at a degree of cornering power sufficient to produce gentle wails from the tyres, even on the wet surface, really convinced me that Mr. Bibendum has something in his metal bound tyres, especially for Bristol cars. Just before St. Flour we stopped for a brief moment while the photographic expert in the party leapt out to take a photograph of Monsieur Eifel's fantastic viaduct. Like so many of us he was unimpressed, as we approached the top of the gorge, seeing the viaduct go straight on out into space, but after descending the steep valley side and realising that the viaduct was still " up there," he was most impressed ! The electric railway that crosses this viaduct had been with us all the way from Millau, sometimes high above us, other times way below, and often at our level. The peculiar arches carrying the electric overhead wires, looked like enormous croquet hoops and were visible many miles away. At one level-crossing a row of tiny bells hung across the road indicating the maximum height that would pass under the electric wires, though quite what one was supposed to do in this desolate, but fertile, countryside if your lorry " tinkled " the bells was not very clear. A lunch stop was made at Gannat, once more out on the open plains of France with long fast roads, and whether it was the excellence of the fare provided by the Hotel d'Agriculture, down a little side turning off the main road, or the reaction to a morning of mountain motoring, I do not know, but the first hour after lunch saw 58 miles go by without ever exceeding 80 m.p.h. At Moulins we joined N7, the road that has such character that it has inspired the writing of a book about it. The 54 kilometres from there to Nevers took 25 minutes, during which time the speedometer was checked at 100 m.p.h. At Nevers we stopped to find an infuriating " tinkling " noise under the bonnet. This proved to be the ferrule on the starting handle, which is kept in clips inside the bonnet. We had agreed to a pact on the outward run that three-figure motoring would be

UP THERE.—Having descended into the valley below the huge viaduct near St. Flour, from the road that was on a level with the railway, the photographer began to appreciate the magnitude of Monsieur Eifel's construction. At the bottom of the valley runs a river that is still farther below the point from which the photograph was taken.

FACE TO FACE.—Bristol-fashion, at Le Touquet.

reserved for the return journey and now the Bristol was beginning to hum contentedly to itself. From Nevers the road follows the river Loire to Briare and undulates in delightful 70-90 m.p.h. sweeps. It has a friendly " English " air about it, after the more severe Massif Central country. The fact that sugar beet industries were beginning to be noticeable again added to this northern look. The Bristol was extremely restful to drive whatever type of going was involved. There was just one fault of which I was beginning to be aware. This was the inadequacy of the brakes for the performance and weight of the car, for the Bristol is not a light motor car and it is fast. There was never a suspicion of not being able to stop at the point aimed at, fade being non-existent, but there was a feeling that having judged the braking point from 90 m.p.h. down to a walking pace, there was nothing in reserve, Therefore when down to 30 or 25 m.p.h. it would not be possible to lock the wheels and slide the car broadside, should an emergency arise. While the pedal pressure was not as heavy as on the 401 it was still quite high for a driver below average stature.

Fontainebleau was reached by 5 p.m. Whilst the passengers admired the Palace a change of drivers was made. The writer had done over 340 miles and felt no more tired than if he had done 30

miles, in fact the only reason for changing was that the co-driver was going to drive in the dark and wanted a few miles to get accustomed to conditions before the light faded. We left Fontainebleau along wide straight roads that run through the great forest. We did two more 100-m.p.h. checks on the speedometer and found it to be a true 97.5 m.p.h. In spite of by-passing Paris on second-class roads, 46 and 48 miles were being covered in the hour for the terrain was now very flat once more, and dull in the extreme after what we had seen in our day's motoring. Amiens was reached in comfortable time for dinner, 460 miles having been covered between the hours of 8 a.m. and 8 p.m. This included the mountains of central France, and the run had not been a " suicidal dice " but a high-speed motoring run. There had never been the slightest chancy moment or risk, in fact it had been touring in the Grand Manner.

Wednesday morning saw rain with us again, but it cleared by the time the airport at Le Touquet was reached, with plenty of time to spare before the Bristol Freighter took off. We were feeling very satisfied with our motoring trip until we met our fellow aeroplane passenger, an Australian, who had just ridden from Bagdad on a motor-cycle and sidecar. The trouble about travelling is that you can never finish and there is always someone who has been farther !

The hour we lost on our arrival in France was now regained, when we landed on English soil. This enabled us to lunch near Charing, on the A20, and report at the office in time for afternoon tea. We had covered 1,851 miles and used 103 gallons of petrol, which is as honest an 18 m.p.g. as one could wish for; the amount of oil used was one pint going into Spain and a further pint on our arrival home.

I have always felt that the word " motoring " was not really adequate for this present age, for when Mr. Citizen in his " Universal Eight " goes motoring when he drives down to the local, or takes his family to the sea in a long queue of " mimsers " creeping along the arterial road. Racing is a word one reserves for the like of Fangio and Ascari, so it is difficult to convey the right impression of the type of travel which cars in the 403, Aston Martin, Continental Bentley or Lancia GT category offer; it is not high-speed motoring, for that is the group covered by the Mille Miglia competitors, so I feel that if we spell " motoring " with a capital " M " it will convey the idea of the trip which the Barcelona Grand Prix afforded me. If you have had the opportunity to go " Motoring," I think you will see what I mean.—D. S. J.

The Lister-Bristol— Continued from page 101

passenger's seat, and some attention to the air intake, I feel that something like 140 m.p.h. would be available. Even in its present undeveloped form it reaches 130 m.p.h. with a couple of hundred revs. in hand, which is terrific motoring for a 2-litre. Messrs. George Lister & Sons, of Cambridge, have certainly produced a very fine little motor.

SPECIFICATION AND PERFORMANCE DATA

Car Tested: Lister-Bristol sports two-seater. Price, chassis only, less engine, gearbox, tyres and tubes, £465, plus tax.

Engine: Six cylinders in line, 66 mm. x 96 mm. (1,971 c.c.). Pushrod operated inclined valves in light alloy head. 142 b.h.p. at 5,750 r.p.m. 9 to 1 compression ratio. Three downdraught Solex carburetters. Delco Remy distributor, Lucas coil.

Transmission: Borg and Beck single dry plate clutch. Four-speed gearbox with short central lever. Ratios: 3.73, 4.8, 6.7, and 10.7 to 1. (Alternative final drive ratios of 4.1 and 4.56 also available.) Salisbury hypoid differential unit, driving rear hubs through Hardy Spicer universally jointed half shafts.

Chassis: Three-inch T.45 seamless drawn steel tubing with fabricated uprights. Independent front suspension by equal length wishbones with long threaded king pins. Forward mounted rack and pinion steering. De Dion tube rear axle, located by sliding block and parallel radius rods. Helical springs all-round, embracing Woodhead-Monroe telescopic dampers. Dunlop racing wire wheels with knock-on caps, fitted 5.50 in. x 16 in. racing tyres. Girling hydraulic brakes with 11 in. x 1¼ in. Al-Fin drums, 2LS in front, inboard mounted at rear.

Equipment: 12-volt lighting and starting. Speedometer, rev. counter, oil pressure gauge, oil and water temperature gauges.

Dimensions: Wheelbase, 7 ft. 6 ins.; track, front 4 ft. 2¼ ins., rear 4 ft. 2 ins. Weight of complete car without fuel or oil, 12 cwt.

Performance: Maximum speed, 129 m.p.h. Speeds in gears: 3rd 94 m.p.h., 2nd 66 m.p.h., 1st 41 m.p.h. Standing quarter mile, 16.2 secs. Acceleration: 0-50 m.p.h. 6 secs., 0-60 m.p.h. 7.6 secs., 0-70 m.p.h. 10.4 secs., 0-80 m.p.h. 13.8 secs., 0-90 m.p.h. 17.4 secs., 0-100 m.p.h. 21.8 secs., 0-110 m.p.h. 26.6 secs.

Fuel Consumption: 22 m.p.g. (approx.).

The 1955 Lister Spor

EXCITING for these Cambridge schoolboys (above) is the first appearance of a newer, sleeker, Lister-Bristol with an advanced aerodynamic body. In these photographs its low build is well seen, and the tail fins and horizontal fences above the front wheel arches are interesting features to note.

L AST season the Lister sports-racing machin came into prominence by virtue of man successes on British circuits in the hands Archie Scott-Brown. A 2-litre, Bristol-powere machine was developed from the earlier Liste M.G. prototype, and it is this car which h provided the basis for the new series-productio Listers.

Thom Lucas, an aerodynamacist from th Bristol area, was called in to design a con pletely new body. After careful wind-tunn tests, the new shape emerged as a very work man-like open two-seater, having the re stabilizing fins as developed on pre-war Au Union and Mercedes-Benz record attem machines, and brought to a finer stage of pe fection by Porsche and the Bristol Aeropla Co., Ltd., in post-war years, for their spor racing cars.

The Lister differs from any other British-bui aerodynamic design in that it employs hor zontal fences at the top of each front whe arch; there is a complete absence of vertic fences at th front. The stabilizing fins at th rear are unique in that they have very marke converging angles. The wind-tunnel tes proved conclusively that this type of fin pro motes a much smoother air flow at high spee than certain other contemporary designs, well as having a very definite effect on stabilit

The very ticklish problem of extracting th air from under the bonnet has been solved b Thom Lucas. He has evolved some very cleve ducting, which permits a practically 100 pe cent. non-restricted entry and egress of th cooling air stream. Driver comfort has bee

PHOTOGRAPHY

CONSTRUCTION: George Tyrrell is seen (above) assembling the front suspension of the new car. A forward steering layout is used.

CONCEPTION: Brian Lawrence (left) at work in the Lister drawing office on a brake pedal assembly design.

MODIFICATION: Don Moore (below) is responsible for power unit development and is seen here giving attention to a Bristol cylinder head.

Racing Car

★

New Aerodynamic Body and Revised Suspension for Successful Bristol-engined 2-litre Machine

★

carefully considered, fresh air being directed into the cockpit via a separate duct. One of the 1954 cars is at present being modified to the latest standards.

In view of the admirable performance of the Lister-Bristol last season, it was thought unnecessary to make any major alterations to the rear end. However, detail modifications resulted in considerable weight saving and still further improvement in the already excellent road holding. A glance at the accompanying illustrations will show that the rear springs are now mounted at an angle, instead of vertically, and that a welded tubular structure replaces the more massive assembly used originally.

Braking has been much improved and the 1955 cars have 12 ins. x 2¼ ins. drums, as opposed to the 11 ins. x 1¾ ins. units of last season. The drums are manufactured by Jack Turner, with axial-type cooling fins; they are constructed of "Elektron". Brian Lister, Ltd., are also experimenting with disc units, but, so far, have found the drum brakes to be more than capable of stopping the machine from speeds well in excess of 130 m.p.h.

All Bristol engines fitted in Lister chassis receive the personal attention of Don Moore, who is responsible for tuning and development of power units for the concern.

There is little doubt that the new Lister-Bristol will be a strong challenger for sports-car honours both at home and abroad. It is designed not only for circuit racing, but to take part in the long-distance events of 1,000 kilometres and over, which qualify for the World Sports Car Championship.   G.

GEORGE PHILLIPS

MACHINE SHOP scene (above) of George Palmer pictured boring the front suspension boxes that carry the double wishbones.

★

ARC - WELDING the tubular chassis members (right) is Bob Gawthrop.

REAR HUBS are being turned (left) by John Heward.

★

CHASSIS design has not been greatly altered this year, but tubular uprights (below) replace the box structures used previously. The helical springs are now canted inwards.

★

REAR VIEW (left) of the Lister emphasizes the wind-cheating body design. The tail fins are set to converge rearwards, aiding directional stability, and extensive wind-tunnel tests were made before the design was made final.

119

THINK OF A NUMBER!

THERE IS A SUSPICION OF WITCHCRAFT ABOUT 405

By MICHAEL BROWN

"THIS time," I say to myself sternly, "you must be your age." And then along comes another Bristol, the colour of old burgundy (like the last, which was a 404), and I have lost my heart again. For the next thousand miles I think only of a number—405—and the tenth commandment must remain in abeyance until that streamlined and finned tail has disappeared along the Bath Road for Bristol.

You can approach this car in the cold light of reason, which reveals six cylinders, 1,971 c.c. of capacity, and a long stroke of 96 mm. The bore is 66 mm and the overhead valves in the hemispherical combustion chambers are operated from a single side camshaft through vertical and diagonal push-rods. The compression ratio is 8.5 to 1 and there are three carburettors ready to respond to the accelerator. They do. This is a unit which is positively angelic in its response to the driver. It will make the fairly heavy car (2,712 lb) trickle through a city on a silent third gear; it will thrum up through the gears to 70 m.p.h. and then waft the car almost noiselessly along the open road in overdrive, or it will take over the job of accelerating up to a hundred with a throaty hammer that sets the fingertips tingling excitedly. The Bristol 405 is the litmus paper that decides whether a driver has a soul or not. If he dismisses the car as a high-efficiency 2-litre with a good aerodynamic shape he is absolutely right, but that is all. The 405 is a car to gloat over, whereupon the litmus shows a positive response.

Escape of a Commuter

I used this car for two or three days over the normal commuting route. Then, on a starlit Friday night we headed west for Wales, and on a sunny Saturday it was driven hard round the Principality and back to Hereford, to detour gently back to London on Sunday via Malvern. By that time it was a wrench to hand it back.

The Bristol provides motoring of a type that is inseparable from the traditional heavy-membered chassis. Once the separate chassis goes such motoring disappears, and only two or three production cars remain to exploit its virtues. The Bristol is one of the finest exponents of them. It sits down solidly on the road, feels entirely in one piece, and allows its wheels to respond to the ups and downs instead of its passengers. If the suspension (transverse leaf in front, torsion bars behind) cannot cope entirely, the body makes a brief and grudging up and down movement, quickly damped out, that upsets no one, not even the passenger asleep at 90 m.p.h. The ratio of sprung to unsprung weight is high, in other words, Al-Fin brake drums and light alloy wheels doing their share in keeping it so. Once the car is steered off the straight line and centrifugal force begins to thrust a shoulder against one side or the other, further appreciations grow. The weight is concentrated as low down as possible (the almost underslung and very roomy luggage locker is a brilliant example of thought in this context) and its disposition is excellent. The spare wheel is in the wing just aft of the left-hand front wheel, and the battery balances it over the other side. Polar moment of inertia

has been carefully considered and the reluctance of the car to slide is assisted by a longish wheelbase—9ft 6in—and the fitting as standard of Michelin X tyres. The 405 is leechlike on corners; presumably it slides at some combination of velocity and steering radius, but it is a point of departure that I have no wish to reach.

One starts to throw this car into corners after a very few miles of driving. The high-geared steering (transverse rack and pinion) responds to the single quick turn of the two-spoked wheel, and the 405 goes round, as uncompromisingly upright as a Calvinist pastor, and with the cunningly shaped luxury of the seats holding the occupants against a radial acceleration that feels like g plus. ·

I cannot fault this steering. Castor action, road response (through the X tyres, remember) directional accuracy—all are just right; for me, at any rate. You can put on a pair of sun-glasses at leisure on the straight at eighty, though anyone outside the Bristol's body, which seems a light alloy haven of safety at such speeds, would probably be horrified to observe your doing so. The only feature that I would criticize that is even remotely connected with the steering is the stiffness of the central boss horn switch, which makes the informative "pip" of the horn difficult; the triviality of such a criticism serves to emphasize the general excellence.

Two litres are not many, in contemporary motoring terms, with which to provide the performance of which the Bristol is capable, and the work on the engine has obviously been crafty and thorough. When it is turning over at 5,000 r.p.m. the output exceeds 100 b.h.p. and the driver is given every means by which to make best use of the power. There is a freewheel on first gear, with the result that first is usable, and should be used, with the utmost freedom for low-speed acceleration. The short, rigid gear lever, remotely controlling the box and falling exactly to the left hand, has a precise and satisfying movement through the gears until it comes back—usually at around 60 m.p.h.—to the penultimate ratio, which is top. After that there is the overdrive, controlled by a miniature facia lever on the right of the main instrument panel.

The operation of this is delightful. Once the car is

"Everything is there, to hand, working silently and efficiently"

THINK OF A NUMBER!

" Fine stone-grey leather, piped with black "

in top the lever can be moved upwards and the over-drive comes in automatically; the movement is feather-light to the finger. The rev counter needle swings back about 500 r.p.m. and the crankshaft then loafs around to a just-audible high-pitched croon from abaft the gear box, where the overdrive is located. If you wish to return to top gear, then the facia lever is flicked back and a slight increase of throttle will smooth the transition. But if you want an indirect gear then you merely change down and the overdrive automatically cuts out, which I find a good thing, being merely embarrassed by the avail-ability of overdrive indirects. The Bristol satisfies in a way that few things in life do.

If you are going to send an aerodynamic shape along a road at 90 to 100 m.p.h., then you will need good brakes to stop it, for the wind resistance is low and therefore unhelpful in deceleration. On the 405 there are 168 sq in of brake lining getting a grip on the Al-Fin drum interiors, a two-leading grip in front, and a leading and trailing one at the rear. The resultant friction heat is dissipated with the aid of the brake drum finning and holes in the light alloy wheel discs, and not once did this Lockheed system give any cause for disquiet. Even the hand brake inspires confidence, with a hefty central lever topped by a black plastic handle and thumb-operated ratchet. It holds—tight—no matter what the slope. Pedal pressure for the brakes is medium until the dog runs

out when the speedometer needle is over-centre, and then you must tread good and hard for the really drastic stop.

Cheltenham, Gloucester, Ross, Hereford, Kington and Cross Gates—average main road, finishing up and around the Radnor Hills; the spring sun streamed down, the spring colours—green, primrose yellow and wild hyacinth blue—streamed by. It was noon when we started up A483, which jinks and winds alongside the burbling and, on that Saturday, sunlit Ithon. The 405 clung resolutely to the route, darting like a trout up the contour of the stream. I would have liked to have seen it from an aircraft, a ruby arrow on that yellow ribbon of road through a green countryside. To climb above the car is to confirm how absolutely right-looking the shape is from every angle.

Overlooked

After a picnic lunch in a sunny and wind-sheltered ravine (from which an eye could be cocked to the shapely visage of the Bristol, peering over the lip) we went farther north until, at four o'clock, Snowdon was high on the left, Llyn Gwynant shimmered behind us and the Pen-y-Gwryd hotel lay in front on the Capel Curig road, with its aura of splendid tragedy in high places—Mallory and Irvine, gone these thirty years on the last terrible thousand feet of Everest. The road that runs through Capel Curig to A5 is wavy, and the speed had to stay below 60 m.p.h., but once A5 had roared in from Holy-head only its curves and the Saturday traffic held the car back. The 130 miles that lay between us and a bottle of Volnay at the friendly Green Dragon at Hereford were covered at over 46 m.p.h. and one grew almost con-temptuous of a mere eighty.

All this in a silence and comfort that add up to luxury, a luxury that breeds confidence and contentment, one of my passengers assures me. " Ninety is like 60 in other cars." How well one knows the phenomenon! The fine stone-grey leather, piped with black, the excellent visi-bility all round, the twin-speakered radio—all of them pander to the sybaritic in man. The controls flatter his power complex. Everything is there, to hand, working silently and efficiently. At night the seven dials of the main instrument cluster glow softly at the behest of the rheostat. The black leather surround leaves the screen reflection-free and so nothing distracts from the clean swathe of the head light beams; the foot dip interposes a sharp cut-off and then the speed must come down from the highest ranges, but otherwise this car is as happy at night as by day. Indeed, the 405 seems positively cal-culated to make its occupants happy. The car is a joy in the way that beautiful things always are, and that is why its high price is acceptable. By building into it such artistry, the Bristol company transform their product

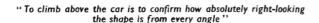

" To climb above the car is to confirm how absolutely right-looking the shape is from every angle "

THINK OF A NUMBER !

" Snowdon was high on the left "

from the mundane to the creative; the 405 is at one with Tompion clocks, Van Goghs and Wren churches; a work of art, a masterpiece. You cannot put a price on the intangible in these things, but you must acknowledge its enormous value if you have any æsthetic perception whatsoever. If not, then the litmus paper hasn't responded and you might as well buy a family ten.

In any case, once the owner has faced up to first cost, the Bristol should prove economical in operation. I would imagine that with fast but considerate driving in open country it is fairly easy to get 25 m.p.g., and the quality in the materials and workmanship should make everything long-lasting. The car will not "date" (it is, in any case, about ten years ahead of most in its lines) and it is in that category of possessions that retain their beauty even when they are antique. However, when a car shape is functional aerodynamically, it is difficult to

see how it can be supplanted unless there is a move back to aerodynamic inefficiency for the sake of other considerations—hardly a likely contingency.

How functionally aerodynamic is the Bristol? The driver can only guess, but my guess—assuming that I was unaware of the work that went into the body shape—would be that it is better than any other British saloon at the moment. The uncanny way in which a falling leaf will follow the contour of the front, about an inch from the cellulose, until is disappears over the roof peak, is one proof; the undeviating line in high winds is another. The absence of wind noises is a third and the delightful freedom of the car's gait a fourth.

Perhaps the most impressive aspect of the Bristol 405 is its all-round efficiency. The car provides a judiciously balanced mixture of all the motoring virtues, achieved with only two litres of engine size. Sometimes you can hear a motorist criticize the engine size and demand something bigger. In the same way people will say that the Morris Minor would be so much better if it had a 1½-litre engine. The argument, to me, is nonsensical. A designer sets out to achieve a certain object; he decides that he can do so efficiently with an engine of a certain size and proceeds to do it. He can, admittedly, achieve *another* object—higher speed, greater acceleration and suchlike—by using a larger engine, but there is no virtue in installing a larger engine unless the sights are deliberately so raised. The 405 achieves its object with a unique completeness, as far as I am concerned, by giving me a motoring experience that moves the car to the top of the list of those that I most covet.

" Finishing up and around the Radnor Hills "

The A-B competition model has abbreviated windshield and stark interior to minimize weight.

Arnolt's Sports Car

The 6-cyl. engine with relay rocker mechanism, inclined valves, and vertical intake ports.

THERE IS a man in Warsaw, Indiana, who got his start in business by marketing the "Mighty Mite" marine engine. No mite himself, S. H. Arnolt (weight: about 200 lbs) went on to bigger and better things such as importing cars. That, in turn, led to the importation of *unusual* cars—cars like the Alfa-Bertone B.A.T.-5, for example. And so it happened that "Wacky" Arnolt got his nick-name, as well as experience in dealing with the strange psychology of of doing business with Italian auto makers.

The Arnolt-Bristol-Bertone sports car was almost inevitable. Mr. Arnolt knew the fame of Bristol, Frazer Nash and its German predecessor, the BMW. He also wisely understood that many frustrated Americans had given up all thought or hope of owning a beautifully styled Italian car. Why not combine the sterling qualities (no pun!) of the potent two-litre Bristol with the impeccable flair of Italian styling? Of course this meant months of negotiating, even though he happens to be vice-president of Carrozerria Bertone, but eventually the details were arranged. Bristol was to ship the chassis to Turin, Bertone agreed to a realistic price, then the completed cars were to be shipped to America.

Two models were offered, the stark competition model at $4750 and the deluxe version for an extra thousand. All of the initial order have been sold, and during the past season the name of Arnolt-Bristol has frequently appeared well up in class "E" competition results.

Horsepower costs just so much per dollar in American iron. But in sports cars the cost per horsepower increases as the engine size classification gets smaller. In class E you get 90 bhp for $2500, 130 bhp for $4750, or 175 bhp for $12,000. The Arnolt-Bristol fits into the middle category of Class E sports cars, but is by no means middling in performance. ●

Tufted strings attached to body demonstrate airflow direction.

Such aerodynamic testing results in "low coefficient of friction."

BRISTOL

THE BRISTOL Aeroplane Company created its Car Division shortly after the end of World War II in anticipation of reduced peacetime demand for its jet and piston-type engines for aircraft.

Bristol cars were originally patterned after BMW products, but the new Bristol 405 drophead coupe is distinctively Italian in flavor. A four-door sedan is also produced.

The 405 is powered by a two-liter engine, patterned after the pre-World War II BMW. It is a six-cylinder, in-line type, equipped with three downdraft carburetors. With a displacement of 120.23 cubic inches, it develops 105 horsepower at 5000 rpm. Compression ratio is 8.5 to 1. Overdrive fifth gear permits fast cruising at a modest engine rpm and, with the clean aerodynamic lines of the body and consequent absence of wind roar, makes for quiet motoring throughout the entire speed range. Maximum speed, stock, is about 80 miles per hour.

Fuel consumption is good, about 24 miles to the gallon at normal cruising speed.

The Bristol 405 pressed-rail chassis is sound-proofed inside the frame. Independent front suspension is by leaf springing, while the rear suspension is achieved on a rigid axle by torsion bars. The car is built on a 114-inch wheelbase with an overall length of 189 inches; weight is 2720 pounds dry. Instruments are attractively grouped in a cowled panel to eliminate reflection. Interior of the four-passenger car is handsomely finished in quality leather and trim; a large luggage compartment with a 17.7-cubic-foot capacity provides a distinct advantage over some of the smaller European sports cars. Price is $5880 at the factory.

In the 405, the Bristol factory is close to its ultimate goal of producing an all-purpose vehicle for the enthusiast who wants a quality, roadable car capable of excellent top speeds.

BRISTOL 405

ARNOLT-BRISTOL

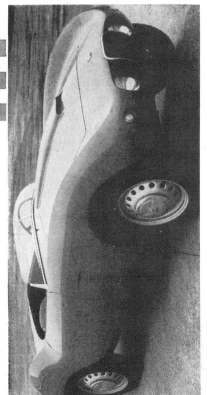

ARNOLT-BRISTOL

THE BRISTOL Aeroplane Company of England and Bertone of Turin, Italy, collaborated with S. H. Arnolt to produce the Arnolt-Bristol two-seater sports car. The car is built primarily for U.S. import and sells for about $4500.

Arnolt-Bristol successes in sports car racing include a near-sweep in the two-liter class in the 1955 Sebring Grand Prix—first, second, fourth, and fifth, plus the Overall Team prize. At the Cumberland National SCCA, it was first in the two liter class and second in the overall class of the Cumberland Businessmen's Trophy.

The car is available in two models, a deluxe and competition car. Walt Woron, editor of *Motor Trend* magazine, had an opportunity to get some first-hand driving impressions of a stripped-down Arnolt-Bristol recently. He said, "What you can do with the Arnolt-Bristol on a road course is little short of phenomenal. It was my pleasure to throw it into deliberate slides on asphalt, on dirt, and on loose gravel. Never once did I become leery of the car's handling characteristics. The more I drove it and the harder I pushed it through the turns, the more confidence I got until I fairly exuded it.

"Choppy surfaces don't seem to affect the Arnolt-Bristol any more than flat ones. Body lean on curves is practically negligible; passengers have no complaint on this score, for the contoured bucket seats hold onto you like some giant hand.

"What makes it handle so good? It's a well-thought-out design, incorporating some of the best features of suspension and chassis engineering. Front wheels are independently sprung, using wishbones at the top and transverse springs at the bottom. Torsion bars are used at the rear, running fore and aft; with a triangular bracket at the top of the banjo housing, these locate the rear axle. Double-acting telescopic shocks are at all four wheels. Steering is rack and pinion with only three turns lock-to-lock, making for quick and accurate steering. The rigid frame is made of box sections of 6½-inch depth with three crossmembers for good measure.

"Driving position is good with the steering wheel set just a trifle high. Both the steering wheel and seat are adjustable for your height. The steering column telescopes.

"The six-cylinder Bristol is only a two-liter engine; that's only 120 cubic inches. Out of that comes 130 horsepower, being pulled out by three Solex carbs, overhead valves, a compression ratio of 9 to 1, and revving it up to 5500 rpm. That's a lot to ask of an engine half the size of a Chevy six (which develops 136 hp). This 130-hp engine pulls around the Arnolt-Bristol weighing 2000 pounds, which gives it a power/weight ratio of around 1 to 15.

"On the driving test, these times were posted: 0 to 60 mph, 9.19 seconds; standing start ¼-mile, 17.5 seconds with 85 mph at the top end. Top speed is 120 mph.

DON MACDONALD

ARNOLT-BRISTOL

STRICTLY FOR COMPETITION was the Arnolt-Bristol roadster Don Mac-Donald and I had for a week during my recent Detroit stay. Prepared and driven by S. H. ("Wacky") Arnolt at the last Sebring event, this combination of Bristol of England (engine and chassis), Bertone of Italy (body), and Arnolt of Indiana (designer and marketer) was tuned for top-end running. At almost anything under its top speed of around 120 mph, it spit and snorted, complaining that it was leaned too thin at the bottom end, but bragging it would run like a scared jack-rabbit at the top end. I therefore arranged with Wacky to put another car at my disposal after my return to the West Coast.

This was subsequently done by Henry Hinkle, West Coast Sales Manager for Rootes Motors (Arnolt West Coast distributors), enabling me to give you a more complete story on the roadster. Like the other car, it was stripped (no top, no bumpers, a cutdown windshield, no wipers —which you *can* get as accessories, tho). It's one of 3 models (selling for $3995); there's a deluxe model fitted with top, rugs, plusher seats, bumpers, etc. (going for $4995), and a coupe (at $5995).

What you can do with the Arnolt-Bristol on a road course is little short of phenomenal. It was my pleasure to throw it into deliberate slides on asphalt,

on dirt, and on loose gravel. Never once did I become leery of the car's handling characteristics. The more I drove it and the harder I pushed thru the turns, the more confidence I got, until I fairly exuded it.

On our road course that we use to test roadability, it was a joy to start to spin, correct the wheel, all the time keeping my foot on the throttle, and have it follow the groove around the turn. The correction required is very slight even in a power slide; a flick of the wheel and I was once more pointed in the direction I wanted to go. When it broke loose, the rear end would go 1st. I would correct the wheel to keep it from swapping ends, and it would move into a 4-wheel drift, which I could then easily control. I forced it into a turn, cramped the wheel hard over and hit the brakes to really make it break loose. Then off the brake, full on the throttle, and I was back into a controlled drift.

Choppy surfaces don't seem to affect it any more than flat ones. On gravel I could whip the wheel, start to spin sideways, push the front wheels into the slide and the slide would peter out. And all

the while, body lean is practically negligible; passengers have no complaint on this score, for the contoured bucket seats hold onto you like some giant hand.

On a straight road, cruising at high speeds, I had the same assurance I had on winding curves. I always felt like I had complete mastery of the car, and that it would obey my every whim. It has an almost uncanny sense of wanting to go *exactly* where you point it. It did this even when I whipped the wheel from side to side; it seemed to think I wanted to turn, therefore *it* turned from its straight course, returning only when I commanded. Personally, I would like a little more incline to the kingpin, which should give it a better straightline corrective action.

What makes it handle so good? It's a well-thought-out design, incorporating some of the best features of suspension and chassis engineering. Front wheels are independently sprung, using wishbones at the top and a transverse spring at the bottom. Torsion bars are used at the rear, running fore and aft; with a triangular bracket at the top of the banjo housing, these locate the rear axle. Double-acting telescope shocks are at all 4 wheels.

Beauty queen of all Arnolt-Bristols is fastback, jewel-like Bertone coupe ($5995)

126

Tiny but mighty is 2-liter Bristol engine; its 3 Solex carbs, 9 to 1 compression, 6 cylinders put out 130 horsepower

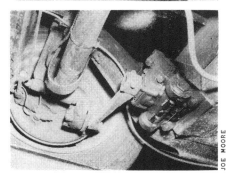

Steering is rack and pinion, with only 3 turns lock to lock, making for quick and accurate steering. The rigid frame is made of box sections of 6½-inch depth, with 3 crossmembers for good measure.

Driving position is good, with the steering wheel set just a trifle high. Both the steering wheel and seat are adjustable to your height; the column telescopes; the seat can be unbolted and placed in the most convenient location for you (it slides on the deluxe). There's lots of legroom, with considerable space at left of the clutch. You can rest your throttle leg against the transmission housing during long drives.

Unlike that of some short-wheelbase cars, the ride of the Arnolt-Bristol is not choppy. The ride is definitely firm, but in a competition sports car, you wouldn't want to have it any other way. Nor would I complain about such a ride in the deluxe model, or even a stock car with a wheelbase longer than this 96 inches.

Before I tell you how the Arnolt-Bristol goes I'd like to preface my remarks with a thought you should bear in mind: the 6-cylinder Bristol is only a 2-liter engine. That's only 120 cubic inches. Out of that comes 130 horsepower, being pulled out by virtue of 3 Solex carbs, overhead valves, a compression ratio of 9 to 1, and revving it up to 5500 rpm. That's a lot to ask of an engine half the size of a Chevy 6 (which develops

136 hp). This 130-hp engine pulls around a car weighing 2000 pounds, which gives it a power/weight ratio of around 1 to 15. (The hottest American stock sedans are now down around 1 to 16 and 17.)

Except for the fact that a replacement of the Bristol engine with one like the Chevy V8 or Ford V8 would take the Arnolt-Bristol out of the 2-liter racing class, it would be interesting to see what such a combination would bring. Certainly one advantage would be less high-revving to get its peak output, while another could well be astounding performance. Maximum torque of the Bristol engine comes at 5000 rpm (considerably

higher than comparable 2-liter engines also employing 4-speed gearboxes). Getting this torque down to an rpm of around 2500 would be a big help in getting the car off the mark and accelerating out of a turn. As it is now, there's a very definite time lag from 0 to 3000 rpm before you feel a surge of power that cuts in like a blower. Taking off from a standstill I probably lost a good second in the 0 to 60 mph and ¼-mile times. Even so, they're hardly anything of which to be ashamed.

With 2 of us sitting in the foam-cushion bucket seats, we posted these times:

0-60 mph (64 mph speedo reading; 1st & 2nd gears only)	9.9 secs.
Standing ¼-mile (turning 85 mph at end)	17.5 secs.
30-50 mph (using 2nd gear only, up to 5000 rpm)	4.1 secs.
50-80 mph (using 3rd gear only, up to 5200 rpm)	8.9 secs.

I tried several different ways to keep from getting the hesitation in 1st gear, but got it nevertheless. The best times were achieved with a slow-rolling start, revving up to 5500 rpm in 1st and 2nd, snapshifting in between gears, and taking it up to 5200 rpm in 3rd, where I crossed the ¼-mile mark and hit 85 mph simultaneously. The transmission has an easy shift pattern and good ratios: 1st is 11.4, 2nd is 7.12, 3rd is 5.04, and 4th is 3.9. The 8-pound clutch seems adequate, altho more torque at the low rpms would be a big assist.

You can't complain too much, tho, when you have a car that's able to nab 1st and 2nd in its class on a tricky course like Watkins Glen, and turn in other impressive performances. It's a real handling fool.

Deluxe roadster abounds in recessed accessories, but competition model is austere and intended only for connoisseurs of high-level, thoroly enjoyable driving

Space in rear of either roadster is nearly nil. This is not a car for shopping

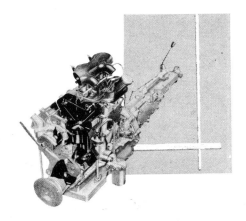

SOMETIME back in 1945, while the giants of Britain's automotive industry struggled to assemble a handful of their pre-war models for the 1946 market, the Bristol Aeroplane Company, Ltd., made a decision to offer their interpretation of a machine for the connoisseur. Considering that these formative years faced a market clamoring for cheap to buy and even cheaper to maintain transportation, survival of the mark appeared to be an extremely doubtful proposition. The Bristol, from inception, was a specialized machine which pretended no concessions to price, engineering perfection or design and solely based on rather expensive and idealistic principles.

Nevertheless, a Car Division was duly formed under the instigation of one George White, a speed conscious soul best known as Britain's outstanding holder of speedboat records during pre-war years. Now a director of the Bristol firm, White pioneered the Car Division project and selected Major G. H. Abell for charge of the operation. Major Abell, a former director at Invicta and Connaught car manufacturers, managed to conjure up a design team together with small groups of men and factory space "borrowed" from other divisions of the parent company.

Having decided to adapt an existing engine to suit their needs and specifications, these men selected the basic 6-cylinder Type-328 BMW of 1971 cc. as a foundation. Even then this power unit was rather advanced in featuring inclined overhead valves operated by a unique pushrod arrangement and incorporating hemispherical combustion chambers. In standard form it developed 80 hp.; after preliminary modifications by the Bristol engineers 85.4 hp. as the first engine ran on the testing bench in May of 1946. Principal changes were the use of three S. U. carburetors and an experimental cam shaft. However, if the engine proved to be peppier than expected, it also turned out to be rougher. A touring series cam was promptly evolved and 75 hp. became standard power while the experimental cam was offered as an option to buyers willing to sacrifice smoothness for the additional nudge of 10 horses.

Introduced at the 1947 Geneva Show, the Type-400 scored immediate favor and was soon in limited production. Further attention was soon drawn to the newcomer when, a little over a year following the show, a privately-owned 400 emerged class victor in the 14th Polish National Rally

Bristol: *businessman's*

At Le Mans, 1954, the Bristol 450 team arrives 1, 2, 3 in class and in numerical order.

128

in August of 1948. The drivers apologized for not winning the event outright, explaining that only because they had never driven the course before and competed with drivers familiar with the country were they prevented from making better use of their machine. Almost simultaneously a Belgian driver took top honors in the race for touring cars at the Course de Cote de la Sarte. A few months later, the Polish Rally class winners copped third in general classification and finished first among British entries in the 1949 Monte Carlo Rally. Several days later this same car, having been pushed at 5500 rpm. in second gear for over an hour during one stretch of the Monte Carlo route, headed for exhibition in England. Stopping at the famous Montlhery track near Paris on the way, the Bristol averaged over 92 mph. for 100 kilometers. The course was frozen at the start and still wet at the finish of this run and the Monte Carlo engine seals were still intact, the total mileage of the car being more than 45,000.

Even in those earliest years, the Bristol set out to prove by doing rather than by claiming. Second in class for the Targa Florio of 1949, a merciless grind surpassed only by the Mille Miglia, a car breaker in which Bristol finished third in touring category only four minutes behind the winner. First in class at Como Lario; second on the pen Hill Climb; fifth and sixth in the 1949 Alpine Rally; first in touring class of the Tuscany Cup; third in class for the Stella Alpina and many, many lesser honors. And, as if this were not proof enough of Bristol's adaptability, a Canadian owner chose to set a new record for the transcontinental crossing at a time when Canada had little to offer in the way of a paved route. Certainly an imposing record for the two-year-old upstart and, as we shall see, merely a token of things to come.

What magic had the men of Filton applied to their offspring to provide it with these unorthodox capabilities? By and large, the answer is simply their relentless and enthusiastic devotion to detail. This attitude was directed primarily towards the engine and began with improvement of the optional equipment offered in alternative to the standard 75 hp. unit. This modified engine, designated the 85/A, differed from standard mainly in the sports cam with an 80-degree overlap and delivered 10.4 hp. extra at 4,750 rpm. Perhaps a major figure in the shaping of Bristol's course at this stage was Colonel D. A. Aldington of Frazer-Nash who, having co-driven Bristol entries in

express

Larry Kulok and his Le Mans replica Frazer-Nash after winning 3 out of 3 starts.

At Rheims in 1954 Bristol finished second, third and fourth ahead of Maseratis and Gordinis again in sequence with only Ferrari ahead.

Anthony Crooks' Bristol-engined Frazer-Nash was the first attempt to adapt the power plant to track events and from the record the car and driver have established the merger has been most successful.

129

the Targa Florio, Mille Miglia and Alpine Rally, was more than a little in on developing an engine for his most successful machines. To suit Aldington requirements, the F.N.S. series engines received a compression hike to 8.5:1, whereas the standard and 85/A engines held to 7.5:1; three Solex carburetors replaced original S. U. equipment and 100 hp. spun the clutch at 5,500 rpm. Initially offered as a second alternative to really hairy tourists, the F.N.S series was adapted specifically for Frazer-Nash cars about March of 1949 when the alteration of inlet port diameters alone stepped power up to 126 at the same engine speed. That the right thing was done to the right place at the right time is indicated by the interesting fact that inlet port area was increased by 26.5% and the resultant horsepower gain amounted to exactly 26%! The F.N.S. series also received larger oil sumps for improved cooling and bolt-on crankshaft counterweights permitted finer balancing. Powered by this unit, Norman Culpan's Frazer-Nash went out that year to secure third place in both the index of performance and general class for the 1949 Le Mans. And, during 1950, a replica of the Culpan machine carried Larry Kulok through a particularly successful season of sports car racing in this country.

If further reference be required regarding the importance of Bristol's attention to detail, a few F.N.S. engines built to individual order received highly polished heads and the carburetor or butterfly valves were streamlined to a razor edge which added 4 hp. and the similar streamlining of correction jets produced another 1.5. Inserting circular deflectors in the air cleaners to straighten the flow of air into the carubretors and a 9.5:1 compression brought the overall dividend to 10 valuable horsepower! This persistent concern for the seldom dramatic, but most essential detail has now brought Bristol well past the threshold of a very promising future in the racing as well as the passenger car world. For the very attitude which doggedly pries after every elusive fractional horsepower has also created a highly regarded competition package for the hard to please amateur and professional alike. If we devote so many words to the engineering aspect of Bristol, it is to impress upon the reader the constant quest for the ultimate being carried on by the men behind this quietly fabulous automobile. Few other machines can claim to be nearly so versatile as those bearing the Bristol hallmark.

Seeking still further efficiency from the F.N.S. unit,

intensive experiments were carried out to deal with the "tuning" of the exhaust system by various combinations, lengths and diameters of piping. Also under observation was a new super-sports camshaft of still greater overlap and the combined modification resulted in 122 hp. at 5,500 rpm. at only 7.5:1 compression and on pump fuel. Raising the compression to 9.5:1 with racing fuel, power leaped to 145 hp. at 5,750 rpm. Catalogued the B.S.1, the design was promptly adopted by the Cooper concern for their Cooper-Bristol; the new E.R.A. and a single-seater Frazer-Nash model all doing battle under the 1951 Formula II rules of 2-liters unblown. The "production" B.S.1 later developed 132 hp. and was beefed up to enjoy the stress of grand prix workouts, acquired packed valve springs to control high rpm. bounce, a larger oil pump and lighter push-rods and rocker assemblies. In this form, Mike Hawthorn's Cooper-Bristol immediately snatched two firsts and a second place from a 4.5 Ferrari. Hawthorn eventually returned his engine to Filton for the 9.5:1 compression which, with other minor changes, returned a total of 149.8 hp. Several more recent applications of the Bristol power plant to specialist cars are noteworthy, the Kieft and Lister adaptations in particular. The Kieft-Bristol is almost monotonously consistent in finding a berth among the first few finishers of most contests entered and the Lister-Bristol success closely parallels that of the Bristol itself. Handled by W. A. Scott-Brown, the Lister-Bristol garnered a class win at its debut in the 1954 British Grand Prix of Silverstone, taking fifth in general classification ahead of ten larger engined cars and seven class contenders. Incidentally, second and third class honors were awarded a Cooper-Bristol and the Bristol-powered Warrior.

Meanwhile, Bristols continued to make good account of themselves in races and rallies throughout Europe. Due to his successes with Bristol cars, Count "Johnnie" Lurani was declared Italian Champion. Others took first, third and team prizes in the Production Touring Car Race at Silverstone; first place in both '52 and '53 International Tulip Rallies and first in Touring Class of the Rallye Soleil at Cannes. 1953 was also the year the Bristol factory began looking upon the Sarthe circuit at Le Mans as a testing ground and produced a weird factory team car with a straight from Mars appearance. Less than six

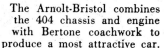

The Arnolt-Bristol combines the 404 chassis and engine with Bertone coachwork to produce a most attractive car.

months off the drawing boards, these entries are best described as technically advanced mechanically, aerodynamic to the point of utilizing immense stabilizing tail surfaces and compact enough to require their being tailored to fit the drivers. The Filton folk are still fairly stingy about releasing much information on the 140 mph. laboratories, but the stated wheelbase of 97½ inches justifies the guess that there are much modified 404 bits and pieces involved. First introduced at the 24-hour classic, these machines represented a full scale attempt to test many ideas heretofore prohibited in the production machines because of appearance, cost, convenience and many other factors. The previously mentioned exhaust system development, for example, evolved strange shapes and lengths of plumbing which hardly befitted the passenger models regardless of the theoretical advantages offered and here was another chance to test by trial. Super streamlining ideas culminated in the usual body lines highlighted by the ugly, if effective, twin tail fins. Most likely powered by a B. S. type engine of something over 150 hp., the two cars were popular fvorites for 2-liter honors until mysteriously igniting themselves on the 29th and 70th laps, respectively.

A quick double check and then off to Rheims for the 12-hour annual where they more than made a comeback. Here the 450 placed first in class and fifth overall behind four cars of substantially larger engine capacity. Then back to the drawing board once more. A year goes by and 1954 finds the Bristol team anxious to vindicate the previous Le Mans chagrin. Even further reduction in frontal area had been attained and the channel between the rear fins was altered to minimize turbulence. The three cars lapped with monotonous regularity and added little drama to the event until but 45 minues from the finish. Trying to avoid a smaller entry, one of the team cars took to the hills quite rapidly. The nose contours were considerably altered. However, the pit was reached and, after seven frantic hammer-flying minutes, it zipped out again to rejoin its team. Thoroughly shattering Gordini hopes, the three green Bristols finished 1-2-3 in their class and 7-8-9 in overall classification, established a new 2-liter distance and average speed record and were the only team to finish intact!

And, to rub the salt still deeper, the 450 proceeded to Rheims and acquired second, third and fourth places behind Ferrari while mastering Maserati and Gordini competition, yet still found time to establish another 2-liter

lap record for the course three weeks later.

Then, in March of this year, spectators at the Sebring 12-hour race watched a team of three Arnolt-Bristols glide into first, second and fourth positions in class. These hybrids, sired by the imagination of S. H. "Wacky" Arnolt, Italy's carozzeria Bertone and the blessings of Filton, came home ahead of much larger engined competition including a Kurtis-Buick, several XK140 Jaguars and Mercedes. That this unique mark has attracted enthusiastic attention is witnessed by the immediate appearance of several Arnolt-Bristols in domestic lineups at Thompson, Cumberland, and so on.

Could Bristol hold this pace and repeat the hat trick at Le Mans for 1955? By all means, say the records as the trio of 450 cars swept home 1-2-3 in their class and 7-8-9 overall for the second year. The only team to be placed, their leader's average of 95 mph. was but 12 mph. below that of the winning Hawthorn-Bueb Jaguar. Holding down fourth class position was Frazer-Nash which actually gave Bristol engines the first four places in the 2-liter contingent. These entries were basically identical in mechanical specification to the 1954 models. However, the ungainly double tail coupe bodies have been replaced by a much cleaner looking open version sporting a single fin directly behind the driver. All of the clutter marking the 1953 450 has been moulded into unusually smooth lines and it is possible that the additional visibility afforded explains why the leading Bristol covered nearly 100 miles greater distance during 24 hours than last year. Even the third place 450 returned a higher average speed than did the 1954 leader. The reliability and complete absence of excitement within the Filton team is fast becoming legendary and even the most enthusiastic account was limited to comparing the entry with "a Sunday afternoon parade."

Thus, in less than 10 years, the Bristol mark has developed from a wishful thought aimed towards pleasing the tourist-sportsman to a respected entry in all phases of competitive motoring. Although the interest in competition began mainly as a means of subjecting prototype models to the most rigorous of testing, it would now appear that the tail commences to wag the dog as Bristol propels more and more victors over the finish line. Whatever the outcome of this delightful Frankenstein, Bristol and the world of motorsports stand to gain immeasurably.

—☆—

The 1955 version of the 450 Bristol on its way to repeating the 1954 sweep in class.

Exposed wheels, sharp-creased fenders give the car a taut, rugged look.

arnolt-bristol coupe

DOES THE OPEN two-seater you purchased so blithely last spring look a bit "old hat" this fall? Does your wife complain that, with the more formal winter season approaching, she no longer will tolerate having her hair tossed about like a mixed green salad? If these are among your motoring problems, you will be interested in the first of the 1956 foreign sports cars to reach these shores—the new Arnolt-Bristol two-litre two-seater sports coupe!

American-designed, British-powered, and Italian-styled, this little car comes from the combined talents of designer Arnolt of Chicago, the Car Division of the Bristol Airplane Company of England, and body-builder Bertone of Turin, Italy.

The engine: Most R & T readers are familiar with the various versions of this unique six-cylinder, cross-over pushrod engine in the pre-war BMW's and the post-war Bristols and Frazer-Nashes. The version in the coupe is the 3 Solex down-draft carburetor job which with 9:1 c. r., develops 130 bhp at 5500 rpm and 128 ft. lbs of torque at 5000 rpm. It is built with such details as centrifugally-cast austenitic alloy steel inserts for valve seats, chrome-nickel steel inlet valves and austenitic chrome-steel exhaust valves.

The chassis: Like the engine it is by Bristol and offers a 96-inch wheelbase, wishbone transverse springing in front and torsion bar springing in the rear; large hydraulic telescopic shocks; rack and pinion steering; a light but strong sheet-steel box frame with 6½-inch longitudinal members and 3 cross members; and on this model the new Borrani steel wheels with magnesium alloy rims appear.

The body: The unique creased fenders, completely exposing the wheels, and the high-clearance but definitely aerodynamic lines of the all-aluminum body combine to give the car an exceptionally sturdy, utilitarian look. In fact, the car might almost look ugly were it not so beautifully finished both inside and out.

The car weighs in at about 2,100 pounds, will do an estimated 125 mph and yet offers all the comforts of home; the going price is $6000.   JOHN F. FELLOWS   ●

Fog, beam and headlights are a development of experience gained from racing at Sebring.

Comfortable seats, good leg-and-foot room.

Rear trunk contains spare, little else, but luggage space behind seats is adequate.

LOOKING AT LAKELAND PASSES WITH A BRISTOL 405

A British 2 - Litre Saloon of Outstanding Luxury and Performance

TYPICAL LAKELAND SCENE.—The Bristol 405 photographed at the top of Wrynose Pass with the way ahead winding down beside the river to the commencement of the climb over Hard Knott Pass, into the hills veiled in mist.

WHEN I was a schoolboy, obliged to do all my motoring on paper, I used to be intrigued by those reports in the motor papers of 30/98 Vauxhalls, Silver Ghost Rolls-Royce and other fine cars tested in the Lake District. Usually such reports included pictures of these high-speed touring cars parked picturesquely on those hump-back stone bridges which abound in Cumberland and Westmorland, which seemed excitingly remote to a small boy reading his *Autocar* in London.

When, early this year, a Bristol 405 came along for appraisal I pondered on where to go in it. It then occurred to me that, although I am reasonably familiar with most parts of the British Isles, the Lake District were less well known to me, so why not drive there in the Bristol. We might even be able to photograph it on a hump-back stone bridge, for old times' sake !

So it came about that, moderately early one Tuesday morning, we set off up A 1, bound for Windermere. This so-called Great North Road proved as restricted and traffic-infested as ever, but we were cheered to discover that at all events other drivers of fast cars were out on it, for soon after leaving London we encountered four DB Aston Martins, a 300SL Mercedes-Benz and an Austin-Healey, while, higher up, we met two XK Jaguars and a TR2.

The Bristol 405 made light of the difficult going to such good effect that we were in Yorkshire in comfortably under three hours, the average speed, notwithstanding the usual slow start, thus being better than 50 m.p.h. On two occasions the speedometer needle stood steady on 110 m.p.h. and the habitual cruising speed was between 80 and 90 m.p.h. This 405 saloon possessed an overdrive, controlled by a little lever convenient to the driver's right hand, which had the effect of reducing engine speed by some 900 r.p.m., so that 80 m.p.h. can be held comfortably at a mere 3,100 r.p.m. in this 3.28-to-1 gear, instead of at 4,000 r.p.m. in the normal 4.22-to-1 top-gear ratio. This overdrive operates only from top gear and a change to a lower ratio automatically puts the overdrive out of action, so that when the next change-up to the highest ratio is made it is to normal top, thus obviating a big change in engine speed.

Mention of overdrive brings me at once to the excellence of the Bristol gearbox. Controlled by a rigid remote central lever, which is most conveniently positioned, if a trifle farther forward than one expects, the changes can be made instantaneously, and so quiet are the indirect ratios that it is easy to mistake third gear for the direct

drive. Moreover, a free-wheel operating in bottom gear entirely eliminates the gear drag frequently experienced when engaging the lowest cogs in the box, and when, later on this journey, I had occasion to snatch bottom on 1-in-3 gradients, this feature truly proved to be a blessing. The Bristol gear ratios consist of an emergency bottom gear, in which the car will start smoothly on freak gradients, and three considerably higher ratios, of which the driver employs the synchromesh second and third frequently in order to obtain continuous high-performance from the high-efficiency 2-litre six-cylinder engine. 5,000 r.p.m. comes up easily in third gear, representing a speed of 80 m.p.h., and at any speed under 40 m.p.h. a drop is made into second gear. With a gear-change, and gear ratios, of such merit, no regret is occasioned that the Bristol engineers continue to use a 1,971-c.c. power unit, for were an engine of three or more litres installed there might be less excuse to swap cogs, and to connoisseurs of motoring this would be a loss indeed ! Some engine noise intrudes, because the Bristol power unit is so frequently accelerating to beyond 4,000 r.p.m., but this is scarcely objectionable, is reduced considerably as overdrive is brought in, and in any case is a small penalty to pay for the excellent fuel economy, of which more will be written later in this report.

The general impression of the Bristol 405, as we forged along A 1, was that it is a tireless car in which to drive fast over long distances, the passengers being able to relax in great comfort and luxury, while the driver enjoys himself with the excellent controls and the sense of exceptional security provided by good roadholding, steering and brakes. It possesses, moreover, interesting items of detail. Thus the instruments are all grouped on a fully-hooded walnut panel directly before the driver, from which he can check at a glance that the oil temperature is at the normal 55 deg. C., the water temperature happy at 80 deg. C., and that the oil pressure reads between 40 and 75 lb./sq. in. according to engine speed. A neat black-dialled 140-m.p.h. speedometer and 7,000-r.p.m. rev.-counter, with white figures, the former incorporating trip and total mileage recorders, the latter a small clock, ammeter and a fuel gauge, flank the smaller dials. The minor switches comprise neat black knobs, in most cases with a white letter to indicate their function. To the driver's right there are knobs controlling the excellent fog-lamps, a rheostat-control of the panel lighting, the self-parking, two-speed screen-wipers, and the very powerful Lucas spot-lamp within the radiator

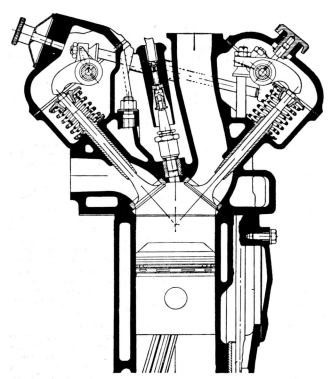

THE VALVE GEAR OF THE BRISTOL 405 seen in section, showing the cross push-rod actuation of the inclined o.h. valves and downdraught inlet ports.

cowl. Above these, on a separate walnut panel, is the aforesaid lever controlling overdrive (it is moved up to engage, down to disengage overdrive, a change out of top gear causing it to fall automatically), together with the push-button for the screen-washers, which deliver for a period corresponding to the length of time the button is depressed. Beneath the dash shelf are further controls operating the starter, mixture control, bonnet release (by push-button), ignition advance-and-retard, and hand-throttle; below these are the usual tiers of control levers for the interior heater. When being started the engine likes the ignition retarded, but otherwise this control is ignored, no "pinking" being evident on permanent full-advance. The lamps-switch-cum-ignition-key is normal, a passenger's grab-handle is provided, a lever depending from the screen sill works the self-cancelling flasher-type direction-indicators (which have a reminder light on the main instrument panel), while—full marks!—a reserve petrol supply of two gallons can be switched on by the driver, a blue light reminding him that this has been done.

After lunch (best forgotten!) just north of Doncaster, Scotch Corner came up in seemingly no time at all, and then mist closed in across Bowes Moor, persisting as we skirted Lake Windermere at tea-time. The Old England Hotel loomed up out of the darkness, so in this spacious and pleasant Trust House flanking the lake we paused for the night.

This high-speed winter journey had been accomplished very pleasantly, due to the commendable appointments of this British 2-litre saloon. Luxury is imparted to the occupants by the comfort of the seats, which have the merit of deep Dunlop foam rubber cushions, smooth upholstery in real hide, and squabs which are adjustable in respect of angle and shaped to provide support while the car is cornering in traditional Bristol fashion. These seats, bucket-type at the front with Leveroll adjustment, may not be perfect (indeed, no mere motor car seems quite to compare with a good air-liner for seat-comfort) but they deserve considerable praise, especially as when adjusted to provide 100 per cent. leg room there is still fair leg space for those occupying the back seat.

Other simple but commendable points of detail enhance the luxury of the Bristol 405. The wide shelf beneath the polished walnut dash is extremely useful, being far more commodious than any cubby-hole. With rigid pockets in all four doors, pockets in the backs of the front seats and a shelf behind the back seat in addition, one could hardly wish for more interior stowage space. A map light within the dash shelf, operated by a tiny on-off push-switch before the front-

seat passenger, crash padding above the dash, arm-rests on each door with a centre rest for the back seat, leather "pulls" on the doors, high-geared window-winding handles, useful front ventilator window panels, and opening rear lights, further enhance the well being of those who travel in a Bristol 405. For smokers there are covered ash-trays in the rear-door arm-rests and another in the windscreen sill (which, however, reflected in the windscreen).

The driver is particularly well provided for, because the positioning of two-spoke steering wheel and pedals is really satisfactory, while both the massive front wings are in full view. Visibility is ensured by the use of thin screen-pillars, and the diminishing-rear-view mirror is excellent. The big front wings and high, plain bonnet with carburetter air intake, however, make the car seem rather wide, and in sunlight there is a good deal of reflection from this unbroken paintwork. Further luxury is evident in the reversing-lamp operated by the gear-lever (reverse is beyond first gear, easy to engage and unlikely to be selected inadvertently).

From the servicing viewpoint the one-shot chassis lubrication system, operated by pressing a pedal adjacent to the clutch pedal, is notable; this feeds oil to the front suspension and, as the rear suspension is lubricated by oilways from the differential casing, the only nipples seeking occasional application of a grease-gun are those on the propeller-shaft universal joints and pedal bushes.

It is inevitable that, having driven in a Bristol 404 up to Scotland last summer, we should compare this now-defunct model with the current 405; in doing so we mourned the passing of such items as the push-button door handles, which have given place to normal levers, and the substitution of a separate key for the petrol-cap flap, whereas on the Bristol 403 and 404 an interior knob operated this flap, so that, with the doors locked, the petrol was automatically rendered tamper-proof. The external door handles and other plated protrusions, such as rain-deflectors, seem to have spoilt somewhat the aerodynamic lines of the 405, for above about 80 m.p.h. there is considerable wind-whistle round the screen pillars. Castor-action in the rack-and-pinion steering, while still vigorous, is less so than on the 404, so that the steering is correspondingly lighter, although this isn't really light steering by today's standards. Vibration, and sharp reaction from the road wheels, is transmitted to the driver's hands over bad surfaces, and the steering is not so positive as that on the 404. It is geared exactly three turns, lock-to-lock, which provides sufficiently good control without perceptible effort, and lost-motion was virtually absent. The steering-wheel rim and its two horizontal spokes are well provided with finger-grips.

The car we had for test was shod with Michelin SDS tyres, and these scarcely ever protested, even when cornering at high speed. Under these conditions the Bristol is roll-free, and the cornering tendency is pleasantly neutral, neither under- nor over-steer characteristics intruding. The suspension is sufficiently firm to resist roll, yet provides a very high degree of comfort over all normal surfaces, although at times the rigid back axle can be felt tramping about slightly.

In assessing this latest product of Bristol Cars Limited, I am in the happy position of having very little with which to find fault. The presence of a tubular interior lamp (there is one on each front door-pillar, switched on by the driver) exactly where the front-seat occupant rests his or her head when trying to sleep is *not* appreciated, any more than a smell of petrol which was sometimes noticeable inside the car after it had been standing—presumably a leak

HANDSOME LINES.— The Bristol 405 outside the highest inn in England, at Kirkstone Pass, 1,500 feet up. Note the typically Bristol radiator cowl and air intake on the top of the bonnet for the triple Solex downdraught carburetters.

STEEP ! — The handbrake holds the Bristol effectively at a 1-in-3 corner on Hard Knott Pass, from which point the car restarted without difficulty.

from the float chambers. The clutch pedal requires some pressure to depress; a slim foot can just be rested beside it, but otherwise the foot has to be placed beneath it. The headlamp dimmer button works with a commendably positive action, like the other controls, but it is somewhat awkwardly located below the clutch pedal and would be better placed above it. The excellence of the gear-change, which has already been strongly emphasised, makes it doubly unfortunate that occasionally the lever moves too far over when second gear is sought, muffing a clean change.

The luggage boot is lined and is unobstructed by the spare wheel, for this lives in the near-side front wing, balanced by the battery and reservoirs for the screen-washer in the off-side front wing. The boot lid can be locked with the petrol-filler flap key and the lid is spring-loaded. The luggage capacity is 17¾ cu. ft. and fitted suit-cases can be supplied, the shape of the boot being appropriate to them. Under the bonnet another little luxury is apparent in the lead-lamp, which can be plugged in should illumination be needed for tyre-changing, etc.

The Bristol can be accepted as one of today's fine cars, capable of an excellent performance from an engine of modest size. The maximum speed of over 100 m.p.h. is certainly usable in this country, for the well-chosen gear ratios result in useful acceleration. What is especially noticeable is the absence of vibration and exhaust noise, the Bristol engine running up smoothly to 5,000 r.p.m., and showing no symptoms of distress when switched off after prolonged fast running. The composite wood and metal body, panelled in light alloy, is free from rattles and the deep doors shut easily and quietly.

On the second day of the test I received proof that, apart from being a swift car on main roads, the Bristol 405 is unperturbed by long spells of low-gear collar-work. Up the short but interesting Kirkstone and Honister Passes, and on the long, impressive haul over Wrynose and Hard Knott Passes, it needed bottom gear on more than one occasion and interminable work at the steering wheel to swing it round the hairpins, but the needles of the water and oil-temperature gauges never altered appreciably, the occupants remained extremely comfortable, and in some 200 miles of this kind of going, with overdrive engaged very infrequently, the unexpectedly good petrol consumption of 19.9 m.p.g. of Esso Extra was recorded.

Incidentally, these Lakeland passes are worth a visit if you have never driven over them. Any car longer than the Bristol would be exciting to take round the 1-in-3¼ hairpin corners of Hard Knott, which climbs impressively along a ledge in the hillside, taken from the Wrynose end, Wrynose itself being a stiff two-mile 1-in-3½ proposition, the road, as seen from the summit, zig-zagging away in the distance towards the foot of Hard Knott. Honister was short and not quite so steep, Buttermere seems to have vanished from B 5289 (or else wasn't discernible in a Bristol!), and Kirkstone and Whinlatter Passes were not really exciting, although we took them from the less difficult directions. We were able to complete this morning tourlet of the lakes—Windermere, Ullswater, Derwent-water, Crummoch Water, Bassenthwaite, Thirlmere, Buttermere, and Ennerdale Water—on less than a tankful of fuel, the Bristol's range a useful one of nearly 300 miles under the worst conditions before the reserve supply has to be brought in.

Meeting vintage vehicles always enlivens these journeys in modern cars, but on this occasion, apart from a nice Bentley tourer which we overtook going at a good 60 on A 1, afterwards seeing it refuelling at Boroughbridge, a Bean encountered in Retford, and a gay Austin Twenty with van body in Keswick, they were conspicuous by their absence.

Another aspect of the car which our rapid embrace of nearly all the Lakes which tourists like to visit underlined was the absence of fading of the Lockheed brakes. These brakes, 12 in. by 2¼ in. 2LS at the front, 11 in. by 1¾ in. at the back, in light-alloy drums, are quite vice-free, pulling the car up strongly and progessively in a straight line without a sound. They call for fairly heavy pedal pressure. The hand-brake, the lever of which lies horizontally on the propeller-shaft tunnel between the front seats, is equally deserving of full marks, for it is convenient to use and holds the car securely on gradients of 1 in 3.

The English Lake District, seen in winter, with most of its hotels closed, seems decently remote, especially when, stopping at a likely-looking hostelry before 2 p.m., you are curtly informed that " luncheon finishes at 1.30." This remoteness was emphasised by the presence of damp mist which seems to cling more to the Windermere than to the Ambleside area. We were reminded even here of the march of civilisation, however, by having to follow Ultra Radio Television vans along the narrow roads, and because Ullswater recalled Donald Campbell's jet-propelled achievements with " Blue-bird." Kirkstone Pass, like the others we ascended, was easy-meat to the Bristol and, pausing at the summit, 1,500 feet above sea level, for our first photograph, I was pleased to observe that even here there is a pump supplying Clevecol—my favourite petrol.

Leaving the Lake District without appeasing our hunger, we came down A 6 into Liverpool, past Aintree race circuit—was motor-racing ever conducted in more drab surroundings ?—and through the Mersey Tunnel—where the illumination is a pleasant change from the murk outside—to spend the night in the quaint old town of Chester, with its two-storey shopping centre. Just before Bolton-le-Sands an XK120 Jaguar two-seater, with the hood up, had accelerated past us before turning off the main road, but apart from this, and a 4.3 Alvis saloon doing 80 along the Chester road, nothing overtook the Bristol during this three-day outing. Lan-caster seemed sordid, seen in the mist of a January twilight, and Preston more so, especially when we followed a fingerpost marked " Liverpool " and immediately became hopelessly lost !

Incidentally, the A.A. weather service was operating on A 6, a mile or so north of Preston, and must have proved its worth the next day, for although we left Chester in sunlight, putting 54 miles into the first hour's running, in spite of traffic halts, thereafter the fog clamped down, lorries ran into other lorries on the frozen surface of A 5, and the average speed fell as low as 14 m.p.h. for the next half-hour, and remained at little better than 33 m.p.h. all the way to London. Thus our intention to carry out a fast main-road fuel-consumption check was thwarted, but driving for miles in the lower gears, and using the performance to the full, up to 100-m.p.h. maximum when brief clear patches permitted, quite the worst conditions for low petrol consumption, we recorded 21 m.p.g., convincing emphasis indeed of Bristol economy. No water and very little oil were consumed in over 1,000 miles' driving, and the only mechanical set-back was when the extension for zero-ing the trip

CONTINUED ON PAGE 287

ONE OF THOSE BRIDGES.—A Lakeland stone bridge carries the Bristol over a stream not far from Derwentwater.

A racy red-and-white paint job adds zest to the fleet lines of the aluminum body.

ROAD TEST:

THE *Arnolt-Bristol*

FOR COMPETITION

Three Solex carburetors and six-branch manifold are features of the 1971 cc engine. The cockpit interior offers broad leg-and-foot space with commendably large pedals.

IN EARLY 1954, New York was treated to the first U.S. showing of a new and different-looking sports car. It represented the combined efforts of James Watt of England's Bristol Aeroplane Co., Bertone, one of Italy's famed bodybuilders, and S. H. Arnolt, well-known Chicago automobile importer. Destined entirely for the American market, the Arnolt-Bristol (Bertone gets his name and crest on the side) reached New York the long way: the engine and chassis, built at Bristol, were shipped to Turin, where Bertone fitted the body and sent the completed car on across the Atlantic. The complicated production arrangements seemed to work out fairly well without pushing the final selling price out of reason, and in the 1954-55 U.S. racing seasons the car has shown itself to be a top Class E performer, as much at home in the short, fast sprint races as in the long endurance grinds such as Sebring.

The Arnolt-Bristol comes in two versions, the bare competition car and a luxuriously outfitted touring model (coupe or convertible) for about $1000 more. We selected the competition model for a road test because of its relatively modest price and superior performance, and the test car, a "veteran" of 5000 racing miles, was kindly provided by Williamson Motors of Los Angeles. For the actual performance data, given in tabular and graphic form at the right, we make no apologies. The car was in good average condition, although perhaps not as "hot"

photography: Poole

as some examples we have observed in recent races. It was equipped with a quiet muffler for road use, which undoubtedly hampered top-end performance, but, however, the zero-to-60 acceleration time and maximum speed figure are the best we have ever recorded for a two-litre machine, and we have tested every popular, available make except one (the AC Ace).

As can be expected with any automobile designed specifically for racing, our car offered a minimum of comfort and furbelows (no top, stubby windshield, etc.) and an engine that didn't really get its throat cleared below 3000 rpms. Also noted was a strong tendency to foul plugs within a few minutes of city driving. After 100 miles of normal highway cruising to the testing grounds, it was necessary to change plugs before putting the car through its paces. The rack-and-pinion steering was extremely quick and positive, but also extremely heavy at lower speeds, and although three turns of the steering wheel are required from lock-to-lock, the front wheels will cramp sharply enough to produce a turning circle only 31 feet in diameter.

During the acceleration trials, the car was definitely slow off the mark; this was due partly to slightly oversize tires on the rear wheels and partly to the fact that the cam does not begin to "bite" until above the low-rev range—once over 3000 rpm there is a very satisfying "surge" in 1st and 2nd gears. The gear-box was a pleasure to use, and shifts, up or down, are virtually foolproof. In fact, we gained the strong overall impression that in all operational departments—steering, shifting, braking and general roadhandling—the Arnolt-Bristol is the most "forgiving" competition car we have ever encountered, and an aspiring novice could hardly find a better vehicle in which to try out his wheels.

Mechanically, the car has an interesting ancestry. As is well known, the Bristol engine and chassis had its origin in Germany before the war, as the BMW type 328. The present Bristol-built engine is, however, a very much refined design, developing more horsepower with considerably greater reliability than the old "328". Although there is some technical objection to its obsolete bore/stroke ratio, the proven stamina of this engine demonstrates once more that a few years of development often give a better power unit than a new "ideal" design. The unusual relay-rocker mechanism which operates the inclined valves from a camshaft mounted low in the cylinder block also rates some criticism from the "dohc-or-nothing" purists, but it works very well up to at least 6000 rpm, and there is no long timing drive-chain problem. In addition this arrangement is accessible and easy to service.

The body styling of the Arnolt-Bristol has caused considerable comment one way and another—obviously, Mr. Arnolt approves. The creased fenders, unusual grille with the buried headlights, and high rear end do combine to give the car a kind of taut, fleet look, but the wheels, however practical, are on the drab side. Like them or not, the contours are such that the car's identity is not easily mistaken; but for anyone who contemplates taking up The Sport in a serious way but who lacks grand-scale financing, the Arnolt-Bristol competition sports car is one sure way of garnering a mantelpiece full of Class E trophies. ●

ROAD AND TRACK ROAD TEST NO. F-2-56

ARNOLT-BRISTOL

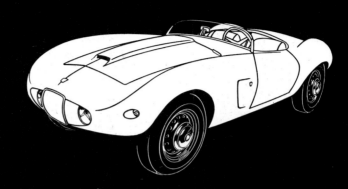

SPECIFICATIONS

List price	$4245
Wheelbase	96.2 in.
Tread, front	51.9 in.
rear	54.0 in.
Tire size (not std.)	6.00-16
Curb weight	2185
distribution	50/50
Test weight	2475
Engine	6-cyl.
Valves	inclined ohv.
Bore & stroke	2.60 x 3.78 in.
Displacement	1971 cc
Compression ratio	9.00
Horsepower	130
peaking speed	5500
equivalent mph	115
Torque, ft/lbs	128
peaking speed	5000
equivalent mph	105
Mph per 1000 rpm.	20.9
Mph at 2500 fpm	83.0
Gear ratios (overall)	
4th	3.90
3rd	5.04
2nd	7.12
1st	11.4
R&T performance factor	49.1

PERFORMANCE

Top speed (avg)	107.1
best run	108.8
Max. speeds in gears—	
3rd (5500)	89
2nd (5500)	63
1st (5500)	39
Shift points from—	
same as above	
Mileage	17.5/22.0 mpg.

ACCELERATION

0-30 mph	4.0 secs
0-40 mph	5.8 secs
0-50 mph	7.8 secs
0-60 mph	10.1 secs
0-70 mph	13.9 secs
0-80 mph	18.3 secs
0-90 mph	26.2 secs
Standing ¼ mile—	
average	17.7 secs
best	17.6 secs

TAPLEY READINGS

Gear	Lbs/ton	Mph	Grade
1st	off scale	—	—
2nd	430	at 51	22%
3rd	290	at 60	15%
4th	220	at 68	11%
Total drag at 60 mph, 124 lbs			

SPEEDO ERROR

Indicated	Actual
30 mph	29.0
40 mph	38.8
50 mph	48.6
60 mph	60.6
70 mph	70.5
80 mph	80.2
108 mph	108.8

ARNOLT-BRISTOL "COMPETITION"

Acceleration thru the gears

ROAD and TRACK

The Bristol 405 is a deluxe sedan with true sports car performance and handling

a photo story by Joe H. Wherry

The well-appointed cockpit with nicely arranged dashboard which includes complete instrumentation

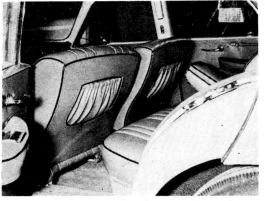

Upholstery is leather of marvelous quality and fine detailing. Notice the tremendous width of doorway

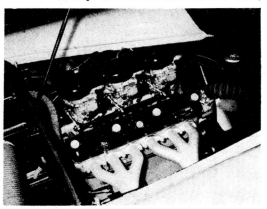

OUTSIDE of a handful or 2 of Rolls-Royce and Bentley models annually, this country sees comparatively few examples of British cars that can truly be characterized as belonging to the fine car class. So it's refreshing to see an importer taking the bit in the teeth and bringing in something off the beaten track.

The car concerned reflects considerable aircraft background. It should, for this very sportive 4/5-seater sedan is the product of the Bristol Aeroplane Co., whose aircraft and engines have attracted considerable attention and note for close on 5 decades. Several years ago Brewster brought in several of the 401 and later the 403 2-door models; these were supplemented by the competition-bred 404 coupe that was built on a close-coupled chassis to appeal chiefly to enthusiasts.

The Model 405 is indicative of a new appreciation on the part of Bristol that aerodynamic design can be mated to pleasing styling. The new lines stem from the 404 coupe back as far as the windshield, but aft of this location the needs of the family man who desires comfort as well as distinction have been far more

successfully catered to than in any previous Bristol sedans. Whereas the previous *saloon* models once held great resemblance, in the front, to contemporary B.M.W. (German) passenger cars, the new 405 now has a style line of its own. If this car owes anything to any other make, it can only be the heritage of the power plant which is, after many changes and improvements, now only a very distant cousin to the pre-1953 B.M.W. engine. So the Bristol engine has taken a separate identity thru successive developments and it has been installed successfully in Frazer-Nash, A.C., Cooper competition cars, and others.

A tried and true 6-in-line, the Bristol plant remains traditionally a long-stroke design with hemispherical combustion chambers. The valves are inclined at 80 degrees, the inlet valves operating directly from pushrods and rockers while horizontal pushrods actuate the exhaust valves. For several years Bristol engines have featured triple carburetors but recently the compression ratio of the stock engines has been increased (from 7.5) to 8.5 to 1. Together

The sleek lines of the Bristol 405 shroud a wondrous collection of unusual features. An example is the location of the spare, which is concealed behind a section of the fender just to the rear of the left front tire

Trio of carburetors tops the famous overhead valve, single-overhead-cam, 6-cylinder Bristol powerplant

BRISTOL 405

with improved ignition and manifolding, this has upped the output from 85 to 105 bhp at 5000 rpm. The exhaust system, at 1st glance, seems to be a dual unit. However, the dual-appearing triple header units converge near the crankcase into a single pipe with a muffler designed to minimize back pressure and effectively silence as well.

Much use has been made of aluminum alloys, as might be expected from an aircraft firm which recently made the Car Division a more or less autonomous subsidiary. The head, according to modern practice, is aluminum while the body, even for a relatively low-production car, uses a lot of the lightweight metal. The chassis is a box section unit of sheet steel with the rear floor and luggage compartment attached in integral fashion. The chassis components are soundproofed internally and treated to resist rust. Said to be extremely resistant to torsional stresses, this chassis unit could probably be more correctly termed a stub frame.

One of the cleanest passenger bodies existent, developed of course in Bristol's own wind tunnels and also extremely light in weight, graces the car. Exponents of conformity will no doubt dislike the lack of a notch back, but a fast drive in this car proves the efficiency of the streamlining in reducing wind noise. Aluminum alloy, 18-gauge for the most part, covers a body which is built of seasoned ash framework. That wood should still be used in modern passenger car body construction may seem strange to many, but the practice is still quite in vogue in England in the fine car field, the exponents claiming that little if any strength is lost by such methods. Forward of the passenger compartment, the aluminum sheet contours cover a steel framework while the doors and pillars and the luggage bin, as previously noted, are steel.

Not a small car in the true sense of the term, the 405 has a wheelbase of 114 inches; but very moderate front and rear overhang hold the overall length to just a hair over 189 inches, or a shade under that of the current Rambler. Passenger comfort in the legroom department is generous and compares favorably with that of all the popular domestic cars. Leather upholstery without blemish or seam fault is used thruout the interior except for the plastic headliner. The driver and each passenger has an armrest and an additional folding rest in the rear seat makes way for a 5th person when the need arises. Previous Bristol sedans used

only pushbuttons for opening the doors and the trunk could only be opened by means of a pull toggle in the rear passenger space; now, tho, the more positive door handles have returned and the trunk opens conveniently by key. The entire effect is that of luxury and practicality in good taste. Chrome is used sparingly.

The front seats are individually adjustable. Altho low, they are most comfortable and long trips should be as restful as one could hope for. The steering is rack and pinion, has a lock of just 3 turns, and the wheel which happily lacks a horn ring is adjustable to 3 positions. A driver who likes to know the mechanical score will delight in the instrument panel which lacks nothing. The instruments, all non-reflecting and legible at a glance with dull black backgrounds, are set directly in front of the driver in a polished walnut dashboard. A tachometer and matching full-circle speedometer are supplemented by genuine oil pressure and oil temperature gauges as well as a radiator thermometer and a fuel gauge that is remarkably accurate. There's a one-shot chassis lubrication pedal, a reserve fuel switch, and a mixture control that should guarantee long cross-country jaunts with relatively consistent performance, regardless of altitude or climate changes. Of course there's a clock and a combination heater and fresh air unit. The hood, bonnet if you prefer, opens from beneath the dash while the turn signals are controlled by

a timed toggle on the top of the dash. The latter control would be much handier on the steering wheel, but then the Bristol is one of those cars which puts efficiency and detail uppermost. "His Master's Voice" radio is well toned and at high speeds can be heard with the volume low.

Tossing the floor-mounted stick shift around is a joy, there being no remote linkage to snafu the fastest shifts. Unfortunately this car had less than 200 miles on the odometer so the test run was taken at conservative speeds in spite of

the fact that all Bristol engines are given a fairly thoro breaking-in on the block before installation. Therefore, it was *verboten* to make any acceleration runs. From previous experience in a 1953 Model 401, tho, I believe I can give a reasonable idea of how this no-heavier-but-more-powerful car can be expected to perform. The new engine over-revs very easily, with virtually no noise and without sign of strain; the book says that 4th gear is good for 18.56 mph per 1000 rpm, while overdrive (operative by toggle on the dash and only after 4th is engaged) delivers 23.9 mph. At 2500 feet per minute piston speed, the top speed in overdrive is 94.7 mph, which takes place at considerably less than full and safely developed revs (5000), so it would appear that the century mark is easily surpassed.

The old 401 was often clocked above 96 mph with its considerably less moxie, would go to a corrected 60 mph in 17.8 seconds, would cruise effortlessly at 60 mph and deliver a good 18 mpg of regular fuel. It would seem reasonable to assume an ability of the new 405 to top an easy 105 mph (corrected) with little difficulty in view of the rapidity with which this more efficient engine winds up.

Acceleration thru the gears is very rapid and is felt in the seat of the pants without exceeding 3000 rpm, which was the requested limit on this new car. With extension of the revs to a sustained 5000 from the former 4500, 405 should easily break 14 seconds from a standing start to a true 60. The instrumentation, being of the highest order, was extremely accurate up to 80 mph on the old 401. While no attempt was made to determine the extent of speedometer inaccuracy on this car, it seems unlikely that more than 3 mph error at an indicated 60 would be tolerated by Bristol. When broken in and competently driven, the quick-shifting box will probably make a true 80 mph possible in 24 seconds. The brakes, which showed great resistance to fade on several hard stops, should make this a good mount for the driver who wants both fast and safe transportation and plenty of room.

In 4th gear at highway speeds, a relaxation of the throttle produces less than the usual amount of engine braking. Coasting out of gear further testifies to the efficiency of the streamlining. The front suspension is by a transverse spring and wishbones plus an anti-roll bar, while the rear suspension is by longitudinal torsion bars. Additional torsion arms locate the rear axle and there is a stabilizing unit which firms the differential cage. The result is an extremely smooth ride combined with near-perfect handling. Sway on corners is non-existent and roll is so little as to be noticeable only by an almost complete absence. Sharp rises and dips have very little effect. It's a *sports sedan* for sure and a connoisseur's delight—for a bit over $7000.
                                    —J.H.W.

SCI

tests the
Arnolt - Bristol

Gracefully designed by the Bertone coachbuilding firm of Turin, Italy, the aerodynamic body of the Arnolt-Bristol stands a mere 44 inches in height.

IT WAS 5 a.m. in the desert. The air temperature was a frigid 35 degrees, and the car hadn't been tuned since it left the factory many months before. I had already discovered that the stock plugs, fine for Britain's lower-grade fuel but not for premium U.S. gas, were misfiring, and that three of the brakes were dragging. The time and place were wrong for taking corrective measures, and I didn't expect much.

To start the car I went by the book. I pulled out the mixture-control lever and pressed the starter button. One spin of the crankshaft and the cold

engine fired, ticking over at a fast warm up idle of 1500 rpm. The water temperature rose to a good operating level within three minutes, but the oil temperature was slow. After 10 minutes' warm up and five miles of tooling along below 2000 rpm, though, the oil stood at 40 degrees Centigrade. Now, according to the book, I could go ahead and use whatever the engine had to give.

First, the standing quarter-mile. I revved the engine to 5000 with clutch in and shift lever in first cog, popped the clutch and stood on the throttle. Low gear was quite high (low numerically) by touring car standards, and for

a full second very little happened. The car started forward, moving like a rocket, slowly at first, gathering momentum. The tach needle crept around to 3000. Suddenly the racing cam effect came in. Within two seconds the needle was swinging past 5000, the speedometer read 40 and the valve gear was screaming its tension.

With foot hard on the throttle I punched the clutch, whipped the shift lever down to second and snapped the clutch out again, keeping the revs above the thrusty 3000 mark. I wound past 4000, listening to the *haawnk* of great volumes of air ripping through slender venturis become louder and stronger. Now the tach read 5000, and as it approached 6000 at 65 mph I popped another shift, still keeping the throttle pinned to the floorboards. There was the ascending engine note in second, the sudden descent, then as the clutch bit, the start of another, lower-keyed ascent. I wound on out in third at 6000, indicating about 95 mph, and threw the final shift into fourth. The engine, losing only a few revs, continued to drone its song of pure power. In 17 seconds flat I'd spanned the standing quarter, indicating nearly 90 mph in 1320 feet with a 120 cubic inch engine!

This, friends, is a *car:*

The Arnolt-Bristol is one of the finest real *high*-performance sports cars I've ever driven. Its engine and chassis have European lineage of unique distinction, and its beautiful body is one of Bertone's best. In competition form the car costs just $3995. Yet you can buy one without having to sweat out a long waiting list, and this is the fact that astonishes me. By all that's rational, hot-eyed enthusiasts ought to be snatching these machines off the boats as fast as S. H. Arnolt can produce them. The reason they aren't, apparently, is that there's a widespread notion that the A-B is some sort of cobbled-up U. S.

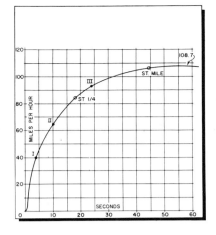

The razor-sharp edges of the Bertone coachwork are attained by careful finishing of the metal. Large airscoop helps accommodate tall engine and ducts cool air to three Solexes.

All parts including the short rockers are polished to a near-mirror finish on the Bristol BS-1 Mk II engine. Transverse pushrods actuate the exhaust rockers. In effect and in operation, this arrangement acts as a direct overhead camshaft.

Speedometer of the A-B indicated from 70-75 mph as the aerodynamic two-seater sped around test bend.

Weight distribution, and stable suspension geometry permit high cornering speeds with slight drift.

jalopy that happens to use the Bristol engine. This is far from true.

The Arnolt-Bristol is a purebred sports car. Its sweeping class win at Sebring in '55 proved that it's every bit the machine that Bristol-powered cars are across the Atlantic — cars that can win their class 1-2-3 at Le Mans and sustain over 125 mph for 200 miles at Montlhery. In the U.S., A-B's have finished ahead of two-litre Ferraris, 300-SL's and Jaguar XK140M's. There's nothing in the two-litre production class that can keep up with them.

The A-B is magnificent for short, straight road courses. It has a top speed of about 112 mph and it's geared to reach the maximum right away. The top speed it can achieve theoretically on a long desert highway is actually beside the point. What *is* the point is the fact that within a mile, from a standing start, it can come within a hairsbreadth of its potential maximum.

It thunders through first so fast that you need all your alertness to keep it from yielding its limit right there. Second and third ratios arm you to cope with any situation of acceleration, ascent or descent. Fourth is a dream. You can use it to pull smoothly from 20 mph or you can use it where it's happiest:

cruising between 80 and 100 mph. Here the engine runs with a free and totally frictionless feel. This is a car that hungers to prance at 105 mph at only a nudge from the driver. Only at the bitter end of its top limit does it begin to tighten up.

The bodies Bertone has built for Arnolt are beautiful, and that's a deliberate understatement. The lines are essentially the same for all the body styles. Our test car was the simplest, the competition two-seater, which has a racing windscreen, and no top, side curtains or bumpers. Next in price is the Bolide model, which has full weather protec-

141

tion and a price of $4250. The De Luxe model, with top, side curtains, bumpers and an elegantly finished interior, sells for $4995. And finally there's the Coupe at $5995, which has roll-up windows and interior appointments that are really luxurious.

All these models derive their lines from Bertone's brilliant B.A.T. series of aero-dynamic body forms. No matter from what angle you view the Arnolt-Bristol, it has beauty, harmony, and integrity of line. At a three-quarter rear view, for example, the sharply sculptured curve of the front fender harmonizes faultlessly with the curves of windscreen and airscoop. The body is light, strong and practical. The doors are so light, so well-balanced and lightly-hinged, that I thought they must be made of aluminum. But they're of steel sheet, and so are all the panels except the hood and rear deck. This is good from the standpoint of strength, and strength has been an important consideration in the laying out of this body.

Welded-in steel-sheet wheel wells give the body's front and rear extremities a boiler-plate solidness. Because of the structural strength you can haybale an A-B and pay for the damage without too much strain. For one reason or another two of these cars have been rolled in West Coast races. They came to rest on the high points of their fenders and the repair costs, including paint, ran between $150 and $175.

In the past I've seen some sad examples of "fine Old World craftsman-

TEST CAR:
Arnolt-Bristol 2-liter Competition model. Bristol 404 chassis, B.S. 1 Mk. II engine.

TEST CONDITIONS:
Number aboard.....2, weight of passengers and instruments 340 lbs.
Top position..........Down (no top on competition model)
Temperature..........Top speed, 36°F. Acceleration, 74°F
Miscellaneous..........No wind, top speed taken at sea level, acceleration at 950 ft.

PERFORMANCE

TOP SPEED:
Two-way average........107.3 mph
Fastest one-way run.....108.7 mph

ACCELERATION:
From zero to:
30 mph..................2.9 sec.
40 mph..................4.0
50 mph..................6.2
60 mph..................8.7
70 mph..................11.7
80 mph..................16.0
90 mph..................21.3
100 mph..................27.9
Standing ¼ mile..........17.0   (avg. 52.9 mph)
Speed at end of
    quarter..................82 mph
Standing mile..............44.3 secs.   (avg. 81.4 mph)

CHASSIS:
Wheelbase...................96 ins.
    Front Tread.............51.25 ins.
    Rear Tread.............54 ins.
Suspension, front........Transverse leaf and A-arms
Suspension, rear..........Rigid axle, longitudinal torsion bars
Shock absorbers..........Hydraulic double-acting telescopic
Steering type................Rack and pinion
Steering wheel turns
    L to L.....................3
Turning diameter.......32 ft. 10 ins.
Brake type....................Lockheed hydraulic; two leading shoes at front
Brake lining area........148 sq. ins.
Wheel studs,
circle diam...................Five 9/16 in. studs; 4¼ in. bolt circle
Tire size.........................5.50 x 16
Rim width
    (outside) ....5⅞ ins.

GENERAL:
Length.....................167 ins.
Width.........................68 ins.
Height.........................44 ins.
Weight, test car..........2120 lbs. with full fuel tank
Weight distribution,
    F/R.....................49/51
Weight distribution,
    F/R with driver
    and passenger..........47/53
Fuel capacity—
    U. S. gallons.............18.5

With excellent grouping of instruments, adjustable bucket seats, precise location of shift lever and handbrake, ample leg room for the lanky, the A-B cockpit leaves little to be desired.

Partial cutaway exposes valve train and operation. Single camshaft in block actuates intake valves by push-rods and rockers. Exhaust valves are activated by transverse rods impelled by bell cranks on intake rocker shaft.

ship" in which the sheet metal was just a rough base for a sculptor's skill with many pounds of body putty. This was the first thing I looked for in the Bertone body, but I could find nothing but paint and well-formed sheet metal. The razor edges of the fenders are areas that even the least cynical observer would be likely to suspect. But if you reach up under the body and feel inside you find that the razor edge was achieved by steel alone, and not by lead, putty or any other substitute for competence in metal-shaping.

The aerodynamics of this body are notable. If you're of average height — say from 5 ft. 6 ins. to 5 ft. 11 ins. — you ride in total comfort. The airstream gives you a gentle scalp massage and rips up and over the racing windscreen to deflect insects and other airborne impediments harmlessly. But extend your arm to make a turning signal and you discover how efficient the streamlined packaging is. You can almost break a wrist by testing the airstream too boldly at high speed.

The big airscoop in the hood is no dummy. Without it the car would have to be a good deal higher than it is, to accommodate its tall engine. The scoop channels cool outside air to the three Solexes that mix the engine's fuel and air.

The passenger space is one of the most acceptable I've found. Bertone's bucket seats are perfectly form-fitting and give superb lateral support to pas-

RATING FACTORS:

Bhp per cu. in.............1.08
Bhp per sq. in.
    piston area..............4.07
Torque (lb-ft)
    per cu in...................1.05
Pounds per bhp-
    test car   16.3
Dry weight ....1990 lbs.
Piston speed @
    60 mph.................1850 ft. per min.
Piston speed @
    max bhp..................3465 ft. per min.
Brake lining area
    per ton (test car) ....140 sq. ins.

SPEEDOMETER CORRECTION:

Indicated	Actual
30	29
40	38
50	47
60	56.5
70	66
80	75.6
90	82.5
100	92

FUEL CONSUMPTION:

Hard driving.............16.5 mpg
Average driving
    (under 60 mph) ......24 mpg

BRAKING EFFICIENCY:

1st stop.........................71 percent
2nd stop........................71 percent
3rd stop.........................71 percent
4th stop.........................76 percent
5th to 10th stop...........73 percent

SPECIFICATIONS

POWER UNIT:

Type:...........................In-line six
Valve Arrangement.....Vee-inclined ohv, pushrod operated
Bore & Stroke
    (Engl. & Met) ....2.59 x 3.77 ins. 66 x 96 mm
Stroke/Bore Ratio...... 1.455 to one
Displacement
    (Engl. & Met.) ....120.2 cu. ins., 1971cc
Compression Ratio.....9.0 to one
Carburetion by............3 single-throat Solex type 32B1
Max. bhp @ rpm.........130 @ 5500
Max. Torque
    @ rpm......................128 @ 5000
Idle Speed....................600 to 900 rpm
Ignition by...................Lucas coil and single-breaker
                              distributor

DRIVE TRAIN:

Transmission ratios I	Overall	Gearbox
I	11.4	2.92
I	7.12	1.83
II	5.04	1.29
III	3.9	1.00

Front running gear detail. Eleven-inch brake drums lack finning and ventilating ports for cooling, but in spite of simplicity endure harshest treatment with impunity. Note concertina-type seals shield rack and pinion.

Front underchassis view of plumbing for Bristol chassis' excellent one-shot lubrication system. All running gear friction surfaces are sealed from dirt either by neoprene seals or by leather covers secured by straps and buckles.

Arnolt-Bristol

sengers under the hardest cornering. Leg-room is unusually ample. The seats have five stages of positively-locked adjustment. My height is 5 ft. 10 ins., and with the driver's seat in the next-to-longest notch I was barely able to touch the front floorboard with either foot. In the competition body there are no interior panels to the car's doors. But there is a metal strip about 1½ inches deep along the bottom inside of each door. This adds to the doors' rigidity and also makes a useful parcel-storage area in each door. There's no partition between the passenger compartment and the luggage space at the rear. Thus this space is accessible both from behind the seats and through the rear deck lid.

The A-B's complement of instruments is very complete. There are a big speedometer, a tachometer of equal size, and gauges for oil and water temperature, oil pressure, ammeter and fuel supply. The tach includes a clock and the speedometer a trip odometer. Warning lights are used to indicate high beam of headlights (Italian "warning" style), two-gallon fuel reserve, direction indicator and battery discharge. Controls include hand throttle and automatic mixture control for starting. The pedals are nicely dimensioned and spaced for feet of average size and the hand-brake lever is ideally placed between the seats. The shift lever is long and on the springy side. If you insist on the last word in refinement you can get a special remote shift linkage from Arnolt.

The 96-in. wheelbase chassis is based on a rigid, light, box-section frame with front suspension by a single transverse leaf and upper wishbones damped by steeply inclined, double acting tubular shocks. The rear axle is solid, with its differential housing offset to the right. Suspension is by longitudinal torsion bars, and the axle is positively located by a triangular stabilizing bracket that anchors final drive housing to frame. There are four shock absorbers at the rear and fabric slings to prevent excessive axle travel during rebound.

Steering is by rack-and-pinion that is dead-positive and impeccable. It appears to be completely non-reversible —

that is, although the steering wheel The A-B's first is good up to 40 mph.

First has no synchromesh, but you directs the road wheels very sensitively, there is no playback from road wheels to steering wheel. The system responds as quickly as the most demanding driver could want. A wheel movement of just an inch or two is enough to execute most changes of direction, and gentle road curves need only a fraction of an inch. The steering has what I consider an ideal amount of fuel — it's slightly heavy even at high speeds. Because of this you can set the wheel on the straightaway or in a constant-radius turn, take your hands off and enjoy the rare experience of having your car "remember" your command long after you gave it.

The A-B is one of the fastest-cornering cars I've ever handled, and this includes many quality road machines capable of far greater top speed. Its fore-and-aft weight distribution is very close to being equal and is slightly tail-heavy. Its tread is wide, its wheelbase short, and its suspension geometry is very stable. Under heavy side loading the rear wheels slide outward just the right amount to permit fast and effortless cornering. At high cornering speeds in big-radius bends the car drifts ever so slightly. Its natural cornering stance is flat and rock-steady and it stresses its tires hardly at all. It tracks true and perfectly at almost any speed. Once you learn not to use too much tiller, you can steer it with something very close to a centaur-like sense of oneness with the mount — especially when you gauge the wheel-setting for any curve precisely in advance, set the wheel with a single motion, and let the car do the rest.

The Bristol gearbox is a near approach to perfection. Its bottom cog has obviously been chosen for racing. It's low in terms of numerical ratio and therefore makes the car slow in getting away from the line. There's a good second lost between letting the clutch out and meaningful forward acceleration. But if it had a higher numerical ratio the engine would peak sooner.

You only start once in a race, but there will probably be many times when you can use a broadly useful low-gear range.

can downshift to it with no clash or noise by using elementary Model A Ford double-clutch technique. The other gears are synchronized and can be changed with a delicious degree of silence and certainty if you will make the change "slowly"—taking about one-tenth of a second to pass from gear to gear, while never lifting your foot from the throttle. A similar pause insures silent downshifts. You can make them more rapidly, with less stress on the mechanism, by double-clutching and blipping the throttle with the clutch out.

The brakes are terrific. I pulled a wheel to inspect one of the brake drums and was totally unimpressed by the sight of the simplest sort of non-finned, non-ventilated drum. Yet these brakes are all you could ask for. During our ten-stop fade test they lost not a bit of their massive stopping power. These are brakes to race with — which means they're the kind of brakes you don't mind entrusting with your life.

So let's summarize. In terms of performance, the Arnolt-Bristol is a thoroughbred racing car fit to be stabled with Ferraris and Mercedes. Its acceleration is shattering and any point on the acceleration curve can be reached in a matter of instants. You can get tremendous speed in the space of a few watch-ticks, then downshift and brake and be creeping along in Second split-minutes after you were indicating 110 mph. The engine's power is nothing short of a revelation. It forces you to take a second look at all the scholarly arguments in favor of the short-stroked engine. In terms of hand-work and fine finish on mechanical components, there are few machines in the world that can compete with the Arnolt-Bristol. It's a goer and a winner, a full fledged racing machine that can blow off others far out of its displacement class and worlds apart from its price class. It's a car the enthusiasts ought to be fighting to buy.

I'm thoroughly convinced that you'll find no car with more performance per dollar than you can get in the A-B. It's a Golden Age-type sports car, the sort of combination of fierce racing car and obedient road machine that survives here and there only in the high price-brackets. **G B**

Servo-boosted disc brakes are used on all four wheels of the new Type 406 which has a very attractive two-door body by Beutler.

BRISTOL

An "Export Only" 2¼-litre Type 406

DESPITE rumours which have been published in American magazines to the effect that the Bristol Aeroplane Co., Ltd., is to abandon its small-scale production of cars, a new Bristol type is being shown at Paris and London. Listed as being for export only, the Type 406 is being shown with two-door saloon bodywork by Gebr. Beutler, of Thun, Switzerland.

With a background of use in racing, a bigger version of the well-proven Bristol engine is introduced for the Type 406, enlargement of the cylinder bore from 66 mm. to 68.69 mm. and an increase in piston stroke from 96 mm. to 99.64 mm. stepping up the swept volume from 1,971 c.c. to 2,216 c.c. Maximum power output remains at the

same figure of 105 b.h.p. as with the smaller swept volume, but is attained at 4,700 r.p.m. instead of at 5,000 r.p.m. in consequence of improved torque. In conjunction with the four-speed gearbox, an overdrive is provided, and with the 4.27 : 1 hypoid-geared rear axle used in place of a 4.22 : 1 spiral bevel unit to lower the transmission line of this model a highest gear ratio of 3.28 : 1 becomes available.

Improved braking performance is promised by the adoption of Dunlop disc brakes for the Type 406, with a servo pump to boost the hydraulic operating pressure. Suspension continues to be independent at the front by

a transverse leaf spring and wishbones, torsion bar springs being used in conjunction with a rigid axle at the rear. Bolt-on wheels with wide-base rims carry tyres of 5.75-16 size, the wheelbase of the new model remaining the same as that of the Type 405 at 9 ft. 6 in. but the rear track increasing from 4 ft. 6 in. to 4 ft. 8 in.

Weighing an estimated 22¾ cwt. in comparison with the 24½ cwt. of the Type 405 four-door saloon, the Type 406 two-door saloon illustrated on this page will be seen to feature exceptionally slim roof pillars and large areas of glass, slight tail fins emphasizing its modern character.

Great Britain BRISTOL

BRISTOL AEROPLANE CO., LTD., FILTON, BRISTOL, ENGLAND

BRISTOL 405 DROPHEAD COUPE

The Bristol 405 saloon and drophead coupe are unchanged from last year. With a reputation for building quality cars, the Bristol Aeroplane Company has built a car which provides a good performance with economy, at a rather high initial cost. The car is powered by the Bristol two-liter engine, which is a six-cylinder powerplant with 120.3 cubic inches displacement. It is rated at 105 bhp at 5000 rpm with a compression ratio of 8.5 to 1. It has three downdraft carburetors. Its transmission is a four-speed unit with overdrive standard equipment, which accounts for its economy. The overdrive unit has an unusual feature of a

freewheel in first gear only. Thus, the gear lever can be moved into first gear without use of the clutch. The car is mounted on a pressed-rail frame and uses independent front suspension. Rear suspension is on a rigid axle with the use of torsion bars. The car, streamlined in design, is built on a 114-inch wheelbase with an overall length of 189 inches. Its dry weight is 2720 pounds. Instruments are grouped directly in front of the driver, cowled to eliminate reflection, in a polished walnut panel. The front end has a low sloping hood and a road light mounted in the center of the grille shell, a rather unique arrangement. ∎

ARNOLT-BRISTOL

DRIVING IMPRESSIONS BY OUR ART EDITOR

THE ART EDITOR must be content (usually, at least) to get his thrills via the drawing board. All too often I've looked out the office window, watched with envy as the MOTOR TREND test crew prepared to depart for a day of road testing. With reluctance I would return to page layouts.

This time it was to be different. After a luncheon jaunt in the Arnolt, Walt Woron suggested, "You take it — see what you think of it. After all you've got a T-Bird, like good-lookin' cars."

So it was arranged. Next day Bob D'Olivo, our chief photographer, and I started, equipped with wrenches, extra set of Lodge plugs, drawing paper and India ink. When pictures of this car first came across my desk, I took notice — now I was going to meet the rig in person. On the way to the dragstrip, I could sense this Arnolt-Bristol had performance. After finding out how it can eat up corners, I was sure.

To the artist the lack of needless embellishments is refreshing. The aerodynamic lines are clean and appealing. Bucket seats are exceptionally comfortable. I told Bob, "This beats the chairs in our front room."

At first glance the Arnolt-Bristol looks too potent for ordinary street use. Actually it can be as docile as a Persian cat, or cheetah-like when the throttle is depressed. You can drive the Arnolt-Bristol to the local drug store on Friday night, and then be in the thick of a road race during the weekend — kinda Jekyll-Hyde style. Run off and hide from the pack. If you want a sports machine that is a cut above the ordinary and still not priced out of this world, then this Bertone-bodied bomb is it.

Now — back to my layout chalks and T-square. It was a great experience seeing how our cars are put through their paces.

I'd say Arnolt of Chicago has done the leadfoot fraternity a real favor in making this sports car available on the American market . . . **J. Bryce Gillespie.**

Fast cornering is the Arnolt's forte.

Distinctive styling makes it a crowd-stopper

Esthetic profile is unusual and appealing

Plenty of torque for fast ta[...]

Its aviation heritage is evident in the cockpit

NOW THE BRISTOL 406

The brilliant 406 is the latest of Bristol's high-performance cars. It has all the fine qualities of its predecessors—plus new features.

These include:

Larger, more flexible 2.2 litre engine

Servo-assisted disc brakes by Dunlop on all wheels

Two-door body

Increased interior room and comfort

Even larger luggage boot

The enduring high performance and smart appearance of the earlier models bear witness to the durability of Bristol cars—and to the pride and enthusiasm these cars inspire in their owners.

Bristol-engined cars continue to win races all over the world. Two out of the five British cars to complete this year's gruelling Le Mans 24-hour race were powered by Bristol engines.

BRISTOL →
406

BRISTOL CARS LIMITED

The New

BRISTOL

406

**1959
CARS**

A Luxury Two-door Saloon with Larger Engine, Disc Brakes and Improved Rear Suspension

SKILLED man-hours are, perhaps, the most expensive commodity in the post-war Western world. That fact accounts for the progressively greater price gap which exists between the good, the better and the best. In the automobile field in Britain, the third of these categories has always been associated with large size in accordance with a natural tradition carried down from the spacious days before World War I.

It is the belief of Bristol Cars, Ltd. (a subsidiary of The Bristol Aeroplane Co., Ltd.), that modern conditions have brought about a widening of the scope for quality of the highest order and that, just as a luxury penthouse may be more appropriate than a country mansion to the needs of some, so a medium-sized car designed in accordance with modern techniques and built to the highest standards of quality and behaviour may hold the greatest appeal for some motorists.

This thinking lies behind the latest production from Filton, which is announced today—the new Type 406 Bristol saloon, which supersedes the "405." The new model is a two-door saloon of medium size but surprisingly roomy accommodation, with superb finish and furnishing, built on a chassis that largely follows familiar Bristol practice, but differs in having an enlarged engine producing considerably more torque in the low and medium speed ranges, disc brakes all round, re-designed rear suspension and an all-steel frame for the aluminium-panelled body.

The price is £2,995 which, with £1,498 17s. Purchase Tax, brings the total cost to £4,493 17s.

*　　*　　*

Mechanically, the chassis follows the specification of the export-only "406 E" design shown at the Earls Court last October

Engine dimensions				Oil capacity	12 pints (sump)	Wheel type	Bolt-on pierced disc;
Cylinders	...	...	6	Cooling system ...	Pump, fan and		wide-base rims
Bore ...	...	...	68.69 mm.		thermostat	Tyre size	6.00—16
Stroke	...	...	99.64 mm.	Water capacity ...	16 pints	Steering gear ...	Rack and pinion
Cubic capacity	...		2,216 c.c.	Electrical system ...	Lucas 12-volt		
Piston area	...	...	34.5 sq. in.	Battery capacity ...	51 amp./hr.	**Dimensions**	
Valves	...	...	Inclined o.h.v.			Wheelbase	9 ft. 6 in.
			(pushrods)	**Transmission**		Track:	
Compression ratio	...		8.5	Clutch	Borg and Beck s.d.p.	Front	4 ft. 5 in.
				Gear ratios:		Rear	4 ft. 8 in.
Engine performance				Top (s/m)	4.27 (overdrive 3.32)	Overall length ...	16 ft. 4 in.
Max. power ...	...		105 b.h.p.	3rd (s/m)	5.52	Overall width ...	5 ft. 8 in.
at ...	...	...	4,700 r.p.m.	2nd (s/m)	7.79	Overall height ...	5 ft. 0 in.
Max. b.m.e.p.	...		144.5 lb./sq. in.	1st (freewheel) ...	15.42	Ground clearance ...	6½ in.
at ...	...	...	3,000 r.p.m.	Rev.	12.34	Turning circle ...	37 ft. 6 in.
B.H.P. per sq. in. pis-				Prop. shaft	Open	Dry weight	26⅞ cwt.
ton area ...	...		3.04	Final drive	Hypoid bevel		
Piston speed at max.						**Performance factors**	
power ...	...		3.070 ft./min.	**Chassis details**		(at dry weight)	
				Brakes	Dunlop disc	Piston area, sq. in.	
Engine details				Brake disc diameter	11¼ in. (pads 2⅛ in. dia.)	per ton	25.6
Carburetters	...		Three Solex down-	Friction lining area		Brake lining area,	
			draught (B32 P.B.1/7)	(disc brakes) ...	31.8 sq. in.	sq. in. per ton ...	23.6 (disc brakes)
Ignition timing con-				Suspension:		Top gear m.p.h. per	
trol...	...	...	Centrifugal and manual	Front	Independent (transverse	1,000 r.p.m. ...	18.8 (O/D 24.2)
Sparking plugs	...		K.L.G. P.Ten.L.70		leaf; anti-roll bar)	Top gear m.p.h. per	
Fuel pump ...	...		AC mechanical	Rear	Torsion bar (rigid	1,000 ft./min. piston	
Fuel capacity	...		18 gall. (incl. 2 reserve)		axle and Watt linkage)	speed	28.8 (O/D 37.1)
Oil filter ...	...		Vokes full-flow	Shock absorbers ...	Telescopic hydraulic	Litres per ton-mile ...	2,625 (O/D 2,030)

The New
BRISTOL
406

with a Beutler body. The increase in engine size by 245 c.c. to 2,216 c.c. has been brought about by a change in both bore and stroke. A cylinder block of substantially the same design is used, but the bore of the dry Brivadium cylinder liners has been increased by 2.69 mm., whilst the stroke has gone up by 3.64 mm. by the use of a new four-bearing counterbalanced crankshaft with longer throws.

Although the compression ratio remains unchanged at 8.5 to 1, new pistons are fitted to provide a more efficient combustion space. Instead of being of simple dome shape, the crowns are now more in the form of a truncated cone which, in conjunction with the hemispherical head, gives a better-shaped combustion space. The new pistons have three compression rings and one scraper, and also differ from the former design in that the ribs under the crown now run from boss to boss, whilst the skirt is split.

The familiar Bristol arrangement of direct pushrods and rockers to operate the inlet valves, with additional rockers from horizontal pushrods across the top of the light-alloy cylinder head to operate the exhausts, is retained. No change has been made

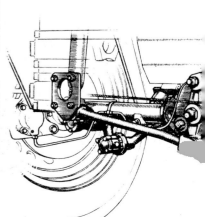

Left: The driving compartment has hooded instrument dials in front of the driver and walnut veneer facia panel and door cappings. Padded rolls above and below the facia are supplemented by a crash pad above the screen.

Right: Rear axle location is now by means of a transverse Watt linkage pivoting on a central casting and anchored to the chassis through mounting plates; a single fore-and-aft radius arm links the axle to a cross-member.

Right: Changes in the inclined-ohv engine include a four-bearing crankshaft with longer throws, and truncated-cone piston crowns to give a better-shaped combustion space.

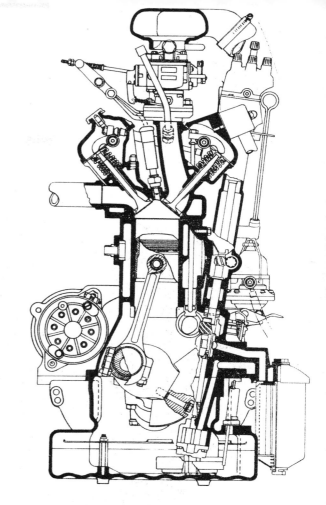

in either timing or valve size, as the whole object in the new engine has been to provide increased torque in the low and medium r.p.m. ranges rather than to improve top-end performance. Thus the maximum power output remains at 105 b.h.p. but is now delivered at 4,700 r.p.m. in place of 5,000 r.p.m., whilst the torque at 2,000 r.p.m. has gone up from 100.9 lb. ft. to 113.4 lb. ft., and at 3,000 r.p.m. from 115.3 lb. ft. to 130 lb. ft. As one would expect, these changes in characteristic were found in a brief drive to have made an enormous difference to top-gear performance.

Incidental engine improvements include the use of a new timing-chain tensioner, which is of the rubber-slipper type actuated by hydraulic pressure, and a new and very much more accessible dipstick.

The gearbox remains as on the 405 model, together with the Laycock-de Normanville overdrive which is applied to top gear only and controlled by a switch on the facia so arranged that when a change down into third is made, the switch reverts to the direct-drive position automatically. Now of Salisbury manufacture, the rear axle has a ratio of 4.27 to 1 in place of the former 4.22 to 1. In practice, this very slight lowering of the overall ratios is compensated for by the fitting of 6.00-16 tyres in place of the former 5.75-16 size. The tyres are the new Dunlop Gold Seal or Michelin, but Dunlop Road Speed covers can be supplied if required.

The interesting point about the rear axle is its new location arrangement. As before, longitudinal torsion bars coupled to the axle by transverse links are used as the springing medium, but in place of the former central A-bracket, the new design incorporates a Watt linkage for lateral location and a single central arm to provide for torque. For this purpose, the normal axle cover plate is replaced by a light-alloy casting which, in the centre, has a mounting for the transverse Watt linkage, the extremities of the links being anchored to a new stout pressing which connects the up-swept side members of the chassis and also provides a medium for carrying the new enlarged petrol tank (18 gall. in place of 16).

continued overleaf

Left: A gaitered transverse leaf-spring forms the lower link in the i.f.s. system, the upper wishbone straddling an inclined telescopic damper and having an anti-roll bar anchored to it through bushed pivots.

Right: Reutter reclining seats are used, a special Bristol addition being the hinged top of each squab, which can be swung up to form a head-rest when the seat is in the reclining position.

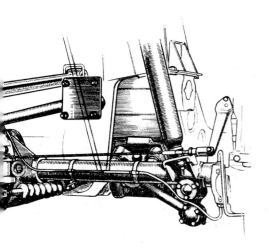

Right: Extra elbow room in the wide rear compartment is provided by recesses above the armrests which also provide deep pockets illuminated by concealed dual-purpose reading lamps.

The New BRISTOL 406

The deep, fully-trimmed boot has a flat floor and an absence of ob-structions. Auto-matic illumination is provided.

At the top of the axle cover plate, a boss is formed to accommodate a single central fore and aft torque arm, the forward end of which is anchored to a cross member. Rubber bushes are employed throughout so that no additional maintenance is introduced.

The new Dunlop disc brakes are of the now-familiar self-adjusting type, with vacuum servo boost to their hydraulic pressure and separate callipers for the handbrake. An interesting point is the use of a pair of pulleys in the handbrake cable to avoid employing a curved enclosed cable with its inevitable friction.

The servo unit is well protected, being located in the offside front wing compartment which it shares with the battery and screen-washer reservoir. A similar compartment on the near-side houses the spare wheel, this novel arrangement of swing-up front wing valances being retained from the 405; a detail improvement, however, lies in the use of a carriage-lock plus a safety catch.

The new body has an all-steel frame panelled in aluminium and, in accordance with normal Bristol practice, is welded to the very stout box-section chassis. Particular care has been taken with sound insulation, Mutacel sound-deadening material being used on all surfaces liable to drumming, whilst the entire under-chassis is treated with Novaseal.

As will be seen from the accompanying photographs, the new body, whilst still retaining typical Bristol characteristics, is both more modern and more elegant as well as being distinctly roomier than before. Although the wheelbase remains at 9 ft. 6 in. the overall length has gone up from 15 ft. 9¼ in. to 16 ft. 4 in., this enabling both head and knee-room in the rear seats to be increased considerably without sacrifice of harmonious proportions. Wider internally, the body is unchanged in external breadth. Actually the track has been increased slightly (mainly to accommodate the disc brakes), but the real gain has been obtained by reducing the tumble-in at waist level, so giving 4 in. more width to the upper structure. This has enabled a broader windscreen and rear window to be used, which, together with the absence of central pillars, give quite exceptional all-round vision.

So far as seating is concerned, these changes have made a big difference in elbow room, the width across both front and rear seats now being no less than 55 in. At the rear, even more elbow room is offered because the trim is recessed to take a deep pocket

behind the arm rest on each side, and the upper portion of this pocket provides something like 6 in. additional elbow room; the pocket itself is sufficiently deep to "swallow" a large vacuum flask in an upright position.

The front seats are of the Reutter type in which the squabs can be instantly adjusted to any position from near-upright to fully-reclining merely by the operation of a small lever. In the case of the Bristol, a further refinement is that the upper sections of the squabs are hinged and can be swung forward to provide a head rest in the reclining position.

Wide, but not cumbersome, doors make entry easy to both compartments and it is, in fact, easier to enter and leave the rear seats of the two-door 406 than the four-door 405 model.

In addition to the two deep pockets already mentioned, there are useful map pockets on the doors and a lockable cubby hole in the facia board, together with a small shelf ahead of the driver. At the rear, there is a very commodious boot.

Automatic illumination is arranged for the boot and there are also interior lights for both the cubby locker and the rear-seat pockets, all being arranged so as to provide a reading light for the adjacent occupant without dazzle to the driver. In addition there is a normal roof light above the centre of the screen, controlled both by courtesy switches in the doors and a separate over-riding switch.

Exterior illumination is equally thorough. The Marchal head-lamps give an asymmetrical beam in the dipped position for easy overtaking, whilst both a fog lamp and a long-range lamp are situated in the nose recess in front of the new grille. A distinctive touch is given by a small hidden lamp which illuminates this recess when the sidelamps are alight. Flashing amber direction indicators are supplemented by small amber beacons on the roof above the doors.

Detail Refinements

As one would expect, the range of instruments on the "406" keeps the driver unusually well informed of what is going on. All the dials are grouped in a hooded panel clearly visible through the two-spoke, finger-grip wheel and they comprise a speedometer (designed to have no "flatter"), rev. counter, oil-pressure gauge, clock, water and oil thermometers, ammeter and fuel gauge. Instrument lighting is rheostat-controlled and an ignition advance-retard, a hand throttle and a reserve petrol switch are provided. The heater and demister controls are also unusually comprehensive and allow, when required, for cold-air demisting with a warm air supply to the body.

Other refinements include a telescopic steering column, a cigar lighter, a windscreen washer (which, at the press of a button, serves both to squirt water on the screen and operate the wipers for sufficiently long to clear the glass, when they automatically switch themselves off), ashtrays for all four passengers, and twin universally-mounted vizors.

The whole interior finish is beautifully carried out in the highest grade leather and a note of luxury is provided by walnut veneer for the facia panel and door cappings. A sensible safety feature is the provision of padded rolls both above and below the facia panel and also a safety pad above the screen.

Excellent vision is a feature of the new Type 406, as this picture shows: note the thin screen pillars, absence of door pillars and large rear window.

BRISTOL 406 with four-wheel disc brakes

Typically Bristol in line the new 406 is roomier and although the overall length is greater the wheelbase remains the same as that of the model it supercedes. Visibility is helped by large rear window and windscreen with very slim pillars

FOR some years Bristols have been producing high performance 2-litre sports saloons of medium size equipped in luxurious fashion. The new Type 406 is a logical development of the previous range of models, but the price of the new car has increased by £807 over that of the Type 405 which it replaces.

Main differences in the new car are an increase in engine size bringing the capacity up to 2,216 c.c., the fitting of Dunlop disc brakes on all four wheels (instead of to the front wheels only), improved rear suspension and a new body giving greater accommodation without increase in width. The chassis of the new model is similar to that of the "406 E" car with the Beutler body shown at Earls Court last year. Increased capacity engine has been effected by increasing the bore by 2.69 mm. and the stroke by 3.64 mm. by using a new longer throw four-bearing crankshaft. Maximum power remains at 105 b.h.p. but is obtained at 4,700 r.p.m. instead of 5,000 r.p.m.; the new engine produces more torque lower down which should improve top gear performance, and a figure of 129 lb. ft. at 3,000 r.p.m. is quoted. The compression ratio remains the same at 8.5 : 1 but combustion chamber design has been altered.

The rear axle which is now made by Salisbury has a ratio of 4.27 : 1 in place of the previous 4.22 : 1 but the overall gearing is unaltered since 6.00 × 16 tyres are fitted in place of 5.75 × 16. Location is improved and is now by Watt's linkage for lateral location and a central radius arm linking the axle to a chassis crossmember. Longitudinal torsion bars are still used as the suspension medium.

Dunlop disc brakes are of the self-adjusting type and are assisted by a vacuum-servo boost system. The servo unit is located in a special compartment in the offside front wing together with the battery and screen washer reservoir. The spare wheel is also kept in the nearside wing. A feature of the 406 is that a carriage lock as well as a safety catch is used to retain the valances.

The new body is built in the normal Bristol fashion—aluminium panelled steel frame and is of typical Bristol line. The overall length has been increased from 15 ft. 9¼ in. to 16 ft. 4 in. but the wheelbase remains the same at 9 ft. 6 in. Width is unchanged externally but internally has been increased by 4 in. giving more elbow room which is further improved at the rear where the trim is recessed providing a pocket behind the armrest some 10 in. deep. Visibility is greatly improved by the use of very thin screen pillars and by a wide windscreen and a large rear window. Two very wide doors permit easy entry into the car which has Reutter type front seats. These have squabs which can be adjusted for angle by the operation of a small lever. A Bristol touch is the provision of retractable headrests on top of the seat squabs which fold flat when not in use.

Maps and oddments can be accommodated in the door pockets, in a lockable cubby hole on the dashboard and in a tray ahead of the driver. Illumination is provided in the boot, in the cubby locker and in the pockets in the rear seat arms, and the latter is arranged to provide a reading light for the rear seat occupants without dazzling the driver. A roof light above the centre of the screen is controlled by courtesy switches in the doors.

Instruments are very comprehensive and are situated in a binnacle in front of the driver, lighting is controlled by a rheostat. An advance/retard ignition lever is fitted. Among the other refinements are a telescopic steering column, a cigar lighter, and a windscreen washer which at a touch of the button both squirts the windscreen and switches on the wipers.

Finish is in true luxury fashion, walnut veneer covers the dashboard and door cappings; the dashboard is provided with rubber padding as a safety measure. Fine quality carpet covers the floor and upholstery is in high grade leather.

In all, a very good looking and sensible motor car the Bristol 406 will appeal to the more affluent enthusiast for performance and luxury.—D.S.   ★

Driving compartment of the new 406 showing the luxurious Reutter seats with adjustable squabs and with retractable headrests. Comprehensive instruments are arranged before the driver in a binnacle in the walnut dashboard. Note rubber crash padding above and below panel

Very slim pillars and the absence of quarter vents ensure excellent vision

*New Bristol Type 406:
Two-Door Saloon
with Increased Space:
Engine Capacity
Raised to 2.2 Litres:
Dunlop Disc Brakes*

SEVENTH OF THE LINE

TO replace the Type 405 four-door saloon which was introduced by Bristol Cars, Ltd., in October, 1954, a new Type 406 two-door saloon is announced. A departure has been made from the previous policy of manufacturing the bodies within their own works, for the coachwork is constructed by Jones Brothers, of Willesden, to Bristol design. It is much roomier, with increased headroom, and better appointed, and the engine capacity has been increased from 1,971 c.c. to 2,216 c.c. by enlarging the bore and lengthening the stroke. The object of this has been to make the new car more tractable than its predecessor, without sacrifice of performance.

Basically the chassis is unchanged, but an improved method of rear axle location has been adopted, as have Dunlop disc brakes for all four wheels. Much thought has been given to passenger comfort, as can be judged from the fact that no optional extras are listed other than a radio to choice, but there has been a considerable increase in price, the new model costing £2,995 basic, to which purchase tax of £1,498 17s is added for U.K. buyers, making a total of £4,493 17s ex works. The policy of the company is to produce this one model, and no drophead version is projected at present.

Engine capacity has been increased to the maximum possible within the framework of the previous design without altering cylinder centres. As the unit utilizes a four-bearing crankshaft, the spacing between Nos. 1 and 2, 3 and 4, and 5 and 6 cylinders is narrower than that between Nos. 2 and 3 and 4 and 5, where the in-

termediate crankshaft bearings are placed. These narrow lands were the limiting factor in deciding the bore size which could be used; they have not been reduced by the amount of the increase in bore size, for the cylinder bores are fitted with Brivadium (high nickel content) dry liners, and these are thinner in section than previously. The dimensional increase of the bores is from 66 mm (2.598in) to 68.69 mm (2.705in). Stroke has been lengthened from 96 mm (3.779in) to 99.64 mm (3.923in).

A feature of the crankshaft is that it is manufactured from nitriding steel, which enables the journals to have almost glass hardness without any fear of distortion during the hardening process. Copperlead, steel-backed bearings are used for the mains and big-ends, and there are bolt-on balance weights, for relief of main bearing loads, placed on each side of the intermediate main bearings and on the inside of the front and rear mains. There is a torsional vibration damper on the front of the shaft.

On the exhaust side of the cylinder block the water jackets run the entire length of the bore, but on the inlet side the jacket length is reduced to provide clearance for the tappets, which are inserted through a hole in the side of the crankcase, and enclosed by a cover plate. In the longitudinal plane of the cylinder block, water space is provided between those bores where a main bearing panel occurs, i.e., between Nos. 2 and 3 and Nos. 4 and 5, and at the ends of the front and rear cylinders.

Hemispherical combustion chambers are formed in the aluminium alloy cylinder head, and the valves, which operate on austenitic steel inserts, have an included

angle of 80 deg, equally disposed on either side of the vertical centre line. These valves are operated from a single, side-mounted camshaft. The inlet valves are operated directly by means of vertical pushrods and rockers. For each exhaust valve there is an intermediate bell-crank rocking lever and a secondary near-horizontal pushrod which operates the valve rocker.

Vertical intake ports are retained, and these are fed by three Solex 32 PBI/7 downdraught carburettors. There is much to be said for the vertical inlet type of port, for it permits of good filling, but it does raise engine height, and hence bonnet line.

A minor change is incorporated in the carburettors of this new type 110 engine. A feature of this basic model of Solex carburettor is the use of an enrichment pump to provide an extra injection of fuel at the change-over point from slow running to main jets; it usually takes the form of a feed pipe into the main choke area. Development work revealed that the Bristol engine did not require this device, but there was a slight occasional hesitation at this change-over point. The enrichment pump is, therefore, retained, but the fuel passages in the carburettor have been re-routed, so that the function of the pump is to maintain the level of fuel in the slow running or pilot feed chamber at the change-over point.

There are individual exhaust ports in the cylinder head which connect to two three-branch manifolds, the outlet pipes of which lead to a single silencer with one tailpipe.

Maximum power output of the enlarged engine is the same as that of the previous 2-litre unit, at 105 b.h.p., but arising from the longer stroke it now occurs at 4,700 r.p.m. instead of 5,000 r.p.m. Of more importance is the fact that the torque curve is fuller and smoother throughout its range, and its peak, which occurs at 3,000 r.p.m. instead of 3,750 r.p.m., is raised from 123 to 129 lb/ft.

No changes have been made to the gear box, which is in unit with the engine; it has four forward speeds, with synchro-

This unusual aspect emphasizes the clean lines. Air intake for the ventilating system is the flush grille in the rear edge of the bonnet

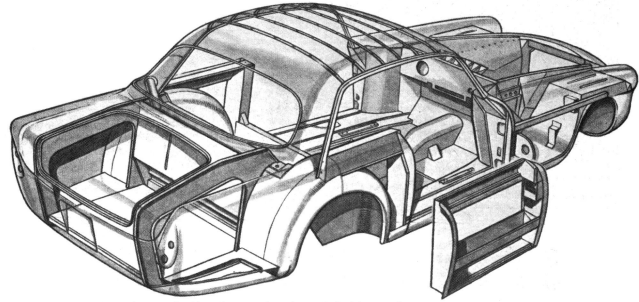

The body is constructed entirely in metal, with steel structural members and aluminium panels. This drawing shows the stress-carrying members before the panels are fixed in position

mesh of the baulk-ring type on the upper three ratios. Control is by a remote central lever. A feature of bottom gear is the use of a freewheel, which permits easy engagement on the overrun without the use of the clutch. A Laycock de Normanville overdrive operates on top gear only. It is selected by an upward-action tumbler switch on the facia. If a change-down to third gear is made with overdrive top selected, this switch drops out of engagement automatically, so that on the subsequent change-up direct top is available. This is a very desirable feature, and it is surprising that it has not been more widely adopted on other cars with overdrive.

No changes have been made in the basic chassis frame which, as hitherto, is assembled within the Bristol works; the side members are widely spaced, and of box section. The main floor is welded directly to the frame, as is the superstructure at the rear for tank mountings and that portion forming the framework of the luggage compartment.

At the front the two side members taper inward and terminate in tuning-fork arms to which the complete front assembly is bolted. A transverse leaf spring, in conjunction with a long upper wishbone at each side, are the main elements of the front suspension.

Forward of the leaf spring is the rack and pinion steering unit, with a steering rod at each end connecting directly to the forward-facing steering arms. An increase in roll stiffness has been achieved

by enlarging the diameter of the front anti-roll bar from $\frac{1}{16}$in to $\frac{13}{16}$in. The front spring is fitted with gaiters to retain lubricant, and the only points on the chassis which need the attention of a grease-gun are the propeller shaft and pedal bushes, the remainder being looked after by a one-shot lubrication system. This is foot-operated by a plunger head, mounted above and between the brake and accelerator pedals.

Considerable changes have been made in the method of location for the rear axle, which is now of Salisbury manufacture, the earlier types being of Bristol design with gears made by E.N.V. As previously, the suspension medium is a torsion bar placed beneath each chassis side member, and operated by an arm and drop link from the outer ends of the axle casing.

Formerly the axle was located in both planes by an A-bracket mounted from the top of the banjo casing. It has been replaced by an H-section light alloy torque link for fore and aft location, with thick rubber bushings at each end. Transverse location is by means of a Watts linkage with rubber bushes, the free link being in the centre, and the anchorage points attached to each side of the steel superstructure beneath the fuel tank. The anchorage points for these linkages on the axle are formed on a special cast light alloy cover for the differential gears; the balance link for operation of the hand-brake is also

A lift-up panel behind the right front wheel encloses the battery, screen wash bottle and electrical controls: the spare wheel is in a similar compartment on the left side

(Right) The veneered facia and cowled instrument panel: shock absorbing, leather-covered rolls are used on upper and lower edges of the facia. There are five outlets for demisting the screen. Below (left): the passenger's seat in a reclined position with the head rest raised; (centre): there is a central folding arm rest in the rear seat, with a courtesy light above each side pocket; (right): the wide doors open to right angles and the windows have separate frames

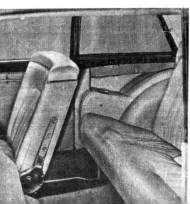

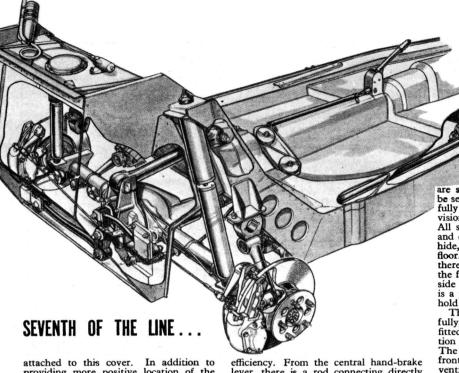

SEVENTH OF THE LINE...

attached to this cover. In addition to providing more positive location of the rear axle, this new rear-end layout has lowered the roll centre at the rear by 4½in which, it is claimed, noticeably improves the handling.

Dunlop disc brakes of 11⅛in diameter are fitted front and rear. Each caliper contains a circular pad of 2⅛in diameter on each side, and servo assistance is of the Lockheed suspended vacuum type. Separate, mechanically operated calipers are used at the rear for the hand-brake, and much thought has gone into eliminating friction from the linkage to improve efficiency. From the central hand-brake lever, there is a rod connecting directly to a cable which passes over two pulleys to connect to the operating lever attached to the rear axle. From here, a cable at each side operates the wheel calipers, and thus the use of conduit is avoided throughout the linkage.

The new body is unmistakably Bristol in character, but it is very much more roomy than the 405 and, as might be expected, the finish and detail equipment are of the highest order. Earlier Bristol models have had rather pronounced shoulders but these have now been eliminated, with the result that the screen is 4in wider, and approximately the same amount of extra width has been provided in the rear seats. Replacement of the A-bracket for location of the rear axle has enabled the seats to be lowered and, in conjunction with the raising of the roof contour line by 2in, between 4in and 5in of extra headroom is made available. These rear-end changes have also provided more fore and aft latitude so that, even with the front seats in their rearmost position, adequate room is available for the rear passengers' knees.

Reutter individual front seats are standard equipment. Their backs can be set to any position between vertical and fully reclining; a refinement is the provision of a hinged headrest on each squab. All seats are upholstered with Dunlopillo and covered in best quality crushed grain hide, and there is Wilton carpet on the floor. Pockets are provided in each door, there is a large, lockable compartment in the facia on the passenger's side, and beside each side arm-rest at the rear there is a pocket, sufficiently deep and wide to hold a Thermos flask.

The windows in each door wind down fully, and no front quarter-lights are fitted—an aid to good vision, in conjunction with noticeably slim screen pillars. The rear passengers' side windows are front-hinged for ventilation. Heating and ventilation provision is most comprehensive. There are four controls—to regulate the amount of heat, to vary the amount of air directed to the screen for demisting, for general distribution internally, and for direct entry of cool air.

A full range of instruments is housed in a separate, cowled panel immediately in front of the driver, and clearly visible through the two-spoked steering wheel. Main controls, such as ignition switch and lights, are on the right side of the steering column, with the auxiliary switches on the lower edge of the facia on the right-hand side.

Steel framework is used throughout for body construction, this framework being welded to the chassis frame. It is panelled entirely in aluminium, and the doors are constructed wholly in this material. Hinged panels in the front wing valances give access on the left to the spare wheel, and on the right to the battery, screen wash bottle, fuses and junction boxes, and the brake vacuum servo unit. Because the spare wheel is kept out of the luggage locker, storage space is considerable, for side panniers, formed in the sections behind the wheels, provide useful storage for soft baggage.

At the rear there is a vestigial fin at each side, with the grouped rear lights below. There are three turn indicator lights, a miniature one being provided on

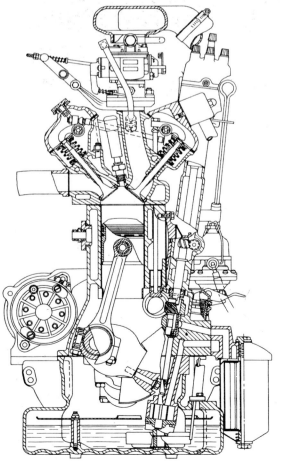

Engine cross-section, showing how the valve gear is arranged to operate opposed valves in a hemispherical combustion chamber from a single side camshaft

ENGINE

No. of cylinders	...	6 in line
Bore and stroke	...	68.69 x 99.64mm (2.70 x 3.92in)
Displacement	...	2,216 c.c. (135 cu in)
Valve position	...	Opposed, in hemispherical combustion chamber, pushrods and rockers
Compression ratio	...	8.5 to 1
Max. b.h.p. (nett)	...	105 at 4,700 r.p.m.
Max. b.m.e.p. (nett)	...	144 lb per sq in at 3,000 r.p.m.
Max. torque (nett)	...	129 lb ft at 3,000 r.p.m.
Carburettor	...	3 Solex B 32 PBI/7 Downdraught
Fuel pump	...	A.C. mechanical
Tank capacity	...	18 Imp. gallons—including 2 reserve (82 litres)
Sump capacity	...	12 pints (6.8 litres)
Oil filter	...	Vokes full flow
Cooling system	...	Fan, pump and thermostat
Battery	...	12 volt 51 ampere hour

TRANSMISSION

Clutch	...	Borg and Beck s.d.p. 8in dia.
Gear box	...	4 speed (overdrive on top). Synchromesh on 2nd, 3rd and top (freewheel on first). Central gear lever.
Overall gear ratios	...	Overdrive top 3.32; top 4.27; 3rd 5.52; 2nd 7.79; 1st 15.42
Final drive	...	Hypoid bevel, 4.27 to 1

CHASSIS

Brakes	...	Dunlop discs with Lockheed vacuum-servo assistance
Disc dia., shoe width		11.25 dia. F. and R. (2.25in dia. pads)
Suspension: front	...	Independent with upper wishbone and lower transverse leaf spring; anti-roll bar
rear		Torsion bars with rigid axle controlled by torque arm and Watts linkage
Dampers	...	Telescopic F. and R.
Wheels	...	Pressed steel (5 studs)
Tyre size	...	6.00 x 16in Dunlop Gold Seal
Steering	...	Rack and pinion
Steering wheel	...	2 spoke, 17in dia.
Turns, lock to lock	...	3

DIMENSIONS

Wheelbase	...	9ft 6in (289.6 cm)
Track: front and rear		4ft 5in (134.6 cm) F, 4ft 8in (142.2 cm) R.
Overall length	...	16ft 4in (498 cm)
Overall width	...	5ft 8in (172.7 cm)
Overall height	...	5ft 0in (152.4 cm)
Ground clearance	...	6.5in (16.5 cm)
Turning circle	...	37ft 6in (11.43 m)
Kerb weight	...	3,010 lb—26.9 cwt (1,365 kg)

PERFORMANCE DATA

M.P.H. at 1,000 r.p.m.	...	Top 18.8 O/d top 24.2
Torque lb ft per cu in engine capacity	...	0.956
Brake surface area swept by linings	...	520 sq in
Weight distribution (kerb weight)	...	F. 50.6 per cent R. 49.4 per cent

each side of the roof panelling, and all are amber-coloured. Marchal lamps are fitted, the main lights being augmented by fog and long-range lamps placed in the air intake, forward of the new concave grille. The filler for the fuel tank, in the left-hand rear quarter panel, has a lockable flap, and the total tank capacity is 18 gallons, including two reserve.

Brief Impressions

During a short run in one of the early prototypes, it was immediately apparent that the increased engine capacity, in spite of a slight increase in the car's total weight, has improved flexibility. One example is that the car will pull away quite smoothly in top gear without protest from about 23 m.p.h. All-round vision is excellent, and seat comfort very good indeed. It was not possible to obtain any performance figures; the manufacturers state that they tally almost exactly with those of the previous Type 405, which had a claimed top speed in excess of 100 m.p.h.

In producing this latest version of an established design, the manufacturers have aimed for more luxury and comfort; they appear to have succeeded, but at the cost of a substantial increase in price.

Polished nave plates with ventilation holes are fitted to the wheels. There is a reversing light on each side of the rear number plate

The 1960 Bristol has relocated fog and spot lights, now behind the front bumper.

Bristol

Production of the latest Bristol car, known as the type 406, remains unchanged for 1960. The model, a two-door four-seater sedan, introduced last year, is powered by a 2.2-liter engine developed from the famous Bristol two-liter which is still in production for the A.C. Ace and Aceca automobiles. The higher-powered engine in the 406 (developing 105 hp) gives increased performance and improved torque in the lower engine speed range. In the 1960 model shown, the fog and spot lights have been repositioned behind the front bumper.

The body, giving an increase in interior space, still maintains the aerodynamic design characteristic of previous Bristol cars. An adjustable steering column and sliding bucket seat insure that the driver can be at ease. The instruments are grouped directly in front of the driver, in a protruding panel which eliminates reflections. The driver in this car sits on the right side.

The luxurious seats, finished in crushed grain hide over foam rubber, provide superb comfort for long distance and high-speed travel. Good lateral support for all passengers has received particular attention and excellent rear vision has been provided by a large wrap-around window.

The provision of Dunlop servo-assisted disc brakes on all wheels provides greatly improved and fade-free braking at the high speeds of which the car is capable.

Incidentally, the type 406 model replaces the type 405 four-door sedan which was originally introduced by Bristol in 1954. The coachwork is constructed by Jones Brothers to Bristol design. The car features very slim pillars, and the absence of side vent-window posts insures excellent vision. Actually, the chassis is unchanged basically, but an improved method of rear axle location has been adopted. Maximum power output of the overhead valve six-cylinder engine is 105 bhp at 4700 rpm. No changes have been made to the gearbox, which is in unit with the engine; it has four forward speeds with synchromesh on the upper three gears. A feature of the bottom gear is the use of a freewheel, which permits easy engine engagement without the use of the clutch. A Laycock de Normanville overdrive operates from top gear only. It is operated by a toggle switch on the instrument panel. If a change down to third gear is made with overdrive top selected, this switch drops out of engagement automatically, so that on the subsequent change-up, direct top is available. This, according to reports, is a very desirable feature.

Interesting is a lift-up panel located behind the right front wheel which encloses the battery, window-wash bottle, and electrical controls; the spare wheel is in a similar compartment on the left side.

For the comfort of passengers, the front seats can be reclined and the built-in headrest raised. A central folding armrest is located in the rear seat, with a courtesy light below each side pocket. The wide doors open to right angles and the windows have separate frames, similar to convertible-type construction. ■

Bristol Cars, Ltd., P.O. Box 3, Filton House, Bristol, England.

USED CARS on the Road

No. 153—1952 BRISTOL 401

PRICES: Secondhand £875; New—basic £2,270, with tax, £3,533

Acceleration from rest through gears:

to 30 m.p.h.	6.0 sec	20 to 40 m.p.h. (top gear)	13.2 sec
to 50 m.p.h.	13.3 sec	30 to 50 m.p.h. (top gear)	18.6 sec
to 60 m.p.h.	18.6 sec		
to 70 m.p.h.	26.2 sec	Standing quarter-mile	21.0 sec

Petrol consumption	18-23 m.p.g.
Oil consumption	negligible
Mileometer reading	87,667
Date first registered	April 1952

Provided for test by Francis Motors, 393, Humberstone Road, Leicester, Leicestershire. Telephone: Leicester 66304.

The smooth shape of the Bristol is unbroken by door handles: push buttons are used, which still work well despite weakening in the door springs A button, concealed by the rear armrest, opens the luggage locker lid

QUALITY cars may generally be expected to survive a high mileage without too extensive mechanical deterioration, and to be rattle-free and still pleasant to drive after extended use. With a mileometer reading of 87,667, this Bristol is certainly in the "high mileage" class—although it has averaged little more than the usual 10,000 miles a year—yet it remains comfortable to travel in, feels pleasantly taut and rigid, and is capable of covering the ground rapidly in safety.

It is likely that overhaul work has been carried out on the engine at some time, although no evidence of recent attention to it was seen under the bonnet. The engine—a six-cylinder, long-stroke unit of 1,971 c.c.—starts well and warms up rapidly from a cold start. Valve gear noise is audible throughout the speed range. For smooth torque, particularly at low speeds, use should be made of the ignition control on the facia to retard the spark. Above 2,000 r.p.m. the engine pulls strongly, and the car performs well provided the driver is not reluctant to take full advantage of the excellently-spaced ratios of the four-speed gear box. The central, floor-mounted gear lever is very light to operate.

On all three upper ratios the synchromesh is effective, enabling rapid upward or downward gear changes to be made, and on first gear there is an automatic freewheel. This enables bottom to be engaged (on the overrun) without use of the clutch while the car is on the move. The intermediate gears are quiet but, when the engine is pulling, a pronounced whine is audible from the back axle. Slight clutch judder sometimes occurs when moving off from rest.

Some weakness is evident in the spring dampers. On rough surfaces the passengers are considerably jolted, and there is often a degree of high frequency pitching. The suspension is independent at the front, using a transverse spring, and by torsion bars at the rear. Directional stability and cornering are very good, and on wet roads the car gives confidence to the driver; there is a slight tendency to understeer. Benefits of the aerodynamic styling of the car are felt in terms of the low level of wind noise, but the Bristol is not immune to the effects of cross winds. Steering, by rack and pinion, is light and very precise; there is a strong self-centring action.

For the Bristol's ability to cruise at 80 m.p.h. when road

The seats are readily adjustable for reach or squab angle. As the Bristol has only two doors, the seat squabs are arranged to hinge forward for access to the rear compartment. Chassis lubrication is by one-shot pedal

conditions permit, the brakes are adequate. Pedal loads do not have to be excessively high and, in normal motoring conditions, fade was not experienced. The hand brake is conveniently placed between the individual front seats, and it holds the car effectively on a steep gradient.

As far as appearance is concerned, the car still looks graceful and dignified from outside, despite a measure of deterioration of the black paintwork. Some corners and bodywork edges have been retouched, and elsewhere the finish has faded slightly, and lost its glossy lustre. The chromium has been polished away on parts of the window surrounds, but elsewhere it is spoilt only by shallow scratches; for the age of the car the lack of rust on the chromium and bodywork is commendable.

Light beige is the colour of the interior leatherwork of the seats and door trim; the leather shows fewer signs of wear than one would expect. Maroon seat covers, now in the luggage locker, have protected the seats, but are themselves in need of cleaning before further use. The seats are not particularly well shaped, and give little lateral support, but they do not become uncomfortable on a long journey. Wear on the floor carpets is mild, and the roof lining, of hard plastic, has lasted well. Slight weathering of the wooden fascia panel is noticed.

The instruments are well placed, although the general arrangement is not neat. The speedometer and rev counter needles swing at low speeds, but settle down to steady readings as the car accelerates. Probably the least satisfactory feature of the Bristol is its poor visibility. The side windows are large, but the tiny rear window and divided windscreen (enclosed by thick pillars) give a poor view of the road behind and ahead of the car. There is a full length crack in the left section of the windscreen. Unpleasantly near to the front occupants' heads are roller sun blinds—standard on the new car—and there is a rear window blind, now very soiled.

An oil temperature gauge is standard on the 401; this happens to be the only part of the Bristol's equipment which is not working. There are also a reasonably powerful fresh-air heater, a windscreen washer and a radio among the accessories added to the car. The radio—an H.M.V. set—is faulty, and lacks volume except when tuned to the Light Programme (long wave).

With the exceptions of a jack and wheel nut spanner, there are no tools on the Bristol. The car has a starting handle, housed on the right of the engine compartment. It is well shod, having four Michelin X tyres, less than half-worn. The spare, housed in a hinged tray below the luggage locker, is well worn.

Probably an early casualty on the Bristol will be its battery. The dynamo charge rate is scarcely sufficient to cope with the radio and head lamps; after a night run the battery was exhausted and would not operate the starter. The head lamps, incidentally, had to be adjusted so that the car could be used at night without dazzling oncoming drivers; even then other road users obviously were troubled by the scatter of light from the dipped beams.

In many small ways the Bristol reveals its age; but remembering its eight years one can only admit that it has lasted well, and it remains a satisfying car to drive. In the same way the price asked for the car, which may seem high now, should be related to the original cost in 1952.

New Cars

**The season for new cars has arrived as manufacturers prepare
for the salons**

*The restyled walnut fascia of the Bristol 407 with pushbuttons
for the Chrysler Torque-Flyte automatic transmission
visible at the right*

Bristol 407

*The smooth lines of the 406 body remain almost
unchanged*

*Biggest deviation from earlier Bristols is this 5,130 cm³
Canadian built Chrysler V8 engine—it develops 250 bhp
gross at 4,400 rev/min and has a maximum torque of
340 lb ft—this gives the car over 100 per cent power
increase for less than 20 per cent weight increase*

Motor cars are such complex pieces of machinery that every manufacturer has to rely on outside suppliers for some components, and small volume producers by necessity have to buy in more of their running gear than the industry giants. The history of car manufacture is so riddled with bankruptcies that those small companies which stay in business do so by building individualistic cars around relatively common or garden mechanicals. The use of a proprietary engine/gearbox assembly has kept many from falling off the economic tightrope, but the penalty of this compromise for these companies — most of them at the prestige and performance end of the market — has been having to settle for insufficient power.

Back in the early sixties, they began to discover American V8 engines. There was much to commend the solution: these V8 engines were highly developed, built in huge numbers, smooth, powerful, inexpensive, unstressed, reliable . . . and available. The first two British companies to hit on the idea were Bristol and Jensen, beginning a trend which would be imitated by Gordon Keeble, AC, Sunbeam, TVR, De Tomaso, Iso, Monteverdi and others.

The launch of the 5.1-litre Chrysler V8 powered Bristol 407 in 1961 was a radical step for a company noted for its conservatism. Its visually identical predecessor, the 406, looked very different from the anglicised BMW lines of the first car from Filton, the 400 of 1947, but under the skin it used a 2.2-litre straight-six engine descended from the BMW unit of the first car. While this relatively modest engine, in 2-litre form, had endowed Bristols through the fifties with 100mph performance, many lesser saloons had now developed to the point where Bristols were no longer so superior in speed and flexibility. More power was badly needed: an American V8 was the obvious solution, offering the smoothness essential for a relaxing Grand Tourer.

Careful work

Bristol worked carefully on the Chrysler engine, substituting solid tappets for hydraulic ones to allow higher engine speeds, fitting a special high-lift camshaft and four-barrel Carter carburettor, and installing twin electric fans to reduce noise and save space. An output of 250bhp at 4400rpm was quoted, but when road testers got their hands on the car they felt that this may have been an exaggeration. Whatever the real figure, it was good enough to propel the 407 to 125mph and give sprightly acceleration, borne out by a 0-60mph time of 9.2secs. If there was a drawback, it was that front suspension and steering changes meant that a less precise Marles worm-type steering box replaced the previous rack and pinion system, but no road testers at the time commented adversely.

One might have expected the motoring press to be a little circumspect about a car which typified traditional British virtues, but used, of all things, an American engine. But they sung the 407's praises loudly. The Motor summarised its feelings like this: 'Sheer performance is combined so well with quiet comfort and smooth controllability in the new Bristol 407 that this English car with a Canadian power unit provides some of the best motoring that money can buy.' The approval of the big Bristol's refinement, smoothness and silence was no surprise, but John Bolster, writing in Autosport, was especially appreciative of the car's finesse at speed: 'The riding and handling are much more in the tradition of British sports cars. Initially, the springing feels quite hard, though it gives a comfortable ride at speed. The car oversteers slightly but is well balanced, and there is enough power to slide the rear end when this is convenient.'

Bristol's policy of gradual evolution meant that the 407 had only a two-year innings before being replaced by the 408, whose main differences were cosmetic. The 'hole in the wall' grille which had been a Bristol feature since the 404 was replaced by a wider, criss-cross patterned intake incorporating an auxiliary pair of headlamps and giving a more angular frontal aspect.

Through the fifties, Jensen had been aiming for much the same market, although their cars always cost about 25 per cent less than Bristols. In terms of

How well did the Bristol 408 and Jensen C-V8 combine the New World's V8 power with the Old World's design and craftsmanship? Mark Hughes reports

refinement, performance, equipment and accommodation, the Jensen 541 introduced in 1953 was very close in flavour to the Bristols of the period. In other ways, though, the Jensen approach was different. The philosophy at West Bromwich was more pioneering in spirit, for the 541 was the first production four-seater in the world to go for corrosion resistance through glass-fibre rather than aluminium, while the later 541 de luxe was the first production vehicle with disc braking on all four wheels. While Bristol used a sophisticated small capacity engine, Jensen opted for a 4-litre six-cylinder Austin unit which was offered variously with twin or triple SU carburettors. Like Bristol, Jensen found towards the end of the decade that they were not offering sufficient performance for such an exclusive price tag, and that a Chrysler V8 engine, this time of 5.9-litres capacity, was the most cost effective way to answer that deficiency.

Using the basic body shape of the nine-year-old 541, Jensen launched the C-V8 at Earls Court in 1962. There was a new ladder frame chassis and revised nose and tail treatment, but to the casual observer the result was a heart transplant for an ageing body. The road testers were as ecstatic about the new Jensen as they had been about the Bristol 407 a year earlier, although there was a more notable reservation — unanimous dislike of the rather oriental frontal appearance.

The 5916cc engine was an awesome unit delivering 305bhp at 4800rpm, and mated, as in the 407, to a

Bristol: grouped dials, joystick-style steering wheel

Jensen: dials are more spread out, scuttle is higher

three-speed Chrysler Torqueflite automatic transmission (although Jensen made a few cars with the three-speed manual option). Performance had the expected edge over the 407, with 0-60mph taking just 8.4secs, the standing quarter mile elapsing in an almost unbeatable 16.0secs, and a top speed of comfortably over 130mph. Those figures, in the words of The Motor, added up to '. . . one of the fastest cars we have ever tested, and certainly the fastest full four-seater.'

In the introduction to its test, Autocar stated: 'It is gratifying to be able to report that the Jensen C-V8 is right first time in all the major factors necessary with a notably fast sporting saloon . . . There is no doubt that it represents a definite advance over the six-cylinder 541S.' The Motor subjected a C-V8 to 4500 miles of European motoring, and particularly liked its handling: 'With its nearly even weight distribution (almost 50/50), and fairly high-geared rack and pinion steering, the Jensen handles in a precise, responsive, almost sprightly way that suggests a much smaller car . . . it invited quite forceful driving.' Back to Autocar for its conclusion: '. . . here, indeed, is a car that more than fulfils great expectations.'

To find two cars for our comparative test 20 years on, we went to the Bristol Owners Club (new members should contact Lou Bates, Membership Secretary, Unit 21, Monument Farm Industrial Park, Chalgrove, Oxon OX9 7RW) and the Jensen Owners Club (Doug Mason, Membership Secretary, Glendale, Broad Street, Green Road, Heybridge, Maldon, Essex). In order to make the comparison as directly contemporary as possible, we opted for 'second generation' V8 models from both marques: a 408 and a C-V8 Mk II. No road test of the 408 has ever appeared, but the differences over the 407 were small. The only changes under the surface were the adoption of Armstrong Selectaride dampers at the rear and a modified ventilation system. Similarly, most road test reports of the C-V8 were of the Mk I, but in order to assess one of the best surviving cars in the country we went for a Mk II, which boasted a larger 6276cc engine.

First Bristol

'Our' Bristol was provided by the club's chairman, Colin Selvin, a chartered surveyor who bought the 408, his first Bristol, three years ago. A Bristol enthusiast since childhood, he confesses that he is disinterested in most other marques except Aston Martin and Jaguar, and that he had nurtured the ambition to own a Bristol for many years. He bought UU666 on impulse "because I happened to hear that there was a good one for sale at a reasonable price", and has since covered 15,000 miles to take its total to over 100,000. It is entirely original apart from its sunshine roof and black vinyl roof covering, and has had one re-spray — "not a very good one, because poor preparation has meant that the paint is pulling away from the aluminium panels in places" — in the original ivory white while in a previous owner's hands.

Dave Nash, who works in the music business, has owned his C-V8 for rather longer, having bought it for £900 13 years ago with 40,000 miles on the clock, thinking that it would be an interesting car for daily use. Its fuel consumption soon forced him to turn to something more economical (a Morris Minor), but his fondness for the C-V8 encouraged him to embark on a ground-up restoration, which took most of the seventies! It has been a remarkable job, Dave having done all the work himself apart from a re-spray in Jensen Sun Bronze and £600 worth of re-carpeting to the original pattern. All the mechanical work was done at home, and it scores top marks on originality. As an example of his painstaking efforts, Dave has even reconditioned the Selectaride dampers. The rewards for all this effort have been many concours awards, the most treasured being the Master's Class at the Thoroughbred & Classic Cars national concours at Donington in 1982, and the Jensen Owners Club President's Cup in the same year. Concours activities are fewer these days, but CPX 605B remains one of the finest C-V8s in the country.

Although both cars were designed as high speed Grand Tourers, the difference in their interiors gives

the right impressions about their contrasting characters. The 408 is a true gentleman's carriage, the lofty driving position giving a commanding view over miles of bonnet. All trim — even the door coverings — is of pale grey leather, the only vinyl being in the recesses behind the armrests in the rear. The seats are superbly comfortable, although their flatness suggests that the car is intended more for high speed cruising than fast cornering. The rear seats are, if anything, even more comfortable, and there's plenty of legroom. Generous glass area and slim pillars accentuate the spacious feel and the driver's feeling of command, while the instruments could not be more tidily grouped in the single binnacle behind the adjustable steering wheel, which features Bristol's joystick style pair of spokes linking rim to centre. On the facia by the driver's right hand is a row of buttons which one could take to be a radio at first glance, but which in fact are the automatic transmission selectors. It's a neat arrangement, although the driver must momentarily take his eyes off the road if he wants to select a hold in first or second gear. Luxury, quality and functionalism pervade the interior — it's sumptuous, but there are no frills.

The instant impression within the C-V8's cockpit is that this car is much racier. For a start, the colours — red leather seating, beige carpeting — shout excitement rather than sobriety. The seats are more bucket-shaped, especially those in the rear, where two adults can sit comfortably but without being able to stretch out Bristol-style. Nor would the Jensen's inferior boot capacity lend itself so well to touring 'four-up'. The driver sits far more within the car: he climbs up into the Bristol, but bends himself down into the Jensen. Once installed, he feels surrounded by car, not by space: to the left the transmission tunnel is taller, to the right the door is closer, in front the scuttle is higher, and to the rear the view in the driving mirror is narrower. The wood-rimmed steering wheel is as large as the Bristol's and similarly adjustable, but sportier in flavour with its three drilled aluminium spokes. The instrumentation is just as comprehensive, but only the speedometer and tachometer are

sited before the driver, the smaller dials being grouped centrally on a facia trimmed with a cheaper veneer than the Bristol's walnut burr. The view over the bonnet is dominated by curves and wings rather than the gentle planes of the Bristol, but it's just as imposing.

The build quality of both cars is magnificent, the clunk of a closing door announcing solidity. The gaps between the Bristol's aluminium panels are like hairline cracks, while the Jensen's glass-fibre is heavy and thick. Dimensionally the cars are both large, but the Bristol is *very* large!

Muscular

On the road, both cars are muscular performers, whether using top gear torque or kick-down urgency. With at least 80bhp extra and less weight, the Jensen is definitely quicker, but the Bristol is no sluggard. With identical Torqueflite transmissions, they have the expected similarities with a good, sharp take-off from rest, and a jerkier change when using kick-down instead of manual hold. Both will trickle along in top at 1000rpm yet accelerate smoothly and briskly from that speed — the Jensen's power peak at 4600rpm is a little higher up the scale than the Bristol's 4400rpm, but both are beginning to sound busy at that speed.

There is more contrast in ride and handling, with the Bristol leaning towards touring smoothness and comfort, the Jensen towards sporting firmness and precision. The first impression when making cautious progress with the Bristol is that it's a heavy, understeering pig of a car. Squeeze the throttle a little harder through the corners, though, and it becomes poised. Give it some more and it becomes clear what a finely balanced car this is, for the steering lightens up, the rear wheels take a wider line and cornering becomes effortless. Drive with the good old-fashioned balancing on the throttle routine and it tucks itself into the chosen line beautifully. There is some roll and one slithers on the seat, but there's a big, stout steering wheel (with no power assistance) to hang on to!

The Jensen has such heavy steering that parking

manoeuvres are a real effort, but it too becomes lighter — although the change is not as great — with speed. Neither is the handling so throttle dictated, for gentle cornering on trailing throttle is more neutral, while harder cornering under power does not provoke quite the armfuls of opposite lock which one might expect from 330bhp. There's much less roll, but the ride is correspondingly less pliant, even on the softest of the four Selectaride settings.

Both cars have magnificent, inspiring brakes, with those on the Bristol, if anything, more efficient. Neither car is quiet when pressed but noise levels in the Bristol are generally lower, apart from a whine from the rear axle which Colin says is not unique to his car. With subdued engines, good sound insulation and fine engineering, both cars allow normal conversation at a relaxing 80-100mph.

In terms of practicality and attention to detail, both have myriad thoughtful touches. The Jensen, for example, boasts a small first aid kit in a locker beneath one of the rear seat arm rests, and the seat belt mounting on the B-post is a long tube which allows the belt to slide up and down so that it sits at a height to suit the driver. Following traditional practice for the Filton company, the Bristol's spare wheel could not be more conveniently mounted under the hinged panel behind the nearside front wheel arch, while the battery and servo unit are sited in the same cubby hole on the other side of the car.

The Bristol 408 and the Jensen C-V8 are closely comparable as early applications of lazy American V8 engines in traditional British Grand Touring cars, but it is remarkable how such a different pair of characters were created in two cars designed to the same concept. I would hate to pick a winner as is the custom in this feature, and would prefer to sum up the contrast as gentleman's carriage versus businessman's express, or as traditional versus progressive, or even — dare I say it! — as aristocratic versus *nouveau riche*. Regardless of which is the more apt description, I thank Colin Selvin and Dave Nash for their generous co-operation.

SPECIFICATION	BRISTOL 408	JENSEN C-V8 Mk II
Engine	V8	V8
Bore stroke	98mm × 84mm	108mm × 86mm
Capacity	5130cc	6276cc
Valves	ohv (pushrod)	ohv (pushrod)
Compression ratio	9.0:1	10.0:1
Power	250bhp @ 4400rpm	330bhp @ 4600rpm
Transmission	Chrysler Torqueflite Automatic	Chrysler Torqueflite Automatic (three-speed manual option)
Brakes	Dunlop discs	Dunlop discs
Suspension front	Ind by wishbones, coil springs and dampers, anti-roll bar	Ind by wishbones, coil springs and dampers, anti-roll bar
Suspension rear	Live axle, torsion bars and Selectaride dampers, trailing link above prop-shaft, Watts linkage	Live axle, semi-elliptics and Selectaride dampers, Panhard Rod
Steering	Marles worm type	Engineering Productions rack and pinion
Body	Box section frame, aluminium body	Tubular/box section frame, glass-fibre body
DIMENSIONS		
Length	16ft 5½ins	15ft 3¼ins
Width	5ft 9ins	5ft 8ins
Height	4ft 10½ins	4ft 7¾ins
Wheelbase	9ft 6ins	8ft 9ins
Kerb weight	32½cwt	30cwt
Tyres	6.00 × 16	6.70 × 15
PERFORMANCE		
Max speed	125mph	130mph
0-60mph	9.2secs	7.8secs
Standing ¼ mile	17.3secs	14.6secs
Average mpg	15-18mpg	13-17mpg
PRODUCTION		
Years built	1964-5	1964-5
Numbers built	300	250
Price when new	£4460	£3491

Jensen C-V8's slightly dated appearance was inherited from the 541 launched in 1953

Huge air cleaner hides 5.1-litre Chrysler V8

Jensen's V8 was larger: 6.2-litres, 330bhp

Timeless lines with generous glass area are Bristol hallmarks which last to this day

PROFILE

BRISTOL
Sixes

*Chris Balfour explains why the
400-406 saloons were unique in
terms of engineering skill and
dedication. Pics: Nathan Morgan*

All too infrequently in the history of the human
race, circumstance, tradition, personal vision
and chance have combined to produce an
occasion or artefact of outstanding merit. Thus it
was with the Bristol 400 introduced to the world at
the 1947 Geneva Show.

Circumstance was the end of the 1939-45 war
when the Bristol Aeroplane Company found themselves with unused factory space, and extra
employees needing work. Tradition was the spirit of
West Country engineering, different to the Midlands,
nurtured and developed by the White, Verdon-Smith
and White-Smith families to meet the demands of
aviation (initial customers should not be expected to
complete the testing process in the air!), and
rigorously disciplined by Roy Fedden during the
development of the war-time sleeve-valve radial
engines.

The personal vision came from George White and

Reginald Verdon-Smith, who believed there was a market for a sporting saloon built to aircraft standards, and who gained the support of the older generation. The company already employed designers and craftsmen who were able to turn the vision into metal.

And finally there were two chances, both car accidents. Towards the end of the war, Don Aldington of AFN (the company responsible for the pre-war Frazer Nash-BMW) had come to grief in his Singer Le Mans, been invalided out of the Army and posted to the Bristol office of the Ministry of Aircraft Production. There he heard of Bristol's plans, and alerted his brother, which led to HJ Aldington demonstrating a 327/80 BMW to the Bristol directors. Second, HJ had happened to crash at Hamburg in 1939 so that his own 328 had been left at the BMW works for repair. This provided one good excuse for those '45 Aldington visits to Munich which eventually

led to that Stirling bomber's return to Filton loaded with BMW drawings and parts. And in time Fritz Feidler (who with Rudolph Schleicher had been responsible for the 326 and subsequent models) came to work with AFN, and acted as consultant to Bristol on the 400.

Bristol believed there was a market for a sporting saloon built to aircraft standards

The Frazer Nash-Bristol was announced in the press in September 1946, but, as the differences between the Aldington and White philosophies became apparent, it was decided that the car should be a Bristol and that components should be supplied to AFN for their own products. The aircraft factory

made most of the parts, *The Autocar* reporting "that only electrics, clutch, brakes, propeller shaft and tyres were bought from outside." An engine was installed in the Verdon-Smith pre-war BMW by mid '46, and in *The Autocar*, December 6, 1946 there is a photograph of "the new Bristol saloon in Milan while on one of several long-distance continental test runs". The 400 was built with the close-coupled wood-framed steel body from 1947, priced at £2724 for those who could obtain one. The Government was then insisting on priority for exports, as witnessed by another photograph of "a batch of Bristols destined for Australia, Belgium, Brazil, Czechoslovakia, South Africa and Switzerland".

Meanwhile the indefatigable HJ had been visiting the Italian coachbuilders. He persuaded the Filton men that a few bodies should be commissioned from Superleggera Touring and Farina. Dudley Hobbs, the Bristol designer, was already working on an aerodynamic successor, and the 'aerodyne' 401 appeared in 1948 using the Superleggera principle of small-diameter welded steel tubing round which aluminium panels were wrapped. This roomier body, full of ingenious details like push-button releases, and the bumpers with their 1½-inch retraction, is a constant source of pleasure to engineer-owners.

Gradually more vehicles became available for the home market: Enter Tony Crook, who was now the Surrey distributor. After leaving the RAF he had worked with Raymond Mays and Peter Berthon at Bourne for one season and then acquired his own garage at Caterham. He had already been involved through his successful racing activities with Bristol and BMW-engined cars. In the fifties he also had a showroom in Esher High Street before moving to the Hersham site, which later became Woking Motors. Other distributors were University Motors, AFN, and Kevill-Davies & March in the London area; the Cedar Service Station in Fareham, Bolton of Leeds, Bob Gerard Cars in Leicester, James Galt in Scotland and, later, RF Fuggle at Bushey Heath.

There were now accounts of these cars giving satisfactory service in many lands and the 401 was gaining a strong following, amongst those who could afford it, as a desirable and efficient sporting saloon. The 403 followed on in May 1953. Some refer to it as the 401 'put right' with its Alfin brake drums and 100bhp 100 A engine. The price stood at just below £3000 compared with the Aston DB 2/4 at £2620 and the Mk VII Jaguar at £1616.

It had been nearly a decade of prodigious effort. As well as the saloons, the drophead 402 and the short chassis 404 coupe had been produced in smaller numbers, and the Arnolt chassis was going to Chicago via Bertone. Engines in the FN, BS and D series were being supplied to AC, AFN, Cooper, Lister, Lotus and others for their sports and racing cars. The later BS 4A delivered 155bhp at 6000rpm. Bristol themselves appeared at Le Mans and elsewhere with the 450 and the BCE engine, which gave 170bhp in its final form.

The four-door wood-framed 405 (together with a two-door drophead) was introduced at the London

FOR:
Engineering integrity, spares availability, aluminium bodies (except 400), reliability, easy routine maintenance

AGAINST:
Brakes on pre-disc cars, rear visibility 400-403, repair costs, cooling in long traffic jams

Motor Show in 1954. Overdrive as standard gave the quieter cruising at lower revs which had been so much appreciated when fitted to later 403s. Owners delighted in testing their skills and that precise gear change to get the best out of the efficient small engine. But, with still only 2 litres and priced at £3386 by the middle of 1955, potential new customers could now purchase 7 Jaguar litres (ie two MkVIIs) for the same price.

Obviously the directors were fully aware of this price comparison and had already commissioned the successor – the type 160 3.65-litre engine. By the end of 1954 the replacement type 220 chassis with all independent suspension was being road tested. All seemed set fair for another generation of Bristol-engined saloons to please the steadily growing band of Bristol devotees. But it was not to be. The graceful de Havilland Comet airliner had been dropping out of the skies. The salvage operations showed that the testing procedures for pressurised aircraft would have to be extensively revised. No aircraft producing company could escape, and at Bristol this led to the cessation of all development work and the cancellation of projects 160 and 220.

In 1956 the Car Division became a separate subsidiary known as Bristol Cars Limited. Tony Crook joined the board with George White as managing director and Frank Derham as company secretary. The 405 was in production till 1958 and was replaced by the 2.2-litre 406 with metal-framed body built by Jones Brothers of Willesden, but still

trimmed and finished at Filton. In 1961 the parent company became part of the British Aircraft Corporation (BAC) and George White and Tony Crook bought the car company. With no 220 it was realised that the 406 could still be the basis of a new range. After investigating other possibilities, they settled on the Chrysler V8, which leads onto another story.

I have stressed the vision and work of Sir George White (as he became in 1963 after his father's death) because without him there would have been no initial

It was realised the 406 could be the basis of a new range, with a larger engine – the V8

Bristol Cars. What bad luck that he was seriously injured in an accident in 1969, which led to his retirement. Tony Crook acquired the White holdings in 1973 and since then has been the sole owner of the company. It was he who argued that the original spares should be kept, and took responsibility for the storage costs when they were moved from a hangar at Filton to Chiswick.

He reasoned that, when the inherent worth of the cars was realised, the value of these spares would be appreciated. Today the company holds £1½ million pounds worth and continues to commission new costly batches of some items. Where they have not been able to make provision, the specialist restorers have tried to fill the gaps. Tony Crook's life-long dedication and shrewd business philosophy has borne fruit. The V8s, vehicles still in the Bristol tradition, remain in production. The Company's continuing interest in the Sixes, the service it and the specialist restorers provide, and the support available from the Owner's Club, all add to the unique experience and pleasure of Bristol ownership.

Left: Stunning view of streamlined rear sweep of 403. Note tiny curved rear screen. Below: Split-screened 403 interior offers spacious leg-room; walnut dash liberally splattered with knobs and fifties squared dials.

The saloons are often categorised by their shapes: the BMW look-alike, the 'aerodynes' and the cars with the Brabazon-inspired air intake. But it is easier to take the 400 as the original and the 406 as the final development of the 400 concept. If the 400 represents the charm of an initial relationship (adjustments have still to be made), then in the 406 maturity has been achieved:– Disc brakes, Watts linkage, overdrive, ventilation and heating, a larger back seat, big windows and wide doors. Yes: the years have added weight, but is maturity ever achieved whilst retaining all the agility of youth? Thus the 401-3 and 5 are seen as stages on the journey, each with their particular delights, but also with deviations from the path.

The 401, and even more the developed 403, have that appealing shape, which still looks good today, and the mix of qualities that have always made them so useable: but the deviation is the rear tank and spare wheel which, together, detracted from the ultimate handling. For some the 405 was the most stunning looker of them all, purposeful and lithe, with those fenestrated flanks sweeping down between svelte fins. The deviation is the wooden frame and the four small doors, all of them a bit of a squeeze.

But there still remains the components common to all the cars. The frame is (and remains today in the V8) a deep box section with tubular cross-members. The rear springs are torsion bars running back from the central cross member to the two transverse axle linkages, which keep the rear wheels vertical. What is so clever is that there is enough controlled movement to give a comfortable ride with the appropriate shock absorbers and settings. And sideways movement is kept in check by the third attachment point, in the form of an A bracket running from the propshaft tunnel to the final drive housing. (This was changed to Watts after the 405).

The front suspension is mounted in a separate box section, which can be detached as a complete unit. The wheels are independently sprung by a transverse leaf spring. The spring eye forms the lower, and the wishbone radius arms the upper link for the stub axle and swivel pins. On the early cars, 400, and 401s up to chassis 1006, the inner attachment of the wishbones is the central component of Bristol's own rotary shock absorbers. When those delectable devices were discarded – it was too difficult to set up and maintain valve operation – the empty damper housing remained to provide the bush for the wishbones. In their place large telescopics were mounted from the lower link to new upper brackets. For the 405, turrets at each end of the suspension box replaced the old damper housing. By meticulous attention to all design details, castor angle, pin inclination, spring and wishbone angle and steering offset, a masterly combination of ride and roadholding was achieved.

The steering rack is mounted on top of that box. The pinion assembly is adjustable for both thrust and mesh. Lubrication is by the same one-shot system which feeds the suspension. Correctly set up and lubricated, the feel of this steering is one of the features which can turn owners into Bristol Six addicts for the rest of their lives. It should not be heavy on any car except under extreme parking conditions.

The engine is based on the pre-war BMW but made use of materials and processes developed in the aircraft factory. It is short and compact so that there is sufficient torsional stiffness with only four main bearings. From the single low camshaft, driven by a short chain, vertical push-rods operate the inlet valves. Further transverse push-rods, each contained in a separate alloy tunnel, take the movement across the aluminium cylinder head to operate the exhaust valves.

Over the years there have been references to

Ten things you didn't know about Bristol and the Bristol Sixes

1. After the war the factories at Filton were also producing pre-fabricated houses.

2. The prototype of the Fedden sleeve-valve radial rear-engined car, which crashed on test at Stoke Orchard, was built by a separate company after Sir Roy had left Bristol.

3. Major George Abell OBE, general manager of the Car Division until 1954, had previously been manager of Invicta.

4. Before the war Sir George White raced speed boats. He held six world records and only stopped after a bad crash in Poole Harbour in 1938.

5. If a half-shaft breaks on the earlier cars, they can still be driven! The axle is designed so that the broken parts bind themselves together.

6. Ronnie Parkinson survived the Alpine crash to the bottom of a 200ft ravine. Touch wood, there

have only been two fatalities in the six-cylinder cars.

7. The main runway at Filton was extended to two miles for the take-off of the 224-seat Brabazon. It was an appropriate testing facility for the car company.

8. Tony Crook drove a 401 with higher axle ratio from Caterham to Montlhèry, recorded 104 miles in one hour from a standing start, and was back at Caterham the same day.

9. After Pierre Levegh's devastating crash at Le Mans in 1955, Bristol gave all their prize money for winning their class to the disaster fund for the 83 victims.

10. The records of the two clubs show that there are now more 400s accounted for in Australia than in the UK.

'forests of knitting needles'. But, with Bristol achieving the manufacturing tolerances which do not allow those rods to wander, Rudolf Schleicher's design is an elegant and economical solution. The carburettors are mounted high and central. With small 10mm plugs there is sufficient room to bring the fuel mixture almost straight down into the well-shaped combustion chamber.

Time has demonstrated the value of this layout. The engine was progressively developed from the 80bhp of the early 400s, through the 100bhp of the 403 to the 105bhp of the 405 and enlarged 406. (There were still higher outputs in sports and racing applications). The gearbox is conventional with free wheel on first. The Laycock overdrive was added for the 405.

Not all cars will fit this description. Filton added modifications as they became available and some owners, instead of changing, had earlier cars updated with the later improvements. Amongst several permutations there are 403s with overdrive, and 401s with 403 brakes.

DRIVING IMPRESSIONS

Everything about the Bristols suggests 'large', from the solid, heavy body, through the 406's wide doors, to the spacious interior. Tony Crook was known to say that the 406 was designed so that four 6 feet tall gentlemen could depart for an enjoyable and comfortable golfing weekend.

Clambering into the Bristol you settle back into the large leather seats. Hands rest easily on the large steering wheel which dominates the walnut dash, itself generously spattered with various black knobs. In the 403, the dials are very 'fifties' in their squared-off shape and large numerals.

The Bristol is about as reliable as they come. Provided it is used regularly, the engine is a willing starter, even from cold. All it takes is a gentle pressure on the starter button and the engine fires immediately, burbling happily at a steady 1000rpm.

Moving away, in either the 406 or 403, first gear is very low, lower in fact than reverse, and considered the weak point in the gearbox. No marks for a sprint from the traffic lights, although it 'will take you up a

brick wall'. First is also alarmingly close to reverse. Otherwise, the gear changes are precise, snicking neatly through the narrow gate. Having swiftly changed up to second, you can quite happily wind the engine up 30mph (or 60 in the 403 before the engine starts screaming). From third up the scope of acceleration is seemingly endless. And as for cruising, the temptation in the 403 to flick into overdrive and then pretend it's an automatic. Cruising at 70-80mph is where the Bristol is happiest.

Driving at speed with the windows down, the Bristol's heritage and good breeding shines through. On both the 403 and 406, the streamlined shape of the body is such that the wind rushes past the windows, leaving those four gentlemen (and ladies) calm and unruffled.

The styling is not all good news in the 403. Visibility is appalling. The curved split windscreen is narrow, the diminutive rear-view mirror reflects a miniature view through the tiny rear screen. Rear three-quarter vision is nil, in comparison to the 406, whose thin front pillars, generous rear and front screen allow extremely good all-round vision.

Above left: 2.2-litre 406 engine with centrally mounted carburettors happily provides 70mph at 3000rpm. Above: 406 cockpit is light and airy. Dials now grouped behind thin-rimmed steering wheel, knobs neatly lined up to left. Note period radio. Left: On open roads, 406 gives effortless ride

PRODUCTION HISTORY

March 1947: 400 introduced at Geneva show. 85A engine. Early cars had tubular bumpers, top-hinged boot with spare wheel inside.
1948: Later cars had bottom-hinged boot, spare mounted externally and opening rear window, pressed sheet bumpers and over-riders (already fitted to some earlier cars). 85C engine, 3 Solex, available.
March 1948: Superleggera Touring cars at Geneva Show.
October 1948: 401 introduced at Earl's Court Show. 85C engine. Yellow Bristol badge. Rear lights recessed into bumpers. Ridge each side of car between wheel and bottom of doors only in early cars. Cars from chassis 696 had rear lights set in wings and Newton rear shock absorbers. Cars from chassis 1006 had Borg Warner synchromesh and Newton front shock absorbers.
1949: Beutler 401.
May 1953: 403 introduced. 100A engine. Alfin brake drums and modified leverage, silvered radiator grille, red Bristol badge, 403 numerals on bonnet and boot lid. Later cars had side lights on top of the wings, and a remote control gear lever.
October 1954: 405 introduced Earl's Court Show. 100 B2 engine, overdrive. Later cars from chassis 4037 have a tubular AC — Delco air filter replacing the earlier Vokes unit.
October 1957: Beutler 406 E at Earl's Court.
August 1958: 406 introduced. 110 2.2-litre engine. Watts linkage. Dunlop disc brakes. First cars had auxiliary lamps within air intake aperture and grille with vertical bars. No over-riders. The grille was then changed to a mesh of horizontal and vertical metal strips, auxiliary lamps moved to bumper supports and over-riders fitted. Later cars had rounded off corners on door-to-dash pocket and radiator grille made from chromed wire.

PRODUCTION FIGURES

400	471
401	601
400/401 Touring/Beutler	4
403	275
405	297
406 Beutler	1
406 prototype (TLN)	1
406	168
Based on incompleted Owners' Club research	

Triumphant Treybal (left) and Dobry (right) with Bristol 400, hold aloft their trophies, having taken 3rd (1st Brits home) in the Barclays Bank Challenge Cup, Monte Carlo, 1949

CLUBS

Bristol Owners' Club: Offers 12 sections and around 800 members including those from Belgium, Canada, France, Germany, Holland, Hong Kong, Mauritius, Oman, Scandanavia, Sri Lanka, Switzerland and USA. (Includes V8 owners). The club produces a quarterly bulletin and the next meeting will be the Annual Bristol Day in Kensington Gardens on Sunday, September 16 starting at 11.00am. Membership secretary: John Emery, Vesutor Ltd, Marringdean Road, Billingshurst, West Sussex RH14 9RH. Tel: 0403 784028 (day) 0903 814630 (evening). There are around 200 members of the Australian Club. For more details contact secretary Jeff Hase, PO Box 215, Niddrie, 30/42 Victoria, Australia.

BOOKS

Bristol Cars & Engines by L.J.K. Setright. Published by Motor Racing Publications, 1974. Now out of print, but specialist bookshops suggest £25-£30 if obtainable.
Bristol: The Quiet Survivor by Charles Oxley. Published by Oxley-Sidey Publications, 1988 (£19.95).
Bristol Cars Gold Portfolio 1946-1985. Published by Brooklands Books (£10.95).
From Chain Drive to Turbocharger – The A.F.N. Story by Denis Jenkinson. Published by Patrick Stephens (£19.95).

SPECIALISTS

Bristol Cars Ltd. Head Office: 368 Kensington High Street, London W14 8NL. Tel: 071-603 5555.
Bristol Cars Services Ltd. Service & Spares. The Baltic Centre, Great West Road, Brentford, London TW8 9BT. Service, tel: 081 568 8998. Spares, tel: 081 568 8999. (It is sensible to first check with Bristols to see what is available. Ask for Teresa Daniels. As Bristols themselves say "they are continually financing the remanufacture of slow moving parts which ties up capital, but without which cars would be off the road. The more this service is used, the easier it is to keep prices down."
T.T. Workshops. 127 West Wilts Trading Estate, Westbury, Wiltshire. Tel: 0373 823603.
Brian May. Peterbrook, 497 Peterbrook Road, Shirley, West Midlands. Tel: 021 430 3767.
Spencer Lane-Jones. 20 Deverill Road, Sutton Veny, Warminster, Wiltshire BA12 7BY. Tel: 0985 40534.
Anthony Smith. 9 Heathside, Hinchley Wood, Esher, Surrey KT10 9TD. Tel: 081 398 5731.
Liberty Classics, Unit 3, Devil's Lane, Thorpe Road, Egham, Surrey TW20 8HD. Tel: 0784 466707.

Performance? The 406 is a big car to depend on a 2.2-litre engine so don't expect miracles, but, as with the 2-litre 403, having climbed through the gears, the ride is effortless and the handling confident. The car sits squarely on the road, bumpy surfaces and corners are treated with relative disdain. Tight cornering in the 403 can provoke tail slide due to the weight of the petrol tank and spare wheel behind the rear axle but it's not easily done.

Once rolling, the steering is feather-light, just a finger's pressure on the wheel is swiftly relayed to the wheels with not a hint of shudder or speed loss. But trying to park a 16ft 7in 406 in a parking space designed for a Mini Metro, the steering is very heavy. Driving through town is quite a different experience to the open roads. Constant gear changes and braking can become quite wearing on the legs. The clutch is quite heavy and the brakes only respond to a firm pressure. If you need to stop in a hurry, only by booting the pedal will you get the reaction you need.

CONTEMPORARY REPORTS

The Autocar, September 6, 1946: 'This car can travel at 30mph over road surfaces so bad that a normal chassis would shake its occupants badly, and only inspection of the road after the trip shows… the test to which it has been subjected. Its cornering at speed is refreshingly good, and the steering is as positive as anything that has ever been built.'
The Motor, May 19, 1948: 'The Bristol 2-litre is a car with quite exceptional ability to suit itself to the mood of driver and passengers. If haste is required it will give speed and road holding which might be the envy of many a super-sports model. If, on the other hand, the mood is leisurely, it will drift quietly along in the most comfortable touring fashion.'
The Autocar, February 25, 1949: 'The resultant loss of time completely dismayed us and never in my life have I driven a car with such violence in an attempt to liquidate the debt. Over inferior mountain roads, with one hairpin following another with appalling frequency and surfaces coated in ice in many places, it was necessary to average some 46mph. Luckily for us, nocturnal visibility prevented us from realising the appalling dangers of the precipices flanking many of the hairpins. For over an hour the Bristol was in and out of second and third gears without a single top-gear respite, the engine repeatedly reaching and holding 5500rpm. As we approached Digne it was realised… that the seemingly impossible race against time had been won. (*Zdenek Treybal writing of his Monte Carlo drive.*)
The Motor, January 10, 1951: 'The particular merit of the 401 is a combination of virtues which may not be equalled in any other motorcar in the world. It will comfortably carry four people, it will swallow an almost fabulous volume of luggage. It will sustain 80-90mph from dawn until the cows come home; and then on into the night.'
The Autocar, April 27, 1951: 'The chance came in August when business called me to Eastern Canada and I decided to take the Bristol… to go all-Canadian

although my Vancouver friends insisted there was no passable road round the north of Lake Superior. Beside the turbulent Frazer the road is partly surfaced. It is a supreme test of cornering, as the road winds along the side of the great canyon… soon after Calgary we had our first taste of prairie roads, the surface was atrocious in places and one just had to let the car take it on the snubbers… the surface to the Saskatchewan border was bituminous with pot-holes several feet long caused by the winter frosts. We reached home on Sunday evening having completed the 7100-mile round trip at an average running speed of 46.8mph.' (*Jack Lawson writing of Canadian motoring in his 401*).
The Motor, May 11, 1955: 'Until the last minute of the last race first place was in doubt… in the second, Marten's Fiat streaked away lapping at a speed which would have won outright, and then with two laps to go retired with a slipping clutch… in the ninth Bill Banks, sixth last year and the year before announced as first until another car's disqualification, drove the Bristol saloon faultlessly and was leading. Finally came Tak in the Mercedes, his engine failing and almost out of oil… at four laps he dropped to 2min.9sec. with time still to be made up, smoke poured from the exhaust, the engine was sick and

To climb above the car confirms how absolutely right-looking the shape is

sounded like it. Somehow he picked up, his times went back to 2mins.6sec. per lap, stayed there, and the Rally was won.' (*Tulip Rally Report*)
The Autocar, May 20, 1955: 'The 405 clung resolutely to the route, darting like a trout up the contour of the stream. I would have liked to have seen it from an aircraft, a ruby arrow on that yellow ribbon of road through a green countryside. To climb above the car is to confirm how absolutely right-looking the shape is from every angle. Perhaps the most impressive aspect is its all-round efficiency. The car provides a judiciously balanced mixture of all the motoring virtues, achieved with only two litres of engine size.

COMPETITION HISTORY

The 1948 Monte Carlo Rally was cancelled owing to petrol shortages, but *Autocar* had a drawing by Gordon Horner depicting the 400 as the sort of British car which might have done well. Appropriately, in 1949 Zdenek Treybal and F. Dobry took third, just four marks behind the second place Hotchkiss, which in turn was only four marks behind Trevoux's winning Hotchkiss. Pretty good for a 2-litre when you realise the Hotchkiss was a 3.4-litre and the 4th-placed Allard, nine marks behind the Bristol, was a 3.6-litre. *The Motor* referred to the complicated calculations and that, whilst waiting for the results, there had been talk that Treybal might even have won. Two months later Count Lurani and HJ Aldington achieved second place (with NHX 115) in the Touring category of the Targa Florio despite a growling back axle. In May the same crew and car entered the Mille Miglia, took third in the Touring category, and 13th overall.

Four Bristols were entered in what was described as a 'gruelling' Alpine. Treybal, in a 400 borrowed via AFN (not the Monte car), was one of only 32 (out of 92 starters) who completed the formidable first night section through the Alps Maritimes without loss of marks. He then beat everyone (including the over 3-litre class) in a splendid run (88.9mph) on the timed 5km flat-out Autostrada section before coming to grief after the Rolle Pass. *The Autocar* blamed the brakes this time and the car disappeared over a precipice. The Czech driver was flung clear but his co-driver, Parkinson, was seriously injured.

The Wisdoms were also doing well when they had

Left: Alpine Rally, 1949, the Wisdoms' 400 tight-cornering near Menton shortly before full-frontal crash. Right: Tony Crook at Hersham. Below: George White at Filton

a full-frontal incident with a non-competing car. The third 400, driven by Don Aldington, with David Murray, lost marks on that first section but subsequently caught up to come 4th in the class. HJ, with Alan Marshall in the Pinin-Farina cabriolet, was 5th, and fastest up the timed Stelvio climb. Private owners, Maurice Falkner at Sestrieres, O'Hara Moore in the Alpine, Newton and Bolton amongst others at Monte Carlo, campaigned the 400 into the fifties.

The 401 then took over and made a speciality of the Spring Tulip Rallies. In 1952 Ralph Sleigh, with Pointer and Martin, trounced the Aurelias, Alfas and Citroëns to win the 2-litre class and come 8th overall. In 1953 Bill Banks (the Koni importer), who had been out of action after a Monte crash the previous year, and his co-driver Porter, were acclaimed as overall winners. But then the 1½-litre class leader was disqualified and, under the Tulip marking system, the new class leader received extra points which put him just ahead of the Bristol.

In 1954 Banks and Sears took an Alvis to 6th place, and then the following year returned to the fray with a Bristol and, teamed with Meredith-Owens, achieved another fine 2nd place just behind the winning Mercedes 300 SL. So, remember, if you find yourself having to defend the Bristol's valour, that these comfortable 2-litre saloons were within an ace of winning both the Monte and Tulip against all comers.

On the track the 2-litre cars consistently won their class in the Silverstone Producting and Touring car race. Tony Crook was usually to the fore and, in the last year of entry, 1955, conducted the four-door 405. The 406 was not raced or rallied, but like all the earlier models, has shown its worth in recent retrospective runs and rallies.

BUYER'S SPOT CHECK

The cars that come on the market will range from the expertly restored, through those that were 'botched' when values were low, to those basically still original vehicles which will have suffered in different degrees the ravages of time, climate, use and abuse. The botched ones are the most difficult, too often patching the struture with miscellaneous materials has accelerated decay in adjacent areas.

Think before you visit a possibility. Do you want a car which can be driven soon after purchase? How much work can you and are you prepared to do yourself? Control the emotions if a car looks good and sparkling. Instead, work steadily through the potential problem areas and if you are unsure of your capacity to do this, the safest course is to have a full survey by an expert.

Chassis: Get under the car or put it onto a lift. Carefully examine those extensions at both ends of the main frame ❶. At the front they support the bumper mountings. Take particular note of the extensions which support the top shock absorber mounting and the rear of the body on the 405 and 406 ❷. Are the bump stops still there? Also, look where the front anti-roll bar attachments are secured

to the frame (403 and after) ❸, at any metal side extensions carrying the wider bodies (eg 406) ❹, and tap the lower surface of the rear U of the frame, especially beneath the propellor shaft ❺. Rust damage usually starts from within and is worse than first appears.

Bodies: First the ever delightful 400, the only one with a steel body. Look at the underside of those long flowing front wings. Because there were no rubber flaps or inner linings, corrosive salt spray can be thrown right back to the point where the front wing joins onto the bottom of the rear wing.

You are on safer ground with the aluminium skins of all other saloons. Being softer they bend easily, but they only corrode where they are in contact with the steel sub-structure by which they are joined to the chassis. On all cars examine the inner steel wheelarches, the luggage boot floor, boot and bonnet water channels and the bottoms of the door pillars ❻. On 405 and 406 also examine the lower surfaces of the battery and spare wheel compartments ❼. Provided the chassis is OK, it is not too difficult (just time and patience) to cut out the corrosion and weld in new metal. History and chance seem to be the determinant of wooden frame condition in the 400 and 405. As this isn't visible to the eye, smell is some guide. Sniff the front pillars and below the windscreen, sniff the area below the rear window. It may be possible to push something like a darning needle into exposed woodwork. On the 401 and 403 those steel frame tubes can also corrode if damp and moisture has penetrated at the edge openings in the shell – windows, screens, etc. As a general statement it is usually easier to replace the 401/403 tubes than the 400/405 woodwork.

Remember that all this is written as a warning, not to dishearten. It is now increasingly worthwhile, as a long-term exercise, to salvage a rough saloon now that their inherent worth is more widely recognised. Too many have already been scrapped to provide mechanical bits for ACs and Frazer Nashes.

Interiors: The story here isn't different to other

luxury cars of that period. Leather, woodwork, carpets can all be refurbished or replaced according to the pocket and preference of the purchaser. It is worth looking under the carpets to check on damp.

Paintwork: Find out what has been done to a repainted aluminium shell. Is it a re-spray on a sound base? If it was taken back to base metal, were all the correct aluminium primers properly applied? If an imperfectly-adhering base has been re-sprayed, the top coat will soon crack and bubble.

Engine and transmission: It is suggested that you drive a running and taxed example out of town for at least 45 minutes. Using full choke (and priming the pump if the car has not been run for some hours) the engine should start on the first turn. On spring and summer days there should be a clear exhaust and on most cars the choke can be pushed in, first to the half-way position, and then fully home, within 30 seconds. Whilst cold, the oil pressure will soar to between 70 and 80psi. It is important that higher revs above 3000rpm are not used until the oil temperature reaches 40°C. This may take as long as 10 minutes. If possible, then drive the car on a

PARTS & REPAIR COSTS

Bristol Cars have supplied many of these prices. They have not increased in proportion to the values of the cars and many are reasonable compared with the costs for other vehicles of this calibre. Other prices have been supplied by the specialist repairers.

Crankshafts	c. £2500	Valve spring	each £7.36
Big end bearings	set £122.66	Gasket set full	£104.06
Main bearings	set £447.20	Gasket set decarb	£63.62
Camshafts	£638.88	Starter ring gear	each £140.00
Camshaft bushes	set £100.17	Exhausts	£250.00
Water pumps	£301.21	Engine rebuild depending on condition	£5000-£8000
Water pump repair kit	£78.08	Front spring	£450.00
Oil pumps	c. £250.00	King-pins	each £193.43
Oil filter conversion kit	£58.75	Top pins	each £37.27
Oil filter	£3.37	Bottom pins	each £37.27
Valve guides	each £21.29	Handbrake cable	£49.83
Valves	each £14.88	Windscreen 401	£171.00
		Windscreen 405	£587.00
		Wings: front 401/403	each £1469.74
		Wings: front 405	each £1100.25
		Bare-metal respray	£5000-£8000
		Interior re-trim	£5000-£6000

motorway or main road for at least 20 minutes. Check that oil pressure is still at or near 60psi at 3000rpm with water and oil temperature around 70°C.

How do you establish the problem areas? The bottom end, originally made from high quality materials, should last for at least 150,000 miles if it has been properly treated (oil and filter changes) or, if rebuilt, correctly done. Some will tell you that the cause of top end rough running stems from the three carburettors being unsynchronised. In the same way ignition difficulties (points, plugs, etc.), or air leaks into the fuel flow, can soon be rectified. The valve gear lasts well, provided people have not tampered. If it is noisy, the cam followers are likely to be worn. Piston rings and pistons, particularly some replacements, do not last for ever.

The last point is to look beneath the exhaust on the off side ❽. A hand mirror helps. Because you can't drain the last drop of water via the taps, the cylinder walls are prone to crack on all engines, but most will have now been rectified. Does a repair look sound? Are the core plugs oozing? Is there any weep from the gasket ❽? If the car is running, falling oil pressure is the best clue to potential problems. If not, see if there is a starting handle clipped to the bulkhead and try and feel the compression of the cylinders.

Check that the insulation is in place over the gearbox. The unit should be quiet. The well-worn phrase "like a knife through butter" is still an apt description of the agreeable feel, particularly of the closer ratio Borg Warner synchromesh introduced to later 401s. Check if the freewheel on first gear is still operating. Sharp engagement followed by hard acceleration can lead to the rollers hammering and breaking the gear shell, and the mechanism may have been replaced by a fixed gear.

Rear axles don't always last 'for ever'. The later ENV gears on the 405 and the complete Salisbury hypoid axle on the 406 tend to become noisier than the spiral bevels on the 400, 401 and 403. It is only on the Salisbury that the hub bearings have to be separately greased. Look for leaks at the front of the housing ❾. It's sensible to check oil lever (however difficult the removal of the plug) ❿ before a long journey in a car you don't know.

Steering & suspension: Correctly set up and with a light touch on that sensitive wheel, the car will not wander. But, if you are thrown off course and react with a tight grip, you may find yourself overcorrecting and veering from side to side. Let the car correct itself. The 401 and 403, with their rear tank and low spare, have the greater tendency to oversteer. Swivel pins, and pin and wishbone bushes will eventually wear and upset the geometry. Check that there is oil in the one-shot reservoir. Press the pedal above the footbrake, look inside the front wheel ⓫. Oil should be seeping out from the bottom of the stub axle. One learns to park where offence will not be caused: much better than no sign of oil which indicates the system may not be functioning. This would be confirmed by heavier steering. Check the four bolts under the centre of the spring ⓬. They can work loose. To end with another warning: transverse spring leaves can break after a high mileage, if they have become dry or the car has been run without gaiters ⓭. Taking off and replacing the gaiters is a fiddly and dirty business, but it has to be faced in order to grease those leaves and keep them in good condition.

SPECIFICATION	400/85A	401/85C	403/100A	406/110
Engine	Six in-line	Six in-line	Six in-line	Six in-line
Bore/stroke	66 × 96mm	66 × 96mm	66 × 96mm	68,7 × 99.6mm
Capacity	1971cc	1971cc	1971cc	2216cc
Valves	Pushrod & rocker ohv	Pushrod & rocker ohv	Pushrod & rocker ohv	Pushrod & rocker ohv
Compression ratio	7.5:1	7.5:1	8.5:1 (late cars)	7.5:1
Power	80bhp at 4200rpm	85bhp at 4500rpm	100bhp at 5000rpm	105bhp at 4700rpm
Torque	96lb/ft at 3000rpm	107lb/ft at 3500rpm	117lb/ft at 3500rpm	129lb/ft at 3000rpm
Carburettors	3 SU-D2	3 Solex 32Bl	3 Solex 32B1	3 Solex 32B1
Transmission	Bristol gearbox 4-speed manual	Bristol gearbox 4-speed manual	Bristol BW/CR/5 gearbox 4-speed manual	Bristol BW/CR/9 gearbox 4-speed & overdrive
Brakes	4-wheel drums	4-wheel drums	Alfin front drums	Discs
Front suspension	Transverse leaf	Transverse leaf	Transverse leaf, anti-roll bar	Transverse leaf, anti-roll bar
Rear suspension	Torsion bars A bracket	Torsion bars A bracket	Torsion bars A bracket	Torsion bars Watts linkage
Steering	Rack & pinion	Rack & pinion	Rack & pinion	Rack & pinion
Body/chassis	Steel (aluminium doors & bonnet) wood frame. Separate chassis	Aluminium on steel tubes. Separate chassis	Aluminium on steel tubes. Separate chassis	Aluminium steel frame. Separate chassis

DIMENSIONS	400	401	403	406
Length	15ft 3in	15ft 11½in	15ft 11½in	16ft 4in
Width	5ft 4in	5ft 7in	5ft 7in	5ft 8in
Wheelbase	9ft 6in	9ft 6in	9ft 6in	9ft 6in
Height	4ft 11in	5ft	5ft	5ft

PERFORMANCE	400	401	403	406
Max speed	95.7mph	97.3mph	106mph	102mph
0-60mph	14.7sec	15.1sec	13.5sec	n/a
Standing ¼ mile	19.7sec	19.9sec	n/a	n/a
Fuel consumption	21-28mpg	20-26mpg	20-25mpg	20-25mpg

PERFORMANCE COMPARISON	Bristol 400	Bristol 401	Alvis 3 litre	Bentley MkVI (4½)	Lagonda 2½	Riley Pathfinder
Max Speed	95.7mph	97.3mph	90mph	102.3mph	90.9mph	100mph
0-60mph	14.7sec	15.1sec	15.5sec	15sec	17.6sec	16.8sec
Standing ¼-mile	19.7sec	19.9sec	20.5sec	19.7sec	21.7sec	20.8sec
Overall fuel consumption	21.4mpg	20.8mpg	19.5mpg	16.5mpg	17mpg	19.5mpg

PRICES

All those to whom we talked, including the manufacturers, stressed the difficulty of calculating a representative value. The easy way out is to say between £20,000 and £30,000 for cars in good condition, which will not need immediate expenditure, with the 400 a little more and the 406 at present a little less than the mean. Exceptional vehicles, with a known good history, either properly restored or original, have sold for higher prices.

The task in trying to evaluate a car in poor or mediocre condition is to first work out an approximate repair cost (see Spares & Repairs) and then subtract this from the following hesitant guide.

400 – £28,000	403 – £27,000	406 – £24,000
401 – £25,000	405 – £27,000	

eg. the value of a 401, needing an engine rebuild with new parts (£8000), bare metal respray (£6000), interior trim (£5000) and sundries (£3000) will be £25,000 – £22,000 = £3000. If this paragraph causes concern it is specifically written to underline the pitfalls for the unwary. There are cars around in less than good condition which do not require work in all these areas.

A sound purchase may still become a valuable asset as well as a source of pleasure.

Elegant Bristol 400 in the hangar at Filton, 1948, in front of the ill-fated over-sized Brabazon airliner

OWNER'S VIEW

Christopher Balfour's enthusiasm for Bristols extends through 30 years of ownership. His favourite is the 406.

"Driving back from Andorra last Autumn, three up plus luggage, in my Bristol 405 proved typical of the adventures I have had over the years of Bristol ownership.

"The Catalonian authorities were re-routing that lovely road from Seo de Urgel to Bourg-Madame, and, missing a deviation sign, we suddenly found ourselves trapped amidst the heavy lorries rumbling along the new section to Puigcerda. Resisting the temptation to turn round we had an experience on that still unsurfaced stretch comparable to the 1946 *Autocar* description (Contemporary Reports), and a reminder of why Bristol owners in Africa and Australia had been so enthusiastic in the fifties.

"The adventure was not yet over either. Over the Col de Puymorens, high pass of the Pyrenees, we ran into an out-of-season snow storm. The front-wheel drivers were searching in their boots – were last Winter's chains still in the garage? – but the 406, with its good traction, ploughed steadily to the summit. Then it was downhill all the way from Hospitalet, through Foix and past Pamiers, and for an hour we pretended the car had that prototype 160 engine! Those 105 horses suffice, but another troop would not go amiss. Next day we were driving on the deserted roads of Aquitaine and Poitou-Charentes. As we had appreciated the ride in Spain, so now we appreciated the steering and roadholding on those superb French surfaces. Driving skills were matched against the natural contours of the land, not against the cut and thrust of other traffic.

"It's a journey like this which confirms that these cars are still practical, useable transport, especially in the less densely populated parts of the world. There is room, the seats are comfortable, visibility, ventilation and brakes are all still satisfactory. On the autoroutes you can waft along in overdrive, revs right down with little noise or vibration. But things are not so rosy in crowded south-east England. The cooling system was designed for optimum cruising performance, not for hour-long traffic jams. In the fifties, when the French, *not* the English, roads were the stuff of adverse comment, the Filton designers could not have conceived that local authorities would so drastically reduce their highway maintenance budgets. The car is not at its best coping with this deteriorating undulating tarmac.

"I was given a weekly subscription to *The Motor* at school after the war. The magazine's description of the 400 in November 1946 was followed by the road test in May '48, and the desire for future ownership

was implanted. It was 12 years later when I read the advertisement for a 400 in the *Hampshire Chronicle* and £375 quickly changed hands. LHT 716 was an exceptional car built for Sir William Verdon-Smith and willed to his doctor. Eric Storey, service manager at Filton, had watched over it from its creation and supervised the fitting of the later 85c engine and B/W synchro box.

"This heather grey beauty (a 'metallichrome' which glowed maroon in sunlight) was a supremely enjoyable and useable driver's car. It still had those Bristol rotary shock absorbers in working order. (Has the combination of ride and handling ever been surpassed?) Having then moved to Gloucestershire, the half-yearly servicing vists (and subsequent trouble-free motoring) are one of life's treasured memories. I remember the car lined up between the surviving 450 and a black 405, still covered in red African dust, which had gone off the road in Kenya and been shipped back for rebuilding.

"Count Lurani, who had extensively campaigned an early 400, referred to it as "that good car with the impossible brakes". Filton improved matters by a servo and harder linings, but, as traffic density

increased in the early seventies, one had to press harder and harder to cease from forward motion. I had a session with TLN 246, the 406 prototype then still at Filton, whilst the 400 was receiving attention, but was very conscious of the bulk for that small engine, and there wasn't the agility of the 400. However, the disc brakes were a revelation.

"Eventually I took the plunge and became the owner of my current 1285 AP. The car had a history of regular use and maintenance with the paint and chrome blemishes of a working vehicle – I did not want the worry of immaculate coachwork. After several visits to Bill Banks' place at Crowland I managed to regain that agility with Konis all round. But in later years (with an imperfect spine) I have come to prefer the mixture of Konis at the front and Spax at the back. This is more comfortable at the expense of a little agility.

"Seventeen years later I still do not regret the change to a 406. My experiences seem to confirm that a six-cylinder Bristol is best considered as a long-term proposition. Because the car will potentially last a lifetime, it is worth getting details like the driving position as you want them and, when a mechanical component does wear, it is worth the time and money to achieve the best refurbishment. The pleasures of ownership do not come from Aston or Ferrari-like speed potential. They are more subtle. There is the soothing effect of handling the work of skilled craftsmen. There are nuts and bolts and plated screws, not plastic clips. There are carefully formed pieces of wood and metal, not plastic mouldings. There is leather, and wool carpet, rather than factory-made materials.

"If a car is set up properly, it will not let you down. If there is a minor engine malfunction, components under the bonnet are easily seen and reached. There is satisfaction in knowing how to cope yourself. It is how these machines go about their work, not ultimate performance, that satisfies. Any six-cylinder Bristol can be a pleasing artefact both to use and have in the garage. ✄

Our thanks to: Tony Crook, Teresa Daniels, Brian Cuddigan (403), Richard Fuggle, John Giles, Tony Hutchings, Spencer Lane-Jones, Bill Limb, Brian May, Charles Oxley-Sidey, Ron Grantham (406) and Anthony Smith for all their help. Special thanks to the Shuttleworth Collection at Old Warden for providing the fine 1917 Bristol fighter for the main picture.

CLUB CLASS

The Alvis TF21 and Bristol 406 took
the drawing room to the road.
Richard Heseltine tries two truly
British takes on luxury motoring

TONY BAKER

There's something intrinsically English in rooting for the underdog, as exemplified by those excruciating Norman Wisdom falling-down-a-manhole-before-getting-the-girl flicks. We love egging on our hapless hero, flying in the face of adversity and heartily cheer as he defies the odds – or so you will have been led to believe.

But forget all that island race benevolence: we're beasts, gorging on the goonish fate of others. View Britain's motor industry – the few remaining slivers that haven't been lifted by Johnny Foreigner – and try not to be jaundiced about the future. Many of the firms that have escaped the clutches of multinationals are addled with incipient senility, so obscurity invariably beckons. But, for all this defeatist talk, you can guarantee that when fossil fuels have been exhausted and cars have become mere relics to be studied in the Natural History Museum, Bristol will still be building idiosyncratic sporting carriages.

How this quintessentially British firm has survived, let alone prospered, is a mystery to

Alvis red triangle used from 1922, originally with wings; Bristol badge is city coat of arms

many but it could be because Bristol has never pandered to public whims and fancies, eschewing fashionable trends for its own blend of bespoke old-world charm. Take this 1959 406. With that gaping chasm for a grille cavity, protruding headlights and oddly cropped tail fins, it can never be described as pretty – or even attractive – but there lingers that intangible quality of presence: you could never mistake it for anything other than a Bristol.

In period, the 406 was an exclusive machine for wealthy 40-somethings to whom a Bentley was too staid, and a Jaguar Mk2 too common. The characteristic Bristol owner was the sort of foppish goober to whom the phrase 'New Labour' meant another bar steward installed at his club; a man outwardly untroubled by image but secretly vying to stand out from the crowd. And there was little to tempt him away from Filton's finest.

If Bristol had anything resembling a rival during this period it was Alvis. Both had backgrounds in the aero industry, automobile output a relatively small, yet important, concern. But if Bristol's clientele was seemingly made up of pinstriped city types, Alvis's T-series was the car of choice for the tweedy set who appreciated the car's coachbuilt construction and lusty 3-litre power.

Though each was the price of a decent house when new, both cars are now within the reach of the great unwashed. The last of Bristol's 'sixes' is something of a compromise. Outwardly, the car lacks the sporting pedigree of its ancestors, the new look being fatter and more upright than earlier efforts. Gone are the

Classic pricey Brit brightwork – twin headlights first appeared on TE21 of 1963

hallmark swooping curves, in their place slab sides and an elevated bonnet line. The styling apes that of Swiss *carrossier* Beutler's one-off 405 shown at the '57 Paris and Earls Court motor shows and is of all-steel-framed construction rather than the composite timber/metal arrangement of previous efforts.

The Alvis – this is a late-model TF – is infinitely more attractive than its rival, but isn't above criticism, the Graber style being rakishly handsome, but with a rear overhang long enough to give a Winnebago an inferiority complex. Despite the Swiss styling, the overall

form is thoroughly British in feel, the swage line that fades out as it runs forward and those sharp-edged wing tops conspiring to produce a silhouette that's in thoroughly good taste. Detailing is beautifully discreet such as the chrome bootlid strake that effectively obscures the jutting handle.

This sense of restrained elegance is carried over to the delightfully old-fashioned cabin. There's nothing ostentatious: no thumping great clods of timber, no non-essential frippery, just modest, gently curved walnut fillets which carry through to the centre nacelle, home to a

Alvis TC/TD/TE/TF21

WHAT TO LOOK FOR

1 Rust is the most serious problem but virtually all body panels are available – at a cost. Ensure car is structurally sound, paying particular attention to the timber A-posts and sills. Going rate for restoration is about four grand a corner
2 Chassis can corrode around the outriggers but replacement frames are out there **3** ZF 'boxes are sturdy but can wear with age and repairs could be expensive. BMW-type Getrag gearbox can be substituted **4** Shouldn't burn oil excessively but check for blue smoke on start up. Could mean the piston rings are on their way out **5** Ensure all the chrome jewellery is in place; body trim is becoming hard to find, and expensive

FACTFILE AND PRICES

Construction steel platform with steel and alloy body over steel/part timber frame
Engine 2993cc pushrod ohv in-line straight-six, 104/115/130/150bhp @ 4000rpm
Gearbox four/five-speed manual, auto option
Suspension front: independent by wishbones, coil springs, telescopic dampers, anti-roll bar; rear: live axle, semi-elliptic leaf springs, telescopic dampers **Brakes** front: Lockheed discs; rear: drums (discs from TD21 S2) **Steering** power-assisted ZF rack and pinion
Length 15ft 8½in **Width** 5ft 6in **Height** 5ft ¼in
Weight 3450lb **Top speed** 115mph (TF21)
0-60mph 10.5 secs **Mpg** 22
Number made 1534 (all types)
Price new £2910 12s 3d **Now** £14,000

Seats comfortable, very slidy; hard to believe huge engine is only 3 litres; lots of understeer

complement of white-on-black instruments. ep aboard the Bristol and it's immediately ent that more emphasis was placed on ence-led civility than sporting pretensions, e no fewer than four cigar ashtrays, and up headrests atop the German Reutter rs. High-quality crushed grain hide and ut veneer dominates, the distinctive steer-wheel with its finger indentations ideally ed ahead of the oh-so-stylish fascia.

o 406 was ever fully road tested by the s at the time, Bristol perhaps being cious that the extra 5bhp gained by upping

the displacement to 2.2 litres wasn't enough to haul the additional weight (288lb) faster than the 405 it replaced. No wonder the firm swiftly switched to Yankee V8 power for all subse-quent models. On paper, the Alvis has its opponent on the ropes in the performance stakes, meaning the Bristol should float like a bee and sting like a butterfly by comparison. But, although in ultimate performance terms the Bristol is on to a loser, the bald statistics of 0-60mph in 13. 9 secs and a top speed barely scraping over the ton don't tell the whole story.

Heading north on quiet Oxfordshire back

Marchal main and driving/spot lamps, stock Lucas units rear, nestling under vestigial fins

Idiosyncratic interior, wheel good to hold; aircraft-inspired styling; pre-war design 'six'

Bristol 406
WHAT TO LOOK FOR
1 Bristols are fairly durable but check inside of wheelarches and the boot floor as they may have corroded. Most panels are still available from the factory **2** Engines are robust but carbs are prone to leaking needle valves which won't always be obvious until you accelerate hard **3** One-shot lubrication system is simple but oil on the outside doesn't necessarily mean that it's getting to where it should. It might be worth removing the kingpins to see if everything's being lubricated **4** Steering should feel taut and responsive – if not, bushes could be worn **5** Ensure that all the cabin trim is in place and small items are getting increasingly scarce, in particular switches and door furniture

FACTFILE AND PRICES
Construction box-section steel frame, steel and alloy body
Engine 2216cc pushrod ohv in-line straight-six, 105bhp @ 4700rpm, fed by three Solex carbs
Gearbox four-speed manual with overdrive
Suspension front: independent by transverse leaf springs; rear: live axle with torsion bars, central torque arm and Watt linkage **Brakes** Dunlop discs all round, vacuum servo-assisted
Steering Marles worm and roller
Length 16ft 6in **Width** 5ft 8in **Height** 5ft
Weight 3010lb **0-60mph** 13.9 secs
Top speed 104mph **Mpg** 22
Number built 174
Price new (1962) £4368 18s 11d
Now £10,000+

The rivals

ALFA ROMEO 2000/2600 SPRINT

Sold from 1960-'66 (7699 built) 1975/2584cc, 115/145bhp, 112/124mph, 0-60mph 9.7 secs
Price new (1962) £3221 4s 9d **Now** £9500

Styled by 21-year-old Giugiaro during his stint at Bertone, Alfa's luxury supercoupé is an attractive car from most angles and fast too. Sadly it doesn't feel especially sporting with ludicrously heavy steering and excessive body roll. Rhd from '64.

JAGUAR XK150

Sold from 1957-'61 (9398 built) 3432cc/3781cc-190/210/220bhp, 124-138mph, 0-60mph 8 secs
Price new (1959) 1694 **Now** £25,000

Essentially a stop gap until the E-type was ready, the lardy XK150 lacks the purity of line of its forerunners but remains curvaceously sexy. Vivid

acceleration but wayward handling and choppy ride let the side down. Straight-six sounds good though, and cabin a joy despite gripless seats.

BMW 3200CS

Sold from 1961-'65 (approx 538 built) 3168cc, 160bhp, 106 mph, 0-60mph 13.2 secs
Price new (1961) £2782 13s 7d **Now** £5500

Marriage of BMW 502 running gear and Bertone

styling flair should have been annulled but the firm persisted with this stylish coupé and lost a fortune. V8 soulless and car surprisingly slow.

FIAT 2300/2300S COUPE

Sold from 1961-'68 (approx 7500 built) 2279cc, 115/130bhp, 115-120mph, 0-60mph 10.7 secs
Price new (1964) £2993 **Now** £6500

High on '60s Latin chic but low on driver involvement, Ghia-styled Coupé an effective

disguise for corpulent 2300 saloon. Sold in the UK from '62, with unnecessary and chintzy makeover in '65. Virtually extinct in Britain.

LANCIA FLAMINIA COUPE

Sold from 1959-'67 (5284 built) 2458/2775cc, 119/136bhp, 105-117mph, 0-60mph 11.5 secs
Price new (1962) £2836 17s 3d **Now** £9000

Aping the lines of Farina's glorious Florida II show

car, the Flaminia Coupé was beautifully made and loaded with goodies, justifying the high price over the saloon. Few takers in the UK.

---

roads, your mood is soon in tune with the car's unflustered pace. Acceleration is leisurely, but, at cruising speeds, the car responds eagerly, the engine happier at mid-range with the overdrive only required for relaxed main-road progress. The smooth ride and refined handling inspire from the outset, sophisticated poise in true Bristol fashion. Over undulating surfaces, the 406 nonchalantly soaks up bumps. Guiding the rack and pinion steering is a joy, with only minimal input required for direction changes. Unlike the Alvis, its ZF power rack feels fearfully light at high speed and unnervingly vague through twisty country lanes.

The Coventry machine sprints off the line with haste, the turbine-smooth straight-six proffering a delicious deep bass burble. It doesn't have the same well-oiled feel of the Bristol unit, but there's an appropriate robustness and flexibility that's predictably impressive. A feeling that's accentuated by the long-throw five-speed ZF 'box that demands a forceful shove on the elegant chrome lever, but is reassuringly positive compared to the Bristol's plodding unit. Ride quality is soporific, if

perhaps a little soggy and under-dampened, but attack corners and the Alvis's delicate equilibrium is easily unsettled. Turn in and your reward is masses of understeer, the TF ploughing on like a wayward shopping trolley.

Driven with suitable decorum, the Alvis is a delight but you're constantly aware of its vast tonnage. It's not a sporting chariot – not even close – but as a dignified tourer it convincingly melds the best of traditional and modern. The Bristol, however, for all its lack of alacrity, ultimately comes out on top. While it might resemble a squatting toad and has trouble getting out of its own way, the actual driving experience is almost soothing. This is a car for the connoisseur: someone who'll appreciate it for what it is – an idiosyncratic, infuriating yet utterly intoxicating blend of almost Bohemian variety. Ideal transportation for the charming eccentric with no love of committees. ◆

Thanks to Malcolm C Elder & Sons for the loan of both cars (01869 340999) and Bristol specialist Brian May for his assistance (0121 430 3767)

Bristol loses the contest on looks, but outhandles Alvis on bumpy roads and corners

Externally there is little difference between the 2·2-litre Bristol 406 and the 5·1-litre 407 model which now supersedes it. The waist moulding has been extended along the sides of the car and there is some embellishment around the name badge on the grille. Bodies are made by Park Royal

Selector buttons for the automatic transmission are on the right of the instrument panel. Polished walnut is used extensively for the redesigned facia and the controls for the heater-demister have been simplified

Bristol 407

5·1-LITRE VEE-8 ENGINE:
AUTOMATIC TRANSMISSION:
NEW FRONT SUSPENSION

WITH the introduction of the new Bristol 407 there has been a break with tradition in the fitting for the first time of a power unit made outside the organization. Since 1947, when the first Bristol 400 appeared, the high-efficiency six-cylinder, long stroke 2-litre engine with opposed valves, based on a BMW design, has proved most successful not only in Bristol cars but also in other makes as well.

Three years ago when the Bristol 406 was announced, the capacity of this unit was increased to 2·2 litres. It has now been decided that, as no further increase in capacity can be made with this design and it is at the limit of its development, its production for Bristol cars will be discontinued and a more powerful engine installed to enhance performance. Spare parts for the 2- and 2·2-litre units, of course, will be available for many years to come.

Basically this latest Bristol is very similar to the 406 model, except for the Canadian-built vee-8 Chrysler engine and automatic transmission which has been installed. This engine has a capacity of 5,130 c.c. and develops a maximum gross power of 250 b.h.p. at 4,400 r.p.m., and a maximum torque of 340 lb. ft. at 2,800 r.p.m.. Compared with the 2·2-litre engine there is

an increase of approximately 110 per cent in power and 140 per cent in torque. As kerb weight is increased by under 20 per cent the performance of the latest car is very considerably higher, and at a recommended maximum crankshaft speed of 5,100 r.p.m. the road speed is 122 m.p.h.

The Chrysler engine is representative of current American practice and has over-square bore-stroke proportions of 98·55mm × 84·07mm. A single five-bearing chain-driven camshaft with high lift cams operates the valves by mechanical tappets, push-rods and rockers. The valves operate directly in the iron cylinder heads without guides, and inlets and exhausts are staggered. The inlet valves are inclined towards the centre of the vee at an angle of 19 deg. to the cylinder axis, giving an improved induction port shape and better breathing. This results in a part wedge, part bath-tub form for the combustion chamber, the sparking plug being located as close as possible to the inlet valve. Five main bearings support the crankshaft and lubrication is from a rotor-type oil pump driven by skew gears from the crankshaft. Carburation is by a Carter four-choke downdraught instrument with automatic choke and the air cleaner has a paper element.

A special radiator has been made by J. W. Lawrence, designed to withstand an operating pressure of 15 p.s.i. In its bottom tank is a tubular heat exchanger for cooling the oil of the automatic transmission. Two Kenlowe electric fans are mounted in front of the radiator and are arranged to cut in under the control of a thermostat in the cooling system. Very few altera-

Bristol 407 . . .

tions to the engine have been necessary to make it fit the Bristol chassis, but the dynamo has had to be repositioned. Existing engine mountings are employed, bonded rubber-to-metal types supporting the engine in shear at the front, with a single mounting consisting of a stiff vertical coil spring and opposed rubber snubbers beneath the gearbox.

Acknowledged to be one of the finest automatic transmissions now produced, the Chrysler Torque-Flite consists of a three-element torque converter having a maximum multiplication of 2·2 at stall (1,810 r.p.m.), and a gearbox with two planetary gear sets providing three forward speeds and reverse. The driver has push-button selectors in place of the usual lever, and intermediate gear can be held up to a road speed of 70 m.p.h. by pressing the appropriate button. There is also the usual kickdown control incorporated in the accelerator linkage. Low may be selected by a button, but this is an emergency gear and there is no automatic upchange to intermediate. There is the usual inhibitor switch which prevents the engine from being started unless the neutral button has been pressed first; no transmission lock for parking is provided.

On the propeller shaft of the Bristol a splined coupling has been dispensed with, the front universal joint permitting axial, as well as angular movement. Initially of Detroit design, but manufactured by Hardy Spicer, it is a type of de Dion pot joint in which spherical bushes, mounted on needle roller bearings on the arms of the joint, and thrust buttons, engage with two slots machined in the input member. The construction is shown in an illustration. A heavier-duty Salisbury rear axle with hypoid bevel final drive is now fitted and one effect of this is that the rear track has been reduced by 1·5in.; on the previous model the rear track was 3in. wider than the front. A controlled slip differential is not considered necessary on this car.

In appearance the chassis frame is very similar to that of the Type 406 although it has been strengthened. It has two widely spaced deep box-section side members braced by three cross-members and the main floor is welded directly to the frame. At the rear a fabricated superstructure, supporting the 18-gallon fuel tank and the framework of the luggage compartment is integrated with the chassis.

Luggage space is increased by housing the spare wheel ahead of the left front door and there are separate compartments for tools between the hinges of the counterbalanced lid. The rear number plate is no longer recessed into the tail panel

▼

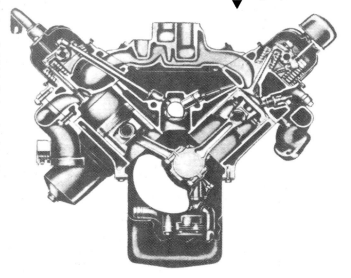

At the front of the frame, however, there is a new massive box-section cross-member to support the wishbone and coil spring front suspension assemblies. This is a change for Bristol who hitherto have fitted a suspension with a transverse leaf spring and upper wishbones only. The new wishbone layout, adopted because of the car's increased weight and performance, consists of forged upper and lower wishbones of unequal length mounted at their inner pivots on rubber bushes. The lower forgings are extended inwards beyond the pivots to act upon rebound rubbers. A coil spring is seated in a pressing bolted to the lower wishbone and has a concentrically mounted Armstrong telescopic damper.

An unusual feature of the front suspension is that the vertical link supporting the stub axle is cast in aluminium alloy, the shaft being pressed into a machined bore in the link and secured by a self-locking nut. This gives a valuable reduction in unsprung weight. Both upper and lower swivels are spherical joints of Engineering Productions (Clevedon) manufacture. Since these have sealed nylon sockets and the wishbones have rubber bushes, there are no greasing points on the front suspension.

Although previous models had rack and pinion steering gear, this has now been changed to a Marles cam and roller gear, manufactured by Adamant Engineering; it has been possible to obtain more accurate steering geometry with a conventional three-link track rod in conjunction with the new suspension. The ball joints of this steering linkage also have nylon sockets and require no greasing.

In the rear suspension there are only minor changes to the layout, which comprises longitudinal torsion bars connected to the axle side tubes by arms and pivoted drop links. These

The front portion of the chassis has been redesigned to accommodate wishbone and coil spring front suspension. A shroud plate protects the inner faces of the brake discs from road grit

SPECIFICATION

ENGINE

No. of cylinders ...	8 in 90 deg vee
Bore and stroke ...	98.55 x 84.07mm (3.88 x 3.1in.)
Displacement ...	5,130 c.c. (313 cu. in.)
Valve position ...	Overhead, pushrods and rockers
Compression ratio...	9 to 1
Max. b.h.p. (gross)...	250 at 4,400 r.p.m.
Max. b.m.e.p. (gross)	164 at 2,800 r.p.m.
Max. torque (gross)	340lb. ft. at 2,800 r.p.m.
Carburettor ...	Carter 4-choke downdraught AFB 3131S
Fuel-pump ...	Carter mechanical
Tank capacity ...	18 Imp. gallons (81 litres), including 2 gallons (9 litres) reserve
Sump capacity ...	10 pints (5.6 litres)
Oil filter ...	By-pass
Cooling system ...	Pressurized, pump and thermostat, two electrically driven fans, thermostatically controlled
Battery	12-volt, 72 ampère hour

TRANSMISSION

Coupling	Three-element torque convertor
Gearbox	Planetary type, three forward speeds and automatic control. Push button selectors on facia
Overall gear ratios...	Top 3.31; 2nd 4.80; 1st 8.10; Reverse 7.28 to 1
Final drive	Hypoid bevel, 3.31 to 1

CHASSIS

Brakes	Dunlop discs, vacuum servo
Disc diameter ...	11.25in.
Suspension: front ...	Wishbones and coil springs
rear	Live axle, longitudinal torsion bars, central torque arm; Watts linkage lateral location
Dampers	Armstrong telescopic
Wheels	Pressed steel, five studs, 5K rims
Tyre size	6.00—16in.
Steering	Marles cam and roller
Steering wheel ...	Sprung two-spoke, 17in. dia.
Turns, lock to lock	3.75

DIMENSIONS (Manufacturer's figures)

Wheelbase	9ft 6in. (290cm)
Track: front	4ft 5in. (135cm)
rear	4ft 6.5in. (138cm)
Overall length	16ft 7in. (505cm)
Overall width	5ft 8in. (173cm)
Overall height	5ft 0in. (152cm)
Turning circle	39.5ft (12m)
Ground clearance ...	6.5in. (16.5cm)
Kerb weight	3,584lb—32cwt (1,626kg)

PERFORMANCE

Top gear m.p.h. per 1,000 r.p.m.	23.7
Torque lb. ft. per cu. in. engine capacity	1.09
Brake surface area swept by linings	520 sq. in.
Weight distribution, dry ...	F. 53 per cent; R. 47 per cent

two arm-and-link assemblies, together with a forged aluminium-alloy torque arm between the chassis frame and the rear of the final drive casing, locate the axle longitudinally and absorb torque reaction. As before, lateral location is by a Watts link pivoted at the rear of the final drive casing. Rubber bushes are now fitted between torsion-bar arm and drop link, and the telescopic dampers are fixed so that their upper mountings can be detached without requiring access from inside the body. Rebound check straps are now fitted.

As before, Dunlop 11.25in. disc brakes, with a Lockheed tandem vacuum servo, are fitted front and rear. A new pad material—Ferodo DA2—is used which is less prone to squeal. A magnesium alloy casting on the bulkhead supports the pendant brake pedal which pivots in Glacier DU dry bushes. These bushes are also used in the steering idler assembly. Previously a centralized chassis lubrication system was fitted but this is now no longer necessary.

The body is built by Park Royal Vehicles and has aluminium panelling over a steel framework welded to the chassis. There has been much attention to sound deadening; inside surfaces of pressings and panels are sprayed with Aquaplas and there are Revertex barrier mats on floor areas and bulkhead. Like the previous model, the finish and equipment are to the highest standard. One of the few changes that have been made is that the facia has a new and simpler layout. There are now two controls only for the heating-ventilating system, whereas previously there were four. Headroom for the rear seat passengers is increased; they have ample leg room even when the front seats are adjusted fully back. These front seats are of Reutter type, the backrests of which can be adjusted to any angle, including a reclining position. Crushed grain leather is used throughout for seat covering and trim.

Weight distribution (dry) is 53 per cent front and 47 per cent rear, compared with an almost 50-50 balance on the 406 model.

A short drive showed that the new car has good handling characteristics, almost neutral but with a slight bias towards understeer, and as the suspension rates have been lowered a little the ride is softer. It accelerates very rapidly indeed and gear changes take place particularly smoothly. The brakes are light to operate and require a very small pedal movement. Altogether an extremely high standard of refinement and quietness has been achieved on this new model which is priced at £3,525 basic, and the total, including British purchase tax, is £5,141 17s 3d—an increase of £773. The only optional extra in this very fully equipped car is an H.M.V. radio with twin speakers.

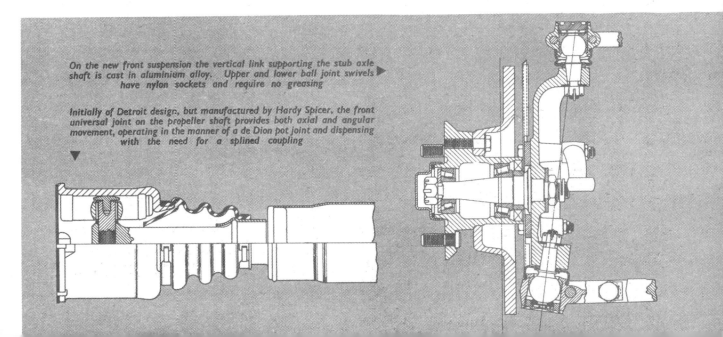

On the new front suspension the vertical link supporting the stub axle shaft is cast in aluminium alloy. Upper and lower ball joint swivels have nylon sockets and require no greasing ▶

Initially of Detroit design, but manufactured by Hardy Spicer, the front universal joint on the propeller shaft provides both axial and angular movement, operating in the manner of a de Dion pot joint and dispensing with the need for a splined coupling ▼

The Bristol 407

Luxurious British Sports Saloon
with a 5.2-litre V-8 Engine
from Canada

1962 Cars

IN its classical British sports saloon appearance, the new V-8 Bristol type 407 differs little from the type 406 which it supersedes. In its speed and refinement however, this new car with a Canadian-built 5,130 c.c. engine and torque converter transmission represents an enormous leap forward. Our full Road Test Report, to be published next week, will show how quickly, quietly and controllably this comfortable saloon can exceed 120 m.p.h.

Our artist's drawing and the accompanying photographs show that this Bristol's handsome and very practical two-door saloon bodywork is based on a straightforward box-section chassis frame. In more than doubling the size of their engine, the Bristol designers have not needed to make any fundamental changes in the layout which served so well on their 406 model, other than re-designing the independent front wheel suspension to use coil springs and ball-jointed transverse wishbones in place of a transverse leaf spring. In its essentials, the proven chassis reinforced by a steel body frame, the Dunlop disc brakes which

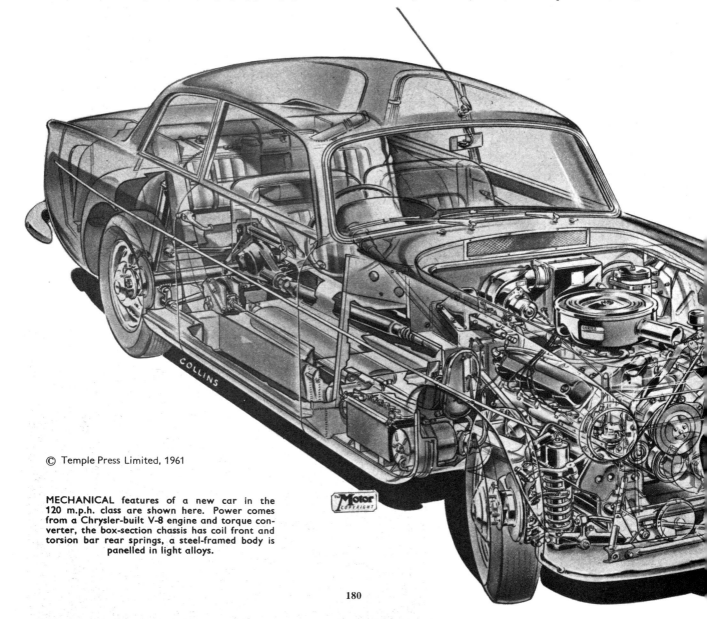

COLLINS

MECHANICAL features of a new car in the **120 m.p.h. class** are shown here. Power comes from a Chrysler-built V-8 engine and torque converter, the box-section chassis has coil front and torsion bar rear springs, a steel-framed body is panelled in light alloys.

The Motor
COPYRIGHT

LONG and slender lines of the new 407 Sports Saloon are shown in these two photographs. Foglamps, reversing lamps and radio are standard items of equipment.

have ample cooling air space around them thanks to retention of 16-inch wheels, and the torsion bar rear suspension system with a Watt straight-line linkage to locate the axle laterally, have required only detail refinements. Increasing engine displacement by 130%, torque by 160% and peak power by 135% has involved a weight increase of only about 20%.

Power for this very new kind of Bristol comes from a V-8 engine built in a Canadian factory of the Chrysler Corporation. Slightly over-square in its ratio of bore to stroke, this 5,130 c.c. unit is commendably light in weight, American foundrymen being world famous for their accuracy in producing relatively thin-walled iron castings. A compression ratio of 9:1 makes 100-octane preferable for sustained hard driving but not essential, the camshaft is a high-lift design operating with mechanical tappets, and a four-choke downdraught carburetter has the throttle butterflies opening successively in pairs. Adapting this engine to the Bristol chassis has involved only such minor alterations as new cooling water outlets, and provision of an oil pressure gauge connection. The engine-driven fan is eliminated in favour of two side-by-side electric fans which come into action if necessary at low car speeds. Pulley alignment checks at Bristol ensure reliable belt drive to the water pump and Autolite D.C. generator at high engine r.p.m.

The Chrysler 3-speed torque converter transmission with which this engine was designed to operate has been standardized for the Bristol 407. It may be left to operate quite automatically, or a line of press-buttons identified as 1, 2, D(rive), N(eutral) and R(everse) on the facia just to the right of the steering wheel may be used to select any gear manually. The hydraulic torque converter which provides a 2.2/1 multiplication of effort when starting from rest operates to a diminishing extent up to about 2,500 r.p.m. in any gear, and provides effortlessly lively top gear

performance; a "kick down" change into an indirect gear, or "press-button" selection of 1st or 2nd gear, turns liveliness into really dynamic acceleration such as few saloon cars built anywhere in the world can match. Cooling for the torque converter fluid in traffic or slow hill-climbing conditions is by an oil-to-water heat exchanger in the bottom tank of the engine radiator.

Independent front wheel springing on the Bristol 407 is to a new design using pairs of unequal-length transverse wishbones, widely spaced rubber bushes forming the inner wishbone pivots whereas Clevedon nylon-lined ball joints form the outer steering and suspension pivots. Vertical coil springs enclose Armstrong telescopic dampers, and there is an anti-roll torsion bar. Extremely rigid mounting of a Marles steering gear on the front suspension cross member is a detail typical of this carefully planned chassis, which has been under test on the road for more than a year and needs greasing only at 10,000 mile intervals.

The unusual rear suspension follows proved Bristol lines, and has been refined only in a few details which eliminate unwanted friction. Fore-and-aft torsion bars have short arms on their rear extremities shackled to the axle, these arms and a trailing link above the propeller shaft locating the axle fore-and-aft. A Watt linkage behind the axle ensures true lateral stability. Built within the perimeter of an aircraft factory although now the responsibility of an independent company, this Bristol uses light-alloy forgings for several unsprung parts such as suspension links and the front stub-axle carriers. To eliminate propeller shaft splines which might bind under the torque of a big engine, a Detroit needle roller bearing universal joint which permits axial as well as angular deflection has been used at the front of a single-piece propeller shaft.

Bodywork for the new Bristol is being built and trimmed by Park Royal Vehicles Ltd., using light alloy panels over a steel

CONTROLS shown here include the exclusive Bristol steering wheel, to the right of which are five push-buttons permitting manual selection of any ratio in the automatic gearbox. Full instruments, including an electrical r.p.m. indicator, are on a wood veneer panel.

The Bristol 407

COMFORTABLE rear seat accommodation for two men is provided in the two-door saloon body, and the leather-upholstered front seats have reclining backrests.

POWER for vivid acceleration and effortless 100 m.p.h. cruising comes from this Canadian-built engine and torque converter. Twin Kenlowe electric fans ahead of the radiator operate when required, no engine-driven fan being fitted.

frame. Of two-door design but long enough to be an uncramped four seater, this body has a rear luggage locker extending across the full width of the car behind the rear wheels. Fuel is carried in an 18-gallon tank directly above the rear axle (a reserve tap guards the last 2 gallons), a compartment in the left front wing conceals the spare wheel, and in the right front wing the battery, brake servo and reservoir are accommodated. A considerable weight of sound absorbent material is used above the chassis and inside body panels to make this a really quiet car in spite of its outstanding performance.

Traditionally British design is evident inside the body, with high quality leather upholstery and veneers wood of sober colour. Individual front seats have reclining backrests, there is leather-covered crash padding above and below the facia as well as flexible sun visors, and the familiar Bristol steering wheel with one arched pair of spokes is retained. Fresh-air interior heating and de-misting is fitted as standard, and there is an inbuilt push-button radio with speakers above the windscreen and on the rear parcel shelf.

With its heater, radio, screen washers, twin foglamps and other items of a full specification, this remarkable new Bristol's basic price is £3,525, purchase tax and the present tax surcharge lifting the total to £5,141 17s. 3d. A full road test report on this newcomer to the ranks of the world's fine cars will be published in *The Motor* next Wednesday.

BRISTOL 407 SPECIFICATION

ENGINE

Cylinders	...	90° V-8 with 5-bearing crankshaft.
Bore and stroke	...	98.55 mm. × 84.07 mm. (3.875 in. × 3.3125 in.).
Cubic capacity	...	5,130 c.c. (313 cu. in.).
Piston area	...	94.6 sq. in.
Compression ratio	...	9.0/1.
Valvegear	...	Overhead valves operated by push-rods and rockers from one chain-driven camshaft.
Carburation	...	Carter AFB 3131 S downdraught 4-barrel (progressive) carburetters, fed by Carter mechanical pump, from 18-gallon tank (2 gallons in reserve).
Ignition	...	12-volt coil, centrifugal and vacuum timing control, 14 mm. K.L.G. or Autolite sparking plugs.
Lubrication	...	Chryco by-pass filter and 8-pint sump.
Cooling	...	Water cooling at 14 lb./sq. in. pressure with pump and thermostat: twin Kenlowe electric fans operated by temperature sensitive switch: water capacity (including heater) 36 pints.
Electrical system	...	12-volt 72 amp/hr. battery charged by 35 amp generator.
Maximum power (gross)	...	250 b.h.p. at 4,400 r.p.m., equivalent to 144 lb./sq. in. b.m.e.p. at 2,425 ft./min. piston speed and 2.64 b.h.p. per sq. in. of piston area.
Maximum torque (gross)	...	340 lb. ft. at 2,800 r.p.m., equivalent to 164 lb./sq. in. b.m.e.p. at 1,545 ft./min. piston speed.

TRANSMISSION (Chrysler Torqueflite automatic)

Clutch	...	Hydraulic torque converter, maximum multiplication 2.2/1 at approx. 1,800 r.p.m. with car at rest.
Gearbox	...	Epicyclic 3-speed and reverse, operating automatically or with push-button selection of 2nd and 1st ratios.
Overall ratios	...	3.31, 4.8 and 8.1; rev., 7.28; Torque converter operates with all ratios.

Propeller shaft	...	Detroit single-piece open, with front universal permitting axial movement.
Final drive	...	Salisbury 4 HA hypoid bevel.

CHASSIS

Brakes	...	Dunlop discs on all wheels, hydraulically operated with Lockheed vacuum servo assistance.
Brake dimensions	...	Front and rear discs 11¼ in. dia.
Brake areas	...	31.8 sq. in. of lining working on 520 sq. in. rubbed area of discs.
Front suspension	...	Independent by ball-jointed transverse wishbones of unequal length, coil springs enclosing Armstrong telescopic damper, and anti-roll torsion bar.
Rear suspension	...	Rigid axle located by torsion bar arms, trailing top link and transverse Watt linkage. Longitudinal torsion bars controlled by Armstrong telescopic dampers.
Wheels and tyres	...	5-stud steel disc wheels with 5K rims and 6.00-16 tubed Dunlop road speed tyres.
Steering	...	Marles worm gear with 3-piece track rod.

DIMENSIONS

Length	...	Overall 16 ft. 7 in.; wheelbase 9 ft. 6 in.
Width	...	Overall 5 ft. 8 in.; track 4 ft. 5 in. at front and 4 ft. 6½ in. at rear.
Height	...	5 ft. 0 in.; ground clearance 6½ in.
Turning circle	...	39 ft. 6 in.
Kerb weight	...	32 cwt. (without fuel but with oil, water, tools, spare wheel, etc.).

EFFECTIVE GEARING

Top gear ratio	...	23.8 m.p.h. at 1,000 r.p.m. and 43.1 m.p.h. at 1,000 ft./min. piston speed.
Maximum torque	...	2,800 r.p.m. corresponds to approx. 66 m.p.h. in top gear.
Maximum power	...	4,400 r.p.m. corresponds to approx. 105 m.p.h. in top gear.

THE AUTOCAR, 6 OCTOBER 1961

BRISTOL

407

Simplicity and cleanliness of line make the Bristol an out-standingly smart, prestige car

AFTER the last war, Bristol obtained the rights and patents of the well-known 2-litre, 328 BMW engine. Besides selling this engine to other concerns, these famous aircraft manufacturers turned to the construction of their own car. From the original 400 model to the 405 the 2-litre engine was used, and for the 406 its capacity was increased to 2·2 litres. As might be expected from such a firm, the car was of the highest quality.

Even so, it had become obvious that the character of the engine was strictly limiting the scope of the car. Accordingly it was decided to replace this power unit, and look for a proprietary engine for the new model, the 407. Their choice, the Canadian-built 5,130 c.c. vee-8 Chrysler engine, seems to have been a particularly happy one. Most American-designed vee-8 power units are noted for their power and smooth running, and automatic transmissions for mechanical refinement. Both these properties are very much in keeping with the fine appointments and high-quality finish of this latest Bristol, of which the price places it in the luxury bracket. Since, however, it is a two-door saloon it remains basically an owner-driver car.

As might be expected with a power unit developing 250 b.h.p. at 4,400 r.p.m., the performance is outstandingly good, although the car is no lightweight. A standing-start quarter-mile is covered in 17·4sec, and 100 m.p.h. can be reached from standstill in 26·6sec. The maximum speed of the car, 122 m.p.h., can be attained in under 50sec. This maximum represents the engine speed limit of 5,100 r.p.m. which the manufacturers had requested *The Autocar* to respect. The ease with which the engine reached this limit in top gear indicated that a still higher maximum was available for the irresponsible. A higher rear-axle ratio could be fitted advantageously for, in spite of the loss in ultimate acceleration, there would be gains in lower engine revolutions at a given cruising speed and improved fuel economy.

To provide adequate cooling, a special radiator pressurized to 15 p.s.i. is fitted to this model. This means that the temperature at which the coolant water boils is raised to approximately 120 deg. C. As well as this there are two Kenlowe electric fans mounted in front of the radiator. On the test car, the thermostatic switch, still in the experimental stage, controlling these fans did not work correctly, as they often failed to start operating even when the temperature had passed 105 deg. C. Normal running temperature was 85 deg. C. but use of full throttle, high speed cruising or long delays in traffic resulted in the temperature rising to well over 100 deg. G. When this happened, excess heat beneath the bonnet affected the carburation, causing irregular running of the engine at tick-over or low speeds. More cold air round the carburettor and inlet manifolding might well cure this.

Hot or cold, the engine never hesitated to start immediately. At the first start in the morning, even if the rather lengthy starting instructions in the driver's manual were followed

Deep pile carpets, supple crushed grain leather and polished walnut veneer give the interior of the Bristol an attractive and inviting look. Only the radio was an extra on a very well-equipped car

BRISTOL 407 . . .

meticulously, some of the plugs were inclined to wet, and misfiring—chronic on one occasion—usually occurred. The manufacturers are well aware of this trouble and are seeking to remedy it with the help of a sparking plug manufacturer.

In many ways the manner in which this car performs is even more impressive than sheer performance in terms of figures. The refinement of this high-powered magic carpet is greatly assisted by the Chrysler Torque-Flite automatic transmission. Two slight criticisms can be levelled at it; firstly, a jolt that occurred when selecting a gear from neutral; secondly, an uneven surge on full-throttle changes-up or when the kick-down switch was operated. This latter complaint can be eradicated by attention to driving technique. On changes-up the surge is avoided by slight easing back of the accelerator just prior to the automatic change-up point. In the case of kick-down, smoother driving is achieved by selecting the appropriate button of the transmission controls. The kick-down, however, is there for emergencies, but its switch has sufficient resistance to prevent accidental actuation.

Controls for the transmission consist of five buttons; reverse, neutral and three forward selection—Drive, which automatically uses all three ratios, Low hold and Intermediate; the last holds the middle ratio, irrespective of speed or throttle opening, up to 70 m.p.h. and changes down to it again at 60 m.p.h. It was possible to kick-down from Intermediate to Low below 27 m.p.h., and from Top to Intermediate up to 59 m.p.h. Full throttle changes with Drive selected occurred at 38 m.p.h. and 71 m.p.h. In Low hold the r.p.m. limit of 5,100 is equivalent to 49 m.p.h.

The usual safety lock prevents accidental engagement of reverse; when moving forward at high speeds Neutral is engaged if the reverse button is selected mistakenly. The starter will operate only if the transmission is in Neutral.

Hand in hand with this performance goes superb braking. Dunlop discs are fitted at front and rear, and more than one member of the road test staff considered their operation as fine as they had ever experienced. They are powerful and progressive, and instil complete confidence when quick stops have to be made from any speed. As so often happens with disc brakes, the test figures obtained from 30 m.p.h. do not seem to warrant such glowing praise; but at this low speed their retardation effect was marred by a tendency for the right front wheel to lock prematurely, a fault not apparent at high speeds.

The hand-brake, mounted between the front seats, held the heavy car on the 1-in-3 test hill, from which angle only a dab at the throttle was needed to make the car rocket forward. The transmission does not incorporate a parking lock.

Overall fuel consumption for the test was 14·1 m.p.g., but with gentler use of the throttle and by not exceeding 3,000 r.p.m. a figure of 20 m.p.g. could be returned. Very fast cruising is the *métier* of this particular vehicle and naturally consumption rises abruptly with speed. A constant-speed fuel consumption of 19·5 m.p.g. at 70 m.p.h. is certainly good for this car, and must be attributed to the aerodynamic shape of the body and the large engine doing little work at this speed. There is an 18-gallon fuel tank—two of these gallons are in reserve and are obtained by a facia-mounted switch. Even driven hard, therefore, the range of this car would be nearly 200 miles. Three pints of oil were added to the engine during the 1,016 miles of the test.

Pleasant Handling

Handling of the Bristol is at its best on open, sweeping bends, and on such roads it is a joy to drive. Through tighter corners, on narrow roads, the car feels more cumbersome, partly because the steering becomes much heavier at slower speeds. Even so, at no time could the steering be called other than good. That it cannot be placed in the outstanding class is perhaps because the final degree of precision has been sacrificed to gain complete freedom from road shock and tremor at the steering wheel.

The 407 understeers under all conditions, but not severely on dry surfaces. With so much power available, however, it is easy to bring the tail round by judicious use of the throttle pedal. Directional stability is not beyond criticism, and when the car is cruising fast a cross-wind will make it lurch slightly.

Certain combinations of bumps and road surface catch out the rear suspension and on a corrugated "washboard" surface

Power plant. The Chrysler vee-8 fits snugly into the space that used to be occupied by the 2-litre Bristol engine; The large air-cleaner hides a vast four-choke downdraught Carter carburettor

it has the unusual property of being smooth at 30 m.p.h. and 70 m.p.h. but suffering vibrations in between these critical speeds. The ride is a curious mixture of soft and firm and the comfort varies very much with the road surface. At all times the front-seat occupants have a smooth ride, but those sitting in the back are not always so lucky. Although the ride is almost devoid of roll or pitch, vertical movements can become quite pronounced under certain circumstances.

Similar to that of the 406, the 407's frame has been strengthened wherever necessary. Certainly it is very rigid, as is the bodywork—aluminium panels on a steel framework. There is no trace of scuttle or body shake regardless of how bad the road surface might be. The almost complete absence of road and mechanical noise is uncanny; Park Royal Vehicles, who build the body, have been highly successful in the attention they have paid to sound-deadening.

First quality leather covers the seats and trims the insides of the doors. The front seats are by Reutter and have adjustable squabs. They are extremely comfortable and, like any well-designed seat, will fit a person of almost any shape and stature. Shorter people complained that they sat too low for a good driving position, but the purchaser of such a car could have the seat adjusted to his own requirements. Plenty of leg-room is left for the rear-seat occupants, even when the front seats are fully back on their runners. There is a central

Although only a two-door saloon, its doors are sufficiently wide to allow easy access to the rear seats. An ashtray is provided on each outside arm rest and there is room for immediate wants in the side pockets

Above: A clever use of space in the front wings to stow the spare wheel allows more room in the boot for luggage; Below: Deeper than this photograph implies, the boot is also a good shape for the conventional types of suitcase. Either side of the number plates are reversing lamps

fold-down arm rest, and it would be possible to fit three people into the rear seat.

As might be expected from a concern closely related to the aircraft industry, the layout of the driving controls and instruments is exemplary. To the right of the steering column are grouped the transmission control buttons and the starter-ignition switch. On the steering column is a turn indicator switch which incorporates headlamp flashers. To the left there is a row of switches—fuel reserve, windscreen washers and two-speed wipers, main and auxiliary lamps, instrument panel light with rheostat, courtesy light and heater and ventilation controls with two-speed fan. These switches are well separated and, although they are initially slightly confusing, it would not take a driver long to learn them. Two of the switches were not very precise in their operation.

Visible through the upper segments of the steering wheel and above its crescent spokes are the instruments—rev counter, speedometer, gauges for oil pressure, water temperature and fuel, ammeter and electric clock. Four different-colour tell-tale lights indicate headlamp high beam, ignition, fuel reserve and turn indicators. All these instruments are simple and legible and tell at a glance, without resorting to any 'gimmickry', all the driver could need to know.

For this two-pedal car Bristol have not adopted a wide brake pedal; yet it is easy to use either left or right foot for braking. There is a foot-operated dip-switch. The main headlamps are excellent and the auxiliary spot and fog lamps are standard. The built-in reversing lamps are also powerful and very effective.

Great care has been taken to avoid reflections in the windscreen from the instruments and steering wheel, so it is a pity that the two small ashtrays mounted above the facia cause particularly bad reflections.

Effective Heater

Changes have been made to the heating system since the 406 and it now works very effectively. Even on maximum boost the fan runs very quietly. Fresh-air ventilation, however, is still inadequate, and the opening of any window, including the hinged rear extractors, results in considerable wind noise—an irritation in a car which otherwise is almost silent. The quality of the overcentre clips on the extractors is scarcely in keeping with the rest of the car. All-round visibility is good and the pillars have been kept to a praiseworthy slimness. A larger rear-view mirror would take better advantage of the big back window.

The interior of the car is plentifully provided with storage space; there is a pocket in each door, and one in the back of each front seat. Beneath the sill of each rear side window there is a small well where articles can be stowed. A large, slightly sunken platform lies beneath the rear window and an ample locker is in the left of the facia. For larger luggage there is a deep, well-shaped boot. This will certainly carry all the luggage two people could ever need and enough for four in most circumstances. In a shelf between the hinges of the bootlid there is a toolroll with a selection of high-quality spanners.

Much space has been gained in the boot by the mounting of the spare wheel in the left front wing. A lid, opened by a carriage key, hinges upwards, and in here, with the spare wheel, are housed the jack and wheel brace. In a similar compartment on the right-hand side are mounted the battery, fuses and brake servo mechanisms.

Few owners of this car are likely to carry out their own servicing, but for the mechanic most items for routine inspection or adjustment can be reached easily. The bonnet lifts

backwards and is spring counter-balanced. The release lever for the bonnet catch is beneath the fascia.

This latest Bristol is for the wealthy man who prefers to drive himself, but does not appreciate bulk and swagger. Certain small criticisms have been made, but this is a car whose price and quality are such that the most minor faults become prominent. It is comfortable, refined, beautifully made, and its well-balanced performance makes it very fast and safe transport. Certainly this car's fine low-speed torque, superb acceleration in the middle ranges, powerful, responsive brakes, predictable roadholding and compact overall dimensions allow the miles, and other traffic, to be passed in effortless and smooth luxury.

BRISTOL 407

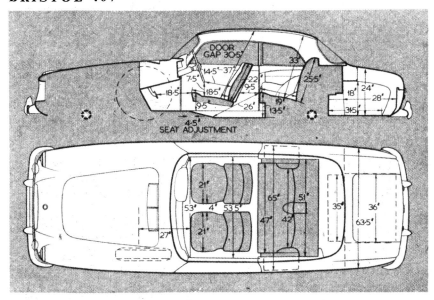

DOOR GAP 30·5
SEAT ADJUSTMENT

------------ PERFORMANCE ------------

ACCELERATION TIMES (mean):

Speed Range, Gear Ratios and Time in Sec.

m.p.h.	Top	Intermediate	Low
10—30	—	4·3	2·6
20—40	5·4	4·0	2·7
30—50	5·5	4·7	—
40—60	6·5	5·1	—
50—70	7·4	5·1	—
60—80	8·6	—	—
70—90	9·4	—	—
80—100	10·0	—	—
90—110	13·5	—	—
100—120	20·8	—	—

Gear ratios: Top, 3·31; Intermediate, 11·66-4·8; Low, 17·6-8·0.

From rest through gears to:

30 m.p.h.		3·4 sec.
40	„	4·8 „
50	„	7·4 „
60	„	9·9 „
70	„	12·5 „
80	„	16·6 „
90	„	21·4 „
100	„	26·6 „
110	„	34·9 „
120	„	47·4 „

Standing quarter mile 17.4 sec.

MAXIMUM SPEEDS ON GEARS:
(At manufacturer's limitation of 5,100 r.p.m.)

Gear	m.p.h.	k.p.h
Top	122	196
Intermediate	71	114
Low	49	79

TRACTIVE EFFORT (by Tapley meter):

	Pull (lb per ton)		Equivalent gradient
Top	405 ...	...	1 in 5·4
Intermediate	585 ...	...	1 in 3·7

BRAKES (at 30 m.p.h. in neutral):

Pedal load in lb.	Retardation	Equiv. stopping distance in ft.
25	0·18g	177
50	0·53g	56
75	0·80g	37
85	0·93g	32·2

FUEL CONSUMPTION (at steady speeds in top gear):

30 m.p.h.	28·4 m.p.g.
40 „	26·0 „
50 „	23·7 „
60 „	21·7 „
70 „	19·5 „
80 „	17·9 „
90 „	15·7 „
100 „	13·8 „
110 „	11·7 „

Overall fuel consumption for 1,016 miles, 14·1 m.p.g. (20.04 litres per 100 km.).

Approximate normal range 14-20 m.p.g. (20-14 litres per 100 km.).

Fuel: Super Premium.

TEST CONDITIONS: Weather: Dry and sunny, 10 m.p.h. wind.

Air temperature, 65 deg. F.

Model described in *The Autocar* of 8 September, 1961.

SPEEDOMETER CORRECTION: m.p.h.

Car speedometer ...	10	20	30	40	50	60	70	80	90	100	110	120
True speed	10	20	30	39·5	49	59	70	80	90·5	101	111·5	122

------------ DATA ------------

PRICE (basic), with saloon body, £3,525. British purchase tax, £1,616 17s 3d. Total (in Great Britain), £5,141 17s 3d. **Extras:** Radio. Price not available.

ENGINE: Capacity, 5,130 c.c. (313 cu. in.). Number of cylinders, 8 in 90 deg. vee. Bore and stroke, 98·5 × 84·1 mm (3·87 × 3·21in.). Valve gear, overhead, pushrods and rockers. Compression ratio, 9 to 1. B.h.p. 250 (gross) at 4,400 r.p.m. (B.h.p. per ton laden 140·9). Torque, 340lb.ft. at 2,800 r.p.m. M.p.h. per 1,000 r.p.m. in top gear, 23·8.

WEIGHT: (With 5 gal fuel), 32·5 cwt. (3,640lb). Weight distribution (per cent); F, 52·9: R, 47·1. Laden as tested, 35·5cwt (3,976lb). Lb per c.c. (laden), 0·77.

BRAKES: Dunlop disc hydraulic, servo assisted. Disc diameter: F and R, 11·25in. Swept area: F, 260 sq. in., R, 260 sq. in. (292·9 sq. in. per ton laden).

TYRES: 600—16in. Dunlop RS5. Pressures (p.s.i.): F, 28; R, 28 (normal). F, 33; R, 33 (fast driving).

TANK CAPACITY: 18 Imperial gallons. Oil sump, 10 pints. Cooling system, 36 pints.

STEERING: Turning circle, Between kerbs: R, 37ft. 7·5in.; L, 36ft. 10in. Between walls: R, 39ft. 9·5in. L, 39ft. 0in. Turns of steering wheel from lock to lock, 4.

DIMENSIONS: Wheelbase, 9ft. 6in. Track; F, 4ft. 5in.; R, 4ft. 6·5in. Length (overall), 16ft. 7in. Width, 5ft. 8in. Height, 5ft. 0in. Ground clearance, 6·5in. Frontal area, 21 sq. ft. (approximately).

ELECTRICAL SYSTEM: 12-volt; 72 ampère-hour battery. Headlamps, 60-45 watt bulbs.

SUSPENSION: Front, wishbones, coil springs and telescopic dampers with anti-roll bar. Rear, live axle located by central torque arm and transverse Watts linkage, telescopic dampers.

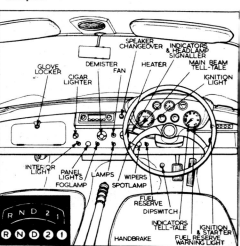

BRISTOL GETS A V8

Abandoning the famous old Bristol 2.2-litre engine, the new Bristol 407 car is now powered by a large capacity and very powerful Chrysler V8 unit.

AMONG the few individually built specialist cars for 1961 is the Bristol 407 with a new Canadian-built 5-litre Chrysler engine and Torque-flite automatic transmission with manual push-button control.

Although the new engine is two and a half times greater in capacity than the power units of the earlier series of Bristols, it remains a comparatively economical car.

The engine is a V8 with angled valves in polyspherical combustion chambers operated by rockers and cross over pushrods. Bore and stroke are 98.55 by 84.07 mm giving a swept volume of 5130 cc. Compression ratio is 9 to 1 and power output is 250 bhp at 4400 rpm. There is a Carter four choke downdraught carburettor, automatic choke for cold starting and a large paper element air cleaner/silencer. Twin electric fans operated by a thermostat control,

ensure maximum cooling irrespective of engine speeds.

Chrysler designed the Torque-flite automatic transmission with torque converter has three speeds and reverse and there is an intermediate gear hold to allow engine braking. Gear ratios are 8.1, 4.8, 3.31 and reverse 7.28 to 1.

The chassis has been redesigned and there is a new front suspension with wishbones, coil springs, telescopic dampers and an anti-roll bar — and no lubrication is required. Rear suspension is by hypoid rear axle, torsion bars, Watts linkage and telescopic dampers. Steering is the Marles worm type and the Dunlop disc brakes are servo assisted.

Fuel tank holds 18 gallons including two gallons in reserve. Reserve switch is on the instrument panel and there is also a lockable filler cap.

Body is similar to previous model with light alloy panels, two doors, separate front seats with fully re-

clining back rests. Rear seats hold two people and have a centre folding arm rest. Upholstery is in leather over foam rubber cushions and backs.

The facia panel and door cappings are in walnut but the facia panel is padded at top and bottom. There is an illuminated lockable glove box and deep pockets at each side of the rear seats. The rear quarter lights open and the roof light is operated by opening the door or by a switch on the facia panel. The steering column is adjustable and the push-button gear selector panel is within a few inches of the steering wheel. Instruments are grouped in a cowl in front of the driver and include rheostat controlled illumination, speedometer with trip recorder, tachometer, electric clock, fuel gauge, oil pressure gauge, water temperature gauge and ammeter. There are warning lights for ignition, headlamp main beam, direction indicators, brake fluid level and fuel reserve. #

187

The Motor Road Test No. 34/61

Make: Bristol **Type:** 407

Makers: Bristol Cars Ltd., Filton, Bristol.

Test Data

CONDITIONS: *Weather: Warm and dry with light wind for most tests, cooler with drizzle during maximum speed runs. (Temperature 66°-73° F., Barometer 29.9 in. Hg.) Surface: Smooth concrete and tarred macadam. Fuel: Super-premium grade pump petrol (approx. 101 Research Method Octane Rating).*

INSTRUMENTS

Speedometer at 30 m.p.h.	3% slow
Speedometer at 60 m.p.h.	1% slow
Speedometer at 90 m.p.h.	3% slow
Speedometer at 120 m.p.h.	3% slow
Distance recorder	5% slow

WEIGHT

Kerb weight (unladen, but with oil, coolant and fuel for approx. 50 miles) ... ... 32½ cwt.
Front/rear distribution of kerb weight 53/47
Weight laden as tested ... ... 36¼ cwt.

MAXIMUM SPEEDS

Flying Mile

Mean of four opposite runs ... ... 125.2 m.p.h.
Best one-way time equals ... ... 129.0 m.p.h.
N.B. Recommended engine speed limit of 5,100 r.p.m. is exceeded beyond approx. 122 m.p.h.
"Maximile" Speed. (Timed quarter mile after one mile accelerating from rest.)
120 m.p.h. reached in approx. 1 mile from rest.
Speed in gears (Automatic upward changes at full throttle.)
Max. speed in 2nd gear ... ... 70 m.p.h.
Max. speed in 1st gear ... ... 36 m.p.h.

FUEL CONSUMPTION

27½ m.p.g. at constant 30 m.p.h. on level.
25½ m.p.g. at constant 40 m.p.h. on level.
24 m.p.g. at constant 50 m.p.h. on level.
22 m.p.g. at constant 60 m.p.h. on level.
20 m.p.g. at constant 70 m.p.h. on level.
18 m.p.g. at constant 80 m.p.h. on level.
16½ m.p.g. at constant 90 m.p.h. on level.
14 m.p.g. at constant 100 m.p.h. on level.
Overall Fuel Consumption for 889 miles, 58.2 gallons, equals 15.3 m.p.g. (18.5 litres/100 km.)
Touring Fuel Consumption (m.p.g. at steady speed midway between 30 m.p.h. and maximum, less 5% allowance for acceleration), 17.5 m.p.g.
Fuel tank capacity (maker's figure), 18 gallons, including 2-gallon reserve.

STEERING

Turning circle between kerbs:
Left ... ... 34¼ feet
Right ... ... 34½ feet
Turns of steering wheel from lock to lock 4

BRAKES from 30 m.p.h.

0.99 g retardation (equivalent to 30½ ft. stopping distance) with 100 lb. pedal pressure.
0.80 g retardation (equivalent to 37¾ ft. stopping distance) with 75 lb. pedal pressure.
0.55 g retardation (equivalent to 54¾ ft. stopping distance) with 50 lb. pedal pressure.
0.24 g retardation (equivalent to 125 ft. stopping distance) with 25 lb. pedal pressure.

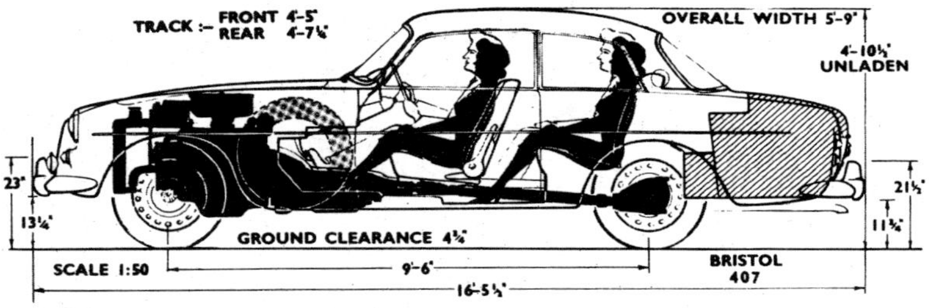
TRACK :- FRONT 4'-5" REAR 4'-7¼"
OVERALL WIDTH 5'-9"
4'-10½" UNLADEN
23"
13¼"
21½"
11¾"
GROUND CLEARANCE 4¾"
SCALE 1:50
9'-6"
16'-5½"
BRISTOL 407

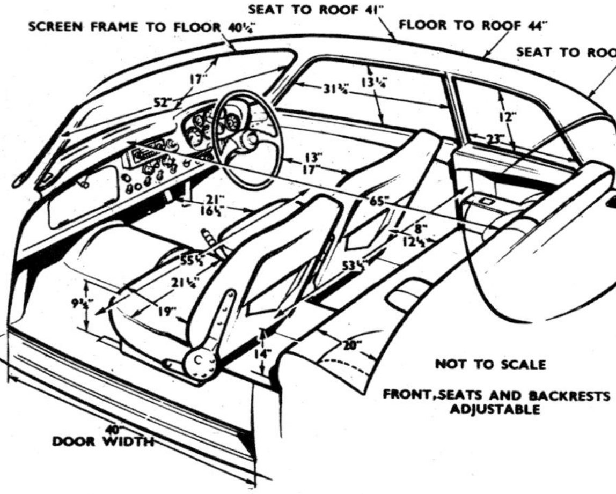
SEAT TO ROOF 41"
SCREEN FRAME TO FLOOR 40½"
FLOOR TO ROOF 44"
SEAT TO ROOF 38½"
NOT TO SCALE
FRONT, SEATS AND BACKRESTS ADJUSTABLE
40" DOOR WIDTH

ACCELERATION TIMES from standstill

0-30 m.p.h.	3.0 sec.
0-40 m.p.h.	4.7 sec.
0-50 m.p.h.	6.8 sec.
0-60 m.p.h.	9.2 sec.
0-70 m.p.h.	12.1 sec.
0-80 m.p.h.	16.2 sec.
0-90 m.p.h.	20.8 sec.
0-100 m.p.h.	26.3 sec.
0-110 m.p.h.	32.9 sec.
Standing quarter mile	17.3 sec.

ACCELERATION TIMES on upper ratios

	Top gear	"Kick Down" Range
0-20 m.p.h.	—	1.7 sec.
10-30 m.p.h.	—	2.2 sec.
20-40 m.p.h.	—	2.9 sec.
30-50 m.p.h.	5.1 sec.	3.8 sec.
40-60 m.p.h.	6.2 sec.	4.5 sec.
50-70 m.p.h.	7.1 sec.	5.3 sec.
60-80 m.p.h.	7.8 sec.	7.0 sec.
70-90 m.p.h.	8.7 sec.	8.7 sec.
80-100 m.p.h.	10.0 sec.	10.0 sec.
90-110 m.p.h.	12.1 sec.	12.1 sec.

HILL CLIMBING at sustained steady speeds

Max. gradient on top gear, steeper than 1 in 5 (Tapley exceeds 450 lb./ton).

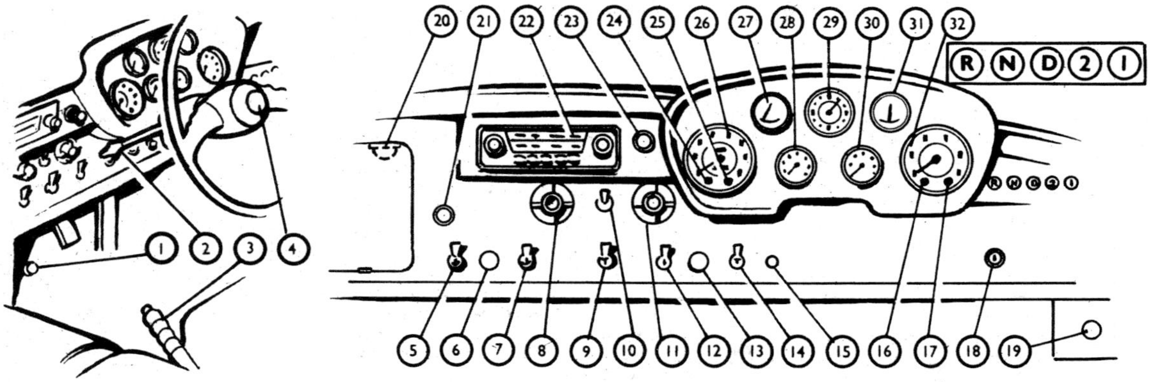
R N D 2 1

1, Dip switch. 2, Trafficators and headlamp flasher control. 3, Handbrake. 4, Horn button. 5, Interior lights switch. 6, Panel light rheostat control. 7, Fog-lamp switch. 8, Demist and defrost control. 9, Main lighting switch. 10, Blower switch. 11, Heating and ventilation control. 12, Spotlamp switch. 13, 2-Speed wipers control. 14, Reserve petrol switch. 15, Trip reset. 16, Trafficator warning light. 17, Fuel reserve warning light. 18, Ignition and starter. 19, Bonnet release. 20, Map reading and locker light. 21, Cigar lighter. 22, Radio. 23, Radio speakers balance control. 24, High beam warning light. 25, Ignition warning light. 26, Speedometer. 27, Fuel gauge. 28, Water temperature gauge. 29, Clock. 30, Oil pressure gauge. 31, Ammeter. 32, Rev. counter.

The BRISTOL 407

SPORTS SALOON lines of the new V-8 Bristol are shown here. The bonnet is long but over-all width is conveniently moderate, and body pillars are slender in the modern manner.

Rocket-age Performance in a Quiet Traditional Sports Saloon

LAST week the select company of really fine cars which are built in modest numbers by a very few countries of the world gained a new recruit. Sheer performance is combined so well with quiet comfort and smooth controllability in the new Bristol 407 that this English car with a Canadian power unit provides some of the best motoring that money can buy.

Large engines from the New World have been put into British or Continental chassis before now, and have almost invariably produced extremely high performance. This Bristol is by no means a light car, and there is no sign of its power unit being in any extreme state of tune, yet it contrives to produce performance even superior to expectations. Within a quarter mile of starting from rest it exceeds 80 m.p.h., a second quarter mile sees it doing a quiet 100 m.p.h., and only a mile after starting it can be doing about 120 m.p.h. Whilst we timed it at a mean speed of just over 125 m.p.h. in wet and windy weather,

driving at much more than 120 m.p.h. with the normal axle ratio involves going beyond the recommended engine speed limit of 5,100 r.p.m.

Most Bristol 407s are likely to come into the hands of mature drivers who will be unworried by a 120-m.p.h. speed limit but very appreciative of being able to cruise quietly at 100 m.p.h. on modern roads with little or no regard to wind or gradient, to check their speed promptly and surely when other traffic blocks the way, and to be back again at their cruising speed within a very few seconds of getting a clear road once more.

In its proportions the new 5,130-c.c. Bristol is long and lean like its 2-litre predecessors, seating its passengers further back along the wheelbase than is currently fashionable. Save for the length of bonnet which momentarily impedes driving vision over the most acute sort of hump-back bridge, traditional sports-car proportions which make this a handsome car do not seem to restrict its amenities, partly because they leave room for such things as the spare wheel and the battery inside the front wings instead of in the rear luggage locker. Four men can be very comfortable, individual seats in front where there is only a very low gearbox cover, and a cushion-height transmission hump in the rear, discouraging three-abreast travel for which room might otherwise be found. Extending down to the bottom of the car and sideways into both rear wings, the luggage locker is surprisingly capacious. Long-limbed drivers might wish to specify a rather greater range of adjustment for the variable-rake driving seat, whereas the steering wheel and instrument panel are high enough for short drivers to have to peer over them.

Well furnished with fine leather, pile carpets and polished woodwork of a fairly dark tone, the interior is pleasing without being decorative, and thoroughly practical. A lockable glove compartment of reason-

able size is supplemented by four pockets in the doors and behind the front seats, parcel wells on each side of the rear seat and a recessed shelf below the rear window. Full instrumentation is provided on the facia, but the electrical r.p.m. indicator on our test car at times fluctuated in its readings more than the over-run behaviour of a torque converter would explain. Neatly arranged tumbler switches would have been appreciated more fully at night if the main lighting switch had differed in shape as well as in position from five others above and on each side of it, but the arm of the direction indicator switch is, of course, arranged to flash the headlamps when squeezed towards the wheel rim.

Engineers at the Bristol factory emphasize the care with which friction has been eliminated from their suspension system, using coil springs at the front and torsion bars at the rear, and over most of the minor irregularities of British highways this 407 model rides with almost uncanny smoothness and freedom from road noise. In certain more adverse conditions it

SAVING space at the back of the body for luggage, the spare wheel, jack and wheelbrace are stowed inside the left front wing. A similar locker on the opposite side of the car houses a large-capacity battery.

In Brief

Price £3,525, plus purchase tax £1,616 17s. 3d., equals £5,141 17s. 3d.
Capacity ... ... 5,130 c.c.
Unladen kerb weight ... 32¼ cwt.
Acceleration:
20-40 m.p.h. in kick-down range ... ... 2.9 sec.
0-50 m.p.h. through gears ... ... 6.8 sec.
Maximum top gear gradient: steeper than 1 in 5.
Maximum speed: 125.2 m.p.h. (engine r.p.m. limit reached at 121-122 m.p.h.)
Touring fuel consumption: 17.5 m.p.g.
Gearing: 23.8 m.p.h. in top gear at 1,000 r.p.m.; 43.1 m.p.h. at 1,000 ft./min. piston speed.

The BRISTOL 407

behaves less well, the tyre pressures advised for this very fast car (from 28 to 33 lb., according to whether it is to be run at below or above 105 m.p.h.) making potholes or similar sharp bumps very audible. Also, and especially when several passengers are being carried, humps or awkward combinations of bumps encountered at speed can set the rear suspension moving more than is comfortable for back-seat passengers, the modern tendency to have lower-frequency front than rear springs not appearing to have been followed. Nevertheless, as a civilized car for civilized roads, this Bristol rides superbly at most times.

Stable at Speed

Softly sprung and quiet, the 407 is not built for road racing, but it is so fast that cornering qualities which fell far short of excellence would be very irksome. One could wish for even more positive steering mechanism when making small changes of course on a cambered and not entirely straight road, but once in a corner this car has exceptionally strong self-centring feel in very frictionless steering. Thoroughly stable at speed, the Bristol corners without much roll and with no sideway whatever, thanks to the Watt linkage which gives positive and symmetrical control of rear axle side-float, the tyres seldom making themselves heard unless fiercely provoked. Cornering in the wet, adhesion may reach its limit at the front rather than at the rear unless some of the great power is being used.

Vast though the available power is by European standards, it is delivered very smoothly and quietly indeed, thanks to progressive carburation which opens the four throttles of a single big carburetter two-by-two in succession, and to a very fine automatic transmission. With the accelerator pushed down to the floor, the Bristol surges away from rest, with no

wheelspin on a hard surface and a deceptive lack of fuss, second gear engaging smoothly after less than 4 seconds at about 35 m.p.h. and top gear equally smoothly at 70 m.p.h. only about 12 seconds after the start from rest. On a whiff of throttle, the getaway can be as gentle as the driver wishes and top gear will have engaged unnoticed by the time 25 m.p.h. is reached. At 30 m.p.h., the accelerator can be depressed until the kick-down switch is felt, and whilst the engine speed indicator will swing round to 2,500 r.p.m. as the hydraulic torque converter does its job, speed will jump up from 30 to 50 m.p.h. in only 5.1 sec. without a change out of top gear—away up the speed range, acceleration from 90 to 110 m.p.h. takes only 12.1 sec.! Kick-down pressure

on the accelerator will engage first gear at any speed below 25 m.p.h., or second gear at anything between 25 and 60 m.p.h., to produce even more vivid medium-speed acceleration.

For the keen driver, push buttons (lit internally at night) are provided to the right of the steering wheel rim, and second gear may be selected almost imperceptibly for gentle braking or in anticipation of the need for utmost acceleration (with this button pressed, top gear engages only above 70 m.p.h. and disengages as soon as the speed drops to 60 m.p.h.) or first gear can be selected for powerful engine braking (perhaps inevitably much less smooth) down a very steep hill. Whether press-buttons are preferable to the usual quadrant for operation by "feel" without the driver taking his eyes off the road is a moot point, but they certainly work very well.

Engine braking need not normally be depended upon, the Dunlop disc brakes

190

with vacuum servo operation being ample in size and well provided with air cooling. From high speeds, or for slow descents of precipitous Welsh mountain roads, the brakes were smoothly and quietly competent, slight "sponginess" in the servo being felt only at very low speeds in traffic. A brake pedal position which required the driver to lift his foot several inches from the accelerator was disappointing, and should be capable of improvement. The handbrake would hold the car on a 1 in 3 test hill, its adjustment screws being readily accessible through ventilation holes in the rear wheels—no parking pawl is incorporated in this particular automatic transmission. Since the torque converter enables this amply-powered car to potter steadily up a 1 in 5 hill in top gear, ability to re-start anywhere that there is wheel-grip goes without saying, and whilst radiator temperatures can rise to 100° C. in slow-speed hill climbing before the twin electric fans switch themselves on, this with a pressurized radiator leaves a safe margin before boiling could occur—only by stopping the engine at the top of a steep Welsh mountain by-way was a slight loss of water induced.

A Quiet Car

With all windows closed and a fair intake of fresh air through the scuttle vent, this is a quiet car right up to its top speed, but some little warmth seems to penetrate into the bodywork from the big V-8 engine, and with outside air temperatures above 70° F. it is preferable to open a window and put up with some wind noise. We did not have cold weather in which to sample the heater's full power, but late at night it proved controllable when slight warmth was needed. Starting on summer mornings was prompt, though the starter was the noisiest thing on the car, and the engine's automatic choke gave temperament-free

DOMINATED by the carburetter air filter which almost totally eliminates power roar, the Canadian-built Chrysler V-8 engine of 5,130 c.c. displacement fits neatly into the Bristol chassis. Sparking plugs are invisible, but reasonably easy to change.

warming up: hot, the engine distinguished itself from some other V-8 units by being an easy and reasonably prompt starter.

Two conventional headlamps of sealed-beam type gave quite a good spread of light for ordinary night driving, on both main and dipped beams, but lacked the range to encourage really fast cruising after dark. Of the two additional lamps provided as standard equipment, one gives a flat beam for fog, whilst the pencil beam of the other comes from too low a position to augment

headlamp beam length very usefully.

The present 10% surcharge on an already high purchase tax which has lifted its price over the £5,000 mark emphasizes that this Bristol is a car for the fortunate few. We use the word fortunate quite deliberately, this remarkable new all-rounder being one of the pleasantest and least tiring to drive of all the world's very fast cars.

Specification

Engine

Cylinders	V-8 at 90°
Bore	98.55 mm.
Stroke	84.07 mm.
Cubic capacity	5,130 c.c.
Piston area	94.6 sq. in.
Valves	o.h.v. (pushrods)
Compression ratio	9/1
Carburetter	Carter AFB 3131 S 4-choke downdraught, with automatic choke
Fuel pump	Carter mechanical
Ignition timing control	Centrifugal and vacuum
Oil filter	Chryco by-pass
Max. power (gross)	250 b.h.p.
at	4,400 r.p.m.
Piston speed at max. b.h.p.	2,425 ft./min.

Transmission (Chrysler Torqueflite automatic)

Clutch	Torque converter, maximum multiplication 2.2/1
Top gear	3.31
2nd gear	4.8
1st gear	8.1
Reverse	7.28
Propeller shaft	Detroit open, with needle roller universals
Final drive	Salisbury hypoid bevel
Top gear m.p.h. at 1,000 r.p.m.	23.8
Top gear m.p.h. at 1,000 ft./min. piston speed	43.1

Chassis

Brakes	Dunlop disc type, with vacuum servo
Brake disc diameters	11¼ in., front and rear
Friction areas	31.8 sq. in. of pad area working on 520 sq. in. rubbed area of discs
Suspension:	
Front:	Independent by transverse wishbones, coil springs and anti-roll torsion bar.
Rear:	Rigid axle, longitudinal torsion bars, trailing link above propeller shaft and transverse Watt linkage.
Shock absorbers	Armstrong telescopic
Steering gear	Marles worm type
Tyres	Dunlop Road Speed RS5 (tubed) 6.00-16

Coachwork and Equipment

Starting handle ... ... None
Battery mounting: In right-hand front wing (external access panel).
Jack: Smiths bevel-geared pillar type
Jacking points: 2 sockets on frame side members used through trapdoors in floor.
Standard tool kit: Jack, wheelbrace, tool roll containing pliers, 6 open-ended spanners, sparking plug spanner, screwdriver, pliers, feelers, brake bleeder and wrench.
Exterior lights: 2 headlamps, 2 sidelamps/flashers, spotlight, foglamp, 2 stop/tail lamps, 2 reversing lamps, rear number plate lamp.
Number of electrical fuses 2
Direction indicators: Self cancelling flashers (white front, amber rear).
Windscreen wipers: Electrical two-speed twin-blade, self parking.
Windscreen washers: Trico, operated from wipers switch.
Sun visors ... Two, universally pivoted
Instruments: Speedometer with total and decimal trip distance recorders, r.p.m. indicator, clock, fuel contents gauge, oil pressure gauge, coolant thermometer, ammeter.
Warning lights: Dynamo charge, headlamp main beam, petrol reserve switched on,

direction indicators, handbrake on or brake fluid level low.
Locks:
With ignition key: Ignition/starter switch and driver's door.
With other keys: (a) luggage locker and glove box; (b) fuel cap.
Glove lockers ... One on facia, lockable
Map pockets: 2 inside doors, 2 behind front seats.
Parcel shelves: Behind rear seat; also parcel wells on each side of rear seat.
Ashtrays: 2 on windscreen rail, 2 in rear compartment.
Cigar lighters ... ... One on facia
Interior lights: Roof lamp with courtesy switches on doors, light inside glove box, light inside luggage locker.
Interior heater: Fresh air heater and screen de-mister fitted as standard.
Car radio: Optional extra twin-speaker Radiomobile.
Extras available ... ... Radio
Upholstery material ... ... Leather
Floor covering: Pile carpets with felt underlay
Exterior colours standardized: 4 plain and 3 metallic colours, or duotone combinations.
Alternative body styles ... ... None

Maintenance

Sump: 8 pints plus 2 pints in filter, S.A.E. 10W/30 or 20W/30.
Gearbox and torque converter: 16 pints, fluid type "A" Automatic Transmission.
Rear axle: 3 pints, S.A.E. 90 hypoid gear oil
Steering gear lubricant ... S.A.E. 90 EG gear oil
Cooling system capacity (including heater): 36 pints (1 drain tap and 2 plugs)
Chassis lubrication: By grease gun every 6,000 miles to rear hubs and handbrake mechanism.
Ignition timing: 10° before t.d.c. at 500 r.p.m.
Contact-breaker gap ... 0.014-0.019 in.
Sparking plug gap ... ... 0.035 in.
Valve timing: Inlet opens 13° before t.d.c. and closes 55° after b.d.c.; Exhaust opens 51°

before b.d.c. and closes 17° after t.d.c.
Tappet clearances (Hot):
Inlet: 0.010 in.
Exhaust 0.018 in.
Front wheel toe-in ... ... ⅛ in.
Camber angle ... Zero at kerb weight
Castor angle ... ... 1°
Steering swivel pin inclincation ... 6½°
Tyre pressures: Front and rear, 28 lb. normal or 33 lb. for sustained speeds over 100 m.p.h.
Brake fluid ... ... Dunlop disc brake fluid
Battery type and capacity: Lucas BT 11A, 12 volt 72 amp. hr.
Miscellaneous: Every 2,000 miles wash air filter on engine oil filler, oil ignition distributor, generator and manifold heat valve. Also adjust handbrake.

Bristol 450: Great Unknown

The terse success story of the Bristol Car Company's three-year campaign in two-liter racing is almost unknown outside the small circle of factory personnel and racing enthusiasts who witnessed it, yet it was one that produced the wildly imaginative Bristol 450's, a prime example of which is the 1954 coupe shown on this page. This is due to the hitherto tight-lipped policy of the Bristol Aircraft Company's car-making branch. The breach between making cars and aircraft is not as great as it seems. Saab and Rolls-Royce operate successfully in both today, and racing gave Bristol a chance to show its cars were as dependable as its aircraft. Nevertheless, in the 1953-to-1955 period, interest in two-liter cars was far from great. And while a three-car sweep class win is doubly impressive when it is scored twice in two successive years, as Bristol did at Le Mans with the 450's, finishing in seventh, eighth and ninth overall positions rarely make many headlines. CAR AND DRIVER's request for information on the 450s' racing record was warmly received and we are pleased to present on these and the following two pages descriptions and histories of all three 450 models. The reasons behind Bristol's entrance into sports-car racing are not clearly defined, but there can be little doubt that the prospect of competition success to underscore the basic quality of the Bristol line of fast sports-tourers enticed George White, son of the aircraft company's founder and head of its car-building offshoot. Under White's direction, Bristol began production of cars just after World War II. At the London Motor Show in November, 1952, he announced that Bristol would be represented at Le Mans in 1953. His directive, with only eight months of working time ahead, put Vivian Selby, the firm's sales manager, in charge of the crash program. Apart from their engines and transmissions, the heavy and luxurious Bristol passenger cars didn't offer a basis from which to work. Since time did not permit evolution of an all-new chassis, an important short cut was authorized: Bristol bought from E.R.A. (English Racing Automo-

The Bristol sports-tourers provided the engine for the 450 racing cars. It was essentially a low-compression version of the aluminum-headed rockerbox six that Bristol had been supplying to Cooper, E.R.A., Frazer-Nash and others for Formula 2 racers, and traced its beginnings to the pre-World War II BMW 328 engine. Bristol paid homage to its power source by designing the grilles of its early sedans after that of the BMW, as is shown on the next pages. While full specifications are shown in the table at the right, there are other significant details to note. The cutaway drawing shows that the engine was almost lost under the Bristol's broad hood. It was flanked by side-mounted fuel tanks which contributed to the broad-shouldered stance of the 450's. In addition, while E.R.A. had converted its engines to dry-sump operation, Bristol retained an oil pan. However, a 2¼-gallon tank in the left front fender was used to replenish the supply as it was consumed and gave rise to the fallacy that the 450's had dry sumps too.

The wide stance of the Bristols was no illusion. Their width, in both coupé and roadster versions, was 65 inches, although the overall length shrank more than a foot when the open car replaced the 176-inch coupé for 1955. The 450s' engines were developing 142 bhp at 6,000 rpm when they began racing in 1953 at Le Mans. Refinements raised it to 155 at 6,000.

SPECIFICATIONS BRISTOL Type 450	
Manufacturer:	Bristol Car Company Ltd. Filton, near Bristol, England
ENGINE	
Displacement	120 cu. in. 1971 c.c.
Dimensions	Six cylinders, 2.59 in. bore, 3.78 in. stroke
Valve gear	Overhead valves inclined at 80 degrees included angle, operated by pushrods and rocker arms from single camshaft in side of block.
Carburetion	Three Solex DC
Power	155 bhp @ 6,000 rpm
CHASSIS	
Wheelbase	97.5 in.
Tread	F 51 in., R 52 in.
Overall length	176 in.
Transmission	4-speed Bristol, in unit with differential.
Brakes	Lockheed hydraulic 12-inch drums, inboard.
Tankage	33 gallons
Curb weight	1826 lbs.

biles), the Hodkin-designed chassis of its G-Type. This car had shown promise in the then-current two-liter Formula 2 racing category. As may be seen in the cutaway drawing at the bottom of the page, Bristol's adaptation of the E.R.A. frame maintains its key features: tubular side members of massive cross section, splaying slightly toward the rear. Just ahead of the rear axle, they angled sharply upward to provide abutments for the coil spring/shock absorber units. While the 450's chassis heritage is evident in the cutaway, it had some dissimilarities from the E.R.A. original. The main difference was that the Bristol frame used round steel tubes of 4½-inch diameter for its main members in place of the 6-inch-diameter aluminum tubes used by E.R.A. In addition, the frame of the 450 was about three-and-one-half pounds heavier than E.R.A.'s. Bristol used five crossties, including one a few inches from the rear suspension riser. The rectangle it formed was crisscrossed by two small-diameter diagonals to carry the differential unit. The side-view picture of the second 450 clearly shows the startling top line which has been compared to that of a Bactrian camel. Its very long hood and the pronounced tail fins were evidence that Bristol Cars had been tested in Bristol Aircraft's wind tunnel. The body panels, supported by small-diameter tubes, were made of thin aluminum. Sprayed British racing green, the cars were pronounced ready for Le Mans.

THE BRISTOL 450's

First 450 had startling styling when it appeared at Le Mans.   After its success at Reims, the

450's Bright, Brief Career

The first edition of the Bristol 450 (two appeared at the Le Mans 24-hour race in June, 1953) showed a curious mixture of inventiveness and styling abandon. This was probably a result of the great pressure put on the firm's racing crew to produce a great car at first try. The front of the car (above left) was marred by protuberant headlight and driving light nacelles, haphazard slotting and slatting and the presence of an exposed oil radiator. At the rear, the fender lines were broken by the taillights sticking out from them.

The 450s' first Le Mans was a failure. Both cars retired in the ninth hour of racing. Some reports at the time said it was due to faulty "connecting rods," that forced retirement of the Whitehead/Macklin car and "fire" as the cause of Wisdom/Fairman's retirement. Both are true, but neither was the whole truth. Actually, the shedding of crankshaft balance weights led to connecting-rod breakages and in the case of the Wisdom/Fairman car a rod punctured both the block and exhaust pipe, causing the oil fumes to catch fire. One of the Bristols had been averaging almost 95 mph. Considering that '53 was the first year Le Mans was won at over 100 mph, its performance is a credit to all concerned. Apart from the drivers, these included Dave Summers, who headed the design team, chief mechanic Stan Ivermee, Percy Kemish, an ex-Bentley racing mechanic, and Sammy Davis, one-time Le Mans winner, who acted as consultant to Selby on team management. Furthermore, pit work was excellent. At Reims, the same year, the outcome was much more encouraging. The two cars ran the 12-hour race, one retired with clutch trouble and the other won its class. This was followed by a rash of record breaking at Montlhéry with

new two liter marks set for 200 and 500 miles, 500 and 1000 kilometers, and three and six hours at speeds up to 126 mph. The 450s were finally rolling so Bristol made sure the project gathered no moss in the nine months between this Montlhéry spree and Le Mans, 1954. After Reims, the bodies had been smoothed off at the front end (see above center) and the side panels just behind the front wheels were depressed for better ducting of hot air away from the brakes.

At Montlhéry it had been found that the body area between the tail fins was setting up a local vacuum, so it was filled in, with a 14 per cent reduction in overall drag. The bulge over the vertical carburetors was opened at its forward end to form a cold-air scoop. The engine had demonstrated its reliability, but the need for more power was apparent. A new cylinder head, with separate intake

Ten years of Bristols, starting with the 1946 400 model, far right, include, right to left, the

194

450's contours were refined.

The ultimate 450 was the 1955 roadster which was the fastest.

ports, was produced, and fed by three dual-choke Solex carburetors. This raised the output from 142 to 155 bhp, still at 6,000 rpm.

The developments paid dividends in the form of the 450s' best racing performance to date. In addition to producing the lithe coupe, better performance resulted with more victories. In spite of heavy rain, Le Mans, 1954, saw Wilson and Mayers first in the two-liter class, seventh overall with a 90.76 mph average. Wisdom and Fairman were second in class and eighth overall, while Keen and Line took a class third and ninth overall. Theirs was the third three-car team to finish intact in the longest of road races, an achievement in itself. Pitwork was again outstanding, with the fastest Bristol spending only a total of 15 minutes out of 24 hours on stops. The Wisdom/Fairman car spun out in the last hour. While repairs were being made, one of the officials, with the delicate tact and forbearance only they can exercise when they feel like it, picked up

an unauthorized jack the mechanics were using and walked away with it without a word. For 1955, Bristol sawed the tops from the coupés to form roadsters. There were no significant engine changes, but the removal of the top and its lowering effect on the frontal area increased top speed while decreasing fuel consumption. One of the cars was timed at 150.34 mph on the Mulsanne straight at Le Mans in 1955 and had gasoline mileage as high as 15 miles per gallon. The original plan for 1955 was to contest the Reims 12-hours and skip Le Mans. But Reims was cancelled, so Bristol decided to run the 24-hours. The result was that the same three-man team as the previous year, paired identically, occupied the same class and overall positions: 1, 2, 3 in class and 7, 8, 9 overall. The team increased its aggregate distance by 307 miles to over 6,775, even though they were told by their pit crew to slow down for the last four hours. It has never been disclosed, until now, that Bristol donated its

winnings to the fund for relatives of victims of the Pierre Levegh crash in which 82 were killed (See CAR AND DRIVER, January, 1962, page 34). Cornering power had been augmented in the roadsters through a revised rear suspension, the work of Dave Summers, who evolved a system he described as "part Watts, part Summers." One of its features was that it could be set to give zero rear-wheel steering effect. Fairman had the most experience with the 450's although the future world champion, Jack Brabham, was a reserve driver in '55. Fairman says the '53 cars were fierce understeerers, but would change suddenly to oversteer. By 1955, the handling was viceless, he said.

Why did Bristol stop racing when its efforts were showing big returns? Probably because there were other fancy fish in the pan, big, flying fish like the Britannia airliner. Will Bristol cars make a comeback? They doubt it. But it was wonderful while it lasted.

401 coupé, the 403 convertible and sedan, the 404, the 405 coupé and convertible, and the 450.

Close-Up:
BRISTOL'S 407 GT ZAGATO

A US-engined challenger for the Aston Martin DB4

A YEAR ago Sports Car World was tipping that the change of ownership at Bristol Cars would bring back performance into the range. Anthony Crook, who with managing director George White has brought the firm from the aircraft combine that gave it its name, is a racing driver whose achievements with Bristols and Bristol-engined racing cars went a long way towards putting the marque on the map. For nearly two years before the takeover Crook has been trying to keep alive the Bristol sporting tradition by offering coachwork from his Milanese friend, Gianni Zagato, both on new 406 chassis and on reconditioned earlier ones.

But it had been a losing fight: the Filton factory kept getting further and further away from the original GT concept and the BMW-derived engine itself was steadily going out of date. Even with Zagato's ultra-lightweight bodywork, the 406 would not keep up with competitors costing far less.

In fact, the Bristol had become a bit of an enigma. There was a car with a racing tradition and a competition-bred engine, offered with expensive super-luxury bodywork on a chassis that rode like a pre-war two-seater. Everybody knew there would be a change as soon as Crook and White got control, but which way would they swing?

One of the world's finest-looking fast cars, new 5.2 Zagato offers unusual stability thanks to tremendous wheelbase. It is a foot shorter overall than 407 sedan.

Tail view shows the new car's superb wind-tunnel form. This is one of the few GT cars which manage to look right with disc wheels. Another is Maserati's famous 3500.

Story: DOUG BLAIN

Photographs: GEOFFREY GODDARD

The answer, briefly, is every way. Performance is back all right, yet the standard Bristol is more luxurious than ever. And now Crook, through his own concern Anthony Crook Motors, is offering a GT variant that promises to be one of the fastest all-out sports cars in the world.

Heart of the revamped 407 is Chrysler's medium-size all-iron 5130cc 90-deg V8, as used in the Detroit — and Canadian-built — Dodge Dart and Plymouth Fury. The engine slots into the very long (9ft 6in wheelbase) Bristol chassis complete with its own three-phase automatic transmission. Naturally, a powerplant like that transforms the big car's performance. It becomes an immediate competitor in a cut-throat field, at least on acceleration and top speed.

To make sure the improvement carries through to the rest of the car, White and Crook have given the coachwork contract to Lord Brabazon's Park

Frontal treatment is simple, dignified, with low penetration point to help high-speed stability. Grille resembles that on Zagato's much smaller OSCA 1500 GT coupe.

Royal Vehicles, builders of the celebrated London buses, and authorised a complete revision of bodywork standards. The changes bring the Bristol up with the world's best-made cars, although they do involve a penalty in weight (574lb) and in price, which stands now at more than £A4000 in England before tax.

In fact the 407 saloon, although it is much, much faster than the 406, has become even less sporting. It is now a swift and silent luxury car, with supple suspension and first class roadholding to back up its beautiful traditional coachwork.

But to hold up the firm's sporting reputation there's this GT of Anthony Crook's. It is not, of course, the first Bristol to have lightweight bodywork by a Continental specialist. The earliest model to get that was the 401, for which Touring of Milan designed a rather Alfa-like shell as long ago as the early '50's. After that there was a gap, during which Bristol itself offered and later withdrew the famous 404 "Businessman's Express". Then Anthony Crook, at that time a Bristol main dealer without any active connection with the firm, decided to get Zagato to build them a series of close-coupled four seaters on the 406 chassis, introduced in November 1958.

The first Zagato-Bristol appeared for the 1959 Earls Court motor show. It was a handsome but not wildly beautiful machine weighing little more than a ton and a quarter. With the 2216 litre triple-Solex engine installed, slightly tuned and complete with Abarth exhaust, it would carry four passengers up to 110 mph or so with ease. But the price was high, and the acceleration far from shattering.

Crook's next idea was to recondition a number of older 400 and 401-3 Bristols, strip off the bodies and send the chassis to Milan. When they came back with the same Zagato bodies as the first car had, he did some sums and found he could offer them at around £A1500. Interest was strong enough, but the idea had come a little late; used 404s and 405s had dropped in value by that time to a comparable figure, and people proved more anxious to snap them up than to risk trouble with an older chassis. The result is that some of the cars are still sitting in the showroom, shopsoiled but otherwise unused.

Then for the 1960 show Zagato came up with another effort, this time on a shortened 406 frame. The body was a stylish two-seat coupe, and because of the lopped and lightened frame this promised to be the fastest Bristol yet. Crook thought he would sound out the market and set a price accordingly, after the show. Maybe it was the thought of that smallish, hard-working engine;

Bristol-Zagato engine is 250 bhp 90 deg V8, with inclined valves in iron heads and 9 to 1 compression. Crank is statically and dynamically balanced. Carb is four-barrel Carter.

perhaps it was just the look of the front end, which in spite of all Zagato's skill was still far too high (because of the engine's stroke) for modern taste; whatever the reason, the car didn't take and after he sold the prototype Anthony Crook gave it up.

But that was the model that set the rumors flying. What a machine it would be, people said, if only Bristol would come up with a new engine!

The wish was closer to the mark than most observers thought. The same idea had occurred to Crook, who of course was now part owner of the firm, and George White had been thinking along similar lines for some time — not so much about the Zagato car, however, as of a completely transformed saloon.

Bristol's design department had been hard at work on an engine itself, but as the design progressed it occurred to someone that the new powerplant was getting mighty like one of Detroit's V8s. Why not drop everything now and see about peeling off a tiny slice of Chrysler's low-cost production run; if the arrangement went through, think of the extra money they could spend on chassis development and bodywork . . .

Everyone knows what happened. The 407 appeared and, as predicted in SCW, one of the first chassis found its way to Zagato's factory at Milan. Pressmen covering the 1961 London show got their first view of the new Crook-Zagato project on preview day. The car had just arrived, and it looked unfinished. British journalists are all too ready to assume all Italian work is like that: most of them took a quick peek and passed on to the GT Mini-Minor. So Zagato had stuck another makeshift body on a Bristol: so what?

As the show progressed, Crook's staff found time to put right the more obvious omissions on the rushed (10 weeks, a dream to reality) prototype shell. A big, bronze Bristol badge on the nose gave the frontal styling a finished look, hub-caps on the silver-sprayed wheels made a big difference to the side elevation and a clean-up inside brought out the simple, functional elegance of the traditional Zagato decor. Correspondents who took a second look revised their judgment, but still the

Single deep console houses all instruments and most minor controls right ahead of driver. Alloy wheel obscures innermost dials in dead-ahead position. Interior is spacious, with room for children behind seats and lots of space for legs.

Shallow but very long boot runs right through to cockpit, with carpet to cover gap when required. 18 gal fuel tank lives under spare. Car needs greasing at three points every 6000!

new car's significance seemed to escape the British Press. Few reporters ever bothered to ask the price; they would have been staggered to learn that it is around £A650 less than for the coach-built saloon at just over £3000 sterling without tax — £380 sterling more than the basic DB4 Aston Martin.

How does the Bristol-Zagato compare with the Aston in other ways? A hard look at the specification shows that this newcomer really does belong among the world's fastest cars. Nobody has got around yet to putting the prototype on the scales, but it is unlikely to weigh much more than 3000lb. The DB4 scales in at the same figure, in standard form. Although it is shorter by roughly 16 inches in the wheelbase, the Aston has four seats to lug around, and its Touring-planned bodywork is bulkier.

Most of the Bristol's weight, incidentally, comes from its tremendously rigid box steel chassis and from the Chrysler engine-transmission unit, which is roughly 180lb heavier than the far less powerful ex-BMW six. Zagato's bodywork is certainly the lightest of its standard in the world.

The Aston Martin has a slight advantage in gross output, with 263 bhp against the Bristol's 250. Yet the new car's peak delivery point is more than 1000 rpm lower down the scale at just 4400 rpm, and it yields a whopping 340lb ft of torque instead of 240 at no less than 1500 fewer revs. All this should help to make the Bristol-Zagato a real fireball away from the lights, automatic transmission or not.

Even the bulky 407 saloon shows up most sports cars. Pulling roughly 4000lb laden and coping with something like 21 sq ft of frontal area, it will whisper through from a standstill to its recommended maximum of roughly 122 mph in well under a minute. Running over Chrysler's engine rev limit of 5100, it will reach an honest 130 mph with no trouble on the same axle ratio.

Crook is offering his lightweight variant with a faster rear end ratio — 2.9 to 1, against 3.31. That should allow a corresponding 12 percent increase in top speed, assuming the same trespass

on Detroit's rather conservative engine ceiling. Theoretical maximum becomes at least 145 mph, to the DB4's 143 on test, and considering the Zagato body's typically tiny proportions and highly functional shape there seems no reason to doubt that the car will do it.

Engine position is well back in the frame, a hangover from the old transverse leaf suspension layout. Yet the wide, bulky V8 fills its space to the brim, and Crook's engineers are having a tough time finding room for a remote air cleaner to replace the pancake type fitted as standard (there is, of course, no room for it under the Zagato bonnet). The wide, slanted radiator has twin electric fans mounted just ahead of the core.

The torque-flite box drives to a Salisbury hypoid final drive and rigid axle via a unique Detroit-designed, British-built forward pot-joint.

Suspension in front is by nylon-bushed wishbones and coil springs, with a torsional roll bar. Longitudinal torsion bars at the back connect to the axle housing through arms and links, with locational help from a hefty Watt linkage and a central forged alloy torque arm. Brakes are 11.25 in Dunlop discs all around, generously servo-boosted. Steering is by Marles cam and roller, with 3¾ turns lock to lock and a 34ft turning circle.

Although suspension rates are unchanged, the GT takes the road with just a nice natural increase in hardness because of its lighter body. The long wheelbase, combined with the rearward engine position and near 50/50 weight distribution, should make for first class handling. The 407 saloon understeers quite markedly, but indications are that the GT will have neutral characteristics along with a strong tendency to keep going where you point it.

Bristol is anxious to see how the automatic transmission goes down as a rigidly standard item in the 407. Anthony Crook is even more anxious to find out what the sports car public thinks of a GT with a lemon-squeezer as stock.

CONTINUED ON PAGE 287

Bristol built—but air inspired

A. G. Pritchard, B.L., outlines Bristol cars, including competition ones, from their introduction after the war until the present time

Flight-Lieutenant Anthony Crook at the wheel of a 328 BMW, the car which formed the basis for the first Bristol

One of the first three production models is seen below, competing in the Eastbourne rally, 1947

To the man in the street, the name Bristol summons up visions of ships and aircraft, but to the knowledgeable it also means motoring expressed in its highest form. It was only in 1945 that the Bristol Aeroplane Company commenced car manufacture, but in these few years the make has secured a reputation second to none. Plant and machinery formerly occupied by heavy wartime contracts was then free and the need for diversification was clear. Since then Bristol have made a name not only as car manufacturers, but also for plastic products which include Lotus Elite body/chassis units and Nobel 3-wheeler bodies.

At first only a small area of factory space was taken over for car production and a period of research followed. Bristol, rather wisely, decided not to start completely from scratch so the pre-war BMW was used as a working basis. The initial product, the 400, was a mixture of BMW ideas, based on the 326 chassis with the 328 power unit and coachwork similar to that of the 327 Autenreith saloon. The BMW 328 had been one of the most eminent and successful sports cars of the immediate pre-war period and in streamlined form had won the 1940 Mille Miglia.

In the design and development of the 400, Bristol collaborated closely with Frazer-Nash Cars who had been the pre-war concessionaires for BMW and the assemblers of Frazer-Nash-BMW; post-war "Frashes" were powered by Bristol engines until 1957 and the firm was for some time distributors for Bristol cars.

Work was put in hand on a number of complete sets of parts; of these two were assembled as chassis and tested as such, four were to be fitted with bodies and become the first prototypes and the remaining set was retained for spares. By early 1946 the first Bristol-built engine was running on the test bed; not long afterwards the first chassis was running on test. The final selection of body-style depended to a large extent on the results of wind-tunnel tests and these tests have since formed a major factor in the development of all the various Bristol body designs. The initial cars were almost 100% Filton built, but sub-contracting was gradually introduced until Bristol became like most manufacturers, in reality, car assemblers.

The 400 was announced to the public at the Geneva show in 1947 and production continued until 1950. The Bristol gained an early competition success by winning the 1948 Polish International Rally and followed this by third place in the 1949 Monte-Carlo Rally.

In many respects the 400 was an attractive model; radio, one-shot lubrication and a free-wheel on first gear were standard fittings (the latter remained so until the

The type 401 model being driven 104.78 miles in one hour by Tony Crook at Montlhery

A few drophead versions of the 401 were made, and designated the 402. Here film star Jean Simmons, who bought the first one, tries it for size

introduction of the 407). There was a choice of 75 or 85 bhp engines and top speed was around 90 mph. This was, apart from the 404, the lightest Bristol and also the most compact. The body was constructed with a steel frame and a combination of steel and aluminium panelling. The very high quality of these cars is testified by the fact that so many are to be seen today in such excellent condition. A '400' will still cost around £350, which is far from cheap for a car 12-15 years old, but it is nevertheless a very satisfactory investment.

The Bristol 401 entered production in late 1949. The coachwork was styled by Superleggera Touring of Milan and was of steel hoop construction panelled in aluminium. The 85 bhp engine was standardised in this model. The body was the as-then ultimate in aerodynamic efficiency and the chassis was commendable for its torsion bar front suspension and rack-and-pinion steering. Only in small ways does the 401 show itself a little démodé today, such as the small window area, the divided windscreen, the rear window and roller sun blinds. The maximum speed of this model was 97 mph, 80 mph was possible in third and 0—60 took 18 secs. all this in a full 5-seater saloon weighing 25 cwt and at a fuel consumption of around 23 mpg. An eight year old 401 tried with some 80,000 miles to its credit was found to be still capable of 0-60 in 18 secs, and the steering and brakes were still sufficiently good for the car to be driven for sustained periods at any speed up to its maximum. The brakes of this car, in accord with the reputation of the model, were first class but required very considerable pressure to achieve maximum retardation. A well maintained 401 is still a joy to own and in the writer's opinion a good long term investment. Current price?—anything between £350—£600 dependent, naturally, upon condition. Production ceased in 1953.

From 1949 to 1950, a drophead coupé version was marketed in very limited numbers. This was known as the 402 and was indentical to the 401 in chassis design and general styling, but was of two-light design and had a smoothly contoured hood which folded completely out of sight.

The next Bristol model, the 403 was introduced in 1953 and was in simple terms, a refined and much faster version of the 401—a good car made even better. The majority of 403s had the 100A engine with a 7.5 : 1 compression ratio, but the last few had the 8.5 : 1 100B unit and some have been converted to this by Anthony Crook. Performance was considerably increased and a top speed of 104 mph with acceleration times of 0—60 in 13 secs and 0—70 in 17 secs were obtainable. Gear noise, audible

at high revs. in the 401 was completely eliminated and an anti-roll torsion bar reduced the slight oversteer tendencies of the 401; the 403 had ideal neutral steering characteristics. Modifications to the shock-absorbers gave a softer ride and new, light-alloy brake drums combined better heat dissipation with a considerable reduction in pedal pressures. This model is distinguishable from the 401 externally only by the chrome radiator grille, Bristol name medallions low down on the front wings and the numerals 403 on the sides of the bonnet.

Although the Bristol is rather too expensive a piece of machinery for most people to risk in competitions, a 403 was rallied with considerable success by J. W. E. Banks of Koni fame and A. Meredith-Owens; their most notable success was second place in the 1955 Tulip Rally. Rally.

The 403 was perhaps the nicest Bristol, with excellent handling, performance and brakes. Prices are rather steep and range from £650 to £900 for a late model fitted with disc brakes and overdrive by Crook. Undoubtedly, such a car, in sound order, will give many years of faithful and reliable service; further it should be remembered that although expensive to purchase, the heaviest depreciation has been suffered before coming into your hands.

During the 1952 season, the re-formed ERA Company had been racing, with limited success, the 'G'-type formula 2 car, powered by a Bristol engine, and during that season mainly driven by Stirling Moss. The Bristol Aeroplane Company purchased the car, design rights and equipment and during the winter of 1952 and the following spring there was evolved the 450, an experimental sports/racing car. The body style was a rather revolutionary fixed-head coupé with twin tail fins. This was one of the first competition cars to have such fins and the side windows were of curved plastic to blend in with the general body lines. These fins were intended to increase the directional stability and to prevent the car being deflected by side winds. Only projecting fuel and oil fillers midway along the sides of the front wings spoilt the general aerodynamic effect. To minimise the effect of change in weight distribution as the car consumed fuel, the tanks were mounted on each side of the body well within the wheelbase. The fuel supply itself was unusual, coming from the left tank only and the filler was in the right tank, with a non-return valve between the two so that centrifugal force on right-hand bends caused the fuel to be thrown into the left tank where it was trapped by a valve. The filler

The three Bristol 450 competition cars finishing in line ahead to take second, third and fourth places in their class at Rheims in 1954 ('Motor' photograph)

Rara avis—the beautiful type 404 being driven by Tony Crook in a production car race at Goodwood

cap on the 1½-gallon extra oil tank was held in place magnetically. In addition the car was fitted with neat glass inspection panels in the rear wings so that the driver could keep a check on tyre wear.

The Company entered two cars for the 1953 Le Mans race driven by Lance Macklin/Graham Whitehead and Tom Wisdom/Jack Fairman respectively. They were ill-fated: by the end of the fourth hour the Macklin/Whitehead car had caught fire because of an obscure electrical fault and left the road. Some 4 hours later a precisely similar fate overtook Wisdom, who suffered sufficient injuries to detain him in hospital for a while.

In the Reims 12-hour race the two cars were again entered. One car retired with transmission trouble, but the other, in the hands of Fairman and Wilson, won the 2-litre class and finished 5th overall, defeating Ferrari, OSCA, Gordini and Frazer-Nash opposition. In the October of the same year a 450 was taken to Montlhery and set up six new class records in International Class E (1501-2000 cc). The drivers were Macklin and Fairman and the records ranged from 125.87 mph for the 200 miles to six hours at 115.43 mph. At the completion of the record runs, Fairman then took the car round at over 126 mph to demonstrate that it was still in fine fettle. Slight external modifications were discernible in the smoother outline of the nose of the car. The records were completely trouble-free apart from the failure of a bonnet catch which was wired down to prevent its opening at speed.

The policy of limiting entries to Le Mans and Reims was continued in 1954 and entries for the former were this time three cars driven by Fairman/Wisdom, Wilson/Mayers and Keen/Line. The Bristols proved to be the epitomy of reliability, finishing first, second and third in their class. The leader, Wilson/Mayers, covered 2,203 miles and the team was seventh, eighth and ninth overall. The fastest lap by a Bristol was 99.7 mph in the hands of Wilson, and the car was timed at 132.29 mph on the Mulsanne straight. The cars were largely unchanged from the previous year, but had slightly modified rear suspension, greater engine power and the depth of the channel between the rear wings reduced.

At Reims the three 450 coupés again appeared in what was to prove an uneventful race. The race started at 12 pm and by 10 am, in a Jaguar dominated race, the Keen/Line Bristol was leading the 2-litre class, but they were pipped for a class victory in the closing hours of the race by the Picard/Pozzi Ferrari and had to be content with second.

The team again entered for the two French sports car events in 1955, the first of which was the tragic Le Mans event won by the Hawthorn/Bueb Jaguar after the withdrawal of the Mercedes team. The cars had been converted to open 2-seaters with a single tail fin and the reason for this is fairly clear to see. Drivers have always preferred open cars to the cramped, noisy and possibly fume-filled interior of a coupe. Even now the problem of making a wiper that will clear the screen of a really high speed car has not been solved. The cars proved to be both infinitely quieter than the coupes and also somewhat faster. They finished in the first three places in the 2-litre class in the order seventh (overall) Wilson/Mayers, eighth Keen/Line and ninth, Wisdom/Fairman. As a result of the strong anti-motor racing feelings following the Le Mans disaster, the Reims 12-hour race was cancelled and Le Mans was the last race appearance of the 450.

To a very limited extent the 404, introduced at the

1953 Motor Show reflected racing experiences. The "Business Man's Express" as the car became known from its inception, employed the basic mechanical components of the 403 in a chassis of very short wheelbase. The body was a carefully chosen compromise between the ideals of aerodynamic efficiency and luxurious accommodation for two to the standards of a private study. There was the option of 105 or 125 bhp engines. The bodywork was framed in a combination of hardwood, steel and light alloy and panelled in aluminium alloy. The 404 was one of the first production cars to have tail-fins, but these were as much for the demands of styling as for aerodynamic reasons and were purely vestigial. In my opinion this is one of the few cars on which fins have looked attractive. An interesting point was the fitment of dual master cylinders in the hydraulic brake system so that there was in fact a separate fluid system for each pair of wheels. No journal in this country tested the 404, so precise performance figures are not available, but they may be equated with those for the Aceca-Bristol, which is somewhat lighter, but has the same choice of power units and a slightly greater frontal area. The short wheelbase was supposed to lead to handling problems, but having seen Tony Crook drive a 404 in club events with considerable verve, I am not of that opinion.

Also to be seen at the 1953 Show was a very handsome 404 drophead coupé by Abbott. This lacked the straight-through lines of the coupe and had a smoothly curved rear-wing outline and no tail-fins; the body was constructed in 16 gauge light alloy, hand beaten. British coachbuilders have often been criticised for failure to keep abreast with modern trends. It would not be inappropriate to mention the many excellent post-war Abbott products on such chassis as Healey, Bentley, Ferrari, Jensen, Connaught and Jowett. Unfortunately the 404 dhc did not enter production and the coupe itself was withdrawn in late 1955 together with the 403. Only a small number of 404 were produced and it is something of a rare bird; a second-hand example costs around £1100.

Since then Bristol have concentrated on a single model policy, and until 1958 this consisted of the 405 introduced at the 1954 Motor Show. This was a development of the 404 having the more usual wheelbase of 9 ft 6 in and four-door coachwork (this is the only 4-door Bristol). Construction was similar to that of the 404 and it employed the same 100B engine. This was a very fine handling of extremely elegant lines, and Anthony Crook raced even this model in club events. The 405 was a design in which the concentration of weight was kept as low as possible; as with the 404 the spare wheel was stowed behind a flap in the wing to the rear of the nearside front wheel and balanced on the offside by the battery. Unsprung weight was kept to a minimum by the use of light alloy road wheels and Al-fin brake drums. The rack and pinion steering (fitted on all models prior to the 407) was simply superb, holding a dead straight line at high speeds, high geared yet light. Overdrive was fitted as standard to the 405 and was very desirable to reduce top gear revs, for something like 5,000 rpm was reached at a speed of 100 mph in direct top gear. With its superb aerodynamic shape and the use of overdrive a fuel consumption of up to 25 mpg was obtainable. A drophead version by Abbott was also available and similar in all major aspects to the saloon, but 2-door coachwork was fitted. Certain examples of the 405 have been fitted with disc brakes by Anthony Crook.

The 405 remains a superb example of the efficient motor car—it combines the virtues of a largely unstressed, medium sized engine of good power output with a beautifully constructed body, aerodynamically efficient and not excessively heavy. To obtain the best from the car the revs must be kept up and this demands frequent use of the gearbox—but this is all part of the pleasure of driving a Bristol.

Such a car as the Bristol is often criticised by motorists who demand a large engine. I do not regard this as logical since a designer aims at a certain object, and with the 405, he has achieved it with a 2-litre engine. To increase the engine size would imply an increase in performance and that means that the designer has now set his aim at a different object. The emphasis of the 405 was on sporting luxury, in contrast with the 407 a high speed

The type 405 Bristol—"emphasis on sporting luxury"—shown in two-door drophead coupe form

406 Bristol with Zagato body specially commissioned by Anthony Crook Motors made its appearance at the 1959 Earls Court Motor Show

luxury touring car. The emphasis has thus changed.

Early in 1958, a prototype Bristol known as the 406E was shown with neat 4-seater coachwork by the Swiss Coachbuilder "Beutler", who had previously executed bodywork with considerable success on Bristol chassis; however this was vastly different from the finalised production 406. This had a large engine of 2.2-litres, increased in both bore and stroke and a power output of 105 bhp. There was no increase in performance as the 406 was both less aerodynamic and heavier than its predecessors. The rakish lines were lost and replaced by a form of rather superior platform styling. Dunlop disc brakes on all four wheels were standard and for the first time the coachwork was constructed by an outside builder, Jones Brothers of Willesden, but naturally to Bristol design. Although the chassis was very similar to that of the 405 the coachwork was of entirely metal construction with steel structual members and aluminium panels.

During the production life of the 406, Zagato, in conjunction with Anthony Crook, produced a number of lightweight bodies on the standard chassis, but short chassis versions were also available and some bodies were built on earlier but reconditioned chassis. These special versions are now offered on the current 407 chassis. The Zagato bodies are of most attractive appearance, curved but not bulbous—a pleasing contrast to the majority of current models—and superbly finished. but the price is astronomical.

Comparative data of Bristol cars

BRISTOL ENGINES

Car type	Engine	BHP	RPM	Comp. ratio	Valve timing	Carburetters	Identification means
400	85A	75	4200	7.5:1	10,50,50,10	Solex dual d/draft	Oil cooler in block
401 400	85B	85	4500	7.5:1	10,50,50,10	Triple S.U. D.2. or Solex	Oil cooler in block on early models.
401 402	85C	85	4500	8.5:1	10,50,50,10	Triple Solex 32B.1	Cylinder liners, no oil cooler in block
403	100A	100	5000	7.5:1	Valve timing—15,65,65,15. Carburetters—Triple Solex 32B.1.			
403 404 405	100B	105	5000	8.5:1	Larger stepped sump, increased diameter crank-pins, larger inlet valves, light tappets.			
404	100C	125	5500	8.5:1	Identical to 100B except for sports type c/shaft			
406	(2.2lt) 110	105	4700	8.5:1	15,65,65,15	Triple Solex 32B.1.	
Ace and Aceca	100D2	128	5750	9:1	15,65,65,15	Triple Solex 32B.1.	

RACING ENGINES

BS 1 Mk 2		130	5500	9:1	Valve timing—40,80,80,40. Carbs.—to choice.
BS 1 Mk 3		142	5750	9:1	
BS 1A Mk 3		148	5750	10:1	There were many variants available, such as magneto or coil ignition, timing drive by chain or gears, breather arrangements.
BS 4 Mk 1 and 2		142	5750	9:1	
BS 4A Mk 1 and 2		155	6000	11:1	

BRISTOL MODELS.

Model	Years built	Wheelbase	Length	Width	Height	Weight	Price (inc. p.t.)	Coachwork
400	1946-50	9 ft. 6 in.	15 ft. 3 in.	5 ft. 4 in.	4 ft. 11 in.	2580 lb.	£2374 (1948)	2 dr 2/4 st. sal
401	1949-53	9 ft. 6 in.	15 ft. 11½ in.	5 ft. 7 in.	5 ft. 0 in.	2700 lb.	£2995 (1950)	2 dr 4/5 st sal
402	1949-50	9 ft. 6 in.	15 ft. 11½ in.	5 ft. 7 in.	5 ft. 0 in.	2700 lb.	£3245 (1949)	2 dr 4/5 st dhc
403	1953-55	9 ft. 6 in.	15 ft. 11½ in.	5 ft. 7 in.	5 ft. 0 in.	2788 lb.	£2976 (1955)	2 dr 4/5 st sal
404	1953-55	8 ft. 0¼ in.	14 ft. 3¼ in.	5 ft. 8 in.	4 ft. 7¾ in.	2290 lb.	£3330 (1955)	2 dr 2 st fhc
405	1955-58	9 ft. 6 in.	15 ft. 9¼ in.	5 ft. 8 in.	4 ft. 9¼ in.	2712 lb.	£3188 (1955)	2 dr 4 st dhc 4 dr 4 st sal
406	1958-61	9 ft. 6 in.	16 ft. 4 in.	5 ft. 8 in.	5 ft. 0 in.	3010 lb.	£4244 (1960)	2 dr 4 st sal
407	1961—	9 ft. 6 in.	16 ft. 7 in.	5 ft. 8 in.	5 ft. 0 in.	3584 lb.	£5142 (1962)	2 dr 4 st sal

The Zagato cars were, and are, built only in very limited numbers, but the Bertone-bodied Arnolt-Bristol was a full-scale production model introduced in late 1953 for export to the U.S.A. The chassis was essentially 404, but with the BS1 Mark II engine, giving 130 bhp at 5,500 rpm and eleven inch brakes all round, as opposed to the twelve inch size fitted to the front wheels of the 404. The chassis, made in left-hand drive form only, was shipped to Italy for the body to be fitted. The bodies were of striking appearance and although compact had generous curves and with a razor-edged peak to the wings, giving just a glimmer of traditional English styling. Although the Bristol power unit is rather deep, it was neatly installed in this car of low overall height. Two versions were available—an open 2-seater which achieved limited competition success in the States, including first, second, fourth and fifth places in the 2-litre class of the 1955 Sebring 12-hour race; the second version was a neat fixed head coupé. This model was both inspired by and marketed by S. H. Arnolt, one of America's leading sports car specialists. Production ceased in 1958.

In 1961 Bristol Cars Ltd became divorced from Bristol-Siddeley Engines Ltd., the car and engine division of the newly formed Bristol/Hawker-Siddeley Group. It is now run as an independent concern with Mr. George White (former managing director of the old Bristol Cars) and Anthony Crook as directors and production continues to be centred on Filton.

Since that date, substantial changes have been made in the company's policy. It was decided to discontinue production of the Bristol engine for the company's own use, although it would continue to be supplied to A.C. Cars Ltd, who were by then the principal users. Spares facilities for all Bristol engines will continue to be available for many years. The Bristol engine has built up a superb reputation in the post-war years, the acme of development being attained eight years ago in the Formula 2 Cooper-Bristol. But modern high-speed luxury cars such as Jaguar, Facel Vega and Daimler were now capable of speeds well in excess of 120 mph and Bristol could not hope to compete in terms of sheer performance if reliability was to be retained.

It was, therefore, a courageous if inevitable step to lay aside an engine of so many years development and fit the 5.1-litre Canadian-built Chrysler unit. The cost of development and production of a suitable alternative would have been prohibitive and the Chrysler unit is a good choice. It is nevertheless surprising that fitting this mass-produced unit should raise the price of the 407 by an amount in excess of the price of a complete Chrysler car in the country of its origin!

The Bristol 407 is basically the 406 fitted with the new power unit. There is a considerable increase in the weight carried on the front wheels, and this has undoubtedly affected handling to a certain extent. The Chrysler engine develops 250 bhp at 4,400 rpm, an increase of approximately 110 per cent in power. Chrysler Torque-flite automatic transmission is fitted as standard, and this is one of the finest of such transmissions available. The driver has push-buttons instead the normal lever; intermediate gear can be held up to a road speed of 70 mph by pressing the appropriate button. The body is built on exactly the same lines as the 406, but the actual coach-builders are now Park Royal Vehicles. Performance is outstanding: a top speed in excess of 120 mph and 0—60 in only 9.9", 0—80 16.6" and 0—100 26.6". Fuel consumption is comparatively heavy (as might be expected) at around 14—15 mpg.

Latest of a long line: the superb 1962 Bristol-Zagato Grand Sport, derived from the 407 with 5-litre Chrysler engine

Production of Bristol cars continues but inevitably rising costs and competition from mass-production rivals are increasingly difficult to combat. The place of such cars on the motoring scene is somewhat problematical, but for sheer quality they are without equal.

AUTOMATIC GT

FORECAST FOR THE FUTURE?

BY DOUG BLAIN

PHOTOS BY
GEOFFREY GODDARD

Refusal to compromise either airflow pattern or r

WITHOUT FUSS OR FANFARE, the world has gained another really fast car. While the newcomer's final form is still undecided, it will surely be a sizzling performer.

Three great car firms had a hand in the conception: Chrysler of Canada, Bristol of England and Zagato of Italy. The progeny, broadly speaking, is a glamorous GT with a stack of baggage space, room for kids behind the seats, power to burn and—wonder of wonders in a European product—automatic transmission as stock.

How come no trumpet blast? It's hard to say. Put it down to British conservatism and you'll come as close to the truth as anybody is likely to get. Back in October, pressmen covering the motor show at Earls Court in London noted on Zagato's unpretentious stand in a corner behind the trailer-homes a long, sleek and unfamiliar shape labeled Bristol-Zagato. The car was an obvious rush job. British journalists, too ready to assume *all* Italian work is rather impulsive, took a quick peek and walked on. So Zagato had stuck another makeshift body on a Bristol. So what?

It was an old story. For the past two years the Milan house had been showing special Bristol bodies, all commissioned and handled by Gianni Zagato's English friend Anthony Crook. Crook had first put the west-of-England marque on the racing map and has been number one Bristol dealer right from the beginning in 1946. But his and Zagato's early efforts had never been really pretty, largely because the long-stroke Bristol six called for a hood line that was far too high to suit Gianni's characteristically spare styling. The cars never had much performance either. The 2000 and 2200-cc sixes, fine enough powerplants in themselves, just couldn't cope with the weight and bulk involved.

What so many people failed to consider last October was that the '62 coupe prototype no longer used the 28-year-old BMW-based engine. In the year since the previous show Anthony Crook and George White, the firm's long-time president, had bought Bristol cars lock, stock and locomotion from the giant aircraft combine from which it got its name. In the same period White and Crook had scrapped the superb but now sadly outdated six and had standardized on Chrysler of Canada's all-iron 5130-cc V-8, along with the celebrated TorqueFlite transmission.

This engine, by the way, has no current American equivalent; it is a bored-out version of an earlier Chrysler-Plymouth V-8 engine which featured "poly-spherical" combustion chambers, not to be confused with the still earlier pure hemispheres. (Bore and stroke are 3.875 in. x 3.31 in.) And although the Zagato car is still officially an Anthony Crook project, these and other changes show up both in specification and in presentation.

The newcomer, in fact, was designed to look and to go like the expensive catalog model it is. At last Bristol was to have a product worthy of world attention, and as the Earls Court show progressed it became obvious that the thinkers really had done their homework. By the time Crook's staff had taken care of the more obvious omissions on the rushed (10 weeks, dream to reality) Zagato shell, there just wasn't a finer looking car in the hall.

The more you examine the Bristol-Zagato the more you realize that this all-new international project really does belong right up in the top bracket, on performance as well as looks. Nobody, at this writing, has had time to make a proper check on official curb weight, but it is unlikely to go much over 3000 lb in spite of the Chrysler engine's extra 180 lb or so on the early six. That puts the newcomer right on a level with the stock Aston Martin DB-4, at just under 3000 lb. Although the Bristol boasts one of Europe's beefiest box steel chassis along

Wide wheel spokes hide oil gauge and ammeter in otherwise excellent cockpit.

Front end treatment exudes performance.

...ibility produced huge rear window.

with a wheelbase some 16 in. greater than the Aston's, the legendary lightness of Zagato's coachwork saves it handsomely. In fact the normal 407 weighs 3740 lb at the curb and still does 0 to 100 mph in 26.6 sec—no mean performance. This lighter version should chop nearly 6 sec off that with ease.

The American ironmongery, suitably painted as a sop to British taste in such things, snuggles neatly into the massive Bristol chassis well aft of the front wheel axis. Ahead is a wide vertical-flow radiator, fed according to a thermostat's demands with cool air from a pair of electric fans mounted right in the nose. The 3-speed TorqueFlite transmission has close ratios and the inclusion of a variable ratio torque converter gives very nearly the effect of 5 speeds forward.

R&T suggested to Anthony Crook that it might be a big help if the factory were to offer a good 4-speed manual box as an extra, much as Jensen does with its 541-R. We were told around the workshop that a box actually exists, but Crook assures us he isn't going to install it.

A half-hour run over mixed roads in a Bristol 407 did show us, though, that the torque converter has more possibilities in a decidedly sporting European chassis than many enthusiasts might imagine. TorqueFlite is acknowledged everywhere to be one of the most efficient of all such systems, and certainly its ability to snap from one range to the next without "marking time" gives it a sporting appeal that is absent elsewhere. Actual experience on a racing circuit (Goodwood) with a similarly prompt auto-drive setup (British Hobbs) in a Cosworth-tuned Stage Three Lotus Elite has already convinced us that there is little danger in shiftless competition driving, provided you choose good equipment. Actually, auto-drive cuts the chances of costly mistakes and gives you extra time to choose your lines. And disc brakes, of course, remove the old objection about the increased chances of fade.

Driving position is first class, with everything just where you want it. The twin hide-upholstered seats are scanty but comfortable. They offer 3-way adjustment, but little sideways support. The wood-rimmed Nardi wheel is set high and square ahead, with a nicely shaped console beyond it for instruments and minor controls, most of which are toggles set within finger-reach of the wheel. Aside from the console, paired heater-defroster controls and the internally illuminated transmission buttons are the only items on the entire crackle-finished dash panel.

Although the traditional Zagato eagerness to "add lightness" shows up in a nice sort of way wherever you look, the cockpit is not sparsely furnished. The floor has a thick pile carpet, and each of the wide doors gets an armrest and two map pockets. The head-lining is padded black leather. A small trunk in the tail communicates direct with the cockpit when you unclip a piece of carpet covering the gap. The two tiny but usable occasional seats have padded backrests that fold up individually, Porschefashion, out of the recesses that form the cushions.

Visibility from inside is good, although the rear view mirror gets in the way a little. The prototype is just a shade short on headroom for anyone over six feet, so Zagato has arranged that future cars should get an extra inch of roof height.

Production will depend on demand. At present Zagato has a stock of chassis and the factory has merely to cable him when an order comes through. Delivery date in London works out to about 10 weeks after that, with a proportionate increase for America. Price in London for the complete car is around $9500.

Just a final word about the choice of a U.S. engine. Bristol is the second actual and at least the fourth prospective European (as distinct from Euro-U.S.) builder of performance cars to swing to American propulsion in the past year. We were interested to learn that the firm actually had had a new unit of its own well in hand as a replacement for the veteran straight six, but as the design developed it occurred to someone that the new engine was getting mighty like Chrysler's medium-bracket offering. From there the process was easy, because Canada's trade agreement with Britain makes importation from Chryco's northern branch a relatively inexpensive and straightforward thing. The Bristol engine therefore joins the growing pile of similar British projects on a high and dusty shelf, while the mass-production Chrysler continues performing with the best. 🏁

Trunk lid support is small hydraulic ram.

JOHN BOLSTER TESTS THE
BRISTOL 407

SOME years ago, I always looked forward to testing the latest Bristols. Their quality of construction was unsurpassed and they could achieve the magic 100 m.p.h. when this was a speed only associated with the fiercer sports models. Subsequently, many 100 m.p.h. saloons were produced and the Bristol, having an engine of only 2-litre capacity, was surpassed for acceleration and flexibility by cheaper cars with bigger cylinders.

Now, the famous name is back, right at the top of Britain's quality cars. The Bristol still has its traditional aluminium-panelled body, with doors that shut with the gentlest "clunk" and a perfection of finish that recalls past glories of British coachbuilding. Most important of all, it has regained its performance leadership, for it now has 5.2-litres to propel it.

The heart of the Bristol 407 is a Chrysler V8 engine, specially built for the car. Big American engines have become so highly developed that there is probably nothing to

touch them for smooth power production and compact size overall. Furthermore, their characteristics perfectly match the efficient automatic gearbox with which they are generally fitted. The typical automobile from U.S.A. is far from ideal for British roads, however, and American styling lacks the restraint which is considered good form over here.

For these reasons, there is a great deal to be said for the idea of powering a traditional British luxury car with an American power unit. This is precisely what has been done in the case of the new Bristol. The over-square engine has a special high-lift camshaft but hydraulic tappets are not used, as they tend to limit the revs. A four-barrel Carter carburetter is fitted and 250 b.h.p. is developed at 4,400 r.p.m. The engine unit is surprisingly compact, having regard to its considerable piston swept volume, and the use of twin electric fans for the radiator saves space as well as reducing noise.

This very effective piece of machinery is

allied to a torque converter and a three-speed automatic gearbox. During hard acceleration, the up-changes occur at 37 and 70 m.p.h., but top gear may be engaged at very low speeds if the driver is light on the accelerator. A press-button system of gear changing allows second or first gear to be selected at will, which is useful when braking for a corner or driving on bad roads. There is a "kick-down" on the accelerator pedal which will engage second gear below 60 m.p.h. or first gear below 29 m.p.h.

Thus, the transmission is fully automatic but can be used as a manual box whenever convenient. The power is transmitted through an open shaft to a hypoid axle, which is located by a Watt's linkage and a central radius arm, with torsion bar suspension. With a relatively heavy car like this, there would be no great advantage in deleting the axle beam. In front, the independent suspension is orthodox.

Naturally, a coachbuilt body must be mounted on a separate chassis, and the frame of the Bristol is a suitably massive structure. With the considerable speed potential and substantial weight, the best brakes are needed and large Dunlop discs have been chosen. The car is a luxurious four-seater with a capacious luggage boot, but no attempt has been made to achieve the maximum accommodation, for this is a two-door speed model, in spite of its length of 16 ft. 7 ins.

The interior of the car is upholstered in crushed grain leather over foam cushions, and the heavy pile carpets have felt under-lays on a sound-proofed floor. The separate front seats have adjustable backs and may be let right down to the fully reclining position. There is a comprehensive heating and ventilation system and the rear quarter lights may be opened for air extraction. Very fine walnut is used for the instrument panel, facia, and door cappings, and there is a splendid array of round, black dials.

The big Bristol is as silent and smooth as one would expect. The riding and handling, however, are much more in the tradition of British sports cars. Initially, the springing feels quite hard, though it gives a comfortable ride at speed. Similarly, the steering tends to be heavy at the lowest speeds but becomes delightfully sensitive at the higher velocities.

One would not attempt to fling so heavy

Bristol's 250 b.h.p.! There is absolutely no sensation of fierce acceleration, but the speedometer, which is accurate at 60 m.p.h. and actually slow at maximum speed, hurries round the dial in a most impressive manner. The acceleration does not fall off at the top end. the car going from 100 m.p.h. to 120 m.p.h. very quickly. During the timed runs, I attained about 5,000 r.p.m. in top gear, which is bordering on the red part of the dial. It would certainly seem that the axle ratio is exactly right for maximum performance. 100 m.p.h. is a very lazy cruising speed which can be attained on any reasonable straight. As would be expected, the fuel consumption is not light at the higher speeds, and I averaged 12½ m.p.g. during the test.

For me, a proper array of round instruments adds greatly to the pleasure of driving, and the rev counter tells the full story of what is happening in the automatic gearbox. The push-button system is excellent for choosing one's own gears, and avoids the possibility of missing the right notch, which is always present when the usual quadrant selector is employed.

The Bristol 407 is very well equipped and its manufacturers do not regard such essential things as the heating installation as being outside the quoted price. My only criticism concerns the rear window, which

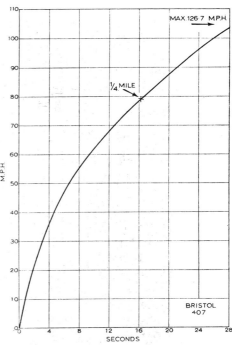

ACCELERATION GRAPH

THE BATTERY lives in a special compartment in the offside wing; the spare wheel has a similar compartment on the other side of the car.

a car as this round sharp corners in the way that one might be tempted to handle a light sports two-seater. On the faster curves, though, the big machine becomes very nimble. For example, I found it easy to take one particular curve in a rousing drift, which I entered at 120 m.p.h. The car oversteers slightly but is well balanced, and there is enough power to slide the rear end when this is convenient. The controllability remains good on wet or icy surfaces and the brakes, though powerful, do not tend to lock the wheels unexpectedly. In spite of the weight, strong winds can deflect the car appreciably.

The very rapid acceleration is achieved effortlessly, and the well-located rear axle glues the tyres to the road, so there is literally no wheelspin. How different from many cars with only a fraction of the

might well be provided with some form of demisting in a car of this calibre. A very good point is the storage of the spare wheel in one of the front wing valances, balanced by the battery, which is similarly positioned on the other side. In both cases, the doors can be opened very easily for instant access, but they are cleverly concealed. This gets two bulky objects out of the way, leaving more space for other things, such as luggage.

It would be difficult to find another car to equal, let alone surpass, the sheer perfection of the bodywork on this Bristol chassis.

SPECIFICATION AND PERFORMANCE DATA

Car Tested: Bristol 407 two-door saloon, price £4,259 18s. 7d., including P.T.

Engine: Eight-cylinders 98.55 mm. × 84.07 mm. (5,130 c.c.). Push-rod-operated overhead valves. Compression ratio 9 to 1. 250 b.h.p. at 4,400 r.p.m. Carter four-choke downdraught carburetter. Coil and distributor ignition.

Transmission: Automatic gearbox with fluid torque converter, ratios 3.07, 4.41, and 7.45 to 1. Torque converter stalled ratio 2.2 to 1. Push-button control. Open propeller shaft. Salisbury hypoid rear axle.

Chassis: Welded-steel box-section frame. Aluminium panelled coachbuilt body. Independent front suspension by wishbones and helical springs with anti-roll torsion bar. Marles worm-type steering gear. Rear axle supported on short arms and fore-and-aft torsion bars, with lateral location by Watt's linkage and torque arm above differential case. Telescopic dampers all round. Dunlop disc brakes on all four wheels with Lockheed servo. Bolt-on pierced disc wheels fitted Dunlop RS 5 6.00 × 16 ins. tyres.

Equipment: Speedometer. Rev counter. Oil pressure, water temperature, and fuel gauges. Ammeter. Clock. 12-volt lighting and starting with spot, fog, and reversing lamps. Windscreen wipers and washers. Heating and demisting. Flashing direction indicators. Extra: Radio and record player.

Dimensions: Wheelbase 9 ft. 6 ins. Track (front) 4 ft. 5 ins.; (rear) 4 ft. 6½ ins. Overall length 16 ft. 7 ins. Width 5 ft. 8 ins. Turning circle 39 ft. 6 ins. Weight 1 ton 12 cwt.

Performance: Maximum speed 126.7 m.p.h. Standing quarter-mile 16.2 s. Acceleration: 0-30 m.p.h., 3 s.; 0-50 m.p.h., 6.6 s.; 0-60 m.p.h., 9.2 s.; 0-80 m.p.h., 16.6 s.; 0-100 m.p.h., 25.9 s.

Fuel Consumption: 12½ m.p.g.

Acceleration from a standstill to 100 m.p.h. in 25.9 seconds will take care of the opposition very nicely, and the easy controllability will flatter the driving of the lucky owner. This is the kind of car which will certainly appeal to the man who demands the highest quality but who would find chromium-plated decoration intolerable.

BRISTOL 407

ENGINE CAPACITY: 313.75 cu in, 5130 cu cm;

FUEL CONSUMPTION: 18.2 m/imp gal, 15.2 m/US gal, 15.5 l x 100 km;

SEATS: 4; **MAX SPEED:** 125.2 mph, 201.6 km/h;

PRICE: list £ 3,525, total £ 4,260.

ENGINE: front, 4 stroke; cylinders: 8, Vee-slanted at 90°; bore and stroke: 3.88 x 3.31 in, 98.5 x 84.1 mm; engine capacity: 313.75 cu in, 5130 cu cm; compression ratio: 9 : 1; max power (SAE): 250 hp at 4400 rpm; max torque (SAE): 340 lb ft, 46.9 kgm at 2800 rpm; max number of engine rpm: 5100; specific power: 48.7 hp/l; cylinder block: cast iron; cylinder head: cast iron; crankshaft bearings: 5; valves: 2 per cylinder, overhead, with push rods and rockers; camshaft: 1, at centre of Vee; lubrication: rotary pump, filter on by-pass; lubricating system capacity: 5.4 imp qt, 6.5 US qt, 6.2 l; carburation: 1 Carter down-draft 4-barrel carburettor; fuel feed: mechanical pump; cooling system: water; cooling system capacity: 18 imp qt, 21.7 US qt, 20.5 l.

TRANSMISSION: driving wheels: rear; gear box: Torqueflite automatic, hydraulic torque convertor and planetary gears with 3 ratios + reverse, max ratio of convertor at stall 2.2; gear box ratios: (I) 2.45, (II) 1.45, (III) 1, (Rev) 2.20; push button control on facia; final drive: hypoid bevel; ratio: 3.31 : 1.

CHASSIS: box-type ladder frame, long members; front suspension: independent, wishbones, coil springs, anti-roll bar, telescopic dampers; rear suspension: rigid axle, longitudinal torsion bars, Watt linkage, telescopic dampers.

STEERING: worm and roller; turns of steering wheel lock to lock: 4.

BRAKES: disc, vacuum servo.

ELECTRICAL EQUIPMENT: voltage: 12 V; battery: 72 Ah; ignition distributor: Autolite; headlights: 2 front and reversing.

DIMENSIONS AND WEIGHT: wheel base: 114.00 in, 2896 mm; front track: 53.00 in, 1346 mm; rear track: 54.50 in, 1384 mm; overall length: 199.00 in, 5055 mm; overall width: 68.00 in, 1727 mm; overall height: 60.00 in, 1524 mm; ground clearance: 6.50 in, 165 mm; dry weight: 3584 lb, 1626 kg; distribution of weight: 53 % front axle, 47 % rear axle; turning radius (between walls): 19.7 ft, 6 m; tyres: 6.00 - 16; fuel tank capacity: 18.00 imp gal, 21.65 US gal, 82 l.

BODY: saloon; doors: 2; seats: 4; front seat: double, adjustable backrests.

PERFORMANCE: max speed in 1st gear: 39.8 mph, 64 km/h; max speed in 2nd gear: 70.2 mph, 113 km/h; max speed in 3rd gear: 125.2 mph, 201.6 km/h; power-weight ratio: 14.3 lb/hp, 6.5 kg/hp; useful load: 706 lb, 320 kg; acceleration: standing 1/4 mile 17.3 sec, 0 — 50 mph (0 — 80 km/h) 6 sec; speed in direct drive at 1000 rpm: 23.8 mph, 38.3 km/h.

PRACTICAL INSTRUCTIONS: fuel: petrol, 100 oct; engine sump oil: 5.0 imp qt, 6.0 US qt, 5.7 l, SAE 20 (winter) 30 (summer), change every 3000 miles, 4800 km; gearbox oil: 8.0 imp qt, 9.6 US qt, 9.1 l, change every 10000 miles, 16000 km; final drive oil: 1.5 imp qt, 1.8 US qt, 1.7 l, EP 90, change every 10000 miles, 16000 km; steering box oil: EP 90; greasing: every 6000 miles, 9600 km, 2 points; tappet clearances: inlet 0.010 in, 0.25 mm hot, exhaust 0.018 in, 0.46 mm hot; valve timing: (inlet) opens 13° before tdc and closes 55° after bdc, (exhaust) opens 51° before bdc and closes 17° after tdc; tyre pressure (medium load): front 29 psi, 2.1 atm, rear 29 psi, 2.1 atm.

VARIATIONS AND OPTIONAL ACCESSORIES: Viotti Convertible; Zagato GT body, 2 + 2 seats, dry weight 2968 lb, 1346 kg, axle ratio 2.8 : 1.

Crisper shape for the nose, a lower flatter roof-line, additional styling strips and the Bristol badge on each side identify the new 408

Bristol 408

IMPROVEMENTS INCLUDE FACE LIFT AND RIDE CONTROL

PRICE

	Basic	Total (inc. P.T.)		
	£	£	s	d
408 Saloon	3,690	4,459	6	3

TWO years ago the Bristol 407 was announced with a Canadian built Chrysler vee-8 engine replacing the high-efficiency six-cylinder 2-litre unit which had powered all Bristol cars since the 400 model. At the time, the steel-framed aluminium body, by Park Royal, was retained with little change. Now, with the introduction of the 408, there has been a further break with tradition in that a wide, shallow air intake with a stainless steel grille has taken the place of the familiar air scoop which has been the hallmark of Bristols for some years. To complete the transformation two extra, 5·75in. headlamps are built into the ends of the grille.

The flatter bonnet needed with the new grille is matched by giving the roof above the cantrails a hard line and by reducing the curvature of the roof. The general effect is to make the car look longer and lower although it is in fact shorter overall. This low line is emphasized by an extra body side moulding and by a deep embossed, stainless kick strip along the body sills. The Pegasus motifs, used on 1963 models, have been moved up from the bottom of the scuttle panels to a new position in line with the side mouldings, forward of the door.

Mechanically the main change is the adoption of Armstrong Selectaride shock absorbers in the rear suspension. They are controlled by a dial on the facia panel, to the right of the steering wheel, and may be adjusted to give good variation in ride without affecting the safe handling characteristics in the softest setting.

A wider ventilating air intake, located forward of the windscreen, is now practically the full width of the scuttle. This allows the fresh air ducts at either side of the heater intake to be nearly double the previous size, the extra volume of fresh air being controlled by a lever under the middle of the facia.

With its four-barrel carburettor and high lift camshaft, the 5,130 c.c. vee-8 engine develops 250 b.h.p. (gross) at 4,400 r.p.m. This was sufficient to propel our road test car at 122 m.p.h. and to accelerate it to 100 m.p.h. in 26·6 seconds (*Autocar*, 6 October, 1961). Power is transmitted through a Chrysler Torqueflite three-element torque converter with pushbutton hold-down for first and second gears. This power unit and transmission combination remains unchanged in the 408.

The deception of shortening the car and yet making it look longer has been remarkably successful. Additions to the specification have necessitated a price increase of almost £200, the new price including purchase tax now being £4,459 6s 3d.

Dimensions

Wheelbase	...	...	9ft 6in. (290cm)
Track: front	...	...	4ft 5in. (135cm)
Track: rear	...	...	4ft 6·5in. (138cm)
Overall length	...	...	16ft 1·5in. (491 cm)
Overall width	...	...	5ft 8in. (173 cm)
Overall height (unladen)	...	4ft 11in. (150cm)
Ground clearance (laden)	...	6·5in. (16·5cm)
Turning circle	...	...	39ft 6in. (12m)
Kerb weight	...	...3,584lb-32cwt(1,626kg)

Left: Facia remains unchanged except for the addition of the Selectaride and air-intake controls mounted to the right of the steering wheel. Right: At the rear there are no alterations

The BRISTOL 408

1964 Cars

THE new Bristol is a logical development of the 407. A redesigned body gives an up-to-date shape still in the tradition of the Bristol 400-series. A new frontal treatment houses four headlights while at the rear a revised lamp cluster and a wrap-round bumper help to distinguish the 408. A slightly squared roof-line gives an overall height an inch less than the 407.

Interior planning is unchanged, with reclining front seats and very comfortable back seat accommodation for two; seat belt attachment points are provided, but choice of make is left to the owner. The dashboard, with lockable glove pocket, is of polished wood with a separate nacelle housing a comprehensive set of instruments.

Cold air is ducted from a large plenum chamber which is supplied from a grille at the rear of the bonnet; hot air is provided by a Smiths heater which also draws from the plenum chamber.

The rear shock absorber settings can be varied by the Armstrong Selectaride system, operated by a four-position switch on the facia. A live rear axle is controlled by torsion bars and Watts linkage with telescopic shock absorbers; independent front suspension uses coil springs and transverse wishbones. Dunlop 11¼ in. disc brakes are fitted all round and are operated through a Lockheed tandem vacuum servo unit. Dunlop RS5 (6·00-16) tyres are fitted as standard.

The relatively light engine, incorporating the latest American thin-section cast iron foundry techniques, is basically a 313 Chrysler 5·13-litre V-8. Different camshaft configurations and an inlet manifold to take the four-choke Carter carburetter, give the Bristol version 250 b.h.p. (gross) at 4,400 r.p.m. and 340 lb. ft. torque at 2,800 r.p.m. This is coupled to the Chrysler Torqueflite 3-speed automatic transmission, as designed for this power unit.

Engine cooling is assisted by two thermostatically controlled Kenlowe electric fans which are accessible, with the horns, through an easily removed front grille.

A short test demonstrated the effectiveness of the adjustable shock absorbers over varying road surfaces and the suitability of the Chrysler units. Acceleration on automatic could not be bettered by holding the individual gears and gear changes were scarcely noticeable. Wind tunnel testing of the body shape was justified by the absence of wind roar; the handling was steady and precise at all speeds, although the steering was a little heavier than might be expected. This test also served to confirm the probability of the manufacturer's figure of 0-100 in 26 seconds.

(Above) the treatment of the four headlights is different, and the roof line is squarer and one inch lower than the 407. There is plenty of room for baggage in the large boot (left), and the revised lamp clusters remind one of the Humber Sceptre. The wraparound bumper is also new.

PRICE: Secondhand £1,185 ; New–Basic £2,995, with tax £4,244

Petrol consumption	20-24 m.p.g.	*Date first registered 25 March 1960*	
Oil consumption	*negligible*	*Mileometer reading*	20,552

"IF you're rich enough to run one, you can afford to buy one new" is a simple maxim which goes a long way to explaining the poor demand on the used car market for certain exclusive quality cars, and which accounts for the shattering depreciation which goes with them. Although a rare car with enthusiast appeal, this Bristol 406 illustrates the point by a price drop of £3,000 in four years. It is the last of the line to be powered by the long-lived Bristol six-cylinder engine, enlarged for this model to 2¼ litres, and replaced by the 5·1-litre Chrysler engine in 1961.

Outwardly, the engine resembles a twin-overhead camshaft unit, and does in fact have inclined valves in hemispherical combustion chambers; but they are operated by vertical and horizontal pushrods with a single side camshaft. Although the valve gear is somewhat noisy, the engine is efficient, and gives unexpectedly lively performance in this relatively large car. It starts reliably and warms up very quickly. Three Solex downdraught carburettors are used, and to judge from the even 500 r.p.m. tickover, clean throttle response, and good performance and economy, they are evidently in correct tune.

The engine is still very fit; it does not object to repeated revving up to 5,000 r.p.m. in acceleration testing, and oil consumption is negligible. Some vibration from the clutch thrust race is felt through the pedal in gear changes at high revs. It is understood from the vendors that the mileometer has been replaced, and shows only about half the true mileage of 39,000.

Overdrive Standard

The Bristol's extremely good gearbox, with quiet indirects and a precise central change, is rare in having a freewheel on bottom gear, which is extremely useful in city traffic. The 406 also featured the first self-cancelling overdrive, and this, too, is still working correctly. A small chromed lever to the right of the steering column engages overdrive on top gear only, at the same time closing a circuit to energize a small electromagnet in the switch, which holds its lever in the up or "on" position. When the gear lever is moved out of top, the circuit is broken, switching off the electro-magnet, and the overdrive lever drops to the off position by gravity.

A slightly "vintage" feel is given to the car by firm, rather ponderous suspension, with a lot of high-frequency jogging over bad surfaces. The rack-and-pinion steering is precise and is not unduly stiff in spite of fairly high gearing, but it does transmit some rattle, suggesting wear in the front suspension king pin bushes. The lock is good, a help when manoeuvring this rather long car. The suspension design is an odd mixture—transverse leaf spring at the front; and live axle with Watts linkage, torque arm, and torsion bars connected to the ends of lever arm dampers, as well as telescopic dampers, at the rear.

By today's standards, rather heavy brake pedal loads are needed, but the brakes—discs all round—have real bite, and easily take care of comfortable 80-90 m.p.h. cruising speeds.

Completely resprayed in dark green, with black on the roof, the bodywork has almost the appearance of a new car, and although there are quite a lot of scratches and marks on the chrome, especially the bumpers, they do not detract from the overall impression of a very clean car. Inside, considerable creasing and a few small tears in the pale green leather upholstery

and trim give a more travel-worn appearance, but carpets, polished wood facia and p.v.c. roof linings are in good shape.

Two well-worn and three practically new tyres are fitted, and jack, wheelbrace and starting handle are with the car. The spare wheel lives in a compartment built into the rear part of the left front wing, and a similar compartment on the right reveals the battery and the windscreen washer reservoir.

When the Bristol was collected for test, Alan Day Ltd. explained that it had not been passed out as ready for sale, but said that any faults discovered would be put right, regardless of what they were. In fact, nothing major was found to be wrong with the car, but a number of minor troubles came to light. The radio was permanently on long wave, and its loudspeaker, the cigarette lighter, temperature gauge, left instrument lighting and one of the reversing lamps, were not working. New windscreen wiper blades were needed, and the windscreen washer was out of action. All these matters are being put right, and two other weaknesses—scratches on the windscreen, and a smell of petrol leakage when the 18-gallon tank is brimmed—also merit attention. New king pins also will be fitted before sale.

Often this sort of exclusive car, praised to the heavens by enthusiasts, simply fails to "ring the bell" in used car assessment; it is not so with this Bristol 406, and one can well understand reasons for being starry-eyed about it. In appearance alone it is impressive, it has a feeling of solidity and craftsmanship in its construction, and it is essentially a car that is different from the run-of-the-mill.

Very full equipment includes an oil thermometer, a small foglamp, two wing mirrors, cigarette lighter and radio; and there is an effective fresh-air heater. The front seats have reclining backrests, and the top section can be released and hinged forward to serve as a headrest

PERFORMANCE CHECK
(Car not previously Road Tested)

0 to 30 m.p.h.	..	5·5 sec	0 to 80 m.p.h. ..	30·0 sec
0 to 40 m.p.h.	..	7·2 sec		
0 to 50 m.p.h.	..	11·0 sec	**Standing quarter-mile**	20·4 sec
0 to 60 m.p.h.	..	16·8 sec	20 to 40 m.p.h. (top gear)	9·1 sec
0 to 70 m.p.h.	..	21·5 sec	30 to 50 m.p.h. (top gear)	10·6 sec

Car for sale at: Alan Day Ltd., 341-347 Finchley Road, London, N.W.3. Telephone: HAMpstead 1133.

BRISTOL 408

ENGINE CAPACITY 313.76 cu in, 5,130 cu cm
FUEL CONSUMPTION 18 m/imp gal, 15 m/US gal, 15.7 l × 100 km
SEATS 4 MAX SPEED 122 mph, 196.4 km/h
PRICE list £ 3,690, total £ 4,459

ENGINE front, 4 stroke; cylinders: 8, Vee-slanted at 90°; bore and stroke: 3.88 × 3.31 in, 98.5 × 84.1 mm; engine capacity: 313.76 cu in, 5,130 cu cm; compression ratio: 9; max power (SAE): 250 hp at 4,400 rpm; max torque (SAE): 340 lb/ft, 46.9 kg/m at 2,800 rpm; max number of engine rpm: 5,100; specific power: 48.7 hp/l; cylinder block: cast iron; cylinder head: cast iron; crankshaft bearings: 5; valves: 2 per cylinder, overhead, push-rods and rockers; camshaft: 1, at centre of Vee; lubrication: rotary pump, filter on by-pass; lubricating system capacity: 11 imp pt, 13.11 US pt, 6.2 l; carburation: 1 Carter AFB 3131S downdraught 4-barrel carburettor; fuel feed: mechanical pump; cooling system: water, 2 automatic thermostatically controlled fans; cooling system capacity: 36 imp pt, 43.13 US pt, 20.4 l.

TRANSMISSION driving wheels: rear; gearbox: Torqueflite automatic, hydraulic torque convertor and planetary gears with 3 ratios + reverse, max ratio of convertor at stall 2.20, possible manual selection; gearbox ratios: I 2.45, II 1.45, III 1, rev 2.20; push button control on facia; final drive: hypoid bevel; axle ratio: 3.31.

CHASSIS box-type ladder frame; front suspension: independent, wishbones, coil springs, anti-roll bar, telescopic dampers; rear suspension: rigid axle, longitudinal torsion bars, trailing lower radius arms, upper torque arm, transverse Watt linkage, electrically adjustable telescopic dampers.

STEERING worm and roller; turns of steering wheel lock to lock: 4.

BRAKES disc (diameter 11.25 in, 286 mm), vacuum servo.

ELECTRICAL EQUIPMENT voltage: 12 V; battery: 72 Ah; alternator; ignition distributor: Autolite; headlights: 2.

DIMENSIONS AND WEIGHT wheel base: 114 in, 2,896 mm; front track: 53 in, 1,346 mm; rear track: 54.50 in, 1,384 mm; overall length: 193.50 in, 4,915 mm; overall width: 68 in, 1,727 mm; overall height: 59 in, 1,499 mm; ground clearance: 6.50 in, 165 mm; dry weight: 3,584 lb, 1,626 kg; distribution of weight: 53% front axle, 47% rear axle; turning circle (between walls): 39.6 ft, 12.1 m; tyres: 6.00 × 16; fuel tank capacity: 18 imp gal, 21.6 US gal, 82 l.

BODY saloon; doors: 2; seats: 4; front seats: separate, reclining backrests.

PERFORMANCE max speeds: 40 mph, 64.4 km/h in 1st gear; 70 mph, 112.7 km/h in 2nd gear; 122 mph, 196.4 km/h in 3rd gear; power-weight ratio: 14.3 lb/hp, 6.5 kg/hp; carrying capacity: 706 lb, 320 kg; acceleration: standing ¼ mile 16.2 sec, 0 — 50 mph (0 — 80 km/h) 6.6 sec; speed in direct drive at 1,000 rpm: 23.8 mph, 38.3 km/h.

PRACTICAL INSTRUCTIONS fuel: 100 oct petrol; engine sump oil: 10 imp pt, 12.05 US pt, 5.7 l, SAE 20 (winter) 30 (summer), change every 3,000 miles, 4,800 km; gearbox oil: 16 imp pt, 19.24 US pt, 9.1 l, automatic transmission fluid, change every 10,000 miles, 16,100 km; final drive oil: 3 imp pt, 3.59 US pt, 1.7 l, EP 90, change every 10,000 miles, 16,100 km; steering box oil: EP 90; greasing: every 6,000 miles, 9,700 km, 2 points; tappet clearances: inlet 0.010 in, 0.25 mm hot, exhaust 0.018 in, 0.46 mm hot; valve timing: inlet opens 13° before tdc and closes 55° after bdc, exhaust opens 51° before bdc and closes 17° after tdc; tyre pressure (medium load): front 29 psi, 2 atm, rear 29 psi, 2 atm.

VARIATIONS AND OPTIONAL ACCESSORIES 408 GT Zagato, 2 + 2 seats, 2.80 axle ratio, dry weight 2,968 lb, 1,346 kg, power-weight ratio 11.9 lb/hp, 5.4 kg/hp.

BRISTOL 408

ALTHOUGH BORN of a fairly long line of cars whose appeal is in the connoisseur class, the Bristol 408 is comparatively little known. Perhaps because of this, it somehow seems to invite comparison with others that are known to set standards. Let us fall in with this idea by saying that in quality of manufacture it bears comparison with the best products of other British manufacturers of luxury cars, while in performance it is surely sufficient to remark that it will hold a 250GT 2+2 Ferrari over a standing half mile.

In many of its constructional details the 408 is obviously derived from the earliest Bristols, but the least traditional thing about it is what, if any one thing be singled out for the honour, gives it its effortless superiority. We refer, of course, to the specially modified and adapted Chrysler engine, a hemispherical-head V8 of 5,130 c.c. capacity. Built in Canada to special order, and modified at Filton, it is typical of the best transatlantic engines in having high volumetric efficiency (the peak bmep is 164 lb/in^2) and delivering a tremendous amount of torque over a wide range of engine speeds.

A faultless starter, the engine warms up quickly with the aid of an automatic choke that can be kicked into submission if one is in a hurry to take to the road: the 1,300 r.p.m. idle given by the choke is altogether too fast for safe driving. Even without its aid, warm-up is still fast, for airflow through the radiator is controlled by two Kenlowe electric fans with their usual sensitive thermostatic control.

Mated to the engine is a standard Chrysler Torqueflite transmission, comprising a three-element torque convertor with a stall ratio of 2·2 to 1 and a planetary gear train giving three forward speeds. Conventional fully automatic transmission is available if number 3 of the row of buttons on the facia to the right of the steering wheel be pressed, but more control over the workings of the gearbox can be exercised. Button 1 limits the car to bottom gear only; button 2 works similarly on second gear, but if acceleration is continued a change up to top gear will automatically be made at 4,700 r.p.m., second being automatically resumed as soon as speed has slackened sufficiently. This type of gear-hold is useful when winding roads have to be negotiated as fast as possible, but for all

In a manner which has become traditional on Bristol cars, the spare wheel (below) is accommodated in a recess in the nearside front wing which is hinged to permit ready access.

practical purposes the fully-automatic drive, with its kick-down selection of the lowest suitable ratio for full accelera-tion, is perfectly satisfactory. In any case, every gear change is very smooth indeed regardless of throttle opening, only a slight lurch intruding if button 1 is pressed while travelling

too quickly. Left to itself, the transmission makes upward changes during full-throttle acceleration at 35 and 68 m.p.h.; conversely, the car can be made to trickle along in top gear, so wide is the spread of useful power.

Liberal use of the 250 b.h.p. made instantly available by this responsive transmission might be expected to lead to trouble; but it was in fact almost impossible to make either rear wheel spin, even on damp roads. Some of the credit for this doubtless belongs to the Avon Turbospeeds with which the test car was shod (Dunlop RS5 are regulation issue), but it is clear that the unusual suspension linkage for the rigid rear axle plays a major part in absorbing torque reactions. Perhaps because of this, a limited-slip differential is merely an optional extra instead of being mandatory.

Wheel adhesion is helped by good suspension geometry and seemingly well-judged spring rates, the ride being firm enough for good control without ever being hard. The rear dampers are Armstrong's electrically adjustable Selectaride, a knob on the facia controlling their firmness. How much this control is used will depend on the sensitivity of the individual driver; even when only lightly laden, the car seemed quite happy to be kept at the hardest setting.

Like the ride, the seats are comfortable but firm, especially at the edges where they support the thighs well. The seats and squabs are if anything a little too wide, but this is scarcely a fault, for they are so shaped and upholstered that the occupant is automatically centred and supported against lateral sway. The individual front seats are adjustable for reach and, through Reutter controls, for rake right back to the fully reclining position. No attempt has been made to create a cavernous seat-five-or-six-at-a-pinch interior, but the head and leg room available in all the seats justifies the makers' claim that the car will comfortably accommodate four six-foot men. Unless they be immodest in their requirements it should also take their luggage, for the boot is vast. Its great depth is made possible by the absence of petrol tank (further forward over the rear axle, where changing fuel levels will have less effect on weight distribution), spare wheel (in the nearside front wing) or battery (in the offside front wing). There are thus no awkward nooks and crannies, just a lot of very useful space. The Bristol designers, always sticklers for structural stiffness, have been unable to resist the temptation to build a high sill across the rear of the body shell, and this is responsible for the only fault in the luggage boot: the high lift necessary to clear the sill makes loading and unloading rather heavy work.

Within the passenger compartment there is plenty of provision for storing odds and ends. Each occupant has a big rigid pocket near at hand, as well as ample shelf space, and there is a lockable cabinet in the facia. It is tempting to list all the detail niceties of this body, to enthuse over such things as the polished woodwork or the elegant-shape and fine 'hand-made' fit of the catches for the pivoting rear windows. However, space only allows that we summarise it as being up to the best standards of London coachbuilders. Perhaps it should be added that, since this is a compact fast four-seater rather than a mobile drawing room, there is a transmission hump down the middle of the floor; footroom is still more than adequate.

Just how fast the Bristol is can be difficult to appreciate, so utterly fuss-free is it at all speeds. Even when accelerating hard,

the silence of the engine and the slickness of the transmission mask much of the drama, but the push in the back can certainly be felt. It is not just a jerk, it is a long sustained push that tells of acceleration being maintained and hints at the meaning of a 470 lb/ton Tapley pull in top gear—higher, just to put the car in perspective, than that of an E-type Jaguar. There is no marked falling-off in acceleration even well beyond the century mark, which can be reached along any short straight.

When such speeds are possible, braking calls for good judgement and intelligent anticipation. In the Bristol 408 it also calls for moderately high pedal pressures, for the very powerful Dunlop discs are not extravagantly servo-aided, lest they be locked by a panic application. By a happy choice of servo ratio and lining material the brakes have been made quite sensitive enough for low-speed stopping, often the bugbear of discs on fast cars, while a force of about 100 lb. (pretty heavy, but not *too* much for a lady) at the pedal will produce 1g retardation as often as desired. The balance of braking effort between front and rear wheels is just about ideal when the car is fully laden, but when travelling light there is a tendency for the rear wheels to lock a shade prematurely.

Any resultant directional instability is well within the power of the steering to correct. Never unpleasantly heavy, the steering becomes lighter and seemingly more precise as speeds rise. In traffic the driver may be conscious of its low-geared response, for $3\frac{3}{4}$ turns of the wheel are needed to go from one extreme to the other of a $39\frac{1}{2}$ ft. turning circle. He may also, if his standards are particularly high—if for example he is used to the earlier rack-and-pinion Bristols—feel that the steering lacks the "feel" and hairline accuracy that is the mark of a real thoroughbred. This feeling soon passes, presumably because his brain adjusts itself, and he can thereafter begin to take the 408 round all manner of bends, corners and assorted traffic hazards in a way that belies its size. The car is very well-balanced, with just enough understeer for directional stability at high speed, and there is enough power on tap for some fairly advanced cornering techniques to be used. Steady drifts through long fast curves or rapid attitude reversals in roundabouts can all be included in the repertoire; but in practice the limits of cornering are imposed by consciousness of that £4,459 price tag!

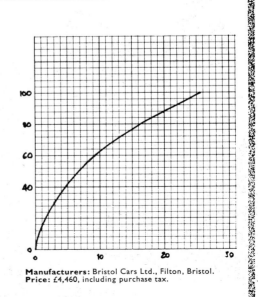

Cars on Test

BRISTOL 408

Engine: Eight-cylinder (90 degree V) 98·55 mm.× 84·07 mm. (5,130 c.c.); pushrod-operated overhead valves in hemispherical heads; compression ratio 9 to 1; Carter 4-choke downdraught carburettor; 250 b.h.p. at 4,400 r.p.m.
Transmission: Chrysler Torqueflite transmission; torque convertor and three-speed epicyclic train; fully automatic with kickdown and manual over-ride.
Suspension: Front, independent, wishbones and coil springs; rear, live axle located by Watt linkage and central torque arm, sprung by longitudinal torsion bars. Selectaride dampers.
Brakes: Dunlop $11\frac{1}{4}$ ins. discs to all four wheels, with vacuum servo assistance.
Dimensions: Overall length, 16 ft. $1\frac{1}{2}$ ins.; overall width 5 ft. 8 ins.; height, 4 ft. 11 ins.; ground clearance, $6\frac{1}{2}$ ins.; turning circle, 39 ft. 6 ins.; dry weight, 32 cwt.

PERFORMANCE

	m.p.h.			secs.
MAXIMUM SPEED	—128	ACCELERATION	0–30 —	3·0
			0–40 —	4·7
			0–50 —	6·6
Speeds in gears—see text			0–60 —	9·1
			0–70 —	12·0
			0–80 —	16·3
			0–90 —	21·0
			0–100 —	25·5
		Standing quarter mile		—16·1

Manufacturers: Bristol Cars Ltd., Filton, Bristol.
Price: £4,460, including purchase tax.

A lighter swifter Bristol

Model 409 with many detail improvements

The Bristol 409

A FIRM like Bristol Cars with a small labour force hand assembling about four cars a week does not bother to make changes for the sake of change. The many detail improvements on the new 409 are all worth while and they make the Bristol that much better a car. The price, including tax, is £4,849 (basic, £4,012).

Logical rationalization between Chrysler Canada and Chrysler America has increased the engine capacity by 81 c.c. but the quoted power figures remain the same—250 b.h.p. at 4,400 r.p.m. and 340 lb. ft. at 2,800 r.p.m. The engine is a special unit for Bristol and not just another Chrysler option, the main difference being a special cam and mechanical tappets. A Chrysler alternator is now fitted in conjunction with a smaller Dagenite battery, negatively earthed; this battery has a larger than usual electrolyte reserve capacity, allowing longer periods between checking the levels.

The latest Chrysler Torque-Flite 3-speed automatic transmission is smaller and lighter, with an aluminium housing. The unit has been modified to allow second gear to be held until you select third, instead of the previous arrangement which selected third automatically—there is a rev. counter—giving full manual overriding control. The 409 is slightly lighter than the 408, and it was felt that the raised axle ratio would not affect acceleration, but give better fuel consumption and around 10 m.p.h. extra maximum speed—the makers claim about 132 m.p.h. The radiator is smaller to take advantage of improved air flow through a slightly different intake.

To improve the ride the front suspension has been softened by 10% and all damper settings have been changed, including the Armstrong Selectaride adjustable ones at the rear. In theory the softer springs would lead to higher roll angles but this has been taken care of by raising the front roll centre by 2 inches with a different front hub carrier but the same inboard wishbone mountings.

Some people thought that the brake servo assistance came in too suddenly on the previous models, so the "crackpoint" (pedal pressure at which assistance starts) has been lowered to give a more progressive feel to the brakes; these are Girling disc units all round with a separate, self-adjusting pair of handbrake calipers. Bristol's fade acceptance test includes 30 $\frac{1}{2}$-g stops from 70 m.p.h. at 30-second intervals—rather more severe than in *Motor's* road tests. There is also a transmission parking brake.

The silencers have been redesigned to last longer and to eliminate shell noise—vibration of the casing. An inspection of 408 silencers which had failed revealed that it was at one or more of only three points—the perforated tube, the baffle or the inner casing. The new Burgess design has stainless steel replacements for these parts but retains the outer mild steel casing with an asbestos sandwich which does the sound damping.

The rear screen now has electric demisting as a standard fitting.

In character the Bristol has changed very little over the years relative to the successive eras of each model; each new series is an indication that the designers move with the times and take good advantage of any new development without actually pioneering it. To do otherwise in such a small production could be a costly error.

The 409 is the latest development of the full four-seater luxury carriage, able to cruise comfortably and silently at over 100 m.p.h.—now just under 4,000 r.p.m. The maker's address is Bristol Cars Ltd., Filton, Bristol. **M**

Brief Specification

Engine.
V-8. 5,211 c.c.; bore and stroke 99.31 x 84.07 mm.; 250 b.h.p. at 4,400 r.p.m.; 340 lb. ft. at 2,800 r.p.m.; sealed cooling system with twin thermostatically-controlled electric fans.

Transmission.
Three speed and torque converter—Torque-Flite—with ratios 3.07, 4.45, and 7.52; m.p.h. per 1,000 r.p.m.—25.9; Avon Turbospeed tyres 6.00 x 16.

Suspension.
Front: independent with double wishbones and anti-roll bar with coil springs. Rear: live axle with twin lower and single upper radius arms with transverse Watt linkage, torsion bars.

Brakes.
Girling disc brakes front (10.9 in. dia.) and rear (10.66 in. dia.) with vacuum servo.

Chassis.
Closed box section welded steel with deep bracing cross-members.

Body.
Welded steel structure with aluminium alloy panelling.

Dimensions.
Wheelbase, 9 ft. 6 in.; track front and rear—4 ft. 6 in. and 4 ft. 6$\frac{1}{2}$ in.; overall length 16 ft. 1$\frac{1}{2}$ in.; width 5 ft. 8 in.; height 4 ft. 11 in.; ground clearance 6$\frac{1}{2}$ in.; kerb weight 31$\frac{1}{2}$ cwt.

BRISTOL 409

Identification of the Bristol 409 is by the curvature of the top and bottom of the radiator grille surround

ONE of the first British cars to be equipped with a lightweight American vee-8 engine was the Bristol 407, introduced in 1961. Two years later, some styling changes and suspension improvements appeared for the 408. Since then, Bristol Cars have not been content to "leave well alone," but have made a host of detail improvements to the mechanical side which are now revealed on the Bristol 409.

At a casual glance there are no styling changes. However, the radiator grille surround has been revised, now being radiused at top *and* bottom.

Perhaps the most significant move is the adoption of a Girling all-disc braking system (Dunlop on the 408), possibly because Dunlop interests have been taken over by Girling. A Lockheed servo and Ferodo DS31 pads are specified. A parking lock has been added to the

Torqueflite automatic transmission.

Subtle changes to the suspension geometry have raised the roll centre and allowed softer springs to be used. Damper settings have been adjusted to suit; Armstrong Selectaride control of the rear dampers is retained.

To meet certain U.S.A. and Canadian requirements, the Chrysler engine size has been increased slightly to 5,221 c.c. (91·31 × 84·07 mm), from 5,130 c.c.; no changes in power or torque outputs are reported. The Chrysler Torqueflite transmission is much smaller and more compact than before, with an integral aluminium torque converter housing, and the back axle ratio has been lowered to 3·07 from 3·31. In addition to the transmission lock already mentioned, there is provision for each intermediate gear to be "held" if needed for maximum performance. An alternator and a

pre-engaged starter complete engine changes, and a new exhaust silencing system is aimed to cut down corrosion and noise.

In view of the specialized nature of the car, it is only fitting that an electrically heated rear window is now standard, and that literally any body colour, to individual customer's requests, can be provided without extra charge.

The change in axle ratio, together with the mechanical refinements, and some improvement in aerodynamics (partly due to a smaller, more efficient radiator) have raised the maximum speed claimed from 122 to 132 m.p.h., with a small though significant improvement in the fuel consumption. The new 409 is priced at £4,012 basic or a recommended total figure of £4,849 7s 11d, including U.K. purchase tax. ∎

BRISTOL 409

ENGINE CAPACITY 317.98 cu in, 5,211 cu cm
FUEL CONSUMPTION 18 m/imp gal, 15 m/US gal, 15.7 l x 100 km
SEATS 4   MAX SPEED 132 mph, 212.5 km/h
PRICE IN GB basic £ 4,260, total £ 5,238

ENGINE front, 4 stroke; cylinders: 8, Vee-slanted at 90°; bore and stroke: 3.91 × 3.31 in, 99.3 × 84.1 mm; engine capacity: 317.98 cu in, 5,211 cu cm; compression ratio: 9; max power (SAE): 250 hp at 4,400 rpm; max torque (SAE): 340 lb ft, 46.9 kg m at 2,800 rpm; max engine rpm: 5,100; specific power: 48 hp/l; cylinder block: cast iron; cylinder head: cast iron; crankshaft bearings: 5; valves: 2 per cylinder, overhead, push-rods and rockers; camshafts: 1, at centre of Vee; lubrication: rotary pump, full flow filter; lubricating system capacity: 8.50 imp pt, 10.15 US pt, 4.8 l; carburation: 1 Carter AFB 3131S downdraught 4-barrel carburettor; fuel feed: mechanical pump; cooling system: liquid, sealed circuit, 2 automatic thermostatically controlled fans; cooling system capacity: 32.50 imp pt, 39.11 US pt, 18.5 l

TRANSMISSION driving wheels: rear; gearbox: Torqueflite automatic, hydraulic torque convertor and planetary gears with 3 ratios + reverse, max ratio of convertor at stall 2.2, possible manual selection; gearbox ratios: I 2.45, II 1.45, III 1, rev 2; push button control: on facia; final drive: hypoid bevel; axle ratio: 3.070.

CHASSIS box-type ladder frame; front suspension: independent, wishbones, coil springs, anti-roll bar, telescopic dampers; rear suspension: rigid axle, longitudinal torsion bars, trailing lower radius arms, upper torque arm, transverse Watt linkage, electrically adjustable telescopic dampers.

STEERING worm and roller; turns of steering wheel lock to lock: 4.

BRAKES disc (front diameter 10.91 in, 277 mm, rear 10.60 in, 269 mm), vacuum servo; area rubbed by linings: total 420 sq in, 2,709 sq cm.

ELECTRICAL EQUIPMENT voltage: 12 V; battery: 64 Ah; generator type: alternator, 430 W; ignition distributor: Chrysler; headlamps: 4.

DIMENSIONS AND WEIGHT wheel base: 114 in, 2,896 mm; front track: 54 in, 1,372 mm; rear track: 54.50 in, 1,384 mm; overall length: 193.50 in, 4,915 mm; overall width: 68 in, 1,727 mm; overall height: 59 in, 1,499 mm; ground clearance: 6.50 in, 165 mm; dry weight: 3,528 lb, 1,600 kg; distribution of weight: 52% front axle, 48% rear axle; turning circle (between walls): 39.5 ft, 12 m; tyres: 6.00 × 16; fuel tank capacity: 28 imp gal, 33.5 US gal, 127 l.

BODY saloon/sedan; doors: 2; seats: 4; front seats: separate, reclining backrests.

PERFORMANCE max speeds: 50 mph, 80.5 km/h in 1st gear; 90 mph, 144.9 km/h in 2nd gear; 132 mph, 212.5 km/h in 3rd gear; power-weight ratio: 14.1 lb/hp, 6.4 kg/hp; carrying capacity: 706 lb, 320 kg; acceleration: standing ¼ mile 16.2 sec, 0 — 50 mph (0 — 80 km/h) 6.6 sec; speed in direct drive at 1,000 rpm: 25.9 mph, 41.7 km/h.

PRACTICAL INSTRUCTIONS fuel: 100 oct petrol; engine sump oil: 6.50 imp pt, 7.82 US pt, 3.7 l, SAE 10W-30, change every 2,000 miles, 3,200 km; gearbox oil: 16.50 imp pt, 19.87 US pt, 9.4 l, automatic transmission fluid, change every 30,000 miles, 48,300 km; final drive oil: 3 imp pt, 3.59 US pt, 1.7 l, EP 90, change every 20,000 miles, 32,200 km; greasing: every 20,000 miles, 32,200 km, 2 points; tappet clearances: inlet 0.010 in, 0.25 mm hot, exhaust 0.018 in, 0.46 mm hot; valve timing: inlet opens 13° before tdc and closes 55° after bdc, exhaust opens 51° before bdc and closes 17° after tdc; normal tyre pressure: front 31 psi, 2.2 atm, rear 31 psi, 2.2 atm.

VARIATIONS AND OPTIONAL ACCESSORIES power-assisted steering; electrically controlled windows.

MR EDITOR BLAIN SAYS THAT BECAUSE MY PRESENT car is a Bristol, about which I am too enthusiastic, and because my previous car was also a Bristol, about which I was nearly as intolerable, I am unfit to write about the 409 which is the current model from the Filton factory. Biased, he says I am. *I* say that there is nothing like long experience with a make to encourage an objective test of the latest model. Nothing, perhaps, unless it be a price tag of £5150, which is guaranteed to encourage one to be very objective indeed.

One thing is clear. The Bristols they make today are not like the Bristols they used to make in the old days. If you saw a Bristol on the road in the early or middle 1950s there was no mistaking it for anything else. Bristols in those days, idiosyncratic in shape as few other cars have ever been, were unmistakably the work of an aircraft manufacturer. Today you could see a 409 coming towards you on the road and mistake it for a puffed-up Oxbridge model (unfair to Pininfarina—*Ed*). It looks long and lean and messy in profile, but it still does not look like an aeronaut's idea of how to travel on four wheels. Today, on the other hand, the car is a lot faster, you do not have to row it along with a gearlever, and the noise level approximates to that of a well-carpeted morgue instead of the three-score maladjusted sewing machines that seem to be accommodated beneath the bonnet of the old two-litre wagon.

The fact of the matter is that, while maintaining their standards in most things, Bristol have changed their ideas about the market to which they try to appeal. Chaps who want to rush about in juvenile exuberance can jolly well go and buy the Astons and Ferraris that they were always tempted to buy anyway. Chaps who want something in the Bentley Continental class but prefer it to be faster, quieter, much better handling and equally well made may profitably indent for a Bristol instead—and will presumably not be greatly upset by saving more than £2000 in the process.

Because of this change in marketing appeal, one can go too far in the comparison of old Bristols and new. For example, the old ones had quite narrow windscreens and superstructure because, since they were built to accommodate four adults, there was no need for full width construction there. They were not, however, ideal cars for claustrophobes, whereas four adults who did not like each other very much could sit in a 409 without finding the degree of intimacy more disturbing than in any other luxury saloon.

Still, many things about Bristols have not changed. They have always been among the best-made cars in the world, because they are put together by people with aircraft manufacturers' standards in design, manufacture and inspection. In quality of finish they are probably better now than they ever have been, although in quality of workmanship they may be inferior to the cars of the early 1950s when there were at Filton 20 or so of the finest tinsmiths working anywhere. Don't ask me where they are now; when the government reorganised the aircraft industry so that the Bristol Cars Division had to be hived off into a separate private company, quite a lot of people and plant were prized away and they rather tended to throw out the baby with the bath water.

Today, it needs no more than an examination of the suspension and the pains taken to eliminate friction from all its joints to impress upon one the care with which Filton still makes its cars. Then again, Bristols have always been amply fast by the standards of the day without being in the front rank of the out-and-out speedsters; they have always been big enough to make travel elegant

Not-so fashionable BRISTOL

So long as you are
on the inside
it's splendid
LJK SETRIGHT

rather than indecorous; and they have always had handling qualities of a very high standard, usually up to the best sports cars. Broadly speaking, therefore, they represent one of the best possible compromises among all the conflicting demands made of a car.

In this exists a summary of all that is the 409. Of course there are several cars that are faster, but 132mph is a not unsatisfactory speed and the 409 can do it easily. Of course there are many cars that are more compact, but I can think of few that will take four 76in men and their luggage in real comfort—in fact the Bristol is the first car I have encountered for a long time in which I can, as it were, sit behind me when I am driving. Again, too, there is a multitude of cars that are bigger and perhaps more opulent, but the ones that can be hustled along winding roads with the calculated abandon possible in the 409 can be numbered on the thumbs of one hand. I have also encountered some cars that are quieter . . . but the latest of them was made in 1937.

I can even think of a number of cars that are considerably better looking. There are some really gawky and uncomfortable angles about the 409: the slab front of the wings may produce a nice flat surface upon which mounting of lights is child's play, but it betrays a stylistic crudity that would not have been out of place in a Panzer regiment. As for the staccato streaks of brightwork along its flanks, and the immodest Pegasus emblem bulging therefrom, there can be no excuse save the fact that the car would look even more gross without them. Other apparent crudities are better explained away. The shape of the radiator air intake is roughly the same as that of the cooling matrix behind it—a rare enough thing nowadays. The angular section of the roof produces some curious semi-razor edge styling in some unexpected places, but makes the thing roomier and slightly lower. And if the whole car looks high and narrow, at least it can be put through traffic with greater assurance, gives room with a view, and is fairly easy to enter and leave.

Nevertheless, with these peculiar proportions the 409 appears undoubtedly old-fashioned. In fact it looks considerably less advanced than the models that preceded it. One might also be tempted to criticise the mechanicals as old-fashioned too, for there is a rigid axle at the rear, and every savant will tell you that nowadays a rigid

axle is hopelessly obsolete. The fact remains that when I put the car on to full lock and then did a full throttle bottom-gear take-off on a wet road there was no wheelspin—the brute simply moved away in the appropriate direction, and moved away right promptly. A rigid rear axle that is properly located by Watt linkages and radius arms need neither hop nor tramp, and it never introduces worries about varying wheel camber.

Then again there is that chassis—admittedly very strong, having been blessed with a life of 21 years without any major change to the basic frame. But really, a *chassis* in this day and age? The Bristol answer to this is quite simple: they reckon that a car is safer with a chassis like this than without it. Certainly, it provides sufficient stiffness for the various components to be assured of a precise spacial relationship, and the accident record of Bristols suggests that it is also a good thing to have around in a crash. For all their good handling, Bristols have been crashed in fair numbers, but so far as is known only three fatalities have ever occurred in them in all the thousands of cars produced since 1946. And at least one of those deaths could not be blamed on the car.

Another thing that looks old-fashioned is those skinny-tyred wheels, 16in affairs carrying mere six-inch Avons. The comeback here is that the carrying capacity of a 6.00/16 tyre is no less than that of a 6.40/ or 6.70/15, but the rolling resistance is less, the tendency to spin is less, and the self-aligning torque is less—all things that it is good to minimise. It is also true that the amount of rubber in contact with the road is likely to be less—but 1*g* braking, and cornering that approaches the same limit (Bristols were recording 1*g* sideways in 1951, and I have had my own car up to 0.85*g* in the wet, which is more than standard Minis, Imps and DB6s will do in the dry) suggests that there is no marked inadequacy.

Where the Bristol *is* old-fashioned is in being built by hand, one at a time, three a week, and don't come agitating for rapid delivery because the thing has to spend over a fortnight in the paint-shops getting its 20-odd coats. Hand-fangling techniques are of course responsible for a lot of things apart from the price, possibly even for the unconcealed screw heads which abound and which so offend the eye of Blain. Quite why he should so take offence I cannot understand, for a screw head seems an honest enough thing. I can only suppose that, being a delicately nurtured individual with a marked sense of propriety (you have noticed the reserve and decorum of his writing, no doubt?), he finds such blatant display of vital parts immodest.

Personally, the only fault I have to find with the finish is that the leather of the seats is too slippery. The seats are also too big, evidently being dimensioned to suit the behinds of fat company directors rather than waisted playboys. So, although they are designed to give lateral support by arranging for the body so to sink into the softer upholstered central parts as to be partially embraced by the firmer edges, there is still room for the more willowy figure to slide about a bit, and at three-quarters of a *g* that is not a good thing. Otherwise the standard of appointment is frankly terrific with headroom and legroom before and behind, good wood, and beautifully located and eminently legible instruments, though the minor switches are not sufficiently distinguished from each other. The steering wheel is like all past Bristol steering wheels since the 401 model—rigid, too large in diameter, and almost vertical. The driving position is like that of a good vintage racing car, which is precisely how the earlier Bristols felt. The adoption of a big V8 engine forced a change from rack and pinion to Marles mechanism, which is all very well for GT Ferraris and the like but hardly good enough for a long-term confirmed Bristolian. At least it is being improved; changes in geometry, weight distribution and steering box mechanism have made the 409 not only lighter than the 407 and 408, but also somewhat more responsive. It is still not quick and precise enough for dodgy manoeuvres at city speeds, but fat company directors seldom treat Piccadilly as a slalom course. For high jinks on the more open of roads the steering is quite good.

Power steering? Bristol spent six years saying 'Certainly not!' while secretly trying to evolve a system that would be satisfactory. Most lately they have been sorting out the ZF servo box, and at last they have got the valving right. The power steering now available is no less precise than the unassisted variety, gives no less feel, and is no higher geared. It just needs less effort.

Cars that are as fast as the Bristol (oh, yes, it is fast; I am coming to that) are dangerous without good handling qualities. There are several cars as fast as the Bristol and a lot of them *are* dangerous. Since the Bristol is not bought for its looks, it is presumably bought to be driven—so it has to behave. Three things are primarily responsible for the fact that it behaves as well as it does: first, the suspension, which may be jolly firm by luxury car standards but is reassuringly stiff; second, the absence of roll, almost incredible in a car so apparently high and ungainly; third, and probably

most important of all, the near-perfect weight distribution. With a moderate load of crew and fuel aboard, the weight of the car is almost exactly halved between front and rear wheels. Various brilliant stratagems have made this so: the spare wheel, for example, is under the nearside wing amidships instead of cluttering and messing up the boot. The battery is in a similar compartment on the offside, along with things like the brake servo and all the fuses and electrickery neatly displayed for examination whenever they might be required. The gearbox is a new lighter version of the Chrysler Torqueflite, the engine has been moved back a bit, and minor changes in the shape of the radiator air intake have improved the air flow figure to a point where a smaller radiator matrix can now be employed, which makes for

photographs: Charles Pocklington

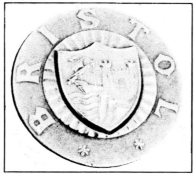

further front-end weight saving. In sum, half a hundredweight has been removed from the front wheels and from the car as a whole since the 408, which only had 53percent of its unladen 32cwt up at the front anyway.

Whatever you feel about the looks of the thing there is no gainsaying the fact that the greatest change in the character of the Bristol has been wrought by the substitution of a whacking great Chrysler V8 for the peppery little two-litre six-cylinder engine that lurked under the high bonnet in the days when Bristols were Bristols. This is one of the best transAtlantic engines there are, but it doesn't find its way into the Bristol until it has been modified in several respects to make it fit for the job. For instance, the hydraulic tappets are replaced by solid lifters, riding a special high-lift camshaft. The capacity is 5.2litres, the power output a very conservative 250bhp, and the torque a compulsive 340lbft. All this is funnelled through a three-speed automatic transmission with torque converter, one of the smoothest there is.

Push buttons control the box from the facia in a way that denies too much independence to the hydraulic slaves down below. Button D gives full automation, with changes occurring at the ideal time for optimum acceleration if you keep the throttles wide open. Button 2 and button 1, on the other hand, will respectively engage middle or bottom gear and hold it, regardless of revs or anything, so that you can let the engine whizz round to 6000 and fall apart. It is quite safe to maintain 5100, which is 132 mph.

Acceleration can best be summed up by saying that the Bristol can hold a Ferrari 250GT 2 + 2 over the standing half-mile, which may explain why Ferrari started building the 330 instead. Full power for 26 seconds from a standing start realises 100 mph. The driver realises it only from scrutiny of the unfashionably accurate speedometer, for there is no noise, no great sensation, just a couple of neat white pointers gyrating rapidly inside some attractive matt black instrument bezels. On my favourite drag strip I have had higher terminal velocities from the Bristol than from Austin Healey 3000, 3.8 Jaguar and the like. The secret lies in the fact that with all that torque and the nicely calculated gearing, the Tapley pull in top gear is even greater than, say, that of a 3.8 E-type.

Maybe the Bristol is one of the few real practical motor cars left. So long as you are on the inside, it is splendid. Not exciting, mark you—everything happens with such a complete absence of drama that the car becomes almost a bore to drive, in marked contrast to the sensual delights of older two-litre Bristols such as my own. I will not launch into a long description of the thrills attendant on the driving of my 405; all you need do is to consult the March issue of CAR. The 409 is nowhere near as absorbing: you simply set the needle on the dial to any desired speed up to 132 and then get back to thinking about the big business that must concern you if you can afford all that money. ✳

JOHN BOLSTER tests

THE BRISTOL 410

THE Bristol car holds a position which is certainly unique. Manufacture started after the war, and at once we knew that this was a very special sort of car, built to aircraft standards and bearing no relationship to the popular mass-production vehicle. The firm served its apprenticeship in competition, and Bristol engines powered numerous successful racing and sports cars of other makes, notably AC, Cooper, ERA, Frazer-Nash, Lister and Lotus. Yet the Bristol cars themselves tended more and more to swing towards the luxurious and sophisticated side of motoring.

Wonders were performed with the small six-cylinder Bristol engine, but it became apparent that more litres were necessary if the performance of the future was to be allied with traditional luxury. A big V8 was the answer, and so the Chrysler engine was adopted, in this case a specially prepared 5.2-litre unit with solid tappets and a high-lift camshaft. A box-section chassis frame of welded steel construction was

designed to give immense rigidity, without calling upon the body for bracing, and to provide a stronger protection for the occupants in the event of a crash than probably any other car.

With power to spare and a chassis immune from distortion it was up to the body builders to choose the most suitable construction in the coachbuilders' repertoire. They decided that, when price is no object, there is nothing to beat a tubular steel framework with aluminium panels. Disc brakes were used all round, with wishbones on helical springs in front and a fully located axle on torsion bars behind. This larger car, the 407, was built to the same standards of quality as the models from 400 to 406 had been.

Having tested all the earlier Bristols, I put the 407 through its paces in 1963. I was greatly impressed by its air of quality and effortless performance and I timed the car at 126.7 mph. It was obvious that, by the bold step of adopting a much larger

engine, Bristols had regained their former performance leadership while setting still higher standards of quality.

Since then, 408 and 409 have come and gone, so I was delighted when Tony Crook offered me the latest 410 for a full continental road test. The new model has more modern styling and is a little lower, and the engine, outwardly similar, has a small bore increase. A considerably lighter automatic gearbox with an aluminium case is mounted in unit with the engine, which has been moved back a considerable distance in the chassis in the interest of weight distribution. Among other improvements are the provision of twin brake master cylinders and electrical adjustment of the rear dampers on the Armstrong Selectaride system.

The brakes are still discs all round but are now by Girling, while there is more rubber on the road by courtesy of Avon. Power-assisted steering is now standard instead of being an extra, as it is becoming a normal piece of equipment for cars of this calibre. When I tested the 407 I criticized the tendency of the rear window to mist up, so electrical demisting is now installed, and very effective it is, too.

The coachwork is of the highest standard and there is satisfaction in merely closing the doors. The walnut veneer is finished to perfection and the leather upholstery is of top quality. The front seats have fully reclining backs and the driver's seat can be raised or lowered to match the stature of the individual, the position of the steering wheel being set to suit the purchaser on delivery. From my point of view, one of the greatest improvements is the neat central gearlever for the automatic gearbox, though the earlier press-button system is still available for clients who want an unobstructed floor for ease of entry from either side to the driving seat.

Electric fuel pumps are used, and when a red warning lamp glows one switches on the reserve 2.5 gallons, the total capacity being 18 gallons. With this type of fuel supply, the carburetter is full before the starter turns the engine and from dead cold the unit springs to life instantaneously. The Chrysler V8 is a naturally silent piece of mechanism; also the body panels are treated with anti-drumming material in addition to full undersealing of the chassis, and it is possible to forget that the engine has been left running when the car is parked, so quiet is it.

The Bristol is a big, substantial car, but the torque of the Chrysler makes light of it. The acceleration is very fine indeed, and it seems to go on, right up the range. Almost incredibly, the performance figures in the data panel were taken on a wet road. At this time of year it is rare indeed to find a dry road, and many cars can hardly be tested at all because they are martyrs to wheelspin. The rain was actually falling when the test figures were taken but, as they are better than those which I obtained from the 407, it shows that traction was not being lost to any extent.

The new gearlever gives complete control of the gearbox, and once a lower gear has been selected the revs can be taken right into the red if desired. By letting the rev-counter touch the red in first and second gears, it is actually only possible to make a small improvement on the acceleration figures obtained in full automatic operation. The manual selection is ideal for changing down on entering a corner, the little gearlever being just as delightful to use as that of a good synchromesh box.

A genuine 120 mph come up on a fairly short straight. At 130 mph the rev-counter needle is going into the red, although it is possible that the car could go even faster on a long straight road if conscience did not call a halt. 100 mph is a good cruising speed but so is 120 mph, though the fuel consumption is then beginning to rise.

The slight oversteering tendency of the 407 has been eradicated by the revised weight distribution and broader tyres. Perhaps the car understeers initially, but it is well balanced during normal fast driving. The power-assisted steering is not of the ultra-light variety and a good feel of the road is retained, yet the big machine may be parked without effort. The disc brakes seem to ignore the substantial weight and they do not become overheated during hard driving.

An occasional glance at the unusually accurate speedometer is perhaps advisable, because the high-speed cruising of the 410 is somewhat deceptive. Not only does the engine show no sense of effort, but the absence of pitching and rolling gives an almost unnatural ease to the performance. Though the ride is adjustable, it is always firm rather than soft, but sharp bumps are well absorbed and there is a marked absence of wind noise.

The Bristol is a big impressive car, and naturally the four occupants have plenty of headroom and generous space to stretch their legs. There is a roomy luggage boot with compartments for the tools, and the left wing valance swings open to reveal the spare wheel, behind which the jack and brace are concealed. The right valance also opens, revealing the battery, fuse box and twin brake servos. This unique employment of space which is usually wasted leaves the boot free for luggage and improves the accessibility of the engine. There is quite a large locker in the fascia panel, and the two storage spaces ahead of the rear wheel arches are useful.

I must admit that I have a great affection for hand-built quality cars. The modern quantity-produced car is an excellent vehicle, and it gives many owners all that they require, but for people much as myself the pleasure of using a craftsman-built car is so great that it is a different kind of motoring altogether. To the man requiring a big, dignified car of very high performance, the Bristol brings a pride of ownership that abundantly justifies its considerable price.

Even after cudgelling one's brains, it is difficult to find any points for criticism. Trivial matters are the electric horn button, which sometimes causes an unexpected blast when the back of the driver's seat is folded forward, and the channel in the protective strips along the bottom of the car, which tends to hold mud that can soil ladies's stockings. The Bristol 410 is full of safety features, ensuring protection for the occupants in the event of an accident, but its acceleration, brakes, and roadholding are the best safety insurance of all.

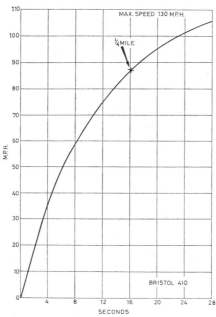

SPECIFICATION AND PERFORMANCE DATA

Car tested: Bristol 410 two-door saloon, price £5673 1s. 10d. including PT.

Engine: Eight cylinders in 90 deg Vee, 99.31 mm x 84.07 mm (5211 cc). Pushrod-operated overhead valves. Compression ratio 9:1. 250 bhp at 4400 rpm. Carter four-choke downdraught carburetter. Coil and distributor ignition.

Transmission: Torque converter and three-speed automatic gearbox, open propeller shaft and hypoid rear axle, overall ratios 3.07, 4.45, and 7.52:1. Torque converter stalled ratio 2:1.

Chassis: Separate steel reinforced box-section frame. Aluminium panelled body on tubular framework. Unequal length front wishbones with helical springs. Power-assisted recirculating ball-type steering with three-piece track rod. Rear axle suspended on torsion bars with Watt's linkage and torque-resisting member. Telescopic dampers all round with Armstrong Selectaride system at rear. Girling servo-assisted disc brakes all round with twin master cylinders. Bolt-on disc wheels with wide-base rims, fitted Avon Turbospeed 6.70-15 ins tyres.

Equipment: 12-volt lighting and starting with alternator. Speedometer. Rev-counter. Ammeter. Oil pressure, water temperature, and fuel gauges. Clock. Heating, demisting, and ventilation system, with electrically demisted rear window. Two-speed windscreen wipers and washers. Flashing direction indicators. Reversing lights. Radio with adjustable twin speakers (extra).

Dimensions: Wheelbase 9 ft 6 ins. Track (front), 4 ft 6 ins; (rear) 4 ft 7 ins. Overall length 16 ft 1½ ins. Width 5 ft 8 ins. Weight 1 ton 11 cwt 56 lb.

Performance: Maximum speed 130 mph. Standing quarter-mile 16.2 secs. Acceleration: 0-30 mph, 3.3 s; 0-50 mph, 6.2 s; 0-60 mph, 8.8 s; 0-80 mph, 13.6 s; 0-100 mph, 23 s.

Fuel consumption: 12 to 16 mpg.

BRISTOL 410

ENGINE CAPACITY 317.97 cu in, 5,211 cu cm
FUEL CONSUMPTION 18 m/imp gal, 15 m/US gal, 15.7 l × 100 km
SEATS 4 MAX SPEED 130 mph, 209.3 km/h
PRICE IN GB basic £ 4,614, total £ 5,673

ENGINE front, 4 stroke, Chrysler; cylinders: 8, Vee-slanted at 90°; bore and stroke: 3.91 × 3.31 in, 99.3 × 84.1 mm; engine capacity: 317.97 cu in, 5,211 cu cm; compression ratio: 9; max power (SAE): 250 hp at 4,400 rpm; max torque (SAE): 340 lb ft, 46.9 kg m at 2,800 rpm; max engine rpm: 5,100; specific power: 48 hp/l; cylinder block: cast iron; cylinder head: cast iron; crankshaft bearings: 5; valves: 2 per cylinder, overhead, push-rods and rockers; camshafts: 1, at centre of Vee; lubrication: rotary pump, full flow filter; lubricating system capacity: 8.50 imp pt, 10.15 US pt, 4.8 l; carburation: 1 Carter AFB 3131S downdraught 4-barrel carburettor; fuel feed: mechanical pump; cooling system: liquid, sealed circuit, 2 automatic thermostatically controlled fans; cooling system capacity: 32.50 imp pt, 39.11 US pt, 18.5 l.

TRANSMISSION driving wheels: rear; gearbox: Torqueflite automatic, hydraulic torque convertor and planetary gears with 3 ratios + reverse, max ratio of convertor at stall 2, possible manual selection; gearbox ratios: I 2.449, II 1.449, III 1, rev 2.199; selector lever: central; final drive: hypoid bevel; axle ratio: 3.070.

CHASSIS box-type ladder frame; front suspension: independent, wishbones, coil springs, anti-roll bar, telescopic dampers; rear suspension: rigid axle, longitudinal torsion bars, trailing lower radius arms, upper torque arm, transverse Watt linkage, electrically adjustable telescopic dampers.

STEERING recirculating ball, servo; turns of steering wheel lock to lock: 3.25.

BRAKES disc (front diameter 10.91 in, 277 mm, rear 10.60 in, 269 mm), independent front and rear circuits, vacuum servo; area rubbed by linings: total 420 sq in, 2,709 sq cm.

ELECTRICAL EQUIPMENT voltage: 12 V; battery: 64 Ah; generator type: alternator, 430 W; ignition distributor: Chrysler; headlamps: 4.

DIMENSIONS AND WEIGHT wheel base: 114 in, 2,896 mm; front track: 54 in, 1,372 mm; rear track: 55 in, 1,397 mm; overall length: 193.50 in, 4,915 mm; overall width: 68 in, 1,727 mm; overall height: 59 in, 1,499 mm; ground clearance: 6.50 in, 165 mm; dry weight: 3,528 lb, 1,600 kg; distribution of weight: 52% front axle, 48% rear axle; turning circle (between walls): 39.5 ft, 12 m; tyres: 6.00 × 16; fuel tank capacity: 18 imp gal, 21.6 US gal, 82 l.

BODY saloon/sedan; doors: 2; seats: 4; front seats: separate, reclining backrests.

PERFORMANCE max speeds: 53 mph, 85.3 km/h in 1st gear; 90 mph, 144.9 km/h in 2nd gear; 130 mph, 209.3 km/h in 3rd gear; power-weight ratio: 14.1 lb/hp, 6.4 kg/hp; carrying capacity: 706 lb, 320 kg; acceleration: standing ¼ mile 16.2 sec, 0 — 50 mph (0 — 80 km/h) 6.6 sec; speed in direct drive at 1,000 rpm: 25.5 mph, 41 km/h.

PRACTICAL INSTRUCTIONS fuel: 100 oct petrol; engine sump oil: 6.50 imp pt, 7.82 US pt, 3.7 l, SAE 10W-40, change every 2,000 miles, 3,200 km; gearbox oil: 15.50 imp pt, 18.60 US pt, 8.8 l, automatic transmission fluid A Suffix A, change every 30,000 miles, 48.300 km; final drive oil: 3 imp pt, 3.59 US pt, 1.7 l, EP 90, change every 20,000 miles, 32,200 km; greasing: every 20,000 miles, 32,200 km, 2 points; tappet clearances: inlet 0.010 in, 0.25 mm hot, exhaust 0.018 in, 0.46 mm hot; valve timing: inlet opens 13° before tdc and closes 55° after bdc, exhaust opens 51° before bdc and closes 17° after tdc; normal tyre pressure: front 32 psi, 2.2 atm, rear 32 psi, 2.2 atm.

VARIATIONS AND OPTIONAL ACCESSORIES enlarged sump, lubricating system capacity 10.50 imp pt, 12.68 US pt, 6 l; electrically controlled windows.

THE BRISTOL 411

Producing the Chrysler-powered Bristol 411 is more a hobby than a business for one of the board members of the Bristol Aeroplane Co., Ltd., but the car has a steady if small following at around $16,000. Emission and safety regulations ended their availability in the U.S.

Europe's supersonic Concorde jet airliner is being built in two plants at Toulouse, France and Bristol, England. Right inside the walls of the Bristol factory there's a small group of buildings owned privately by one of the Board of Directors where Bristol cars are built by hand to aerospace industry standards of quality — and of cost. The operation started after World War II with a design based on the 1940 BMW layout. Then, a rather larger car was designed around a V-8 Plymouth motor, and the Bristol 411 for 1970, which costs only 15 percent less than a Rolls Royce, is the latest development of this theme.

In comparison with a Rolls the Bristol is small, despite being designed to seat four tall men. Its wheelbase is 114 inches, its tread only 55 inches. Also in comparison with a Rolls it is a simple car that is free from gimmicks, but it scales 3724 pounds at the curb.

Solid quality is the "Bristol fashion" of car building. The products are ship-shape rather than airy-fairy, Bristol having been a seaport centuries before it built aeroplanes. For example, Bristol are proud that their bare chassis weighs fully 350 pounds before they start to mount the steel frame for aluminum body panels, or any mechanical elements. Sound deadening in front of and under the passenger compartment is achieved by sheer weight of insulation, and there is enough to make the Bristol one of the world's quietest cars.

Engine size is up for 1970, with 383 cubic inches instead of 318. The 335 horsepower motor with one four-barrel carbureter still comes from Chrysler, though, complete with the excellent Torqueflite three-speed automatic. Axle gearing is chosen to give 25 mph per

Main change between the 411 and the 410 that preceded it is the bigger (383 versus 318 inch) Chrysler engine, wrap-around bumpers and less liberal use of chrome trim. Bodies are built by the factory of aluminum.

1000 rpm, allowing a reasonable factory claim for a top speed of 138 mph at 5500 rpm.

Behind the Detroit (or more precisely, Windsor, Ontario) powerplant, the car is British traditional. There's lots of walnut veneer highly polished, deep pile carpet and leather armchair seats. Power four-disc braking is provided of course, there's power steering of high-speed radial tires and you'll find provision for air conditioning on cars sold to hot countries. A Bristol comes in any color you like, even if you like black. For motorists wanting quality rather than quantity of car for a lot of money, the Bristol aeroplane plant is a good place to go shopping.   *Joe Lowry*

The unostentatious appearance of the Bristol belies its fantastic performance.

Fastest true four-seater touring car

The Bristol holds a unique position among cars of the highest quality. It is manufactured literally without regard for cost by the most painstaking craftsmanship. In a world where ostentatious appearance and flashy decoration are demanded by most wealthy car buyers, the Bristol relies on the custom of the few who prefer quiet good taste. It is pleasant to record that there are enough discerning purchasers to keep the factory going to full capacity, who are happy to pay for intrinsic quality rather than outward show.

The latest model, the 411, retains the immensely sturdy separate chassis which has always been a feature of the *marque*, with a tubular framework to carry the aluminium body panels. This construction is not only far superior to the usual integral pressed-steel body in resisting corrosion, but it gives much greater protection to the occupants in the unfortunate event of a crash.

Based on the 410, the body has been considerably restyled. The windscreen and rear window are deeper and more gradually sloped, with a re-shaped tail giving a wider lid to the luggage boot and a lower scuttle and bonnet line. The front grille is less conspicuous and the badge has been removed

from the bonnet, as have the double bright strips from the side of the car, only the minimum rubbing strips for protection remaining. No vulgar, shiny lettering mars the rear panel and only the name of the car, in very small letters, appears in front and behind. The wheelbase is long to give ample leg room to the rear passengers and no attempt has been made to give the body a "fastback" rear treatment, for ample head room is essential on long journeys and the Bristol is a full four-seater, *not* a 2 + 2.

Some suspension changes have been made and radial-ply tyres adopted, but I leave the greatest change until last; the engine size has gone up from 5211 cc to 6277 cc, the unit still being a Chrysler. This change was made partly because the bigger unit has hydraulic tappets and it was thought desirable to remove valve adjustment from the periodical servicing jobs—Bristols have always specialised in the longest possible service intervals, in the interest of owners living in remote districts.

Thus, almost accidentally, the Bristol has become the fastest genuine touring saloon, beating the Mercedes-Benz 300SEL 6.3 both for maximum speed and acceleration. It is

interesting that it is also faster than other cars of more sporting appearance which have similar power units. The Bristol's dignified body has an unexpectedly low drag coefficient, as a result of much wind-tunnel work at Filton. More important, the designers have resisted the temptation to widen the track, as is the modern fashion, and the 3 ins or so saved in overall width give an appreciable reduction in frontal area. It is curious, too, how one notices that the car is narrower than other luxury automobiles, those few little inches making an astonishing difference when threading crowded roads.

Everything about the 411 breaths an air of quality, which is even emphasised by the way in which the doors shut. The furnishing of the interior simply cannot be faulted and everything is in the right place. As I drove away from Tony Crook's showroom near Olympia at a strictly legal 29 mph, I at once felt that the machine was handling perfectly and that this was going to be a memorable road test. How right I was !

The 411 is quite firmly sprung at low speeds and it never gives the soft, floating ride that some big cars do. Yet it is extremely comfortable for all the occupants and there is a most reassuring feeling of stability. The sensitivity of the steering is not marred by the unobtrusive power assistance, which takes all the work out of low-speed manoeuvres but does not make the control too light for fast cornering.

A neutral handling characteristic is maintained and the rear end behaviour is exemplary; there is no hopping of the back wheels during a wheelspin start or on bumpy corners. The level of road noise is very low, only such things as cats eyes producing radial thump, and the absence of wind noise is most noticeable—that wind-tunnel again ! The all-disc brake installation stands up well to hard driving, in spite of the substantial weight.

The acceleration is terrific and the figures given in the data panel were obtained with fully automatic operation of the gearbox. It is possible that even more dramatic results could be achieved by making manual changes and the rigid little lever is available for those so inclined. The engine is equally silent whether turning fast or slow and has phenomenal torque in the middle ranges. A red section of the rev-counter dial starts at 5,500 rpm, which is equivalent to a

The 411 has the greatest maximum speed and acceleration of any genuine touring saloon.   41-8-2

theoretical 138 mph. This I was able to achieve, but though I was willing to use the Nelson touch to get a timed 140 mph, the big Chrysler refused to compound the felony. It was happy to run at 5,500 rpm as long as I asked it, but it politely declined to be over-revved and that was that.

With its dignified appearance and the luxury of its spacious interior, the Bristol might give the impression of being a silent town carriage. It soon becomes clear to the driver, however, that this is above all a high-performance car. The firm and stable ride, the surge of power, and the capacity to go from a standstill to 120 mph in less than half a minute—all these things make it very clear that this is a machine for going fast all day, preferably from one end of Europe to the other.

The details are all so right. There are no fewer than four adjustable face-level air inlets and great trouble has been taken to obtain silent operation of the fan that boosts them. The switches are well placed so that you cannot for example, turn off the lights instead of the windscreen wipers. A carpet of white light makes fast night driving a delight. The few trivial criticisms that I have made of previous Bristol cars have been removed and instead I am going to place great emphasis on something that is so rare as to be almost unique these days—*the speedometer is accurate !*

In the past, I have tested many costly cars that made me glad I am a poor man. The Bristol 411 is a car for the very wealthy but it has many special virtues which render it as desirable to the young sports car enthusiast as to the more mature and experienced driver. This is a modern quality car of traditional British excellence.

SPECIFICATION AND PERFORMANCE DATA

Car tested: Bristol 411 two-door saloon, price £6,997 including PT.
Engine: Eight cylinders 107.9 mm x 85.72 mm (6277 cc). Pushrod operated overhead valves. Compression ratio 10 to 1. 335 bhp (gross) at 5,200 rpm. Carter four-barrel downdraught carburetter.
Transmission: Chrysler Torque-flite transmission with fluid torque converter and three-speed automatic gearbox, open propeller shaft and hypoid rear axle with limited-slip differential. Overall ratios: 3.07, 4.45 and 7.52 to 1. Torque converter stalled ratio 2 to 1.
Chassis: Separate steel reinforced box-section frame. Aluminium panelled body on tubular framework. Unequal length front wishbones with helical springs and torsional anti-roll bar. Power assisted recirculating ball-type steering with three piece track rod. Rear axle suspended on torsion bars with Watt's linkage and torque-resisting member. Telescopic Koni dampers all round. Girling disc brakes on all four wheels with servo assistance and twin master cylinders. Bolt-on disc wheels with wide-base rims, fitted 185-15 Avon radial-ply tubed tyres.
Equipment: 12-volt lighting and starting; speedometer; rev-counter; water temperature, oil pressure and fuel gauges; ammeter; clock; heating, demisting and ventilation system; two-speed windscreen wipers and washers; flashing direction indicators with hazard warning; reversing lights. Extra: radio and tape player.
Dimensions: Wheelbase, 9ft 6ins; front track, 4ft 6ins; rear track, 4ft 7ins; overall length, 16ft 1in; width 5ft 8ins; weight, 1 ton 13 cwt 1 qr.
Performance: Maximum speed, 138 mph. Standing quarter-mile, 15 s. Acceleration: 0-30 mph, 2.2 s; 0-50 mph, 5.1 s; 0-60 mph, 7.0 s; 0-80 mph, 11.8 s; 0-100 mph, 18.8 s; 0-120 mph, 29.2 s.
Fuel consumption: 13 to 17 mpg.

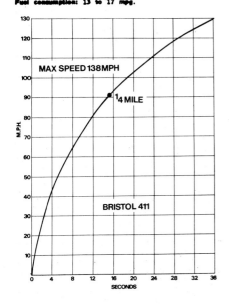

The engine and spare wheel are both easily accessible.

The dashboard is comprehensibly equipped and the switches are well placed (above). The 6.3 litre V8 Chrysler engine fits snugly under the long bonnet.

BRITISH AS BOILED BEEF

TODAY THERE ARE just two cars in the world which offer a cost-regardless blend of four seater luxury, ultra-high performance and hand-crafted quality.

One is the Swiss Monteverdi and the other, the Bristol of Britain.

"Bristol?" you ask, "didn't it die years ago." The answer is no, not quite, though the hourglass production rate of three a week makes the Aston Martin and Jensen equivalents look like peak hour at Ford.

The Bristol is really the ultimate to the motoring perfectionist and in England is considerably more prestigious than a Rolls-Royce.

With a top speed of 143 mph, boardroom appointments and hand-finished aluminium coachwork, the car is a conservative statement of success and good taste.

It could only be a British car, made by British craftsmen for British drivers. There is no left hand drive version because home market orders exceed production. And the output will not be increased to meet demand.

If you wish to buy a Bristol in Australia, Italy, America — in fact anywhere outside the sole central London showroom — then you must contact the factory to place your order.

There are no Bristol dealers as such. The factory believes it is only organisation capable of giving its product the sales attention it deserves.

Besides, every Bristol is made on order, not on spec. After a recent British Budget set-back the factory found itself with four unsold cars and things were thought to be pretty grim.

Of course, not very far away Aston Martin had 70 unsold DB6 models . . .

Yet despite its very British aura and club atmosphere, this Bristol is a hybrid. Under the hand-beaten aluminium bonnet lies an American heart in the form of a lusty 6.3 litre 335 bhp Chrysler V8 engine linked to a three-speed automatic transmission.

It is identical to the engine fitted to the latest Jensen Interceptor and it would be hard to imagine a smoother and more suitable powerplant for the large, two-door *saloon.*

But when the firm forsook its traditional 105 bhp 2.2 litre six cylinder power plant in favor of the then 5.2 litre, 250 bhp Chrysler V8 nearly 12 years ago. many Bristol enthusiasts were horrified.

At that time the firm had just been bought from the Bristol Aeroplane Company by its former managing director, Sir George White, and its original distributor and racing driver, Mr

Variations on a theme. British registration number "100 MPH" or closely relating numbers have been used for years on Bristol factory demonstrators.

Anthony Crook, and the current model was the attractive, but heavy and underpowered 4.6 saloon.

A new, bigger and more powerful six cylinder engine was then under development at the Bristol works, but with somewhat courageous foresight, Anthony Crook saw that this power plant would still not re-capture the good performance of the early Bristols.

He found that the firm could obtain the Canadian-made 5.2 litre Chrysler V8 engine to fit the car, with a number of detail modifications to suit the British market. It came with an excellent automatic transmission which he felt would be needed to sell such a car in the 1960s and so the plunge was taken.

In 1961 the 406 was replaced by the 407 model with the V8 as a standard fitting and the locally-designed engine was shelved. The model was certainly viewed with some suspicion.

With the Chrysler Torqueflite transmission as a standard fitting — all previous Bristols had been available only with four speed manual gearboxes — even the new directors were not completely sure of the reception. Anthony Crook confesses to having bought a number of manual gearboxes from the French Pont-a-Mousson firm which supplied Facel Vega in case there was resistance to the new format. But not one was needed.

Walnut, white-on-black instruments and plenty of them, leather upholstery and deep pile carpets create traditional British appeal for 411.

BULLDOG BRISTOL

Words like traditional, handcrafted and businessman's express come to mind, writes MIKE BROWNING, who enticed one of the latest 411s away from the factory for a couple of hours.

BULLDOG BRISTOL

"A drive in the car was all that was needed to convert the sceptics," he said.

The emphasis was changed from that of a sporting saloon with four seater comforts, to that of a luxurious four seater with sporting performance and attributes. And it is along these lines that the five V8 models since have been developed.

The decision to go V8 gave economic stimulus to the small firm just as it did to Jensen. And there are many people who say that Aston Martin would not be in its current financial mess if David Brown had swallowed national pride and gone Stateside for his V8 engine instead of embarking on the costly local development program.

Anthony Crook is the first person to admit that a lot of British pride had to be swallowed to abandon the traditional powerplant in the 407.

"It was simply a matter of providing our customers with what they really wanted," he said. "In all fairness to the 406, it was asking a lot of a 2.2 litre engine to give a 3000 lb car the sort of performance the Bristol name stood for.

"But I think these days the motor industry as a whole needs to work together to produce cars. Even Rolls-Royce has an American GM automatic transmission and pays patent royalties to Citroen. You can see the name Citroen written under the bonnet.

"However British coachbuilding is an art in itself and we like to think we are offering our buyers the best of all mechanical worlds in terms of reliability, easy servicing and good power combined with the very best in roadholding, steering and appointments."

Certainly Bristols are still built on traditional lines.

As with all models except the first 400, which had a steel-panelled centre section and alloy doors, boot and bonnet, the latest 411 is panelled in 16 gauge aluminium attached to a strong welded steel-closed-box-section.

This box section, with three sturdy cross members, forms a chassis with great strength. In fact Anthony Crook says it will be "over my dead body" that Bristol ever forsakes its chassis.

"We are building really strong cars which will comply with any crash tests — not throw-away cars which will simply fold up," he says. "In 26 years of Bristols we have only had three people killed in the cars."

Resplendent British Bristol with Anthony Crook, the man responsible for the marque and its future.

The 411 model complies with all the world crash test requirements except, of course, its bumpers and a number of other minor features would not be acceptable for the American market.

This does not worry the men at Bristol as they have no American market anyway. The last of the cars to go to US was in 1969 and this 410 has already covered more than 70,000 miles towing a Can-Am sports car.

Being in such limited production, the Bristol buyer can to a large extent have his car "tailor-made".

Although about 12 cars are under construction at any given time, there is no time schedule on production. If one car should take longer for any particular reason then the whole line slows. There is no hurrying along to meet deadlines as a Bristol buyer will wait about six months for his car anyway and a week or two more will hardly matter.

Until quite recently Bristol proudly claimed to offer its customers a free choice of color and trim, but this has now been limited to a wide color range and an equally broad choice of best quality British hide.

Anthony Crook explained that the free choice of paint brought problems, as special tints were very hard to match. And then you had people wanting to match the color of their Rolls-Royce or Bentley. One chap brought in his Cambridge University tie and wanted a car the same color!

Bristol styling is something else. Although the design appears to have changed very little from the 1959 406 model, only the doors remain in the 411, which itself has had three facelifts.

With its own styling department and the low production volume, the entire design of the Bristol can be changed at a couple of months' notice. A change of style is generally decided at a round table conference and I'm sure Anthony Crook was quite genuine when he said he didn't know what they could do to the model next.

The latest version was introduced in July, 1972 and features a new "toaster element" grille and other minor external changes although a number of detailed running changes were also made

Inside, the 411 is very British, with an unmistakable drawing room quality created by rich leather, pile carpeting and a generous spread of walnut veneer. However, the curved central selector for the automatic transmission is also unmistakably Chrysler and the interior door handles are mainstream Leyland Austin-Morris for the sake of easy repair and maintenance.

CONTINUED ON PAGE 288

AND NOW, A QUICK LOOK AT SETRIGHT'S BRISTOLS

Yes, he's done it again. That most devout Bristol follower, LJK Setright Esq., has bought another one . . .

THE TROUBLE WITH MANY OTHERWISE attractive cars, such as the Fiat 124 coupe, the Jaguar E-type, the Porsche 911 or the Bristol 405, is that they are too common. There is no holding a motor manufacturer who has hit upon the right formula for producing a particularly popular design. So in the course of only about four years, Bristol built no fewer than 297 examples of their only four-door saloon, the two-litre 405. I had to invest in a set of admirable but expensive Minilite wheels just so that I could tell which one was mine in the car park. Now that a number of Bristol owners have done likewise, it really is not good enough.

After more than 280,000 hard miles the Setright 405 is itself not really good enough. The body has been looking shabby for some time, mainly as a result of a visit to one of those paint-a-car establishments, where the world's toughest paint is sloshed on after the world's worst preparation. Some of the internal woodwork has suffered too: For some unaccountable reason Bristol chose a wooden structure for the framing of the 404 and 405 bodies above the waistline, and after a dozen years or so this wood (laminated ash, painstakingly worked) begins to deteriorate unless great care is taken to keep it bone dry. The upholstery is no longer such as would inspire the pride of the Connelly Bros and Dunlop. The weather seals around the doors and boot lid have failed, and even the massive and almost incorruptible chassis and running gear are showing slight signs of old age here and there. A bit of a poor show, really: After all the car is only 19 years old, has never been driven faster than 123mph, nor cornered harder than 1.06g. It has not even suffered a hard career in sporting competition: When I drove it in the VSCC Pomeroy Trophy event three or four years ago, I was content for it to prove itself the best and fastest saloon there, rather than force it into contention with the likes of the V8 Morgan, Michael Bowler's Frazer-Nash or Neil Corner's racing GTO Ferrari. The saloons were only Bentley Continentals and Aston Martins, a Jensen, and that sort of thing, so the car was not really used hard. Thus it seemed rather unjust that

by the middle of 1973, after only eight years ownership of the 405, I should have to admit that I needed another car.

Not *any* other car, of course; it had to be another Bristol. Apart from a selection of the latest Ferrari models which are beyond my pocket anyway, there is no other car I know so fastidiously produced and gratifying to drive.

Many a Bristol owner has long debated the question of the model with which to replace a 405. For me it was particularly difficult, for my specimen was mechanically, if not cosmetically, one of the better ones, with disc front brakes, adjustable dampers, and what is probably the best two litre Bristol engine in the country. It is not, I am forced to admit, the car's original engine. That was wrecked by the attentions of a village bodger who undertook a decoke for the previous owner. My engine is one of the rarest BS4 series, with geared drives to the camshaft and distributor instead of the usual chain, with one of those lovely Le Mans crankshafts that are polished all over, and with a number of other refinements of the sort that are only of concern to another Bristol owner. This engine was assembled from new parts by John Dennis, who used to be racing mechanic to Anthony Crook who today is one of the partners in Bristol cars, and a driver who would never be beaten by another car of equal performance 20 years ago.

No ordinary Bristol is going to be very satisfying after an experience like that. I toyed with the idea of a 404, the short-chassis two-seater of which Bristol made 40 examples, and which with one of the more sporting engine variants can be made to perform very satisfyingly indeed. I even bought one with the hope of restoring it, but with the high pressure of nose-application to the grindstone insisted upon by the likes of Mr Editor Fraser, there was simply no time to undertake the work—and in any case, I really needed a four-seater which would accommodate the whole family.

Four suitable four-seaters exist. They are all that remain of an original batch of six type 406 chassis that were bodied by Zagato in 1960 and 1961. By this time the 406 had been in production for two years, bringing with it the first noticeable change in character in the Bristol car since the first Bristol type 400 made its debut at the 1947 Geneva Show. It was a bigger, heavier and more luxurious Bristol than ever before; but if it was less lively than a 405 beyond 70mph, it would out-accelerate it up to that speed, thanks to the magnification of torque produced by enlarging the engine to 2.2litres. However, despite its additional height and weight, it was as proficient around the corners as the earlier models. The 406 was the first production car to have a Watt linkage to provide lateral location of the rear axle; it also fixed the rear roll centre at hub level—lower than before and to good purpose—yet allowing the torsion-bar-sprung axle to retain the strictly incorruptible geometry of motion that Bristol had from the beginning insisted was a prerequisite for good handling. On the way into a corner the 406 was even better, having four large disc brakes. It was an excellent car, in fact, but it still was not what I wanted. The Zagato version was! Lighter and smaller and with a tuned version of the 406

engine, it put more emphasis on speed and handling without impairing reliability and whilst still retaining reasonable rear-seat accommodation.

Apart from its wheels and its overall proportions, it looked nothing like a Bristol. In Milan, where two of Mr Crook's men were sent to make sure that the Italians committed none of the solecisms for which they are notorious, Zagato created an angular lightweight saloon that wore its panelling stretched around it as tightly as a matador's trousers, keeping the frontal area to a minimum. The car was supposed to weigh only 21.5cwt (the 405 was 24, the 406 was 27), and was built to be a good deal stronger than it looked. Extensive steel tubular cage work, especially in the tail, supplemented the already sturdy chassis and acted as a foundation for the bodywork which featured such niceties as flush doorhandles and frameless windows that somehow contrived to be proof against rain and dust. The windscreen was no wider than it should be, the roof no higher than it need be—which meant putting an Abarth-style crease down its middle,

since nobody would be sitting in th[e] middle. In fact the car was five inche[s] narrower and five inches lower than th[e] standard saloon, as well as being a l[ot] lighter. Moreover, the engine ha[d] within it the 300deg sports camsha[ft] and a compression ratio raised to 9.[?] to one, and with the aid of an Abar[th] exhaust system of proven effectivenes[s] it yielded 130bhp at 5750rpm, whic[h] compared favourably with the 105 [at] 4700 of the standard car.

It ought to go, and it went: Joh[n] Dennis had the job of checking the ca[r] before sale and verified a speed of [at] least 122mph over a measured mil[e.] But although the 406Z was a quick ca[r] when fitted with the sports camsha[ft] the customers were reluctant to use th[e] necessary revs, so the milder cam [of] the standard 406 was substituted. [In] this form the car did 115, in the over[-] drive that supplemented the peerles[s] Bristol gearbox. More to the point, [it] handled better than any previous Bristo[l,] which is saying a very great deal.

This, then, is what I wanted. Ther[e] were six made, and two had bee[n] written off—the last one by a gyratin[g]

guar only about three years ago. Of
e remaining four, I knew the owners
 two. One, Mr Robinson, could not be
rsuaded to part with his; the other,
 Brownhill, eventually might. He
ved his car and looked after it as
ough it were a baby. Although the
ctory stipulated oil changes at 3000
les, he did his at 1500. The car was
pt in a heated garage, never used in
ndon or for short journeys or on salted
ads, and never driven hard. The three
rburettors were regularly cleaned
th alcohol and the ignition system
pt *au point*, which partially explains
y on more than one occasion the car
is able to travel from Switzerland to
ndon on one 18-gallon tankful of
trol at an average of 31mpg.

This was the exact car I wanted. The
ck seats were perfect for my children,
e size of the car perfect for me, its
aracter equally satisfying for my
fe, who drives the Bristol just as often
d nearly as hard as I do. Two years
o I told Mr Brownhill that if he should
er decide to part with the car I would
ve to have it; in the late summer of
73 he finally agreed. Here I am with a

1960 car that has only done 140,000
miles and is without serious blemish.
I have had to do very little so far: new
dampers and tyres were due, but these
presented no problems. Koni have
always excelled in providing dampers
to suit Bristols, so I ordered a set
without a moment's hesitation. The
tyres virtually chose themselves, too.
Nothing bigger than a 6.00V16 Avon
Turbospeed would fit, and nothing less
than this magnificent high-speed cross-
ply tyre would do the car justice. These
tyres made a remarkable contrast with
the fat radials of my 405. The initial
response to steering input is a lot
softer, but control at the limit is a lot
sweeter and there is no gainsaying the
tenacity of their grip. They are in fact
very close relations of the tyres that
were used in racing when the Zagato
was new, but exploiting all the benefits
of advanced polymer chemistry that
have made tread compounds so much
better in the interval.

So far we have only done about 6000
miles in the car. Although it takes a long
time to learn how to drive any Bristol
properly, we definitely like it. It is not as

fast as it was in its youth, but that is
only a temporary objection, for even now
the 405 is away having its previous
engine removed and overhauled by
Mr Dennis before being installed in the
Zagato. The more flexible 406 engine
will then be put in the 405, which can
continue to serve as a hack for the daily
chores of shopping, taking the children
to school, or popping up to town. The
younger, better, and faster car can then
be kept for better things. The changes
will be completely in character: the
Zagato begs for a crisp high-performance
engine, while Bristol themselves produced a few 405 saloons with 406
engines and proved them to be generally
better.

There is untold satisfaction in owning
a car of such distinctive merit. Any
Bristol in good condition is a superb car,
but this one is better than most, and
there are not too many of them. Admittedly, the last two Bristol Owners'
Club meetings I have attended found my
car being parked alongside its sister
owned by Mr Robinson. But he has had
his fitted with Minilite wheels so that he
can identify it in the car park. ●

BRISTOL: SIMPLE SUPERIORITY?

LJK Setright argues that Britain's finest high-performer is not the Rolls-Royce Camargue nor Aston Martin but the new Bristol 412. It is probably pertinent to note that it could also be our last fling in open-topped exotica

JOHN HUSS, ABOUT TO BE BURNED AT THE stake 560 years ago, watched a peasant in his innocent labours bring more fuel to add to the fire. Being an open-minded fellow (which was why he was being removed from circulation) his reaction was not at all subjective: all he said was 'O holy simplicity!' One can imagine a similarly envious attitude on the part of various lately condemned manufacturers of cars in the specialist category, remarking as they go to the stake that Bristol survive in a life of blessed simplicity and modest sufficiency. While all about them dabble with new fancies, finding themselves hopelessly enmeshed in their own elaborations, Bristol have quietly persevered with their original objects, which were to make cars that were entirely roadworthy without being uncomfortable, fast enough without necessarily being the fastest, and luxurious in quality without any ostentatious display of the fact. They have been at it for practically 30 years, and the extraordinary number of features common to the first Bristols and the latest demonstrates the possibilities inherent in steady and continuous development. The old saying 'Be good, sweet maid, and let who

will be clever' might have been coined for the especially as they display a virginal naivete wh tiptoeing through the market and attracting n admirers from all sides.

The latest models, the 411 series 5 saloon a the 412 convertible, are every bit as Filtonian ever. Fuel consumption apart, all the differenc are improvements: the first Bristols had qu superb steering, and so do the current ones but now there is no need for muscle in parkin nor any kickback to accompany the feel at hi speeds. Accentuating the positive and elimina ing the negative shows up in the suspension, to the 400 was outstanding in its day for combination of roadholding, handling, and ri comfort over bad surfaces covered at high spe — and the current self-levelling cars are just remarkable by the standards applied today. for fuel consumption, the Chrysler clean-air may not match the efficient breathing and econ mical burning of the old Bristol six, but becau the Bristol body is an aluminium one and son shaped with the aid of a wind tunnel and son very clever men, the give-and-take consumptic of 15mpg is better than you can expect in

ilarly detoxed Jensen or Rolls or Mercedes or
juar V12 or Lamborghini or anything else with
ich it can fairly be compared.

After driving the 412 for a while, comparisons
d to be forgotten, for there is nothing like it.
e driver must not be too short, for like its pre-
cessors the new Bristol is one that you have to
rn to drive. At first it feels high and narrow; and
figures show that it is, but the reason is not
deep chassis frame (the virtues of which are
ugh to justify it) but the blessedly con-
ient housing of the spare wheel in the near-
e wing behind the front wheel arch, a 21-year
stol feature that improves weight distribution
d liberates the entire tail for luggage space.
w well worth the sacrifice when you realise
t in the 412 there is as much room for four big
n, and as vast a luggage boot, as in the R-R
margue, but in a car that is 9in shorter, 6in
rrower, 12cwt lighter and immeasurably more
ful. The narrowness soon ceases to be a
irce of worry: the car rolls very little, and
ponds to the steering with the low-speed
ger of a Citroen SM and the high-speed
curacy of a Ferrari.

It is high-geared steering, three turns of the
little offset wheel reaching round to turning
circles that would be the envy of many a shorter
car. It is also very light and entirely accurate, so
what you do with your fingertips is immediately
and wholly translated into movement of the fat
front tyres. It is not meant for sneezers and
shufflers: nudge the wheel and the car nudges
simultaneously. At first, as when coming new to
the SM, it is almost frightening in its response,
and you wonder how you will manage at high
speeds; but the faster you go, the more feel
comes through the wheel, until you are ready to
acclaim this the most polished steering gear you
have ever met. It is not a matter of fighting
growing understeer, for the car seems neutral
right into the three-figure bracket: it is more like
the feel given by steering that passes a fixed proportion of tyre self-aligning torque through to the
driver and filters out everything else, a
characteristic I once noted in the Ferrari
Daytona. The 365 GT4 2+2, and perhaps the
current Espada, have similar ZF servo systems,
but neither is geared anything like so high.

Along with the fast steering goes fast

cornering. The car can be tracked clinically
through bends at very high speeds, and I got the
impression (though not the opportunity to prove)
that it could be flung through them sideways if
desired. It takes time to learn, as I said, but the
eventual outcome is surprising. In a long bend
that I use as a regular test, there are some ripples
halfway through that sort the soggy and the
supple and the stiff with cruel candour. A Volvo
144 was intimidating at 70mph, a Camaro felt as
though it were on the rack at 90, and I have never
dared take a motorcycle through at more than 95.
The best I have ever managed was 120 in an
Urraco, roll-rocking on its stiff torsion bars. The
Bristol goes through at 110mph; and that is
praise enough, is it not?

Not many Bristol customers drive that fast. The
provision is there for those who do, and is part of
the safety package for the remainder. Mr Chairman Crook tells me that safety looms large in
buyers' minds these days: a few minutes devoted
to that impregnable chassis, the Avon safety
wheel that he proved at 144mph recently and is
now standard equipment, the excellent MIRA test
results, the roll-over cage built into the 412 top,

and all the standard details like high-intensity rear lamps, clever but not unsightly interior padding, rail-located inertia belts and a petrol tank well out of harm's way, are enough to convince the most timorous. If not, there remains the fact that Bristol's brake testing is still the toughest in the industry.

They are not the sort of brakes that pitch you through the windscreen when you look for the pedal. As always, pedal pressure is enough to make check braking jerkless and emergency braking safe, but the power is there when wanted. And it may easily be, for this is a very fast car for those customers who want it that way. Most of your driving can be in utter silence, but if you can bear a slight and low-pitched moan of ardour from the engine, tread the accelerator right down and the Bristol leaps away in a display of clean-limbed power that erases all doubts about the engine or the drive-line. The Torqueflite transmission is still, to my surprise, the smoothest of them all: at full power, just as at a trickle, its gear-changes are quite undetectable unless you watch the rev-counter. Eschew the kick-down and use the lever, and the results are the same,

both in smoothness and in acceleration.

Just accept, if you please, that the Bristol will give you all the performance and handling you are likely to want, even if you are a man accustomed to the Italian exquisites — and all the luxury and quality you could appreciate, even though you had been brought up on Royces. You will have to accept that neither facet of its character shows, for that would be out of character: the speed and roadworthiness are incidental outcomes of the quest for efficiency and safety, and Bristol quality is not to be sought in mirror-plate paint but in detail design and materials selection, in the work of inspectors and testers who are acute and unforgiving. These are the things that make the Bristol one of the best cars in the world.

For years I have been saying that there was no best car, in defiance of Mr Boddy's views on the Mercedes-Benz and Rolls-Royce's view of themselves. After driving the latest Bristol I may have to do what Jan Hus (that was his real name, for he was a Czech even if his last words were in Latin) burned for refusing to do: recant. If the 411 series 5 is not the best car in the world (the 412 is

mechanically the same, but it has not the prodigious lighting of the saloon) it can only be because the new 450 SEL 6.9 Mercedes-Benz is good enough to rival it. The only advantage of the Merc is the theoretical one of its much greater technological density; but that is a two-edged thing with practical disadvantages. The Bristol, simple device that it is, is less likely to go wrong and easier to work on if it does.

On the other hand, you will not find a friendly Bristol dealer nearby if you run into trouble on a dark night in Caithness or Cordoba, even though the factory will cater for the special needs of far-flung clients with, for instance, a limited-slip diff for icy climates. The standard car does without a self-locker now, the rear suspension being good enough to make it unnecessary and the handling being better without it: the SEL has one because in theory it should. That is the difference — or rather part of it, the remainder being the social fact that most representative Bristol-owning gentlemen would prefer not to be seen in anything that looked like the swanker from Stuttgart. You will look in vain for brightwork on either of the new Bristols. They do not need to advertise.

FLAT-OUT BLOW-OUT

**How Bristol tested
the Avon Safety Wheel,
by L. J. K. Setright**

Demonstrations of the Avon safety wheel are not news. We have grown used to the idea of a car rushing along at 60 or 70 mph until a bang announces that a charge has been detonated to blow one of the front tyres.

The car continues on its way with surprisingly little waywardness despite the flatness of the tyre which, try as it might, cannot leave the rim of the special Avon wheel with its occluded well. The whole stunt is rather taken for granted, even as a between-races bill-filler at Silverstone; but when Bristol considered the wheel for fitment to the 411, they opted for something rather different.

Like blowing the tyre at 140 mph plus. With all respect to Avon, deliberately to burst a tyre at twice the motorway speed limit is potentially hazardous, the

sort of undertaking for which other manufacturers might use some hapless but expendable hired hand. In Bristol's case, the boss did it.

Anthony Crook, erstwhile racing driver and now sole proprietor since the retirement of Sir George White Bt a year ago, is probably a better driver than any other boss in the car industry (including Chapman and probably Agnelli) and is not the type to shirk a task like this.

So he flew his little *Aero-spatiale* (made by the collaborators in the Concorde, which is surely the most beautiful Bristol of them all) into RAF Keevil where a 411 waited, on a runway with a surface similar to that of a decent secondary road. Taking the car for a quick sprint down the runway to try it for size, he went back to the beginning and

**Top: Anthony Crook poses with
car, flat tyre, and detonator.
Above: the car turns before doing
trick shots for television**

set off again at full throttle.

When the rev-counter showed 5700 rpm (which, even allowing for converter slip, is equal to 144 mph) Mr Crook, steering with one hand, pressed the bell push he held in the other. . . . In the quiet interior of the 411, the loudness of that tyre-ripping explosion was disconcerting, he said; but nothing else was. There was a slight tremor in the steering, as though the offside front wheel had lost a balance weight, but nothing more.

After a couple of seconds of undisturbed progress, Mr Crook braked the car to 50 mph in a straight line. There was then, he

said, a trace of tramp before he swerved to the left of the runway for a tyre-howling right-about to take him back in the return direction. There were some TV cameras to be entertained, so he drove the Bristol towards them in a blood-curdling slalom that should, in the words of one onlooker, have had all four tyres off their rims, let alone the deflated one.

After all this the tyre was pretty hot, but it was still there. The rim of the Avon wheel was almost unmarked. Within an hour the guv'nor was back amid the paperwork in his London office, where he confirmed that the wheel would be approved for optional fitment to the 411—and the Avon publicity team were complaining that it had all looked so undramatic.

SPECIFICATION—BRISTOL 412 CONVERTIBLE

ENGINE

Manufactured for Bristol Cars by Chrysler. Eight cylinder, 90° Vee with overhead valves—pushrod operated. Bore 110.28 mm. (4.342 in.) Stroke 85.72 mm. (3.375 in.) Capacity 6556 c.c. (400 cu. in.) Compression ratio 8.2:1. Chain drive high performance camshaft, hydraulic tappets. Full flow oil filter. Carter 'Thermoquad' 4-barrel downdraft carburettor, automatic choke for cold starting. Manifold heat control valve for rapid warm-up. Large paper element air cleaner/silencer. Cooling capacity 29 Imp. pints (16.5 litres) pressurised 15 p.s.i. Twin electric fans automatically controlled by thermostat ensure optimum cooling irrespective of engine speed. Engine incorporates 'Cleaner Air System' which reduces concentration of hydro-carbons and carbon monoxide in exhaust gas. Speedhold when switched on provides electronic control of the throttle so that under cruise conditions the car's speed is held constant with absolute minimum of correction being applied.

TRANSMISSION

Chrysler Torque-flite, three forward speeds and reverse automatic transmission, with fluid torque converter, gives variable ratio drive incorporating intermediate gear hold permitting engine braking. Gears selected by floor mounted selector lever with six positions—P (Park), R (Reverse), N (Neutral), D (Drive), 2 (Second) and 1 (Low). Ratios (overall)—Low 7.52, Intermediate 4.45, High 3.07, Reverse 6.75. Torque converter stalled ratio 2:1.

CHASSIS

Closed box section welded steel construction with three cross members forming a very robust structure of great protective strength. Open propeller shaft.

SUSPENSION

Front—Independent by wishbones of unequal length with coil springs, telescopic hydraulic dampers, torsional anti-roll bar. Rear-torsion bar springs with Watts linkage. Self-levelling rear suspension. Adjustable dampers on front and rear suspension.

STEERING

Power assisted, recirculating ball type, 15.7:1 ratio. Sealed ball joints. 15'' three spoke steering wheel with an energy absorbing steering column designed to collapse axially at a predetermined rate. Anti-theft steering column lock operated by ignition key.

BRAKES

Separate front and rear hydraulic systems operated by tandem master cylinders. Failure warning device connected to lamp on instrument panel. Self-adjusting, servo-assisted Girling disc brakes on all wheels. Handbrake employs separate clamps operating on rear discs. Pull up type lever, mounted on floor between front seats. Warning light indicates

'handbrake on' position and also checks failure of warning circuit function. Mechanical parking lock working through transmission operated by gear-change lever.

WHEELS

Avon Safety type wheels. 6'' wide rims. Tubeless Avon Radialply tyres 205 x 15VR.

ELECTRICAL SYSTEM

12-volt negative earth system. 71 amp./hr. battery. High performance alternator charging system with electronic voltage control. Electronic ignition system eliminates need for contact breaker points, increasing reliability and reducing maintenance.

BODY

Full four seater convertible with welded steel structure, roll over bar and aluminium alloy panelling. Two doors hinged on front pillars have burst proof locks and are fitted with armrests, ashtrays, window lift switches and grab handles. Electrically operated windows. Individual fully adjustable front seats with fully reclining backs, which tip forward to allow easy access to rear. Front centre armrests. Front seats have ramp type seat runners providing height adjustment. Individual rear seats accommodate two persons in comfort and have folding centre armrest. Interior upholstered in top quality hide over foam rubber cushions and backs. Protective padding above and below fascia panel. Walnut veneered fascia panel and instrument panel. Pile carpet with soundproof underlays. Lockable glove box. Pockets on rear of front seats and sides of rear seats, courtesy roof light operated either by the doors or independent switch. Five ashtrays. Two cigarette lighters. Full width front and rear bumpers with rubber cappings. Windscreen in laminated plate glass; door lights and quarter lights in toughened plate glass. Spare wheel housed in unique compartment in left hand front wing. Similar compartment in right hand side houses battery, twin brake servos and fuse panel. Luggage boot, 22 cu. ft. capacity with tool stowage shelf. Underside of body fully undersealed. Inside of body selectively treated with anti-drumming material, detachable centre hood piece, easy stow rear hood.

HEATING AND VENTILATION

Through-flow system provides fresh air at desired volume and temperature without necessity of open windows. Air is fed to heater and/or four individually adjustable cold air face level vents from opening below the windscreen, minimising intake of traffic fumes. Four slots at base of windscreen for demisting and defrosting. Manually controlled foot level ventilation.

INSTRUMENTS, LIGHTING AND CONTROLS

Instruments, grouped in cowl in front of driver, have rheostat controlled illumination and include a 4'' dia. speedometer with trip recorder, a 4'' dia. tachometer, a battery condition indicator, water temperature gauge and electric clock. Warning lights for headlamp main beams, direction indicators, brake fluid level, petrol reserve, handbrake and manual override switch for cooling fans. Warning lights provided for hazard and "rearguard fog lights". Sealed beam headlamp system, including side lamps; foot operated dip switch. Direction indicator lamps. Twin combined tail stop and direction indicator lamps incorporating reflectors. Twin automatic reversing lights. Rear number plate lights. Two "rear guard" fog lamps. Automatic luggage boot light. Dual 2-speed, self-parking windscreen wipers. Windscreen washers. Twin windtone horns. Interior convex driving mirror. Safety type dipping. Combined direction indicator, horn and headlamp flash switch mounted on steering column. Control stalk type switch for "engage", "faster" and "resume" of Speedhold control. Rheostat controlled, subdued fascia illumination; hazard warning system.

FUEL SYSTEM

Tank mounted behind rear seat, separated from car interior and boot by steel bulkhead. Capacity 18 gallons (Imp.) (82 litres) including 3½ gallons (16 litres) reserve supply controlled by switch on fascia panel. Lockable filler cap.

COLOURS

Bodywork: a wide range of colours is available.

Upholstery: the interior is upholstered in specially selected leather hide of the finest quality.

OVERALL DIMENSIONS

Wheelbase: 9' 6'' (2.9m). Track—front 4' 6½'' (1.38m.) Track—rear 4' 7'' (1.39m). Overall length: 16' 2½'' (4.9m). Overall width 5' 9½'' (1.77m). Overall height 4' 8½'' (1.44m). Ground clearance 5'' (12.5cm). Kerb weight 3780 lb. (1714 Kg.).

PERFORMANCE DATA

Top gear m.p.h. per 1000 r.p.m. 26.0 m.p.h. (41.80 k.p.h.). Top gear m.p.h. per 1000 ft./min. 45 m.p.h. (72.4 k.p.h.). Acceleration 0-70 (0-112 k.p.h.) 9.5 sec. 0-100 (0-160 k.p.h.) 19 secs. Speed 140 m.p.h. (225 k.p.h.) @ 5500 r.p.m.

AT THE TIME OF GOING TO PRESS MAY 1st, 1975, THE STATEMENTS IN THIS BROCHURE ARE CORRECT BUT THE MANUFACTURERS RESERVE THE RIGHT TO ALTER THE SPECIFICATION AT ANY TIME.

NEW BRISTOL 412

' Dignified travel for four 6ft people '

Complementing their existing 411 saloon, Bristol Cars have announced a cleanly-styled, full four-seater convertible complete with massive chassis and roll-over bar.

The company (now nearly 30 years old) is happy to produce only a small number of cars each week to maintain high standards and exclusivity—and both these qualities are promised with a total price of £14,584 for the new 412!

Production of the 411 (now the Series V priced at £12,587) continues with several improvements including restyled nose and rear seats, self-levelling suspension and Avon safety wheels, as on the 412.

Luxury, space, economy and safety are the chief selling points of the new model. The interior is said to be upholstered in the finest hide, selected walnut is used for the facia, the reclining front seats have individual arm rests and all cars have power steering and Torque Flite automatic transmission.

Despite a modest width of 5ft 9½in, Bristol say that the car will take four 6ft occupants in comfort and access to the rear is particularly easy for a two door car. Behind them is a 22 cu ft boot with a tool shelf but without a spare wheel (Bristols carry them in the nearside front wing; the offside contains the battery, twin brake servos and fuse panel).

Although the car is powered by the company's adopted 6556cc Chrysler V8 (now with electronic ignition) it is not likely to be as thirsty as most cars in this capacity/price class. An average of 15 mpg on two-star fuel is claimed and an electronic steady speed device (also calculated to reduce driver fatigue over long distances) is, no doubt, a help. Bristol also point to the light aluminium body as an asset to economy, though like the 411, the weight of the chassis is still considerable and the new car tips the scales at a quoted 3780 lb (kerb weight) compared with the saloon's 3775 lb.

Basis of the new car is the same as that of the saloon—a closed box section steel chassis with three crossmembers. Front suspension is by unequal length wishbones and coil spring dampers, while the rear is by torsion bars, springs and Watt links. Adjustable dampers are fitted all round and the rear suspension is self-levelling. Girling disc brakes are fitted front and rear.

Extra protection in an accident situation is provided on the 412 by the welded steel roll-over bar which is neatly incorporated into the styling; features small opening side windows and provides a mounting point for the separate rear hood and detachable front hard-top. Although electrically operated windows are fitted, the rear hood is described as " one-hand operated " but does not pro-

trude far from the body when folded. There is a through-flow ventilation system with face-level outlets for use when the car is closed.

A steel bulkhead runs across the body behind the rear seats to separate the passenger compartment from the boot and 18 gallon fuel tank, which includes a 3½ gallon reserve supply.

Bristol claim to have solved the problem of rear seat passengers leaving the car by installing unique inertia belts for the front seats. A rail on the floor mounting enables them to be pushed out of the way of rear seat passengers. This device is also fitted to Series V 411 saloons.

ROAD IMPRESSIONS

As with the 411, the 412 produces probably very little tyre and road rumble, though what mild resonance there is has a slightly deeper timbre in the convertible. The 6556cc Chrysler V8 has the same discretion, the same gusty response to kickdown, the same streakaway output. There is a new electronic " speedhold " (a touch of the brake pedal overrides it) designed to maintain a selected pace at optimum butterfly openings. At a steady 70 mph, 21 mpg has been attained, though Chairman Tony Crook quotes 15 mpg as a realistic average return.

On my brief outing I listened carefully for wind noise from the hood. On a two-way run I got hustle at 40 mph in one direction and nothing at 70 in the opposite direction—airflow direction is all, therefore, but even normal conditions the 412 must produce little wind fuss.

The *de ville* hood section behind the rollover bar takes down easily in seconds by hand, dropping neatly into a space provided, and re-erects just as quickly. Between the screen top and rollover bar a hatch lifts out.

The prototype hatch is in heavy steel—a light glassfibre one will be fitted to the production cars (14 being built now), and when this is stowed in the huge square 22 cu ft boot—or left in the garage—a sort of rollerblind affair will pull out of the rollover bar and clip to the screen top for summer soft-top motoring.

A lot of clever new detail sustains the enormous feeling of well being and the traditional Bristol walnut and hide luxury you get for your £14,584.   E.F.

SINCE the end of World-War-Two the Bristol has earned a great reputation as a car manufactured to immaculate engineering standards, such as would be expected of a product of a leading British aircraft company. Originally it used a better made and properly adapted version of the 328 BMW power unit, this making the 400 to 406 models outstanding 2-litre luxury sporting motor-cars (the 406 was actually a 2.2-litre). From the Bristol 407 to the present 411 and 412 models the power has been provided by large Chrysler V8 engines, again specially adapted to Bristol's purpose.

Whereas Rolls-Royce intend to step-up production of "The Best Car in the World", Bristol Cars Ltd. are content to protect their exclusiveness by keeping to an almost ridiculously small output of cars which some people believe to be the best-engineered high-quality cars available anywhere.

It was to look into the reputation enjoyed by Bristol of Filton that I went to the factory recently and had things explained to me by Mr. Anthony Crook, the Chairman and Managing Director. I was conducted round in the company of Mr. Dudley Hobbs, the Chief Designer and Stylist, Mr. Dennis Sevier, the Chief Engineer, and Mr. Syd Lovesay, the Production Manager.

The Company was originally part of the Bristol Aeroplane Company and, although in 1961 it passed into private ownership, the original factory buildings on the Filton airfield are retained and many of the personnel are ex-aircraft employees, so that production and inspection methods to the highest standards prevail. Not only that, but the excellent facilities of such an important airfield are available to the car company on a contract basis, and Tony Crook is able to commute between there and White Waltham in his four-seater Aerospatiale Minerva light aeroplane, which enables him to move urgent spares, carry personnel, etc. in this convenient and quick manner and to bring his showrooms in Kensington High Street, London, and the Bristol factory within an hour's travel-time. Recently the old Hudson Motor Company's premises on the Great West Road were acquired as the London Service Depot of Bristol Cars and it is significant that stocks of spares are held for every model, right back to the 400, in the form of

engine parts, body shells, axles, etc., down to small components. Apart from which, excellent servicing and crash-damage repairing facilities are available to owners of more recent Bristols.

I was soon immersed in the care and conscientious standards used in the manufacture of Bristol cars, which owe so much to the enthusiasm and extensive knowledge of Anthony Crook who, as is well known, has a long and successful record of racing Bristol-engined Cooper and Frazer Nash cars and who drives a modern Bristol when not flying his aeroplane. His nonchalant one-hour-run at 104 mph with a Bristol 401 saloon at Montlhéry in 1950 has not been forgotten. Since becoming Chairman of the new Company Mr. Crook reckons to do a 60-hour week in the service of Bristol.

The factory is a single storey white building, with workshops leading off the frontal office block. Small, but very impressive, is the Inspection Department where Mr. Radford is in charge. Here a 100% check of all mechanical parts is made, as it is of all the glass and chromium-plated items used in the cars. Bought-out components, such as the Salisbury back axles, Girling disc brakes, etc., are inspected individually if the need arises, but in any case 20% of outside supplies go through this Department.

The 6,556 cc (400 cub. in.) F-series Chrysler engines are shipped to Avonmouth and brought to the factory in Bristol's own trucks. These engines have been tested in America, but at

Filton every one has its sump pan removed for an inspection of the bearing bolts, etc., and Bristol put their own gaskets between engine and gearbox bell-housing. Moreover, before the Chrysler engine was adopted, Bristol made very careful tests and altered certain aspects of this excellent 90 deg. V8. For instance, a fuel pump test-rig was used to measure the time various Chrysler pumps took to pass a pint of fuel at delivery pressures of up to 5 lb./sq. in., so that the most suitable one, for the high speeds Bristol engines would be required to maintain, could be fitted. The Chrysler Torque-flite 3-speed automatic transmission was likewise altered to meet Bristol's exacting requirements. The part-throttle kick-down has been eliminated, as not giving a sufficiently smooth action, and the full-throttle kick-down adjusted to suit the lower weight of the Bristol against that of a massive Chrysler sedan. Otherwise the power units of the Bristol 411 and 412 are standard Chrysler, apart from changes in the engine mountings, dip-stick, etc., for installation purposes. These blue-painted power packs come over in batches of 100 and seven at a time are kept beside the Bristol assembly line.

The Bristol 411 and 412 have a separate chassis frame of great rigidity; therein lies the durability, in conjunction with all-aluminium body panels, of the car, and its impressive strength from the crash-impact aspect. The frame is made at Bristol and undersealed before any components are fitted to it. It may, indeed,

Anthony Crook, Chairman, Managing Director and proprietor of Bristol Cars Ltd., flanked by Dennis Sevier, Chief Engineer (left) and Dudley Hobbs, Chief Designer and Stylist. New 411s take shape behind them.

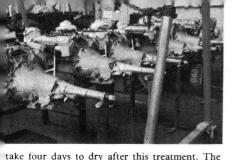

take four days to dry after this treatment. The rear suspension assemblies, with the self-levelling mechanism which has it own engine-driven pump, are then fitted, after which the frame is turned over on its stands by the operatives, for the engine and front suspension assembly to be mounted. Engines are brought to the chassis on a small hand-operated crane. Two assembly bays are in use for the production of axles, suspension units, etc. Bristol use their own castings and do their own machining for such parts but the broaching for the torsion bars of the rear suspension is done by an outside specialist. The suspension units are checked very carefully on their own jigs for hub alignment and balancing, etc. Mr. Jenkins is in charge here and if one ex-aircraft fitter completes his check in, say, half-an-hour, whereas another fitter takes half-a-day, this is regarded as quite in order, the aim being to ensure that the assemblies are absolutely right before being mated to the chassis. Much testing was undertaken to eliminate the parasitic effect of rubber bushes, reducing the front wheel rate from 118 to 76 lb./in. and the lateral frequency of the front suspension from 39 c.p.s. to 20 c.p.s. This made the action more compatible to radial-ply tyres. The iron hubs were subjected to 60,000 cycles with a maximum cornering overload of 1.75 on a Dunlop-Wohler fatigue machine, and showed no sign of failure or cracking. When Armstrong self-levelling was applied to the rear suspension the effective travel was increased from 8″ to 10¼″, which enabled superior damper-settings to be used. Extra pre-setting of the torsion bars was introduced to absorb the increased stresses involved.

In the same conscientious way, when Tony Crook finally agreed to permit power steering to be used, exhaustive tests of the ZF units were made to ensure that the action would be acceptable to Bristol drivers and that it would remain consistent under oil temperature variations of from 20 to 90 deg.C. The original two-stage metering control was unacceptable to the Filton engineers because it gave a noticeable difference in steering feel when changing lanes at high speed on a Motorway. Careful development of the pump and the employment of hoses of differential diameter eliminated the problem. In the same way as they developed the steering, the

Chrysler 6,556 c.c. V8 engines with Torque-flite transmission await installation.

most careful investigations were carried out to make certain no exhaust fumes could enter the car, by making observations using a Redex/paraffin smoke-screen, and it should be noted that the silencers have stainless steel baffles to obviate condensation corrosion after short periods of use. Such is the detailed near-perfection they aim for at Filton.

Engines, having already been tested by Chrysler, are not bench-tested at Filton. But any small adjustments needed are done there, such as replacing a non-standard valve spring, etc. In fact, Bristol have the best possible working relationship with Chrysler, who have taken up improvements instituted in the first instance by the Bristol Cars. After the chassis is complete the body is assembled onto it in sections, being welded to the frame. Any dents incurred are removed by operatives using mallets, etc., and the body is then taken on a hoist to the paint shop. The entire inside of the shell is first rust-proofed, and the exterior finish is then applied. This latter is a very thorough process involving sanding the undercoat, using a plastic filler to remove cavities, applying six or seven coats of polyester, flattening down, spraying on three coats of surfacer and a guide coat, followed by further flattening down, treating any exposed parts with a surfacer, and finally using four colour coats, followed by further flattening down, before doing the final polishing.

The paint is baked in the single-car booth under a 140 deg.F infra-red arch, which automatically traverses above the car. Only three of these De Vilbiss dryers are thought to be in use in this country. They ensure a uniform finish and do the job with three traverses, representing a time of from 25 to 35 min., depending on whether the paint finish is plain or metallic. Bristol offer 15 different colours but do not encourage special finishes, as these can be disappointing to the customer on completion and therefore detrimental to the car's reputation. The finished cars are inspected for blemishes under uniform lighting. If satisfactory they then emerge through double doors into the trim shop. Here the head lining, soundproofing, veneered facia (from an outside supplier), etc., are fitted but not the seats, because a slave seat is used during the initial road testing, as are slave wheels and tyres. I was amused to be shown in the trim shop, amongst the later Singer sewing machines, one which was originally used by the British & Colonial Aeroplane Co., fore runner of the Bristol Aeroplane Co., before 1914, presumably for making fabric wing covering. Incidentally, 261 pieces of Connolly's finest hide are used for the seats and door trim of each Bristol. The matt roof covering of the 411 can be scrubbed if it gets soiled and it goes without saying that the most searching final inspection of the paint and trim is undertaken.

Before the carpets and seats are fitted two test drivers have been out on the road, first doing 30 miles, then two spells of 20 miles each, with a final ten miles, any rectifications required being made between these runs. The completed cars are then ready for delivery to London – there were three waiting to go while I was there. They now receive yet another road test, because a chauffeur

Leather and veneer luxury reminiscent of older Bentleys and Rolls-Royces (left). The 140 deg. F. infra-red arch of the De Vilbiss dryer bakes one of a 411's many coats of paint (right).

who has been with the Company for many years, or perhaps Tony Crook himself, will drive the car up to London, keeping to a maximum of 2,000 rpm, and if any further attention is deemed necessary on arrival this will be done at the London Service Station where the car's accessories are installed. The car is now ready to be run-in by the customer, who is advised not to exceed 2,000 rpm for another 1,000 miles.

Briefly, that is how this small factory, making these highly exclusive cars, operates. The 411 body was deliberately designed to be compact and even self-effacing, which is the Bristol hallmark. The doors are protected by the side structure of the 14 gauge chassis member and the required rigidity is maintained in the 412 drop-head by a gusset-plate under the chassis, apart from stiffening afforded by the roll-over protection. The detachable top of this ingenious body is stored in the boot when the cabriolet hood of the car is opened up; this steel roof-panel is regarded as too heavy for a lady to remove easily and is to be replaced by a fibre-glass panel.

It is unique that Bristol have no agents, selling every car themselves. Output of the 411 exceeds that of the new 412 d/h by more than 2 to 1 at present but 17 of the new coupes, the styling of which was finalised by Zagato, were on the way at the time of my visit. Output is pleasingly small, as befits such an exclusive car – 145 to 170 a year; say three per week, on average. The American safety requirements have made Bristol close this market down but sales to Malaysia, Switzerland, Canada and the Middle East absorb the export section of the market.

Driving the Bristol 411

Following my factory visit I was sent away for a weekend in a 411 Series V saloon. It was registered MPH 100, which seemed likely to act as a magnet to any prowling Police cars, so I was fairly pussy-footed; anyway, this is a misnomer, for the top speed of the Bristol is around 140 mph. Its acceleration from 0 to 100 mph is variously quoted as occupying from 16 seconds to under 20 seconds. This is the sort of performance to be expected from the big Chrysler engine, for which no hp figures are normally quoted. The car achieves all this in an absolute hush, a quietness the equal of any other top luxury car. The Bristol runs so quietly, in fact, that you can hear the seats creaking. It comes as a surprise to find that the engine runs on 2-star petrol, economical consumption of which is aided by several factors. Firstly, the axle ratio is 3.07 to 1. Then, the engine is encouraged to run hot, safeguarded by two special electric fans which blow air through the radiator (Jensen suck it through with their Chrysler installation) if the temperature rise becomes too high, while a facia control enables the thermostat of the fans to be over-ridden in conditions of extreme heat. Then

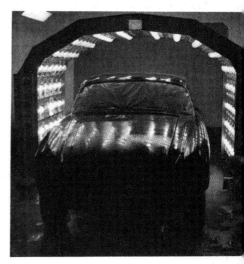

This delightful 412 coupe is the latest Filton product. The juxtaposed version of the famous registrations adorned the road test 411.

there is the Speedhold, that enables any speed from about 24 mph upwards to be held automatically, at the most economical throttle-settings, without using the accelerator. A touch on the brakes puts this out of action but it can be re-set at a touch on the slender rh stalk. The lh stalk is for turn-indicators, lamps-flashing and the horn, lamps dipping being by a foot-operated switch. Whereas R-R use an American speed-hold, Bristol buy theirs in Coventry.

The two-door body on the 9' 6"-wheel base chassis is deliberately somewhat old-fashioned but is beautifully made, so that doors, boot-lid etc, fit and shut impeccably. It was amusing to hear the MOTOR SPORT photographer say, after being shut in the 411's boot while changing a film, that he had never before been in greater darkness in a car's luggage compartment . . . Extensive rig-testing of torsional and bending stresses has eliminated "Motorway shake" from the body, built up by radial-ply tyres, and Bristol are proud that whereas in compulsory crash-tests many cars produce in excess of 80g. decelerations, which far exceed those the human body can withstand, the maximum reading obtained from five decelerameters fitted to various parts of the Bristol body was 30g., while its steering-column moved only 0.9" and there was no visible rearward movement of bulkhead and toe-boards in a stop which reduced the length of the car by two feet. Electro-magnetic vibrators were used to check that the shell was also rigid from the viewpoint of not transmitting resonance or vibrations from the transmission drive-line.

I have probably written sufficient to show how well a Bristol car is made. This is reflected in the pleasure derived from driving one. As soon as you sit in the 411 the quality and practicability is evident and this is clearly a car to enjoy by appreciating its ingenious layout and skilled design, before so much as starting the engine. Since the 404 model, the spare wheel has been accommodated under the near-side wing, with the jacking-up apparatus, while the battery, wiper motor, twin brake servos and fuse-box are under a matching panel on the o/s, thus improving weight distribution, luggage space and keeping these components cool. These panels are opened with a carriage-key, neatly stowed before the driver's right leg.

The leather seats and high-gloss facia veneer are reminiscent of the older Bentley and Jaguar cars or a pre-Camargue Rolls-Royce. The smell as well as the feel of the seats is a luxury worth having! In a veneered binnacle before the driver are the seven Smiths instruments, black with white needles and digits, as befits a car of class. They comprise 160 m.p.h. speedometer, 6000 r.p.m. tachometer, clock, and heat, fuel and battery gauges. On the right of the facia, sensibly apart from other switches, are the lamps and wipers controls. If the hazard-warning switch is required in a hurry, there it is, as the driver's left hand falls directly onto it, behind the gear selector lever. Every switch is very clearly lettered (not labelled) and is conveniently to hand. The controls for the quiet and smooth electric window-lifts are recessed in the doors, with neat covered ash-trays ahead of them. There is a similar ash-tray on the screen sill. The two rotary heater controls in the centre of the facia are clearly lettered, one for defrosting or demisting, the other for car heat or ventilation; there are four fascia vents and *it is possible for warm air to*

go the driver's side of the car while cool air is delivered to the passenger's side, and vice versa. This is a notable refinement, but I can also mention two minor ones, typical of the thought that has gone into the Bristol – the two-speed heater fan is inaudible on the slow setting and you hear only a slight hiss of air when it is running fast, and the petrol low-level light does not wink, it is either on or off. And there is, of course, a facia controlled, 3½-gallon, reserve fuel supply. There is rheostat control of instrument lighting and a cigar-igniter each end of the facia. Air-conditioning is a £600 extra.

Space precludes going over this enthralling motor-car in further detail. But let me say that it is handsome in a completely unobtrusive way, that there is ample head room in the back seat, which has its own two seat-headrests and folding centre arm-rest (each front seat also possesses a little folding arm-rest), and that the Bristol looks very generously shod, with those 205 x 15VR Avon tyres on Avon Safety wheels, which Tony Crook so bravely tested and demonstrated in a high-speed tyre burst at R.A.F. Keevil not long ago. The rear of the car is rendered exciting by the four exhaust outlets and I was intrigued to discover that each of the two silencers is flexibly slung on rubber-links. The exhaust system generates a good deal of heat, noticed as you step out of the car, but on a hot day the water thermometer showed 92 deg.C and oil pressure was steady at 74 lb./sq.in. The boot takes more luggage than external appearance suggests, its lid and the bonnet self-prop, and there are internal stowages in the doors, on the back of the front-seats squabs, and in a large lockable cubby. In brief, the Bristol 411 is endowed with all the convenience and luxury the most discerning owner could require. The Radiomobile radio has an automatic aerial with its own little switch, front/rear speakers and incorporated tape player. There are red warning lamps in the edges of the doors and night driving is simplified by the four Lucas halogen headlamps.

The automatic transmission has two hold-positions but acceleration is normally more than adequate in "D"! I have never sat behind a smoother or better behaved automatic box, and its cranked-rearwards selector lever is well placed, with clear P, R, N, D, 2 and 1 indications. The suspension is firm, on fast corners, ground clearance is excellent, vision good, and the power steering nearly as pleasing in feel as the best and quick-3 turns, lock to lock. Fuel thirst came out

at 15.4 m.p.g.; the tank, with lockable cap, holds 18 gallons. I felt I needed a long Continental journey to do full justice to MPH 100 but in this country it was virtually faultless. There are still times when it is good to be British . . .

If any criticism can be levelled, it has to be qualified by the job the Bristol is designed to do. It is a long-distance express, faster than a sporting saloon. The front coil-spring, rear torsion bar, live axle suspension is not flabby, so some lurch and bump-thump sometimes arises but the 411 corners as a fast touring-car should; it hasn't quite the precision of a sports car or some lighter saloons.

The floor of the boot gets exceptionally hot. I got somewhat confused by the four keys, although an owner shouldn't, because they are of different sizes and shapes. I would have appreciated an outside mirror. That is the sum total of rather niggardly adverse comment. Further items on the credit side – a Triplex laminated windscreen is fitted and electric windows and horn function with the ignition switched off.

The 411 sells for what I can only call a modest £12,587 (£2,875 less than an admittedly more spacious Silver Shadow) and the openable 412, which can be said to be in the Corniche class, costs £14,584 (the Corniche convertible is £22,792). Nowhere else, surely, can such old-style quality and dignity allied to such exclusiveness and high-performance be obtainable for this kind of value-for-money, as in the modern Bristol twins? – W.B.

Marking out trim panels in best quality Connolly hide.

CONVERTIBLE BRISTOL

Bristol has moved into the realms of wind - in - the - hair motoring. Douglas Armstrong reports.

HIGH fuel prices, economies, conservation or no, there are quite a few new big-engined cars rearing their beautiful heads, and the Bristol 412 is certainly the most unusual of them. And it costs the equivalent of $26,800!

What, I think I can hear some of you saying, is a Bristol? Well, you might well ask, for only a handful are built a month, in a works virtually in the shadow of the Concorde construction hangar at Bristol (where else?), and they are hand-made. I mention a handful a month because the current 411 saloon has been in production for several years, and like the 412 Convertible, is Chrysler V8-powered.

The new model (like the saloon) has a sturdy steel box-section chassis, and the bodywork is aluminium-panelled. The rear suspension is self-levelling (with a live axle) and there are disc brakes all-round. Under the long bonnet is a 6556 cm³ Chrysler engine of around 170 kW, which demands only 92 octane petrol, yet performance is immense — and the silence and flexibility noteworthy. The 412 comes complete with electric windows, removeable top, and real stretch-out legroom for tall rear seat occupants. Fuel consumption is a claimed 18.83 lit/100 km (15 mpg) but if you can afford that sort of car the figures are purely academic.

A little more about the marque's background. The Bristol Aeroplane Company decided to go in for motor manufacture after the war (aircraft weren't exactly in big demand), and there is no doubt they were aided and abetted by the Aldington brothers of AFN Ltd (manufacturers of Frazer-Nash cars) who desperately needed a powerful two-litre motor for their post-war range of sports cars.

Before the war of course, the Aldingtons, besides making their own chain-driven Frazer-

Nashes, imported the full range of BMW models from Munich, and sold them as "Frazer-Nash-BMWs". Among the imports was the ahead - of - its - time Type 328 open two-seater which set the fashion for modern-day sports cars. H. J. Aldington ("Aldy" to the *cognoscenti*) was a very fine driver, and besides scoring many race wins with specially-prepared 328s, had a big hand in the development of that amazing six-cylinder pushrod ohv (with hemispherical combustion chambers) engine.

Even after the war the two-litre in-line six design was still advanced, and the Aldington brothers talked the Bristol Aeroplane Company into making that self-same "BMW" engine, the scheme being that Bristol would have a fine motor for their own saloon, and Frazer-Nash would have that same super-motor for their post-war sports cars.

Well, it worked out, and Bristol went into production with the motor, their car was a success, and the engine was so good it was used by Cooper, AC, Tojeiro, ERA, Kieft, Lister, and many other sports and racing marques, as well as Frazer-Nash.

The latter, by the way, won a post-war *Targa Florio* (1950) with a Bristol-powered "Le Mans Replica", the only British car so to do.

Mike Hawthorn started his racing career with a Formula 2 single-seater Cooper-Bristol, and so did Jack Brabham. Bristol's own team raced with distinction at Le Mans, Rheims, and all over the place.

To cut this story down to size, I will say that after about 10 years of car and engine manufacture (at a guess), Bristol decided to cease automotive production, and Anthony Crook, a keen Frazer-Nash racer and ex-RAF fighter pilot (WW2) took over the car side, and the name, and began to manufacture what were virtually the same cars but with 5.2-litre Chrysler V8 engines under the bonnets, designated 409.

Then came the 6.3-litre 411, followed by the 6.5-litre 411, and recently the 411 Series V. Power steering, limited-slip diff, automatic transmission, tinted glass etc all come as standard on the Bristols, and in spite of many hardened traders saying that Anthony Crook could never make it with such an expensive, small-production car, that worthy has kept steadily on. Maybe it's because it *is* so expensive and exclusive.

The 412 doesn't slavishly follow the current wedge fashion, but is rather chunky. With a width of 1.77m, and a length of 4.9m the new Bristol accommodates four full-size adults in comfort — in fact, the Company's slogan for the model is "Dignified Travel for four 6ft people". In addition

there is a 523 litre (22 cu. ft.) luggage boot — an enormous cavern which will accept the four adults' baggage, and part of the reason for the realism of the boot is the fact that the tools and spare wheel are carried in the nearside wing. The offside wing contains the battery, fuse panel, and twin brake servos.

The car is out of the ordinary, and so is the company, for the cars are never advertised (by the manufacturers), and rarely is anyone let into the factory where the cars are painstakingly made. Selected walnut is used for the fascia, finest quality Connolly hide for the upholstery, and the hand-applied paint (by spray-gun of course) goes on as 22 coats. The reclining seats have individual armrests, and all is babylonian luxury within.

The bodywork incorporates a steel roll-over bar which blends well with the lines, the rear compartment has its own little hood which folds (almost) out of sight when not in use, and the front section's roof clips on or off. When the hood is not being carried (it can be left in the garage when weather is good) there is a flexible roller blind affair which pulls out of the roll-over 'howdah'.

The engine has hydraulic tappets, and an electronic ignition system (no contact breaker points) so servicing should be at a minimum. There is also an electronic "Speedhold" which permits a constant speed to be set (on motorways) irrespective of wind, gradient etc, with optimum fuel economy. With such luxury and 225 km/h on tap the Bristol 412 has to be one of the most In cars today.

BRISTOL FASHION

It is 15 years since *Motor* last tested a Bristol. In fact not a single member of the present staff had even driven a modern one until now. So it was with more than usual interest that we approached the sumptuous targa-topped 412. Have Bristol played hard to get all these years for fear we'd burst the bubble about their cars' exclusive dynamic qualities? We never doubted the 412's workmanship, luxury or performance. But how well would it fare on the road? Rex Greenslade and photographer Maurice Rowe bring to an end *Motor's* barren Bristol era with a report that starts after the colour section

IN THE 30 years of its existence, Bristol cars have made no more than 6000 vehicles. Today its Managing Director, ex-racing driver and Second World War RAF pilot Anthony Crook, still stubbornly resists any suggestions that he should increase the production rate to more than three cars a week. For he sees Bristol's two greatest assets as exclusivity and excellence of manufacture, both of which could be harmed by such a move. Bristol build cars for those that can appreciate — and afford — the best. Considering that you'd only receive 62p change from £18,000 for the 412 there's no disputing that only the very rich can realistically contemplate owning a Bristol—despite its use of 2 star fuel.

Such attitudes may seem ever more out of place — but all the more laudable — in a society that increasingly demands computer-designed plastic-wrapped characterless products, be they washing machines or televisions. Bristol's prosperity is proof enough that there are people who still desire something which has been manufactured with great thought, care and skill, and more importantly that there are people who are prepared to pay dearly for it.

But is mere finish and workmanship sufficient? I think not, for history has proved that few companies can survive on those two qualities alone. Without true excellence in the performance of the car (and I mean performance in its broadest sense, including the car's ride, handling, comfort, reliability and refinement as well as how fast it goes), the queue of waiting customers is apt to dwindle quickly in times of austerity as Jensen, for instance, found to their cost.

If there is any justice left in this world there should be no danger of that happening to Bristol for the 412 is every bit as good when judged by

today's standards as the original 2 litre was in 1948. It is no coincidence that the character of these two cars, though separated by nearly 30 years, is almost identical. The first paragraph of *The Motor*'s road test on the 2 litre is as good a summation of what Bristol cars are all about as any, and equally applicable to the 412 today. I quote: "The Bristol 2 litre . . . is a car with quite exceptional ability to suit itself to the mood of the driver and passengers. If haste be required it will give speed and roadholding which might be the envy of many a super-sports model. If, on the other hand, the mood is leisurely it will drift quietly along in the most comfortable touring fashion."

With a distinctive (though to my eyes not especially pretty) body styled by Zagato the 412 attracts a good deal of attention, yet not attention of the embarrassing type. Passers-by are intrigued, people who "know about cars" look with envy, and perhaps most interestingly of all, Rolls-Royce owners regard you with barely concealed jealousy. One of the reasons for this is that you can cut so many different dashes with the 412. Perhaps it and the R-R Corniche are the only large convertibles now being made, but the 412 is much more besides.

In what Bristol call its winter guise, the 412 is a superb, weatherproof saloon, draught- and rattle-free. Indeed so much so that it comes as something of a revelation that the Targa-like centre section (light glassfibre and stowable in the boot) and the steel hardtop behind the rollover bar can be removed completely, giving all the joys of open motoring.

For summer, the rear hardtop can be replaced with a folding hood, easy to erect should a sudden storm appear. You can run around with the car as a "Targa" (centre

removed, hood up), as a "de Ville" (centre in place, hood down), as an open sportster, or a saloon. If you're a man of many moods, there can be few cars that offer you as much freedom of expression as the 412.

More importantly, this Bristol excellence reaches much deeper into the car than such esoteric devices as hoods and hardtops. Like all Bristols before it and notably the new 603 as well, the 412 has a separate box frame chassis — a type of construction particularly suited to low volume production — which carries a welded steel body structure with aluminium alloy panelling. The front suspension is quite conventional with double wishbones, coil springs and an anti-roll bar — but that at the rear is pure Bristol.

The engineers at Filton regard a sophisticated independent rear suspension as unnecessary in a car of this class and weight and are not convinced that the camber and bump steer effects inherent in most such layouts can be satisfactorily eliminated. The 412 therefore has a live axle, albeit one that's extremely well located. Longitudinal torsion bars provide the springing medium connecting to the axle via drop arms which serve to locate the latter in a fore and aft direction. Further location is provided by a torque reaction arm running forward from the top of the differential and by a transverse Watts linkage.

The result is handling that belies the car's size and compares favourably with any car in the world. The power steering — a ZF system re-engineered by Bristol's engineers — is responsive, direct, ideally weighted and possesses true feel. If you detect a faint air of surprise in that statement, there is. For if feel means the ready ability for you to detect a lightening in the steering force at the wheel rim as the front wheels lose adhesion, then it is the first time in five years' testing that I have detected such a characteristic in a power steering system. Many seem that they have feel; only the Bristol truly has.

With adjustable dampers front and rear, and incidentally pump-fed self levellers at the rear to maintain a level stance whatever the load, an owner can alter the ride/handling compromise to suit his own needs. The car is supplied with the dampers on their softest setting, and it was in this condition that we tested the 412, so that the slight floating on undulations and modicum of lurching when transferring from one lock to the other could have been ironed out by winding the dampers up a couple of clicks. Nevertheless, these are our only criticisms of what is otherwise excellent behaviour on smooth and bumpy roads, slow and fast corners alike. In the main, the 412 understeers gently, so that stable, stately, yet extremely brisk progress can be maintained with ease. Of course, in the wet there's enough power to send the tail scuttling out of line if you're indiscreet with the throttle, but even then such a slide is easily caught.

Another Bristol strong point is its power train. Purists may have cringed when Bristol adopted an American V8 on the demise of their beloved straight six, but it was a

decision that's been justified hundredfold. For there can be few more refined and less obtrusive engines, and certainly no automatic transmission that's smoother.

Don't believe that such a stately machine is sedate. With the throttle floored and the box left to its own devices, the Bristol will whisk its occupants from rest to 60 mph in 7.9 sec, and to 100 mph in 21.0 sec, with no more than a throaty warble from under the bonnet. Delaying the upward gearchanges to the red line of 5500 rpm (normally full throttle changes are at 4000 rpm) reduces these acceleration times to 7.4 and 19.3 sec respectively. To put those times in perspective, they add up to performance that's equivalent to an XJ12, to the fastest, but most unreliable, of all the Jensens, the SP, and, dare I say it, performance that will leave an R-R for dead.

Unfortunately within our limit-ridden isle we couldn't verify Bristol's claim of a 140 mph maximum but spot checks revealed that the engine would run up to 5300 in top with no signs of running out of steam. That's equivalent to 138 mph so it seems that Bristol's claims are, if anything, slightly conservative.

Of course, if you use all the performance, the fuel consumption does suffer, though not to the degree that we'd expected. One of the reasons for this is that the engine is built by Chrysler to Bristol's own specification using the latter's camshaft and carburetter and ignition settings; it isn't one of the US's thoroughly emasculated units. We achieved 12.2 mpg overall, driving very hard for the most part. Neglecting use of the second bank of carburetter chokes, which causes such an increase in acceleration that it can easily be mistaken for a downward gearchange, and employing the Speedhold to cruise gently at 60 to 70 mph we returned 16.7 mpg.

One of Bristol's idiosyncrasies is the stowage of the spare wheel, jack and wheelbase in the nearside wheel arch. It's so logical and obvious that I can't understand why others have not followed suit unless they're frightened lest they spoil the body shell with the extra shut line that must result. But the gains in boot space are enormous. Despite the short overhang at the rear the 412 must surely have the largest boot of any car in the world, certainly any that we've tested.

With two doors and its sporting overtones, the 412 is clearly aimed at the sporting owner/driver, rather than the person who wants to be chauffeur-driven. So the rear seats aren't as large as, say, a Silver Shadow or Mercedes 450 SEL, but they are true seats for adults — unlike the Jensen Interceptor's — if lacking a little headroom and space for your knees when the front seats are pushed fully back. But as the front seat room is so lavish that should be a rare occurrence indeed.

It is the interior that most exemplifies the traditional British workmanship that goes into the making of this marque. I'm in a minority in the office for liking facias of polished walnut, with lots of small dials and switches. Unergonomic, perhaps, but to my eyes extremely pleasing. There are some stray reflections

The seats were one of the few items we weren't very impressed with: they lacked lateral and lumbar support. The 603's vastly better seats cost an extra £980. Below: rear seat access is good

If leather trim and a walnut facia are to your liking then the Bristol won't disappoint. Some of the switchgear and minor dials are rather unergonomic but Bristol will bespoke-fit items to your choice

Chrysler's V8 is specially built for Bristol and horsepower and torque figures are described as 'more than adequate', which they are

from the instrument faces, true, but they are attractively calibrated, clear and easy to read, extremely accurate (the speedometer was bang on up to 100 mph) and all grouped directly in front of the driver. The facia-mounted wash/wipe control is an anachronism, of course, but for £86 Bristol will fit a foot operated wash/wipe system and move the dipswitch to the steering column stalk.

This bespoke approach is typical of Bristol. The options and changes that can be, and often are, made to suit customers is far too long to print here. Suffice to say that you can have cloth upholstery instead of the normal leather for no extra charge, or even cloth inserts in the centre of the seats for no premium. We weren't very keen on the standard 412 seats, most of our drivers feeling that they lacked lateral and lumbar support. For a hefty £980 extra you can have 603 type seats which look much more modern and are infinitely better shaped. For £1208 the 603 seats come equipped with electric servo motors for height, tilt, reach and even backrest angle.

Everywhere there is evidence of meticulous attention to detail. The electrically powered windows rise into channels in the Targa top when they're closed, in an attempt to cut down noise (this is only a partial success for hissing from the windows is the car's poorest feature).

Operating the door handle to open the door, from inside or out, causes the window to wind down an inch or so to clear the roof channels; small switches near the door locks allow you to close the windows from outside when locking the car. Then there's the battery/fuses/brake servo compartment in the right hand wheelarch that leaves the engine compartment uncluttered; the cable release for the boot should the lock jam; the provision of no less than five ashtrays; the seat belts whose lower ends are mounted on rails so they can be slid out of the way when

rear seat passengers are entering or leaving.

I could go on further, but I won't. Let me just cite one more example: the heating and ventilation system. One of Bristol Cars' major assets is that it can still call upon the services of engineers employed by BAC. Apparently the same designers that built Concorde's air conditioning system penned the most important parts of the 412's heating and ventilation system. An air conditioner is available, but Tony Crook actually tries to dissuade people from buying one, and we can see why. It simply

isn't necessary in this country, for the 412's heating and ventilation system is one of the best available regardless of price. So often the heater is the Achilles Heel of a car made by a small specialist manufacturer. The excellence of the 412's is proof of the skill that Bristol put into each and every car.

Anthony Crook has been selling Bristols from the outset of the company. Yet he says that doing so is one of the easiest jobs around: the cars are so good that they sell themselves. After 15 years wait, we now see what he means.

Above and left: panels in the rear of both front wheelarches lift to reveal the respective locations of spare wheel and battery — so simple that we're surprised other firms don't make use of similar space in their cars

Left: the roll cage windows open. Above: button beside the door lock enables the windows to be closed from the outside

PERFORMANCE

MAXIMUM SPEEDS	mph	kph
Speed in gears (at 5500 rpm):		
1st	58	93
2nd	99	159
3rd	140*	225
*Estimated		

ACCELERATION FROM REST

mph		sec	kph		sec
0-30	.....	2.8	0-40	.....	2.3
0-40	.....	4.0	0-60	.....	3.7
0-50	.....	5.5	0-80	.....	5.5
0-60	.....	7.4	0-100	.....	7.9
0-70	.....	9.7	0-120	.....	10.7
0-80	.....	12.1	0-140	.....	14.2
0-90	.....	15.2	0-160	.....	19.2

0-100 ..... 19.3	0-180 ..... 26.0	
0-110 ...... 24.8		
0-120 ...... 32.7		
Stand'g ¼ 15.9	Stand'g km 29.2	

ACCELERATION IN KICKDOWN

mph		sec	kph		sec
20-40	.....	2.3	40-60	...	1.4
30-50	.....	2.8	60-80	...	2.0
40-60	.....	3.8	80-100	...	2.6
50-70	.....	4.3	100-120	...	2.9
60-80	.....	4.7	120-140	...	3.8
70-90	.....	6.4	140-160	...	5.7
80-100	....	8.4	160-180	...	7.4
90-110	.....	10.3			
100-120	....	14.3			

GENERAL SPECIFICATION

ENGINE

Cylinders	V8
Capacity	6556 cc (400 cu in)
Bore/stroke	110.3/85.72 mm (4.342/3.375 in)
Cooling	Water
Block	Cast iron
Head	Cast iron
Valves	Pushrod ohv
Valve timing	
inlet opens	21° btdc
inlet closes	67° abdc
ex opens	79° bbdc
ex closes	25° atdc
Compression	8.2:1
Carburetter	One carb 4-barrel "Thermo-quad"
Bearings	5 main
Fuel pump	Carter mechanical
Max power	Not specified
Max torque	Not specified

TRANSMISSION

Type	Chrysler Torqueflite 3-speed automatic
Clutch	Torque converter
Internal ratios and mph/1000 rpm	
Top	1.00:1/26.0
2nd	1.45:1/18.0
1st	2.45:1/10.6
Rev	2.20:1
Final drive	3.07:1

BODY/CHASSIS

Construction	Welded steel body on separate chassis frame; aluminium alloy body panels
Protection	Complete underbody sealant

SUSPENSION

Front	Ind. by double wishbones, coil springs, adjustable dampers and an anti-roll bar
Rear	Live axle located by Watts Linkage, longitudinal torsion bars and top link. Adjustable dampers and self-levelling

STEERING

Type	Recirculating ball
Assistance	Yes
Toe in	⅛ in
Camber	0°0'
Castor	1°0'
King pin	6½°

BRAKES

Type	Discs all round
Servo	Yes
Circuit	Dual: split front/rear
Rear valve	No
Adjustment	Automatic

WHEELS

Type	Avon (safety rim) alloy 6in × 15in
Tyres	Avon 205 VR 15
Pressures	28 psi F and R (normal; 32 psi F and R (high speed)

ELECTRICAL

Battery	12V, 71Ah
Polarity	Negative
Generator	Alternator
Fuses	8
Headlights	2 60/55W Quartz halogen

Western expansion

Bristol 411 replaced by new-style 603

TO CELEBRATE their 30 years as builders of luxury sports saloons, Bristol have announced the 603 fast-back, four-seater coupé. This replaces the 411 Series V saloon, and joins the 412 Convertible

Saloon, which was a very surprising eve-of-Show launch at last year's Earls Court, albeit in prototype form. Like the 412, the 603 uses a massive separate chassis, with a wheelbase of 9ft 6in, and front and

rear tracks of 4ft 6½in and 4ft 7in respectively. The two-door bodywork is in aluminium, with neat blade-type bumpers and pressed steel 6in. wheels running on Avon 205VR15in. tyres. Suspension is basically unaltered from the 411, using unequal length wishbones and coil springs at the front, and a rear live axle, with torsion bars and a Watt linkage at the rear; dampers fore and aft are adjustable.

Two engines are available. For the 603-S, there is the 5.9-litre version of the Chrysler V8, fitted with a Carter four-choke carburettor, while the 603-E (for Economy?) uses the 5.2-litre V8, with a twin-choke carburettor. Both engines run on 2-star fuel, and the tank holds 18 gallons, with 3½ in reserve. The same Chrysler Torque-Flite

automatic transmission ratios are shared by the models, but the smaller-engined 603-E has a larger diameter torque converter, with a lower stall ratio. Automatic cruise control is fitted as standard.

Inside, the standard of trim is well up to Bristol's usual high standard, with electrically-adjustable front seats, a walnut veneered facia, with crash padding top and bottom, air-conditioning, pile carpet and a choice of either leather or wool cloth trim as standard. Boot space is huge, as the spare wheel is stowed, in traditional Bristol fashion, behind a panel just aft of the left-hand front wheel. A similar panel on the right covers the battery, dual brake servos and fuse box. The price has yet to be announced. □

NEW BRISTOL 603

Long, narrow and British

Like a good deed in a naughty world, the Bristol is built to the standards of the upper-crust cars of the good old days. There's no nasty pressed steel to rust, for the body is panelled in aluminium, and if some upstart in a cheap car is so foolish as to collide with the big machine, the immensely

strong chassis will ward off the blow with contemptuous ease.

Although the quality of the Bristol has always been acknowledged as almost incomparable, some prospective buyers regarded the appearance as a little too formal. Now, all that is altered, for the

603 is a very pretty car. Like all Bristols, it has its dignity, and it carries four people and their luggage with a lot of room to spare, but its lines are altogether more pleasing then those of previous models, of which the good points are retained, such as the compartments in the front wings for spare wheel, battery, and tools.

The V8 engine and transmission are specially made for Bristol Cars by the Chrysler Corporation and two power units are now offered: 'High Performance', 5900cc with four-barrel carburetter, and 'Economy', 5211cc with two-barrel carburetter. Wishbone-type independent front suspension is used, with an anti-roll bar and power-assisted, recirculating-ball steering. At the rear, the axle is sprung on torsion bars, with a self-levelling arrangement and lateral location by Watts linkage. The servo-assisted, dual-circuit brakes are discs on all four wheels, with separate calipers for the proper pull-up brake lever between the front seats.

Full marks must be given to the manufacturers for avoiding the modern disease of excessive width, which can be such a nuisance in traffic driving. The Bristol is 5ft 9½ins wide, but its wheelbase of 9ft 6ins ensures ample leg room for all the occupants. The overall length is 16ft 1in.

This is a craftsman-built car of the highest class and will remain exclusive because of limited production; the existing 412 convertible saloon will also be on the stand at the motor show. I hope that I may be given the opportunity to road test the new 603, for all the previous models have had an air of quality about them that is such a welcome change in these days of mass-production.

JVB

Not exactly a slave to the modern idiom, the new Bristol certainly stands out from the crowd.

THE HYPERTOURERS

Ferrari 400 Auto, Bristol 412 and Aston Martin Lagonda

A personal investigation of ends and means: If time is the rarest commodity, shouldn't the ultimate four-seat GT be the one that best preserves it?

BY L.J.K. SETRIGHT

Putting maximum hyper in hypertouring (clockwise from left): Aston Martin Lagonda, Ferrari 400A, Bristol 412.

PHOTOGRAPHY: TOM NORTHEY

• When vanity and indolence first drove me into the writing business many years ago, I discovered a strange practice among librarians. In their classification systems they lump together such seemingly uncompanionable topics as radio, ships, aircraft, telegraphy and cars, all on the grounds that these strange bedfellows are modes of communication. To a librarian, it makes no difference whether you drive yourself to visit someone or convey your ideas to him by telephone, no difference whether you attend a drive-in cinema or watch the same thing on your home television set, nor whether a communication be of words or of people or of goods and chattels. The end is the communication; the means to that end must be secondary. As surely as time is history divided by geography, a car is just a means to an end.

Some cars are ends in themselves. A

(since we can neither earn nor steal more of it than we are given), it is the everyday four-seater, which most motorists drive most of the time, that needs to be quick.

The very word *tourer* suggests some amiable potterer, fit only for a family fortnight meandering through country lanes while the occupants gaze in awe at the wonders of nature. Of course it should be amenable to this, just as it should be able placidly to endure the torpor of urban crush-hour traffic. But its repertoire, if it is to be much use as a car, must extend beyond the uses of *paterfamilias* with his wife and children aboard or of *homo agonistes* lonely on his crowded way to work: It may be pressed into service to whisk four businessmen, tycoonly fat, across the city to visit their bankers or across the state to visit a factory. With no less speed, stamina or surefooted-

Dino 246 or a Lotus Seven is not a car that one drives to a destination, but surely a car that one drives to distraction, just as one should drive a Daimler to the peal of bells or a Bugatti to the greater glory of God. If one has the means to indulge in such ends, there is no effective substitute for such a car, but neither is such a car an effective substitute for the everyday motor. That is the trouble with sports cars: They do not pretend to the *quoti diurnal* utility of the tourer. There is nothing nonsensical in the vast majority of the world's cars being four-seaters, for the needs of the same majority of the world's motorists make four seats a necessary provision. What *is* nonsensical is that we should assume that a four-seater is and must be a touring car, and thence to reason that in exchange for the roominess one must trade rapidity. As surely as time is the most precious commodity of all

ness, it must be able to take four chums soaring up into the mountains for a weekend's recreation. And if its trunk will hold a cello, so much the better for string quartets. All these things and more it must be able to undertake as fast as anyone can drive it, for time is worth more than money; as quietly and comfortably as a cherished passenger might merit since dinner or the opera must be approached in the right frame of mind and as easily and untemperamentally as you might require when wheeling down the road to post a letter since no man should be a slave to his possessions, automotive or otherwise.

It sounds a tall order, because so few manufacturers have tried it, but it is not an impossible one, for a precious few have done it. How few they may be in number is a matter of opinion, not a matter of fact: There is no clear line of demarcation for this class of cars. There are some smugly opulent saloons so redoubtable that they demand consideration: With a little more agility and a little less built-in burden, the V-12 Jaguar and the 450 Mercedes-Benz (especially the mighty 6.9) might make the grade. Of those that unquestionably qualify, three or four rank supreme—and the fourth, the Lamborghini Espada, is now so nearly out of production that it cannot be taken much more seriously than, say, the Monteverdi. That leaves Ferrari, Bristol and Aston Martin, whose Lagonda is just going into production.

Each of them is a four-seater of impeccable flexibility and luxurious appointment, outstandingly roadworthy and very fast: Each can accelerate from standstill to 60 mph in seven seconds and press on to a maximum speed beyond 140. Yet they are all very different in character, offering as varied a choice of means to an end as you could hope

---

Hypertourers must be outstandingly roadworthy, impeccably flexible, luxuriously appointed and very, very fast.

---

for in so small a class. The Bristol is simplicity itself, a classical statement of strict classical concepts; the Ferrari is intricate, a classic expression of romantic ideas; and the Lagonda is elaborate, a romantic through and through.

By this reckoning the Ferrari is the most equivocal of the three, and a passing familiarity with Ferrari history is enough to explain why this should be. Ferrari's preoccupation has always been with engines. In the past this has sometimes left its cars seeming rather primitive in comparison with those of certain rivals that never made such a gorgeous noise, but which would go reasonably well and steer and stop a good deal better. After 30 years of little spikey cars, big hairy ones and one or two distinctly woolly ones, Ferraris still give the impression that their engines are all that mattered to their creator, that the rest of each car was little more than an afterthought that was intended to earn revenue to pay for the Grand Prix racers and that their bodies were therefore made to look beautiful rather than to be practical—presumably on the grounds that the average rich man can see a good deal

Efficiency breeds efficiency: The long Lagonda aids airflow—and its passengers.

more clearly than he can think.

Certainly the latest version of the GT4 2 + 2 body, created by Pininfarina in 1968, is surpassingly beautiful. No other four-seater can compete with it for looks—but the Ferrari is a cheat, because it turns out not to be a proper four-seater at all. There is nothing whatever wrong with the front seats, in which I found I could distribute my 75 inches pretty comfortably in a driving position that was quite good by Italian standards. It is the rear seats that let the car down since they have neither the headroom nor the legroom to accommodate a respectably grown man. It may serve well enough for family outings or for jaunts with another couple, but only if you put both the ladies in the back—a working-class practice that would strike a jarring note in a car costing as much as a Rolls-Royce. I would not go so far as to dismiss the car simply because its luggage boot will not take a cello, but neither in stowage nor in seating does this immensely promising and incomparably beautiful motorcar qualify as a genuine tourer, high-performance or otherwise.

Notwithstanding its inability to carry four ninety-fifth-percentile American males, the Ferrari deserves further investigation because there may be some suitably rich customers among the wee folk and because it sets some standards that any other contender for the hypertourer title would do well to match. I am bound to admit that all my driving has been of the immediately precedent 365: Neither in Britain nor in Italy was there one of the new 400 Automatic models that could be driven when I went in pursuit, though I was able to pry deeply into

the first British 400A. In most essentials the cars are very similar, the only difference being an increase in piston stroke expanding the engine displacement from 268 to 293 cubic inches. With the breathing and piston area unchanged, so is the power output, and the engine could hardly be more flexible than it was already. It is a paragon of an engine, inspiring an enormous pride of possession when you fling open the bonnet before many envious admirers, but when the car is on the road its most impressive asset is not its engine but its suspension.

Each wheel is independently suspended by its own four-bar linkage, the rear ride height being kept constant by road-pumped, self-energizing Koni damper struts. The whole system is so beautifully tuned that the ride is perfectly flat and absorbent while the roadholding is tremendous. The tires and wheels undoubtedly help, the 215/70VR-15 Michelin XWX radials being tautened by 7.5-inch rims. Withal, the expected alacrity of response is missing. And despite the short wheelbase (which is what cramps the nursery quarters in the rear), the Ferrari is a heavy car with a high polar moment of inertia, a ponderous clumsy turning circle and accurate but curiously dead powered steering. In fact the whole thing feels like a detuned version of the 365 GTB4 Daytona, that late, lamented gentleman's sports car, except that it does not entice its driver to go faster and try harder as the seductive Daytona did. Mark you, this 365 2 + 2 was no car for a lady; its clutch pedal required far too much effort. It is in this respect that the latest version has taken the biggest step forward, for the 400A at long blessed last may be ordered with automatic transmission, which I consider essential in a high-powered tourer. The box comes from General Motors (as it does for Rolls-Royce), and if the engine be wound up to its permitted 6500 rpm the car does 61, 101 and 149 mph in the three successive gears. Hyper? Indubitably. Tourer? It depends on the size of your passengers.

The Aston Martin Lagonda inspires no such doubts. If the Ferrari 400A is a Daytona masquerading as a four-seater, the Lagonda is a Cadillac pretending to be a TR7. Its styling, by William Towns, contributes towards this illusion by acknowledging some contemporary fashions :in American bodywork, but with the note-

> Like Bugattis, hypertourers
> should be driven
> not to destinations, but
> to distraction and
> the greater glory of God.

engineering and, as installed in the Lagonda and in the two-door Aston Martin, it probably develops 345 bhp, though the firm will admit nothing. All it claims is that the car will do 140 mph; when I drove the prototype I did not seek to prove my point, but I reckon it will go significantly faster.

I could hear more of the engine when I drove the Lagonda prototype than I thought proper in so luxuriously appointed an interior, but in the circumstances it was excusable. The car was carrying test instruments galore, with wires and capillary pipes running from them through the bulkhead to the engine compartment, and it was inevitable that some noise should come through the holes made for their passage. When the Lagonda made its debut last autumn, the feature that attracted everybody's attention was the elaborate electronic instrumentation, with ribbon and digital displays by gas-plasma illumination and touch-sensitive proximity switches for all minor controls. With a miniature computer to process all the information handled, it was possible to change the

Ferrari 400A owners get a beautiful car with a paragon of an engine, superb suspension and small, cramped back seats.

worthy difference that it is aerodynamically very efficient, minimizing lift and generating a laudably low coefficient of penetration of only 0.36. I suspect this is the product of another impressive coefficient, this time of what I can best describe as the ballistic one, a figure that I deduce by dividing the square of the car's length by its frontal area. The Lagonda is a very long car, so these sums work out in its favor with the welcome corollary of—for once—ample room for an adult entourage.

Given these wind-cheating proclivities and a weight that is competitive with that of the Ferrari (because the body paneling is aluminum), no extravagant power is needed to propel the Lagonda very quickly. Its four-camshaft V-8 engine is not a work of art, but it is a fine piece of

Ferrari formula: 340-hp, 293-cu. in. V-12.

speedometer display at will from miles to kilometers per hour and even to integrate the speed, time and fuel flow to show average speed and fuel consumption on the journey. It was all very dramatic and trendy, but it has not been passed for production without some modifications, and the prototype car in which I went driving with Aston Martin's development man Bill Bannard (an old friend, a very practical engineer and a formidably fast and demanding driver) was shorn of all this electrickery.

I was much more interested in what the car was like to drive. Knowing that the steering needed only two turns of the wheel from lock to lock, and that this long-wheelbase luxmobile had a tighter turning circle than either of the two cars under review, I expected it to feel ner-

Bristol 412, as old-fashioned as virtue: Zagato styling, Chrysler power, a steel chassis, aluminum body and a live axle in back.

vous and twitchy, perhaps a little like a Citroën SM. On GR70VR-15 Avons wrapped around seven-inch rims there would be no shortage of grip, after all.

My expectations were confounded. The steering was soft and easy, accurate but not a bit nervous. Thanks to that, to progressive brakes and to the eternally blessed Chrysler TorqueFlite transmission, the car was blissfully easy to manage. Moreover, considering that it represented the original thinking of chief designer Loasby straight off the drawing board, its ride was wonderful—so good that Bannard feared that the suspension would never be allowed any development at all. Like the Ferrari, the Lagonda has self-levelling struts to control its helical rear springs, but unlike the Italian car its rear wheels grace a De Dion axle given precise lateral location by a Watt linkage and tolerable longitudinal location by parallel trailing arms. At the front the

insulated sub-frame originally postulated has proved unnecessary, and the whole thing will probably be made solid.

The whole car feels solid in the nicest possible way. Its torsional stiffness is quite respectable for so long a structure, but this ceases to be a surprise when you look at the elaborate boxing of the chassis platform. Thanks to this the wheels do not stray from their appointed angles, and when pushed towards its roadholding limits the Lagonda hangs on well. I found a big circular roundabout that was not too busy and lost count of the number of laps I did (it was well over two dozen) with the four tires howling most of the time and with occasional tweaks of steering or throttle to break their grip. It took a lot of provocation and a lot of speed and power, and even then the car was surprisingly docile in being brought back onto course, revealing no vicious reactions to variations in tractive

effort or in braking while cornering. One did not feel the roll either, though the camera showed it to be considerable. All I felt was a mounting understeer as the cornering speed increased on a constant radius and a mounting backache as I strove to stay in my seat despite the massive lateral-G forces.

They are comfortable seats normally, upholstered in deliciously soft Italian veal leather that is unlikely to be durable; it will probably be replaced by the latest ultra-soft Connolly hides as supplied to Rolls-Royce for the Camargue. There are one or two other things likely to be changed before production settles down in the proud little factory at Newport Pagnell, but Aston Martin already has a long list of firm orders for the car, and this promise of success could not be made to nicer or more deserving people.

Leather by Connolly is as automatic a choice for the seats of the Bristol as wal-

HYPERTOURER DATABASE: SOURCES OF THE MAGIC

	Ferrari 400A	Bristol 412	Aston Martin Lagonda
Engine displacement	293 cu in	400	325
Piston area	95.8 sq in	118.7	97.3
Stroke/bore ratio	0.963:1	0.776	0.85
Maximum power	340 bhp @6500 rpm	265 @ 4800	345 @ 5800 (est.)
Equivalent Brake Mean Effective Pressure	141 lb/sq in	109	145
Maximum Torque	NA lb/ft	335	385
Equivalent BMEP	NA lb/sq in	126	169
Vehicle weight (full tank and two adults)	4261 lb	4229	4329
Weight/power ratio	12.54 lb/bhp	15.96	12.55
Frontal area	25.23 sq ft	27.43	25.45
Power/frontal-area ratio	13.48 bhp/sq ft	9.66	13.56
Ballistic coefficient (length²/frontal area)	9.83	9.58	11.8
Overhang ratio (length/wheelbase)	1.78	1.70	1.81

Bristol style: Connolly hide and walnut.

nut for the fascia, for despite the unusual styling of the 412 body by Zagato (the saloons are designed by Bristol's own ex-aircraft engineers), the car is as old-fashioned as virtue. It looks narrow and high, which is unfashionable but justifiable: What fixes its proportions is not the lightweight aluminum body but the heavyweight steel chassis, substantially unchanged for over 30 years. When the Bristol did its barrier-crash test, it achieved results matched by no other car that I know to have passed, and the reason lies in the basic structure. Many cars pass the test although maximum decelerations (lasting longer than five milliseconds) measured internally have ranged from 80 to 200 G, far in excess of the 40 G that represents the human body's limit for such a length of time. The dummy in the Bristol suffered only 30 G, and *nothing* fell off.

Yet the chassis *is* old-fashioned. It retains a live rear axle, which would make any properly indoctrinated Daimler-Benz or Porsche man laugh himself sick. But that axle is constrained by linkages found in no other car, allowing movement only in the vertical plane. The wheels are only six inches wide, but they have occluded safety wells that prevent the tires from rolling off after deflation. Before they were passed for fitment, the chairman of Bristol personally tested them by firing a charge to burst a front tire while he was steering (single-handed) at 144 mph; everything has to work at all speeds. Likewise, although Girling does not expect its brake-testers to try conclusions above 70 mph, Bristol insists on proving its brakes from twice that speed: Even Stirling Moss had to admit that he could not fade them.

Bristol is old-fashioned because it believes in continuity. It has been in continuous production (usually at a self-imposed maximum of three cars a week) for longer than either Aston Martin or Ferrari, and throughout those 31 years it has quietly persevered with its original objects, which were to make cars that were entirely roadworthy without being uncomfortable, fast enough without necessarily being the fastest, and luxurious in quality without any ostentatious display of the fact. Hence its refusal to be influenced by fashion's demands for cars as wide as the road and as low as the curbstones. Stepping down into the Lagonda or the Ferrari, you accept the logical need to tilt your head and curve your back so as to fit within those domineering body contours. Stepping straight into the Bristol, you assume your ideally alert but unstrained driving position and find that the car fits itself perfectly around you and around the three other six-foot men coming for the ride. In the 412 there is as much room for them and as vast a luggage boot as in the Rolls-Royce Camargue. Yet it seems a compact car, with less bodily overhang than the others. How is it done? The Ferrari spare wheel is in the boot; the Lagonda's is beneath it, but is going inside to keep clean; the Bristol's is behind the left front-wheel arch, out of the way, where its weight is closer to the center, balanced by the weight of the battery on the car's other flank. All the major masses are concentrated within the wheelbase, and all the really heavy ones (the steel chassis and the iron engine) are set very low.

The superstructure may be lightweight, but it is far from flimsy. The rollover bar adds such strength that the car can pass its tests roofless, one of the few openable tourers to survive. The panel over the front seats comes off in seconds and fits inside the boot; the rigid roof section behind the roll-over arch can be left at home, a fold-down substitute being carried in its place. There is no buffeting or windy unpleasantry at 60 mph with the roof off, and there is no change even at 120. Nor do the frameless windows bow outwards at speed or let the rain in: They motor up behind lips on the edges of the roof panel. How do you open the door then? First pull on the doorhandle triggers the motor to wind the window down enough to clear the lip, and then the doorlatch unfastens. To leave the car secure, you press a tiny button after closing the door and the window closes, as resistant to predators as it is to full-speed airflow.

Such speeds are readily reached for the TorqueFlite transmits the urgency of more cubic inches than either of the other cars can boost. The engine itself encourages no boasting: It is a commonplace Chrysler 400 that develops less power than the others (albeit more quietly) and leaves the Bristol the slowest of the three. Likewise, the 205VR-15 tires give it less sheer roadholding grip than the others, so on a race track the Ferrari and the Lagonda would run away from it. On ordinary give-and-take roads it is a different story, for the Bristol's handling is astonishing in a car of this size. It enjoys the best power steering in existence, bar none: Needing three turns from lock-to-lock, it is lower-geared than the Lagonda's, higher than the Ferrari's, but quicker in response and more communicative in feel than either. With the engine set well back in the chassis and with the rear axle behaving itself at the ends of torsion-bars controlled by Bristol's own self-levelling system, the car always feels ready to do as it is told. It is a matter of long wheelbase and short overhang, of low polar moments of inertia in pitch and roll and yaw. It is in fact a matter of proportions, and among hypertourers as in other classes of cars, keeping a sense of proportion is surely what matters most.

That is not the end of it. Perhaps there is no end. A sense of proportion is not an awareness of something absolute, for proportions themselves are just the perception of a reality that matters less than the perceiver. Proportions change with perspective: The beauty is in the eye of the beholder. If you know yourself, you will know which car appeals to you, and only if you know yourself will you have any reference whereby to judge it. The world you tour, or whatever your tiny bit of it, scarcely matters: Many a man has loved his Ferrari who never drove it far enough out of the city to learn what it really feels like to drift through a three-figure bend with life and love leaning heavily on the two fat, drum-taut Michelins that sear their definition of the outside of the curve into your lasting memory. Many a man could bask in the reflected grandeur of the Lagonda though he lived where none might come to see his glory and wonder at it. There are likewise a few men who know that a Bristol is not something to tempt or to flaunt, but something that recalls a wonderful definition of courage as "grace under pressure"—a car that is always a lady, however inhibiting that may sound, retaining her manners where another might be revealed as a bitch. With care and luck, it may never matter; meanwhile, you just go on with your touring, serene at any speed.

The beauty of a car is not, after all, a matter of proportions. Never mind those librarians: The car is not a means of communicating, it is a means of communing, and the beauty is in the communion. Perhaps that is the end of it, in the spirit which illumines these three beauties. It is possible, indeed likely, that they transcend all others that can honestly be used as cars rather than as devotional aids, for the true hypertourers are far between and few. The end does *not* have to justify the means. •

Star Road Test

BRISTOL 603

One of the most exclusive cars in the world. Beautifully finished, to the very highest standards, and with refinement close to that of Rolls-Royce or Jaguar. Very good ride/handling compromise for a live axle car (which can be altered via adjustable dampers), excellent transmission, ventilation and visibility. Performance only average, and instruments and layout of minor controls old-fashioned

IT HAS been a hard life in the last few years for the small, specialist car manufacturer. Fuel crises, crash and emission regulations, the falling value of the pound, have meant that many have fallen by the wayside. Some have survived, but only just, while one at least has sailed confidently on, and that company is Bristol. And one of the main reasons for its success has been the attitudes and ideals of its Managing Director, Mr Anthony Crook.

It is not often we introduce personalities into road tests. They are, after all, an impartial look at a product, not a person. But in the case of Bristol it is all but impossible to separate the car from the man. Each car is stamped with his own strongly held views — and his customers are with him all the way. They are looking for tradition, a magnificent finish, subtlety, solidity, and above all exclusivity.

Roughly three Bristols a week are produced in a small factory within the British Aerospace (formerly the Bristol Aircraft) establishment at Filton, where the Concorde is made. Thus close contact is maintained with the aircraft industry (though Bristol Cars no longer has any direct affiliation with the aircraft side) and it shows in a number of ways — the care and attention to detail, for example, and the thorough testing which each part or new development receives. It is no coincidence that Mr Crook is an ex-World War Two pilot and still a regular flyer.

The basis of the 603, and its sister model the targa-topped 412, is a massive and separate chassis. It is roughly A-shaped, with the apex at the front, and broadens out at the back to a box behind the rear seats which takes the petrol tank and rear suspension. Built onto this is a steel substructure, and the whole is finally encased in alloy external panels. In spite of the light alloy bodywork all this results in a weighty though extremely strong and rigid shell. Power comes from a Chrysler V8, formerly a 6.6-litre engine but now a 5.9-litre unit whose power and torque figures, like those of Rolls-Royce, are "not for publication". In the Bristol application the engine exceeds the 172 bhp (net) at 4000 rpm, and 270 lb-ft (net) torque at 2000 rpm, which Chrysler quote, as Bristol fit a different camshaft and remove much of the emission ancillaries. Matched to this engine is the splendid Chrysler Torque-flite transmission, and in fact it was this excellent combination of power unit and gearbox that led to Bristol making one of the most significant changes in its history back in 1961 when Bristol's own 2-litre, six-cylinder engine was dropped.

As with so many things on this car, the suspension is unusual. Not perhaps at the front, where unequal length wishbones, coil springs, and an anti-roll bar are fitted. But at the back the live axle, located by a transverse Watts linkage and a top link, uses longitudinal torsion bars and Bristol's own form of self-levelling. In addition, the 603 offers what must be rare, if not unique: adjustable koni dampers all round to enable an owner to "fine-tune" the settings to his own desires. In practice, most leave the factory settings (full "soft") untouched. Steering is by a ZF recirculating ball arrangement, but again, specially built and modified to suit Bristol's own requirements. There are massive disc brakes at each wheel, with twin circuits and two servoes. There is a choice of wheels: either all-alloy or pressed steel, but in either case Avon safety bands (well-fillers which prevent the tyre pulling off in the event of a blow-out) are fitted.

But the strong selling points of the Bristol are not just its mechanical components. It behaves like a thoroughbred, even if the performance is not all we expected. The ride/handling compromise can be adjusted to suit personal tastes, as can the seats: the finish is impeccable; the quality unsurpassed; and above all there is the exclusiveness that makes it something rather special, even in the exalted company it has to keep at £29,984.

PERFORMANCE

★★★ We were rather disappointed at the performance figures we achieved. When we tested a 6.6-litre 412 (*Motor*, Mar 5, 1977) we recorded a 0-60 mph time of 7.4 sec. The 603, and its 5.9-litre engine (now used for the 412 also) is lighter, but we could not get this figure below 8.4 sec in favourable wind conditions and the average of runs in opposite directions was 8.6 secs, well down on the 7.6 sec of the Maserati Kyalami and Jaguar 5.3, the 7.9 sec of the Mercedes 450SEL 6.9, and in particular the excellent 5.7 sec of the (manual) Aston Martin V8. The 412 managed 0-100 mph in 19.3 secs: the 603 took 23.3 sec. We were also unable to check the maximum speed, which Bristol claim to be 140 mph.

Subjectively, too, the car did not feel very quick up to about 80 mph, but there was always a reserve of power for rapid and safe overtaking manoeuvres. At higher speeds the car would just keep on accelerating, and 120 mph, with considerably more apparently in hand, was easily achievable on even relatively short stretches of road. Helped by the immaculate changes from the gearbox, progress in the Bristol is just one long, smooth and effortless build-up of speed, and more often than not you find yourself travelling faster than you think you are.

Starting from cold was simple. A prod on the accelerator pedal set the electric choke, and the engine would burst into life at the turn of the key. A few seconds fast idling, a touch on the pedal, and you were ready to move off without drama, as if the warm-up period did not exist. However, until the engine had reached full working temperature, there was a tendency to stall if full steering lock was applied with the air conditioning "on", but a light touch of throttle quickly solved any problem.

Hot starting was not so easy. Emission carburetters are infamous for hot start problems, and when warmed the engine required quite a lot of churning from the starter motor, plus delicate use of the throttle before it would fire.

As with many large American V8s, the Chrysler power unit is, for the most part, quietly unobtrusive in operation. There is not the near total absence of noise that you find in, say, a Jaguar or a Rolls-Royce, but then the muffled noises it makes befit a car with sporting characteristics. Above 4500 rpm this throatiness becomes quite noticeable (with the gearchange left in "D", so the box changes of its own accord, the changes take place at 4300 rpm) and above 5000 rpm up to the red line at 5500 rpm it sounds breathless and hard-working. Since little performance benefit accrues from this treatment, however, such revs are seldom needed.

The engine is very smooth, even when revved, and harshness is totally absent. At 70 mph the engine is turning over at a lazy 2700 rpm, and even at 100 mph you are only using 3800 rpm. The throttle action is nicely smooth and progressive.

ECONOMY

With a lowly 8.0:1 compression ratio, the 603 only requires 91 octane fuel. Bristol say this is two star, but in fact two star fuel can have an octane rating as low as 90, so we would recommend three star. In either case there are some (slight) savings to be made, compared to others which require four or five star petrol.

The overall figure of 13.2 mpg is good for this class of car: it is matched by the Aston and the Mercedes 450 SEL 6.9, and is much better than the Jaguar, Maserati or Rolls-Royce (11.9, 11.6 and 11.6 respectively). The touring consumption is about average at 14.1 mpg, but more interesting than that is the fact that the steady speed fuel graph shows that this heavy car is remarkably economical at low speeds: it does not drop below about 20 mpg until 60 mph is reached, but then does fall off from 18 mpg at 70 mpg to 11 mpg at 100 mph. Thus, driven conservatively, the Bristol should be quite miserly for its class, though by absolute standards it is thirsty: hence the three star rating.

One criticism we would make is that the fuel tank is too small. At 18 gallons it is at least two gallons smaller than any of its competitors, and thus the range, using the optimistic touring consumption, is only 250 miles at best: in practice we found it to be nearer 200 miles,

including the use of the 3.5 gallon reserve.

TRANSMISSION

Chrysler's Torque-flite transmission has long had a good reputation, and to drive the Bristol is to appreciate why. It is of standard construction, with a torque convertor and a three-speed epicyclic gearbox, but has been steadily refined to its present excellence.

Left to its own devices, changes slur quickly, smoothly, quietly and imperceptibly from one gear to another, only a slight change in engine note and a drop in tachometer reading being any indication that something has happened. Manually too, the changes, up or down, are as good: even when changing down so as to bring engine speed up to or near the rev limit, it simply feels as if the brakes have been applied firmly — there is no jerk at all.

Using 5500 rpm, the maximum in the intermediate gears is roughly 60 mph and 100 mph, close to those of the Jaguar and Mercedes — a case of great minds thinking alike. Using the "D" change speed of 4300 rpm the changes take place at 48 mph and 77 mph respectively. Our test car was fitted with a 3.07:1 rear axle ratio, giving a mph/1000 rpm figure of 26.1. An option is a 2.88:1 unit to give 28.2 mph/1000 rpm for more restful and economical cruising.

HANDLING

Any comments about the ride/handling compromise of the Bristol must of course be made in the light of the fact that for the sensitive owner the damping can be softened or firmed up via the adjustable shock absorbers, and thus the characteristics altered almost at will. When we drove the car the settings were slightly firmer than standard, following a comment made in our test of the 412, when the dampers were on their softest settings.

One of the highlights of the car is the steering. Specially made by ZF to Bristol's own specification, it is one of the best power-assisted set-ups we have ever tried. Power assisted systems can offer true "feel", yet if this is defined as the ability to detect a drop in steering force as front wheel adhesion diminishes, then the Bristol comes as close to the true feel as it is possible to get. The whole system is light, direct, nicely weighted and responsive as well: a near perfect compromise.

As set up, we felt that the roadholding was only modest at low speeds — emphasised by the ease with which we could hang the tail out in sharp corners and by tyre squeal, which set in loudly and prematurely and thus deterred spirited cornering around town. By contrast, though, it improved to the point of being very good at high speed. Stiffening the dampers compared to those of the 412 has reduced the tendency to oversteer at low speeds — though, as mentioned, it is still there — and made the handling even more neutral at high speeds, so that it is a joy to drive swiftly through sweeping, open curves, providing

there are not too many bumps or bad undulations which can push the car off line.

One small change we tried — raising the tyre pressures to 32 psi which is recommended for high speed work — had two significant effects: first it reduced the high speed wandering through long, bumpy corners and secondly it reduced the tyre squeal, both worthwhile improvements.

To sum up, the road manners of the 603 befit a sporting but dignified carriage. The steering is the equal of the Mercedes, but it does not have the sheer tenacity or cornering powers of the German car or the Aston. On the other hand it rides more smoothly than the Aston and will easily out-corner the Rolls-Royce.

BRAKES

The 603 is fitted with disc brakes at all wheels and twin circuits (front and rear), each with its own servo. Considering that the system has to dissipate a lot of heat in slowing this heavy (35 cwt) car it works remarkably well. The pedal action is nicely progressive at low speeds but requires a heavy push in an emergency at high speeds — though the car will pull up all square, without drama.

The 603 sailed through our fade test (20 0.5g stops from 90 mph) with only a slight initial increase in pedal loads as the pads warmed up, and returned immediately to normal after a soaking in water. The only time the brakes looked like fading, in fact, was during our acceleration runs, when they were called on to slow the car from speeds near 120 mph in intervals of less than a minute, when they would groan and shudder slightly as well.

The handbrake would not hold the car facing down the 1-in-3 test hill (the rear wheels locked and the car slid bodily down), nor would it lock the rears on the level — but we did record a respectable 0.34g during this latter test.

ACCOMMODATION

Bristol has only ever made one four-door saloon, the 405, and the 603 maintains the two-door tradition. The doors are quite big, but there was criticism that they do not open wide enough, so that entering or leaving the rear seat is not as easy as it should be. But apart from this, it is one of the best two-door cars around in this respect. The aperture is large, and even with the front seat right back it is unnecessary to feed your feet in through a small gap. A neat touch is that the lower mounting of the front safety belt is on a slide, so that it can be moved out of the way of those getting in and out of the back. Considering the size and class of the car, the Bristol is not very wide outside, but a glance at the photographs shows that maximum use has been made of the available width: the "glasshouse" is noticeably wide with little "tumble-home", and the windows are close to the edge of the door. Thus the car belies its looks, and it is very spacious inside: a true four-seater. Passengers need to be very tall before sharing of legroom

front-to-rear is necessary, and there is more than ample knee- and head-room in the back as well. There was one criticism of the rear seats, though: the backrests are too upright. As some compensation the cushions are long and provide plenty of thigh support.

There were no complaints at all about space in the front. Once again there is more than enough head and legroom, while a recent modification has been to lower the front seat mountings, while increasing the amount of vertical travel. They can thus cater for greater extremes of height. The boot is large, taking no fewer than 14.5 cu ft of luggage, usefully square-shaped, and beautifully carpeted throughout. Two plus points here: the lid comes right down to the bumper, so the lifting height is low, and — another unique Bristol feature — the spare wheel is stowed in the nearside front wing. Thus luggage in the boot does not have to be disturbed should it be required. A similar storage space on the offside holds the battery, fuses and brake servos. Inside there is a smallish lockable compartment in front of the front seat passenger, a tape cassette holder between the front seats, a small well on top of the facia (though items placed there reflect annoyingly in the screen), and two neat, lockable compartments on each side of the rear seat passengers.

RIDE COMFORT

Apart from the adjustable dampers, mention must also be made of Bristol's special load-levelling system when the ride is considered. Unlike most other arrangements, which pump up the dampers, Bristol use hydraulics to operate rams connected to the forward end of the torsion bar by arms. Sensors between axle and body note any change in height, and the hydraulics then come into operation rotating the arms and thus alter the pre-load on the torsion bars until the required setting is reached.

As has been said, the 603 came to us with dampers set up roughly half-way between the extremes of softness and hardness. One result is some more — or more noticeable — small bump harshness compared to the 412, but by the same token the slight float over undulations at speed has been diminished. With these damper settings, then, the 603 rides quite firmly and tautly, which we like: others may prefer the softer mode. Compared to such cars as the Rolls-Royce or Jaguar, the Bristol does not absorb bumps and irregularities quite so well. It is, nevertheless, very comfortable and well controlled, with no sway or wallow.

AT THE WHEEL

Some years ago Bristol would invite potential purchasers to Filton to be measured so that the seat fitted to their car would fit them exactly. They found, however, that most owners were happy with (or returned to) a standard shape, so that is what they offer now. Nevertheless they will especially alter the padding to individual requirements if requested to do so: yet another pointer to the personal attention each customer receives.

The seats themselves are big in all respects, and very comfortable. Again after previous *Motor* comments that they could do with more lumbar support Bristol specially increased this in the car we used for our road test to suit our own tastes. In fact, one or two found too much lumbar support after the alterations, others found it perfect. There were no complaints about side (in spite of the width and shallow curvature of the backrest and cushion) or thigh support.

On top of this, of course, there is the adjustment available. Not just fore and aft and backrest tilt either: via a little joy stick on the side of the centre console the seat can be raised or lowered and moved backwards and forwards, while two further switches allow you to raise the front or rear of the seat individually. Thus the perfect driving position, no matter what size or shape you are, can be achieved easily and rapidly.

The major controls are well placed. There is plenty of room around the pedals. They are placed for either left or right foot braking, while on the S3 the gear lever has been modified to make it easier to reach and the radio easier to see. The lever handbrake between the seats is ideally placed.

It is in the layout of the minor controls that the Bristol flies in the face of convention. There are, for example, two stalks either side of the steering column. Common enough, except that, while one works the indicators, flasher and horn, the other operates the cruise control. The dip-switch is on the floor, to the left of the brake pedal — and above it is another push-button pedal for the windscreen washers. It is years since we on *Motor* have seen a floor-mounted dip-switch . . .

The rest of the knobs — rocker switches for the most part — appear to be scattered rather haphazardly around the facia. In fact they follow aircraft practice in being spaced so as to be easily found *by touch once the layout has been learnt*. Thus the lights master switch is a rocker to the right of the steering column, with a rotary switch for the wipers next to it. The rear window demister switch and rear fog switch are located on the centre console between the seats, the electric window switches on the armrests (two for the driver, one for the passenger), the hazard warning, engine fan over-ride and heater fan switches in a row in the centre of the facia, the electric aerial and air-conditioning switches above and to the right of them. The seat controls, boot and fuel filler flap switches are grouped together on the side of the centre console.

Opinions were divided on this layout. Those who lived with the car for any length of time found that, in fact, once learnt, the action to operate any of the switches came naturally: others preferred more modern layouts. Since the Bristol is, in effect, a bespoke car, Bristol will modify some of the arrangements to suit — putting the washer and dip switches on the column, for example. But they find that customers — and many of them are on their third,

fourth or even fifth Bristol — tend to resist such changes. Bristol even admit that a standard Lucas two-stalk system would be cheaper for them than the current layout, but they won't change.

It is worth mentioning, too, how well the cruise control works. There is a master switch beside the driver's right knee, but once that is on all the work is carried out by the stalk. To set it you accelerate to the desired speed, then pull it towards you. The car settles into a constant speed, no matter what hills or dips are met, imperceptibly and smoothly. A touch on the brakes instantly takes it out of operation: once any obstruction is passed you can accelerate using the throttle pedal or simply by pushing the stalk again, when the car will automatically regain the preset speed. You can even use the stalk to accelerate to another desired speed, but the cruise control does not come into operation below about 30 mph, to prevent the car running away when starting up.

All of the switches work beautifully (each is tested before installation) as do all the controls: we can think of only one other car — the Rolls-Royce — where even the feel of a switch is considered important. In addition, each switch is labelled with words, not symbols.

VISIBILITY

★★★ One of the reasons that the 603 feels so small is that the visibility is so good. The glass area is enormous, and the pillars are slim. The initial design called for a smooth slope to the nose, but this tended to hide the edges: thus ridges were added to the top of the wings of the production car to make judging width and corners easier. The rear window is enormous: Bristol are at the moment still trying to find a dipping mirror with a big enough sweep to take in all the view possible. As it is, you can see objects in the road a matter of feet behind the car, though the actual tail is hidden. Also helpful is that the (removeable) rear seat headrests are offset towards the sides of the car. The seat height adjustment was appreciated by the shorter members of staff, for they often find themselves buried down in the depths in big cars.

As befits a car with good high-speed capabilities, the lights are enormously powerful — there is a total of 300 watts on full beam!

INSTRUMENTS

★★★ The styling of the instrument panel, in a binnacle in front of the driver, is "British traditional", with large, clear, white-on-black dials, clear and simple calibrations, and a rock-steady action — the speedometer is absolutely accurate above 40 mph. However, the two outer instruments (petrol gauge on the left, battery condition meter on the right) are hidden by the steering wheel and hands, and though the bezels are matt black and do not therefore reflect, the same cannot be said of the instrument glasses: in strong sunshine they act more as mirrors of the steering wheel and driver.

Above: Luxury to the nth degree, with leather on seats, doors and the top of the facia. The switches on the side of the console operate the seat and open boot and petrol filler flap. Right: Plenty of room in the back, though some felt the backrests were too upright

Two of the instruments have already been mentioned. The others are: a large speedometer and tachometer; smaller matching water temperature and oil pressure gauges; and a clock.

HEATING

★★★ The heater controls are simple to understand and straightforward to operate. There are two slides, one for temperature, the other distribution. Heat output is good and finely controllable, with effective demisting as well. The two-speed fan can be used to increase throughput, but is disappointingly noisy on either of its settings.

VENTILATION/AIR CONDITIONING

★★★ We said in our driving impressions of the 603 that "The throughput of air (of the ventilation system) can be enormous . . . who needs air conditioning?", and these comments still more or less apply. Of course the ventilation system only offers ambient temperatures — hence the fitment of air conditioning for really hot climates.

Taking the ventilation system first, there are four fan-boostable vents on the facia, one at each end and two in the middle. On top of that there are two more down on the wheel well just in front of the door which aim air past the driver's seat to the rear — and yet another two, worked (unlike the others which are of the eye-ball type) by a rotating flap beside the driver's and passenger's shins for yet more air! A total of eight air vents, no less.

Naturally the system can be very finely tuned and adjusted to all tastes, and in fact the problem is one

of perhaps *too* much to learn — but that is one that owners must surely prefer to the reverse situation. The only criticism we can make — and a fairly serious one at that — is that, with all the vents open, there is too much wind noise.

The air conditioning, too, does all that is required of it. There are but two controls, one for the fan speed, the other for temperature, and the cooled, dehydrated air exits from chip-cutter vents either side of these. On a very hot day, with the car sitting for some time, setting the temperature to maximum coldness and the fan to high speed rapidly cools the interior to, if necessary, an arctic chill. But there is a drawback: the fan is too noisy. Even on its slowest setting it is noticeably audible, and on full speed — admittedly only needed very occasionally — it drowns conversation.

NOISE

★★★ If the air conditioning and ventilation system is one of the highlights of the 603, it is also one of the most disappointing, for it is simply too noisy for this class of car. This is a pity, for in other respects the Bristol matches, say, the Rolls-Royce as far as engine noise suppression is concerned. There is very little road roar or bump-thump (except when the tyre pressures were raised to 32psi) and noise from the side windows is virtually non-existent (this follows a change to the position of the rear view mirror). Around town, at low speeds, the Bristol comes close to the epitome of quietness, the Jaguar, but as speed rises, so does the rush from the vents, and at 70 mph it is necessary to turn up the radio quite a bit to hear it properly. At high revs too (though these should seldom be necessary) the engine can become obtrusive.

The massive boot took no fewer than 14.5 cu ft of Revelation suitcases

FINISH

★★
★★

People buy Bristols because of their finish, and to look closely at the car is to see why. External alloy body panels are machine pressed but then hand welded together and rivetted to the body, with a layer of Duralac, a proprietary compound, wherever alloy and steel meet to prevent electrolytic corrosion. The attention to detail is outstanding — just taking one example, the rain gutter blends perfectly into the bodywork where it finishes at the rear. On top of all this goes no fewer than 17 coats of assorted paints, with hand rubdowns in between.

The interior too is the same, from the beautifully finished leather on seats or doors, the perfect fit of the carpets, to the immaculate sweep of polished wood on the facia. The styling is of course traditional — no stylised instruments behind single panes of glass, or plastic mouldings — but that is another reason why Bristols are made the way they are.

There are hidden factors to be considered here too. The car is literally built to aircraft standards: thus there are no fewer than 20 fuses, most controls having their own. In fact there is one member of Bristol's staff who spends a whole day just checking every single switch, lamp, and so on. Yet another example: Bristol also check every single wheel for tolerance, not just random samples. It is this sort of attention to detail that has given Bristol their reputation — and explains why they cost so much.

FITTINGS

★★
★★

Naturally the Bristol comes with a full complement of fittings. Noteworthy are the switches that open the boot and fuel filler flap (on the centre console, beside the seat controls); electric windows; electric seat movement; two cigar lighters and four ashtrays; the walnut dashboard and leather upholstery (cloth is optional, but most customers insist on leather); a laminated screen; the locking cubby holes beside the rear seats; the slide rail to take the belt out of the way when entering the rear seat; four individual interior lights which stay on for a few seconds after the doors are closed; rear fog warning lights; a push-button radio; a separately controlled (electrically operated) aerial; a powerful red warning light built

PERFORMANCE

CONDITIONS
Weather	Occasional showers; wind 5-25 mph
Temperature	61°-69°F
Barometer	29.3 in Hg
Surface	Damp tarmacadam

MAXIMUM SPEEDS
	mph	kph
Banked Circuit	140*	225*
Terminal Speeds:		
at ¼ mile	88	140
at kilometre	110	177
Speed in gears (at 5500 rpm):		
1st	59	95
2nd	99	160

*Estimated

ACCELERATION FROM REST
mph	sec	kph	sec
0-30	3.1	0-40	2.5
0-40	4.6	0-60	4.3
0-50	6.4	0-80	6.3
0-60	8.6	0-100	9.1
0-70	11.1	0-120	12.3
0-80	14.0	0-140	16.5
0-90	17.7	0-160	22.8
0-100	23.3	0-180	32.8
0-110	30.9		
Stand'g ¼	16.5	Stand'g km	29.9

ACCELERATION IN KICKDOWN
mph	sec	kph	sec
20-40	2.8	40-60	1.8
30-50	3.3	60-80	2.0
40-60	4.0	80-100	2.8
50-70	4.7	100-120	3.2
60-80	5.4	120-140	4.2
70-90	6.6	140-160	6.3
80-100	9.3	160-180	10.0
90-110	13.2		

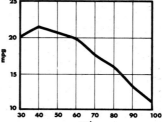

FUEL CONSUMPTION
Touring*	14.1 mpg
	20.0 litres/100 km
Overall	13.2 mpg
	21.4 litres/100 km
Fuel grade	91 octane
	3 star rating
Tank capacity	18.0 galls
	81.1 litres
Max range	254 miles
	409 km
Test distance	1025 miles
	1650 km

*Consumption midway between 30 mph and maximum less 5 per cent for acceleration.

BRAKES
Pedal pressure deceleration and stopping distance from 30 mph (48 kph).
lb	kg	g	ft	m
25	11.4	0.41	73	22
50	22.7	0.90	33	10
70	31.8	1.00†	30	9
Handbrake		0.34	88	27

FADE
20 ½g stops at 1 min intervals from speed midway between 40 mph (64 kph) and maximum (90 mph, 145 kph).
	lb	kg
Pedal force at start	36	16
Pedal force at 10th stop	40	18
Pedal force at 20th stop	42	19

STEERING
Turning circle between kerbs
	ft	m
left	36.7	11.2
right	35.7	10.8
lock to lock	3.2 turns	
50ft diam. circle	1.1 turns	

SPEEDOMETER (mph)
Speedo	30	40	50	60	70	80	90	100
True mph	31	41	50	60	70	80	90	100

Distance recorder: 2.5 per cent fast

WEIGHT
	cwt	kg
Unladen weight*	35.1	1783.2
Weight as tested	38.8	1971.1

*with fuel for approx 50 miles

Performance tests carried out by Motor's staff at the Motor Industry Research Association proving ground, Lindley.

Test Data: World Copyright reserved; no unauthorised reproduction in whole or part.

GENERAL SPECIFICATION

ENGINE
Cylinders	V8
Capacity	5898 cc (360 cu in)
Bore/stroke	101.6/90.93 mm (4.00/3.58 in)
Cooling	Water
Block	Cast iron
Head	Cast iron
Valves	OHV, pushrods
Cam drive	Chain
Valve timing	
inlet opens	18° btdc
inlet closes	54° abdc
ex opens	57° bbdc
ex closes	15° atdc
Compression	8.0:1
Carburetter	Carter 4-barrel
Bearings	5 main
Max power	Not quoted
Max torque	Not quoted

TRANSMISSION
Type	3 speed automatic plus torque convertor

Internal ratios and mph/1000 rpm
Top	1.00:1	26.1
2nd	1.45:1	18.0
1st	2.45:1	10.7
Rev	2.21:1	
Final drive	3.07:1	

BODY/CHASSIS
Construction	Separate chassis, steel superstructure, aluminium body panels
Protection	Complete chassis sealed

SUSPENSION
Front	Ind. by unequal length wishbones, coil springs, adjustable shock absorbers, anti-roll bar
Rear	Live axle, torsion bars with automatic suspension levelling, adjustable shock absorbers, Watts linkage

STEERING
Type	ZF recirculating ball
Assistance	Yes

BRAKES
Front	Disc, 10.91 in dia
Rear	Disc, 10.66 in dia
Park	Rear
Servo	Twin hydraulic servos
Circuit	Twin
Rear valve	No
Adjustment	Automatic

WHEELS/TYRES
Type	Pressed steel 15 × 6J plus Avon safety bands
Tyres	Avon 205 VR 15
Pressures	28/28 psi F/R (normal) 32/32 psi F/R (full load)

ELECTRICAL
Battery	71 Ah
Earth	Negative
Generator	Alternator, 65 Amp
Fuses	20
Headlights	
type	4 Halogen
dip	120 W total
main	300 W total

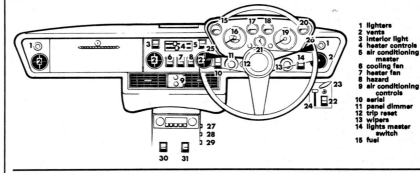

1 lighters		16	speedometer
2 vents		17	water temperature
3 interior light		18	oil pressure
4 heater controls		19	tachometer
5 air conditioning master		20	battery
6 cooling fan		21	clock
7 heater fan		22	cruise control master
8 hazard		23	bonnet release
9 air conditioning controls		24	vent flap
10 aerial		25	indicators/flash
11 panel dimmer		26	cruise control
12 trip reset		27	boot
13 wipers		28	filler flap
14 lights master switch		29	seat controls
15 fuel		30	rear fog guard
		31	rear demist

Make: Bristol
Model: 603 Series 3
Makers: Bristol Cars Ltd, 368/370 Kensington High Street, London W14 8NL
Price: £25627.00 basic plus £2135.58 car tax plus £2221.00 VAT equals £29983.58

 excellent   good    average   poor   bad

Above: traditional British, with gleaming walnut facia. Left: the two outer dials are hidden, and the glasses reflect. Below left: Dipswitch and washer, footwell vent, rear seat vent, ventilation control and cruise control switch in the footwell. Below: the spare is stored in a compartment behind the front wheels

into the rear of the door armrests; the Avon safety bands in the wheels; the cruise control; and the powerful halogen headlamps.

But there are to us some important omissions. Central door locking is optional instead of standard (Bristol believe that with only two doors this is unnecessary and an added complication). The external mirror cannot be adjusted from inside (they say they have yet to find one that meets their wind noise requirements). There is no vanity mirror, or tinted glass — again deliberately, since Bristol say it can cut down on visibility too much for safety. And the heating/ventilation fan has only two speeds.

IN SERVICE

Bristol has no dealers or agents — they deal directly with their customers. They find that most British-based owners bring their cars in for attention to the Chiswick service centre themselves, while those abroad can rely on the extensive Chrysler network.

But also the car is essentially sim-ple to work on, and any competent garage can easily maintain it. Bristol retain a close interest in their customers anyway, and find the personal approach pays dividends — owners stay remarkably loyal, so in practice the lack of outlets or service centres does not appear to be a problem. They also have an enviable stores set-up, being able to supply parts for — literally — any model back to the 400, and at very short notice.

Like many cars nowadays, Bristols need an oil change every 5,000 miles and a service every 10,000. They are guaranteed for a year with unlimited mileage, and the extensive anti-corrosion treatment to the very robust chassis plus the aluminium bodywork and the under-stressed Chrysler mechanicals mean that they have a long life — the number of Bristols still on the road is a very high percentage of all those built. Reliability therefore does not appear to be a problem.

Under the bonnet the engine bay is quite full, but items requiring routine maintenance are easy to get at, and the bay is uncluttered.

Below: lots of belts at the front of the engine, but good access to most ancilliaries

The Rivals

BRISTOL 603 S3 £29,984

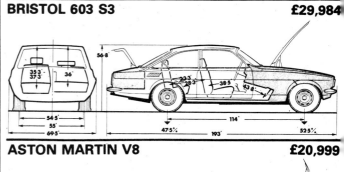

ASTON MARTIN V8 £20,999

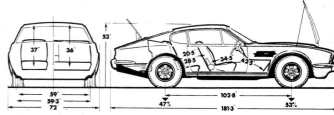

JAGUAR XJ5.3 £12,436

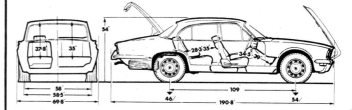

MASERATI KYALAMI £21,996

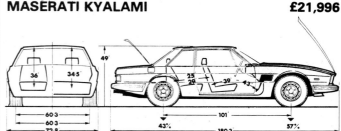

ROLLS-ROYCE CORNICHE £38,879

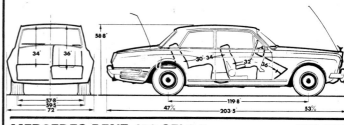

MERCEDES-BENZ 450 SEL6.9 £24,950

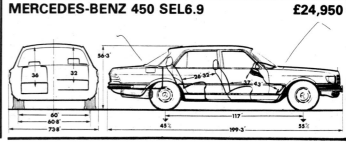

At nearly £30,000 the Bristol is in rare company. Other possible rivals could be the Panther Deville (£39049) or the cheaper BMW 633CSiA (£15370), the Mercedes-Benz 450SLC (£16840), and the Jaguar XJS (£15149)

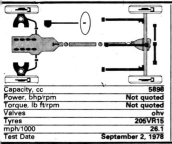

Capacity, cc	5898
Power, bhp/rpm	Not quoted
Torque, lb ft/rpm	Not quoted
Valves	ohv
Tyres	205VR15
mph/1000	26.1
Test Date	September 2, 1978

Exclusive, subtle, magnificently made, beautifully finished, the Bristol exemplifies British craftsmanship at its best. Very good ride/handling compromise aided by adjustable dampers, refinement close to that of Rolls-Royce, superb transmission, high comfort levels, comprehensive ventilation set-up, excellent visibility are plus points: only average performance, old-fashioned instrument and minor control layout, and wind noise are minus points.

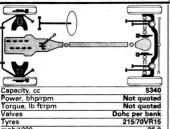

Capacity, cc	5340
Power, bhp/rpm	Not quoted
Torque, lb ft/rpm	Not quoted
Valves	Dohc per bank
Tyres	215/70VR15
mph/1000	26.9
Test Date	October 8, 1973

One of the most exciting cars made today, from a company enjoying a new lease of life. Fantastic performance, superb handling, excellent power steering, impressive brakes are major features. Rear seat accommodation is adequate, though it cannot match the larger saloons in this respect. Economy reasonable too, and quite refined. A most exhilarating car to drive: the Aston is now also available in convertible form — though for export only.

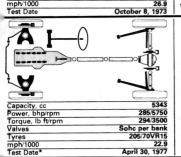

Capacity, cc	5343
Power, bhp/rpm	285/5750
Torque, lb ft/rpm	294/3500
Valves	Sohc per bank
Tyres	205/70VR15
mph/1000	22.9
Test Date*	April 30, 1977

*J5.3 Coupe

One of the world's great cars. Combines unrivalled refinement in terms of noise suppression and smoothness with an exceptional performance — and, like others unfortunately, a thirst to match. Now expensive, but still remarkable value for money — nothing can touch it at the price. Other good points include a smooth automatic transmission and outstanding roadholding and handling except for feel-less, over-light steering.

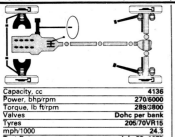

Capacity, cc	4136
Power, bhp/rpm	270/6000
Torque, lb ft/rpm	289/3800
Valves	Dohc per bank
Tyres	205/70VR15
mph/1000	24.3
Test Date	July 22, 1976

Notchback 2 plus 2 has De Tomaso-derived body, but the engineering is pure Maserati. Not as quick as some rivals, but more thirsty. Excellent high speed cruiser, handling good until limit is approached, but ride only fair. Engine less refined than those of many rivals, sounding strained at high revs; gearchange slow. Powerful, progressive brakes. Interior finish leaves much to be desired. A disappointment in some ways.

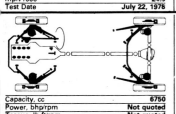

Capacity, cc	6750
Power, bhp/rpm	Not quoted
Torque, lb ft/rpm	Not quoted
Valves	ohv
Tyres	23.5/70HR15
mph/1000	26.9
Test Date	October 4, 1975

The Corniche comes between the Shadow/Wraith and the Camargue. Superb construction and engineering combine with a fabled finish, impressive noise suppression, smoothness and comfort to make an outstanding car. Transmission and brakes are praiseworthy too, but road noise is disappointing and the performance is below others of this class: the ride/handling bias is towards comfort rather than cornering.

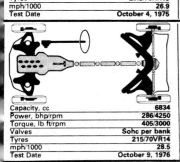

Capacity, cc	6834
Power, bhp/rpm	286/4250
Torque, lb ft/rpm	405/3000
Valves	Sohc per bank
Tyres	215/70VR14
mph/1000	28.5
Test Date	October 9, 1976

Mercedes have managed to combine luxury motoring with four doors and truly sporting road manners in this splendid car. With its magnificent power steering, exhilarating performance and uncannily roll-free, sure-footed handling the Mercedes doubles as a sports car and a limousine. It may not cosset its occupants as well as some rivals, but does whisk them along in style, comfort and utter safety. A car for the press-on, enthusiastic driver.

PERFORMANCE

	Bristol**	Aston	Jaguar**	Maserati	Rolls-Royce**	Mercedes**
Max speed, mph	140†	154.8	145†	147†	116.0	143.9
Max in 4th	—	136	—	134	—	—
3rd	—	112	—	100	—	—
2nd	99	77	100	71	86	97
1st	59	47	60	45	51	62
0-60 mph, secs	8.6	5.7	7.6	7.6	10.7	7.9
30-50 mph in 4th, secs	3.3	5.5	2.7	6.2	4.3	2.7
50-70 mph in top, secs	4.7	6.7	3.4	7.1	6.5	4.3
Weight, cwt	35.1	34.7	36.2	33.3	43.5	39.2
Turning circle, ft*	36.1	38.6	37.2	36.6	34.9	37.4
50ft circle, turns	1.1	1.2	1.1	1.3	1.15	1.0
Boot capacity, cu.ft.	14.5	8.9	11.8	8.9	12.7	15.0

*mean of left and right **automatic—kickdown for 30-50 mph †not measured

COSTS AND SERVICE

	Bristol	Aston	Jaguar	Maserati	Rolls-Royce	Mercedes
Price, inc VAT & tax, £	29984	20999	12436	21996	38879	24950
Insurance group	7	7	7	7	7	7
Overall mpg	13.2	13.2	11.9	11.6	11.6	13.4
Touring mpg	14.1	14.7	—	14.7	13.8	—
Fuel grade (stars)	3	5	5	4	5	4
Tank capacity, gals	18.0	21.0	20.0	22.2	24.0	21.1
Service interval, miles	5000	2500	6000	5000	6000	5000
No of dealers	None	27	350	6	82	95
Set brake pads (front) £*	12.72	36.72	13.41	43.93	11.22	14.54
Complete clutch £*	—	61.36	—	—	—	—
Complete exhaust £*	287.73	218.13	187.38	229.19	669.60	451.21
Front wing panel £*	170.00	343.94	88.99	297.00	270.00	72.13
Oil filter, £*	4.51	4.22	5.88	5.06	5.02	4.29
Starter motor, £*	81.00	90.72	63.12	101.50	82.08	259.18
Windscreen, £*	154.44**	213.25	55.08	216.00**	129.60**	150.09

*inc VAT but not labour charges **laminated †to be decided N/A not available

STANDARD EQUIPMENT

	Bristol	Aston	Jaguar	Maserati	Rolls-Royce	Mercedes
Adjustable steering		●	●	●		
Air Conditioning	●	●		●	●	●
Alloy Wheels		●		●		
Central door locking		●	●		●	●
Cigar lighter	●	●	●	●		●
Clock	●	●	●	●	●	●
Cloth trim	★	★	★	★		
Dipping mirror	●	●	●	●	●	●
Electric window	●	●	●	●	●	●
Fresh air vents	●	●	●	●	●	●
Hazard flashers	●	●	●	●		●
Headlamp washers					●	●
Head restraints	●					●
Heated rear window	●	●	●	●	●	●
Intermit/flick wipe	●	●	●	●	●	●
Laminated screen	●	●	●	●		
Locker	●	●	●			
Petrol filler lock	●	●	●			
Power steering	●	●	●	●	●	●
Radio	●	●	●	●		
Rear central armrest	●	●	●	●	●	●
Rear courtesy light	●	●	●	●	●	●
Rear fog light	●				●	●
Rear wash/wipe						
Rev counter		●	●	●		●
Reverse lights	●	●	●	●	●	●
Seat belts — front	●	●	●	●		●
— rear						
Seat recline	●	●	●	●	●	
Sliding roof						●
Tape player		●	●		●	
Tinted glass		●	●	●		●
Vanity mirror		●		●	●	

★leather

Bristol 412 Convertible V8

★ Well-behaved, silent and very fast. Our international Editor GORDON WILKINS reports on this hand-built car . . .

ROAD IMPRESSIONS

One day an elderly lady from Switzerland asked a London taxi driver what would be a good car to buy. He had his own ideal — hand-built quality, fragrant British leather and figured walnut, effortless performance, and luxurious accommodation for four in a car slim enough to slip easily through heavy traffic; so he took her to the Bristol showrooms in Kensington High Street.

She ordered one. Then it occurred to her that her nephew might like one, so she bought two. Now 82, she still drives herself to and fro between Switzerland and England in her Bristol.

Buyers from faraway places help to keep demand ahead of the three a week which Bristol's craftsmen can produce in the workshops next to those where the

supersonic Concorde airliners are built. They are built to last — cars which have done up to 150 000 km change hands for high prices.

The new 412 is a specially versatile car. Lift off the centre section of the roof, stow it in the trunk and you have the pleasures of open-car motoring without a thrashing wind to ruffle the hair. Rear quarters and rear window can be removed to make it a fully-open tourer, leaving only the strong roll arch which combines with the tough steel chassis to give real accident protection. Or the rear roof section can be replaced by a folding top for the summer.

Rust-proof alloy body panels help to keep the weight down; not that there is any shortage of power, with a 6,6-litre Chrysler V8 which will waft it quietly up to 160 km/h inside 20 seconds.

And it runs on 88–90 octane fuel.

Lockers in the front wings house spare wheel, battery, tools, fuses, and wiper motor, leaving a great deep trunk at the rear free for luggage. Self-levelling rear suspension keeps the beams of the four powerful headlamps steady.

Extremely fast, docile and silent, with excellent power steering and impres-

sive road holding, this is a difficult car to fault. Its Chrysler Torqueflite automatic transmission is one of the best in the world, but for fast driving in mountainous country I would prefer the selector lever to give free movement between Drive and Second, instead of between Neutral and Drive.

The outstanding impression when first driving the Bristol is its silence, lack of mechanical noise, wind noise or road rumble. But very soon it is clear that this is a very fast car indeed, with steering and roadholding to match the performance.

The car I tried had an experimental "economy" axle ratio of 2,8 to 1 instead of the usual 3,07 to 1. Using all the acceleration, but cruising at the legal limits, I got 17,6 to 18,8 litres/100 km (15 to 16 m-p-g). Maximum speed is over 220 km/h.

The past three years have proved disastrous for several makers of expensive high-performance cars, but Bristol have survived by clearly understanding the special niche in the market which they occupy, by limiting their personnel and their output accordingly, and by strictly controlling quality. ●

bespoke express

Mike McCarthy drives the recently revised 603. Pictures by Peter Burn

IT GOES against the grain of a strictly scientific upbringing to admit it, but after years of driving a considerable variety of cars I am convinced that they have individual personalities. The Mini, for example, is quite definitely chirpy and friendly: Jaguars have flair and panache: Citroens suffer from a Gallic arrogance which combines brilliance with irritating quirks: Mercedes do things with a calm and solid efficiency: you see the sort of thing I mean.

And then I met Bristol. The first I drove was a bare six months ago, a 412. The second, a 603, came into my life for a brief few hours last week. First — immediate — impressions of these cars are distinctly misleading, for they are almost all negative. The styling is a case in point: it is so subtle as to be self-effacing. Passers-by invariably notice the number plate (100 MPH on the 412, MPH 100L on the 603) *then* look at the name plate. A 603 could waft past you on the street and you may not notice it, unless your are one of the *cognoscenti.*

Similarly when you climb (these are tallish cars — you don't stoop to enter) into the leather seats. Ahead of you is an instrument nacelle and a polished wood facia, with plain, white-on-black, strictly functional instruments. Traditional, no stylised digits or flashes of chrome or ill-fitting plastic panels. Old-fashioned? Maybe . . .

Start up: a soft whirr from the starter, then the big V8 burbles into life. You can hear it; just enough to know it's there. Slip the gear lever into D, and move off: the engine note rises slightly and the car moves gently forward, the upward changes from the Torque-flite 'box taking place imperceptibly — only a drop in revs on the tacho indicates that valves have opened, oil pressures switched from one feed hole to another, brake bands have been released and/or applied. Impeccable behaviour, no quirks, but no personality as yet, either.

Now go forward a couple of hours, after a drive that encompasses clogged London streets, a portion of motorway, some country lanes — a mixed bag. No wild elation as you dismount, but a very pleasant sense of satisfaction, a feeling that you have been formally introduced to, and have more than just a nodding acquaintance with, a thoroughbred. This is where the personality shows: here is a machine of exquisite manners, that would never stoop to anything vulgar. It is always, discreetly, on *your* side, a veritable Jeeves of a car. But an even more apt simile might be that

Top: even a mini McCarthy sits tall, thanks to the very adjustable seats. Above: the view most motorists will get of the new car. Below: the captain's cockpit

of a beautiful, thoughtful, charming, shy, well-bred, intelligent lady.

Here is a machine that has been designed and assembled with care and loving attention to detail. The switchgear may not be modern ergonomic, but as Anthony Crook, Chairman and MD of Bristol points out, they are sited and shaped on aircraft principles, where touch is more important than looks. Thus the little joystick plus two toggle switches that adjust the seat (the only thing it won't do is move sideways) are on the *side* of the console: one look and from there on you make no mistakes: the action is natural.

These cars reflect Mr Crook's strong influence — and remember he is an ex-World War II pilot and racing driver of some note. He knows what he likes — and, more importantly, he knows what his customers like, though they may not know it themselves. Take the ventilation system. You can, if you want, have your Bristol fitted with air-conditioning. But it shouldn't be necessary. There is basically an air-blend heating/ventilation

system, just like on many other cars, but that in the Bristol is taken, carefully, step by step, to the *nth* degree.

There are four, fan-boostable (by an all but silent blower, naturally) eye-ball vents across the facia, two in the middle, one each end. These are tied in with the heater system and fed from a high-pressure area at the base of the windscreen. But there are more: two, low down beside the door, feeding back to the rear seat passengers under and beside the seats. And yet another two, in the footwells, beside your shins. These are fed by ram from the boxes in the front wings that house the spare wheel and battery. The through-put of air can be enormous . . . Who *needs* air conditioning?

Then there is the steering. Powered, of course, but made by ZF to Bristol's very exacting requirements. It is difficult to tell that it is assisted at all — light, as might be expected, but also direct, responsive and with the nearest thing to true "feel" I have ever encountered. It is at least the equal,

and possibly marginally better than that which I have always previously regarded as the best, the other ZF system as fitted to Mercedes.

Any ride/handling compromise is just that — a compromise. Bristol owners are a discerning lot, some preferring a softer ride, others more taut handling. So Bristol fit adjustable Konis all round — you can literally tailor the handling and ride to your own personal taste. Finesse is the name of the game.

We complained about the seats in the 412: too flat, and lacking in lumbar support. Mr Crook takes criticism to heart, so now all models are equipped with the re-shaped (and, incidentally, lighter) 603 seats. No complaints now — a sufficiency of back and shoulder support, and with the seat tilt facility you can adjust thigh support to suit. Another feature I personally like is the height control. Being of small stature, I hate cars with low seats — I find myself peering over steering wheels, trying to judge hidden corners. No such problems with the Bristol, for you sit up four-square and lordly. It actually makes the Bristol feel *small*, for heaven's sake! Nimbleness in town is but one of the reasons why the Bristol is such a pleasure — you can slip into gaps yet know those precious aluminium panels are inches away from damage.

Care, thoughtfulness, discretion, *subtlety:* that's what a Bristol is all about. Flaws? One or two — excessive wind noise from the exterior mirror is one — but Mr Crook is working on it. He admits the problem: it will be cured. Bristols do change, but gradually, and then only because any modifications are deemed necessary. Change for change's sake? Perish the thought. Pedigrees come from years of careful breeding. . . .

Footwell facing panel controls air distribution, bonnet release and speed hold switch

MILES
Behind the Wheel

THE BRISTOL 412 Convertible Saloon is a fabulously expensive handbuilt — almost bespoke built — machine that has impressed with its mode-for-all-seasons roof arrangement, quality of manufacture, performance, refinement, and road manners. Add by turbocharging possibly another 30 per cent power and torque, carry out some minor suspension modifications, then call it after one of the great wartime Bristol fighter-bombers, and you have the Bristol 412 S3 Beaufighter. . . .

Bristol are one of the few manufacturers remaining to use a traditional chassis. It is a massive box section affair welded directly to the floor-pan and upper structure. Continuing the tradition that was started after the war (when skill and labour were cheap) aluminium is used for the outer body panels, and the spare wheel and battery are cleverly (also space-efficiently) housed in compartments behind the front wheel arches and beneath the car's waistline. Normally the Zagato styled 412 series Bristol has a Targa style hardtop which is stowed in the boot, also a removable rear roof section which can be replaced with a soft ''hood'' in the summer. While the latter feature remains, as does the tough roll-over bar, the Beaufighter has a fixed roof with an inset clear tipping panel which is removable. Other alterations peculiar to the Beaufighter are bigger rear quarter lights, a restyled front end incorporating four headlights, and a subtle rectangular power bulge in the bonnet. The latter is necessary even after lowering the engine and transmission by 1 in. (this has the incidental benefit of lowering the car's centre of gravity) because of the greater engine height resulting from the turbocharger priority valve being interposed between the carburettor and inlet manifold.

Inside the standard Beaufighter specification includes electric driver's seat adjustment, electrically controlled remote boot release and door mirrors, air conditioning, central locking, a redesigned facia and instrumentation modified to reduce reflections incorporating fibre optic illuminated switchgear. In addition to four dash mounted eyeball vents, swivelling footwell outlets also provide fresh air that is ducted through from the spare wheel and battery box compartments. On the Beaufighter fuel tankage is up from 18 to 21 gallons. An extra 10 gallon tank is optional.

Front suspension is conventional with double wishbones, coil springs and telescopic dampers. Bristol rear suspension is unique. A live axle (a loosely set-up limited slip differential is fitted on the Beaufighter) is held laterally by a Watts linkage. Longitudinal location depends at the bottom on long torsion bars with transverse links at their after ends. These connect to the bottom of the axle via drop links. Upper location of the axle is by a single link running from the top of the final drive to the main structure. Self-levelling is cleverly obtained by attaching the forward ends of the torsion bars to hydraulic rams that are activated by a ride level sensor. For the Beaufighter, settings are to be made slightly stiffer, thus revised from the pre-production prototype that I drove. Avon 225-70VR tyres are fitted in preference to the standard 205 section, but still on 15in. dia by 6in. wide Avon safety rims.

The heart of the Beaufighter is Bristol's turbo version of the Chrysler 5.9-litre V8. The conversion has been carried out entirely at Filton, using a Rotomaster blower and also some of their components in the ''Priority Valve'' assembly. Although quite common in the U.S., this is the first time we have seen a PV turbo system on a European car. Instead of all the inlet air/mixture passing through the turbocharger at all times it allows mixture to by-pass the compressor or be directed through it depending on throttle opening. Bristol say that the standard engine running a compression ratio of 8.0 to 1 has needed no internal modifications to withstand the rigours of supercharging at 7psi. Indeed they have run the wastegate set as high as 9psi with no ill effects. A single turbocharger is mounted atop a modified right hand exhaust which is also fed from the left hand one via a cross over pipe running under the sump. The cross pipe provides a convenient mounting for the wastegate, and as the turbocharger sits transversely at just above rocker cover height, the compressor outlet conveniently points straight at the carburettor which is the standard Carter four barrel, suitably rejetted, to richen u the secondary choke circuit.

Now comes the clever bit we have already mentioned, interposed between the carburettor and standard inle manifold is a priority valve. light throttle openings mixtu passes straight through the carburettor and into the manifold in the normal way PV is open). As the throttle is opened wider the valves beg to close as the pressure betw the carburettor and manifold become more equal thus re-directing some of the mixt the long way round through compressor. On wide throttle openings, boost pressure clo the PV completely whereupo all the fuel and air gets compressed before entering engine. Electronic ignition is fitted, but the normally aspirated engine's computerised ''lean burn black box advance curve is discarded in favour of a modified conventional ''bob weight'' distributor. A high capacity fuel pump and large bore lines look after

Return of the
Bristol's new turbo car has power enough for flyi

The turbocharger installation is neatly done. Small bore water pipes heat the priority valve chamber. The diagrams show the gas flow pattern in un-boosted and boosted modes

Beaufighter

n the ground . . . .

Fig a. Priority valves fully open

Fig b. Priority valves fully closed

Priority valve function

reased fuel flow needs. Not unexpectedly, Bristol ve found it necessary to ate Chrysler's Torqueflite omatic transmission. They e done this by fitting the que converter and internal tches normally reserved for with the Chrysler 440 cu in. 2 litres) V8. A stronger pshaft is fitted with larger n standard universal joints.

the road

Bristol follow Rolls-Royce dition in that no engine puts are mentioned. Rest ured there is enough power propel this luxury machine ighing a quoted 34.5 cwt) ently fast. We were unable ake figures during our day but claims of 0-60, 70 and 0 mph in around 6.5, 8.0 17.0 sec hardly seemed to justice to the Beaufighter's ising acceleration and d-range performance. We ve yet to carry out a full otest on a current Bristol so en Bristol chief Anthony ook invited me to spend a few urs with the prototype 412 Beaufighter I happily ored photographer Ron ston's analogous remarks ut a certain wartime aircraft ng prone to ground loop n), and hot footed it to swick.

Okay, the interior of the velopment car did not quite ve the integrated appearance e might have expected in a that will cost so much, but it possessed a hand-tooled ther bound quality that one y finds on the most exclusive chinery. The driving seat, ustable up, down, fore and at the touch of a toggle tch also has micro back ustment so should suit any man frame. There is

somewhat less leg room in the back than in a Jaguar XJ6, but then that car does not have the Bristol's huge boot.

As we headed out of London on the M4, the light airy feel inside and commanding forward visibility over its easy-to-place squared-off bonnet immediately impressed, as did the excellent natural straight line stability and the nicely weighted and geared (3 turns) power steering. Like Mercedes, Bristol show that recirculating ball systems — Bristol use a ZF one — can be made to work beautifully.

The test car seemed somewhat underdamped at the front. Doubtless this contributed to some initial steering vagueness about the straight ahead and a rather traditional feeling of toppliness as one entered a bend with any enthusiasm. Adjustable Koni dampers are fitted as standard so the ride / handling compromise can be altered to suit customers' requirements. "The Beaufighter has yet to have its first service — we will stiffen the front dampers then," commented Crook later.

With no standard car with which to compare mechanical and road noise levels, I felt they were somewhat higher than standards set by Jaguar or R-R, but still very low. Wind noise around the front pillars and / or door mirrors at 70 mph and over was unexpectedly high. Driven on light throttle openings the Beaufighter proceeded in a stately manner, wafting along effortlessly at unmentionable speeds. Snap open the accelerator at any engine speed over 2,000 rpm; all at once the boost gauge flashes round, a hardening engine note combines with a wooshing noise and this enigmatic machine surges forward

breathtakingly. The Beaufighter simply bounds forward.

Left to its own devices the transmission upchanges smoothly at 4,000 rpm (around 30 and 70 mph). Also, bearing in mind the huge power and torque hike, shifts are impressively quirk-free. Kickdown to 2nd is not available until the speedometer is showing less than 65 mph, yet maxima in the lower ratios at the posted 5,500 rpm rev limit are as high as an indicated 55 and 105 mph. In fact, so much torque is available, that once moving briskly overtaking is delightfully instant without resorting to kickdown or manual shifting. It was also noticeable how the torque converter cushioned any throttle lag. If the accelerator was opened suddenly, with the engine revs above 2,000 rpm on a fairly large throttle opening, acceleration response was virtually instant. However, the engine in the test car could plainly be caught out if stooging along gently below 40 mph while, say, waiting to overtake a slow moving truck. When the opportunity came and the throttle was opened — even quite progressively — the engine would protest with a cough and spit back in the carburettor, almost dying on a couple of occasions. The solution at low road speeds was of course to get the engine revving more by changing down manually, then to feed the throttle on progressively. Crook assured us that this characteristic was not endemic and had developed while the car was in another's hands. It did not occur when accelerating from rest, and was a minor niggle that failed to spoil the sheer fun of effortlessly taking overtaking opportunities normally reserved for the supercar.

Our journey took us over quiet Hampshire B roads where, unlike the real thing, this Beaufighter did little to disturb the peace. It is one of those cars

whose refinement deceives the driver into thinking he is going slower than he actually is. As I have said, incorrectly set dampers meant initial handling gave a slightly insecure feeling, especially on damp corners. Also undulating surfaces could produce a fairly lurchy ride. Both belied really excellent manners *in extremis*. In balanced throttle cornering there was a trace of understeer which moderated to neutral balance as the speed increased. Any understeer could easily, delightfully, and predictably be neutralised by kicking the rear out with that huge torque output. The Beaufighter rear end was most impressive. It put the power down well and stayed glued to the road unless upset by a hump large enough to put any car off line. Braking pedal pressures were pleasantly firm — a change from the all too commonly over-servoed kind — and the brakes themselves never gave a moment's worry. I felt the Beaufighter had something of the Rolls-Royce feeling of indestructability, combined with the Jaguar's handling response, but not its ride or quietness. But then the Beaufighter has an open-air capability and goes like the wind.

Assuming the mileage recorder was accurate it averaged approximately 14.0 mpg — no more or less than one might have expected of a normally aspirated 412. Bristol ask "Is this the world's fastest accelerating four-seater?" Subjective judgement suggests that if we leave out the more cramped Aston Martin alternative — it may just be. The price? A mere £37,999.16. □

A soft rear roof section is supplied to take the place of the hard one. The Beaufighter has a tinted tipping and removable roof centre section, rather than a completely removable Targa type. The panel behind the front wheel arches can be clearly seen

SPECIFICATION

ENGINE

Head / block	Cast iron / cast iron
Cylinders	8 in 90 deg V
Main bearings	5
Cooling	Water
Bore, mm (in.)	101.6 (4.0)
Stroke, mm (in.)	90.9 (3.58)
Capacity, cc (in³)	5,898 (360)
Valve gear	Ohv
Camshaft drive	Chain
Compression ratio	8.0 to 1
Ignition	Electronic
Carburettor	Carter four barrel
Max power	Not specified
Max torque	Not specified

TRANSMISSION

Type		Chrysler Torque-Flite 3 speed automatic

Gear	Ratio	mph / 1000rpm
Top	1.00	26.0
2nd	1.45	18.0
1st	2.45	10.6
Final drive gear	Hypoid bevel	
Ratio	3.07 to 1	

SUSPENSION

Front—location	Double wishbones
springs	Coil
dampers	Telescopic
anti-roll bar	Yes
Rear—location	Live axle, with Watts linkage
springs	Torsion bar
dampers	Telescopic
anti-roll bar	No

STEERING

Type	ZF recirculating ball
Power assistance	Yes
Wheel diameter	15 in.

BRAKES

Circuits	2 split front / rear
Front	10.9 in. dia. disc
Rear	10.7 in. dia. disc
Servo	Twin

WHEELS

Type	Avon Alloy
Rim width	6 in.
Tyres—make	Avon
—type	Radial ply
—size	225-70 VR

EQUIPMENT

Reversing lamp	Standard
Hazard warning	Standard
Screen wipers	2-speed + intermittant
Screen washer	Electric
Interior heater	Air blending
Air conditioning	Standard

Blown Bristol Beaufighter

Add a turbocharger to one of the world's most luxurious and exclusive cars and you come up with the fastest accelerating automatic full four-seater production machine made today. And that is precisely what Bristol have done . . .

WHO IN Heaven's name would buy a car costing £38,000, that weighs 35 cwt, that consumes fuel at the rate of 9.4 miles to the Imperial gallon, but which will accelerate to 60 mph in 6.7 secs, on to 100 mph in 17.6 secs, and reach an estimated 140 mph?

A very select group of people, that's who. And for them, Bristol have introduced the Beaufighter, a car of impeccable pedigree, immaculate finish, shattering performance yet with irreproachable manners under all conditions. In short, one of the truly magnificent cars of the world.

The basis of the Beaufighter (full name the 412/S3 Beaufighter) is the 412, an example of which we tested back in March 1977. Thus, mechanically, the two cars are similar. There is, for example, a hefty box-section welded-steel chassis on which is mounted the separate body, consisting of steel substructures and alloy panelling. The front suspension is by unequal-length wishbones, coil springs, telescopic Koni dampers and an anti-roll bar. At the rear there is a live axle with torsion-bar springing and Watts linkage location, plus telescopic dampers again. Except, being a Bristol, the dampers are adjustable to suit personal tastes . . .

There are disc brakes front and rear with ZF power-assisted recirculating-ball steering — modified to Bristol's rather exacting requirements, of course.

All Bristols are fitted with Chrysler engines. In the 412/S2 it was a 6.7 litre V8 (naturally modified and adapted by Bristol), in the Beaufighter it is a smaller 5.9 litre unit. The major difference between the two is that the Beaufighter has a turbocharger as well . . . And, like Rolls-Royce and Aston-Martin, Bristol quote no output figures. In both

cars the engines drive the back wheels via a Chrysler Torqueflite 3-speed automatic transmission and torque converter.

At the front, quadruple headlights in the Beaufighter replace the two of the 412, while the Targa top of the S2 has been replaced with a rigid roof incorporating a tiltable/removable glass sun-roof; the removable rear section is retained, as is a canvas rear hood that can be erected when that rear section has been removed. And there is a discreet "Beaufighter" logo at the back.

To lower the centre of gravity and enhance roadholding the Beaufighter engine and drive line have been lowered and the Beaufighter also has a choice of two rear axle ratios, 3.066:1 for performance, or 2.88:1 for economy. The braking system has a more powerful servo and the tyres are now 225-70 VR 15 instead of 205 VR 15 Avons. The special alloy wheels, with unique well/filler band for safety in case of a blow-out, are retained.

Inside there is an all-new facia, but with traditional clean white-on-black dials set into a beautifully polished walnut facia. The switchgear has been brought into line with current thinking (much to Bristol's MD Tony Crook's disgust!) via twin stalks either side of the steering column for lights and wipers.

Other detail changes include an internal, electrical release for the boot, twin bonnet locks, electrically adjustable front seats (for reach, height and tilt), air conditioning as standard but with revisions to the excellent ventilation system, automatic door locking, a stereo radio and cassette player as standard, twin exterior mirrors adjustable from inside, and fibre optic illumination of the switches on facia and

console from a rheostat-controlled centralised light source. Finally the petrol tank is larger — 21 instead of 18 gallons — useful if you're only doing 9.4 mpg . . .

But of course the big change is under the bonnet. The 412 is naturally aspirated, the Beaufighter turbocharged — but not via a bolt-on kit. Dear me, no: Bristol don't do things that way . . .

They started with a commercially-available blower kit for this engine, manufactured by Roto-Master in America. They took it apart, looked at it, adapted some parts and threw others away. It came, for example, with a water-injection kit to prevent detonation: Bristol found a way around this . . .

The system on the whole works the same way as many others. The turbocharger sucks through the carburetter; there is a conventional waste-gate in the exhaust to limit the maximum boost pressure. But, in addition, there is another component, called a priority valve. This is, in effect, a valve which by-passes the turbocharger compressor, so that at light loads and low speeds the engine acts as a naturally-aspirated unit without the volumetric losses which would occur were the mixture to go through the compressor. As boost rises, however, the valve

closes and the intake manifold then operates under pressure. Interestingly, the Beaufighter engine, despite being turbocharged, has a fairly high compression ratio (8.2:1).

Before going on to describe how all this works, it is only fair to say that the test car was a pre-production prototype, assembled in quite a hurry so that we could be the first magazine in the world to test it (they were still screwing it together the night before we picked it up, and it arrived with a mere 450 miles on the clock).

Many engines fitted with emission-control carburetters tend to be reluctant starters: we had no such problems with the Beaufighter, a quick turn of the key sufficing to get the big V8 burbling away. However, it was necessary to let it idle for a while and warm up a little, otherwise when you gave the accelerator pedal a gentle prod the engine simply hesitated or even stalled.

And that is really the only complaint there is about the performance: the rest is rave reviews. You can trickle in traffic in near silence, then simply surge away at speeds that cause passengers to hold on for dear life. The name Beaufighter is appropriate: it is the nearest thing we know to taking off in an aircraft. The response to the throttle is instantaneous yet utterly smooth: whatever speed you are travelling at, up to 120 mph at least, all you need is a push on the pedal and you vanish into the middle distance. Smoothly, undramatically, and very, very rapidly . . .

Flooring the throttle from a standstill brings 60 mph up in 6.7 secs, 80 mph in 11.0 secs, and 100 mph in 17.6 secs. On paper the Aston Volante is quicker to 100 mph, 17.3 secs, but we must confess that we were forced to take our performance figures under extremely adverse weather conditions, with winds between 20 and 40 mph. Thus our fastest time to 100 mph against the wind was 19.2 secs, but with the wind 16.0 secs. Put the Aston and the Bristol side-by-side on the same day and it would be a close run thing, though the Bristol would definitely be the quicker to 60 mph. Respective figures for the Jaguar XJ12 are 7.6 and 18.4 sec, for the Mercedes 450SEL 6.9, 7.9 and 19.4 sec. Thus we have no qualms in naming the Beaufighter the fastest accelerating full four-seater automatic saloon currently in production. Who said Bristols were staid?

It is usual to talk about turbocharger lag when discussing blown engines but the combination of tremendous low-speed torque from the beefy engine, a turbocharger that comes in at very low revs, and a torque converter to disguise any lag there is means that it just doesn't show up.

Gripes? First of all, noise: there is a loud hissing gurgle when accelerating, while at the same time you can hear the turbocharger and engine working. A check by Bristol showed a gasket leak in the boost system, and in addition the under-bonnet padding wasn't fitted — they have special padding to cope with the high under-bonnet temperature the blower creates, but it takes 36 hours to dry, and there wasn't time if we were to have the car quickly. In addition the idling speed when the engine was warm could creep up to 1800 rpm, but a blip on the throttle brought it down to a more usual 800 rpm or so. Bristol say this is the accelerator pump spring in the carburetter fighting the throttle return spring — and winning. A mod is in the pipeline. Finally, what appeared to be a surge at full throttle and high revs turned out to be a cyclic fluctuation in the waste gate — more heard and seen than damaging.

Allied to the impressive engine is a near-perfect transmission. Changes up were, as one tester put it, miraculously smooth. Kickdown too was instantaneous and equally unnoticeable — just a rise in revs and an increase in urge showed that anything had happened. Allied with a smoothly responsive throttle this makes the Bristol a car that is impossible to drive jerkily unless you down change manually when travelling far too quickly.

The ratios are such as to give 57 mph in first and 97 mph in second if you hold on to the red line. In practice, on full throttle with the selector lever left in D, changes took place at 3800 (1-2) and 4200 (2-3) rpm, and taking the car up to the 5500 rpm red line on the tacho had little effect on improving the accelerative performance: our best times were made by changing up at about 4500 rpm.

Of course you pay for all this performance via an appalling fuel consumption — 9.4 mpg. However, you can

Above left: three-way electrical adjustment for the front seats is standard. Above right: comfortable spacious rear seats Below: polished walnut facia, white-on-black dials — British traditional interior styling

always order your car with the economy diff, or drive gently, though our worst intermediate fuel check — 9.0 mpg — occurred during a period of town driving. Our best was 10.1 mpg . . .

Performance of this type was common back in the "good ol' days" when American "Muscle cars" really did have muscle — but seldom the suspension to cope with it. With the Bristol you need have no qualms on that score. From the steering — a ZF unit modified to Bristol requirements — to the roadholding and handling, the Beaufighter is exemplary. The steering is the equal in feel and general precision to that of Aston-Martin or Mercedes-Benz, systems which are generally regarded as the best around. The Bristol's steering is a little too light for our tastes and lacks feel around the straight-ahead position but it has good feel otherwise. The fat Avons grip up to very high cornering speeds in either the wet or dry, and the handling is to all intents and purposes neutral — most drivers will run out of courage before road. You can, if you are brave enough, hang the tail out, and if you do it is progressive and easily controllable. In spite of a live rear axle the Beaufighter will live with most other cars with more complicated set-ups.

When we drove the 412 we complained that perhaps the dampers were a bit too soft, so for our test Bristol put them on the hardest setting. Having experienced both, we reckon the best setting must be between the two, for the Beaufighter was distinctly firm around town, and thumped over potholes and GPO-Gas Board "road improvements". At higher speeds it rode considerably better, though there was still a trace of the front-end float we found before.

Tony Crook is a tall man, but has a petite daughter: thus the Bristol seating arrangement has to cater for people of all heights, and it does. Both front seats have adjustable backrests and are electrically movable for reach, tilt and height, so that everyone who drove the car was always able to make themselves comfortable. The seats themselves are comfortable, but perhaps a little too wide so that side support is lacking and we had one complaint of too much lumbar support.

It is only when the front seats are right back that legroom in the rear is restricted, and then not seriously. Thus the Beaufighter is a genuine four-seater, with armchair comfort for all.

The new facia is very much English-traditional. There is a row of instruments, from voltmeter on the left to boost gauge on the right, clearly marked in white-on-black, set in a lovely polished walnut facia. Unfortunately, although Bristol claim they are reflection-free, this is not the case: those on the right do pick up reflections through the side windows. All the major controls are ideally placed (the pedals are perfect for left or right-foot braking, for example), and we like the new stalk switch system, even if Mr Crook doesn't (he would still like to see a foot dip switch, for example . . .)

One of the things we cannot really comment on is the heating and ventilation system. We know from the 412 that it can be of the very best in the world at any price. But in the hurry to get the test car completed the heater slides were incorrectly set and the extractor vents covered with tape instead of being properly finished off, leading to a slow heat throughput, and a poorly performing ventilation system.

As tested, with all the uncorrected faults, the Beaufighter was not a particularly quiet car. We have mentioned the turbocharger whistle, which Bristol say is curable. There was some wind noise from around the passenger's door — Bristol say this would have been picked up in one of their pre-

The bottom seat belt anchorages are on a slide so they can be moved out of the way for ease of entry to the rear

The spare wheel is located in the near-side front wing; battery, servo and electrical equipment are housed in the off-side wing

The huge boot takes a massive 15.5 cu ft of luggage

Make: Bristol
Model: 412/S3 Beaufighter
Maker: Bristol Cars Ltd, 368/370 Kensington High Street, London W14 8NL
Price: £30,501.00 basic plus £2,541.75 car tax plus £4,956.41 VAT equals £37,999.16

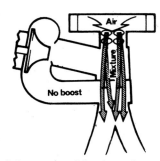
At low speeds and throttle openings (above) the priority valve opens, allowing the mixture to by-pass the compressor, and thus improve throttle response. At higher speeds (below) it closes and the mixture is boosted

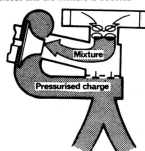

delivery test drives. There was quite a lot of tyre thump, partly due to the extra-wide tyres, partly due to the stiffer damper settings. Tyre roar depended on surface, but on (for example) cross-grained concrete it was quite loud. On the whole the Bristol doesn't match up to, say, Rolls-Royce or Jaguar standards, but it is better than an average quality car such as a Mercedes or BMW.

On the other hand there were no complaints at all about the finish. It is exemplary, with not a flaw in sight, in spite of the rush to get the car finished. This is one of the things for which you pay £38,000, and is what you would expect. And at near enough 35 cwt, you would expect too a solid feel to the car — and you wouldn't be disappointed.

Naturally it comes with all mod cons, plus some others that don't have. Those opening panels in the front wings to hide spare wheel and battery, for example. The removable rear roof section. Real leather upholstery, though we would have preferred cloth ourselves. Slides beside the front seats to take the seat belt anchorages so that the belts slide out of the way to let passengers enter. Powerful red lights in the doors which don't only warn up-coming traffic that they are open, but which also illuminate the interior, and stay on for a few seconds after you get in or out so you don't have to fumble in the dark to find the ignition key-hole. Those safety wheels. We could go on, but why bother? You get the point . . .

How do you sum up the Beaufighter? Built to the highest standards, it is exclusive, with staggering performance, yet total tractability and flexibility. Its roadholding and handling is amongst the most enjoyable in the world and with subtle, deceptive looks it is a car that takes time to get to know but when you do turns out to be a driver's car par excellence, spacious and comfortable inside . . . If not "The best car in the world", could it be close?

Left: a full engine compartment, with the turbocharger prominently mounted

MOTOR FEATURE TEST ●
BRISTOL 412/S3 BEAUFIGHTER

PERFORMANCE

CONDITIONS
Weather	Sunny-High winds (20-40 mph)
Temperature	54-56°F
Barometer	29.25 in Hg
Surface	Dry tarmacadam

MAXIMUM SPEEDS
	mph	kph
Mean (estimated)	140	225
Terminal Speeds:		
at ¼ mile	94	151
at kilometre	115	185
Speed in gears (at 5500 rpm):		
1st	57	92
2nd	97	156

ACCELERATION FROM REST
mph	sec	kph	sec
0-30	2.6	0-40	2.1
0-40	3.8	0-60	3.5
0-50	5.1	0-80	5.0
0-60	6.7	0-100	7.0
0-70	8.6	0-120	9.5
0-80	11.0	0-140	12.9
0-90	13.9	0-160	17.3
0-100	17.6		
Stand'g ¼	15.0	Stand'g km	27.4

ACCELERATION IN KICKDOWN
mph	sec	kph	sec
20-40	2.1	40-60	1.4
30-50	2.5	60-80	1.5
40-60	2.9	80-100	2.0
50-70	3.5	100-120	2.5
60-80	4.3	120-140	3.4
70-90	5.3	140-160	4.4
80-100	6.6		

FUEL CONSUMPTION
Overall 9.4 mpg
30.0 litres/100 km

Fuel grade	98 octane 4 star rating
Tank capacity	21 galls 95 litres
Test distance	750 miles 1200 km

*Consumption midway between 30 mph and maximum less 5 per cent for acceleration.

NOISE
	dBA	Motor rating*
30 mph	63	10
50 mph	65	12
70 mph	72	18
Max revs in 2nd		
(1st for 3-speed auto)	80	32

*A rating where 1 = 30 dBA and 100 = 96 dBA, and where double the number means double the loudness.

SPEEDOMETER (mph)
Speedo								
30	40	50	60	70	80	90	100
True mph								
29	39	48	58	67	75	85	94

Distance recorder: 6 per cent fast

WEIGHT
	cwt	kg
Unladen weight*	34.7	1762.8
Weight as tested	38.4	1950.8
*with fuel for approx 50 miles

Performance tests carried out by Motor's staff at the Motor Industry Research Association proving ground, Lindley.

Test Data: World Copyright reserved; no unauthorised reproduction in whole or part.

GENERAL SPECIFICATION

ENGINE
Cylinders	V8
Capacity	5900 cc (360 cu in)
Bore/stroke	101/90.93 mm (4.00/3.58 in)
Cooling	Water
Block	Cast iron
Head	Cast iron
Valves	Pushrod Ohv
Cam drive	Chain
Compression	8.0:1
Induction	Modified Thermoquad four barrel fed by Rotomaster turbocharger
Bearings	5 main
Max power	Not quoted
Max torque	Not quoted

TRANSMISSION
Type	3-speed, automatic plus torque converter

Internal ratios and mph/1000 rpm
Top	1.00:1	25.6
2nd	1.45:1	17.7
1st	2.45:1	10.5
Rev	2.21:1	
Final drive	3.066:1 (2.88:1 optional)	

BODY/CHASSIS
Construction	Separate chassis, alloy-panelled body
Protection	Underbody sealant, Dinitrol injection in box sections

SUSPENSION
Front	Independent via unequal length wishbones, coil springs adjustable dampers, anti-roll bar
Rear	Live axle located by Watts linkage, and top link, torsion bar springing, adjustable dampers

STEERING
Type	Recirculating ball
Assistance	Yes

BRAKES
Front	Discs 10.91 in dia
Rear	Discs 10.66 in dia
Park	Separate on rear
Servo	Yes
Circuit	Split front/rear
Adjustment	Automatic

WHEELS
Type	Alloy, 15 in × 6 in rims
Tyres	Avon 225-70VR15
	30/30 psi F/R (normal)
	32/32 psi F/R (full load/high speed)

ELECTRICAL
Battery	12V, 71 Ah
Earth	Negative
Generator	Alternator, 65A
Fuses	14
Headlights	
type	Quad Halogen
dip	120 W total
main	260 W total

Bristol Beaufighter

An English gentleman's very high speed sporting carriage!

OWNING a Bristol is much akin to being a member of a very exclusive club. There are so few of them on the road that people automatically turn to examine one as it goes past. That's not because they are ostentatious, quite the reverse, but simply because they are so distinctive, large and obviously upper crust in their whole demeanour. If one accuses Bristol Managing Director Tony Crook of being unashamedly elitist in his approach to building and marketing these cars, he will almost certainly reply that is precisely the reason that Bristol Cars are still in business. Almost absurdly exclusive, Bristols trickle out of their Filton factory at the rate of little more than one a week. And there will always be fifty or so people every year, throughout the country, who are prepared to pay for the incredibly high standards of finish and refinement offered by the current range.

We have recently been trying the turbocharged Chrysler V8 powered Beaufighter, a distinguished four-seater sports coupé carrying the name of one of the Bristol Aeroplane Company's best known fighting machines from the Second World War. It's basically a variation of the distinctive 412 theme; an angular, impressive looking machine built round a substantial closed box section chassis which produces an extremely robust structure onto which the steel framed body, clad with aluminium alloy panelling, is welded. From the moment one climbs aboard the Beaufighter — and I emphasise the word *climbs* because at 4' 8½" height this is certainly no cramped sports coupé — and clunks the heavy driver's door closed, one is aware that this is a very substantial car indeed.

Inside, the Bristol Beaufighter exudes the air of a gentleman's club lounge. If Mercedes and Porsche claim their plain, non-reflective interior finishes to be practical, uncomplicated and ergonomically ideal, then Bristol make no such concession to the latest trends. The Beaufighter's fascia is covered with lustrous, high quality walnut veneer to complement the top quality leather individual front seats. I found the seats tall and broad enough to be extremely comfortable, and although they don't really offer sufficient lateral support for the ungentlemanly practice of hustling the Beaufighter indecorously through tight country lanes, their range of adjustment is magnificent. Drop your fingers down to the side of the transmission tunnel and you'll find small electrical switches which allow one to adjust height, tilt and fore/aft adjustment. I was just about to complain to Tony Crook that I would have liked more support beneath my knees when he pointed out that a paying customer can, of course, have the seat's base positioned at any angle he chooses when he orders his car, thus

SUMPTUOUS and tasteful; the interior of the Bristol Beaufighter is a classic amalgam of wood veneer and top quality leather trim.

THE long flowing wings of the Beaufighter are put to good, practical use. Above left, the flap on the right hand side of the car reveals battery, fuses and servos to be easily accessible. Above right, the left hand compartment stows the spare wheel, thus leaving the large boot free for luggage.

offering a range of adjustment that he wants rather than the one the manufacturer thinks he *ought* to have. I suppose I should have thought of that!

Immediately ahead of the driver is a distinctive, high set three-spoke steering wheel through the top segment of which one can view the discreet 160 m.p.h. speedometer and matching rev. counter. There is a fuel gauge to the left, ominously recording the speed at which the 5.9-litre (101.6 × 90.93 mm.) Chrysler V8 consumes the contents of the Beaufighter's 21 gallon tank. Since the performance of this V8 is boosted by means of an exhaust driven Rotomaster turbocharger which has been specially adapted for this purpose by Bristol, the fuel gauge can register an alarming level of consumption. If one wishes to make use of this Bristol's sub-6 sec. zero to 60 m.p.h. capability allied to a top speed in the region of 140 m.p.h. then a sub-10 m.p.g. thirst can be expected. But during the course of our spell with the Beaufighter we recorded an average consumption of 16.5 m.p.g., which should be pretty representative of the sort of figure an average Bristol owner should be capable of attaining.

Between the speedometer and rev. counter are water temperature and oil pressure gauges plus a large red warning light to remind you when the handbrake is engaged. To the far right of the fascia is a vacuum gauge which indicates whether the turbocharger is operating or not, while just to the left of the steering wheel are the controls for the excellent, very refined air conditioning system which efficiently excludes all road fumes from the interior of the Beaufighter while at the same time providing a delightful freshening breeze in the middle of a hot summer day. In that connection there are also scuttle vents to help the flow of air through the car.

Bristol tradition continues with the spare wheel mounted within a locker in the bodywork behind the left front wheel, while the same aperture on the opposite side contains the battery, servos and electrical ancillaries including the fuse box. This leaves the deep boot helpfully uncluttered and capable of swallowing an enormous amount of luggage for the Grand Tour. We tested the Beaufighter equipped with its superbly trimmed, removable, solid rear roof section attached along with its glass roof panel. But these can be removed in consistently clement weather conditions, leaving the owner with a splendid open luxury four-seater complete with a deeply padded safety rollover bar. As another footnote to the amazing amount of detail thought which has gone into this Bristol, the inertia reel seat belts

CONTINUED ON PAGE 288

Above, Bristol's famous registration could be described as a very conservative label for this superb bespoke motor car. Below, the Chrysler V8's performance is further boosted by an exhaust driven turbocharger. No power output figures are quoted by the specialist British manufacturer!

EXCLUSIVE AND EXHILARATING

Bristol's new Brigand and Brittania models may well be the ideal answer for people fed up with run-of-the-mill Rolls-Royce or Aston Martins. Brian Bennett reports.

WHILE OTHER British manufacturers of exclusive, expensive cars have encountered severe difficulties, or even disappeared altogether, Bristol Cars have remained relatively untroubled, producing their highly individual and characterful products at a consistent rate of approximately two per week. This has ensured that Bristols are a rare sight on British roads — particularly as a large proportion go for export, anyway — but, more importantly, that Bristol have never suffered from large stocks of unsold cars.

The latest models to appear from the Filton-based firm, the Brigand and Brittania, continue the practice, started with the turbocharged Beaufighter, of naming their cars after aircraft produced by the original parent Bristol company. Nowadays Bristol Cars does not have any direct affiliation with the aircraft side but the techniques and practices of aircraft production are still evident in the design and construction of every Bristol, as is the influence of their enthusiastic chairman and managing director, Tony Crook, who is an ex-World War II pilot and still a regular flyer.

The Brigand and Brittania share what is virtually an all-new bodyshell. Only the roof, doors and front and rear screens are carried over from the superficially similar Bristol 603, which still continues in production. The most obvious difference is at the front, where the new cars have lower bonnets which curve down gracefully to a new radiator grille flanked by two large rectangular headlamps. To help in placing the Brigand and Brittania accurately on the road the outer edges of the front wings are kicked up slightly so that they are clearly visible from the driver's seat. At the rear there are large lamp clusters while at both ends there are new bumpers, similar in construction and appearance to those fitted to the Beaufighter.

The Brigand is powered by the turbocharged version of the 5.9-litre V8 Chrysler engine previously seen in the Beaufighter while the Brittania uses the normally aspirated version of the same engine. Like their counterparts at Aston Martin and Rolls-Royce, Bristol do not quote power and torque figures but they reckon that the Brittania should be capable of 140 mph while the Brigand's maximum speed is quoted as approximately 150 mph. Both cars use the well-proven Chrysler Torque-flite three-speed automatic transmission.

In other respects the Brigand and Brittania also follow traditional Bristol practice with just detail changes and modifications. They are built on a separate chassis which supports a steel substructure clothed in the aluminium body panels. Suspension is by unequal length wishbones at the front while at the rear is Bristol's own unique system of a live axle, located by a transverse Watt's linkage and a top link, with springing by longitudinal torsion bars. There is an anti-roll bar at the front and adjustable dampers all round (now Spax, rather than Koni, units) which can be set according to each owner's individual preferences.

Braking is all-disc with fully duplicated hydraulic circuits and separate servos for each circuit. The servos, along with the battery and other electrical equipment, are housed in a compartment in the off-side front wing, while the spare tyre is located in a matching compartment on the other side. Bristol continue to use a ZF power-assisted steering system, modified according to their own exacting requirements.

Apart from their power units, the Brigand and Brittania differ in only minor details. The Brigand has a modest power bulge in its bonnet — to accommodate the extra bulk of the turbocharged engine — and alloy wheels (manufactured by Wolfrace) shod with new 215/70 VR 15 Avon Turbospeed ACR18 tyres and fitted with the Avon safety bands which prevent the tyre coming off the wheel in the event of a puncture. The Brittania makes do with slightly narrower-rimmed steel wheels, also fitted with the Avon safety band, and the new 215/70 VR 15 tyres.

Both cars feature air conditioning (and also separate, comprehensive heating and ventilation systems), centralised door locking, electrically operated, and heated, door mirrors, leather upholstery, and electrically adjustable front seats. The Bristol Brittania costs £46,843.32 while the Brigand is now the flagship of the Bristol range, priced at £49,827.09.

Driving Impressions

Driving an exceptionally powerful car, costing more than £49,000, through London traffic might be considered rather an intimidating experience. In the Bristol Brigand, however, it proved to be an absolute doddle. For a start the driver's seat is adjustable in every possible direction (everything but rake with power assistance) to ensure a perfect, and commanding, driving position, from which you can take advantage of what must be the best all-round visibility available in this class of car thanks to very slim pillars and generous glazing.

Then, once on the move, the delightfully precise steering, with just enough weighting to provide some element of feel, and the absolute docility of the turbocharged V8 when pottering around at town speeds effectively displace any lingering apprehension. In fact its relatively modest dimensions (16ft 1in long but only 5ft 9in wide) are a significant advantage in town traffic, compared with a Rolls-Royce, for example, while the combination of that accurate steering and easily visible front wings make the Bristol easier to place and squeeze through tight gaps than many smaller cars.

Once we had emerged from the tight knot of traffic that generally surrounds Bristol's London premises in Kensington, however, it was possible to savour the other side of the Brigand's character. Transforming the Brigand from docile town car to true sporting thoroughbred (or "businessman's express" as Tony Crook might prefer to put it) requires just slightly more pressure from the right foot. The capable automatic transmission makes all the right decisions, generally imperceptibly, while the turbocharged engine responds without any trace of lag to push it very rapidly towards speeds well in excess of 100 mph.

In our road test of the Beaufighter back in January 1980 we recorded a 0-60 mph time of 6.7 sec and a 0-100 mph time of 17.6 sec. The more aerodynamic Brigand is likely to be, if anything, slightly quicker than this, giving Bristol two of the fastest full four-seater cars currently available. And a full four-seater the Brigand certainly is. Tony Crook's minimum requirement for any of his cars is that they can comfortably, and sumptuously, accommodate four six-footers *and* their luggage; this latter need being helped by the location of the spare tyre in the front wing.

Inside and outside the Brigand is finished to the very highest standards and, of course, it is comprehensively equipped. Worthy of mention, though, are the separate air conditioning, heating and ventilation systems. Each works very effectively and efficiently but the ventilation system is particularly comprehensive with outlets in the facia and the footwells, the latter vents being served by air ducted through the compartments in the front wings.

A fuller assessment of the Brigand's capabilities will have to wait until we can carry out a full road test — and that's something that *Motor*'s hardworked road test staff look forward to with eager anticipation.

BRISTOL BRIGAND

Exclusivity in extremis!

AN outing with a Bristol is like taking a trip back in a time capsule to a more leisured, high-quality way of life; not exactly 1930s, more the studied, unobtrusive good taste of the early 1950s when the rich were still rich, the workers were still workers and life followed a nice, predictable, well-ordered social pattern. Before any of MOTOR SPORT's readers start straining to hear Ivor Novello melodies in the air, and before Tony Crook at Bristol's picks up his phone and asks me why I'm comparing the latest turbocharged Bristol Brigand to something out of the 1950s, let me make it clear that (a) I'm now indulging in an ill-timed bout of misty-eyed nostalgia and (b) I'm not

referring to the engineering technology of the current Bristol cars.

What I *am* saying is the time has passed Bristol by in the most charming way possible. With an absurdly modest output of hand-crafted, high-quality cars, this specialist manufacturer contents itself to occupy an expensive, elite and exclusive *niche* in the high-performance market. "Britain's most exclusive car" proclaims a sign within the company's unostentatious Kensington showroom. A claim that can be made with some justification, we feel, because when we recently spent an enjoyable weekend with the Brigand, we did so in the knowledge that there were barely thirty similar examples of this particular moden anywhere else in the World. That's exclusivity!

Two years ago we enjoyed a test of the square-cut, impressive Bristol Beaufighter, a large drop-head coupé which combined considerable dignity with shattering performance. That recipe is continued with

the Brigand, although most people felt that the slightly softer, more rounded, lines of this latest machine to be more attractive than those of the Beaufighter.

Just to recap for those who may not know the admittedly well-recorded and documented history of this specialist manufacture, the Bristol Car concern was originally an offshoot of the Bristol Aeroplane Company. One of the pioneers of the aviation business, this was founded by Bristol businessman Sir George White back in 1910 and, during the Second World War, over 14,000 aircraft were built for military use, the majority of them being Blenheims (the first British aircraft to operate over enemy territory in 1939). At the end of the War the company found itself with an enormous surplus of engineering capacity, so some of this was turned over to manufacture of specialist cars. By 1956 the Bristol Aeroplane Company had been reorganised into three wholly owned entities: Bristol Aircraft Ltd, Bristol Engines Ltd, and Bristol Cars Ltd. At that point Bristol Cars passed into the ownership of another Sir George White (the grandson of the one who established the aircraft company in the first place) and former racing driver Tony Crook. Production of the cars continued at the firm's Filton factory, as it does to this day, and when Sir George retired in 1973, Tony Crook became Chairman and Managing Director.

Like all Bristol models, the £49,827 Brigand is built round a massively strong chassis of closed box welded steel construction with three cross members and stiff floorpans which are welded into the structure. By any modern-day standards, this gives the Brigand constructional integrity equal (some would say considerably better than) any monocoque structure from a mass manufacturer, and also contributes towards the Brigand's quoted weight of 3850 lb (1746 kg) — more than a ton and a half!

The body is a full four-seater, two-door

TYPICALLY BRISTOL: one of the marque's trademarks has long been the siting of the spare wheel in a separate compartment just behind the nearside front wheel.

saloon of welded steel construction incorporating aluminium alloy panelling. The wide-opening doors have burst-proof locks and a self-locking system — and feel as solid as the bare chassis frame obviously is! Front suspension is by means of unequal length wishbones in conjunction with coil springs, telescopic dampers while torsion bars and a Watts linkage are employed at the rear. Adjustable front and rear dampers are fitted, the steering is a power-assisted recirculatory ball system and self-adjusting Girling disc brakes are employed all round.

As on all the current Bristol range, Chrysler's 5.9-litre V8 engine (101.6 × 90.93 mm) powers the Brigand, in this case equipped with a Rotomaster turbocharger to further boost the "more than adequate" power output. Bristol decline to quote a figure for this unit's brake horsepower, taking a leaf out of Rolls-Royce's book in this respect, but as we said when testing the Beaufighter in 1981, it's quite sufficient to endow the car with a quite outstanding acceleration capability. This 90-degree V8 is equipped with specially developed camshafts, a four-barrel downdraught carburetter and employs electronic ignition. The engine's cooling capacity is 29 Imp pints (16.5 litres) and automatically operated twin electric fans assist engine cooling when required, there also being a manual over-ride switch to control these fans irrespective of engine speed.

Transmission is by means of a Chrysler Torqueflight transmission with torque converter, offering three forward speeds and reverse, with a conventional intermediate hold facility on first and second gears. The Brigand runs on tubeless Avon Turbospeed

THE Brigand interior (left) is an upper-crust mixture of the best hide upholstery, walnut fascia trim and quality carpeting. Right, the slightly "softened" rear end profile makes this large two-door saloon visually more attractive than the rather angular Beaufighter, the last Bristol to come our way.

ACR18 radials (215)70VR15) which incorporate the Avon safety bands to prevent the tyres coming off the Wolfrace-manufactured alloy wheel rims in the event of a puncture at speeds.

So far we have dealt with the Bristol company's background and the bland technical specification of the Brigand. None of this, however, can convey the atmosphere of well-insulated refinement that one experiences when one slips in behind the wheel of one of these bespoke motor cars. To start with, the Brigand's cabin is very high compared with those of most cars on the road today so, inevitably, one is imbued with a feeling of quiet dominance and superiority as you view the world across the seemingly endless bonnet. The Chrysler V8 isn't really quite in the same league for refinement and silence as the Mercedes-Benz V8 or the Jaguar V12, there being a perceptible amount of induction noise, particularly under hard acceleration,

but we're talking in terms of a fine distinction and, by the standards of most large cars, it is extremely refined.

Furthermore, the Brigand continues to startle the driver when one really begins to put one's foot down. It will roar from standstill to 60 mph in six seconds flat and to 80 mph in 10 sec. In terms of top speed, Bristol quotes 152 mph and, during our tests on a privately owned airport runway in East Anglia (taking a leaf out of Tony Crook's book — his cars' performance testing is done at Filton!) the ease with which the Brigand built up to an indicated 145 mph suggested to us that the quoted top speed might be a bit on the conservative side. Of course, harsh acceleration and sustained running at 100 mph-plus speeds will exact a dramatic toll on the Brigand's fuel consumption, but during the course of our three days with the car we averaged out at 17.8 mpg which, under the circumstances, is so outstanding that I had to check my mathematics three times before I was satisfied that my calculations were correct!

At these sort of speeds there is precious little in the way of wind noise and the Bristol Brigand is certainly a supremely relaxing machine to waft about the place at speeds in excess of 100 mph. Such performance would really only be appreciated on long trans-European tours in enlightened countries which enjoy de-restricted Motorway standard roads: even a passing acquaintance with a car such as the Bristol Brigand, endowed with such reserves of performance and handling, reminds one that modern-day technology can easily produce cars that are capable of exceeding the 70 mph limit with absolutely theoretical safety and security. If only most drivers were educated to the same sort of levels, our road safety statistics would make far less worrying reading. . .

Loping along at 100 mph, the Brigand's

Continued on page 316

NEW FROM BRISTOL...

Bristol Cars continue to succeed in their own quiet way, with a production rate of about two cars a week. New at the Show are two models, the Brigand and the Britannia, both based on considerably modified 603 chassis, with lower, sleeker bodies. The Britannia is powered by the normally-aspirated 5.9-litre V8, the Brigand (with a discreet bonnet bulge and alloy wheels, shown here) by the turbo engine of the Beaufighter.

BRISTOL BEAUFIGHTER

Ye Olde English (Turbocharged) Exotic Car

STORY & PHOTOS BY JOHN LAMM

IF YOU'D LIKE to buy a Bristol Beaufighter right now, the price is going to have to include plane fare to London plus the cost of a taxi ride to 368/370 Kensington High Street. This is the site of the only Bristol dealership in existence. With any luck, you'll even meet T. Anthony B. Crook, Bristol's Chairman and Managing Director, because his London office is just off the small 3-car showroom. He is an interesting, unusual man whose cars are likewise.

Though you may never have heard of Crook and his Bristols, be assured they are no fly-by-night organization. Crook, 57, moved from the RAF to the "motor industry" after World War II, and also right into racing. He first drove a BMW 328, then a 2.9-liter Alfa Romeo, various Frazer-Nashes (setting international speed records in one of them) and a very quick Cooper-Bristol in which he not only ran Formula 2 events, but also held the Shelsley Walsh hillclimb record for a time. Crook was obviously no dilettante driver. And he is also a good businessman, so when he retired from racing in 1955 after a very bad accident at Goodwood, he became a director of Bristol Cars.

At that point, Bristol had been building cars for nine years. It had also been constructing airplanes for 45 years, including many during WWII, and it was the excess capacity created when the war ended that drew Bristol to making automobiles. It was decided then to build a car based on the BMW 328. The new Bristol would use a development of the BMW's highly respected chassis with its independent front suspension, and BMW's highly regarded 2.0-liter 6-cylinder engine. Around this would be wrapped an aerodynamic body created in Bristol's wind tunnel. The company was obviously more than a little taken by the BMWs, because its first car, the 400, plus the subsequent 401 and 402 models, even had the BMW-style pair-of-kidneys grille.

In 1961, when the British aircraft industry was nationalized, the Bristol car division was sold off to Crook and Sir George White, grandson of the man who started Bristol in 1910. White retired in 1972 and Crook became head of Bristol Cars Ltd.

The goal of Bristol Cars has always been to build automobiles of quality. Even today you can click-shut the doors on the very first Bristol 400. That attention to quality has covered the 400 Series from the 400 through the 412 and with the 603. The numbering system, which is somewhat confusing, was replaced in 1982 with names from the aircraft company's history—Beaufighter, Brigand and Brittania are now used for the three models.

So why are Bristol cars such a mystery? First of all, they are rare cars, with only around 6000 having been built in the company's history and the present production rate is 150 per year. Your chances of seeing a Bristol on the road in England are about the same as seeing an Avanti in the U.S.

Secondly, Bristol does little to draw attention to itself. Crook's advertising budget for 1983 was all of $3500, the company depending instead on very faithful owners and word-of-mouth to sell cars. It appears to work. Crook tells of the 73-year-old English woman who lived in Switzerland but was on a trip to England when she asked a taxi driver in London what was the best British car. He told her it was a Bristol and at her request took her to Kensington High Street. Once there, she bought a pair of the cars, one for herself and one for her son. Because of her age she requested immediate delivery instead of the usual 2-month wait.

Bristol's factory, which is located in Filton near, quite appropriately, Bristol, England, adds to the car's mysterious image. Though a separate entity for 23 years, Bristol Cars still shares factory space with the airplane company in the same area where the Concordes were once made; the two companies even share some office personnel. Because of the tight security around the aircraft operations, it's rare for any outsider to see Bristol cars being built.

So you'll have to go to 368/370 Kensington High Street, where you'll likely find two new Bristols and one used model on display. Though there are the three current models, they are in two body styles. One is the Britannia/Brigand fastback, the major difference being whether the car has a normal Chrysler V-8 (Britannia) or the turbocharged version (Brigand). The car we are most interested in is the Zagato-designed Beaufighter, which very definitely has the turbo engine.

Incidentally, that third, used Bristol in the showroom could be any of the past models. When I visited there, the board that lists available used models included, among others, a 1953 403 and a 1954 404. And you can be certain the cars are well kept, because Bristol can still supply a part or a body panel for any car it has built. I stopped in at the company's Chiswick repair building and even saw an AC-Bristol having its engine rebuilt. Next to it was a Frazer-Nash and a few rows back was a Bristol 450, a roadster remnant of the 3-car team of very aerodynamic Bristol coupes that won the 2.0-liter class at Le Mans in 1954.

To keep that reputation for quality intact, Bristol insists on basing its cars on a separate frame/body design. Crook also believes there's added structural safety in this system, pointing out that only a few people have died in Bristols, including one who went off a cliff and another who was hit by a 6-ton truck.

Bristol makes the frames itself, along with all the metal suspension pieces except the springs and Girling shocks. These pieces include the unequal-length A-arms and anti-roll bar that go into the coil-spring front suspension, and the top links and Watts linkage that help make up the torsion bar-spring rear suspension. Even the casing for the rear live axle is Bristol made, then fitted with a Salisbury ring and pinion. The brakes are Girling discs at each wheel.

Bristol bodies are of hand-formed aluminum panels, all done at the factory. The design still has the spare tire in a compartment behind the left front tire. The battery, brake servos and fuse panel are in a similar

compartment on the right side.

Most Americans remember Bristol for its engines, as used in the ACs and the Bertone-designed Arnolt-Bristols. Conversely, the major component of the cars that is not made by Bristol these days is the engine, and it is American: a 360-cu-in. Chrysler V-8. The powerplant is shipped from the States complete with a 3-speed TorqueFlite automatic transmission, which is really the reason Bristol uses the V-8.

In the late Fifties, Bristol was developing its own all-aluminum 3.7-liter inline-6 to replace the old BMW-based engine. This change was being made because Bristol customers were demanding more speed and luxury, and the natural extension of this was to also use an automatic transmission. When Bristol asked Chrysler to send one along for evaluation, the gearbox arrived already coupled to a V-8. Bristol decided to put the combination on the test rig and came away as impressed with the engine as with the transmission. They still are and the aluminum six is just a dusty memory.

Bristol decided a few years ago that its cars needed more horsepower to keep up with the likes of Mercedes-Benz, Jaguar and, by all means, the Bentley Mulsanne. So Bristol wanted to turbocharge the V-8. True to the somewhat eccentric nature of its cars, Bristol didn't just order up the usual KKK or Garrett AiResearch turbo, but opted instead for another American design, the unusual Roto-Master Rotocharger.

Basically the Rotocharger works like other turbo systems, except that located between the draw-through carburetor and intake manifold is a pair of "priority" valves. Under light load the air/fuel mixture is drawn in past the open valves and into the manifold, bypassing the turbo. As load increases, air is drawn off into the turbo system ahead of the priority valves, pressurized, and then mixed with the "normal" mixture on the manifold side of the priority valves. Under heavy load, the pressurized charge has picked up enough boost that it shuts the priority valve from the manifold side, routing all the incoming mixture through the turbo.

Tony Crook won't tell us the horsepower of his engines, but it's enough. At light and medium throttle the performance of the Beaufighter is about what you'd expect from a 360-cu-in. V-8 with minimal European emission equipment having to move about 3800 lb along . . . quick and punchy, torquey and no fuss. Stomp on the throttle and

it s another story. Boost buildup and transmission kickdown have been nicely matched to give the Bristol stand-up-and-roar acceleration. From rest that means you get to 60 mph in 6.7 seconds, almost a half-second quicker than the more stately Bentley Mulsanne. According to *Autocar* magazine in England, that puts the Bristol in a league with the European Porsche 928S and Mercedes-Benz 500SE. Just as impressive are the Beaufighter's intermediate times—the ones that really count on the road—such as 30–50 mph in 2.5 sec or 40–60 in 2.9 sec. And still the top speed is around 140 mph.

The Bristol takes its sudden surge of power in what would best be described as a proper and stately manner. I didn't have the chance to really stretch the car's capabilities, but it coped calmly and steadily with its abundance of horsepower, becoming neither twitchy nor uncomfortable. As you might imagine, the ride is not pillow-soft, but firm, though neither rough nor jerky.

Crook insists that his cars should accommodate four adults and a healthy complement of luggage. This, plus the storage area behind the front wheels, says something about why the Beaufighter looks the way it does, Zagato having to work with those difficult requirements. One would never call the Beaufighter beautiful. And yet there are people who feel anything functional is beautiful. There is, in fact, enough room for those four adults and they can take along 22.0 cu ft of baggage, which almost puts the Beaufighter in the station wagon category.

The passenger compartment is done in what you might call old English stately. Walnut stretches the width of the dashboard, with a complete assortment of ye olde English gauges. There's thick-pile carpet underfoot. The seats are

tall, leather-covered and feel capable of carrying you long distances without discomfort. When the weather is foul all this is covered by a 2-piece top, with a fold-down rear portion and a lift-out front section—much the same as the Lancia Zagato sold here several years ago. In place it's a nicely finished roof inside and out, though it isn't what you'd call a casual softtop, and even Bristol says it "adapts to a convertible in summer."

In America, where you would avoid the horrendous taxes the British suffer, a Beaufighter would cost you around $60,000. And you may be able to do that sometime next year. Andrew DeSalvo of North Salem, New York is now attempting to set up a U.S. distribution network for Bristol and aiming to have the car available for sale late in 1985. That would, of course, save you the cost of a journey to 368/370 Kensington High Street, but I'd still recommend the trip for a Bristol owner, just for the fun of it. ◉

EUROPEAN SPECIFICATIONS

GENERAL

Curb weight, lb/kg	3850	1746
Wheelbase, in./mm	114.0	2900
Track, front/rear	54.5/55.5	1380/1409
Length	194.5	4900
Width	69.5	1770
Height	56.5	1440
Fuel capacity, U.S. gal./liters	21.6	82

ENGINE

Type	turbocharged ohv V-8
Bore x stroke, in./mm	4.00 x 3.58 .... 101.6 x 90.9
Displacement, cu in./cc	360 5900
Compression ratio	8.0:1
Bhp @ rpm, DIN/kW	NA .... NA
Torque @ rpm, lb-ft/Nm	NA .... NA
Carburetion	one Carter (4V)

DRIVETRAIN

Transmission	3-sp automatic
Gear ratios: 3rd (1.00)	3.06:1
2nd (1.45)	4.44:1
1st (2.45)	7.50:1
Final drive ratio	3.06:1

CHASSIS & BODY

Layout	front engine/rear drive
Brake system	10.9-in. (277-mm) discs front, 10.6-in. (271-mm) discs rear; vacuum assisted
Wheels	cast alloy, 15 x 6
Tires	Avon, 225/70VR-15
Steering type	recirculating ball, power assisted
Turns, lock-to-lock	NA
Suspension, front/rear: unequal-length A-arms, coil springs, tube shocks, anti-roll bar/live axle, Watts linkage, torsion bars, tube shocks anti-roll bar	

The skinny Michelins didn't stand a chance. The pained screech of rubber on asphalt was far too brief to have the slightest chance of arresting the progress of the slightly tatty Renault 5. Plastic Renault bumper met plastic Peugeot bumper, metal bonnet met metal tailgate with that all-too familiar cacophony of twisting, bending bodywork played to the accompaniment of tinkling glass.

It's not every day you see the classic, flowing lines of a Bristol, especially one sweeping serenely through the circulating mayhem around the Arc de Triomphe. It was all too much for

RU

What better mode of tra
Howard Walker samples th

the Renault driver to take-in in just one glance. The prolonged stare no doubt cost him a nose job and his no-claims bonus.

Then again, I suppose it didn't help that the Bristol's occupants were both sporting full naval attire; the driver wearing a full sea-dog beard and an inflatable plastic parrot on his shoulder, his passenger wearing a diver's face mask.

It was the British at their most eccentric, making a foray deep into France to deliver the finest Lamberhursts and Cuckmeres to Paris. It was *Motor*'s Great English Wine Run, the annual extravaganza that has now become the benchmark for true-Brit lunacy.

I mean, at what other event in the social calendar do you see a

BRITANNIA

...could you have to transport English wine to France than a Bristol?
...ts of the latest Bristol Britannia on Motor's Great English Wine Run

Dorset farmer dressed-up in John Bull outfit driving a 26-year-old tractor and trailer full of manure all the way to Paris; or St Trinian schoolgirls aboard a London bus driving through the Bois de Boulogne?

Tony Crook, erstwhile racing driver, World War 2 pilot and chairman of Bristol Cars was surprisingly enthusiastic at our suggestion that *Motor* should pilot one of his cars to Paris. It has been around four years since anyone from the motoring press had prised a car from him – he simply became tired of hacks referring to his products as "old-fashioned"

"They're not old-fashioned, they're just different. If we changed the shape, our cars would simply look like everyone

else's," he says. "Our customers want something entirely different, but they're not flamboyant; they don't want to display their wealth."

Not that Mr Crook is short of customers willing to hand over upwards of £52,800 for the exclusivity of owning one of the three cars his Filton company builds each week. He never discloses the names of customers, that would be indiscreet, but they include pop tycoon Richard Branson, Environment Minister William Waldegrave, composer Geoffrey Burgon and Lord Kings Norton, Chancellor of the Cranfield Institute of

Walnut facia in front of you (above) and posh leather armchairs to sink into

How to design a Bristol: suspend spare wheel at wheel arch height and build car around it

Technology.

A Britannia was to be put at our disposal – that's the basic model in the three-car range, though "basic" hardly describes this £52,815.85 leather and walnut-clad Grand Tourer. Imagine a more sporting, more exclusive Rolls-Royce and you'd be close to summing up a Bristol.

Bristol's demonstration cars have to earn their keep, so MPH 100 doubles up as a development car, and that's why it is three years old and has currently clocked up just over 30,000 miles – a far cry from the big car makers who swop their demo cars every three months or so.

The Britannia and its turbocharged brother, the Brigand, in effect replaced the well-respected 603 towards the end of 1982. Though the styling was largely unchanged, the bodyshell was virtually all-new with only the roof, doors and front and rear screens carried over. The well-proven construction formula, though, remained the same, with the new cars being built on a massive separate chassis which supports a steel substructure clothed in aluminium body panels.

And each car is very much hand-built, taking between 16 and 20 weeks to craft with no less than 1200 welds painstakingly carried out by the Filton workforce, many of whom have been with the company for

more than 20 years. Robots are unlikely to be part of the Bristol production line for at least the foreseeable future.

While the Britannia may appear to be the ultimate True Brit, the heart of the car actually comes from Detroit. The 5.9-litre V8 and three-speed Torqueflite automatic transmission are straight off the Chrysler production line though modifications are made to the camshaft, carburetter and ignition settings to increase the power. But like Rolls-Royce and Aston Martin, Bristol keep their power and torque figures close to their chest.

Crook is unconcerned at the Detroit connection, pointing to Rover who for so long used the Buick-derived 3.5-litre V8 without criticism. "Our cars are designed for ease of maintenance – we don't have a vast dealer network all over the world, so we have to use components that can be serviced or repaired by the average mechanic. And because the Chrysler engine is so lazy and unstressed, we expect it to be able to last for at least 200,000 miles without serious repair."

The same goes for the suspension; double wishbones, coil springs and an anti-roll bar at the front and a live axle at the rear, albeit a very sophisticated and well-located one. Bought-in components include the GKN-made rear axle, the ZF power steering and the Spax dampers,

though Crook stresses that a great deal of Bristol input is made to the component makers to ensure the parts are right.

"While we build our cars so that they can be serviced by any competent mechanic, we do like to see owners at our service centre in London. And if they come to us, owners know they are getting experience; our junior mechanic has been with us 12 years and the senior fitter 40 years," says Crook.

We reached the heavily fortified Michelham Priory in deepest Sussex just as the September sun was piercing its warming rays through the early morning mist. Here, more than 80 teams carrying around 200 Win Run entrants were lined up ready for the off. "Land of Hope and Glory" was already playing on the "Invade and Conquer France" Society's wind-up gramophone while the "Trucking Falcon and Firkin" pub, mounted on the back of a lorry, was already delivering its first pint.

Our departure time was 8.15 am, which left us just 120 minutes to travel the 60-odd miles from Alfriston to Dover to catch the 10.30 Townsend ferry. Not a demanding task, you may think, but the A27 coast road that we had to use wound its way through Eastbourne, Hastings, Rye and Folkestone before taking us to Dover – and everyone knows that the A27 carries the highest percentage of Morris Minors, Austin A40s

and Reliant Robins in the country.

The flag dropped and MPH 100 burbled its way out of the Priory and on to country roads. The popular image of a Bristol is one of relaxed, restrained cruising – after all 50 per cent of the cars sold last year went to owners who had their own chauffeur. But squeeze the throttle and the Britannia surges away with all the punch of a thoroughbred.

When pressed hard, the Chrysler V8 isn't really in the same league for refinement and silence as, say, a Jaguar V12 or a Mercedes V8, but nevertheless it is muted by the standards of most large executive saloons. Extend the revs past the 5000 rpm mark and the lazy V8 retains its composure, remaining surprisingly smooth and sweet, but the engine note is short on character, somehow betraying its parentage.

Working the engine hard doesn't help the Torqueflite transmission either, for under hard acceleration, the 'box thumps abruptly from one ratio to the next. Accelerate hard in top and again the Bristol wins no prizes for the smoothness of its kickdown, being well short of the standard now being achieved by Mercedes and their silky-smooth four-speed auto.

But drive the Bristol in a style which befits it, and it is transformed into a rich, fluid,

milky-smooth gentleman's sporting carriage. Keep the throttle pedal out of the deep pile carpet and the engine is supremely quiet, the gearchanges nigh-on imperceptible. This is no Escort XR3, and should not be driven like one.

Before long we had caught up with the "Exuberant English" – alias the Holtons of Stony Stratford – in their Union Jack-clad Range Rover. Their Phantom II Roller had blown a head gasket on the way down and had to be dumped unceremoniously in a *Happy Eater* car park. Unfortunately someone had forgotten the road map, so as the Bristol followed the route to Dover, the Range Rover headed off into deepest Sussex.

Time was getting tight and with visions of missing the 10.30 ferry, we decided it was time to press on. The Britannia responded. On some of the long, fast straights between Hastings and Rye, the car would sit comfortably well in excess of the legal limit with not a whisper of wind noise, or roar of Chrysler at work.

The straights on that stretch of A27 are linked by a series of pinch-tight bends that put great demands on a car's braking and handling capabilities. For a car that appears so upright, so dignified to the point of almost being haughty, the Britannia coped well. There's a fair bit of body roll as the car settles into a bend but at no time do you get the impression that the Bristol's fat 215-section Avons will lose their grip.

Less impressive was the ZF steering, which was horribly light and vague around the straight-ahead position at low speed and far too sensitive as the pace quickened. At speeds of around 70 mph on A-roads, the car demanded a very careful touch on the helm to keep the car on the straight and narrow. Later, Tony Crook did point out that his engineers had been experimenting with different valving in the power assistance system and the one fitted gave the highest amount of assistance available.

I was also a bit disappointed with the way the car almost steered itself at the back end when pressing on through a bend, indicating that the bushes in the rear suspension had gone soft or worn out. There were also numerous clonks and groans from the rear suggesting,

perhaps, that after three years, it was time this demonstrator packed up giving demonstrations

But it was surprising just how quickly the Britannia would sweep through a bend, that would leave a new Rolls or even the more sporting Bentley Mulsanne Turbo scrabbling for grip. And for the more sporting Bristol driver, the Britannia's dampers can be adjusted to provide a much firmer, less wallowy ride. Winding the dampers up a couple of clicks would, I feel, have reduced the slight floating on undulations and the slight lurching when transferring from one lock to another.

Having to brake very hard from quite high speed did give the Britannia's all-disc set-up quite a hard time – and it showed. After the third bend, very heavy pedal pressures were needed to slow the 3850 lb (1746 kg) monster down, accompanied by the familiar rumbling and grumbling from all four corners of the car.

The hard driving paid off; we swept into Dover docks at exactly 10.10 am and in tolerable time to join the queue of fellow wine runners destined for *Gay Paris*. The man from TVS television asked why news editor Frater and I were dressed up as naval officers. Simple, we replied, pointing to the car. "This is a Bristol Britannia and Britannia rules the waves – and the roads."

Seventy-five minutes, after we left Dover, *Pride of Free Enterprise* was off-loading us in Calais. We were well on time; now we could sit back, relax and enjoy the Britannia's high-speed motorway cruising ability.

The Britannia is certainly not a short car – at 4.91m (16ft 9in), it's about the same length as a Jaguar XJS. But at a shade over 1.77m (5ft 9in) wide, it's about the narrowest true luxury car you can get. And driving in town, you notice the difference when you start squeezing through gaps. No problem.

The car's wieldiness is increased by the superb visibility the driver gets from his commanding driving seat. Bristol's stylists even designed-in slight lips on the edges of the front wings to act as aiming points for the driver. In addition, the windows are big, the waistline low and the roof pillars surprising slim.

Inside, the seats can't really be described as seats; they're more like the soft leather armchairs you find at posh gentlemen's clubs. The leather work is simply superb and very expensive to get right – Bristol reckons it costs the company a staggering £1100 for the leather they use in one car. And of course there is electrical adjustment in virtually every direction, the controls being mounted on the side of the transmission tunnel. Few drivers would find it difficult to obtain a superb, commanding driving position behind the Bristol's thin-rimmed steering wheel.

Unfortunately, I can't say I'm a great fan of the Britannia's instrumentation. Yes, the walnut dash is superb and the main instruments are very easy to read, but that said, nearly every switch seems to have been thrown on to the facia in a hapazard manner without much consideration for ergonomics. But Tony Crook argues that they are sited and shaped on aircraft

principles where touch is more important than looks. So, the little joystick and two toggle switches that adjust the seat are on the *side* of the console. Once you know where they are the action is natural.

Accommodation inside the car is one of the Bristol's strong points. There's room for four six-foot tall occupants in great comfort, with the rear seats being particularly spacious. With only two doors, getting into the back is certainly not as easy as with a four-door, but that said the doors are enormous and open wide to make access to the back as easy as possible.

One of the Bristol idiosyncrasies is still the stowage of the spare wheel and jack and battery in the front wheelarches. The great benefit of this is that it allows the car to have an enormous boot that's unclattered with spare tyre and battery. It also means that if you do have a puncture and the boot is loaded, there's no need to empty the contents of the boot on the side of the road.

On the *autoroute*, the Britannia was in its element, gliding serenely at a steady 100 mph without the slightest strain on driver or passenger (who was by now fast asleep). Air conditioning was fitted to the car, but the heating and ventilation system is so effective that there hardly seemed any point in using it.

Two and a bit hours later the Bristol was scything through the traffic on the *Périphérique*, *en route* to the finishing yet leisurely run; we had broken no speed records and with the car averaging 15.3 mpg, it hadn't broken the bank either. Bristol don't provide performance figures, but the Britannia should be good for 130 mph-plus.

It would have been interesting to have done the run in a new Britannia, for after all, MPH 100 was getting on a bit. Had the steering been fitted with the right valve to give more feel and had the sloppiness of the rear axle been sorted out, the Bristol would, I'm sure, be a different car.

But I can certainly see the appeal, for there is something very special about the Britannia; whether it is the exclusivity, the hand-crafted bespoke nature of the car, or the subtle, dignified lines, I'm not sure. For the well-heeled enthusiastic driver with absolutely nothing to prove, there is probably nothing else that comes close. [M]

CONTINUED FROM PAGE 135

recorder fell off the speedometer. The demisters, heater and screen-wipers worked admirably under these conditions. The good tone of the H.M.V. radio is relayed from inbuilt speakers in roof and rear window shelf — one merit of which could be that this should dissuade music-loving rear-seat occupants from piling things up until the driver is deprived of rear-vision! It was still possible to make some use of the overdrive, which can be engaged satisfactorily at a mere 40 m.p.h., and that morning had had another demonstration of its value, for on Essolube the Bristol requires some 20 miles' driving before the oil temperature becomes normal, before which 2,500 r.p.m. should not be exceeded—with overdrive engaged it was possible to proceed at 65 m.p.h. without exceeding this engine speed.

As we entered London and drove to the weighbridge to check the Bristol's weight the fog arrived in full measure, so that a normal hour's run home in another car took four times as long and the English Lakes seemed more remote than ever.

Having on previous occasions published a full road-test report on a Bristol 402, an account of a journey to Barcelona in a 403, and a story on a fast drive to John o' Groats in a 404, there remains little to add.

The 100-B engine is a development of that used in the pre-war German 85-b.h.p. B.M.W. 328, with overhead valves inclined at 80 deg. and operated by cross push-rod valve gear and, using triple Solex downdraught carburetters, it develops 105 b.h.p. at 5,000 r.p.m. on the comparatively high compression-ratio of 8.5 to 1. The crankshaft runs in four bearings and is balanced statically and dynamically, while it has a viscous torsional vibration damper. The forged-steel connecting-rods have an internal oil-feed to the gudgeon-pins and the pistons are of diamond-turned forged aluminium alloy. The cylinder head is of light alloy with inserted centrifugally cast austenitic steel valve seats and bronze sparking-plug inserts. The cast-iron cylinder block has Brivadium high-nickel-content-alloy steel dry liners, the chain-driven camshaft runs in four bearings, the thermostatically-controlled pump cooling system circulates 21 pints of water, and the lubrication system uses 12 pints of oil, cir-culating through a full-flow filter. Two three-branch exhaust systems leave the engine on the off side.

THE BRISTOL 405 SALOON

Engine : Six cylinders, 66 by 96 mm. (1,971 c.c.). Cross-push-rod inclined o.h. valves. 8.5 to 1 compression-ratio; 105 b.h.p. at 5,000 r.p.m.

Gear ratios : First, 15.24 to 1; second, 7.71 to 1; third, 5.46 to 1; top, 4.22 to 1; overdrive, 3.28 to 1.

Tyres : 5.75 by 16 Michelin SDS on bolt-on steel disc wheels.

Weight : 1 ton 5 cwt. 7 lb. (ready for the road, without occupants, but with approximately one gallon of petrol).

Steering ratio : Three turns, lock-to-lock.

Fuel capacity : 16 gallons (two gallons in reserve). Range approximately 336 miles.

Wheelbase : 9 ft. 6 in.

Dimensions : 15 ft. 9¼ in. by 5 ft. 8 in. by 4 ft. 9½ in. (high).

Price : £2,390 (£3,586 7s. 0d. with purchase tax).

Makers : Bristol Cars Limited, Bristol, Somerset.

The chassis frame is fabricated from sheet steel, the box-section main members being 6½ in. deep. Front suspension is by transverse leaf-spring and wishbones, rear suspension by torsion-bars. The rear axle has a matched crown-wheel and pinion, and the semi-floating axle-shafts are micro-finished at the registers for the oil seals.

The Bristol 405 is very largely a hand-assembled car; available in saloon and convertible forms, beautifully made and finished, and is, as you have seen, notably pleasant to drive, endowed with well-appointed luxury equipment, and providing high performance for a commendable economy of fuel. If you have £3,600 to spare, this fine British car deserves close consideration and if, in addition to the qualities and amenities described, you crave an exclusive car, there you are—in all those miles we didn't encounter another Bristol !—W. B.

CONTINUED FROM PAGE 199

In theory the idea is unattractive to the true blue enthusiast, especially since the Chrysler setup, unlike several other Detroit transmissions cur-rently in use in European cars, allows almost no effective driver control. If you use the buttons for acceleration you're just wasting time; the box will panic out of any selected indirect range at anything up to 5100 rpm (maker's red line) depen-ding on setting which is where it will change in drive range anyway on the same setting provided you keep the throttle pedal floored. About the only place it can pay to use the manual control is on a long climb, as an anti hunt aid, or perhaps on a long, sharp descent.

A half-hour run over mixed roads in a 407 did show us, though, that the automatic box has more possibilities in a purely sporting European chassis than you might imagine. Torque-flite is acknow-ledged everywhere to be one of the most efficient of all such systems, and certainly its ability to snap through from one range to the next on full throttle without marking time gives it a sporting appeal that is absent elsewhere. Only a very slick hand on a very good gearshift could make a faster change. As for starting from rest, remember that the advantage of a manual box all but disappears with a really powerful car because of the wheel-spin/clutchslip problem; while the keen man is sitting still in first gear burning rubber, his lazy pal is halfway down the strip with his torque converter cannily keeping the balance between power and adhesion. Actual experience, as repor-ted in another issue, with an automatic Lotus Elite has already convinced us that there is no danger in automatic motoring on the limit provided the box is a really good one. And disc brakes, of course, remove the old objection about the in-creased chances of fade.

The Zagato-Bristol's panelling is really beauti-fully finished, and its lines are as fine as those of any current production Grand Turismo car in the world. All the usual cunning Zagato touches are there: The bonnet rises almost imperceptibly towards its trailing edge to clear the top of the carburettor without a bulge, leaving a gap that serves to spill hot air on the screen for defrosting in winter, and at the same time allowing a really low overall profile. Neat alloy ledges along the tops of the side windows double as rain shields and unobstrusive roof gutters. The back window kicks up in the middle, leaving room for a deeper-

than-usual boot lid so that the hinges can be kept clear of the luggage entry. And so on — an exer-cise in originality, without gimmicks.

Driving position is first class. The twin hide-up-holstered seats are scanty but comfortable, al-though they offer little sideways support. The wood-rim Nardi wheel lies high and square ahead, with beyond it a nicely shaped console housing speedo, tach and five minor dials as well as all the detail controls except the paired knobs for the heating system, which dominate the dash centre. The transmission buttons run along underneath the heater knobs; they light up from inside at night. The entire panel is finished in non-reflect-ing crackle enamel.

The cockpit is not sparsely furnished. The floor has a thick carpet, and both the wide doors get armrests and a pair of map pockets — one for the front and one for the pygmies in the back. The headlining is black leather. A small boot in the tail communicates direct with the cockpit, al-though a piece of carpet will clip neatly over the gap. Because the carpet hardly makes an adequate backrest for the tiny but usable occasional seats, each has a padded rest with hinges which folds out of the well that forms its cushion.

Visibility from inside is good, although the dip-ping mirror gets in the way a little and the top corners of the screen are perhaps a shade low for a tall driver. The prototype lacked headroom for anyone over six feet, so Zagato has agreed that future cars should get an extra inch or so in the roof.

Production will depend on demand. At present Zagato has a stock of chassis, and Anthony Crook has merely to cable him when an order comes in. Delivery day works out about 10 weeks after that, in London, where each car is checked on arrival by air from Milan. For when the stockpile in Italy runs out, Crook has an arrangement with Silver City Airways to fly out replenishment at short notice.

And that's the Zagato-Bristol V8. A look at the photographs will tell you more than words can about its superb lines. A couple of simple calcula-tions will convince you that it ought to move. Now, with looks, performance and a price that is far from unreasonable, it seems Bristol is back on the sporting scene with a vengeance. Certainly its hard to think of a more desirable piece of personal transport. ●

There is a magnificent spread of instruments, the main gauges being set into a separate binnacle immediately in front of the driver. The Bristol certainly has one of the best laid-out fascias in the business.

The large individual front seats are comfortable although not very deeply dished for support and they are matched by an equally generous car bench seat.

Bristol makes only a two-door car, because the company feels that with the present concept, four doors would have to be too small for comfort. And certainly with the big openings and the tilting front seats, access to the back is excellent.

The first Chrysler engine fitted to a Bristol was rather special in having a special high-lift camshaft and non-hydraulic tappets as the firm thought its customers would value something "extra".

However, with the adoption of the bigger 6.3 litre engine in 1969, these features were dropped, the firm considering that the hydraulic tappets were quieter and more maintenance-free anyway.

My first impression on driving the new 411 was one of utter smoothness and quietness. Despite traversing some fairly rough sections of bitumen, the car's suspension could scarcely be heard operating and bumps were barely felt.

Although having plenty of home comforts, modern-day Bristols have not forsaken enthusiast drivers when it comes to handling and ride. Unequal length wishbones are fitted at the front while the back suspension is by torsion bar springs with a Watts linkage. The rear suspension is also self-levelling, and there are adjustable dampers on all wheels, operated from a cabin control.

Certainly the Bristol is quieter than its nearest British equivalent — the Jensen. It is faster, too. The Bristol is capable of 138 mph with 143 mph available at 5500 rpm one-way. This is several mph better than the Jensen, which can probably be put down to the Bristol's smaller frontal area, as the cars are identical in engine and transmission.

Acceleration from all speeds is impressive, but quite undramatic. Zero to 100 mph is possible in under 19 seconds.

The ZF power steering system, as fitted to Aston Martins, is standard and is very good, with quite a lot of "feel" even at over 100 mph when it is needed most. Four big disc brakes provide braking to match.

Around town the 411 is completely docile. It has an excellent turning circle for its size and good ventilation, but strangely at 7536 pounds (about $24,000 by the time it reaches us), neither a radio nor air conditioning are included, although both are available as options.

But there are the other Bristol benefits, one of them being a large and very usable boot.

This has been made possible by moving the big 205-15 spare wheel into the rear section of the left hand front mudguard and the power brake servo and battery live in the other mudguard. Both are easily reached by a lift-up panel unlocked with an Allen key kept in a little holster in the cockpit.

Bristol's stated aim is to produce a car of the highest quality with considerable strength, performance and road-holding, capable of carrying four six footers and their luggage in real comfort.

There are enough people in Britain looking for that formula to assure the future of the marque but the aerodynamic aircraft principles used on the first Bristols have given away to a conservative in-breeding.　　　　　　*

Even a Bristol has to suffer the indignity of a barrier crash test. After 30 mph impact the windscreen is still in place and the steering wheel has moved back only 0.9 inches.

BRISTOL BEAUFIGHTER

attach to a runner on the floor which slides forward to allow unimpeded access for the rear seat passengers. Tony Crook sadly confesses that he omitted to patent this clever idea which is now being copied by some other manufacturers.

It's now more than twenty years since Bristol first made contact with Chrysler with a view to engine supply and the relationship has prospered, even though Tony Crook's company uses a very small number of their V8s by the standards of a volume car manufacturer. Interestingly, Bristol was in the process of completing development work on a 3.9-litre d.o.h.c. six-cylinder engine in 1960 and they originally contacted Chrysler to examine the possibility of arranging a supply of their automatic gearboxes. The "sample" gearbox arrived at Bristols complete with V8 engine attached and the decision was taken to experiment with a Chrysler engine installation. From that chance beginning arose the arrangement whereby Chrysler supplied engines for the exclusive coupés from Filton; the six-cylinder engine development was cast aside and they've never looked back from that moment onwards!

Bristol don't talk about vulgar matters such as power outputs. Suffice to say that, bearing in mind its previously mentioned 0-60 m.p.h. time, one can regard the figure as "adequate". The engine is fitted with electronic ignition and cooled by two automatically operated electric fans, this system incorporating a manual over-ride switch

which can operate these fans irrespective of engine speed.

Fire up the Bristol Beaufighter and all you hear is a subdued, muted, distant roar. The three forward speed automatic transmission functions without any snatch, pause or unruly hiccup, even when revving the engine hard. The car's ability between 60 and 90 m.p.h. is truly shattering, making it a very safe car inasmuch as it permits overtaking manoeuvres to be completed without any drama, even on short straights. Front suspension is by means of unequal lenth wishbones with coil springs, telescopic dampers and a torsional anti-roll bar while torsion bars are used at the rear in conjunction with a Watts linkage and telescopic dampers. Initially one might feel the ride a trifle soft, but the steering is so pleasantly positive and well-geared that it doesn't take long to discover that the Bristol may roll a fair deal, but its Avon 225-70 VR 15 radials stay in firm and comforting contact with the road surface. In the pouring rain it's as well to take things relatively gently, although it can be quite an illuminating experience when you suddenly detect a trace of wheelspin in a straight line as the gearbox changes from second to third in such conditions!

With self-adjusting servo-assisted Girling disc brakes on all four wheels, the Beaufighter stops with a reassuring feel. But you can't expect a magical response from just brushing the brake pedal when a car weighing the best part of two tons is well under way. Although we found the brakes effective and fade-free, we were surprised

at the amount of pedal effort required when it's necessary to pull up suddenly.

A high level of auxiliary equipment includes four halogen headlamps, parking lights, twin automatic reversing lights, rearguard fog lamps and twin windtone horns. The windscreen wipers operate in three positions: normal, fast and intermittent; there is a very high quality push button radio / cassette player, an electrical aerial and central locking for the two large doors.

If ever a car offers therapeutic value, then it's this Bristol Beaufighter. After a long day in a London boardroom, it's easy to imagine a Managing Director unwinding behind the wheel of this splendid machine during his drive home. In town traffic it's a bit of a worry because it's so large and so very expensive. But once on the open road, it covers the ground in splendid fashion; unobtrusively, comfortably and remarkably quickly. It is beautifully finished, immaculately trimmed and extraordinarily quiet. For those who love taut-handling Porsches, romantic Ferraris or briskly efficient Mercedes-Benz, the Bristol Beaufighter may have an attraction that is elusive to see. But to judge by the number of owners who have changed from these marques to become Bristol owners over the years, the evidence seems clear. Once you've been bitten by the Bristol bug, it is hard to shake off. If you can afford it, of course! To become the owner of a Bristol Beaufighter will leave you just enough change out of £40,000 to purchase a year's road fund tax. If you've got that sort of money, it would be well spent thus. — A.H.

BRISTOL CARS

THE BEAUFIGHTER
TURBOCHARGED CONVERTIBLE

GENERAL SPECIFICATION

CHASSIS – Closed box section welded steel construction with three cross members plus stiff floor pans forming a very robust structure affording great protective strength. Many Bristol owners have owed their lives to this structure and few, if any, other cars have any chassis at all.

TRANSMISSION – Automatic Torqueflite transmission with torque converter, 3 forward speeds and reverse. Variable ratio drive incorporates intermediate gear hold, permitting manual gear changes and engine braking in all gears. Floor mounted gear lever offers six positions. Park (P); Reverse (R); Neutral (N); Top (D); Second (2); First (1). Transmission fluid temperature controlled by oil cooler built into main cooling radiator. Open propeller shaft drives hypoid gear rear axle.

SUSPENSION – Front: Independent by wishbones of unequal length with coil springs, telescopic dampers, torsional anti-roll bar. Rear: Torsion bar springs with Watts linkage stabilisation and telescopic dampers. Front and rear dampers are adjustable. Sealed balljoints. Bonded rubbers sleeves in mounting bushes for noise insulation.

STEERING – Power-assisted recirculating ball type, 15.7:1 ratio. Sealed ball-joints. Energy absorbing steering column designed to collapse progressively as a safety measure. 15 ins. steering wheel with hand stitched leather covering. Anti-theft steering column lock operated by ignition key.

BRAKES – Separate front and rear hydraulic systems operated by tandem master cylinders. Self-adjusting servo-assisted Girling disc brakes on all wheels. Failure warning device connected to lamp on instrument panel. Handbrake has separate calipers operating on rear discs. Warning lamp indicates "handbrake on" position and also checks failure of warning circuit function. Mechanical parking lock incorporated into transmission is operated by gear lever.

WHEELS – Safety type wheels (to avoid difficulty in controlling the vehicle after a blow-out), pressed steel on Britannia, light alloy on Brigand and Beaufighter.

ELECTRICAL SYSTEM – 12 volt negative earth system. 71 amp/hr. battery. High performance alternator charging system with electronic voltage control. The ignition system is electronic, thus reducing maintenance and improving efficiency and reliability.

INSTRUMENTS, WARNING LIGHTS – Comprehensive range of instruments includes speedometer with trip recorder, tachometer, battery voltmeter, clock, gauges for fuel, water temperature, oil pressure and turbocharging boost (Brigand and Beaufighter only). Warning lights for headlamp beam, cooling fans on manual operation, low fuel level, turn indicators, hazard lights, handbrake/fluid level, rearguard foglamps.

HEATING, VENTILATING, AIR CONDITIONING – Through-flow and ventilating system provides fresh air at variable volume and temperature without necessity of opening windows. Air enters car at base of windscreen and passes through heater to footwells or demist slots above fascia. Ventilation is supplemented by swivel outlets on fascia and side panels of footwells. A comprehensive air conditioning system entirely independent of the heating and ventilation is included in the specification.

LIGHTING, ACCESSORIES – Halogen headlamps, parking lights, turn indicators, rear number plate lamps, stop lamps, twin automatic reversing lights, twin rearguard fog lamps, reflectors, hazard warning lights, twin windtone horns. Main light and interior light switches on fascia. Combined switches on steering column control horns, turn indicators, headlamp beam and flash, windscreen wipers (normal–fast–intermittent), screenwash plus flick wash/wipe facility. Push-button radio cassette, electric aerial, dipping interior anti-dazzle mirror, electrically operated and heated exterior mirrors (on Britannia and Brigand).

TYRES – Avon tubeless radialply 215 X 70.VR15.

FUEL SYSTEM – Tank mounted behind rear seat, protected from impact by strong steel structure. Metal bulkheads separate tank from boot and car interior. Capacity 18 Imp. gallons (82 litres). Low fuel warning light on fascia.

ENGINE – Eight-cylinder 90° Vee. Capacity 5900 cc (360 cu. in). Bore 101.6 mm. (4.00 ins.). Stroke 90.93 mm. (3.58 ins.). Carburation by 4-barrel downdraught carburettor. High performance camshaft with hydraulic self-adjusting tappets operating overhead valves. Ignition efficiency maintained without contact wear or adjustment by electronic system. Cooling capacity 29 Imp. pints (16.5 litres), pressurised to 15 p.s.i. Automatically operated twin electric fans assist cooling when required, manual override switch to control fans if desired, irrespective of engine speed. Engines on Brigand and Beaufighter are boosted by special "Bristol-developed" exhaust driven turbocharging system giving even further power and performance, on demand.

DETAILED SPECIFICATIONS
BRITANNIA and BRIGAND

BODY – Full four-seater saloon with welded steel structure, of great strength, and aluminium alloy panelling. Two doors hinged on front pillars have burst-proof locks and a self-locking system and are fitted with armrests, which have red lights built into the end to serve as a warning to oncoming traffic when the door is open, as well as illuminating the access area to the car with white light, ashtrays, window lift switches and electrically operated windows. Individual front seats, adjustable electrically. Seats tip forward to allow easy access to rear. Head rests on both front seats. Individual rear seats accommodate two persons in comfort and have folding centre armrest. Individual headrests removable when not required. Box forming centre armrest fully padded. On each wheel arch is a deep lockable cubby hole. Interior upholstered in top quality hide. Protective padding above and below fascia panel. Walnut veneered fascia panel and instrument panel. Pile carpet with soundproof underlays. Lockable glove box. Pockets on rear of front seats. Full width rear parcel shelf, courtesy roof lights operated either by the doors or independent switches. Four ashtrays. Two cigarette lighters. Full width front and rear bumpers. Windscreen in laminated plate glass; rear screen, door lights and quarter lights in toughened plate glass. Hinged rear quarter lights. Electrically heated rear screen. Spare wheel housed in unique compartment in left hand front wing. Similar compartment on right hand side houses battery, twin brake servos and fuse panel. Large luggage boot opened electrically, with roof storage shelf. Underside of body undersealed. Inside of body selectively treated with anti-drumming material.

Dimensions: Wheelbase: 9 ft. 6 ins. (2.9 m); Track front: 4 ft. 6½ ins. (1.38 m); Track rear: 4 ft. 7½ ins. (1.41 m); Length: 16 ft. 1 in. (4.91 m.); Width: 5 ft. 9½ ins. (1.77 m.); Height: 4 ft. 8½ ins. (1.43 m.); Weight: 3850 lbs. (1746 kg.).

BEAUFIGHTER

BODY – Full four-seater "convertible". Steel structure welded to the rigid chassis; steel roll-over bar; aluminium alloy panelling. Two doors hinged at front with burst-proof locks are fitted out with internal armrests, ashtrays, window lift switches, grab handles. Door windows electrically operated. Individual front seats accommodate two persons in comfort. All seats have detachable head restraints, specially offset at rear for lounging and good rear vision. Interior trimmed in top quality leather. Walnut veneered fascia panel surrounded by trimming padding for safety. Heat and sound proofing underlays beneath pile carpet. Generous stowage for personal items provided by large glove box (illuminated) in fascia, concealed companion box in armrest between front seats, two large pockets at sides of rear seats, two map pockets in front backrests. Interior roof lamps, front and rear, operated by door switches or independent switch. Four ashtrays. Two cigarette lighters. Laminated safety glass in windscreen, toughened safety glass in side windows. Spare wheel carried in unique compartment in left front wing. Similar compartment in right front wing houses battery, fuse panel, twin brake servos, etc. Both compartments light internally when opened. Boot has 22 cu. ft. luggage capacity, tool stowage shelf, interior light, heat and sound insulation. Front (removable) roof section has large tinted glass panel which may be partly opened for ventilation or removed completely and stowed in the boot. Rear folding hood, adjustable mirrors on both doors. Underside of car fully undersealed and shielded against exhaust heat.

Dimensions: Wheelbase: 9ft. 6 ins. (2.9 m.); Track front: 4ft. 6½ ins. (1.38 m.); Track rear: 4 ft. 7½ ins. (1.41 m.); Overall length: 16 ft. 2½ ins. (4.9 m.); Overall width: 5 ft. 9½ ins. (1.77 m.); Overall height: 4 ft. 8½ ins. (1.44 m.); Weight: 3850 lbs. (1746 kg.).

BRISTOL*fashion*

TRUE BRITS

You buy quality when you buy a Bristol. Open the Britannia's door to climb in (you step *up* to get inside it) and you're almost bowled over by the sweet, hardy smell of fine leather. With slabs of walnut and acres of Wilton, it has a certain period ambience; the Bristol brings to life the aurá of an earlier, more refined era of motoring.

Performance is right up to date, however. Fitted with a normally-aspirated 5.9-litre Chrysler V8, the Britannia we tested (company owner Tony Crook's personal car) hurtles to 135mph, clipping 60mph in around 8 seconds.

Mid-range performance is just as impressive. Power is transmitted via a 3-speed Torqueflite automatic gearbox with well spaced ratios. Hold on to second and acceleration is fierce from standstill to 80mph, when the 'box changes automatically into top. Otherwise kickdown provides all the power needed for effortless overtaking.

If the Britannia will outrun most traffic, it's the unstrained ease with which it goes about it that impresses most. At the legal limit the car is deliciously smooth, and it feels as if you're running at only half that speed. You simply do not hear the engine, and normal conversation can take place without difficulty. As a relaxed continental tourer it would be hard to beat.

Fuel consumption depends on how you drive. On a run 25mpg of unleaded is not inconceivable, although stop-start nightmares on the M25 would drop this to nearer 12mpg.

Suspension is by wishbones, coil springs, telescopic dampers and an anti-roll bar at the front, while the rear is equipped with torsion bars, Watts linkage and dampers. This arrangement certainly soaks up the bumps, reducing even sleeping policemen in the road to no more than a ripple. But it is in no way spongy; indeed, the chassis has a lively, supple feel to it, and the ride is firm, aided by 215/70 VR15 Avon ACR18 Turbospeeds on specially made Wolfrace wheels.

Tight bends cause the car to roll, probably a legacy of its relatively long wheelbase and narrow track. In general it feels immensely secure.

The steering wheel is quite upright and close to the dash, another souvenir of the car's ancestry. But the steering is surprisingly responsive, requiring

● *The style of another era, but instruments are as clear as any*

If the Britannia will outrun most traffic, it's the ease with which it goes about it that impresses

only minute inputs to change the car's direction. By contrast, the all-round disc brakes need a hefty shove, and there's a split-second delay before anything happens. Once they come in, they're effective.

The Britannia has a long, long bonnet. One design tweak has been to mould-in little peaks at the front of the wings to make it easier to judge the car's extremities. They really do help you put the car where you want it to go, and are particularly useful in crowded streets, or for siting down narrow country lanes.

Otherwise, visibility is as good as you'll get; there just isn't a blind spot anywhere. This made us feel a bit self-conscious at first,

with no wide pillars to preserve our anonymity. The Britannia has immense presence on the road; during our tenure of the car, those who didn't turn and stare were the exception.

Inside, the main instruments are housed in a binnacle in front of the driver, and it's a model of clarity. Bristol tried a digital display in the early '80s, but it was quickly abandoned in favour of traditional analogue dials. Other switchgear and controls are a little more haphazard, lacking the coordination of, say, a big BMW.

Electric adjustments to the height and rake of seat squab and back rest make it possible to find an excellent driving position, and the central and door-mounted arm rests ensure a comfortable ride. Ventilation and heating are very efficient, as you might imagine in such a civilised machine, with air conditioning provided.

The Britannia has a surprisingly large boot, helped by a Bristol

● *Bristols have used big American V8s since 1960s — this is a 5.9-litre Chrysler unit*

● *Boot is surprisingly large; overall finish is quite superb*

trademark, the clever stowage of spare wheel and battery in compartments in either wing. The lower sections of the wings lift to give access to the spare tyre, or battery, fuses and brake servoes.

Alongside the Britannia in the Bristol range is the Beaufighter, a targa topped model which features the 5898cc Chrysler V8 in turbocharged guise. The turbo boosts acceleration dramatically, giving a 0-60 time of around 6.5 seconds and top speed of 152mph. Floor the throttle at cruising speed, the engine bursts into life with a roar as the Rotomaster turbo comes in, and you're soon travelling very quickly indeed.

The Beaufighter is quite formidable, but the Britannia was no disappointment, and in fact it was the smoother of the two models.

The Bristol badge is the city's crest, but apart from this colourful logo on the grille the Britannia is refreshingly understated. The most ostentatious item is its numberplate, owned by Crook since the early 1950s.

Finished in beautiful 'Bristol Red', this is a handsome car by any standards. Best viewed from front three-quarters, the Britannia looks tall, long and thin, and from the rear seems to have too narrow a track, as though there's some spare room in the rear wheelarches. At the front, there's virtually no overhang ahead of the wheels.

As you might expect, there are no concessions whatsoever to contemporary aerodynamic aids and no body kits, which would compromise the Bristol's integrity.

In profile the Britannia reminded us of certain 1960s classics such as the Bertone-styled Alfa Giulia coupes, or, in its

own class, perhaps the Ferrari 412. Although it's larger with a longer wheelbase, and completely different in character, the Bristol cannot evade comparison with such classics. It's a sign of maturity, and there's nothing wrong with that.

When it comes to build quality, the Bristol is in a different class, having more in common with a Bentley, because it is superbly finished with up-to-the-minute components. As Tony Crook says, 'We make something in between Rolls-Royce and Aston Martin, and that's our little niche in the market.'

● *Sumptuous leather seats adjust electrically for fine driving position*

● *Spare is housed in one front wing; battery and fuses in the other*

New Bristol shock!

Giles Chapman finds out the secrets of Bristol's latest car, the Blenheim, while over the page Steve Cropley drives it

BUY A NEW BRISTOL Blenheim — revealed today exclusively in *Autocar & Motor* — and you join an arcane and terribly British club. However, it's a question of money rather than connections — £109,000, to be precise.

Become a Bristol owner and this club expects you to behave like one. Respect and promote its principles and club founder and guiding light Anthony Crook will charm you into never wanting anything other than a Bristol. Virgin boss Richard Branson, composer Geoffrey Burdon, cabinet minister William Waldegrave and fashion designer Paul Smith are already enthusiastic members.

If that appeals then you'll love the Blenheim. If, on the other hand, you're mystified as to why anyone would pay a small fortune for a curiously anonymous two-door saloon with an iron-block American engine and a dashboard like a '50s household wireless, you're never likely to enrol.

Tony Crook *is* Bristol. He's real, live English heritage. An RAF flight lieutenant during World War II, he has been closely involved with Bristol since the aeroplane maker diversified into cars in 1946. For pleasure, he raced Bristol-engined Coopers and Frazer-Nashes; for business, his garage sold road-going Bristols.

His liking for publicity and practical jokes endeared him to enthusiasts: one year he'd be driving a Bristol 401 around Montlhéry at a record-breaking 100mph and say afterwards that he was concentrating on a play on the radio and not the driving; the next he'd be pretending to order cars from his rivals at the Earls Court motor show dressed as an Arab prince.

The original, BMW 327-inspired 400 and aerodynamic 401 models evolved into what Bristol called a "businessman's express" — the 404 and 406. In the 407 in 1962 Chrysler's 5.2-litre V8 replaced Bristol's own, expensively machined six-cylinder engine.

In 1961 Bristol sold its car business to Tony Crook and his partner, Sir George White. Since Sir George's retirement 20 years ago, Crook has been chairman, managing director and sole owner. The gaffer.

And the cars? While their basic design principles hark back to the 407 (torque-laden V8 engine and automatic gearbox, hefty separate steel box-section chassis, hand-made aluminium body, four big seats), there have been seven evolutionary models since, plus the Zagato-styled 412/Beaufighter. The Blenheim is a modernised version of the 1982 Brittania/Brigand, itself an update of the 1976 603. From ▶

CHARLES BEST

Blenheim named after another World War II plane

◄ now on it will be the sole Bristol model.

It's named after the World War II Bristol Blenheim fighter-bomber. The name was suggested by Graham Warner, once the proprietor of London's Chequered Flag sports car garage, who has spent years restoring the only airworthy one left in the world.

The car's chassis, suspension, roof and doors are unchanged, but the front and rear bodywork is all new. At the back, the line of the boot has been raised to make an already voluminous boot "ludicrously big", according to Crook. There are big new rear light clusters (from the Vauxhall Senator) and new 'bumpers' of hand-beaten aluminium with rubber strips, which widen the rear without altering the track. "In my opinion," says the proud chairman, "this looks more modern, higher — you can't see the exhaust sticking out any more."

At the front is a Lancia-like

Tony Crook is the gaffer

panel, with a deeply recessed criss-cross grille and four small round headlamps, plus a prominent Bristol badge. Again, it's all hand-made from aluminium, even the chunky front airdam. A swage line running the length of the body looks uneven, but that's because it conceals the shut lines for the flaps in the front wings, concealing a spare wheel on the nearside, battery and fuses on the driver's side — Bristol features since the '50s.

Old-fashioned cabin has an ambience all of its own

Injection for Chrysler V8

Spare wheel hides here

Inside, the Blenheim is identical to the Brittania/Brigand. Crook says a questionnaire sent to present customers ("All the old owners will move up to the new car") confirmed that they preferred to stick with the old-fashioned walnut dash. Bristol's press release sums up what is expected of Blenheim owners: "The various switches and positions, once easily learnt, fall to hand as in any aircraft."

Under the bonnet are more crucial changes. The Blenheim uses a 5.9-litre V8 made at Chrysler's Canadian factory and fitted mainly to trucks these days. But the old four-barrel down-draught carburettors have made way for sequential multi-point fuel injection. It comes with twin catalysts to comply with tough North American smog regulations, but that wasn't good enough to pass British emissions tests. So Bristol fits two more. The engine management system is by pre-programmed dual microprocessors.

Mated to the engine is a new version of Chrysler's venerable Torqueflite automatic transmission, now a four-speed with overdrive.

Fuel economy appears to be impressive, if early and admittedly unscientific figures are a yardstick. Crook claims that on a motorway trip from Bristol's service depot in Chiswick, west London, to its factory in Filton, Bristol, the company's resident chauffeur drove the gentle giant at no more than 70mph and managed 30.9mpg. "We could hardly believe it, but it's true," he enthuses.

Crook is unsure how many Blenheims his company will make: "We can get up to two or three a week," he says, "but we want to make slightly fewer than people want to buy.

"Our new car fills a niche between a Bentley Turbo R and an Aston," Crook explains, adding that the Blenheim is lighter than both. But he hints at another secret of Bristol's top-person appeal: sobriety. "A lot of people have money but don't want to be seen spending it on flashy cars at the same time as sacking chaps."

The Blenheim is the mascot of a club in which many drivers of more contemporary machinery would feel uncomfortable. But Tony Crook and his loyal band of customers don't mind that. They've got a secret — you can tell by the look on owners' face as they glide by.

The Blenheim's illustrious forebears

Bristol 401 (below left) was inspired by BMW 327 and heralded the "gentleman's express"; 407 of the '60s (centre) was the first Bristol to use Chrysler V8; 603 of the '70s is a direct predecessor of the Blenheim

Driving the Blenheim

At 80mph, there's hardly a whisper of wind noise. That would be surprising in a new Mercedes; in the Bristol Blenheim, the lowest of low-volume British coupes and based on models decades old, it's nothing short of astonishing.

You simply can't judge a new Bristol by the criteria you'd use for other cars. Look for the superb manufacturing quality and polish of a BMW 850i, for example, and you'll wonder how the tiny Filton-based company can attract a single buyer. But for the well-heeled who want to hear that individual artisans formed virtually every one of the Bristol's body and interior parts, and that the hand manufacture is gloriously obvious in any inspection of the car, there may be no other car.

Blenheim won't be rushed

On the road the car is a good deal better than I expected, although there are caveats. Governed by very low-rate springs (although the Spax dampers are adjustable), the Blenheim is never going to be a car to throw around. Its adhesion limits are more adequate than tenacious, and any excess of frivolity upsets its composure. It's immediately clear that this traditionalist's coupe expects to be guided through life by understanding hands.

Step into the cabin and the first things you'll notice are the large front seats. Trimmed in red leather in the test car, they sigh deeply when you sit down and step out. They seem extremely comfortable, and the rear compartment has two more, together with adult-sized helpings of headroom and legroom. This is a four-adult grand tourer. One of the few.

Lovers of American V8 low-end torque, plus mechanical smoothness and a woofle from the exhausts, will be at home with the drivetrain, combined with a transmission that's entirely fit for a briskly cruising aristocratic coupe. We didn't take the Blenheim anywhere near a test track but did enough miles to know that the car accelerates briskly (0-60mph in about 8sec, with a top speed of close to 140mph). The transmission has a very tall overdrive ratio that the driver can cut in or out with a switch on the dash. Astonishingly, the engine is ticking over at just 2000rpm at an indicated 80mph.

Show the Blenheim a serious corner and it will understeer, leaning a good deal on the way through. Stiffening the damper settings would have improved its tautness, but then owners can do that themselves. The steering feels accurate and well geared while managing not to be Detroit-light during ordinary manoeuvring.

Tony Crook makes the point — a fair one — that his car is considerably narrower than a Jaguar XJS or a Bentley Continental, and thus easier to hustle along back roads.

The ride is very soft indeed. Ruts are obliterated, but at the expense of some bounce over bigger undulations. Again, you could adjust it, but it would never be stiff. Wouldn't suit the character of the car, anyway.

It's the ambience of the cabin I liked most. True, it doesn't do to examine the details too closely; you might not like the Chrysler auto quadrant or the chrome grin of the air conditioning outlets just above the low console ("I hate consoles that occupy half the car," says Crook). But a lot of it is pure joy. The handsome three-spoke steering wheel is literally machined from solid, then clad in leather. I'd like to hang one on my wall. The instrument binnacle, full of old-fashioned Smiths white-on-black dials, is lovely. Same for the seats.

There are practicalities, too. Air vents route directly into the footwells from outside ("I hate air conditioning, although we have to offer it," says Crook). The facia contains a couple of warning lights linked to the engine room's diagnostic system — the very last feature I thought I'd find on a Bristol. The way the spare wheel stores in a compartment just behind the nearside front wheel still makes sense. And the dash has a special pod near its top surface to contain the radio ("You don't want to be groping for it around your ankles").

For press-on, high-mileage motorists, the Bristol Blenheim is probably exactly the wrong car. It will never be a mile-eating, high-tech showcase like a Mercedes SEC, but it has a unique charm.

As a gentleman's express it performs pretty well, provided the gentleman knows what he's buying. ∎

Soft suspension means plenty of roll through corners

Factfile

Bristol Blenheim

How fast?
0-60mph	6.9sec
Top speed	140mph (est)
MPG: urban	24
56mph	34
70mph	30

All manufacturer's claimed figures

How much?
£109,980 **On sale in UK** from today

How big?
Length	4860mm (191.3in)
Width	1750mm (68.7in)
Height	1440mm (56.6in)
Wheelbase	2990mm (114in)
Weight (claimed)	1746kg (3850lb)
Fuel tank	82 litres (18 gall)

Engine
Max power not given
Max torque not given
Installation front, longitudinal, rear-wheel drive
Capacity 5898cc, V8
Made of iron head, iron block
Bore/stroke 101.6mm/94.9mm
Compression ratio 9.0:1
Valves 2 per cyl
Ignition and fuel electronic ignition and fuel injection

Gearbox
Type 4-speed automatic
Ratios/mph per 1000rpm
1st 39.3/1000 **2nd** 78.6/2000
3rd 117.9/3000 **4th** 157.2/4000

Suspension
Front coil springs, dampers, anti-roll bar
Rear live axle, dampers, anti-roll bar

Steering
Type recirculating ball, power assisted
Lock to lock 3.0 turns

Wheels and tyres
Size 15in **Made of** alloy
Tyres 215/70 VR15

Made and sold by
Bristol Cars Ltd, 368-370 Kensington High Street, London W14 8NL
Tel: 071 603 5556

Writing about William Waldegrave under the heading *Me and My Car* is slightly inappropriate. More accurately it should be Me and My Cars because Waldegrave, MP for Bristol West and Environment Under Secretary, is lucky enough to own two classic Bristols, a 405 saloon and a rare 402 drophead, dating from the late 1940s.

"As somebody who comes from the West Country, I'd always greatly admired the old Bristol Aeroplane Company and remember seeing the Brabazon flying when I was small. In fact, when I was about eight, the then chairman of the board, Sir Reginald Verdon-Smith, took me round the factory at Filton, and I remember 403 saloons being made."

Waldegrave's interest in the cars was also helped by his brother. "He had a 1928 convertible Austin, and I would hold the spanners for him while he worked on it. After that came a Bristol-engined AC Ace, and a car that is now in very good shape, a 1928 Rolls-Royce 20hp Landulette."

Waldegrave's first car was a little more prosaic, being a very secondhand Hillman Imp. "It was a super car, and I thought they were wrong to throw the design away."

He was driving an Alfa Junior, however, when he decided to invest in a Bristol. "I enjoyed the Alfa very much, but knew that I would keep spending money on it and still suffer from depreciation. So I liked the idea of owning a car that I really wanted, which would also hold its value."

As a result, Waldegrave bought a Bristol 405 from Anthony Crook in 1973. During the mid-1950s the 405 was the company's staple product (and its only four-door model), and was powered by a 2.2-litre development of its famous BMW-derived straight-six engine.

"Mine cost £700, which was perhaps a little expensive at the time. Initially, it needed some work on the chassis, and characteristically the ash framing of the windscreen pillars had rotted, so they were replaced. The engine was perfect and has run from that day to this without having to be touched."

Waldegrave had owned the 405 for about two years when he discovered the 402. "I'd got to know Anthony Crook quite well, and had gone to the Bristol depot in Chiswick to see his beautiful

ME AND MY CAR
A BRISTOL MAN

William Waldegrave MP, has childhood memories of the Bristol factory and now owns two of the cars, as Martin Gurdon discovered

Type 450 Le Mans racer. While I was there I found the 402 drophead under some sheeting. It looked amazing."

Only about 20 of these convertibles were built (customers included Jean Simmons and Stewart Granger) and, on seeing this one, Waldegrave was smitten.

"I asked Crook how much he wanted for it. To begin with he wouldn't sell, but I kept pestering him until it was easier to let me buy it than to say no."

So in 1975 the 402 changed hands for £2500. "I went into severe debt as a result, but that Bristol was the best buy I've ever made. It's worth a lot more than £2500 now and it's a lovely car.

"The hood is wonderful: it takes three people about half an hour to put up, and it has a lot of chromed poles, rather like a complicated tent, and looks ridiculous when raised. Lower it, however, and the car has beautiful, clean lines."

At this time Waldegrave was using the more commonplace 405 (about 297 saloons were made) as everyday transport, covering about 10,000 miles a year. After getting married he had access to two Cortina estates and, more recently, a Granada station wagon so the 405 is now kept purely as a pleasure vehicle.

Both it and the 402 are still driven regularly, however, and have, in the main, proved very reliable, although Waldegrave had a few niggles. "Replacing the fan belt on the 405 is very inconvenient, and you need a special tool to change the spark plugs, which always gets lost." He also mentioned that the 405's heating system has a certain period charm. "It works quite well if the outside air temperature gets above 80 degrees."

Wearing his political hat, Waldegrave talked with refreshing candour about the European clean air debate. "I think it's right that lead should be removed from petrol, but we intend that leaded fuel will remain available for

> **"The heating system works quite well if the outside temperature gets above 80 degrees"**

people with classic cars." Did he think that there was a conflict of interests between car manufacturers and governments? "There's a gap between engineers and decision makers which is too wide. You only need to look at some of the terrible things that have happened in America to see that, but I do believe that it's right for governments to push for things like better safety."

We'd hoped to photograph Waldegrave with the 402, but it was wintering at TT Workshops, where its wiring was being seen to. "Last summer the remaining cloth insulation packed up, so the electrics ceased to function, which was rather a bore."

As we looked at the 405 which deputised for it, however, Waldegrave said. "I have a theory that some of the most beautiful things made between 1920 and 1960 are motor cars. Look at the post war Aerodyne Bristols. They might not be art, but I think they're more desirable than the things people buy and sell in Bond Street art galleries." To hear that from a politician is good news indeed . . .

● **Bristol Blenheim** On sale: now

Bristol fashion is still shipshape

Blenheim surprisingly able for a car that owes so much to 35-year-old design. US V8 – once seen as automotive heresy – now an integral part of car's appeal

The Bristol *cognoscenti* wept bitter tears when the 407 – the firm's first Chrysler-powered car – hit the streets in 1961. Bristol had sired a bastard.

Out went the straight six – lovingly crafted in alloy by Bristol itself – to be replaced by an iron V8.

For Bristol – saddled with a unit that was expensive to build – it was the right decision. Top speed rocketed from a shade over the ton to nearly 130 and 60mph arrived in the time it took to light a Montecristo.

Thirty-five years later and Bristol, still steered by Tony Crook, has outlived all its Euro hybrid GT contemporaries

Old-fashioned charm by the bucket

(Jensen, Gordon Keeble, Iso Monteverdi and so on) and Bristol owners have learned to love that big V8.

In a sense, the 407 is still with us in the form of the current Blenheim. The shape has changed but the proportions – tall, slim, long – remain. The 5.9-litre V8 still comes from Chrysler – as does the automatic gearbox – and Bristol still uses the same closed box section chassis clothed by a hand-crafted aluminium two-door, four-seater body.

That separate chassis means you tend to climb up into the car rather than slide down into it. Ensconced on broad but torso-hugging leather seats, you can contemplate a walnut dash that hasn't changed much since the 407, its traditional white on black instruments grouped in a binnacle whose shape echoes that of the grille.

Never raising its voice above a discreet hum, the engine – still using old-fashioned pushrods – is ideally matched to a four-speed auto that exchanges ratios with seamless serenity.

Given its bead with bootfuls of kickdown vigour, the Blenheim feels urgent but never aggressive and the combination

Conservative at best, the Blenheim's looks fail to do justice to its ability

of slender proportions and a lofty driving position make it ideal for threading quickly through traffic.

Loafing in top, you can appreciate inter-stellar gearing: a huge 39.3mph per 1000rpm. At 100mph it's doing just over 2500rpm, at 70 only 1750rpm.

Flick the Blenheim through some turns and you sense class and composure here too – in a vintage sort of way. There is feel and feedback from the weighty power steering, and if the tail feels slightly wiggly over dimples and depressions, you just remind yourself that there is a live axle back there. It all feels commendably together: the Blenheim swoops majestically, and with surprisingly little roll, through fast rural sweepers, and feels refreshingly handy in slower turns too.

Martin Buckley

For Beautifully made, handles much better than it looks, torquey American V8, exclusivity
Against Old-fashioned styling (inside and out) is an acquired taste, high price
Price £109,980 **0-60mph** n/a **Top speed** n/a

Quirky is perhaps too plebeian a word for the Blenheim. Its styling and interior are an acquired taste, like Patum Peperium

Blenheim Palace

The chance to drive a new Bristol comes about as rarely as an earthquake in Wolverhampton. Which, on both counts, is a shame.

In fact, the last time a car magazine was allowed to carry out a full road test on a new Bristol was when the Jensen Interceptor could still have been considered a cutting-edge rival.

Understandably, then, it comes as something of a surprise to receive an invite from Bristol chairman, pilot and ex-Grand Prix driver Tony Crook to

come and have a go in his latest product, the Blenheim II.

Hurriedly scuttling off to the company's solitary showroom on Kensington High Street, west London (it's been there since 1950), I'm greeted by the offer of a cup of tea and the chance to take a gander at the new car.

This latest model is the result of 52 years of steady Bristol evolution. Like its predecessors, it is still hand built in workshops next to Filton airfield in Bristol – home of the original Bristol Aeroplane Company. Development

work is carried out by the same tester responsible for every model to date.

So in common with previous Bristols, the Blenheim II employs a set of six-and-a-half-inch thick steel girders welded to form a separate chassis. The body is crafted from aluminium panels and bonded to a steel frame, just as Bristol once built its planes.

The result is a car that's considerably lighter than other two-door luxury giants such as the Bentley Continental R or Aston Martin V8 Coupe. The intention remains very much for this

latest Blenheim to provide 'dignified express travel for four six-foot persons and their luggage', and hence its body-shape, despite a few tweaks, is still the case of function over form that you see here. The styling revisions over the original '94-on Blenheim are limited to a reshaped nose, larger gas-discharge headlamps and a track widened to help the redesigned wheels do a better job of filling their arches. But that's about it.

Gliding out into west London's traffic, the fact that the Blenheim II's body is narrower than a Mondeo (though

Demonstrating the Bristol's luggage space for us is chairman Tony Crook himself. Now that's what we call personal service

longer than an 8-Series BMW) comes in rather handy. The incredibly tight turning circle also helps out, as do raised corners acting as aiming points at the end of the mile-long bonnet.

As a six foot person, I can tell you that the Blenheim II's plush, Connolly leather-clad cabin more than lives up to its design brief. Those who prefer to drive rather than have their chauffeur do the job for them will be pleased to find that the redesigned seats cosset you superbly. There's plenty of space up front, while there's room for a pair of lanky passengers to relax in the snug but well-padded buckets in the rear.

The boot, similarly, is huge, helped by the spare wheel, battery and brake servo all being located in separate compartments located in the front wings.

The cabin is a smart but distinctly odd space to find yourself in, with a stereo mounted nearly at eye height and fat, shiny switches smattered all over the walnut dashboard with words such as 'air boost' and 'speed hold' written on them. Almost uniquely, the air-conditioning and ventilation systems are completely separate, allowing occupants to simultaneously fry and freeze should the whim take them.

Set far back in the vast engine bay is Bristol's reworking of a 5.9-litre Chrysler V8, uprated from the 237bhp version that's currently found in the fastest Jeep Grand Cherokee. As with any details of his reclusive band of customers (or of sales figures, for that matter) Tony Crook is reluctant to disclose details of power or performance. 0-60 feels like it should come up in a notch under seven seconds, with a top whack

maybe nudging 150mph, though far more relevant is that the Blenheim II cruises with superb composure, makes a nice whoofly noise even at tickover (the rev counter only reads 1,700rpm at 70mph) and thrusts forwards with almost alarming surge when encouraged by a hefty right foot and the four-speed auto box shoved into a low gear.

This is a relaxing and enjoyable car to drive. Despite the fact that few cars this side of a Land Rover Defender or Hindustan Ambassador still come with a separate chassis and a live rear axle, this latest reworking of the Bristol formula rides beautifully, steers lightly, though accurately, and works its way around bends with little in the way of sill-scraping roll. But then it does have 52 years of careful refining behind it.

My time with the Blenheim II is enough to confirm how glad I am that cars like this still exist; I'm also glad that companies like Bristol still exist to make them. For a select bunch of very rich people, the fact that this latest Bristol remains so, well, incomparable, should be enough to please them too.

I'm looking forward to my invite to drive the next new Bristol. Just 30 years to wait, then... □

Story: Peter Grunert
Photography: Derek Goard

FACT FILE	
Model	big posh coupe
Engine	5.9-litre V8, bhp n/a
Performance	'not disclosed'
On sale in the UK	now
Price	£118,953
Rivals	Bentley Continental R, Aston Martin V8 Coupe, Mercedes CL600

There were only two choices in 1975 for a wealthy individual seeking the highest quality from a hand-built British car with four good seats. One, the £13,999 Rolls-Royce Silver Shadow, was the ultimate status symbol on wheels, recognised by most of the world's population. The other, the £9798 Bristol 411, was at the opposite end of the familiarity spectrum, known by only a small core of enthusiasts.

Beyond their spacious seating, country of origin and peerless craftsmanship, the Shadow and 411 share basic mechanical make-up of a massive V8 engine driving through a three-speed automatic gearbox. But there the similarities start to dry up. These cars are complete opposites, so totally different in demeanour that the choice would have been a simple taste preference for anyone able to spend five years' worth of a working man's earnings on a mere car. The character difference remains as clear-cut today, although an ordinary being would now have to work for less than a year to afford a decent example.

Which of the two you lean towards depends on how you like to travel. For peace, comfort and a sense of ease with the world, no other car of the period can touch the veritable drawing-room-on-wheels ambience of a Silver Shadow. For a rather more sporting interpretation of these qualities, with a much higher dose of driver reward, the 411 – like any other V8 Bristol of the '60s and '70s – is equally in a class of its own. On first acquaintance, climbing into these cars and surveying their walnut-veneered dashboards, this contrast is summed up straight away.

The Rolls-Royce takes care of you, removing all unnecessary distraction and effort from the task of conducting yourself from A to B. Dials are scattered almost carelessly across the facia and minimal in the extreme. There's no rev counter because Rolls-Royce travel never involves taking the engine to its limit, while gauges for water temperature and oil pressure are also absent. Having an ammeter at dead centre in your sightline seems odd, but maybe this is because reliability from the multiplicity of electrical equipment could be your biggest concern as the driver. Switchgear is placed randomly and is traditional in appearance, the general look being of stout chromed fittings carrying prominent labels to describe their function.

Befitting a manufacturer with aviation origins, the Bristol provides the comprehensive and tidily arranged instrumentation that a pilot would expect in his cockpit. Big speedometer and rev counter dominate a binnacle that also contains five other dials, all beautifully positioned for clear visibility through the steering wheel. Pleasing rocker switches operate most of the electrical equipment and everything, even the four circular ventilation outlets, seems to be in the right place. What faces you, the driver, is a splendid blend of functional and attractive design.

Both cars offer sublime comfort, but in different ways. The Bristol, narrower in the cabin and more intimate, has beautiful seats that provide enough shape to anchor you well in corners. The Rolls-Royce is altogether more spacious for legroom, height and width, and its seats, more in the nature of sumptuously padded armchairs, are wonderful to sit on. Rear

DAVID SHEPHERD

Lap of Luxury

Luxobarge, sir? Mark Hughes pits the subject of our Best Buy against another opulent contender

passengers are cosseted in both cars: many Shadows were chauffeur-driven when young, while this particular Bristol, unusually, started life with a company chairman who preferred to travel in the back. Both also have enormous boots: the Bristol's is deep enough to carry suitcases upright because no spare wheel gets in the way – that's cleverly stored behind a lift-up panel in the nearside front wing.

The Shadow's finest quality is its silence and unbeatable refinement. Starting the engine, true to cliché, makes no difference to sound levels, to the point where sometimes you turn the key a second time thinking, mistakenly, that the engine hasn't fired. Under acceleration a subtle V8 murmur can be detected, but the only significant sources of noise as speed builds up are the swooshing of big tyres and wind rush that rubber seal

Stately Rolls-Royce is not meant to be thrown into bends. Below: trademark known across the world

technology a generation ago couldn't completely eliminate. The story that the most intrusive sound within a Rolls-Royce comes from the clock is certainly true, but the tick is unusually loud.

The Bristol doesn't offer this sense of isolation from the world outside, and would fail in its role as 'gentleman's sporting carriage' if it did. It's still very refined, but the engine conveys an urgent beat that an enthusiastic driver would enjoy. And what a wonderful engine it is. The first use of a Chrysler V8 shocked some Bristol traditionalists in 1961, but nowadays the crisp

Clockwise from top: a Rolls-Royce driver is cocooned in the plush cockpit; 6750cc motor; polished trim for lights and wheels

response and seamless power delivery of this engine – enlarged to 6556cc for the 411 in Series IV form – overcome any latent prejudice about mass-produced origins. It's rarely necessary, when going through the auto 'box on 'hold', to exceed 3000rpm, well short of the 5500rpm limit, because low-down torque is so substantial.

The aluminium-bodied Bristol has the decisive performance edge promised by its twin advantages of more power (the Chrysler unit's 330bhp at 5200rpm is at least 100bhp more than Rolls-Royce's unspecified output) and less weight (1710kg against 2113kg). Two statistics show the gulf: 0-70mph (the benchmark Bristol's Tony Crook liked to quote) takes 9.5 secs and top speed is 140mph, parallel figures for the Shadow being 14.1 secs and 116mph.

Both cars use brilliant American automatic transmissions, with little to choose between the Shadow's GM400 and the 411's Chrysler Torque-flite. Changes are swift and so smooth that they are almost imperceptible at light throttle openings. The Bristol has a chunky tunnel-mounted shift lever, the Shadow a light-to-operate column stalk that's really only a switch for a servo motor on the side of the gearbox – a typical piece of Rolls-Royce engineering detail.

In other dynamic areas, steering reveals the contrast most strongly. A pre-1977 Shadow's only major drawback is its lifeless recirculating ball system, which is so light that the big two-spoke wheel can be manipulated by gentle

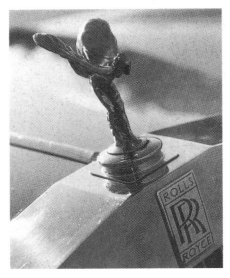

AT A GLANCE

1975 ROLLS-ROYCE SILVER SHADOW
Engine capacity: 6750cc
Max power: 200-230bhp @ 4000rpm (est)
0-70mph: 14.1 secs **Max speed:** 116mph
Restored value today: £15,000-£25,000
Moves with remarkable serenity and presence, but steering poor. Engine/transmission very smooth, brakes exceptional. Main ownership drawbacks are parts prices and potential for monocoque repairs.

1975 BRISTOL 411 SERIES IV
Engine capacity: 6556cc
Max power: 330bhp @ 5200rpm
0-70mph: 9.5 secs **Max speed:** 140mph
Restored value today: £15,000-£25,000
A car of unique virtues: superb dynamics and great performance mixed with fine practicality and quality. Maintenance costs aren't excessive, but tired aluminium bodywork on steel frame can be a problem.

Bristol's Girling system would probably come out on top.

How the rest of the world sees you is another distinction between these cars. The Bristol is discreetly elegant but essentially unobtrusive. The Rolls-Royce, on the other hand, is unmissable, dominating the road through sheer size, presence and status. My eight-year-old son's verdict, after his first Rolls-Royce ride, captured the effect: "Daddy, this is great – people keep looking at us."

I can do without head-turning ability, but with these two cars it was particularly troublesome to separate personal preference from appropriate objectivity. This Bristol really is so much my kind of car that I fell for its exquisite treats of tactile pleasure, all-round performance and fine quality. I like response and intimacy of control too much to want to own a Silver Shadow, but can see why drivers of different inclination aspire to this hallmark of British quality. Taste, such a personal matter when it comes to cars, has to dictate which of these two greats you prefer. ◆

Bristol has sporting feel and is agile on twisty back roads. Below left: delicate grab handle in 411

Thanks for loan of cars to Frank Dale & Stepsons (Rolls-Royce) and Gerry Acher (Bristol). Gerry's 411, bought in 1986 after reading a C&SC article, is his daily car and has covered 110,000 miles in 12 years. Thanks to Martin Barnes of American Car Care Services (0171 278 9786), where the Bristol is serviced

grip between forefinger and thumb. Using both hands is better, however, because free play means that motorway cruising needs regular steering correction to keep the car running straight – a shame when everything else about the Shadow is so relaxed. The big advantage of a Shadow II is that rack and pinion eliminates this flaw. Steering the Bristol gives great pleasure. There's a smaller, sportier wheel with three spokes and a thicker rim, and response is superb. This is a recirculating ball system with power assistance too, but precision, feedback and weight are ideal. The delight in threading the 411 along twisty back roads is also enhanced by the body's relative narrowness, which makes the car feel surprisingly small and agile. Ride firmness and terrific chassis balance complete the Bristol's credentials as a wonderful driver's car. Not a trace of understeer afflicts this big machine but, at the same time, real provocation is needed to unsettle the rear end. Handling is sporting and safe, true to Bristol ethos.

A Silver Shadow isn't meant to be driven like this, so it's pointless to labour its deficiencies of body roll and lethargy when asked to change direction quickly. Instilling outstanding suspension suppleness, complete with hydraulic self-levelling at the rear, was Rolls-Royce's aim, and the result is the equal of any Citroën or Cadillac. Braking is a Shadow strength: being able to stand such a heavy car on its nose is truly impressive. Both cars have all-round discs and, against any other rival the

THE MAIN RIVAL
JAGUAR XJ12 SERIES II
Engine capacity: 5343cc
Max power: 285bhp @ 5850rpm
0-70mph: 9.7 secs **Max speed:** 147mph
Restored value today: £6000-£9000
A brilliant car, but so few remain in good health. Best to go for a late one (Series III continued to 1992 with V12 engine). Refinement and effortless performance (V12 is a jewel) are main strengths, but ride/handling good too. Daimler versions have extra luxury. Rust and neglected maintenance are negatives.

Clockwise from top: walnut veneer on dash of gentleman's sporting saloon; clear dials; aircraft manufacturer; American heart

BRISTOL CREAM

Of all the American-European hybrids that the sixties spawned, only the Bristol models from the 407 to the 411 have had lasting success. Martin Buckley presents our complete guide to them

Even by British specialist standards, Bristol are an exceptional company. Formed in 1945, they have rarely built more than 150 cars a year and since 1961 have produced nothing but big V8 sports saloons based on a chassis that is essentially *pre-war*. By rights, such a car should have died long ago, yet the company continue to supply these bespoke cars to well-heeled devotees who cheerfully pay up to £56,000 for the privilege.

That said, one does not have to be super-rich to enjoy Bristol motoring, because the older breed of the 407-411 models covered by this 'Profile' are grossly undervalued at the moment, and a good example can be picked up for the price of a new Mini. Powerful, luxurious and elegant in their way, Bristols offer aircraft standards of build quality in one of the most exclusive cars on the road. Once bitten, you may not want to own any other type of car again.

The story of Bristol's car division begins at the end of the Second World War when the aeroplane company decided they would utilise spare production capacity and go into the high quality motor car business. Instead of designing a completely new car, Bristol took over the existing pre-war BMW range to create the 400, a vastly improved car using the best components from each model: 326 chassis, 328 cross push-rod six-cylinder engine, and a restyled version of the 327 coupé body.

This is not the place to go into the various permutations of the original 1947 design, but suffice to say that the aerodynamic 401 appeared in 1949, and by 1958, the 406 had evolved, still using the same basic mechanicals and 9ft 6ins wheelbase. The 406 is worth closer examination because it was the last of the six-cylinder cars and used a new two-door

body that would serve until 1976. The preceding 2-litre Bristols had earned a high reputation as drivers' cars, with their superb roadholding, responsive steering and good all-round performance. In all these respects the 406 was no different, but Bristol were now looking towards a more luxurious section of the market, and the relative opulence of the 406 made no secret of their intentions.

Although identifiably 'Bristol' in character, with its Brabazon-inspired front grille, the handsome new body was actually a more square-rigged conventional shape which was wider above the waistline to give better interior space. It was still, of course, built in aluminium (with a wing-mounted spare wheel), but its frame was now all steel. The interior of the 406 had a lot to live up to and as well as being bigger (there was room for four six-footers) the fat front armchairs reclined and sported built-in headrests. Needless to say, wood and leather were much in evidence, and the facia continued to echo aircraft practice with a seven instrument binnacle in front of the driver.

All this incurred a weight penalty, and to compensate, the 406 used a 2.2-litre version of the six-cylinder engine that produced 13 per cent more torque for greater flexibility in the all-important mid ranges. Power output was the same (105bhp NET) but it was produced at lower revs.

The famed Bristol chassis was unchanged in the main, but Dunlop disc brakes were now used all round and the torsion bar suspended live axle had a Watts linkage for better lateral location. This encouraged better roadholding on tight corners.

With the 406, Bristol attempted to move in on the Bentley market but in the process created a car that

was really the 'odd man out'. On the one hand it was still a sporting car, with excellent handling and a superb engine that encouraged frequent use of the lovely gearbox. But these much-loved Bristol features somehow sat uneasily beneath the more dignified new body that obviously lent itself to a big, effortless engine mated to an automatic gearbox. Indeed, by 1960 few buyers would have accepted a luxury car powered by a 2.2-litre engine.

Bristol knew that the old six was at the limit of its development, and had always intended to replace the stop-gap 406 with the sophisticated 220 prototype. Unfortunately, this project was dropped in 1956 and it soon became clear that whatever replaced the 406 would have to continue with the same body and chassis and a much more powerful proprietary engine.

The obvious place to go shopping for more power was North America. The big producers had been building cheap powerful V8s for years, and they had proved amazingly effective. Chrysler engines had always been noted for their quality, and while trying the company's fine Torqueflite automatic transmission, Bristol thought they may as well have a look at the engine it was intended for. The unit with which the Filton engineers were presented was a heavy (but not as heavy as expected) all-iron 5130cc V8 with pushrod operated valves and a Carter carburettor. It produced 250bhp gross, which was probably a true 180 NET installed.

Bristol tried other engines, but were quickly sold on the power and refinement of the Chrysler and decided to use a Canadian-built version of the 'hemi' head. On delivery to Filton, Bristol dispensed with the rev-limiting hydraulic tappets, fitted a high performance camshaft and a bigger sump. A special radiator and twin Kenlowe fans were also used, and in this form the engine probably produced a true 200bhp. Bristol even had the audacity to alter the highly regarded Torqueflite automatic, but although this rather peeved Chrysler at first, they later adopted the changes themselves.

With about 110 per cent more power and 140 per cent more torque, this new power pack couldn't just be slotted into an unchanged 406. The long-serving transverse leaf spring and wishbone front suspension was replaced by a coil spring and wishbone assembly (suspended on a new massive cross-member) and the steering job was taken over by a Marles cam and roller. At the rear, a heavier duty axle put the power down. So it was in this form that the new V8 Bristol appeared in September 1961, logically designated 407. Outwardly, the body was almost indistinguishable from the 406, but once behind the wheel the advantages and disadvantages of the new power source became very apparent.

In one of the few Bristol road tests published, *Autocar's* 407 achieved 122mph, 0-60 in 9.9secs and 0-100 in 26.6secs – figures which put the new V8 firmly into the supercar class of the early sixties. It was the sheer effortlessness of the performance that really impressed. There was no more messing about with a gear lever, just a smooth surge of Detroit horsepower controlled by five press buttons on the dashboard. No wonder *Autocar* called the 407 a 'high powered magic carpet'.

But there was a price to pay for this new vigour, because the once so delicate Bristol steering was now soggy, vague and heavy, even though it had been geared down to 3.75 turns lock to lock. *Autocar*: 'Handling of the Bristol is at its best on open, sweeping bends, and on such roads, it is a joy to drive. Through tighter corners, on narrow roads, the car feels more cumbersome, partly because the steering becomes much heavier at slower speeds'. Certainly, the V8 was no lumbering hulk of a car in the American manner and although the rack and pinion steering and 50/50 weight distribution were gone, few luxury four-seaters could keep up with a well-driven 407. The basic handling characteristic was understeer, but the tail could easily be brought round under power. To all but the most seasoned Bristol enthusiasts, the new car was a success.

It was powerful and refined far beyond any

The basis of all Bristols from the 407 onwards was a massive separate chassis and V8 engine

With the last 407 model, Bristol abandoned their aircraft-inspired nose-cone in favour of a conventional grille – not the most successful of moves …

From 1961 to 1976, the side profile of the staple Bristol production cars changed hardly at all: 407 (above) is nearly identical to 411 (below)

411 (left) and 407 are very much gentlemen's carriages in the old style, although hardly modern

Dashboards in the old-fashioned manner: note Bluemels wheel on 407 (above) and 411 (below) similarity

previous model and many middle-aged Bristol customers would welcome the new-found effortlessness. For the next few years, real agility would just have to take a back seat.

For the next V8, Bristol felt that a complete break from the 407's still traditional front end styling was needed. Thus, the 408 had a rather brutal looking rectangular intake with two auxiliary lamps set into its slatted aluminium grille. This would be the familiar Bristol 'look' for quite a few years to come.

Other 408 recognition points were reduced roof curvature, new side trim and badges and simpler bumpers which reduced overall length by 4ins. The engine and transmission were unchanged, but the 408's rear dampers were the Armstrong Selectaride type, adjustable to four different settings by a dial on the facia. The 408 was perhaps the least desirable Bristol because of its awkward styling.

By the mid-sixties, Bristol Cars, which since 1961 had been owned by Sir George White and Anthony Crook as a separate entity from the aircraft concern, were building a very special product. Fast enough to compare with an Aston Martin but as luxurious as a Rolls-Royce, the V8s were attracting a whole new breed of customer who wanted to cover long distances at speed and in understated luxury. It's true that some customers turned their backs on the V8s and kept their 2-litres, but the company's policy of constant development would eventually begin to win them back.

The process began with the 1965 409. Here was a better balanced car with a larger 5211cc engine mounted further back in the chassis. It was mated to a much lighter, aluminium-housed gearbox. Bristol had noted criticisms of the 407/408 steering and the 409 had a more positive version of the Marles box. The Bristol ride quality had always been very comfortable and well controlled, but the 409 had lower spring rates for an extra degree of softness. Normally, this would have increased cornering lurch, but to compensate the roll centre was raised by 2ins. Hard-charging owners (and there were many) would have appreciated the adjusted Torque-flite transmission, because second could now be held indefinitely for maximum acceleration. Top speed rose to 132mph thanks to the standardised 3.07:1 axle ratio.

For some tastes, the braking servo assistance came in too suddenly, so on the Girling-braked 409 the point at which assistance came in was lowered for better progression. Bristol's brake acceptance test was vry tough. It consisted of 30 ½g stops from 70mph at 30secs intervals.

The 409 was visually near identical to the 408, but the corners of the front grille had been rounded slightly for a softer effect.

Bristol had never favoured power steering but increasing weight and congested traffic conditions were making its adoption seem more and more inevitable. Finally in 1966 a Mk2 409 was introduced with ZF power steering developed in conjunction with Bristol. Adjustable to individual taste, this system was probably the best in existence, and made the car easier to handle in town, yet it was sensitive enough for fast driving.

Embodied in the 1967 410 were a mass of detail improvements, although the body was only subtly different. The bold front air intake was now more at one with the front wings and the car had a lower, sleeker stance thanks to the adoption of smaller 15ins wheels. Later examples had what the Americans call 'radial tuned' suspension, but even the cars shod with Avon Turbospeeds handled noticeably better on the smaller wheels. The push button gear selector was dispensed with on the 410, which now used a more sporting tunnel lever. The car also benefitted from a dual circuit braking system.

By anyone's standards, the 410 was a fast car, but a considerable increase in performance was on the menu when the 411 was unveiled in 1969. Lifting the big rear-hinged bonnet revealed much the same rather uninteresting scene, dominated by two black-painted rocker covers and a big air cleaner. But this unit was different; Bristol had now taken on the 6277cc '383' Chrysler engine, producing a very healthy 335bhp at 5200rpm and a thumping 425lbs ft of torque at 3400rpm. The special high lift cam was still fitted but the hydraulic tappets were retained.

Pressure on the appropriate pedal would now nonchalantly blast this 3726lbs sports saloon to 60mph in 7secs and 100mph in 19secs. Top speed was an impressive 140mph and fuel consumption was typically 15mpg. Considering their performance, the V8s had never been especially thirsty. If you weren't lucky enough to sample the 411's increased urge, then it could be recognised externally by its simpler, finless rear end shape and increased front and rear 'screen rake.

The 411 models, with their better developed suspension and magnificent power steering, were now cross-country chargers of prowess

It's worth noting that the 411 was not only one of the world's fastest full four-seaters, but it was probably also the safest. The aluminium bodywork crumpled progressively on impact and retention of the separate chassis meant there was little intrusion into the cabin. In a skid or tyre blow out situation, the Bristol was a safe place to be, as Anthony Crook proved when he intentionally burst a tyre on a later 411 at 144mph …

With so much power on tap, some felt the 411 needed to put more rubber on the road, so in 1970 what amounted to a Mk2 car was announced, with bigger 205 section tyres on 6ins rims. An automatic self-levelling system was fitted to this version to keep the ride, handling and headlamp beams consistent under load.

Development of the 411 continued apace throughout the early seventies. The Mk3 of 1972 was a decisive facelifting exercise with a smoother full-width front opening dominated by four huge 7ins headlights. American legislation left the Bristol power source wide open to emission strangulation and the beginnings of this could be found on the Mk3's engine which had a lower 9.5:1 compression ratio.

The Mk4 411 took over in October 1973, using an even larger 6556cc 400 engine. The compression ratio had now plummetted to 8.2:1, so this unit could be run on three-star petrol – four-star was by now becoming scarce. For the first time, power outputs were quoted in DIN terms, and the 400 engine produced 264bhp at 4800rpm.

The final version of the 411 series appeared in 1975. Apart from chassis stiffening, measures to reduce vibration and other minor detail modifications, the Mk5 looked just a little more up to date, with its alloy wheels and blacked-out front grille. Inside, the rear seats had built-in head restraints and there was a cruise control.

The 411 models, with their better developed suspension, fatter tyres and magnificent power steering were now cross-country chargers of tremendous prowess. Autocar were reminded of this in a brief assessment of the Mk5 in 1976: 'The 411 may be hustled down a bumpy lane with no trace of bump steer, or any waywardness of the back end. Come what may, it goes where the driver intends it should, the oversteer of the early cars transformed into a

BUYER'S SPOT CHECK

Because of their relatively low market value, some V8 Bristols have fallen into unsympathetic hands. They will often have gone completely unserviced or been maintained by a local garage with limited knowledge of the marque. Luckily, few cars are more sturdily constructed and a Bristol is well able to stand up to years of such treatment before becoming completely unserviceable. Buying such a car is a risky business, because spares prices are in the Rolls/Aston class and specialist services will not come particularly cheap. In the long run, you may be better off going higher up the price scale to an obviously well maintained car with some kind of service history.

The Bristol body is made up of hand-formed aluminium panels over a steel frame (with lagging between the two to prevent electrolytic action) and the standard of construction is extremely high. If you are inspecting an original condition 407, 408 or 409 then you may be struck by the dullness of the paintwork. This is because the cellulose paint used on these early cars aged quickly and was replaced by acrylic on the 410.

The body itself cannot rust in the conventional sense but could be covered in ugly paint blisters, particularly around wheel arches, door bottoms, sills etc. Outer wings could need attention around the headlamps.

One Bristol idiosyncracy is the mounting of the spare wheel in the left-hand front wing, and battery, brake servos and central electrical panel in the right-hand. These boxes are made of steel and usually display a degree of corrosion. Examine the rear inner wheel arches for rust and look at the condition of the boot floor. On 411s, incidentally, the seat belt anchorages can come adrift.

Look at the condition of bumpers, grilles and all chrome trim as prices of certain large items run into hundreds of pounds. If you're looking at an accident-damaged car, it's worth remembering that the average price of a front wing is £1000, but most damage can be beaten out.

The chassis is massively constructed. It consists of two widely spaced deep box section sidemembers, braced by three cross-members. It is very strong and rarely suffers any serious corrosion. First of all, look at the shut-plates between the outriggers which are sometimes rotten, and take a screwdriver to the section over the back axle. Be on the look-out for corrosion around and on the shock absorber mountings, as this is expensive to repair. Look at the state of the area around the bump stops.

The front suspension is a very conventional coil spring and wishbone assembly which, apart from the occasional track rod and ball joint, gives little trouble. If the car looks a little low at the front, the springs have gone soft. Spring seats can break.

It's important that the rear suspension is in reasonably good order because it's a specialised assembly using a live axle, torsion bars, central torque arm, lateral links and a Watts linkage. Torsion bars go soft (they're adjustable) and the various bushes on the Watts linkage, torque arm and so on could be shot. To establish the condition

Specialists can supply many items, and Bristol themselves maintain a strong interest

of the torsion bar roller bearings, drive the car over some good deep pot-holes. If you hear a loud metallic crack then they are due for replacement. This is bad news because the job involves completely dismantling the rear suspension, which is obviously a very costly and time consuming task. Armstrong Selectaride dampers can become inoperative, and on 411s, see if the self levelling is leaking. As for the axle itself, look for leakage around the diff oil seal.

When you try a car without power assistance, look for excessive vagueness in the steering, as the Marles box is now fairly hard to obtain and very expensive. On later models (409 Mk2 onwards), the power steering should be responsive with no 'grittiness'. The 407 and 408 used Dunlop braking systems and some parts are hard to get. Brakes seize if the car has been left standing and the discs corrode. Servoes are prone to leaking.

Power units don't come much more bullet-proof than the 313, 318, 383 and 400 Chrysler engines used in these cars. There are no twin cams, fuel injection systems or alloy blocks to worry about and if regularly maintained, well over 200,000 miles is possible. It's really just a case of looking for obvious signs of wear, such as noisy tappets (pre-411), blue smoke and low oil pressure. A badly maintained car will have the wrong size hoses, fan belts and so on – much to the detriment of the engine's long term well-being. The Torqueflite automatic gearbox is very highly thought of and as long as regular maintenance is carried out (oil changes every 24,000 miles, bands adjusted) it can last for 100,000 miles or more. Needless to say, the change should be very smooth.

The engine/transmission package can be serviced by any reputable American specialist, which is an advantage if you live five hours' drive away from the nearest Bristol specialist. The interior is trimmed in the best British traditions, with walnut veneer on the facia and door cappings, thick seats trimmed in top quality leather and deep pile carpets. On older cars, the veneer can often be faded, cracked or peeling and this can be fairly expensive to restore. Hide food will usually bring dry, cracked leather seats up to scratch but again, if there are any rips then refurbishment will be expensive. Make sure all the gauges are operative, as these are costly items to replace.

The parts situation for these cars is good. Specialists – admittedly they are pretty thin on the ground – can supply many items, and Bristol themselves maintain a strong interest. For instance, at the time of writing, left-hand 411 wings are out of stock and a new batch is being made up.

If you choose your Bristol carefully, it's hard to see where you can go wrong.

gentle, constant, entirely predictable understeer'.

Performance was described as 'crushing', but one of the delightful features of the V8 Bristols is that they never seem to be going as fast as they really are, and *Autocar* made note of this: 'Speedometer checks on some familiar twisty minor roads showed the Bristol was scurrying along faster than almost anything I had previously taken there – yet without feeling particularly quick or in any way ragged … it is worth noting that the 411 speedometer actually *under* read by 1mph at 60; is there any exotic 'GT' that can make the same claim?'

The journal had few gripes to report. The brakes were a little unprogressive, tyre squeal was prominent on some surfaces and although the ride compromise was perfect for the sporting types, it was just a touch firm by Rolls-Royce standards. The tester had his doubts about the car's ability to sit four six-footers in absolute comfort, but the car's refinement was only ruffled when all four chokes of the Carter carb were opened up.

Simultaneously with the 411 Mk5, Bristol announced the 412 'convertible saloon' and they hoped the two models would sell alongside each other in equal numbers (the company had no wish to break its strict three cars a week rule). This was not to be, however, because the 406-inspired shape of the 411 was now very dated, and most buyers were opting for the much more modern (but better looking?) Zagato style of the 412.

To redress the sales balance the company needed a much more up-to-date saloon body and such a car appeared at the 1976 Earls Court show – the 603.

And so ended the first generation of V8 Bristols. With their performance and refinement, they had won the company new friends, yet they had retained that 'something' which makes a Bristol unlike any other car.

PRODUCTION HISTORY

The Bristol 407 was priced at £5141 when introduced in September 1961, an increase of £773 over the 406. The only option was an HMV radio with twin speakers. Externally, this model was almost indistinguishable from the six-cylinder car, except for its flatter bonnet, continuous chrome strip down its flanks and a badge inside the front air intake.

In September 1963, the heavily face-lifted 408 was announced, with Armstrong Selectaride dampers and improved ventilation. At £4459 it was priced

£200 higher than the 407. The last few 408s used the 5221cc engine and lighter gearbox used in the 409. These were known as 408 Mk2s.

The 409 arrived at London Motor Show time in 1965, with the slightly larger '318' engine, aluminium gearbox housing and minor styling refinements. A pre-engaged starter, alternator and better quality exhaust system were also used on this model, priced at £4849. In autumn 1966, a Mk2 specification 409 was announced, with ZF power steering. The £5673 410 was introduced in October 1967, with 15ins rather than 16ins wheels, dual circuit braking system, and a slightly sleeker front end look. Air conditioning could now be ordered as an option, and later examples used Avon radial tyres.

The first manifestation of the 411 series came in October 1969. Outwardly, this car used fewer

The 409 arrived at London Motor Show time in 1965, with the slightly larger '318' engine

chrome accents and lost the vestigial rear fins but under the skin there was Chrysler's '383' engine, producing 38 per cent more power. Bristol finally dispensed with the large Bluemels steering wheel (used since the 401) and the facia was tidied up. The 411 could also claim revised suspension geometry and a limited slip differential. First deliveries of this model were not made until 1970 and the price was £6997 – a £869 increase over the 410. The Mk2 car of late 1970 used bigger 205 tyres and self-levelling rear suspension.

A new, slimmer full-width front grille was a feature of the 411 Mk3 of May 1972, and from the rear the car was identifiable by four exhaust outlets. The engine now ran with a lower compression ratio. In October 1973 the 6556cc Mk4 appeared, and although this car was at first glance identical to the Mk3, the observant would have noticed the flatter boot lid and different rear lamp clusters.

Introduced in May 1975, the Mk5 411 had modernised styling touches (alloy wheels, matt black front grille) and numerous small technical alterations to the fuel pump, exhaust system and so on. The Mk5 remained in the price lists until October 1976, by which time it had risen to £15,924.

According to my figures, Bristol produced 1800 407 to 411 models between 1961 and 1976: that's 1200 407, 409 and 410 variants and 600 411s.

CLUBS, SPECIALISTS AND BOOKS

The Bristol Owners Club was formed in the spring of 1965 as a section of the BMW Car Club. The two split in 1970, and today the club has more than 500 members spread across regional centres in Britain and the USA. A member can obtain technical information and copies of road tests, articles and workshop manuals as well as seeing other Bristols and their owners – a rare experience in itself. The regular bulletin features cars for sale and as might be expected, the club has a close relationship with the factory. For more details write to the membership secretary Lou Bates 'Willowhayne', Burcot, Abingdon, Oxon OX14 3DP (0865 891466).

The classic car scene isn't exactly over-run with Bristol specialists. Bristol's service depot is convenient for London-based owners and as well as undertaking service and repairs they have a good selection of used cars. Their address is Bristol Cars Limited, 368/370 Kensington High Street, London W14 8NL (tel: 01-603 5556).

TT Workshops have been associated with Bristol service and restoration for years and can be found at 127 Engineer Road, West Wilts Trading Estate, Westbury, Wiltshire (tel: Westbury 823603). Performance Auto Services are at Unit 2, Heath Farm, Iron Mould Lane, Brislington, Bristol BS4 5SA (tel: 0272 777685) and specialise in Bristol repair and restoration. They have stocks of new and used parts.

Bradburn and Wedge are actually Nissan dealers, but they can service and restore Bristols of all ages. They can be contacted at 41 Birmingham Road, Wolverhampton (tel: Wolverhampton 58456). American Autoparts are a source of Bristol engine components and their address is 132-134 Brigstock Road, Thornton Heath, Surrey (tel: 01-684 7737).

Bristol Cars and Engines by L.J.K. Setright is the only book that deals with these cars. The oft-quoted 160 pager was first published in 1974 and has been out of print for about 18 months, so it's in short supply. The Bristol story is covered entertainingly in the author's distinctive style with a good deal of text on the V8s. The pictures are of the rather unexciting 'club meet' type (though there are some fair drawings) and there's no colour. A welcome addition promised for publication in the summer by Brooklands Books is a 188 page road test reprint collection, *Bristol Cars Gold Portfolio 1946-85*, at £9.95.

Bristol 407 with 'plane-inspired nose

408 had new grille and brightwork

Brutal-looking 'face' for the 409 model

410 of '67 – smaller wheels, new brakes

Bigger motor and no fins for first 411

Mk5 411 – old shape, modern details

SPECIFICATION	BRISTOL 407	BRISTOL 411 Mk IV
Engine	V8	V8
Bore/stroke	98 × 84mm	110 × 85mm
Capacity	5130cc	6556cc
Valves	Pushrod	Pushrod
Compression	9:1	8.2:1
Power	250bhp (gross) at 4400rpm	330bhp (gross) at 5200rpm
Torque	340lbs ft at 2800rpm	418lbs ft at 3400rpm
Transmission	Three-speed automatic	Three-speed automatic
Final drive	3.35:1	3.07:1
Brakes	Discs all round	Discs all round
Suspension front	Ind by wishbones, coil springs, dampers and anti-roll bar	Ind by wishbones, coil springs, dampers and anti-roll bar
Suspension rear	Live axle, torsion bars, Watts linkage, central torque arm, and dampers	Live axle, torsion bars, Watts linkage, central torque arm, dampers, automatic self levelling
Steering	Marles worm and roller	ZF recirculating ball, power-assisted
Body	Box section frame, aluminium body	Box section frame, aluminium body
DIMENSIONS		
Length	16ft 7ins	16ft 2.5ins
Width	5ft 8ins	5ft 8ins
Height	5ft 0ins	4ft 9.5ins
Weight	3585lbs	3775lbs
PERFORMANCE		
Max speed	122mph	140mph
0-60mph	9.9secs	7.0secs
Standing ¼ mile	17.4secs	15.0secs

RIVALS WHEN NEW

Bristol owners will argue that there is nothing to rival their cars, but during the sixties quite a few small scale producers turned to the American 'big three' for V8 power. Facel Vega were among the first and the Facel II of 1962 also used a Chrysler unit of even greater potency. This exclusive French supercar was a genuine 140mph machine but the typical Bristol buyer may have dismissed it as vulgar. Those with a taste for even greater obscurity may have been tempted by the slightly cheaper ISO Rivolta. Actually, the ISO was quite an agreeable big GT with stylish Bertone looks (room for four) and beefy performance from its 300bhp (gross) GM V8. These cars seem to be completely forgotten today.

The Gordon Keeble GK1 looked very similar to the ISO (it was also by Bertone) and used the same engine yet it cost £1000 less. Its poor interior and glass-fibre body let it down and only 99 cars were built. The Jensen C-V8 was more of a known quantity, but for many, ferocious performance couldn't outweigh its eccentric looks and 'plastic special' image. Pure-bred rivals to the Bristol were much in evidence in the sixties and the super rich may have considered a Rolls-Royce (or Bentley) Park Ward Continental. Very elegant and luxurious, the home grown 6.2-litre V8 was no powerhouse and its handling was barge-like by Bristol standards. Aston Martin were encroaching on Bristol territory with the bigger DB6 of 1965. In manual form, it was as swift and sporting as ever, but the automatic was a bit limp-wristed. They were priced very closely at first, but by the late sixties the Bristol had taken a sizeable price hike.

The glamorous four-seater Ferraris of the early sixties were perhaps a little overtly sporting to bear comparison with the Bristol, but the big 365GT 2+2 of 1967 brought a degree of refinement to the range. Maseratis, though, have consistently offered four-seater alternatives to the V8 Bristols, notably the elegant 4.2 and 4.7-litre Mexico introduced in 1965 and the even faster 4.7-litre, 156mph Indy of 1969-75. Both these glamour cars had handling to match their speed. The glut of American-engined hybrids available in the sixties had begun to dwindle by the beginning of the seventies. The Jensen Interceptor was well established and managed to combine all the C-V8's performance in an elegant all-steel shell. In spite of its low build, this cart-sprung 2+2 never achieved the Bristol's degree of handling poise. The Aston Martin of the seventies was an altogether bigger, more sophisticated beast, and the six-cylinder DBS ran the Bristol close on price and performance. The V8 was a staggeringly fast car but was much more expensive.

The Mercedes 450SLC may have been considered too commonplace and 'low rent' to rival the Filton production, but it was actually more expensive when introduced in 1972. Elegant, quick, but undistinguished, sums up these cars. The mild mannered Rolls-Royce Corniche may not have been fast, but it was still the ultimate in prestige and style.

PRICES

If you want a real bargain V8 Bristol, then look for one of the 407, 408, 409 or 410 models. These come up fairly infrequently, but they are often priced as low as £2500 for an MoT'd car needing a respray and general tidy up. Top condition examples go up to £5500-plus.

The 411 models are in good supply and can be found in fair order for well under £3000. Most of the cars currently for sale seem to be Mk 2, 3 and 4 411s in good to excellent condition, priced between £4950 and £7000. If you want to go all the way and buy the best examples available (short of concours) then you're talking of between £10,500 and £12,000. When you think of the prices being asked for more commonplace classics (offering less performance character), that's very good value indeed.

Hilary Riley (left) and Norman Balaam explain their Bristol passion

The very first Bristols, despite their pre-war BMW origins, were among the most desirable of British high performance cars in the peaceful years following 1945. The BMW 327 and 328 had been race-bred in the Mille Miglia and Targa Florio, and Bristol cars were subsequently raced and rallied and even achieved considerable success at Le Mans with the strange but aerodynamic 450.

The advent of the Bristol 407, however, with its super-smooth Chrysler V8 motor and silky Torque-flite automatic gearbox – operated by push buttons in the true American style – meant that all competition aspirations the marque might have had were lost, and the car matured into a refined gentleman's carriage of considerable distinction, with lots of power but hardly sports car handling. If you were retiring, and couldn't stand the thought of living out the rest of your days in the company of a Vanden Plas 1100, then it would be just the thing.

Believe it or not, this is what Norman Balaam and Hilary Riley have done, and it has to be said that neither the cars nor their owners are showing any serious signs of old age. Hilary Riley, who is now in semi-retirement after a career in mining engineering, owns an immaculate Bristol 407, with the appropriate 407 PF registration number. He came across this amazingly untouched example in a particularly strange way.

"I bought it not meaning to keep it! A local enthusiast died, and his widow wanted to sell all his collection of cars as one batch, and not have to go to all the trouble of selling them off individually. I bought them as a job lot because there was a Mk 2 Jaguar, a 1947 Sunbeam Talbot, a Triumph motorcycle and so on as well as this Bristol. The idea was to buy them all, and then sell off the Bristol to recoup the complete expenditure. Then I drove the thing and liked it so much that I *had* to keep it. Shortly afterwards, I swapped the Triumph for a 408."

Hilary Riley's car is not in absolutely concours condition, but it is totally original. It has never been resprayed, and the paintwork has retained its deep cellulose maroon lustre, bar a few touched-up stone chips here and there. It is obviously a well-cared for car as the 32,000 miles that it had done when Hilary bought the car in 1981 shows.

"It was originally a Tony Crook demonstrator, and I think that it had the 100 MPH number on it at one time or another. It's a 1962 car, and was in near perfect condition when I bought it. It's in general use all through the year – not daily, but certainly weekly. Since I have had the car, I've replaced the petrol pump and that's all! I got the pump for $30 on a trip to the 'States, in Cleveland. It's always had proper servicing, but I have found that for some reason it does get through distributor points, and I always carry a girl's emery-board in the glove compartment just in case."

We went for an all-too-brief drive around the neat suburban avenues of Beckenham, the car seeming very much at home among the lines of trees, neat gardens and 'daily helps' scuttling home in the midday sunshine. Even tootling along, there is masses of power in reserve, while the car has Rolls-Royce standards of silence and build quality. The Bristol was designed with four six foot golfers in mind, for there is lots of room in the front *and* back, and the boot, with the spare wheel safely stowed away in a cavern in the front wing, could easily swallow four sets of clubs, probably a couple of trollies and maybe for long golfing sojourns, an unwilling caddy too!

"It's beautiful to drive in every respect," said Hilary, as the power steering eased us around another corner. "I have no complaints at all, other than it's a bit thirsty. I've had 125mph out of it, still with a bit in reserve, and I felt quite relaxed. I get distinctly nervous doing the same thing in E-type Jaguars …"

That the Bristol V8s we are examining here are timeless designs was brought home to us when we stepped into Norman Balaam's stunning turquoise-blue 411 Mk 2. Ten years separate the two cars, but other than a few concessions to modernity like electric windows and seat belts, you would be hard-pushed to tell the difference between them.

"I bought the 411 from Bristol Cars in Kensington High Street," said Norman, "having traded in my old 408 for it. The car was only three years old then, and the asking price was £5000. The engines always seem to be years out of date – Tony Crook probably buys engines at the end of their production run."

Norman uses his Bristol all year round, although he is now semi-retired from Centronics, where he was an electronics consultant, and it had to stand outside during the rather savage winter from which we are just emerging, the family garage having been 'bagged' by his son for a Triumph GT6 rebuild. He also has a Reliant Scimitar coupé. Like the 407, his 411 is not in pristine condition, which is hardly surprising as Norman uses it every day.

"It's on the road every day, even if it's only pottering around. The car as a whole is very reliable. I've owned this car for ten years now, and the only thing that's gone wrong is when the front suspension packed up. Both servoes have had to be seen to as well. Bristol Cars themselves are very good when it comes to spare parts and can supply virtually everything, but servicing is very expensive indeed. One other thing to remember is that the back axle does need servicing every year without fail, mainly because of the limited slip differential."

It seems that the real attraction of Bristol ownership lies in the fact that it's the sort of exotic car that can be used all year round, which has the subtle image that precludes it from the attentions of vandals, yet remains sophisticated enough not to be out of place at the smartest shoot or cocktail party on a warm summer's evening.

Souls of discretion

Bristol has been in business for 50 years; Martin Buckley drives all its significant models

Buying a Bristol, say those who've had them, is like having your first Saville Row suit made: once you've worn one nothing else will feel quite right. Distinguished yet discreet, fast but not flashy, to its owner the Bristol is a luxury car without an image problem, a quality machine that says the right things to the right people without a hint of ostentation or an ounce of excess.

You couldn't call Bristol a cutting-edge kind of company. Even among British specialist cars Bristol is unique in its perseverance with a massively strong box-section chassis frame whose origins can be traced directly back to the pre-war BMW 327/8, and a live rear axle with torsion bar springing. Rarely has Bristol strayed outside its classic 9ft 6in wheelbase and all the cars, aside from the initial 400, have used an aluminium body.

In precisely 50 years of motor car manufacture, sales figures have yet to break the 10,000 mark. Bristol has no agents (if you want one you buy it from the boss, Tony Crook, at the showroom in Kensington) and doesn't advertise because its reputation has always passed by word of mouth. In any case, the production rate at the Filton factory has never exceeded three hand-crafted cars a week.

The cars have matured with their loyal ownership over the past five decades. The agile 2-litre saloons of the '40s and '50s were favoured by the sporting connoisseur, cars for the man who liked to use the gearbox and get the best out of a sweet, high-efficiency straight-six that was the pride and trademark of the company. It wasn't for nothing that this compact and robust 2-litre engine was favoured by the likes of AC, Cooper and Frazer Nash.

As the age and expectations of the owners increased (and ordinary cars became much quicker) the quest for more effortless, torquey power led Bristol to the Chrysler V8 engine – with attendant auto 'box – which, essentially, is still used in today's Blenheim. For Bristol traditionalists it was a shock to find the classic straight-six banished to the history books. But they got over it, and for 30 years the big, smooth and very reliable Chrysler engine has proved equally addictive in its way, if not such an engineers' delight.

The Bristol Aeroplane Company looked to car manufacture at the end of the 1939-45 war as a way of using spare production capacity. The workforce was highly skilled, yet relatively cheap labour.

By chance Don Aldington of AFN (pre-war importer of Frazer-Nash BMW) was posted to the Bristol office of the Ministry of Aircraft Production and, hearing of Bristol's plans, alerted his brother HJ Aldington who promptly demonstrated a 327 BMW to Bristol directors. They were impressed and the Aldington brothers were soon on a flight to Munich, liberating a planeload of BMW drawings and parts and, later, the BMW engineer/designer Fritz Feidler as the spoils of war.

The steel-bodied, wood-framed Bristol 400 was announced in September 1946, not so pretty, perhaps, as its German alter ego the BMW 327 but beautifully built to close aircraft tolerances and with the best of materials. Despite a £2500 price tag that put it well into the upper-crust luxury bracket, the 400 got rave reviews: it was fast, comfortable reasonably economical and superbly well-wrought with all but a handful of its fixtures and fittings built in-house by Bristol.

TONY BAKER

Driving Simon Draper's 400, oldest of the seven cars assembled in this 50-year celebration of the marque, was a reminder of how roadable the car still is.

Though 400s ran in a mild state of tune to take account of the lousy pool petrol of the late '40s and early '50s, pick-up is eager, highlighting the free-breathing efficiency of the hemi-head design with its big valves and triple SUs. Like all the six-cylinder cars it sounds busy, but well bred. Even on a modest low-compression 80bhp the 400 goes well with a tailored smoothness to all the controls.

Inside, when you're sitting low in torso-cupping buckets behind a massive steering wheel the 400 seems older than its years, with that slot-like rear window and high scuttle. There is little elbow room despite the hollowed-out 'suicide' doors with their sliding windows. Fine detailing abounds too, like the extravagant cantilevered window blinds, and the elegant facia.

Steering – rack and pinion – is precise, light and cornering positive with none of the lumbering understeer and wallow that characterises so many of the 400's contemporaries.

Draper – a Bristol addict who is also custodian of the sole remaining 450 racer – also owns the 403, a freshly-restored car with the late-type remote gearchange. This bold, slippery 'Aerodyne' style was first seen on the 401 of 1949 using Touring's Superleggera principle of small-diameter tubes around which alloy panelling was wrapped, its thickness graded according to function; it was thicker on top of the wings, for instance, where mechanics leant during servicing. On such attention to detail was Bristol's reputation forged.

The shape, inspired by Touring with its elegant teardrop tail and smooth contours, was honed on Bristol's two-mile Filton runway and was truly aerodynamic for the time with low levels of wind noise. Twenty years later only four cars (out of 100) were found to have a lower drag co-efficient when tested in the wind tunnel at MIRA.

The 403, announced in 1953, gained more power from the 100A (100bhp) engine and could easily top the ton: it was fitted with Alfin drum brakes too, for more secure stopping. Tweaked damper settings and the addition of a front anti-roll bar alleviated the tendency towards oversteer, a corollary of the extreme rear mounting of its spare wheel and fuel tank.

Again, it is packed with pleasing details, like the push-button door catches, remote boot release, and the square instrumentation. Even the action of the window winder mechanisms feels smooth, slop-free and well-oiled. Inside it is a bigger, more grown-up car than the 400 with more shoulder room, glass area and rear seat knee room: the 400 was never much better than a generous two-plus-two.

The driving position is commanding, the voluptuous bonnet seemingly vast but there is a delectable feeling of delicacy about the steering; fluid and light yet full of feel and precision. On the move the 403 feels half its size.

The gearchange, a shorter lever now, snicks in and out of ratios with a deliciously light, precise action and the freewheel on first means you can grab bottom for a quick getaway without having to double-declutch. The car feels eager rather than quick, but even in its heyday the forte of the 403 was rapid cross-country progress – or fast, restful top gear cruising – rather than traffic-light drags.

Above: 403 2-litre 'six' has 100bhp for a genuine 100mph.
Left: airy interior of Aerodyne 403 shows superb detail and was first Bristol with sporty remote gearchange.
Below: sleek aerodynamic shape was moulded on Bristol's Filton runway. Spare tyre lives in tail

Breathing through triple high-mounted Solex carbs, the 403 has the throaty, rich timbre of a thoroughbred, a busy snarl that hardens in aggression as the revs climb. It stops better than the 400, with a positive pedal.

The 404, announced in 1953, was a low-volume, short-chassis variation on the 2-litre theme, its wheelbase clipped to just over 8ft to make a compact two-seater coupé.

The styling was new, with a smooth wing line flowing from the brow of the headlights to the pert, rounded tail, its vestigial fins allegedly exerting some stabilising effect at speed. The nose treatment was fresh too, its grille inlet aping the ducts on the wings of the ill-fated Brabazon airliner. Though Bristol never attempted another short-chassis special (unless you count the hybrid Arnolt with its

Bertone body) the timber-framed 404 introduced two Bristol hallmarks that endure to this day: the spare wheel and battery mounted behind either front wheelarch (thus liberating luggage space) and a handsome, shrouded instrument panel directly behind the wheel.

Owner James Calladine, 404 registrar, has owned his car since 1983 when, still a teenager, he bought it from Bristol: "My grandfather used to own them and thought a lot of them. I thought I should carry on the family tradition."

Running the standard 105bhp engine (there was an optional sports cam 125bhp unit) the 404 has the aggression the earlier cars lacked because the weight is lower, the whole feel more nimble with your backside so much nearer the rear axle line.

The steering and gearchange (closer ratio

Original 400 unit uses SU carburettors

Neat binnacle houses dials in '54 405

Top: 404 two-door most sought after 2-litre Bristol though many rate four-door 405, above, as one of the best to drive. Vestigal fins on 404 were meant to help high speed stability. Left: elegant interior of 400

than the 403's) remain superbly slop-free, with plenty of full-blooded oversteer available on tight radii, and generally a more nervous, twitchy feel than the long-chassis cars.

A non-standard Laycock overdrive unit lengthens the gait of the Calladine 404, improving its motorway legs.

For some the pick of the six-cylinder cars from the driver's point of view is the most common of the breed, the four-door 405 of 1954. Its styling themes were developed from the 404 with a near-identical nose and sweeping wing line, but with rear doors and lots of extra glass. Running the 105bhp 100B2 engine, the 405 came with overdrive but lacked some of the classy detailing found on earlier Bristols with its conventional (and rot-prone) bumpers and parts-bin door handles.

Chris Reynolds' 405, bought at the end of 1990, is a well-known car, having belonged to one of the founders of the Bristol Owners' Club. It runs a sports camshaft, a raised compression ratio and stiffened-up suspension with a 406 anti-roll bar, a legacy of its '70s and '80s club competition history.

The freewheel on first, easy to blow if abused, has been deleted which means you have to double-declutch when engaging first. With the high-lift cam the idle is fairly ragged and nothing much happens below 3500rpm: from there on pick-up is crisp and aggressive as the needle shoots round to 5000rpm.

Thrown into a curve, roll is superbly controlled, the fat armchair seats surprisingly hip-hugging as the Michelin X tyres (as fitted to the FX4 taxi) bite into the tarmac. Flip the

slim lever up a cog, fast as you like, blipping the throttle to ease its progress, and you can set the 405 for an aggressive exit out of the next turn with a twitch of oversteer, though its natural posture is confident neutrality. You can feel the back axle working a little, the steering squirming on the folds and undulations of the road yet it is dead positive and free from slop: good steering is a theme that runs through all these early Bristols.

The move from 'six' to V8 was bridged by the 406 of 1958 with its bigger, more luxurious steel-framed body (built outside of Bristol) pointing the way to the plutocrat appeal of the Bristols of the '60s and beyond. What it needed was more power: even with its bigger 2.2-litre engine the fully disc-braked 406, with a Watt linkage to tidy up the handling still

410 has quiet, well-balanced lines with room for four six footers and luggage. Powered by 5.2-litre V8, tops 130mph easily

WHICH IS WHICH?

400: 1946-50 (474 made) Steel body, six-cylinder 2-litre engine. Bespoke and refined, if lacking aesthetic appeal.

401: 1948-53 (611 made) Alloy Superleggera build for this first 'Aerodyne' Bristol. Superb quality, poor vision.

402: 1949-50 (23 made) Elegant Touring convertible based on 401, highly prized but lacks integrity of saloons.

403: 1953-55 (281 made) Much improved 401 with 100A engine, better brakes and front anti-roll bar.

404: 1953-55 (52 made) Rare short-chassis two-seater coupé with new Brabazon airliner grille and timber framing. Chassis twitchy.

405: 1954-58 (285 made) The only four-door Bristol; 100B2 engine and overdrive. Lovely steering, sweet gearshift.

405 Drophead: 1954-56 (43 made) Convertible by Abbot of Farnham. Elegant and much sought-after.

406 Zagato; only 7 made

406: 1958-61 (174 made) Overweight but beautifully contrived with 2.2-litre, 110bhp engine. Luxurious.

406 Zagato: 1960-61 (7 made). Coupé and six 'saloons', some with Abarth-tweaked 110S engine. All but one survive.

407: 1961-63 (88 made) First of the Chrysler V8 cars, same look as 406 but with coil-spring suspension.

408: 1963-65 (83 made) Same 5.2 Chrysler engine but new front-end styling. Pacy.

409: 1965-67 (74 made) Rounded corners on the grille. Improved steering and better weight distribution thanks to moving the engine back.

410: 1968-69 (79 made)

Subtle styling changes give a smoother line. Smaller wheels, floor-shift for auto box.

411: 1969-76 (287 made) Big 6.2-litre engine. 6.6-litre engine followed. 140mph.

412/Beaufighter: 1975-92. Zagato-styled convertible with big double roll-over bar and 6.6-litre Chrysler V8. 1980 model had Rotomaster turbo.

603E/603S: 1976-82 **Brigand/Britannia** '82-92. 'E' was 5.2-litre 'economy' model, S had 5.9-litre engine. Brigand/Britannia replaced 603, Brigand turbocharged with sub-six second 0-60mph.

Blenheim: 1993 on. Latest 5.9-litre Chrysler engine. No turbo but economy impressive.

603E; 'economy' model

further, was a relatively leisurely performer.

With plans for a complex all-new Bristol (Project 220) canned due to lack of funds, new company owners Sir George White and Tony Crook cast around for a new engine to give the 406 the muscle it needed as a '60s motorway express. The 407, with its Canadian-built Chrysler 5.2-litre V8 was the result, catapulting the big four-seater into the 130mph class with standing quarter-mile times equal to the contemporary two-plus-two Ferraris.

Gone was the delicate four-speed Bristol gearbox, replaced by a Chrysler Torqueflite automatic (with flashy push-button selection) and seamless gearchanges. Gone too was that lovely rack and pinion steering, replaced by a Marles worm type unit which, combined with the heavy lump of iron up front, conspired to

make the 407 a less nimble car through tighter turns than its thoroughbred predecessors. Front suspension was new too, coils supplanting the classic transverse leaf.

By the time Roger Stanton's silver early 410 was being produced in 1969, sensitive, high-geared ZF power steering had largely answered that complaint, along with stacks of detail tweaks to the brakes, trim and the styling: the brutal rectangular grille of the 408 was introduced to improve cooling, the tiny fins progressively clipped. The 410 sat lower on wider Avon Turbospeed rubber, and was the first Bristol with the central gear selector for its auto transmission, the last to use the classic 17in Bluemels wheel introduced on the 401. Roger has owned his car since 1989 and finds it easy to live with: only a lack of

secure parking at work prevents him from using it every day.

A gentle-natured, well-mannered device, the 410 feels dark and broody inside and surprisingly narrow, a legacy of the pre-war chassis. Better mannered than a Jensen, less aggressive than an Aston, it has a unique sobriety that could only come from Britain.

Wafting discreetly yet purposefully away on a whiff of throttle, it barely raises an eyebrow when you mash the accelerator into the Wilton for a blast of kick-down aggression that sends the rev counter sweeping around to 4000rpm: keep it there and 60mph should show up in 8.8 secs, 100 in 23 secs and – thanks to Bristol's replacement of the standard Chrysler hydraulic tappets with solid lifters – will pull its 5500 rpm red line in top for a full whack of 130mph.

Barnaby Swire's 411 Series 3 is more of the same but with perhaps the best-looking of the bodies used on the V8 Bristols of the '70s. The 411 series, with its bigger 6.3-litre engine, looked much like the 410 when announced in 1969 but the S3 of 1972 had a much cleaner front-end look with four 7in lamps and an oval 'barbecue' grille. Inside, the drawing-room luxury remained but Bristol was beginning to fit the luxury options expected in its class, like power windows and air conditioning, although the 411's stock ventilation system was already one of the best around.

Swire's car has a non-standard 5.9-litre engine from the 603 fitted 20,000 miles ago along with several other subtle modifications that make it more usable everyday. With dampers adjusted to a soft setting (the self-levelling has long since been disconnected) the 411 rides serenely with just the occasional wiggle from the rear to suggest a live axle. That separate chassis all but eliminates road noise too, though the quiet was occasionally broken by a rustle from the fabric sunroof.

The power steering, with three turns lock to lock, has fine weight and precision for such a big car and the chassis serves up lovely balance through the sort of fast, sweeping corners it is most at home on. On slightly fatter-than-standard Avon rubber there is plenty of grip in hand too.

Like all Bristols it is relatively narrow so in

Elegant 140mph Series 3 411 is swift and refined – best looking of the series

411 interior traditional, well–wrought

Turbo Beaufighter of '80s is very rapid

Chrysler V8 is silent, reliable, docile

town you can thread the 411 through gaps that would stop most other luxury cars, all from a commanding driving position in the big armchair seat.

Even with the gearbox set to change into top at 60mph (with the throttle floored) performance is vigorous: a majestic swell of torque gives the 411 the sort of effortless urge you only get with a really big V8, surging past 100mph without a hint of strain. The engine is always distant, only the Carter carburettor releasing a slight moan when all four chokes are flipped open. This is a fast car but not an especially thirsty one: Swire reports 17mpg on unleaded fuel.

The last of the 411-series cars (Series 5) was joined by the Zagato-styled 412 Convertible in 1975 with its removable targa panel, chunky roll bar and folding fabric rear roof section. It was the first open Bristol production model since the Abott-bodied 405.

The Beaufighter, announced in 1980, was a turbocharged version of the 412 with a new four-light front end and a glass sunroof replacing the targa panel. An American Rotomaster turbo system, specially adapted by Bristol, took the top speed up to 140mph, with 0-60mph in 6.7 secs but Bristol, playing the Rolls-Royce game, wouldn't quote its output.

Whatever, the Beaufighter has massive urge on the road: dump the throttle – fitted with an extra-stiff return spring on this car to keep its lead-footed owner in check – and you get that same effortless swell of power followed immediately by a flick from the boost gauge, a whoosh from the turbo and a giant rush of energy. First will take you to 60mph, second to 115 if you keep your foot planted, all with the same silken gearchanges and precise, delicate steering as the 411. Non-standard alloys shod with fatter rubber fill the Beaufighter's arches but thump more heavily on potholes and ridges than standard. The car doesn't so much glide over bumps as bash them into submission with its sheer mass.

If anything, the driving position is even more commanding, and four-way electric motors in the seat should give anybody perfect posture. The dash had become a flat two-dimensional panel by then, still of polished walnut but somehow not so attractive.

AT THE DRIVING SEAT OF THE BLENHEIM PALACE

At its maximum of 151mph the Blenheim is slipping along at 4000rpm. At 100, you need only a whispering 2300rpm.

At 70mph the sequentially injected 5.9-litre V8 is hardly ticking over in that long, overdriven top. On his regular journeys to Filton, Bristol, from Kensington, Tony Crook reports an amazing 30mpg if he sticks to the speed limit, easy with the cruise control set.

The engine never raises its voice above a polite hum, even when you mash the throttle or

press the button to the right of the binnacle to click out of overdrive, and the wind glides quietly over the screen pillars.

As a town car it works equally well: you sit up high, the view out good thanks to slender roof pillars and plenty

of glass. Gearchanges are shamelessly smooth, the steering emollient yet positive and high-geared with an excellent lock. It's a car somehow aloof from the rabid pack.

Even if the ride lacks the ultimate absorbent smoothness of a Jaguar or Bentley it has a supple, gentle quality few would quibble at. Even at £110,000 the Blenheim undercuts its Rolls and Aston rivals and is far more exclusive, equally well-built. You cannot buy anything else like it anywhere in the world.

The 411 was replaced by the 603 in 1977 with a completely new sided two-door styling on the same chassis as before. The doors were carried over to the Britannia and the turbocharged Brigand in 1982. That line was duly superseded by the Blenheim in 1993.

With radically new front and rear end styling – but again, the familiar 603 doors – and the latest fully managed and sequentially-injected Chrysler V8 with a four-speed automatic box (for a long motorway stride) this car should see Bristol into the next century.

That Bristol has survived into the '90s is an achievement in itself. While 'rivals' like Aston and Jensen faced liquidation and disaster in the '70s and '80s Bristol quietly plodded on simply by staying small (Crook has never planned to produce more than 150 cars per year) and

satisfying a small, but loyal, clientele.

The company maintains a tremendous sense of continuity and Crook has always believed in looking after the older cars. So just think of this: when you drive your 400 or 403 into the Filton factory for an anniversary refit it may well be worked on by one of the men who built it. CLASSIC

Thanks to all the owners mentioned in the feature plus Bob Charlton of the Bristol Owners' Club for his help finding the cars. Thanks also to Martin Barnes of the American Car Care Centre (0171 278 9786) for locating the Beaufighter and Rob Widdows of Goodwood. Goodwood hosts the Festival of Speed on June 21-23 – for advance tickets call the hotline on 01243 787766

Bristol unveils beefier Blenheim

Blenheim has more power and new grille

Bristol is ready to launch a facelifted and more powerful version of its four-seater Blenheim coupe.

The Blenheim 3 goes on sale next month with a new grille and rounder front-end styling, priced £133,950.

Improvements to its air intakes and front spoiler increase its aerodynamic stability and give it a more modern look. Handling and the cabin are also improved.

The Blenheim 3 continues to use the specially adapted 5.9-litre Chrysler V8 engine, but it gets a compression hike, an improved inlet manifold, a camshaft design that allows the engine to breathe more freely at high revs and an exhaust system incorporating two low-restriction catalysts instead of one big one.

Bristol never reveals power figures, but power is up "significantly" to around 350bhp. There is a "noticeable" torque boost, too.

The Blenheim 3 also gets the new-generation Chrysler automatic gearbox, which is lighter and more robust than the previous one. The Bristol keeps its famed long legs for the motorway: top gear gives a remarkable 40.7mph per 1000rpm.

The traditional, hugely strong box-section chassis is unchanged, but new anti-roll bars increase stiffness by 25 per cent front and rear without the need for any increase in ride rates.

The front and rear tracks, widened for the Blenheim 2, are pulled apart a little more, and the car now wears distinctive multi-spoke alloy wheels with Avon Turbospeed tyres.

The new seats give better cornering support and have carefully sculpted rear faces to give rear seat passengers more knee room.

There are new, clearer instruments and the gearbox selector has been modernised.

Bristol chairman Tony Crook claims sales could come close to taxing Bristol's production capacity of 150 cars a year during 2000.

Tony Crook upbeat on sales

BRISTOL BRIGAND

continued from page 277

continued from page 277

V8 engine is ticking over at 3,600 rpm and the atmosphere within the cabin is akin to a West End club. I would suggest that the classic blend of high quality leather upholstery and trim, deep pile carpeting and hand-polished walnut is at least the equal of anything produced by Rolls-Royce. The instrumentation exudes quiet good taste, with white lettering on black backgrounds. Immediately ahead of the driver is a 160 mph speedometer and a matching 7,000 rpm rev-counter which has its warning line at 6,000 rpm. Between the two major dials is a turbocharger boost gauge, and there is a water temperature gauge (105 degrees was normal) and an oil pressure gauge which ran regularly around 55 psi. The fuel contents gauge for the 18 Imp gallon (82-litre) fuel tank is, perhaps thankfully, shielded by one's left hand when one adopts the normal "ten to two" position on the high-mounted, thin-rimmed steering wheel. The car includes in its basic price an excellent air conditioning system and a notably effective combination of heating / demisting and ram-effect ventilation. Not only are there four fresh air vents at face level across the fascia, but there is also one low down on each wheel arch, carefully designed to blow air between the front seats and the doors to cool / warm the rear seat passengers. It is this sort of attention to detail that marks the Bristol apart from even its more expensive and exalted rivals.

Other individualistic touches include rotating vents to admit cooling air from the inside of the compartments behind each wheel arch, those compartments containing the spare wheel (nearside) and the battery, twin brake servos and fuse panel (offside). Once released with the special key, which is normally kept tucked away in a little pouch

on the inside wall of the o/s wheel arch, the lower panels of each front wing swing upwards to reveal these two neat little features which are unique to Bristol's way of doing things.

Aside from its impressive straight line performance, the Bristol Brigand handles remarkably well for a machine which looks so upright and dignified. It rolls a reasonable amount, but at no time does one get the impression that the Avon rubber is about to lose adhesion with the road surface: it hangs on splendidly and, although the ride was, I felt, a touch softer than the Beaufighter's had been, the Brigand can really be hustled through tight corners at an amazing speed. The automatic gearbox was smooth and effective, but crept too much when stationary in "D", while the brakes were not quite as progressive as I would have liked. When one applied pressure to the pedal, they initially felt quite smooth but then seemed to come on too abruptly as the servo effect took over.

It goes without saying that the level of detailed trim and equipment on the Brigand was of a very high order indeed. Windows and front seat adjustment are controlled electronically, the individual headrests are removable when not required, electrically heated rear screen, electrically adjustable door mirrors, pockets on the rear of the front seats, courtesy light with a delay, the luggage boot can be opened electrically by the driver, the whole finished package is undersealed and the inside of the bodyshell selectively treated with anti-drumming material.

There is nothing quite like a Bristol. It's not as common as a Rolls-Royce or Bentley, it's more exclusive than a Jaguar or Mercedes-Benz, less ostentatious than an Aston Martin. It represents a blend of quiet, under-stated good taste allied to a high level of equipment, impeccable finish and dramatic performance. We called the Beaufighter "an English gentleman's very high speed touring carriage," no better soubriquet could be suggested for the Bristol Brigand; it's as simple as that.

A.H.

Not only is Blenheim 3 the last remaining British luxury car, but it is the only traditionally coachbuilt luxury car in series production anywhere to-day.

As with its predecessors it appeals to a most discerning type of owner and the new model incorporates a number of exciting and significant developments that render it more capable, comfortable and desirable than ever.

The new body blends modern elements with traditional Bristol style to give a sleek, rounded silhouette that will look distinguished in any company. The smooth new shape also confers aerodynamic benefits that will be appreciated on long continental journeys or in poor weather conditions at home. Examining Blenheim 3's extraordinary standard of finish and construction gives one immense and lasting pleasure.

Bristols have always been famous for cossetting and calming their occupants in a way that is unparalleled. To this end, Blenheim 3 introduces new "armchair" style seats which are tall and deeply contoured to hold you securely and with unrivalled comfort over any distance. Softly wrapping over these exceptional seats is a new soft, silky and flawless leather specially selected and processed in batches for Bristol Cars. Such quality cannot be found in any rival. Rear passengers can now enjoy concealed lockable storage compartments with veneered fold-out drinks trays or the "town limousine" interior which allows a special slimline front passenger seat to be folded forward when not in use affording effortless entry to the rear seats and almost unlimited legroom.

There is much new for the driving enthusiast to savour. New, clearer instrumentation is matched to improved fascia lighting based on recent scientific research. Optional automatic headlamp illumination and an electronic reversing aid system is available. A restyled centre console with short, precise transmission selector communicates with a new super-smooth highly responsive, electronically controlled automatic transmission. Under the bonnet the new TS3 series engine confers a considerable uplift to the Blenheim's already brilliant performance. Changes include a higher compression ratio, improved cylinder heads, high lift camshaft, more efficient fuel injectors and a new engine management system to ensure that available torque is increased throughout the engine's rev-range giving outstanding performance, engine response and fuel efficiency. Smooth and whisper quiet around town, Blenheim 3 can summon a super car type surge any time the mood takes you.

Enhanced high speed control is assured by a more precise steering linkage and a 28% increase in suspension roll stiffness. The latest tyre developments are incorporated as standard while larger wheels and lower profile tyres are available as options for the first time. A special handling package is available for those who see high speed driving as their primary intent and this uses a new patented variable rate damper, allowing firm high speed control without spoiling the car's low speed ride.

While retaining all Bristol's traditional virtues, Blenheim 3 sets delightful new standards of performance, luxury and style.

Further enquiries may be directed to the head office and showrooms:
Bristol Cars Ltd the manufacturers
368/370 Kensington High Street, London W14 8NL
020 7603 5556 www.bristolcars.co.uk

BRISTOL

A two-seater with 8.0-litre V10 power is not about keeping

Would you like to cruise at 100mph in hand-tailored comfort knowing that you could continue at that speed for four hours without refuelling? Would you relish the thought that the driving process would remain precise and sensually pleasant even at twice that speed?

If you would,then you had better contact Bristol Cars pretty smartly. Orders are already coming in for the new two-seater and the firm expects to make no more than 20 in the first year of production. Do not linger to check with your

bankers that the money will be there; if you have to ask, you probably cannot afford it.

As is part of the firm's unique tradition, Bristol is making no compromises in the design of the projected car and will make none in its manufacture. Functional form will never be subjugated to fickle fashion; everything will be of the highest possible quality, but will entirely ignore popular taste and evanescent modishness.

Bristol standards rigorously exclude any parasitic effects of steering or suspension geometries or mechanisms interfering with the purity and accuracy of steering feel, and no less rigorously exclude anything

but the very best parts of the best Connolly hides from use in the trimming of the cabin.

Most particularly, Bristol will have nothing to do with the senseless aping of racing practice in the design of a car meant specifically for use on the road. The wishbone suspension and inboard dampers, with only one anti-roll bar to tune out variations in roll couple distribution,will echo the layout of Formula 1 racers, but the rising wheel rates and complementary damper settings (Bristol always tests every damper and then fits them in matched sets) are calculated to eliminate the discomforts that may be acceptable in a racing

car, and to ensure a ride that is always supple and quiet.

As in almost every car it has ever made,and as is natural to a firm having its roots in aviation, Bristol attaches enormous importance to aerodynamics: it will have absolutely nothing to do with downforce.It is seen as utterly implausible and downright treacherous in a car running on real roads rather than on billiard-table tracks, and the inducement of downforce always involves a serious drag penalty that (unlike the downforce itself) is manifest at all speeds.

Instead, the car's external envelope is formed by mathematical procedures to

FASHION

...o with the current crop of GTs. It's just the way Bristol does things. By LJK Setright

ensure that attached flow is prolonged and turbulence postponed, that lift and downforce are kept to zero, and drag is kept to a minimum. The one-fifth scale model that is photographed here is so far all that anyone outside the firm has seen of the new project and is destined for the wind tunnel.

There may be modifications to adjust the position of the centre of pressure, but the designers are confident of a drag coefficient in the region of 0.27 and a consistency of behaviour at all speeds and in all weathers.

Noticeable on the model are the provisions for vitiated cooling air to be fed into low-pressure areas in the airstream above the bonnet and tail. Less obvious is that one of the frontal air intakes feeds no heat exchanger at all, but leads into the plenum chamber surrounding the engine where the air picks up some surface heat and, thereby energised, is accelerated through exits at the root of the windscreen to reinforce and steady the flow up and over the roof.

The screen itself is unusual. The centre portion of it is flat, only the ends being radiused: with the driver and passenger sitting shoulder to shoulder, as close to the centre line as possible, the forward view is uncorrupted and the curvature to the sides maintains as nearly as possible a constant radius from the occupants' eyes. Bristol insists on good and undistorted vision. Every Blenheim windscreen is tested (and many are rejected) for the same reason.

Stern inspection has always been part of the Bristol method for ensuring quality; it was part of the inheritance from the aircraft industry. So is the firm's accumulated expertise in lightweight metal structures; it dates back to the '20s, before monocoque structures were feasible.

All Bristol cars to date have had very stiff and strong chassis upon which lightweight aluminium bodies could be mounted. This new one has a vestigial chassis structure of aluminium alloy, forming the basis for a load-bearing hull structure of the same materials, although carbon fibre might be found here and there where appropriate, as it is for the bonnet and gullwing doors.

Continuing an association with Chrysler dating from 1961, when a Canadian-built V8 was adopted for the Bristol 407 saloon, the new two-seater will also be propelled by a Chrysler engine – not a V8 this time, but the mighty 8.0-litre Viper V10.

As always, Bristol modifies it to improve refinement, response and power. Among the most significant changes are ▶

One-fifth scale model reveals shape that makes no attempt to create downforce

◆ Bristol's intake and exhaust manifolds, following similar work (accompanied by new cylinder heads and a different camshaft) on the V8 engine of the latest Blenheim 3 Saloon.

Customers will have a choice of automatic or manual transmissions, and in the latter case the firm aims to recapture (despite the massive proportions needed to cope with the engine's tremendous torque) some of the delicacy and precision for which the Bristol gearbox of the '50s was (and still is) remarkable.

The sense of obligation to tradition is clear at every step. The last Bristol production two-seater was the 2.0-litre Type 404, unofficially nicknamed The Businessman's Express. That was no yahoo sportster, but an elegant coupe in exquisite taste.

The new car is expected to perform the same role for today's Bristol customers, who

seem as discerning as ever.

It will weigh 1400kg, of which 52 per cent will be supported by the rear wheels. Despite the placing of the engine behind the axes of the front wheels, to secure the modest moments of inertia in yaw and pitch which have always contributed to every Bristol's uncannily good handling, the new coupe will still be compact, almost exactly the same as my 2.2-litre Honda Prelude.

The packaging must be clever, for a cramped cabin will not be tolerated. I noticed at the gathering where the model was first revealed that at least half the Bristol owners present were well over six foot, and the same applied to the design engineers. I have also known Bristols happily driven by people 18 inches shorter. The packaging must be *very* clever.

The naming of the car had better be, too. Recent and

current Bristols have been named after famous Bristol aircraft, so for the time being the two-seater project has been identified with the Bristol Fighter, probably the most able and surely the best made aircraft of the First World War. That might sound a bit too aggressive for the market, however, and the production car may well be named after another aircraft: Bloodhound and Bulldog, Bolingbroke and Bisley, these names and many more are available for revival.

Bristol has no wish either to deny the new car's existence or to have its test programmes hampered by the need for secrecy – hence the early announcement of the project. The use, common among bigger manufacturers, of nocturnal testing or grotesque disguises is seen as likely to corrupt test results, and Bristol will have none of that.

There are many things in current motor industry practice Bristol finds objectionable. The intrusive and excessively complex electronically modulated systems fashionable in other high-performance cars are dismissed as a poor substitute for the balance and control that are produced by painstaking basic engineering. No manufacturer tests brakes more severely, none investigates tyres more thoroughly, nor inspects everything more stringently. Getting things right in the first place is judged a better use of engineers' time than correcting errors later.

As for (if you will pardon the expression) styling, a quotation from the firm says all that need be said about innovation and unorthodoxy, whether in the shaping of the skin or what lies beneath: "The company has never been constrained either by custom or its customers." ⦿

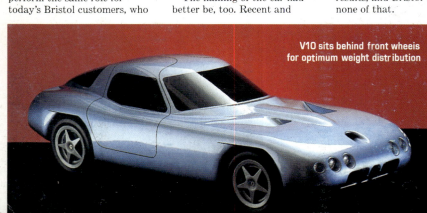

V10 sits behind front wheels for optimum weight distribution

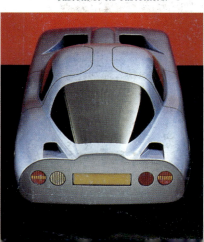